Worlds of History

A Comparative Reader

Volume Two: Since 1400

Second Edition

Kevin Reilly
Raritan Valley College

Bedford/St. Martin's
Boston • New York

To My Teachers: Eugene Meehan, Traian Stoianovich, Donald Weinstein, and the memory of Warren Susman

For Bedford/St. Martin's
Publisher for History: Patricia A. Rossi
Director of Development for History: Jane Knetzger
Developmental Editor: Elizabeth Harrison
Editorial Assistant: Carina Schoenberger
Assistant Editor, Publishing Services: Maria Burwell
Production Supervisor: Jennifer Wetzel
Senior Marketing Manager: Jenna Bookin Barry
Project Management: Books By Design, Inc.
Cover Design: Billy Boardman
Cover Art: Lady Wrapping Her Turban (detail), 1675–1700, M.75.114.3. India, Andhra Pradesh, Golconda. Los Angeles County Museum of Art. Gift of Doris and Ed Wiener. Photograph © 2004 Museum Associates/LACMA; *Woman at the Tailor's.* © Archivo Iconografico, S.A./CORBIS
Composition: Pine Tree Composition, Inc.
Printing and Binding: RR Donnelley & Sons Company

President: Joan E. Feinberg
Editorial Director: Denise B. Wydra
Director of Marketing: Karen Melton Soeltz
Director of Editing, Design, and Production: Marcia Cohen
Manager, Publishing Services: Emily Berleth

For information, write: Bedford/St. Martin's, 75 Arlington Street, Boston, MA 02116   (617-399-4000)

ISBN: 0-312-40201-5 (Volume 1)
       0-312-40202-3 (Volume 2)

Acknowledgments

Preface

Teaching introductory world history to college students for thirty-five years has helped me appreciate three enduring truths that provide the framework for this book. The first is that any introductory history course must begin with the students, as they sit before us in their remarkable diversity. The second is that history embraces all, the entire past, the whole world. The third is that students need to learn to think historically, critically, and independently, and that the subject matter of history can teach them how. With these goals in mind, I have constructed chapters in *Worlds of History* that pique student interest, teach broad trends and comparative experiences, and develop what today we call "critical thinking skills" and the Romans used to call "habits of mind."

The primary and secondary source selections in both volumes of this reader address the question, "What specific topics can imbue a general understanding of world history while helping students develop critical thinking skills?" The reader's format helps students (and instructors) make sense of the overwhelming richness and complexity of world history. First, the reader has a **topical organization** that is also chronological, with each chapter focusing on an engaging topic within a particular time period. I am convinced that students are generally more interested in topics than eras, and that an appreciation of period and process can be taught by concentrating on topics. Into these topical chapters I've woven a **comparative approach**, examining two or more cultures at a time. In some chapters students can trace parallel developments in separate regions, such as the rise of cities in China, Italy, and Egypt in Volume One, or Chinese and European expansion in the fifteenth and sixteenth centuries in Volume Two. In other cases students examine the enduring effects of contact and exchange between cultures, as in Volume One's chapter on the First Crusade in the eleventh century or Volume Two's chapter on the European colonization of Burma, the Philippines, and Nigeria in the nineteenth and twentieth centuries.

A wealth of **pedagogical tools** helps students unlock the readings and extend their critical thinking skills. Each chapter begins with "**Historical Context**," an introduction to the chapter's topic that sets the stage for directed comparisons among the readings. A separate "**Thinking Historically**" section follows, exploring a particular critical thinking skill—reading primary and secondary sources or distinguishing causes of change—that ties to the chapter's selections. These skills increase in difficulty with each chapter so that a student's capacity to manipulate knowledge—to analyze, synthesize, and interpret—builds one step at a time.

"Reflections," a section that summarizes or extends the chapter's lessons, concludes each chapter.

Each volume's fourteen chapters should correspond to general survey texts and to most instructors' syllabi. Understanding that some variation might exist, I have included a correlation chart in the new **online instructor's resource manual** that matches each reading in this text with related chapters in sixteen of the most widely used survey texts. The manual, available at **bedfordstmartins.com/reilly**, also highlights teaching strategies, provides the rationale for the selection and organization of the readings, and includes information about ancillary resources, including films and Internet sites.

NEW TO THIS EDITION

While I am continually testing selections in my own classroom, I appreciate input from readers and adopters and I want to thank them for their many suggestions. Having incorporated some of this feedback, I think those who have used the first edition will find this edition tighter, more interesting, and even more accessible to students. In response to numerous requests, I have added new chapters on gender and women's history in each volume. In Volume One, a chapter on women in the Classical world compares women's lives in India, China, and Rome, enabling students to draw comparisons from classic primary texts. In Volume Two, students read about gender and the family in early modern societies from China to Spanish America, building and evaluating theory as they juxtapose one society with another.

New scholarship has pointed the way to revising other chapters. In Volume One, a chapter on the expansion of Christianity and Buddhism has been broadened to include recent work on the importance of trade along the Silk Road and the expansion of Islam. The last chapter in Volume Two, on globalization, is almost entirely new, benefiting from recent scholarship and post-9/11 interpretations. In other cases, I have added readings of classical scholarship that suddenly give a chapter the focus I have always sought: Fernand Braudel on cities in Volume One and Benedict Anderson on nationalism in Volume Two.

Some of the best new materials in this edition are the illustrations and maps that Bedford/St. Martin's has enabled me to add. In this revision I've introduced brand-new geographic reference maps to many of the chapters' "Historical Context" sections. Not to be "read" as sources themselves, these maps are simply meant to give students a geographic point of reference for readings that span the globe. For example, in Chapter 5 of Volume One, I've provided straightforward maps of the expanding Chinese and Roman empires discussed in the chapter. In Volume Two's chapter on

World War I, I've included a map showing the Allied and Central Powers, as well as the Western Front. As one of my reviewers put it, "Simple maps simply work better"; this has been the inspiration for the new map program.

To emphasize the importance of using nonwritten materials in historical analysis, both volumes now include more visual sources, such as prehistoric Venus statues in Volume One and a global warming cartogram in Volume Two. In some cases, these visuals stand alone to advance the lesson of the chapter: historic Chinese maps of Zheng He's expeditions in Volume Two, for instance. In other cases they are tied to a specific selection and help students better understand the reading, like the graphs depicting the rate of conversion to Islam in medieval Iran in Volume One.

I am not a believer in change for its own sake; when I have a successful way of teaching a subject, I am not disposed to jettison it for something new. Consequently, many of my most satisfying changes are incremental: a better translation of a document or the addition of a newly discovered source. In some cases I have been able to further edit a useful source, retaining its muscle, but providing room for a precious new find. I begin each round of revision with the conviction that the book is already as good as it can get. And I end each round with the surprising discovery that it is much better than it was.

ACKNOWLEDGMENTS

A book like this cannot be written without the help and advice, even if sometimes unheeded, of a vast army of colleagues and professionals. I count myself enormously fortunate to have met and known such a large group of gifted and generous scholars and teachers in my years with the World History Association. Among them, I would like to thank those who were reviewers and questionnaire respondents for this book: Robin Anderson, Arkansas State University; Pierre Asselin, Kapiolani Community College; Martin E. Berger, Youngstown State University; Donna Bohanan, Auburn University; Andrew Clark, University of North Carolina at Wilmington; Franklin M. Doeringer, Lawrence University; S. Ross Doughty, Ursinus College; E. Thomas Ewing, Virginia Polytechnic; Christopher Guthrie, Tarleton State University; Carla Hay, Marquette University; Susan Hult, Houston Community College; Norman Love, El Paso Community College; Justin D. Murphy, Howard Payne University; Patrick Patterson, Honolulu Community College; and Rachel Stocking, Southern Illinois University.

Other friends and colleagues contributed selections, suggestions, and advice for the book in other ways. Among them I would like to thank the following: Michael Adas, Rutgers University; Jerry Bentley, University of

Hawaii; David Berry, Essex County Community College; Catherine Clay, Shippensburg University; Roger Cranse, Norwich University; Philip Curtin, Johns Hopkins University; Ross Dunn, San Diego State University; Martin Gilbert, North Georgia College; Steve Gosch, University of Wisconsin at Eau Claire; Gregory Guzman, Bradley University; Brock Haussamen, Raritan Valley College; Sarah Hughes, Shippensburg University; Allen Howard, Rutgers University; Karen Jolly, University of Hawaii; Maghan Keita, Villanova University; Pat Manning, Northeastern University; William H. McNeill, University of Chicago; John Mears, Southern Methodist University; Gyan Prakash, Princeton University; Heidi Roupp, Aspen High School; Richard Rosen, Drexel University; Robert Rosen, University of California at Los Angeles; John Russell-Wood, Johns Hopkins University; Lynda Shaffer, Tufts University; Anthony Snyder, Brookdale Community College; Leften Stavrianos, University of California at San Diego; Robert Stayer; Peter Stearns, George Mason University; Robert Tignor, Princeton University; Mary Evelyn Tucker, Bucknell University; John Voll, Georgetown University; and Judith Zinsser, Miami University.

I also want to thank the people at Bedford/St. Martin's, especially Joan Feinberg, Denise Wydra, Patricia Rossi, Jane Knetzger, Elizabeth Harrison, Emily Berleth, Nancy Benjamin, Jenna Bookin Barry, Donna Dennison, and Billy Boardman.

While writing this book, memories of my own introduction to history and critical thinking have come flooding back to me. I was blessed at Rutgers in the 1960s with teachers I still aspire to emulate. Eugene Meehan taught me that learning could be both hard work and fun. Traian Stoianovich, who introduced me to the work of his own teacher, Fernand Braudel, demonstrated a vision of history that was boundless, and demanded only originality from this graduate student. Donald Weinstein taught me to listen to students as if they were Stradivarii. And Warren Susman filled a room with more life than I ever knew existed. I dedicate this book to them.

Finally, I want to thank my own institution, Raritan Valley College, for nurturing my career, allowing me to teach whatever I wanted, and entrusting me with some of the best students one could encounter anywhere. I could not ask for anything more. Except, of course, a loving wife like Pearl.

Introduction

You have here fourteen lessons in world history, each of which deals with a particular historical period and topic since the fifteenth century. (A companion volume addresses human history to 1550.) Some of the topics are narrow and specific, covering events such as the Opium War in detail, while others are broad and general, such as colonialism and globalization.

As you learn about historical periods and topics, you also will be coached to think systematically. The "Thinking Historically" passages in each chapter encourage habits of mind that I associate with my own study of history. They are not necessarily intended to turn you into historians but, rather, to give you skills that will help you in all of your college courses and throughout your life. For example, the first chapter distinguishes primary sources (eyewitness accounts) from secondary sources (historical interpretations) — certainly something that historians do. But the true value of this exercise, and of the others that build on it, is in helping you to differentiate between fact and opinion, clearly an ability as necessary at work, on a jury, in the voting booth, and in discussions with friends as it is in the study of history.

World history is nothing less than everything ever done or imagined, so we cannot possibly cover it all. In his famous novel *Ulysses,* James Joyce imagines the thoughts and actions of a few friends on a single day in Dublin, June 16, 1904. The book runs almost a thousand pages. Obviously, there were many more than a few people in Dublin on that particular day, countless other cities in the world, and infinitely more days than that one particular day in world history. So we are forced to choose places and times.

In this volume our choices include some particular days, like the day in 1519 that Cortés and Montezuma met, but our attention will be directed mainly toward much longer periods. And while we will visit particular places like Mexico City in 1519, typically we will study more than one place at a time by using a comparative approach.

Comparisons can be enormously useful in studying world history. When we compare Chinese and European mariners, merchants in Malacca and Persia, science in Japan and England, growing up in Algeria and Nigeria, we learn about the general and the specific at the same time. My hope is that by comparing some of the various worlds of history, an understanding of world history will emerge.

Contents

*Atlantic world that integrated and divided these indigenous peoples. We com-
pare primary sources to understand these first contacts and conflicts.*

3. Asian Continental Empires and Maritime States

Malacca, China, and Muslim Empires, 1500–1700   90

*The rich and powerful continental empires of Asia were alike in some respects,
but important characteristics differentiated land empires from the dynamic
maritime merchant city-states of the new era. In distinguishing the economics,
politics, and cultures of these societies, we learn to understand their differences
and the implications these differences had for their ultimate survival and
success.*

4. Gender and Family

China, Southeast Asia, Europe, and "New Spain,"
1600–1750 135

With the blinds drawn on the domestic lives of our ancestors, one might assume their private worlds were uneventful and everywhere the same. By comparing different cultures we see historical variety in family life and the roles of both men and women.

HISTORICAL CONTEXT 135

THINKING HISTORICALLY
Making Comparisons 136

Reflections 169

5. The Scientific Revolution

Europe, Ottoman Empire, China, and Japan,
1600–1800 171

The seventeenth-century scientific revolution occurred in Europe, but it had important roots in Asia and its consequences reverberated throughout the world. To understand exactly what changed and how, we must study the "before" and "after."

HISTORICAL CONTEXT 171

THINKING HISTORICALLY
Sifting Evidence: "Before" and "After" 171

6. Enlightenment and Revolution

Europe and the Americas, 1650–1850   204

The eighteenth-century Enlightenment applied scientific reason to politics, but reason meant different things to different people and societies. What were the goals of the political revolutions produced by the Enlightenment? A close reading of the period texts reveals disagreement and shared dreams.

HISTORICAL CONTEXT   204

THINKING HISTORICALLY
Close Reading and Interpretation of Texts   205

7. Capitalism and the Industrial Revolution

Europe and the World, 1750–1900   236

Modern society has been shaped dramatically by capitalism and the industrial revolution, but these two forces are not the same. Which one is principally responsible for the creation of our modern world: the economic system of the market or the technology of the industrial revolution? Distinguishing different "causes" allows us to gauge their relative effects and legacies.

HISTORICAL CONTEXT   236

8. Colonized and Colonizers

Europeans in Africa and Asia, 1850–1930   276

Colonialism resulted in a world divided between the colonized and the colonizers, a world in which people's identities were defined by their power relationships with others who looked and often spoke differently. The meeting of strangers and their forced adjustment to predefined roles inspired a number of great literary works that we look to in this chapter for historical guidance.

9. Nationalism and Westernization

The Philippines, Japan, India, and China, 1880–1930   313

Western colonialism elicited two contrary responses among the colonized — the assertion of national independence and the desire to imitate Western

10. World War and Its Consequences

Europe, the Soviet Union, and the Middle East,
1914–1920   354

*The First World War brutally ended an era — the world would never be the
same after such death and destruction. We read historical accounts so we can
begin to understand the war's far-reaching chain of causes and consequences.*

11. Fascism, World War II, and Genocide

Germany, Poland, France, Japan, and China, *1931–1945*   *396*

The rise of fascism in Europe and Asia led to genocide and world war. How could people allow their governments, armies, families, and friends to commit such unspeakable acts? How does the unforgivable happen?

HISTORICAL CONTEXT   *396*

THINKING HISTORICALLY
Understanding the Unforgivable   *397*

12. New States and New Struggles

Middle East, South Africa, China, and Vietnam, *1945–1975*   *434*

New states were created in the wake of colonialism and in the ashes of war, but all too often they were unable to resolve the conflicts that occasioned their creation. What are the fault lines of modern society and culture? Does the present recapitulate the past?

13. Women's World

1950–2000   477

The lives of women in the modern world are as diverse as those of men. Can you find any patterns in these personal accounts and stories? Can you develop any theories about women's lives in the modern world?

14. Globalization

1960 to the Present   516

Globalization *is a word with many meanings and a process with many causes. What are the forces most responsible for the shrinking of the world into one global community? Do the forces of globalization unite us or divide us? We undertake the study of process to answer these questions.*

HISTORICAL CONTEXT   *516*

THINKING HISTORICALLY
Understanding Process   *518*

1

Chinese and European Expansion

China and Europe, 1400–1600

HISTORICAL CONTEXT

Between 1400 and 1500, the balance between Chinese and European sea power changed drastically. Before 1434, Chinese shipbuilding was the envy of the world. Chinese ships were larger, more numerous, safer, and better outfitted than European ships. The Chinese navy made frequent trips through the South China Sea to the Spice Islands, through the Indian Ocean, and as far as East Africa and the Persian Gulf (see Map 1.1). Every island, port, and kingdom along the route was integrated into the Chinese system of tributaries. Goods were exchanged, marriages arranged, and princes taken to visit the Chinese emperor.

In the second half of the fifteenth century, the Chinese navy virtually disappeared. At the same time, the Portuguese began a series of explorations down the coast of Africa and into the Atlantic Ocean. In 1434, Portuguese ships rounded the treacherous Cape Bojador, just south of Morocco. In 1488, Bartholomeu Dias rounded the Cape of Good Hope. Vasco de Gama sailed into the Indian Ocean, arriving in Calicut the following year. And in 1500 a fortuitous landfall in Brazil by Pedro Cabral gave the Portuguese a claim from the western Atlantic to the Indian Ocean. By 1512, Portuguese ships had reached the Bandas and Moluccas — the Spice Islands of what is today eastern Indonesia.

Beginning in 1492, after the defeat of the Moors (Muslims) and the voyages of Columbus, the Spanish claimed most of the Western Hemisphere until challenged by the Dutch, English, and French. European control in the Americas penetrated far deeper than in Asia, where it was limited to enclaves on the coast, and where European nations were in an almost perpetual state of war with each other. Taken together, the nations of Western Europe dominated the seas of the world after 1500 (see Map 1.2).

1

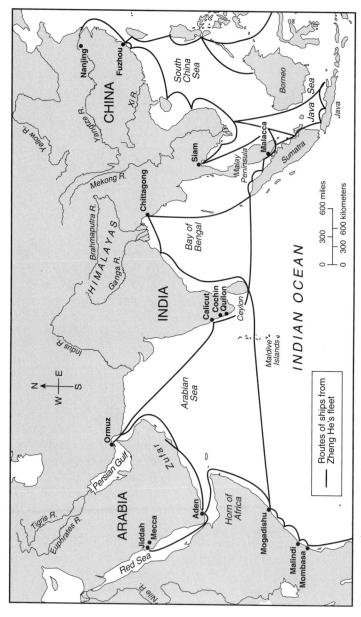

Map 1.1 Chinese Naval Expeditions, 1405–1433.

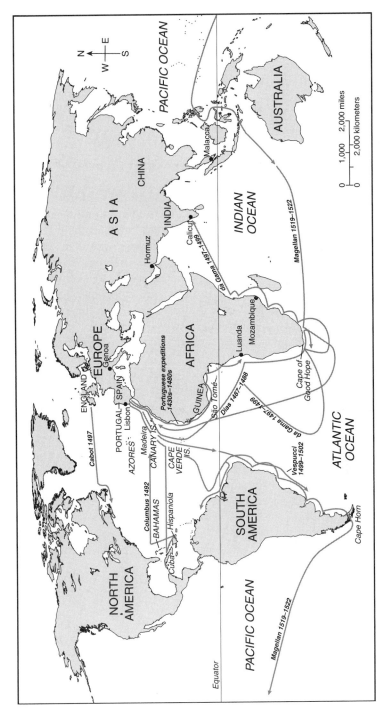

Map 1.2 European Exploration, 1430s–1530s.

What accounts for the different fortunes of China and Europe in the fifteenth century? Were the decline of China and the rise of Europe inevitable? Probably no objective observer of the time would have thought so. In what ways were the expansions of China and Europe similar? In what ways were they different? Think about these questions as you reflect on the readings in this chapter.

THINKING HISTORICALLY
Reading Primary and Secondary Sources

This chapter contains both primary and secondary sources. *Primary sources* are actual pieces of the past and include anything — art, letters, essays, and so on — from the historical period being studied. If a future historian were to study and research students in American colleges at the beginning of the twenty-first century, some primary sources might include diaries, letters, e-mail messages, class notes, school newspapers, transcripts, textbooks, tests, and official and unofficial records. *Secondary sources* are usually books and articles *about* the past — interpretations of the past. These sources are "secondary" because they must be based on primary sources; therefore, a history written after an event occurs is a secondary source.

In your studies, you will be expected to distinguish primary from secondary sources. A quick glance at the introductions to this chapter's selections tells you that the first article is written by a modern historian, and the fifth article, also written by a contemporary author, is taken from a book published in 1991. In contrast, Ma Huan, author of the second selection, recorded his thoughts in the fifteenth century, and Christopher Columbus penned the fourth selection more than five hundred years ago. These latter sources are firsthand accounts of long past worlds. The maps in the third selection date back to the fifteenth and sixteenth centuries.

Having determined whether selections are primary or secondary sources, we also explore some of the subtle complexities that are overlooked by such designations.

THEODORE F. COOK JR.

Zheng He and Chinese Expansion

Cook, a modern historian, recounts the great age of Chinese maritime expansion and the life of the admiral Zheng He, who directed Chinese naval expeditions between 1405 and 1434. Because this era ended so suddenly after 1434, only to be succeeded by the maritime expansion of the Portuguese, Spanish, and other Europeans, historians have frequently tried to explain why the Chinese withdrew their fleets from the southerly oceans. Although this is an interesting question, Cook argues that it assumes that expansion is normal and that only the failure to expand requires explanation. But if expansion is not the norm, we might learn more by asking why China sent out the treasure ships in the first place. In addition, it might be useful to imagine the argument of a Confucian official for ending the expeditions in 1434.

Thinking Historically

This article is clearly a secondary source. It only makes a few direct references to primary sources, but try to imagine what additional primary sources we would need to reconstruct fully this history. One obvious primary source would be the ships' logs and other official records of the Chinese government. In fact, the Confucian opposition destroyed these records after 1434, in their effort to end the expeditions and destroy everything that made them possible. If you were going to write an account of these voyages, what primary sources might you hope to find? How does a lack of primary sources affect our ability to analyze history?

The "Age of Discovery," the "Era of Exploration," the "epoch of European Expansion and Colonialism," have introduced generations of students to the seafaring exploits of navigators, who, from about 1450 to 1600, first set out onto the Western Sea — the great Atlantic Ocean — and then traversed all the oceans of the world. Yet in the previous half-century, nearly fifty years before the Portuguese caravels sent out

---

Theodore F. Cook Jr., "The Chinese Discovery of the New World: Fifteenth Century" in *What If? 2: Eminent Historians Imagine What Might Have Been*, ed. Robert Cowley (New York: Berkeley, 2002), 87–102.

Henry the Navigator crossed the equator on the Atlantic coast of Africa going south, and three-quarters of a century before Vasco da Gama finally reached Calicut in India in 1498, Chinese fleets were poised at the edge of their own explored seas on the other side of Africa. Ready to spread Chinese civilization — economic, cultural, political, and moral values bound together — into what Europeans seemed to regard as their realm of exploitation, Chinese naval forces, sent forth by the Ming emperor himself, had the capability of thrusting themselves into the maelstrom of the history of Western European history as never before.

In the former port of Changle in Fujian Province, on China's southeastern coast, a tablet was erected in 1432 by Zheng He, China's "Admiral of the Western Sea" that evoked a view of the wider world seldom associated with the Middle Kingdom:

> We have traversed more than one hundred thousand li of immense waterscapes and have beheld in the ocean huge waves like mountains rising sky high, and we have set eyes on barbarian regions far away hidden in a blue transparency of light vapors, while our sails, loftily unfurled like clouds day and night, continued their course [as rapidly as] a star, traversing those savage waves as if we were treading a public thoroughfare.

Raised to commemorate the seven great expeditions the admiral had organized and led out to the edges of the Indian Ocean Basin beginning in 1405, the tablet is as much a monument of the spirit of adventure, the thrill of ocean sailing, and the experience of a generation of Chinese seamen who shared their admiral's thrill at visiting lands far from their Chinese home as it was a personal proclamation. In many ways, it was to serve as an epitaph both to the admiral himself and to China's great age of sail. Even before the admiral himself died, the dynasty that had sent him forth was implementing a policy that would call back his fleets, undo the web of diplomatic, trade, and cultural relations he had woven over almost three decades, and, by the time of the arrival of Europeans in numbers in the waters of the Indian Ocean, literally reduce his magnificent sea charts and shipbuilding techniques to ashes.

Yet need it have been so? What if China had discovered Europe?

Zheng He (1371–1433) must rate as one of the monumental figures in any Age of Exploration. His origins and personal history were surely as convoluted and exceptional as the biographies of a Bartholomeu Dias, Vasco da Gama, Christopher Columbus, or Ferdinand Magellan. Moreover, his career was tightly intertwined with the rise to power of the third Ming emperor, Zhu Di, the "Yongle" (or "Perpetual Happiness") Emperor, who ruled China from 1402 to 1424. The emperor entrusted to Zheng He the critical mission of leading what became seven stupendous maritime expeditions between 1405 and 1433. These voyages took him and the name of China into what is today called the South China Sea, through the Strait of Malacca, and past the kingdoms that sought to trade on their geographical control what they saw as "the navel of the world." He was to sail beyond into the Bay of Bengal, to Ceylon, up the Malibar Coast of India to the fabled cities of Cochin and Calicut, to the aptly named Arabian Sea — with its ancient sea route linking India to Mesopotamia and Arabia — into the Red Sea, and by land even unto Mecca. Elements of the fleets sailed down the coast of East Africa, past Zanzibar, perhaps as far as Mozambique and Madagascar. There is some evidence that elements of Chinese fleets may even have touched the northern coasts of Australia after calling at the eastern extremes of the Spice Islands.

The future admiral's origins could hardly have been less auspicious or more difficult. Stories of his youth all agree on the essentials of what was to be an extraordinary rise to power. Born in the land-bound province of Yunnan in southwest China to Muslim parents in this region conquered by Kublai Khan in 1253 to '54, and ruled as a Yuan dynasty province under a Mongol prince until the fall of that dynasty, Zheng He was ten years old when General Fu Youde, sent to subjugate the region for China by the first Ming emperor, completed another of his tasks by gathering a number of boys to be sent to the court for service as eunuchs, a class of public servant most highly prized by the Chinese court. Selected for his alertness and courage by the general himself and marked a "candidate of exceptional qualities," after enduring the excruciating agony of castration by knife (which traditionally removed both penis and testicles), the boy was assigned to the retinue of one of the emperor's sons, the Prince of Yan (Zhu Di's title during his father's reign), at the capital of Nanjing. Trained for military service, largely because of his height, powerful build, and imposing presence, Zheng He served on maneuvers along the northern frontier of China and later in battles of the civil war that culminated with his patron, Zhu Di, deposing his nephew and making himself emperor in 1402.

As one of the most trusted associates of the new Son of Heaven, the eunuch was chosen to create and lead a Ming fleet, augmenting already formidable naval forces engaged in the southern seas. It likely seemed a wise diplomatic gesture to dispatch a Muslim Believer rather than an Infidel as plenipotentiary in sea-lanes then dominated by Arab merchant sailors and to the many countries that were Muslim-ruled. Naval experience was apparently less important than loyalty, although Zheng He soon demonstrated organizational skills and leadership abilities; what was described as an "awesome physical presence," must also have justified the emperor's choice. For a eunuch to command a fleet, or army for that matter, was not unusual in Ming times. Indeed major commands were often entrusted to such men. Yet both Zheng He's success and his closeness to his sovereign were eventually to provoke great jealousy and resentment.

Why the expeditions were ordered is less immediately obvious than the choice of their commander. Their significance must be understood within the broader context of Ming history. Zhu Di became the Yongle Emperor at age forty-two, taking over leadership of the dynasty that his father, Zhu Yuanzhang, the Hongwu Emperor (r. 1368–1398), had founded. The Great Progenitor of the Dynasty, as the founder was styled, had led a successful military rebellion and then military overthrow of the Yuan, or Mongol dynasty, in 1368. A poor peasant who restored native Chinese to the imperial palace by ousting the Mongols and their entourage of Central Asian non-Chinese officials and Chinese sycophants willing to serve at the bottom of the Mongol bureaucratic hierarchy, the Hongwu Emperor's official portrait, now held in the National Museum of China in Taipei, captures his coarse features with his jutting chin, his explosive energy, and potential for violence. The long and bitter battles against the Mongols had entailed military campaigns throughout China and its peripheral regions, and Zhu Di was at the center of these campaigns once he attained his majority.

Zhu Di's usurpation of power from his nephew, and his Shakespearean ambition and simultaneous self-doubts about the morality of his acts, has long fascinated students of what has been called the "Second Founding of the Ming." Using as pretext "the defilement of his father's inviolable institutions" and proclaiming that it was "his duty to rescue the dynasty from the evil ministers exerting undue influence on a young ruler," Zhu Di seems to have sought to equal or surpass the achievements of his illustrious father. Although the former emperor probably perished in the fire that destroyed his palace on July 13, 1402, when Zhu Di's armies stormed Nanjing, his death could not be confirmed absolutely. Fearing that supporters of his nephew might find allies in areas outside the control of the Imperial Government, whether among Mongols yearning for revenge, in the nether reaches to the south, or even across the seas, the Yongle Emperor appears to have decided to make his reign known throughout Asia, to demonstrate that he was now the legitimate ruler of China. Moreover, he determined to invite their rulers to visit his court to offer tribute. His dispatching of fleets under Admiral Zheng He was an essential part of this mission.

What did these "fleets" sent out by Ming China look like? Was it really possible that China could have threatened the coming European domination of the Age of Sail? Indeed, judging from the way China seems to be perceived even today, casual historians of the era may be surprised to learn that China in the first years of the fifteenth century was arguably the world's preeminent maritime power. At the command of the Ming emperors were among the largest and best-equipped fleets the world had yet known.

No more comprehensive description of the expeditions led by Zheng He exists in English than Louise Levathes's *When China Ruled the Seas: The Treasure Fleet of the Dragon Throne, 1405–1433.* Not only did her book bring this extraordinary period in Chinese history to the attention of the wider scholarly and popular world, but her peerless description of the eunuch admiral's world helped rescue from obscurity the grand maritime tradition of China.

China's fleets would have seemed to the Europeans of their day to be gigantic armadas, composed of myriad vessels of undreamt-of size and sophistication. The hardy caravels of the Portuguese or Spanish that made the epic voyages of the last years of the fifteenth century would have been dwarfed by the great "treasure ships" at the heart of the Ming fleet, and surpassed in size and capabilities by many of the other ships in the fleets. Zheng He sailed with an array of vessels specializing in all the needs of expeditions that would sometimes number as many as 37,000 men. He had horse ships, capable of carrying horses both from China for his forces or back in the tribute trade. He had supply and provision vessels, freshwater transport ships especially designed for missions in little-known seas near arid lands. He also had at his command a formidable fleet of combat ships including "floating fortresses," armed with cannon and other weapons well suited for bombardment of recalcitrant enemies, troop transports for his substantial land army, and smaller, faster vessels capable of warding off and running down pirates. They were coordinated at sea by a complex system of flags, drums, gongs, and lanterns, intended to allow the ships to remain in communication with one another, and to relay vital information about navigational or other dangers easily and reliably.

In 1402, the Yongle Emperor ordered his admiral to begin assembling a fleet to dominate the Indian Ocean. By 1420 it had become an imperial armada consisting of about 3,800 ships, 1,350 of which were major vessels capable of combat. Of the combat ships, some 400 were large oceangoing floating fortresses and perhaps as many as 250 were giant "treasure ships." The precise size and shape, as well as rigging and alignment of sails of these ships, which seem to have had as many as nine masts, has long been a topic for debate among students of naval architecture. Not only did the Ming fleets contain vessels larger in size than any wooden ships ever built, but they were extraordinarily seaworthy. They were equipped with the latest technology available, including magnetic compasses, sternpost rudders, detailed maps and charts, compartmentation belowdecks, and staggered masts, so placed as to better capture the wind, with sails of the strongest cloth available. In size, the ships dwarfed their European counterparts. Some displaced 1,500 tons, five times the displacement of the ships Vasco da Gama sailed to India.

Whole provinces were mobilized to build these ships. The effort engaged the minds and skills of the technological cream of the state. More than 400 households of carpenters, sail-makers, and shipwrights were transferred from the maritime regions to the shipyard at Longjiang, and thus perhaps between 20,000 and 30,000 specialists were brought together in one great nexus of shipbuilding expertise. Two shipyards were run at Nanjing — one for the normal boats and one for the huge "treasure ships." The dockyards at Longjiang included seven dry docks, most capable of handling ships 90 to 120 feet in width, with two extra-large ones, 210 feet wide, that could accommodate hulls the size of the treasure ships at the heart of the fleet.

While Western historians often claim that knowledge of wind and sea currents in the fifteenth century was considerably more advanced in the West, thanks to the Portuguese and Dutch, the great caveat must be to add "in the waters they knew." For the Chinese, the regular monsoons of the Indian and Southeast Asian waters, the extensive experience of their own countrymen, and the myriad merchants calling in Chinese ports helped make the charts used by Zheng He marvels of simplicity and practical application. Few have survived to the present day, of course, but they reportedly allowed the admiral to calculate a course accounting for wind, tide, currents, and expected weather, from any major port to any objective, reliable to within hours.

The voyages themselves spanned the period from 1405 to 1433. Zheng He began by making a base at Malacca, from which he could operate into the Indian Ocean. From there he traveled to Ceylon, Siam, Bengal, on to Hormuz and down the east coast of Africa. He forged alliances and used force where necessary. The treasures brought back to China included *quilin,* supposedly sacred animals we would call giraffes, zebras, and other exotic African beasts. These were precisely the kind of signs from nature, the "auspicious animals," that the tradition of Chinese dynastic cycles forecast would appear to indicate Heaven's sanction of a ruler's virtue.

On the first voyage, from 1405 to 1407, for example, Zheng He's fleet consisted of 317 ships accompanied by almost 28,000 armed troops. Many of these vessels were mammoth, nine-masted treasure ships with four decks capable of accommodating 500 or more passengers, as well as massive stores of cargo. Measuring up to 124 meters (408 feet) long and 51 meters (166 feet) wide, these treasure ships were by far the largest marine craft the world had ever seen. On the first three voyages (1405–1407, 1407–1409, and 1409–1411), Zheng He took his fleet to Southeast Asia, India, and Ceylon. The fourth expedition (1413–1415), went to the Persian Gulf and Arabia, and later expeditions ventured down the east African coast, calling at ports as far south as Malindi in modern Kenya. Throughout his travels, Zheng He liberally dispensed gifts of Chinese silk, porcelain, and other goods. In return he received rich and unusual presents from his hosts, including the animals that ended their days in the Ming imperial zoo. Zheng He and his companions paid respect to the local deities and customs they encountered, and in Ceylon they erected a monument honoring Buddha, Allah, and Vishnu, a kind of interfaith Rosetta Stone. Zheng He generally sought to attain his goals through diplomacy. But a contemporary reported that Zheng He walked like a tiger and did not shrink from violence when he considered it necessary to impress foreign peoples with China's military might. He ruthlessly suppressed pirates who had long plagued Chinese and Southeast Asian waters, intervened in a civil disturbance to establish his authority in Ceylon, and made displays of military force when local officials threatened his fleet in Arabia and East Africa. These seven expeditions established a Chinese presence and reputation throughout the Indian Ocean basin. Returning from his fourth voyage, Zheng He brought envoys from thirty states who traveled to China and paid their respect at the Ming court. Thereafter, however, the voyages began to lose central support, and hence the momentum and scale of the next two were substantially curtailed.

At just the moment when Zheng He's fleets seem to have achieved their initial assignment, when China's culture was drawing the attention and respect of rulers and traders throughout the Indian Ocean basin, the expeditions suddenly came to an end. As Emily Mahon has pointed out, many historians have expressed the idea that with the shipbuilding and navigational technology evident in the treasure ships, the Chinese could have met Henry the Navigator in his Portuguese home port. Instead, they apparently turned away from exploration, resuming what Michael Wood has called "their traditional inward focus." The analytical methodology used by most Western scholars has been a negative historical comparison, a "why not?" approach. They ask why *didn't* China develop as the West did? Implicit in such investigations is the assumption that something went "wrong," that the decision made by China's leaders could not have been a reasoned choice made by open-minded men, but was instead one rooted in a cultural uniqueness, reflecting a lack of some vital emotional or economic ingredient that subsequent "Western" success in the first age of imperialism would demonstrate. These arguments will not be refought here, but instead some of the main reasons advanced for them need to be touched on before we look beyond to ask what might have been.

As Zhu Di settled into his imperial role, the need for expensive overseas prestige-building missions seemed to diminish; their fabulous expense was seen increasingly to be drawing off resources needed to meet challenges to security closer to home. When challenges on the northern border from the Mongols became more serious, Zhu Di ordered a reduction in the sea service after the fifth expedition, from 1416 to 1419. There was a single, much smaller sixth expedition in

1421, but Zheng He came back early for the dedication of the new Forbidden City in Peking, the Yongle Emperor's reconstructed northern capital. The admiral presided over a parade of auspicious *quilin*. Disaster struck soon after the dedication, however, when lightning caused a great fire, which severely damaged the new palace. The emperor interpreted it as an ill omen: Had his policies put the world out of balance? He manumitted a substantial number of taxes to reduce the financial burden on the people and temporarily suspended future voyages of the Treasure Fleet. Now old and sick, Zhu Di died in 1424 at the age of sixty-four while on campaign.

His successor was his studious elder son Zhu Gaozhi. No warrior, the new emperor began plans to reverse many of his father's policies including the heavy taxation for military campaigns and public projects. However, Zhu Gaozhi died (perhaps of heart failure, perhaps from poison) after only nine months as emperor, and was succeeded in turn by Zhu Zhanji (age twenty-six) in 1426. The fifth Ming emperor was a combination of his warrior, spendthrift grandfather and his scholarly, fiscally conservative father; his reign was a time of peace, prosperity, and good government. He commissioned Zheng He to accomplish a seventh and final treasure ship expedition in 1430, for increased prestige and restoration of the tribute trade. This was perhaps the largest expedition, with 27,500 men and perhaps 300 ships.

Yet in the mid-1430s, the Ming emperors decided to end the expeditions altogether. Confucian ministers, who mistrusted Zheng He and the eunuchs who supported the voyages, argued that resources committed to the expensive expeditions would go to better use if devoted to agriculture. Moreover, during the 1420s and '30s the Mongols mounted a new military threat from the northwest, and land forces urgently needed financial support. Scholars have blamed the introspective culture of the later Ming period for a decline in many branches of science and technology. Launched on command, China's awesome maritime effort was also shut down from the center. In 1436 an imperial decree forbade the construction of new seagoing ships; the large shipyards consequently deteriorated and naval personnel were reassigned. The ability to maintain the oceangoing ships disintegrated and zealous officials seeking to assure that the expeditions would never be repeated destroyed even the records of the fabulous journeys. Zheng He himself died in 1433, apparently during his last voyage.

By 1474 the fleet was down to one-third of its size in early Ming times; by 1503 just a tenth of its peak size remained. In 1500, it became a capital offense for a Chinese to go to sea in a ship with more than two masts without special permission. Later, officials were authorized to destroy the larger classes of ships. Private merchants and shipwrights fled the maritime provinces and the harsh punishments for engaging in international trade, some finding work along the Grand Canal, and many others establishing themselves in the overseas Chinese communities throughout Southeast Asia that had first become a major feature of the region in the early years of the Ming. Moreover, a suspicion that those engaged in the coastal trade were in contact with non-Chinese beyond the reach of central authority and had a penchant for smuggling led them to forbid coastal people from plying their trades legally. This led in turn to an explosion of piracy along the China coasts, with Taiwan as a major center of activity. This development, often blamed on "Japanese pirates" (who were mostly of Chinese origin) resulted in the population of whole districts being relocated away from the coast both to "starve the pirates" and to shut down smuggling, as well as to destroy the nautical skills needed to engage in it.

What had once been a great fleet operating in response to the Imperial Will had disappeared and become such a minor factor in regional affairs that in 1515 a Portuguese envoy archly remarked that "With ten ships the [Portuguese] Governor of India . . . could take the whole of the China coast." Quite a condemnation!

Need it have been so?

What if, instead of curtailing the great overseas expeditions as it did upon the return of the last of Zheng He's missions in 1433, China's rulers had instead rededicated themselves to bringing to the world beyond eastern and southern Asia the news of China's glorious civilization and extending to yet-unvisited places the benefits of association with the Ming Imperial Court and the Chinese World Order? What if the Chinese emperor, instead of following the advice of his Confucian counselors and fiscal conservatives to abandon what they saw as reckless and unprecedented maritime activity had instead allowed it to continue, or even expanded the effort? What if, rather than yielding to a call to return to the "natural course" of Chinese history through a xenophobic looking inward, China's rulers had run the risk of inviting universal acceptance with its potential rewards as well as its hazards? What kind of world might have resulted had the Ming fleets not been reined in?

Imagine a Chinese fleet, substantially smaller perhaps than Zheng He's last East Africa expeditions, but still dwarfing those of the Portuguese, making a reconnaissance down the coasts of South Africa below Mozambique, around the Cape of Good Hope, into the Atlantic — what would surely have been seen from China's perspective as a second "Great Western Sea." Certainly, there was little to hold their attention in this barren stretch of coast, though the ostrich and other animals that hailed from the area would surely have been welcome additions to the imperial menagerie. But, was there enough to provide incentive for an expedition of discovery, taking a Chinese squadron up the western coast of Africa to Guinea or the Portuguese Atlantic islands before the Portuguese arrived in force? Perhaps there would have been just

enough to carry them into contact. Confronted with a Chinese fleet —
even a smallish one — that had allies and clients along the Angolan,
Congolese, and West African coasts, would the Portuguese have continued to see this route to the East as desirable?

It is of course hard to envision the Roman Catholic Church accepting Chinese fleets as anything but one more instrument of the Devil
sent to torment Christendom. With the Turks ascendant in the Eastern
Mediterranean, the Arabs still powerful in North Africa (though no
longer dominant in Iberia), a significant, sustained pressure from the
south by yet another alien force could hardly have seemed anything
more than another test by god of the Catholic faith. Yet what could the
Portuguese have done to prevent it in the middle of the 1400s? Historically, Portugal only fortified Fort Elmina on the Gold Coast of West
Africa in 1482. One almost certain outcome of a Chinese appearance
on the Cape of Good Hope or the waters of the Atlantic would have
been a greatly solidified Chinese position within the Indian Ocean
basin and a consequent sharp check on Portuguese expansion. Might
not the worst horrors of the Atlantic slave trade been aborted by a halt
to Portuguese expansion along the African coast at this early date?

The Iberian princes, still somewhat unsteady on their own thrones,
may well have been even less inclined to back "mad adventures" than
they were historically. Instead of an East Africa ruthlessly exploited by
the Portuguese as they established their first footholds in Angola on the
western coast and then in Mozambique on the eastern coast of Africa,
Chinese-influenced African kingdoms, perhaps buoyed up in their ability
to resist, might have been able to face the Portuguese down or call on their
"overload" for assistance. Rather than European exploitation of many
areas in the East from bases in Goa, Malaya, and Singapore, and the East
Indies, Chinese control of the Strait of Malacca, even indirectly via a system tributary states rewarded for their obligations to the Dragon Throne,
would have been a tremendous asset to any Ming emperor, and a formidable obstacle to interloping European adventures in the late fifteenth
and early sixteenth centuries. A Chinese presence in Ceylon and the Indian coasts, besides further enriching the remarkable cultural diversity of
those lands, could well have made local rulers less easily intimidated and
less willing to accept the fortified outposts and depots the Portuguese established as a means of asserting their control over routes of trade. Simultaneously, there exists a distinct possibility that the course of Middle
Eastern history might have been altered by a continued Chinese presence
in the Red Sea near Egypt and in the Persian Gulf.

The westward explorations could have had a reverse effect. If Chinese and client merchants had been able to trade and sell goods in Africa
and the West, that Iberian navigators would one day acquire only by sailing halfway around the world, China itself might have been transformed.

Had the constraints and controls of state enterprise been loosened, the dividends could have been enormous. The revenue potential of trade with a world seeking the products of Chinese industry and creativity might have brought about something like a mercantile revolution.

Anyone contemplating the might-have-beens of this scenario must engage in the delightful fantasy of a Chinese discovery of America and a pre-Columbian contact with its peoples. How far-fetched was such a possibility? Certainly it could not have happened until the Chinese had firmly established themselves along the western coast of Africa. Lacking concrete knowledge of a land mass to the west, they would not have had the incentive to brave the devilish currents of the South Atlantic. Moreover, the extensive logistical train that China's approach to naval expeditions had thus far required would not have been suited to a perilous jump into the unknown. But once the entire bulge of West Africa had been incorporated into a Chinese system, probes in the direction of the South American continent would have been more likely. One might imagine a European world in close contact with Chinese fleets along the maritime frontier of Africa forced into a grand strategic defensive in these waters just as it was in the eastern Mediterranean against the Turks, Europe would have had to leave exploration to the Chinese intruders.

An intriguing alternative to the western Africa-to-Brazil route of Chinese maritime expansion might have been a grand trans-Pacific expedition. This would most likely have utilized the northern route, sailing past the Ryukyus, calling at a now still hospitable Japan, and then setting out across the North Pacific to the Aleutians and Alaska. From there, an expedition would have continued down what Europeans would come to call the Canadian shore to California — and beyond. The Chinese could surely have used the trans-Pacific route at lower latitudes, the same one that Magellan's expedition would first exploit in 1521; but, as the Spanish found, while the cross-Pacific route from Mexico to the Philippines was reliable, the reverse direction was much more problematic due to the unreliable currents and vast expanses of empty ocean.

Either route to what would become known as the Americas might have brought peoples of all races of the world under Chinese influence, with local chieftains offering to accept the Ming Son of Heaven as distant overlord in exchange for the wonders of Chinese goods and Chinese recognition. Radically altered diplomatic, cultural, and military exchanges profoundly altering the history of conquest and exploitation that was the fate of the Americas, all raise intriguing possibilities for "Latin" America's course of development. Would the "pre-Columbian" [pre–Zheng He] kingdoms have been wiped out by the diseases of the Old World with the same relentlessness had Chinese been the visitors? Would the Chinese have introduced the horses, guns, and metallurgy, all of which, in the first third of the sixteenth century, might have helped the Aztecs and the Incas keep the Spanish at bay? Or would the Spanish and their militant Catholicism have prevailed, only later in the century? Would smallpox still have tipped the historical balance?

We can be relatively sure that whatever the possibilities for the Chinese beyond Africa, the continuation of maritime and diplomatic efforts in the Indian Ocean basin could have had a great impact on the development of the world along very different lines than the European Age of Discovery we have come to accept as the natural course of world history in the sixteenth century. The Chinese attitude toward the outside world was hardly open-minded, to be sure. Since ancient times, China's imperial rulers had not conceived of their state as a small part of a larger whole — one nation among many others — but as the core of world civilization, and their own place as the "Middle Kingdom," the natural order of Heaven. Chinese rule, when it occurred in such bordering lands as Korea or Vietnam, or even Tibet, could never be described as benign.

Nevertheless, the purveyors of Confucian civilization on the world stage were likely to be less inclined to enslavement of entire peoples than their Iberian brethren and Chinese were not as likely to attempt to cleanse ancient, but newly discovered, civilizations of their essential features and force on them alternative gods as they installed foreign conquerors as their direct rulers. How different the world might have been had the Chinese brought the Old World to the New for the first time.

┌───────┐
│   2   │
└───────┘

MA HUAN

On Calicut, India

Ma Huan was a Chinese Muslim who acted as an aide and interpreter on Zheng He's treasure ship expeditions. In 1433 he wrote The Overall Survey of the Ocean Shores, *a travel account of the lands he visited. This selection, taken from that account, describes his visit to Calicut on the Malabar, or southwest, coast of India. Note that Ma Huan is not always an accurate observer. More familiar with Bud-*

Ma Huan, "On Calicut, India," in *Ma Huan, Ying-yai Sheng-Ian: The Overall Survey of the Ocean's Shores,* ed. and trans. by Feng Ch'eng-Chun with an introduction by J. V. G. Mills (Bangkok: The White Lotus Press, 1970), 137–44.

dhists than Hindus, for example, he mistakes the latter for the former. Nevertheless, he provides some useful information about Hindu-Muslim relations, the spread of the Abrahamic religions (note the story about Moses), the vitality of Indian trade, and the variety of Indian plants, animals, and manufactures. In addition to describing Calicut, what does Ma Huan tell us about the reasons for these expeditions?

Thinking Historically

Ma Huan's account of the treasure ship voyages does not seem to have had an official purpose, but was probably published instead to satisfy the growing interests of a Chinese public hungry for information about foreign lands and peoples. What sorts of things are of interest to Ma Huan? What does this tell us about his audience? How are his interests similar to, or different from, those of a modern traveler? What might be Ma Huan's strengths and weaknesses as a primary source?

The Country of Ku-Li
[Calicut]

[This is] the great country of the Western Ocean.

Setting sail from the anchorage in the country of Ko-chih,[1] you travel north-west, and arrive [here] after three days. The country lies beside the sea. [Travelling] east from the mountains for five hundred, or seven hundred, *li*, you make a long journey through to the country of K'an-pa-i.[2] On the west [the country of Ku-li] abuts on the great sea; on the south it joins the boundary of the country of Ko-chih; [and] on the north side it adjoins the territory of the country of Hen-nu-erh.[3]

"The great country of the Western Ocean" is precisely this country.

In the fifth year of the Yung-lo [period] the court ordered[4] the principal envoy the grand eunuch Cheng Ho and others to deliver an imperial mandate to the king[5] of this country and to bestow on him a patent

---

[1] Cochin, a city in southwest India along the Arabian Sea, 80 miles south of Calicut; Ma Huan made a very slow voyage.

[2] Koyampadi, modern Coimbatore, situated in about 11° N, 77° E, 76 miles nearly due east of Calicut. In giving the distance as 500 *li*, nearly 200 miles, Ma Huan was guilty of an exaggeration.

[3] Now called Honavar, situated in 14° 16′ N, 74° 27′ E; it is on the coast, 199 miles northward from Calicut.

[4] The order was made in October 1407; but, although in nominal command of this, the second expedition, Cheng Ho did not accompany it.

[5] A new king, Mana Vikraman, had evidently succeeded since Cheng Ho was at Calicut in 1406–7 during the course of his first expedition.

conferring a title of honour, and the grant of a silver seal, [also] to promote all the chiefs and award them hats and girdles of various grades.

[So Cheng Ho] went there in command of a large fleet of treasure-
ships, and he erected a tablet with a pavilion over it and set up a stone
which said "Though the journey from this country to the Central
Country is more than a hundred thousand *li*, yet the people are very
similar, happy and prosperous, with identical customs. We have here
engraved a stone, a perpetual declaration for ten thousand ages.[6]

The king of the country is a Nan-k'un[7] man; he is a firm believer in
the Buddhist religion;[8] [and] he venerates the elephant and the ox.

The population of the country includes five classes, the Muslim
people, the Nan-K'un people, the Che-ti people, the Ko-ling people,
and the Mu-kua people.

The king of the country and the people of the country all refrain from
eating the flesh of the ox.[9] The great chiefs are Muslim people; [and] they
all refrain from eating the flesh of the pig.[10] Formerly there was a king who
made a sworn compact with the Muslim people, [saying] "You do not eat
the ox; I do not eat the pig; we will reciprocally respect the taboo,"[11] [and
this compact] has been honoured right down to the present day.

The king has cast an image of Buddha in brass; it is named Nai-na-
erh;[12] he has erected a temple of Buddha and has cast tiles of brass and
covered the dais of Buddha with them; [and] beside [the dais] a well has
been dug. Every day at dawn the king goes to [the well], draws water,
and washes [the image of] Buddha; after worshipping, he orders men to
collect the pure dung of yellow oxen; this is stirred with water in a
brass basin [until it is] like paste; [then] it is smeared all over the surface of the ground and walls inside the temple. Moreover, he has given
orders that the chiefs and wealthy personages shall also smear and
scour themselves with ox-dung every morning.

He also takes ox-dung, burns it till it is reduced to a white ash, and
grinds it to a fine powder; using a fair cloth as a small bag, he fills it
with the ash, and regularly carries it on his person. Every day at dawn,
after he has finished washing his face, he takes the ox-dung ash, stirs it
up with water, and smears it on his forehead and between his two

---

[6] Translated "May the period Yung-lo last for ever."

[7] Probably Ma Huan wrote "Nan-p'i" and meant the upper classes consisting of Brahmans and Kshatriyas.

[8] Ma Huan is mistaken; the king was a Hindu.

[9] Detestation of cow-slaughter is the most prominent outward mark of Hinduism.

[10] It is noteworthy that a Hindu ruler was employing Muslims as great officers.

[11] Since it was the king who made the compact, it would seem reasonable to prefer,
"You do not eat the pig; I do not eat the ox"; thus, they agreed to respect each others' convictions in the matter of diet. It scarcely needs to be said that the pig is anathema to Muslims.

[12] The name might be a corruption of Narayana, a name for Vishnu. All these references
to Buddha, then, must be construed as references to a Hindu deity.

thighs — thrice in each [place]. This denotes his sincerity in venerating Buddha[13] and in venerating the ox.

There is a traditional story that in olden times there was a holy man named Mou-hsieh,[14] who established a religious cult; the people knew that he was a true [man of] Heaven, and all men revered and followed him. Later the holy man went away with [others] to another place, and ordered his younger brother named Sa-mo-li[15] to govern and teach the people.

[But] his younger brother began to have depraved ideas; he made a casting of a golden calf and said "This is the holy lord; everyone who worships it will have his expectations fulfilled." He taught the people to listen to his bidding and to adore the golden ox, saying "It always excretes gold." The people got the gold, and their hearts rejoiced; and they forgot the way of Heaven; all took the ox to be the true lord.

Later Mou-hsieh the holy man returned; he saw that the multitude, misled by his younger brother Sa-mo-li, were corrupting the holy way; thereupon he destroyed the ox and wished to punish his younger brother; [and] his younger brother mounted a large elephant and vanished.

Afterwards, the people thought of him and hoped anxiously for his return. Moreover, if it was the beginning of the moon, they would say "In the middle of the moon he will certainly come," and when the middle of the moon arrived, they would say once more "At the end of the moon he will certainly come"; right down to the present day they have never ceased to hope for his return.

This is the reason why the Nan-k'un[16] people venerate the elephant and the ox.

The king has two great chiefs who administer the affairs of the country; both are Muslims.

The majority of the people in the country all profess the Muslim religion. There are twenty or thirty temples of worship, and once in seven days they go to worship. When the day arrives, the whole family fast and bathe, and attend to nothing else. In the *ssu* and *wu* periods,[17] the menfolk, old and young, go to the temple to worship. When the *wei* period[18] arrives, they disperse and return home; thereupon they carry on with their trading, and transact their household affairs.

[13] Again, a Hindu deity.

[14] "Musa" (Moses). Ma Huan alleges that the incidents occurred at Calicut. Presumably he learnt the story of Aaron and the golden calf from Arab informants. A number of Old Testament characters, including Moses, figure prominently in the Koran.

[15] "Al-Sameri" (the Samaritan), the name appearing in the Koran.

[16] Probably Ma Huan wrote "Nan-p'i," and referred to the upper classes of Brahmans and Kshatriyas.

[17] 9 A.M. to 11 A.M., and 11 A.M. to 1 P.M., respectively.

[18] 1 P.M. to 3 P.M.

The people are very honest and trustworthy. Their appearance is smart, fine, and distinguished.

Their two great chiefs received promotion and awards from the court of the Central Country.

If a treasure-ship goes there, it is left entirely to the two men to superintend the buying and selling; the king sends a chief and a Che-ti Wei-no-chi[19] to examine the account books in the official bureau; a broker comes and joins them; [and] a high officer who commands the ships discusses the choice of a certain date for fixing prices. When the day arrives, they first of all take the silk embroideries and the open-work silks, and other such goods which have been brought there, and discuss the price of them one by one; [and] when [the price] has been fixed, they write out an agreement stating the amount of the price; [this agreement] is retained by these persons.

The chief and the Che-ti, with his excellency the eunuch, all join hands together, and the broker then says "In such and such a moon on such and such a day, we have all joined hands and sealed our agreement with a hand-clasp; whether [the price] be dear or cheap, we will never repudiate it or change it."

After that, the Che-ti and the men of wealth then come bringing precious stones, pearls, corals, and other such things, so that they may be examined and the price discussed; [this] cannot be settled in a day; [if done] quickly, [it takes] one moon; [if done] slowly, [it takes] two or three moons.[20]

Once the money-price has been fixed after examination and discussion, if a pearl or other such article is purchased, the price which must be paid for it is calculated by the chief and the Wei-no-chi who carried out the original transaction; [and] as to the quantity of the hemp-silk or other such article which must be given in exchange for it, goods are given in exchange according to [the price fixed by] the original hand-clasp — there is not the slightest deviation.[21]

In their method of calculation, they do not use a calculating-plate;[22] for calculating, they use only the two hands and two feet and the twenty digits on them; and they do not make the slightest mistake; [this is] very extraordinary.

---

[19] Another observer, Kung Chen, translates "accountant," and adds that the man in question was a broker; Kung Chen further notes that "they wrote out a contract in duplicate, and each [party] kept one [document]."

[20] Presumably the goods were unloaded, unless the Chinese left one or two ships behind; at any rate, on the seventh expedition the Chinese stayed only 4 days, from 10 to 14 December 1432, at Calicut.

[21] This instructive disquisition on administrative procedure illustrates the meticulous care taken to fix the rate of exchange in times prior to the advent of the Europeans.

[22] The abacus, a wooden frame in which are fixed a number of beads strung on parallel wires; used by the Chinese for all kinds of arithmetic calculations upon the decimal system; it came into use in late Sung times.

The king uses gold of sixty per cent [purity] to cast a coin for current use; it is named a *pa-nan;*[23] the diameter of the face of each coin is three *fen* eight *li* [in terms of] our official *ts'un;*[24] it has lines[25] on the face and on the reverse; [and] it weighs one *fen* on our official steelyard.[26] He also makes a coin of silver; it is named a *ta-erh;*[27] each coin weighs about three *li;*[28] [and] this coin is used for petty transactions. . . .

The people of the country also take the silk of the silk-worm, soften it by boiling, dye it in all colours, and weave it into kerchiefs with decorative stripes at intervals; the breadth is four or five *ch'ih,* and the length one *chang* two or three *ch'ih;*[29] [and] each length is sold for one hundred gold coins.[30]

As to the pepper: the inhabitants of the mountainous countryside have established gardens, and it is extensively cultivated. When the period of the tenth moon arrives, the pepper ripens; [and] it is collected, dried in the sun, and sold. Of course, big pepper-collectors come and collect it, and take it up to the official storehouse to be stored; if there is a buyer, an official gives permission for the sale; the duty is calculated according to the amount [of the purchase price] and is paid in to the authorities. Each one *po-ho* of pepper is sold for two hundred gold coins.[31]

The Che-ti mostly purchase all kinds of precious stones and pearls, and they manufacture coral beads and other such things.

Foreign ships from every place come there; and the king of the country also sends a chief and a writer and others to watch the sales; thereupon they collect the duty and pay it in to the authorities.

The wealthy people mostly cultivate coconut trees — sometimes a thousand trees, sometimes two thousand or three thousand —; this constitutes their property.

The coconut has ten different uses. The young tree has a syrup, very sweet, and good to drink; [and] it can be made into wine by fermentation. The old coconut has flesh, from which they express oil, and make sugar, and make a foodstuff for eating. From the fibre which envelops the outside [of the nut] they make ropes for ship-building. The shell of the coconut makes bowls and makes cups; it is also good for burning to ash for

---

[23] Representing the sound *fanam*. The king was an independent sovereign minting his own coinage; but doubtless, as in 1443, he "lived in great fear" of Vijayanagar (Abdul Razzak).

[24] The diameter of the *fanam*, being 0.38 of the Chinese *ts'un* of 1.22 inches, equalled 0.46 of an English inch.

[25] Or "characters."

[26] The gold content weighed 3.45 grains or 0.00719 ounce troy.

[27] Representing the sound *tar* or *tare (tara)*.

[28] If the silver was pure, the silver content weighed 0.00359 ounce troy.

[29] The equivalent of 4 *ch'ih* was 48.9 inches; 1 *chang* 2 *ch'ih* equaled 12 feet 2.9 inches.

[30] The gold content weighed 345.375 grains or 0.7195 ounce troy.

[31] The gold content of 200 *fanam* weighed 690.751 grains or 1.439 ounces troy.

the delicate operation of inlaying[32] gold or silver. The trees are good for building houses, and the leaves are good for roofing houses.

For vegetables they have mustard plants, green ginger, turnips, car-away seeds, onions, garlic, bottle-gourds, egg-plants, cucumbers, and gourd-melons[33] — all these they have in [all] the four seasons [of the year]. They also have a kind of small gourd which is as large as [one's] finger, about two *ts'un*[34] long, and tastes like a green cucumber. Their onions have a purple skin; they resemble garlic; they have a large head and small leaves; [and] they are sold by the *chin*[35] weight.

The *mu-pieh-tzu*[36] tree is more than ten *chang* high; it forms a fruit which resembles a green persimmon and contains thirty or forty seeds; it falls of its own accord when ripe; [and] the bats, as large as hawks, all hang upside-down and rest on this tree.

They have both red and white rice, [but] barley and wheat are both absent; [and] their wheat-flour all comes from other places as merchandise for sale [here].

Fowls and ducks exist in profusion, [but] there are no geese. Their goats have tall legs and an ashen hue; they resemble donkey-foals. The water-buffaloes are not very large. Some of the yellow oxen weigh three or four hundred *chin*;[37] the people do not eat their flesh; [but] consume only the milk and cream. The people never eat rice without butter. Their oxen are cared for until they are old; [and] when they die, they are buried. The price of all kinds of sea-fish is very cheap. Deer and hares [from up] in the mountains are also for sale.

Many of the people rear peafowl. As to their other birds: they have crows, green hawks, egrets, and swallows; [but] of other kinds of birds besides these they have not a single one, great or small. The people of the country can also play and sing; they use the shell of a calabash to make a musical instrument, and copper wires to make the strings; and they play [this instrument] to accompany the singing of their foreign songs; the melodies are worth hearing.[38]

As to the popular customs and the marriage- and funeral-rites, the

---

[32] *Hsiang*, "a box," used for *hsiang*, "side rooms," which in turn is used for *hsiang*, "to inlay."

[33] *Tung kua*, "eastern gourd," the same vegetable as *tung kua*, "winter gourd."

[34] That is, 2.4 inches.

[35] That is, 1.3 pounds avoirdupois.

[36] The tree is *Momordica cochinchinensis*. The editor is indebted to Dr. J. Needham, F.R.S., for the information that *Momordica* seeds were prescribed in the form of paste for abscesses, ulcers, and wounds, as well as in other ways for other affections. The equivalent of 10 *chang* was 102 feet.

[37] The equivalent of 300 *chin* was 394.6 pounds avoirdupois.

[38] Music was cultivated at the royal courts, and numbers of musicians were employed in the temples. Conti, in his account of Vijayanagar city, records solemn singing at religious festivals, and the celebration of weddings with "banquets, songs, trumpets, and instruments muche like unto ours." The instrument referred to by Ma Huan was probably the vina, a fretted instrument of the guitar kind, which was particularly favoured by Indian musicians.

So-li people and the Muslim people each follow the ritual forms of their own class, and these are different.

The king's throne does not descend to his son, but descends to his sister's son; descent is to the sister's son [because] they consider that the offspring of the women's body alone constitutes the legal family. If the king has no elder or younger sister, [the throne] descends to his younger brother; [and] if he has no younger brother, [the throne] is yielded up to some man of merit. Such is the succession from one generation to another.

3

Chinese and European Maps

Figure 1.1 is a Chinese drawing from the Mao K'un collection, which almost certainly dates from the period of Zheng He's expeditions (1405–1434). This map is a collage representing different land masses within and adjacent to the Indian Ocean. Figure 1.2, a translation of Figure 1.1, shows that the large island in the upper right is Ceylon (Sri Lanka); the area in the upper left is the southern tip of India; the central section is the Maldive Islands; and the area at the bottom is a portion of the East African coast. These separate segments are not drawn to the same scale, and a comparison with a modern map shows that the coastlines are only rough approximations. Their placement in relation to each other, however, is relatively accurate, as are the locations identified within each segment. What do these maps reveal about the extent of Chinese maritime exploration during the early fifteenth century?

Figure 1.3 is Sebastian Münster's map of 1544. Notice how close Japan (Zipangi) is to Mexico. What does this map tell you about European knowledge of the Americas in 1544? Figure 1.4 is Edward Wright's mercator projection of 1599. What had Europeans learned of the Americas by this date? What did they still have to learn? Based on these maps, when did the Europeans discover America?

Thinking Historically

These maps are unusual primary sources because their errors and omissions are their most revealing attributes. We can see immediately on an old map what the mapmaker did not know at the time the map was rendered, and sometimes we can ascertain how he viewed the world. What do these maps reveal about their makers?

Figure 1.1 Chinese Collage Map of the Indian Ocean, c. 1420s.

Source: Ma Huan fl. 1414–1451, *Ying-yai sheng-lan. The Overall Survey of the Ocean's Shores* (1433). Translated from the Chinese text edited by Feng Ch'eng Chün; with introduction, notes, and appendices by J. V. G. Mills, Hakluyt Society, 1970.

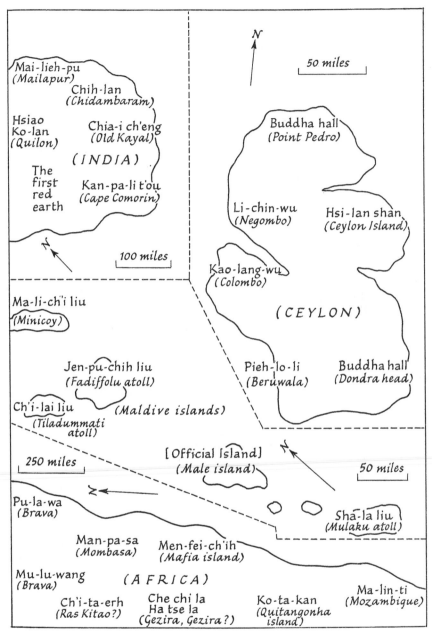

Figure 1.2 A Translation of Figure 1.1.

Source: Ma Huan, fl. 1414–1451, Ying-yai sheng-lan. The Overall Survey of the Ocean's Shores (1433). Translated from the Chinese text edited by Feng Ch'eng Chün; with introduction, notes, and appendices by J. V. G. Mills, Hakluyt Society, 1970.

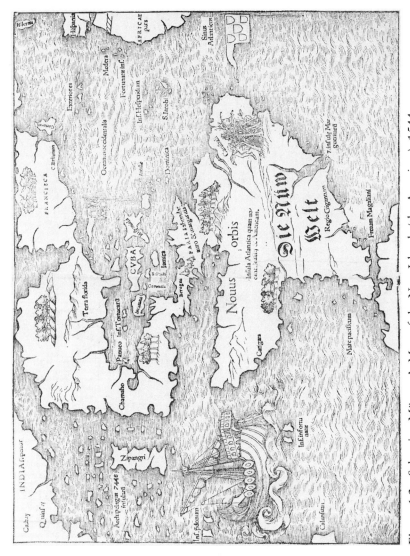

Figure 1.3 Sebastian Münster's Map of the New Islands (the Americas), 1544.
Source: Special Collections, University of Virginia Library.

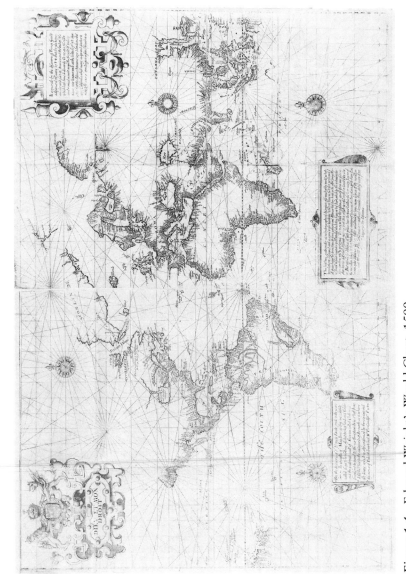

Figure 1.4 Edward Wright's World Chart, 1599.
Source: Special Collections, University of Virginia Library.

4

CHRISTOPHER COLUMBUS

Letter to King Ferdinand and Queen Isabella

Christopher Columbus sent this letter to his royal backers, King Ferdinand and Queen Isabella of Spain, on his return in March 1493 from his first voyage across the Atlantic.

An Italian sailor from Genoa, Columbus tried to make his fortune in Portugal in the 1480s. The Genoese had banking and trading contacts with Portugal, and it is possible that Columbus may have represented one of these contacts. In 1483–84 Columbus tried to convince King John II of Portugal to underwrite his plan to sail across the western ocean to the spice-rich East Indies. Relying on a Florentine map that used Marco Polo's overstated distance from Venice to Japan across Asia and an understated estimate of the circumference of the globe, Columbus believed that Japan lay only 2,500 miles west of the Portuguese Azores. King John II rejected the proposal because he had more accurate estimates that indicated sailing around Africa was shorter. In 1488 the Portuguese navigator Bartholomeu Dias returned with news that he had rounded the Cape of Good Hope, the southernmost point in Africa, which enabled him to sail to the Indies, ending any interest in Columbus's plan.

The new Spanish monarchs, Ferdinand of Aragon and Isabella of Castile, were less knowledgeable about navigation than the Portuguese king. As a result they supported Columbus and financed his plan to sail west to Asia. In four voyages, Columbus touched a number of Caribbean islands and the coast of Central America, settled Spaniards on Hispaniola (Española), and began to create one of the largest empires in world history for Spain — all the while thinking he was near China and Japan, in the realm of the Great Khan whom Marco Polo had met and who had died hundreds of years earlier.

In what ways was the voyage of Columbus similar to that of Zheng He? In what ways was it different? How were the relationships of the explorers with their kings similar and different? Were the motives driving Chinese and European expansion more alike or different?

"First Voyage of Columbus," in *The Four Voyages of Columbus*, ed. Cecil Jane (New York: Dover, 1988), 1–18.

Thinking Historically

Because this document comes from the period we are studying and is written by Columbus himself, it is a primary source. Primary sources have a great sense of immediacy and can often "transport" us to the past intellectually. However, involvement when reading does not always lead to understanding. Think critically about the source and the writer's intended audience as you read. Is the author reliable? Is the information accurate? Might the author represent a particular bias or point of view? We can only determine these things through careful analysis.

First, we must determine the source of the document. Where does it come from? Is it original? If not, is it a copy or a translation? Next, we must determine who wrote it, when it was written, and for what purpose. After answering these questions, we are able to read the document with a critical eye, which leads to greater understanding.

Now, let us analyze this selection. The original letter by Columbus has been lost. This selection is an English translation based on three different printed Spanish versions of the letter. So this text is a reconstruction, not an original, though it is believed to be quite close to the original.

The original letter was probably composed during a relaxed time on the return voyage before its date of February 15, 1493 — possibly as early as the middle of January — and sent to the Spanish monarchs from Lisbon in order to reach them by the time Columbus arrived in Barcelona.

Columbus wanted the readers — let us assume Ferdinand and Isabella — to learn that his voyage from the Canary Islands to the Indies took thirty-three days. Can we believe him? Columbus might have exaggerated his speed or, conversely, the amount of time it took; or a scribe or a printer might have gotten it wrong. As it turns out, we can believe that Columbus's trip took thirty-three days because we have another source that corroborates the information: Columbus's detailed ship's log or diary.

Of course, a close rereading of the opening sentence tells us that the amount of time the voyage took is only part of the message Columbus wanted to impart to Ferdinand and Isabella. First and foremost, he wants them to know that he reached the Indies, that the voyage was a success. And so, the letter's opening sentence tells us something that Columbus certainly did not intend or know. We learn that on his return in 1493, Columbus thought he had been to the Indies when in fact he had not. (It is due to Columbus's confusion that we call the islands he visited the West Indies and Native Americans "Indians.")

We might infer many other things from the first sentence. Did Columbus know that Ferdinand and Isabella were "pleased at the great victory with which Our Lord ha[d] crowned [his] voyage"? No, but we learn that Columbus hoped they would be and that he is writing persuasively. Do we learn that the "Lord ha[d] crowned" the voyage? No, but we learn that Columbus wanted Ferdinand and Isabella to view the voyage as a crowning success and that invoking the name of the Lord was not overreaching in his mind.

Knowing what the author wants a reader to believe is useful information because it serves as a point of reference for other statements the author makes. The success of Columbus's voyage is a case in point. Columbus does not admit to the loss of one of his ships in his letter, nor does he explain fully why he had to build a fort at Navidad and leave some of his crew there, returning home without them. Clearly, Columbus had reason to worry that his voyage would be viewed as a failure. He had not found the gold mines he sought or the Asian cities described by Marco Polo. He thought he had discovered many spices, though only the chili peppers were new. Notice, as you read this letter, how Columbus presents his voyage in the best light.

Every sentence in this letter could be closely analyzed and scrutinized, an exhausting enterprise. As you read the letter, ask yourself the following questions: What does Columbus want the reader to learn? How does he describe his voyage in positive ways? Aside from what Columbus intends, what facts do you learn from the letter about Columbus, his first voyage, and his encounter with the New World? What seems to drive Columbus to do what he does? What is Columbus's attitude toward the "Indians"? What does Columbus's letter tell us about the society and culture of the Taino — the people he met in the Caribbean?

Sir, As I know that you will be pleased at the great victory with which Our Lord has crowned my voyage, I write this to you, from which you will learn how in thirty-three days, I passed from the Canary Islands to the Indies with the fleet which the most illustrious king and queen, our sovereigns, gave to me. And there I found very many islands filled with people innumerable, and of them all I have taken possession for their highnesses, by proclamation made and with the royal standard unfurled, and no opposition was offered to me. To the first island which I found, I gave the name *San Salvador,* in remembrance of the Divine Majesty, Who has marvellously bestowed all this; the Indians call it "Guanahani." To the second, I gave the name *Isla de Santa María de Concepción;* to the third, *Fernandina;* to the fourth, *Isabella;* to the fifth, *Isla Juana,* and so to each one I gave a new name.

When I reached Juana, I followed its coast to the westward, and I found it to be so extensive that I thought that it must be the mainland, the province of Catayo. And since there were neither towns nor villages on the seashore, but only small hamlets, with the people which I could not have speech, because they all fled immediately, I went forward on the same course, thinking that I should not fail to find great cities and towns. And, at the end of many leagues, seeing that there was no change and that the coast was bearing me northwards, which I wished to avoid, since winter was already beginning and I proposed to make from it to the south, and as moreover the wind was carrying me forward, I determined not to wait for a change in the weather and retraced my path as far as a certain harbour known to me. And from that point, I sent two men inland to learn if there were a king or great cities. They travelled three days' journey and found an infinity of small hamlets and people without number, but nothing of importance. For this reason, they returned.

I understood sufficiently from other Indians, whom I had already taken, that this land was nothing but an island. And therefore I followed its coast eastwards for one hundred and seven leagues to the point where it ended. And from that cape, I saw another island, distant eighteen leagues from the former, to the east, to which I at once gave the name "Española." And I went there and followed its northern coast, as I had in the case of Juana, to the eastward for one hundred and eighty-eight great leagues in a straight line. This island and all the others are very fertile to a limitless degree, and this island is extremely so. In it there are many harbours on the coast of the sea, beyond comparison with others which I know in Christendom, and many rivers, good and large, which is marvellous. Its lands are high, and there are in it very many sierras and very lofty mountains, beyond comparison with the island of Teneriffe. All are most beautiful, of a thousand shapes, and all are accessible and filled with trees of a thousand kinds and tall, and they seem to touch the sky. And I am told that they never lose their foliage, as I can understand, for I saw them as green and as lovely as they are in Spain in May, and some of them were flowering, some bearing fruit, and some in another stage, according to their nature. And the nightingale was singing and other birds of a thousand kinds in the month of November there where I went. There are six or eight kinds of palm, which are a wonder to behold on account of their beautiful variety, but so are the other trees and fruits and plants. In it are marvellous pine groves, and there are very large tracts of cultivatable lands, and there is honey, and there are birds of many kinds and fruits in great diversity. In the interior are mines of metals, and the population is without number. Española is a marvel.

The sierras and mountains, the plains and arable lands and pastures, are so lovely and rich for planting and sowing, for breeding cattle of every kind, for building towns and villages. The harbours of the sea here are such as cannot be believed to exist unless they have been seen, and so with the rivers, many and great, and good waters, the majority of which contain gold. In the trees and fruits and plants, there is a great difference from those of Juana. In this island, there are many spices and great mines of gold and of other metals.

The people of this island, and of all the other islands which I have found and of which I have information, all go naked, men and women, as their mothers bore them, although some women cover a single place with the leaf of a plant or with a net of cotton which they make for the purpose. They have no iron or steel or weapons, nor are they fitted to use them, not because they are not well built men and of handsome stature, but because they are very marvellously timorous. They have no other arms than weapons made of canes, cut in seeding time, to the ends of which they fix a small sharpened stick. And they do not dare to make use of these, for many times it has happened that I have sent ashore two or three men to some town to have speech, and countless people have come out to them, and as soon as they have seen my men approaching they have fled, even a father not waiting for his son. And this, not because ill has been done to anyone; on the contrary, at every point where I have been and have been able to have speech, I have given to them of all that I had, such as cloth and many other things, without receiving anything for it; but so they are, incurably timid. It is true that, after they have been reassured and have lost their fear, they are so guileless and so generous with all they possess, that no one would believe it who has not seen it. They never refuse anything which they possess, if it be asked of them; on the contrary, they invite anyone to share it, and display as much love as if they would give their hearts, and whether the thing be of value or whether it be of small price, at once with whatever trifle of whatever kind it may be that is given to them, with that they are content. I forbade that they should be given things so worthless as fragments of broken crockery and scraps of broken glass, and ends of straps, although when they were able to get them, they fancied that they possessed the best jewel in the world. So it was found that a sailor for a strap received gold to the weight of two and a half *castellanos,* and others much more for other things which were worth much less. As for new *blancas,* for them they would give everything which they had, although it might be two or three *castellanos'* weight of gold or an *arroba* or two of spun cotton. . . . They took even the pieces of the broken hoops of the wine barrels and, like savages, gave what they had, so that it seemed to me to be wrong and I forbade it. And I gave a thousand handsome good things, which I had brought, in order that they might conceive affection, and more than that, might become Christians and be inclined to the love and service of their highnesses and of the whole Castilian nation, and strive to aid us and to give us of the things which they have in abundance and which are necessary to us. And they do not know any creed and are not idolaters; only they all believe that power and good are in the heavens, and they are very firmly convinced that I, with these ships and men, came from the heavens, and in this belief they everywhere received me, after they had overcome their fear. And this does not come because they are ignorant; on the contrary, they are of a very acute intelligence and are men who navigate all those seas, so that it is amazing how good an account they give of everything, but it is because they have never seen people clothed or ships of such a kind.

And as soon as I arrived in the Indies, in the first island which I found, I took by force some of them, in order that they might learn and give me information of that which there is in those parts, and so it was that they soon understood us, and we them, either by speech or signs, and they have been very serviceable. I still take them with me, and they are always assured that I come from Heaven, for all the intercourse which they have had with me; and they were the first to announce this wherever I went, and the others went running from house to house and to the neighbouring towns, with loud cries of, "Come! Come to see the people from Heaven!" So all, men and women alike, when their minds were set at rest concerning us, came, so that not one, great or small, remained behind, and all brought something to eat and drink, which they gave with extraordinary affection. In all the island, they have very many canoes, like rowing *fustas*, some larger, some smaller, and some are larger than a *fusta* of eighteen benches. They are not so broad, because they are made of a single log of wood, but a *fusta* would not keep up with them in rowing, since their speed is a thing incredible. And in these they navigate among all those islands, which are innumerable, and carry their goods. One of these canoes I have seen with seventy and eighty men in her, and each one with his oar.

In all these islands, I saw no great diversity in the appearance of the people or in their manners and language. On the contrary, they all understand one another, which is a very curious thing, on account of which I hope that their highnesses will determine upon their conversion to our holy faith, towards which they are very inclined.

I have already said how I have gone one hundred and seven leagues in a straight line from west to east along the seashore of the island Juana, and as a result of that voyage, I can say that this island is larger than England and Scotland together, for, beyond these one hundred and seven leagues, there remain to the westward two provinces to which I have not gone. One of these provinces they call "Avan," and there the people are born with tails; and these provinces cannot have a length of less than fifty or sixty leagues, as I could understand from those Indians whom I have and who know all the islands.

The other, Española, has a circumference greater than all Spain, from Colibre, by the sea-coast, to Fuenterabia in Vizcaya, since I voyaged along one side one hundred and eighty-eight great leagues in a straight line from west to east. It is a land to be desired and, seen, it is never to be left. And in it, although of all I have taken possession for their highnesses and all are more richly endowed than I know how, or am able, to say, and I hold them all for their highnesses, so that they may dispose of them as, and as absolutely as, of the kingdoms of Castile, in this Española, in the situation most convenient and in the best position for the mines of gold and for all intercourse as well with the mainland here as with that there, belonging to the Grand Khan, where will be great trade and gain, I have taken possession of a large town, to which I gave the name *Villa de Navidad,* and in it I have made fortifications and a fort, which now will by this time be entirely finished, and I have left in it sufficient men for such a purpose with arms and artillery and provisions for more than a year, and a *fusta,* and one, a master of all seacraft, to build others, and great friendship with the king of that land, so much so, that he was proud to call me, and to treat me as, a brother. And even if he were to change his attitude to one of hostility towards these men, he and his do not know what arms are and they go naked, as I have already said, and are the most timorous people that there are in the world, so that the men whom I have left there alone would suffice to destroy all that land, and the island is without danger for their persons, if they know how to govern themselves.

In all these islands, it seems to me that all men are content with one woman, and to their chief or king they give as many as twenty. It appears to me that the women work more than the men. And I have not been able to learn if they hold private property; what seemed to me to appear was that, in that which one had, all took a share, especially of eatable things.

In these islands I have so far found no human monstrosities, as many expected, but on the contrary the whole population is very well-formed, nor are they negros as in Guinea, but their hair is flowing, and they are not born where there is intense force in the rays of the sun; it is true that the sun has there great power, although it is distant from the equinoctial line twenty-six degrees. In these islands, where there are high mountains, the cold was severe this winter, but they endure it, being used to it and with the help of meats which they eat with many and extremely hot spices. As I have found no monsters, so I have had no report of any, except in an island "Quaris," the second at the coming into the Indies, which is inhabited by a people who are regarded in all the islands as very fierce and who eat human flesh. They have many canoes with which they range through all the islands of India and pillage and take as many as they can. They are no more malformed than the others, except that they have the custom of wearing their hair long like women, and they use bows and arrows of the same cane stems, with a small piece of wood at the end, owing to lack of iron which they do not possess. They are ferocious among these other people who are cowardly to an excessive degree, but I make no more account of them than of the rest. These are those who have intercourse with the women of "Matinino," which is the first island met on the way from Spain to the Indies, in which there is not a man. These women engage in no feminine occupation, but use bows and arrows of cane, like those already mentioned, and they arm and protect themselves with plates of copper, of which they have much.

In another island, which they assure me is larger than Española, the people have no hair. In it, there is gold incalculable, and from it and from the other islands, I bring with me Indians as evidence.

In conclusion, to speak only of that which has been accomplished on this voyage, which was so hasty, their highnesses can see that I will give them as much gold as they may need, if their highnesses will render me very slight assistance; moreover, spice and cotton, as much as their highnesses shall command; and mastic, as much as they shall order to be shipped and which, up to now, has been found only in Greece, in the island of Chios, and the Seignory sells it for what it pleases; and aloe wood, as much as they shall order to be shipped, and slaves, as many as they shall order to be shipped and who will be from the idolaters. And I believe that I have found rhubarb and cinnamon, and I shall find a thousand other things of value, which the people whom I have left there will have discovered, for I have not delayed at any point, so far as the wind allowed me to sail, except in the town of Navidad, in order to leave it secured and well established, and in truth, I should have done much more, if the ships had served me, as reason demanded.

This is enough . . . and the eternal God, our Lord, Who gives to all those who walk in His way triumph over things which appear to be impossible, and this was notably one; for, although men have talked or have written of these lands, all was conjectural, without suggestion of ocular evidence, but amounted only to this, that those who heard for the most part listened and judged it to be rather a fable than as having any vestige of truth. So that, since Our Redeemer has given this victory to our most illustrious king and queen, and to their renowned kingdoms, in so great a matter, for this all Christendom ought to feel delight and make great feasts and give solemn thanks to the Holy Trinity with many solemn prayers for the great exaltation which they shall have, in the turning of so many peoples to our holy faith, and afterwards for temporal benefits, for not only Spain but all Christians will have hence refreshment and gain.

This, in accordance with that which has been accomplished, thus briefly.

Done in the caravel,[1] off the Canary Islands, on the fifteenth of February, in the year one thousand four hundred and ninety-three.

At your orders.   El Almirante.

---

[1] Sailing ship, in this case the *Santa María*. [Ed.]

After having written this, and being in the sea of Castile, there came on me so great a south-south-west wind, that I was obliged to lighten ship. But I ran here to-day into this port of Lisbon, which was the greatest marvel in the world, whence I decided to write to their highnesses. In all the Indies, I have always found weather like May; where I went in thirty-three days and I had returned in twenty-eight, save for these storms which have detained me for fourteen days, beating about in this sea. Here all the sailors say that never has there been so bad a winter nor so many ships lost.

Done on the fourth day of March.

5

KIRKPATRICK SALE

From *The Conquest of Paradise*

In this selection from his popular study of Columbus, Sale is concerned with Columbus's attitude toward nature in the New World. Do you think Sale's comments are accurate? Are they insightful? Do they help us understand Columbus?

Sale regards Columbus as a symbol of European expansion. Let us for the moment grant him that. If Columbus is distinctly European, what is Sale saying about European expansion? How and what does Sale add to your understanding of the similarities and differences between Chinese and European expansion?

Was Columbus much different from Zheng He? Or were the areas and peoples they visited causes for different responses?

Thinking Historically

Clearly, this selection is a secondary source; Sale is a modern writer, not a fifteenth-century contemporary of Columbus. Still, you will not have to read very far into the selection to realize that Sale has a distinct point of view. Secondary sources, like primary ones, should be analyzed for bias and perspective and should identify the author's interpretation.

Kirkpatrick Sale, *The Conquest of Paradise* (New York: Penguin, 1991), 92–104.

Sale is an environmentalist and a cultural critic. Do his beliefs and values hinder his understanding of Columbus, or do they inform and illuminate aspects of Columbus that might otherwise be missed? Does Sale help you recognize things you would not have seen on your own, or does he persuade you to see things that might not truly be there?

Notice how Sale uses primary sources in his text. He quotes from Columbus's journal and his letter to Santangel. Do these quotes help you understand Columbus, or do they simply support Sale's argument? What do you think about Sale's use of the Spanish "Colón" for "Columbus"? Does Sale "take possession" of Columbus by, in effect, "renaming" him for modern readers? Is the effect humanizing or debunking?

Notice how Sale sometimes calls attention to what the primary source did *not* say rather than what it did say. Is this a legitimate way to understand someone, or is Sale projecting a twentieth-century perspective on Columbus to make a point?

Toward the end of the selection, Sale extends his criticism beyond Columbus to include others. Who are the others? What is the effect of this larger criticism?

Admiral Colón spent a total of ninety-six days exploring the lands he encountered on the far side of the Ocean Sea — four rather small coralline islands in the Bahamian chain and two substantial coastlines of what he finally acknowledged were larger islands — every one of which he "took possession of" in the name of his Sovereigns.

The first he named San Salvador, no doubt as much in thanksgiving for its welcome presence after more than a month at sea as for the Son of God whom it honored; the second he called Santa María de la Concepcíon, after the Virgin whose name his flagship bore; and the third and fourth he called Fernandina and Isabela, for his patrons, honoring Aragon before Castile for reasons never explained (possibly protocol, possibly in recognition of the chief sources of backing for the voyage). The first of the two large and very fertile islands he called Juana, which Fernando says was done in honor of Prince Juan, heir to the Castilian throne, but just as plausibly might have been done in recognition of Princess Juana, the unstable child who eventually carried on the line; the second he named la Ysla Española, the "Spanish Island," because it resembled (though he felt it surpassed in beauty) the lands of Castile.

It was not that the islands were in need of names, mind you, nor indeed that Colón was ignorant of the names that native peoples had already given them, for he frequently used those original names before endowing them with his own. Rather, the process of bestowing new names went along with "taking possession of" those parts of the world he deemed suitable for Spanish ownership, showing the royal banners, erecting various crosses, and pronouncing certain oaths and pledges. If this was presumption, it had an honored heritage: It was Adam who was charged by his Creator with the task of naming "every living creature," including the product of his own rib, in the course of establishing "dominion over" them.

Colón went on to assign no fewer than sixty-two other names on the geography of the islands — capes, points, mountains, ports — with a blithe assurance suggesting that in his (and Europe's) perception the act of name-giving was in some sense a talisman of conquest, a rite that changed raw neutral stretches of far-off earth into extensions of Europe. The process began slowly, even haltingly — he forgot to record, for example, until four days afterward that he named the landfall island San Salvador — but by the time he came to Española at the end he went on a naming spree, using more than two-thirds of all the titles he concocted on that one coastline. On certain days it became almost a frenzy: on December 6 he named six places, on the nineteenth six more, and on January 11 no fewer than ten — eight capes, a point, and a mountain. It is almost as if, as he sailed along the last of the islands, he was determined to leave his mark on it the only way he knew how, and thus to establish his authority — and by extension Spain's — even, as with baptism, to make it thus sanctified, and real, and official. . . .

This business of naming and "possessing" foreign islands was by no means casual. The Admiral took it very seriously, pointing out that "it was my wish to bypass no island without taking possession" (October 15) and that "in all regions [I] always left a cross standing" (November 16) as a mark of Christian dominance. There even seem to have been certain prescriptions for it (the instructions from the Sovereigns speak of "the administering of the oath and the performing of the rites prescribed in such cases"), and Rodrigo de Escobedo was sent along as secretary of the fleet explicitly to witness and record these events in detail.

But consider the implications of this act and the questions it raises again about what was in the Sovereigns' minds, what in Colón's. Why would the Admiral assume that these territories were in some way *un*possessed — even by those clearly inhabiting them — and thus available for Spain to claim? Why would he not think twice about the possibility that some considerable potentate — the Grand Khan of China, for example, whom he later acknowledged (November 6) "must be" the ruler of Española — might descend upon him at any moment with a greater military force than his three vessels commanded and punish him for his territorial presumption? Why would he make the ceremony of possession his very first act on shore, even before meeting the inhabitants or exploring the environs, or finding out if anybody there objected to being thus possessed — particularly if they actually owned the great treasures he hoped would be there? No European would have imagined that anyone — three small boatloads of Indians, say — could come up to a European shore or island and "take possession" of it, nor would a European imagine marching up to some part of North Africa or the Middle East and claiming sovereignty there with impunity. Why were these lands thought to be different?

Could there be any reason for the Admiral to assume he had reached "unclaimed" shores, new lands that lay far from the domains of any of the potentates of the East? Can that really have been in his mind — or can it all be explained as simple Eurocentrism, or Eurosuperiority, mixed with cupidity and naiveté? . . .

Once safely "possessed,"[1] San Salvador was open for inspection. Now the Admiral turned his attention for the first time to the "naked people" staring at him on the beach — he did not automatically give them a name, interestingly enough, and it would be another six days before he decided what he might call them — and tried to win their favor with his trinkets.

> They all go around as naked as their mothers bore them; and also the women, although I didn't see more than one really young girl. All that I saw were young people *[mancebos],* none of them more than 30 years old. They are very well built, with very handsome bodies and very good faces; their hair [is] coarse, almost like the silk of a horse's tail, and short. They wear their hair over their eyebrows, except for a little in the back that they wear long and never cut. Some of them paint themselves black (and they are the color of the Canary Islanders, neither black nor white), and some paint themselves white, and some red, and some with what they find. And some paint their faces, and some of them the whole body, and some the eyes only, and some of them only the nose.

It may fairly be called the birth of American anthropology.

A crude anthropology, of course, as superficial as Colón's descriptions always were when his interest was limited, but simple and straightforward enough, with none of the fable and fantasy that characterized many earlier (and even some later) accounts of new-found peoples. There was no pretense to objectivity, or any sense that these people might be representatives of a culture equal to, or in any way a model for, Europe's. Colón immediately presumed the inferiority of the natives, not merely because (a sure enough sign) they were naked, but because (his society could have no surer measure) they seemed so

---

[1] Given Spanish names. [Ed.]

technologically backward. "It appeared to me that these people were very poor in everything," he wrote on that first day, and, worse still, "they have no iron." And they went on to prove their inferiority to the Admiral by being ignorant of even such a basic artifact of European life as a sword: "They bear no arms, nor are they acquainted with them," he wrote, "for I showed them swords and they grasped them by the blade and cut themselves through ignorance." Thus did European arms spill the first drops of native blood on the sands of the New World, accompanied not with a gasp of compassion but with a smirk of superiority.

Then, just six sentences further on, Colón clarified what this inferiority meant in his eyes:

> They ought to be good servants and of good intelligence *[ingenio]*. . . . I believe that they would easily be made Christians, because it seemed to me that they had no religion. Our Lord pleasing, I will carry off six of them at my departure to Your Highnesses, in order that they may learn to speak.

No clothes, no arms, no possessions, no iron, and now no religion — not even speech: hence they were fit to be servants, and captives. It may fairly be called the birth of American slavery.

Whether or not the idea of slavery was in Colón's mind all along is uncertain, although he did suggest he had had experience as a slave trader in Africa (November 12) and he certainly knew of Portuguese plantation slavery in the Madeiras and Spanish slavery of Guanches in the Canaries. But it seems to have taken shape early and grown ever firmer as the weeks went on and as he captured more and more of the helpless natives. At one point he even sent his crew ashore to kidnap "seven head of women, young ones and adults, and three small children"; the expression of such callousness led the Spanish historian Salvador de Madariaga to remark, "It would be difficult to find a starker utterance of utilitarian subjection of man by man than this passage [whose] form is no less devoid of human feeling than its substance."

To be sure, Colón knew nothing about these people he encountered and considered enslaving, and he was hardly trained to find out very much, even if he was moved to care. But they were in fact members of an extensive, populous, and successful people whom Europe, using its own peculiar taxonomy, subsequently called "Taino" (or "Taíno"), their own word for "good" or "noble," and their response when asked who they were. They were related distantly by both language and culture to the Arawak people of the South American mainland, but it is misleading (and needlessly imprecise) to call them Arawaks, as historians are wont to do, when the term "Taino" better establishes their ethnic and historical distinctiveness. They had migrated to the islands from the mainland at about the time of the birth of Christ, occupying the three large islands we now call the Greater Antilles and arriving at

Guanahani (Colón's San Salvador) and the end of the Bahamian chain probably sometime around A.D. 900. There they displaced an earlier people, the Guanahacabibes (sometimes called Guanahatabeys), who by the time of the European discovery occupied only the western third of Cuba and possibly remote corners of Española; and there, probably in the early fifteenth century, they eventually confronted another people moving up the islands from the mainland, the Caribs, whose culture eventually occupied a dozen small islands of what are called the Lesser Antilles.

The Tainos were not nearly so backward as Colón assumed from their lack of dress. (It might be said that it was the Europeans, who generally kept clothed head to foot during the day despite temperatures regularly in the eighties, who were the more unsophisticated in garmenture — especially since the Tainos, as Colón later noted, also used their body paint to prevent sunburn.) Indeed, they had achieved a means of living in a balanced and fruitful harmony with their natural surroundings that any society might well have envied. They had, to begin with, a not unsophisticated technology that made exact use of their available resources, two parts of which were so impressive that they were picked up and adopted by the European invaders: *canoa* (canoes) that were carved and fire-burned from large silk-cotton trees, "all in one piece, and wonderfully made" (October 13), some of which were capable of carrying up to 150 passengers; and *hamaca* (hammocks) that were "like nets of cotton" (October 17) and may have been a staple item of trade with Indian tribes as far away as the Florida mainland. Their houses were not only spacious and clean — as the Europeans noted with surprise and appreciation, used as they were to the generally crowded and slovenly hovels and huts of south European peasantry — but more apropos, remarkably resistant to hurricanes; the circular walls were made of strong cane poles set deep and close together ("as close as the fingers of a hand," Colón noted), the conical roofs of branches and vines tightly interwoven on a frame of smaller poles and covered with heavy palm leaves. Their artifacts and jewelry, with the exception of a few gold trinkets and ornaments, were based largely on renewable materials, including bracelets and necklaces of coral, shells, bone, and stone, embroidered cotton belts, woven baskets, carved statues and chairs, wooden and shell utensils, and pottery of variously intricate decoration depending on period and place.

Perhaps the most sophisticated, and most carefully integrated, part of their technology was their agricultural system, extraordinarily productive and perfectly adapted to the conditions of the island environment. It was based primarily on fields of knee-high mounds, called *conucos,* planted with *yuca* (sometimes called manioc), *batata* (sweet potato), and various squashes and beans grown all together in multicrop harmony: The root crops were excellent in resisting erosion and producing minerals and potash, the leaf crops effective in providing shade and moisture, and the mound configurations largely resistant to erosion and flooding and adaptable to almost all topographic conditions including steep hillsides. Not only was the *conuco* system environmentally appropriate — "conuco agriculture seems to have provided an exceptionally ecologically well-balanced and protective form of land use," according to David Watts's recent and authoritative *West Indies* — but it was also highly productive, surpassing in yields anything known in Europe at the time, with labor that amounted to hardly more than two or three hours a week, and in continuous yearlong harvest. The pioneering American geographical scholar Carl Sauer calls Taino agriculture "productive as few parts of the world," giving the "highest returns of food in continuous supply by the simplest methods and modest labor," and adds, with a touch of regret, "The white man never fully appreciated the excellent combination of plants that were grown in conucos."

In their arts of government the Tainos seem to have achieved a parallel sort of harmony. Most villages were small (ten to fifteen families) and autonomous, although many apparently recognized loose allegiances with neighboring villages, and they were governed by a hereditary official called a *kaseke* (*cacique,* in the Spanish form), something of a cross between an arbiter and a prolocutor, supported by advisers and elders. So little a part did violence play in their system that they seem, remarkably, to have been a society without war (at least we know of no war music or signals or artifacts, and no evidence of intertribal combats) and even without overt conflict (Las Casas reports that no Spaniard ever saw two Tainos fighting). And here we come to what was obviously the Tainos' outstanding cultural achievement, a proficiency in the social arts that led those who first met them to comment unfailingly on their friendliness, their warmth, their openness, and above all — so striking to those of an acquisitive culture — their generosity.

"They are the best people in the world and above all the gentlest," Colón recorded in his *Journal* (December 16), and from first to last he was astonished at their kindness:

> They became so much our friends that it was a marvel. . . . They traded and gave everything they had, with good will [October 12].
>
> I sent the ship's boat ashore for water, and they very willingly showed my people where the water was, and they themselves carried the full barrels to the boat, and took great delight in pleasing us [October 16].
>
> They are very gentle and without knowledge of what is evil; nor do they murder or steal [November 12].
>
> Your Highnesses may believe that in all the world there can be no better or gentler people . . . for neither better people nor land can there

be. . . . All the people show the most singular loving behavior and they speak pleasantly [December 24].

I assure Your Highnesses that I believe that in all the world there is no better people nor better country. They love their neighbors as themselves, and they have the sweetest talk in the world, and are gentle and always laughing [December 25].

Even if one allows for some exaggeration — Colón was clearly trying to convince Ferdinand and Isabella that his Indians could be easily conquered and converted, should that be the Sovereigns' wish — it is obvious that the Tainos exhibited a manner of social discourse that quite impressed the rough Europeans. But that was not high among the traits of "civilized" nations, as Colón and Europe understood it, and it counted for little in the Admiral's assessment of these people. However struck he was with such behavior, he would not have thought that it was the mark of a benign and harmonious society, or that from it another culture might learn. For him it was something like the wondrous behavior of children, the naive guilelessness of prelapsarian creatures who knew no better how to bargain and chaffer and cheat than they did to dress themselves: "For a lacepoint they gave good pieces of gold the size of two fingers" (January 6), and "They even took pieces of the broken hoops of the wine casks and, like beasts *[como besti]*, gave what they had" (Santangel Letter). Like beasts; such innocence was not human.

It is to be regretted that the Admiral, unable to see past their nakedness, as it were, knew not the real virtues of the people he confronted. For the Tainos' lives were in many ways as idyllic as their surroundings, into which they fit with such skill and comfort. They were well fed and well housed, without poverty or serious disease. They enjoyed considerable leisure, given over to dancing, singing, ballgames, and sex, and expressed themselves artistically in basketry, woodworking, pottery, and jewelry. They lived in general harmony and peace, without greed or covetousness or theft. . . .

It is perhaps only natural that Colón should devote his initial attention to the handsome, naked, naive islanders, but it does seem peculiar that he pays almost no attention, especially in the early days, to the spectacular scenery around them. Here he was, in the middle of an old-growth tropical forest the likes of which he could not have imagined before, its trees reaching sixty or seventy feet into the sky, more varieties than he knew how to count much less name, exhibiting a lushness that stood in sharp contrast to the sparse and denuded lands he had known in the Mediterranean, hearing a melodious multiplicity of bird songs and parrot calls — why was it not an occasion of wonder, excitement, and the sheer joy at nature in its full, arrogant abundance? But there is not a word of that: He actually said nothing about the physical surroundings on the first day, aside from a single phrase about "very green trees" and "many streams," and on the second managed only that short sentence about a big island with a big lake and green trees. Indeed, for the whole two weeks of the first leg of his voyage through the Bahamas to Cuba, he devoted only a third of the lines of description to the phenomena around him. And there are some natural sights he seems not to have noticed at all: He did not mention (except in terms of navigation) the nighttime heavens, the sharp, glorious configurations of stars that he must have seen virtually every night of his journey, many for the first time.

Eventually Colón succumbed to the islands' natural charms as he sailed on — how could he not? — and began to wax warmly about how "these islands are very green and fertile and the air very sweet" (October 15), with "trees which were more beautiful to see than any other thing that has ever been seen" (October 17), and "so good and sweet a smell of flowers or trees from the land" (October 19). But his descriptions are curiously vapid and vague, the language opaque and lifeless:

> The other island, which is very big [October 15] . . . this island is very large [October 16] . . . these islands are very green and fertile [October 15] . . . this land is the best and most fertile [October 17] . . . in it many plants and trees . . . if the others are very beautiful, this is more so [October 19] . . . here are some great lagoons . . . big and little birds of all sorts . . . if the others already seen are very beautiful and green and fertile, this one is much more so [October 21] . . . full of very good harbors and deep rivers [October 28].

You begin to see the Admiral's problem: He cares little about the features of nature, at least the ones he doesn't use for sailing, and even when he admires them he has little experience in assessing them and less acquaintance with a vocabulary to describe them. To convey the lush density and stately grandeur of those tropical forests, for example, he had little more than the modifiers "green" and "very": "very green trees" (October 12), "trees very green" (October 13), "trees . . . so green and with leaves like those of Castile" (October 14), "very green and very big trees" (October 19), "large groves are very green" (October 21), "trees . . . beautiful and green" (October 28). And when he began to be aware of the diversity among those trees, he was still unable to make meaningful distinctions: "All the trees are as different from ours as day from night" (October 17), "trees of a thousand kinds" (October 21), "a thousand sorts of trees" (October 23), "trees . . . different from ours" (October 28), "trees of a thousand sorts" (November 14), "trees of a thousand kinds" (December 6).

Such was his ignorance — a failing he repeatedly bemoaned ("I don't recognize them, which gives me great grief," October 19) — that when he did stop to examine a species he often had no idea what he was looking at. "I saw many trees very different from ours," he wrote on October 16, "and many of them have branches of many kinds, and all on one trunk, and one twig is of one kind and another of another, and so different that it is the greatest wonder in the world how much diversity there is of one kind from the other. That is to say, one branch has leaves like a cane, and another like mastic, and thus on one tree five or six kinds, and all so different." There is no such tree in existence, much less "many of them," and never was: Why would anyone imagine, or so contrive, such a thing to be?

Colón's attempts to identify species were likewise frequently wrongheaded, usually imputing to them commercial worth that they did not have, as with the worthless "aloes" he loaded such quantities of. The "amaranth" he identified on October 28 and the "oaks" and "arbutus" of November 25 are species that do not grow in the Caribbean; the "mastic" he found on November 5 and loaded on board to sell in Spain was gumbo-limbo, commercially worthless. (On the other hand, one of the species of flora he deemed of no marketable interest — "weeds [tizon] in their hands to drink in the fragrant smoke" [November 6] — was tobacco.) Similarly, the "whales" he spotted on October 16 must have been simply large fish, the "geese" he saw on November 6 and again on December 22 were ducks, the "nightingales" that kept delighting him (November 6; December 7, 13) do not exist in the Americas, and the skulls of "cows" he identified on October 29 were probably not those of land animals but of manatees.

This all seems a little sad, revealing a man rather lost in a world that he cannot come to know, a man with a "geographic and naturalistic knowledge that doesn't turn out to be very deep or nearly complete," and "a limited imagination and a capacity for comparisons conditioned by a not very broad geographic culture," in the words of Gaetano Ferro, a Columbus scholar and professor of geography at the University of Genoa. One could not of course have expected that an adventurer and sailor of this era would also be a naturalist, or necessarily even have some genuine interest in or curiosity about the natural world, but it is a disappointment nonetheless that the Discoverer of the New World turns out to be quite so simple, quite so inexperienced, in the ways of discovering his environment.

Colón's limitations, I hasten to say, were not his alone; they were of his culture, and they would be found in the descriptions of many others — Vespucci, Cortés, Hawkins, Juet, Cartier, Champlain, Ralegh — in the century of discovery to follow. They are the source of what the distinguished English historian J. H. Elliott has called "the problem of description" faced by Europeans confronting the uniqueness of the New World: "So often the physical appearance of the New World is either totally ignored or else described in the flattest and most conventional phraseology. This off-hand treatment of nature contrasts strikingly with the many precise and acute descriptions of the native inhabitants. It is as if the American landscape is seen as no more than a backcloth against which the strange and perennially fascinating peoples of the New World are dutifully grouped." The reason, Elliott thinks, and this is telling, may be "a lack of interest among sixteenth-century Europeans, and especially those of the Mediterranean world, in landscape and in nature." This lack of interest was reflected in the lack of vocabulary, the lack of that facility common to nature-based peoples whose cultures are steeped in natural imagery. Oviedo, for example, setting out to write descriptions for his *Historia general* in the next century, continually threw his hands up in the air: "Of all the things I have seen," he said at one point, "this is the one which has most left me without hope of being able to describe it in words"; or at another, "It needs to be painted by the hand of a Berruguete or some other excellent painter like him, or by Leonardo da Vinci or Andrea Mantegna, famous painters whom I knew in Italy." Like Colón, visitor after visitor to the New World seemed mind-boggled and tongue-tied trying to convey the wonders before them, and about the only color they seem to have eyes for is green — and not very many shades of that, either. . . .

REFLECTIONS

Our opening selection by Theodore F. Cook Jr., "Zheng He and Chinese Expansion," was originally titled "The Chinese Discovery of the New World: Fifteenth Century" and published in a book edited by Robert Cowley called *What If?* Cook did not mean to suggest that Chinese treasure ships actually reached America, but historians often like to ask, "what if?" Usually the implication of a "what if" question is that things might have been very different from how they turned out. At the end of his essay, Cook imagines a Chinese presence in Africa preventing the Atlantic slave trade and blocking Portuguese access to Asia. He also imagines the Chinese fortifying the Aztec Empire in Mexico with horses, guns, and immunity from Old World diseases.

Recently, Gavin Menzies, an amateur historian, has taken the "what if" question a few steps further by arguing that the Chinese *did* in fact discover America in 1421. Menzies can make his argument partly because the primary sources for Zheng He's voyages are so thin. Not only were the official records destroyed after 1434, but the great treasure shipyards of Nanjing were leveled, coastal traffic was curtailed, and Zheng He was written out of Chinese history. Thus, Menzies builds his case on a few undigested and often unrelated unknowns. Most historians think that there are sufficient primary sources (two besides Ma Huan's account) to reject Menzies' argument, but *what if* he is right? Certainly, the history of exploration would need a major chapter on China, but the modern world would have turned out the same way. Even if Chinese did settle in Providence, Rhode Island, and Sacramento, California, in 1421, their settlement left no impact that we can discern. Thus, Menzies helps us answer Cook. It is true that *if* China had been radically different, the world might have developed differently. But a Chinese landfall in East Africa or the Americas would not have changed anything if it left no discernible trace.

That Zheng He sailed as far as East Africa has long been part of the historical record. But it was not widely known until the historian Louise Levathes published *When China Ruled the Seas* in 1994. In response to Levathes's suggestion that one of the Chinese treasure ships broke up and sank near the island of Pate off the coast of Kenya, Nicholas Kristof, a *New York Times* reporter, traveled there to look for clues. He discovered Pate islanders who looked a little Chinese and believed that they were descended from the survivors of an ancient Chinese shipwreck.

These clues are primary sources. Chinese African complexions and oral histories are primary sources, even if they are somewhat less reliable than written documents or artifacts. In any case, we know that the occupants of the treasure ships traded, fought, and negotiated with the inhabitants of Southeast Asia, Ceylon, Calicut, and other parts of India, as well as Hormuz, Mecca, and places along the East African coast as far south as Mozambique. But aside from a few exchanged genes and animals for the emperor's zoo, the Chinese did not dramatically transform the regions they visited. The significance of the European encounter with the Americas is that it did not end with Columbus but continued to the point where its impact was unmistakable. All Americans bear evidence of that encounter.

2

Europeans, Americans, and Africans in the Atlantic World

Africa and the Americas, 1500–1750

HISTORICAL CONTEXT

European expansion in the Atlantic that began with Portuguese voyages along the African coast in the 1440s and Columbus's discovery of the Americas in 1492 had by 1750 created a new Atlantic zone of human contact and communication that embraced four continents and one ocean. Until this point, nothing — neither the Chinese contacts with Africa in the early fifteenth century, nor the expansion of Islam throughout Eurasia in the almost thousand years since the Prophet Muhammad's death in 632 — had so thoroughly and so permanently changed the human and ecological balance of the world.

Sub-Saharan Africa had already been integrated into the world of Eurasia by 1450. African populations became more mixed, as peoples from the Niger River area migrated east and south throughout the continent during the fifteen hundred years before the arrival of the Portuguese. Muslims from North Africa and the Middle East had aided or established Muslim states and trading ports south of the Sahara in East and West Africa after 1000. Cultural and technical innovations of the Middle East, like the literacy that came with Islam, penetrated slowly, and the spread of the many plants and animals of the northern hemisphere was slowed by the Sahara and equator. However, microbes traveled swiftly and easily from Eurasia to Africa, creating a single set of diseases and immunities for the peoples of the Afro-Eurasian Old World.

The peoples of the Americas, having been isolated ecologically for more than a thousand years, were not so fortunate. The arrival of Europeans and Africans in the Americas after 1492 had devastating consequences for Native American populations. Old World diseases like smallpox were responsible for millions of Native American deaths — a tragedy far worse in scope than the casualties caused by wars. To work the mines and plantations of the New World, Europeans used Indian labor, but increasingly, especially for lowland plantations, they used African slaves (see Map 2.1). By 1750, the combination of Indian "die off" and African and European migration resulted in vastly different populations in the Americas. On some Caribbean islands and in plantation areas like northeastern Brazil, Indian populations were entirely replaced by Africans. At the same time, European animals (for example, goats, cattle, horses) multiplied in the absence of natural predators, in some cases entirely replacing Native Americans who were wiped out by European disease.

The new Atlantic ecological system was not a uniform zone, however. Coastal regions in Western Europe and towns on the eastern seaboard of the Americas prospered, while American interiors and African populations in Africa stagnated or declined. The Atlantic Ocean became a vast lake that united port cities and plantations with sailing ships that carried African slaves to the Caribbean, Caribbean sugar and rum to North American and European industrial ports, and guns, pots, and liquor to the African "Slave Coast."

Thus, the Atlantic world was integrated with the Old World. Trade routes that began in Boston or Bahia, Brazil, stretched across Eurasia and around southern Africa into the Indian Ocean and the China Sea. Crops that had previously been known only to Native Americans — corn, potatoes, and tomatoes — fueled population explosions from Ireland to China and graced the tables of peasants and princes in between. What began as an effort by European merchants to import Asian spices directly became after 1650 (as European tastes for pepper and Asian spices moderated) a new global pantry of possibilities.

In this chapter, we will read selections that describe some of the first contacts that led to this new global balance. We will read of Europeans in Mexico, North America, and West Africa. We will also explore some of the African and American responses to this European expansion. When reading these accounts, notice how these individuals at the frontier of a new age understand and treat each other. Consider how these initial exchanges, so apparently fortuitous and transitory at the time, changed the face of the world.

THINKING HISTORICALLY
Comparing Primary Sources

By comparing and contrasting one thing with another, we learn more about each, and by examining related works in their proper context, we learn more about the whole of which they are part. In the first chapter

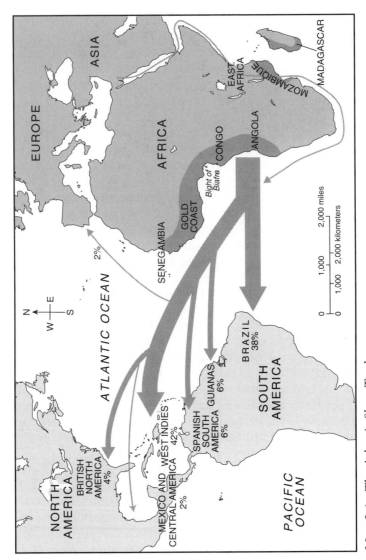

Map 2.1 The Atlantic Slave Trade.

we compared China and Europe or Chinese and European (mainly Spanish) expansion in the fifteenth century. In this chapter we look at the Atlantic world, specifically at Europeans in Africa and the Americas. We begin with two views of the Spanish conquest of Mexico — separate accounts by the Spanish conquistadors and by the Mexicans. The third selection recounts the Dutch conquest of the Algonquin nation in North America (in what is today New York City) and allows us to compare the methods of the Dutch with those of the Spanish.

The final three readings examine encounters between Europeans and Africans and the development of the Atlantic slave trade. Do Europeans treat Native Americans differently than they do Africans? If so, why?

In selection 9 an African ruler responds to the European slave trade. This account contrasts with the encounter of Europeans with the Mexican ruler, Montezuma, in selections 6 and 7. The chapter concludes with an account of a European slave trader and the memoir of an African who was enslaved. Do you notice any discrepancies in these accounts? Which is more believable and why?

6

BERNAL DÍAZ

From *The Conquest of New Spain*

Bernal Díaz del Castillo was born in Spain in 1492, the year Columbus sailed to America. After participating in two explorations of the Mexican coast, Díaz joined the expedition of Hernán Cortés to Mexico City in 1519. He wrote this history of the conquest much later, when he was in his seventies; he died circa 1580, a municipal official with a small estate in Guatemala.

The conquest of Mexico did not automatically follow from the first Spanish settlements in Santo Domingo, Hispaniola, and then Cuba in the West Indies. The Spanish crown had given permission for trade and exploration, not colonization. But the fortune-seeking peasant-soldiers whose fathers had fought to rid Spain of Muslims and Jews

Bernal Díaz, *The Conquest of New Spain*, trans. J. M. Cohen (Baltimore: Penguin Books, 1963), 217–19, 221–25, 228–38, 241–43.

were eager to conquer their own lands and develop populations of dependent Indians.

Cortés, of minor noble descent but a failed student at the University of Salamanca, sailed to the Indies at the age of nineteen, where he enjoyed a sizeable estate on the island of Hispaniola. When he heard stories of Montezuma's gold from an Indian woman who was given to him in tribute, he determined to find the fabled capital of the Aztec empire, Tenochtitlán (modern Mexico City). He gathered more than five hundred amateur soldiers, eleven ships, sixteen horses, and several pieces of artillery, then sailed across the Caribbean and Gulf of Mexico to a settlement he christened Veracruz, and there began the long march from the coast up to the high central plateau of Mexico.

The Aztecs were new to central Mexico, arriving from the North American desert only about two hundred years before the Spanish, around 1325. They settled on an island in the middle of the large lake on the central plain, shunned by the peoples of other cities who thought themselves to be more sophisticated and cultured. In less than two hundred years, this band of uncouth newcomers established dominion over almost all other city-states of Mexico, by 1500 ruling an empire that stretched as far south as Guatemala and as far east as the Mayan lands of the Yucatan Peninsula.

Aztec power relied on a combination of old and new religious ideas and a military system that conquered through terror. The older religious traditions that the Aztecs adopted were those of the classical Toltec culture at the center of which stood the god Quetzalcoatl — the feathered serpent, god of creation and brotherhood. The nurturing forces of Quetzalcoatl continued in Aztec society in a system of universal and obligatory education and in festivals dedicated to life, creativity, and procreation. But the Aztecs also celebrated a god they had brought with them from the north, Huitzilopochtli — a warrior god primed for death and sacrifice. Huitzilopochtli (rendered as Huichilobos in this selection) was given dominant status in the Aztec pantheon by Tlacaelel, an adviser behind the Aztec throne of Montezuma's predecessor, Itzcoatl (r. 1428–1440). Tlacaelel envisioned Huitzilopochtli as a force for building a powerful Aztec empire. Drawing on the god's need for human sacrifice — a need not unknown among religions of central Mexico (or Christians) — Tlacaelel built altars to Huitzilopochtli at Tenochtitlán, Cholula, and other sites. According to the tenets of the religion, the war god required a never-ending supply of human hearts, a need that prompted armies to ever-more remote sections of Central America in search of sacrificial victims and creating an endless supply of enemies of the Aztecs. Among these, the Tlaxcalans, whom the Aztecs left independent so they could be conquered at will for war captives, proved to be an eager ally of Cortés and the Spanish. As the Aztec star waned, other Mexican peoples eagerly joined the Spanish-Tlaxcalan alliance.

With the help of his Indian captive and companion Doña Marina — called La Malinche by some of the Indians (thus, Montezuma sometimes calls Cortés "Lord Malinche" in the selection) — Cortés was able to communicate with the Tlaxcalans and other Indians who were tired of Aztec domination. On his march toward Tenochtitlán, Cortés stopped to join forces with the Tlaxcalans, perhaps cementing the relationship and demonstrating his resolve through a brutal massacre of the people of Cholula, an Aztec ally and arch enemy of the Tlaxcalans. By the time Cortés arrived at Tenochtitlán, Montezuma knew of the defeat of his allies at Cholula.

This selection from Bernal Díaz begins with the Spanish entry into Tenochtitlán. What impresses Díaz, and presumably other Spanish conquistadors, about the Mexican capital city? What parts of the city attract his attention the most? What conclusions does he draw about Mexican (or Aztec) civilization? Does he think Spanish civilization is equal, inferior, or superior to that of Mexico?

Thinking Historically

Díaz gives us a dramatic account of the meeting of Cortés and Montezuma. What do you think each is thinking and feeling? Do you see any signs of tension in their elaborate greetings? Why are both behaving so politely? What do they want from each other?

Notice how the initial hospitality turns tense. What causes this? Is either side more to blame for what happens next? Was conflict inevitable? Could the encounter have ended in some sort of peaceful resolution?

Remember, we are going to compare Díaz's view with a Mexican view of these events. From your reading of Díaz, does he seem able to understand the Mexican point of view? Would you call him a sympathetic observer?

When Cortes saw, heard, and was told that the great Montezuma was approaching, he dismounted from his horse, and when he came near to Montezuma each bowed deeply to the other. Montezuma welcomed our Captain, and Cortes, speaking through Doña Marina, answered by wishing him very good health. Cortes, I think, offered Montezuma his right hand, but Montezuma refused it and extended his own. Then Cortes brought out a necklace which he had been holding. It was made of those elaborately worked and coloured glass beads called *margaritas*, . . . and was strung on a gold cord and dipped in musk to give it a good odour. This he hung round the great Montezuma's neck, and as he did so attempted to embrace him. But the great princes who stood round Montezuma grasped Cortes' arm to prevent him, for they considered this an indignity.

Then Cortes told Montezuma that it rejoiced his heart to have seen such a great prince, and that he took his coming in person to receive him and the repeated favours he had done him as a high honour. After this Montezuma made him another complimentary speech, and ordered two of his nephews who were supporting him, the lords of Texcoco and Coyoacan, to go with us and show us our quarters. Montezuma returned to the city with the other two kinsmen of his escort, the lords of Cuitlahuac and Tacuba; and all those grand companies of *Caciques*[1] and dignitaries who had come with him returned also in his train. And as they accompanied their lord we observed them marching with their eyes downcast so that they should not see him, and keeping close to the wall as they followed him with great reverence. Thus space was made for us to enter the streets of Mexico without being pressed by the crowd.

Who could now count the multitude of men, women, and boys in the streets, on the roof-tops and in canoes on the waterways, who had come out to see us? It was a wonderful sight and, as I write, it all comes before my eyes as if it had happened only yesterday.

They led us to our quarters, which were in some large houses capable of accommodating us all and had formerly belonged to the great Montezuma's father, who was called Axayacatl. Here Montezuma now kept the great shrines of his gods, and a secret chamber containing gold bars and jewels. This was the treasure he had inherited from his father, which he never touched. Perhaps their reason for lodging us here was that, since they called us *Teules*[2] and considered us as such, they wished to have us near their idols. In any case they took us to this place, where there were many great halls, and a dais hung with the cloth of their country for our Captain, and matting beds with canopies over them for each of us.

On our arrival we entered the large court, where the great Montezuma was awaiting our Captain. Taking him by the hand, the prince led him to his apartment in the hall where he was to lodge, which was very richly furnished in their manner. Montezuma had ready for him a very rich necklace, made of golden crabs, a marvellous piece of work, which he hung round Cortes' neck. His captains were greatly astonished at this sign of honour.

---

[1] Chiefs. [Ed.]
[2] Gods. [Ed.]

After this ceremony, for which Cortes thanked him through our interpreters, Montezuma said: "Malinche, you and your brothers are in your own house. Rest awhile." He then returned to his palace, which was not far off.

We divided our lodgings by companies, and placed our artillery in a convenient spot. Then the order we were to keep was clearly explained to us, and we were warned to be very much on the alert, both the horsemen and the rest of us soldiers. We then ate a sumptuous dinner which they had prepared for us in their native style.

So, with luck on our side, we boldly entered the city of Tenochtitlán or Mexico on 8 November in the year of our Lord 1519.

The Stay in Mexico

. . . Montezuma had ordered his stewards to provide us with everything we needed for our way of living: maize, grindstones, women to make our bread, fowls, fruit, and plenty of fodder for the horses. He then took leave of us all with the greatest courtesy, and we accompanied him to the street. However, Cortes ordered us not to go far from our quarters for the present until we knew better what conduct to observe.

Next day Cortes decided to go to Montezuma's palace. But first he sent to know whether the prince was busy and to inform him of our coming. He took four captains with him: Pedro de Alvarado, Juan Velazquez de Leon, Diego de Ordaz, and Gonzalo de Sandoval, and five of us soldiers.

When Montezuma was informed of our coming, he advanced into the middle of the hall to receive us, closely surrounded by his nephews, for no other chiefs were allowed to enter his palace or communicate with him except upon important business. Cortes and Montezuma exchanged bows, and clasped hands. Then Montezuma led Cortes to his own dais, and setting him down on his right, called for more seats, on which he ordered us all to sit also.

Cortes began to make a speech through our interpreters, saying that we were all now rested, and that in coming to see and speak with such a great prince we had fulfilled the purpose of our voyage and the orders of our lord the King. The principal things he had come to say on behalf of our Lord God had already been communicated to Montezuma through his three ambassadors, on that occasion in the sandhills when he did us the favour of sending us the golden moon and sun. We had then told him that we were Christians and worshipped one God alone, named Jesus Christ, who had suffered His passion and death to save us; and that what they worshipped as gods were not gods but devils, which were evil things, and if they were ugly to look at, their deeds were uglier. But he had proved to them how evil and ineffectual their gods were, as both the prince and his people would observe in the course of time, since, where we had put up crosses such as their ambassadors had seen, they had been too frightened to appear before them.

The favour he now begged of the great Montezuma was that he should listen to the words he now wished to speak. Then he very carefully expounded the creation of the world, how we are all brothers, the children of one mother and father called Adam and Eve; and how such a brother as our great Emperor, grieving for the perdition of so many souls as their idols were leading to hell, where they burnt in living flame, had sent us to tell him this, so that he might put a stop to it, and so that they might give up the worship of idols and make no more human sacrifices — for all men are brothers — and commit no more robbery or sodomy. He also promised that in the course of time the King would send some men who lead holy lives among us, much better than our own, to explain this more fully, for we had only come to give them warning. Therefore he begged Montezuma to do as he was asked.

As Montezuma seemed about to reply, Cortes broke off his speech, saying to those of us who were with him: "Since this is only the first attempt, we have now done our duty."

"My lord Malinche," Montezuma replied, "these arguments of yours have been familiar to me for some time. I understand what you said to my ambassadors on the sandhills about the three gods and the cross, also what you preached in the various towns through which you passed. We have given you no answer, since we have worshipped our own gods here from the beginning and know them to be good. No doubt yours are good also, but do not trouble to tell us any more about them at present. Regarding the creation of the world, we have held the same belief for many ages, and for this reason are certain that you are those who our ancestors predicted would come from the direction of the sunrise. As for your great King, I am in his debt and will give him of what I possess. For, as I have already said, two years ago I had news of the Captains who came in ships, by the road that you came, and said they were servants of this great king of yours. I should like to know if you are all the same people."

Cortes answered that we were all brothers and servants of the Emperor, and that they had come to discover a route and explore the seas and ports, so that when they knew them well we could follow, as we had done. Montezuma was referring to the expeditions of Francisco Hernandez de Cordoba and of Grijalva, the first voyages of discovery. He said that ever since that time he had wanted to invite some of these men to visit the cities of his kingdom, where he would receive them and do them honour, and that now his gods had fulfilled his desire, for we were in his house, which we might call our own. Here we might rest and enjoy ourselves, for we should receive good treatment. If on other occasions he had sent to forbid our entrance into his city, it was not of his own free will, but because his vassals were afraid. For they told him we shot out flashes of lightning, and killed many Indians with our horses, and that we were angry *Teules,* and other such childish stories. But now that he had seen us, he knew that we were of flesh and blood and very intelligent, also very brave. Therefore he had a far greater esteem for us than these reports had given him, and would share with us what he had.

We all thanked him heartily for his . . . good will, and Montezuma replied with a laugh, because in his princely manner he spoke very gaily: "Malinche, I know that these people of Tlascala with whom you are so friendly have told you that I am a sort of god or *Teule,* and keep nothing in any of my houses that is not made of silver and gold and precious stones. But I know very well that you are too intelligent to believe this and will take it as a joke. See now, Malinche, my body is made of flesh and blood like yours, and my houses and palaces are of stone, wood, and plaster. It is true that I am a great king, and have inherited the riches of my ancestors, but the lies and nonsense you have heard of us are not true. You must take them as a joke, as I take the story of your thunders and lightnings."

Cortes answered also with a laugh that enemies always speak evil and tell lies about the people they hate, but he knew he could not hope to find a more magnificent prince in that land, and there was good reason why his fame should have reached our Emperor.

While this conversation was going on, Montezuma quietly sent one of his nephews, a great *Cacique,* to order his stewards to bring certain pieces of gold, which had apparently been set aside as a gift for Cortes, and ten loads of fine cloaks which he divided: the gold and cloaks between Cortes and the four captains, and for each of us soldiers two gold necklaces, each worth ten pesos, and two loads of cloaks. The gold that he then gave us was worth in all more than a thousand pesos, and he gave it all cheerfully, like a great and valiant prince.

As it was now past midday and he did not wish to be importunate, Cortes said to Montezuma: "My lord, the favours you do us increase, load by load, every day, and it is now the hour of your dinner." Montezuma answered that he thanked us for visiting him. We then took our leave with the greatest courtesy, and returned to our quarters, talking as we went of the prince's fine breeding and manners and deciding to show him the greatest respect in every way, and to remove our quilted caps in his presence, which we always did.

The great Montezuma was about forty years old, of good height, well proportioned, spare and slight, and not very dark, though of the usual Indian complexion. He did not wear his hair long but just over his ears, and he had a short black beard, well-shaped and thin. His face was rather long and cheerful, he had fine eyes, and in his appearance and manner could express geniality or, when necessary, a serious composure. He was very neat and clean, and took a bath every afternoon. He had many women as his mistresses, the daughters of chieftains, but two legitimate wives who were *Caciques* in their own right, and when he had intercourse with any of them it was so secret that only some of his servants knew of it. He was quite free from sodomy. The clothes he wore one day he did not wear again till three or four days later. He had a guard of two hundred chieftains lodged in rooms beside his own, only some of whom were permitted to speak to him. When they entered his presence they were compelled to take off their rich cloaks and put on others of little value. They had to be clean and walk barefoot, with their eyes downcast, for they were not allowed to look him in the face, and as they approached they had to make three obeisances, saying as they did so, "Lord, my lord, my great lord!" Then, when they had said what they had come to say, he would dismiss them with a few words. They did not turn their backs on him as they went out, but kept their faces towards him and their eyes downcast, only turning round when they had left the room. Another thing I noticed was that when other great chiefs came from distant lands about disputes or on business, they too had to take off their shoes and put on poor cloaks before entering Montezuma's apartments; and they were not allowed to enter the palace immediately but had to linger for a while near the door, since to enter hurriedly was considered disrespectful. . . .

Montezuma had two houses stocked with every sort of weapon; many of them were richly adorned with gold and precious stones. There were shields large and small, and a sort of broadsword, and two-handed swords set with flint blades that cut much better than our swords, and lances longer than ours, with five-foot blades consisting of many knives. Even when these are driven at a buckler or a shield they are not deflected. In fact they cut like razors, and the Indians can shave their heads with them. They had very good bows and arrows, and double and single-pointed javelins as well as their throwing-sticks and many slings and round stones shaped by hand, and another sort of shield that can be rolled up when they are not fighting, so that it does not get in the way, but which can be opened when they need it in battle and covers their bodies from head to foot. There was also a great deal of cotton armour richly worked on the outside with different coloured feathers, which they used as devices and distinguishing marks, and they had casques and helmets made of wood and bone which were also highly decorated with feathers on the outside. They had other arms of different kinds which I will not mention through fear of prolixity, and workmen skilled in the manufacture of such things, and stewards who were in charge of these arms. . . .

I have already described the manner of their sacrifices. They strike open the wretched Indian's chest with flint knives and hastily tear out the palpitating heart which, with the blood, they present to the idols in whose name they have performed the sacrifice. Then they cut off the arms, thighs, and head, eating the arms and thighs at their ceremonial banquets. The head they hang up on a beam, and the body of the sacri-

ficed man is not eaten but given to the beasts of prey. They also had
many vipers in this accursed house, and poisonous snakes which have
something that sounds like a bell in their tails. These, which are the
deadliest snakes of all, they kept in jars and great pottery vessels full of
feathers, in which they laid their eggs and reared their young. They
were fed on the bodies of sacrificed Indians and the flesh of the dogs
that they bred. We know for certain, too, that when they drove us out
of Mexico and killed over eight hundred and fifty of our soldiers, they
fed those beasts and snakes on their bodies for many days, as I shall relate in due course. These snakes and wild beasts were dedicated to their
fierce idols, and kept them company. As for the horrible noise when the
lions and tigers roared, and the jackals and foxes howled, and the serpents hissed, it was so appalling that one seemed to be in hell.

I must now speak of the skilled workmen whom Montezuma employed in all the crafts they practised, beginning with the jewellers and
workers in silver and gold and various kinds of hollowed objects,
which excited the admiration of our great silversmiths at home. Many
of the best of them lived in a town called Atzcapotzalco, three miles
from Mexico. There were other skilled craftsmen who worked with
precious stones and *chalchihuites*,[3] and specialists in feather-work, and
very fine painters and carvers. We can form some judgement of what
they did then from what we can see of their work today. There are
three Indians now living in the city of Mexico, named Marcos de
Aquino, Juan de la Cruz, and El Crespillo, who are such magnificent
painters and carvers that, had they lived in the age of the Apelles of old,
or of Michael Angelo, or Berruguete in our own day, they would be
counted in the same rank.

Let us go on to the women, the weavers and sempstresses, who
made such a huge quantity of fine robes with very elaborate feather designs. These things were generally brought from some towns in the
province of Cotaxtla, which is on the north coast, quite near San Juan
de Ulua. In Montezuma's own palaces very fine cloths were woven by
those chieftains' daughters whom he kept as mistresses; and the daughters of other dignitaries, who lived in a kind of retirement like nuns in
some houses close to the great *cue*[4] of Huichilobos, wore robes entirely
of feather-work. Out of devotion for that god and a female deity who
was said to preside over marriage, their fathers would place them in religious retirement until they found husbands. They would then take
them out to be married.

Now to speak of the great number of performers whom Montezuma kept to entertain him. There were dancers and stilt-walkers,
and some who seemed to fly as they leapt through the air, and men

[3] Green stone. [Ed.]
[4] Plaza or square. [Ed.]

rather like clowns to make him laugh. There was a whole quarter full of these people who had no other occupation. He had as many workmen as he needed, too, stonecutters, masons, and carpenters, to keep his houses in repair.

We must not forget the gardens with their many varieties of flowers and sweet-scented trees planted in order, and their ponds and tanks of fresh water into which a stream flowed at one end and out of which it flowed at the other, and the baths he had there, and the variety of small birds that nested in the branches, and the medicinal and useful herbs that grew there. His gardens were a wonderful sight, and required many gardeners to take care of them. Everything was built of stone and plastered; baths and walks and closets and rooms like summerhouses where they danced and sang. There was so much to see in these gardens, as everywhere else, that we could not tire of contemplating his great riches and the large number of skilled Indians employed in the many crafts they practised. . . .

We carried our weapons, as was our custom, both by night and day. Indeed, Montezuma was so used to our visiting him armed that he did not think it strange. I say this because our Captain and those of us who had horses went to Tlatelolco mounted, and the majority of our men were fully equipped. On reaching the market-place, escorted by the many *Caciques* whom Montezuma had assigned to us, we were astounded at the great number of people and the quantities of merchandise, and at the orderliness and good arrangements that prevailed, for we had never seen such a thing before. The chieftains who accompanied us pointed everything out. Every kind of merchandise was kept separate and had its fixed place marked for it. . . .

When our Captain and the Mercedarian friar realized that Montezuma would not allow us to set up a cross at Huichilobos'[5] *cue* or build a church there, it was decided that we should ask his stewards for masons so that we could put up a church in our own quarters. For every time we had said mass since entering the city of Mexico we had had to erect an altar on tables and dismantle it again.

The stewards promised to tell Montezuma of our wishes, and Cortes also sent our interpreters to ask him in person. Montezuma granted our request and ordered that we should be supplied with all the necessary material. We had our church finished in two days, and a cross erected in front of our lodgings, and mass was said there each day until the wine gave out. For as Cortes and some other captains and a friar had been ill during the Tlascalan campaign, there had been a run on the wine that we kept for mass. Still, though it was finished, we still

---

[5] The temple of the sun god who demanded human sacrifice. [Ed.]

went to church every day and prayed on our knees before the altar and images, firstly because it was our obligation as Christians and a good habit, and secondly so that Montezuma and all his captains should observe us and, seeing us worshipping on our knees before the cross — especially when we intoned the Ave Maria — might be inclined to imitate us.

It being our habit to examine and inquire into everything, when we were all assembled in our lodging and considering which was the best place for an altar, two of our men, one of whom was the carpenter Alonso Yañez, called attention to some marks on one of the walls which showed that there had once been a door, though it had been well plastered up and painted. Now as we had heard that Montezuma kept his father's treasure in this building, we immediately suspected that it must be in this room, which had been closed up only a few days before. Yañez made the suggestion to Juan Velazquez de Leon and Francisco de Lugo, both relatives of mine, to whom he had attached himself as a servant; and they mentioned the matter to Cortes. So the door was secretly opened, and Cortes went in first with certain captains. When they saw the quantity of golden objects — jewels and plates and ingots — which lay in that chamber they were quite transported. They did not know what to think of such riches. The news soon spread to the other captains and soldiers, and very secretly we all went in to see. The sight of all that wealth dumbfounded me. Being only a youth at the time and never having seen such riches before, I felt certain that there could not be a store like it in the whole world. We unanimously decided that we could not think of touching a particle of it, and that the stones should immediately be replaced in the doorway, which should be blocked again and cemented just as we had found it. We resolved also that not a word should be said about this until times changed, for fear Montezuma might hear of our discovery.

Let us leave this subject of the treasure and tell how four of our most valiant captains took Cortes aside in the church, with a dozen soldiers who were in his trust and confidence, myself among them, and asked him to consider the net or trap in which we were caught, to look at the great strength of the city and observe the causeways and bridges, and remember the warnings we had received in every town we had passed through that Huichilobos had counselled Montezuma to let us into the city and kill us there. We reminded him that the hearts of men are very fickle, especially among the Indians, and begged him not to trust the good will and affection that Montezuma was showing us, because from one hour to another it might change. If he should take it into his head to attack us, we said, the stoppage of our supplies of food and water, or the raising of any of the bridges, would render us helpless. Then, considering the vast army of warriors he possessed, we should be incapable of attacking or defending ourselves. And since all the houses stood in the water, how could our Tlascalan allies come in to help us? We asked him to think over all that we had said, for if we wanted to preserve our lives we must seize Montezuma immediately, without even a day's delay. We pointed out that all the gold Montezuma had given us, and all that we had seen in the treasury of his father Axayacatl, and all the food we ate was turning to poison in our bodies, for we could not sleep by night or day or take any rest while these thoughts were in our minds. If any of our soldiers gave him less drastic advice, we concluded, they would be senseless beasts charmed by the gold and incapable of looking death in the eye.

When he had heard our opinion, Cortes answered: "Do not imagine, gentlemen, that I am asleep or that I do not share your anxiety. You must have seen that I do. But what strength have we got for so bold a course as to take this great lord in his own palace, surrounded as he is by warriors and guards? What scheme or trick can we devise to prevent him from summoning his soldiers to attack us at once?"

Our captains (Juan Velazquez de Leon, Diego de Ordaz, Gonzalo de Sandoval, and Pedro de Alvarado) replied that Montezuma must be got out of his palace by smooth words and brought to our quarters. Once there, he must be told that he must remain as a prisoner, and that if he called out or made any disturbance he would pay for it with his life. If Cortes was unwilling to take this course at once, they begged him for permission to do it themselves. With two very dangerous alternatives before us, the better and more profitable thing, they said, would be to seize Montezuma rather than wait for him to attack us. Once he did so, what chance would we have? Some of us soldiers also remarked that Montezuma's stewards who brought us our food seemed to be growing insolent, and did not serve us as politely as they had at first. Two of our Tlascalan allies had, moreover, secretly observed to Jeronimo de Aguilar that for the last two days the Mexicans had appeared less well disposed to us. We spent a good hour discussing whether or not to take Montezuma prisoner, and how it should be done. But our final advice, that at all costs we should take him prisoner, was approved by our Captain, and we then left the matter till next day. All night we prayed God to direct events in the interests of His holy service. . . .

From *The Broken Spears:*
The Aztec Account of
the Conquest of Mexico

This Aztec account of the encounter between the Spanish and the Indians of Mexico was written some years after the events described. Spanish Christian monks helped a postconquest generation of Aztec Nahuatl speakers translate the illustrated manuscripts of the conquest period. According to this account, how did Montezuma respond to Cortés? Was Montezuma's attitude toward the Spanish shared by other Aztecs? How reliable is this account, do you think, in describing Montezuma's thoughts, motives, and behavior?

Thinking Historically

How does the Aztec account of the conquest differ from that of the Spanish, written by Díaz? Is this difference merely a matter of perspective, or do the authors disagree about what happened? To the extent to which there are differences, how do you decide which account to believe and accept?

Speeches of Motecuhzoma and Cortes

When Motecuhzoma had given necklaces to each one, Cortes asked him: "Are you Motecuhzoma? Are you the king? Is it true that you are the king Motecuhzoma?"

And the king said: "Yes, I am Motecuhzoma." Then he stood up to welcome Cortes; he came forward, bowed his head low and addressed him in these words: "Our lord, you are weary. The journey has tired you, but now you have arrived on the earth. You have come to your city, Mexico. You have come here to sit on your throne, to sit under its canopy.

"The kings who have gone before, your representatives, guarded it and preserved it for your coming. The kings Itzcoatl, Motecuhzoma the Elder, Axayacatl, Tizoc and Ahuitzol ruled for you in the City of Mexico. The people were protected by their swords and sheltered by their shields.

The Broken Spears: The Aztec Account of the Conquest of Mexico, ed. Miguel Leon-Portilla (Boston: Beacon Press, 1990), 64–76.

"Do the kings know the destiny of those they left behind, their posterity? If only they are watching! If only they can see what I see!

"No, it is not a dream. I am not walking in my sleep. I am not seeing you in my dreams. . . . I have seen you at last! I have met you face to face! I was in agony for five days, for ten days, with my eyes fixed on the Region of the Mystery. And now you have come out of the clouds and mists to sit on your throne again.

"This was foretold by the kings who governed your city, and now it has taken place. You have come back to us; you have come down from the sky. Rest now, and take possession of your royal houses. Welcome to your land, my lords!"

When Motecuhzoma had finished, La Malinche translated his address into Spanish so that the Captain could understand it. Cortes replied in his strange and savage tongue, speaking first to La Malinche: "Tell Motecuhzoma that we are his friends. There is nothing to fear. We have wanted to see him for a long time, and now we have seen his face and heard his words. Tell him that we love him well and that our hearts are contented."

Then he said to Motecuhzoma: "We have come to your house in Mexico as friends. There is nothing to fear."

La Malinche translated this speech and the Spaniards grasped Motecuhzoma's hands and patted his back to show their affection for him.

Attitudes of the Spaniards and the Native Lords

The Spaniards examined everything they saw. They dismounted from their horses, and mounted them again, and dismounted again, so as not to miss anything of interest.

The chiefs who accompanied Motecuhzoma were: Cacama, king of Tezcoco; Tetlepanquetzaltzin, king of Tlacopan; Itzcuauhtzin the Tlacochcalcatl, lord of Tlatelolco; and Topantemoc, Motecuhzoma's treasurer in Tlatelolco. These four chiefs were standing in a file.

The other princes were: Atlixcatzin [chief who has taken captives][1]; Tepeoatzin, The Tlacochcalcatl; Quetzalaztatzin, the keeper of the chalk; Totomotzin; Hecateupatiltzin; and Cuappiatzin.

When Motecuhzoma was imprisoned, they all went into hiding. They ran away to hide and treacherously abandoned him!

[1] Military title given to a warrior who had captured four enemies.

The Spaniards Take Possession of the City

When the Spaniards entered the Royal House, they placed Motecuh-zoma under guard and kept him under their vigilance. They also placed a guard over Itzcuauhtzin, but the other lords were permitted to depart.

Then the Spaniards fired one of their cannons, and this caused great confusion in the city. The people scattered in every direction; they fled without rhyme or reason; they ran off as if they were being pursued. It was as if they had eaten the mushrooms that confuse the mind, or had seen some dreadful apparition. They were all overcome by terror, as if their hearts had fainted. And when night fell, the panic spread through the city and their fears would not let them sleep.

In the morning the Spaniards told Motecuhzoma what they needed in the way of supplies: tortillas, fried chickens, hens' eggs, pure water, firewood, and charcoal. Also: large, clean cooking pots, water jars, pitchers, dishes, and other pottery. Motecuhzoma ordered that it be sent to them. The chiefs who received this order were angry with the king and no longer revered or respected him. But they furnished the Spaniards with all the provisions they needed — food, beverages, and water, and fodder for the horses.

The Spaniards Reveal Their Greed

When the Spaniards were installed in the palace, they asked Motecuh-zoma about the city's resources and reserves and about the warriors' ensigns and shields. They questioned him closely and then demanded gold.

Motecuhzoma guided them to it. They surrounded him and crowded close with their weapons. He walked in the center, while they formed a circle around him.

When they arrived at the treasure house called Teucalco, the riches of gold and feathers were brought out to them: ornaments made of quetzal feathers, richly worked shields, disks of gold, the necklaces of the idols, gold nose plugs, gold greaves and bracelets and crowns.

The Spaniards immediately stripped the feathers from the gold shields and ensigns. They gathered all the gold into a great mound and set fire to everything else, regardless of its value. Then they melted down the gold into ingots. As for the precious green stones, they took only the best of them; the rest were snatched up by the Tlaxcaltecas. The Spaniards searched through the whole treasure house, questioning and quarreling, and seized every object they thought was beautiful.

The Seizure of
Motecuhzoma's Treasures

Next they went to Motecuhzoma's storehouse, in the place called Toto-calco [Place of the Palace of the Birds],[2] where his personal treasures were kept. The Spaniards grinned like little beasts and patted each other with delight.

When they entered the hall of treasures, it was as if they had arrived in Paradise. They searched everywhere and coveted everything; they were slaves to their own greed. All of Motecuhzoma's possessions were brought out: fine bracelets, necklaces with large stones, ankle rings with little gold bells, the royal crowns and all the royal finery — everything that belonged to the king and was reserved to him only. They seized these treasures as if they were their own, as if this plunder were merely a stroke of good luck. And when they had taken all the gold, they heaped up everything else in the middle of the patio.

La Malinche called the nobles together. She climbed up to the palace roof and cried: "Mexicanos, come forward! The Spaniards need your help! Bring them food and pure water. They are tired and hungry; they are almost fainting from exhaustion! Why do you not come forward? Are you angry with them?"

The Mexicans were too frightened to approach. They were crushed by terror and would not risk coming forward. They shied away as if the Spaniards were wild beasts, as if the hour were midnight on the blackest night of the year. Yet they did not abandon the Spaniards to hunger and thirst. They brought them whatever they needed, but shook with fear as they did so. They delivered the supplies to the Spaniards with trembling hands, then turned and hurried away.

The Preparations for the Fiesta

The Aztecs begged permission of their king to hold the fiesta of Huitzilopochtli. The Spaniards wanted to see this fiesta to learn how it was celebrated. A delegation of the celebrants came to the palace where Motecuhzoma was a prisoner, and when their spokesman asked his permission, he granted it to them.

---

[2] The zoological garden attached to the royal palaces.

As soon as the delegation returned, the women began to grind seeds of the *chicalote*.[3] These women had fasted for a whole year. They ground the seeds in the patio of the temple.

The Spaniards came out of the palace together, dressed in armor and carrying their weapons with them. They stalked among the women and looked at them one by one; they stared into the faces of the women who were grinding seeds. After this cold inspection, they went back into the palace. It is said that they planned to kill the celebrants if the men entered the patio.

The Statue of Huitzilopochtli

On the evening before the fiesta of Toxcatl, the celebrants began to model a statue of Huitzilopochtli. They gave it such a human appearance that it seemed the body of a living man. Yet they made the statue with nothing but a paste made of the ground seeds of the chicalote, which they shaped over an armature of sticks.

When the statue was finished, they dressed it in rich feathers, and they painted crossbars over and under its eyes. They also clipped on its earrings of turquoise mosaic; these were in the shape of serpents, with gold rings hanging from them. Its nose plug, in the shape of an arrow, was made of gold and was inlaid with fine stones.

They placed the magic headdress of hummingbird feathers on its head. They also adorned it with an *anecuyotl*, which was a belt made of feathers, with a cone at the back. Then they hung around its neck an ornament of yellow parrot feathers, fringed like the locks of a young boy. Over this they put its nettle-leaf cape, which was painted black and decorated with five clusters of eagle feathers.

Next they wrapped it in its cloak, which was painted with skull and bones, and over this they fastened its vest. The vest was painted with dismembered human parts: skulls, ears, hearts, intestines, torsos, breasts, hands, and feet. They also put on its *maxtlatl*, or loincloth, which was decorated with images of dissevered limbs and fringed with amate paper. This *maxtlatl* was painted with vertical stripes of bright blue.

They fastened a red paper flag at its shoulder and placed on its head what looked like a sacrificial flint knife. This too was made of red paper; it seemed to have been steeped in blood.

The statue carried a *tehuehuelli*, a bamboo shield decorated with four clusters of fine eagle feathers. The pendant of this shield was blood-red, like the knife and the shoulder flag. The statue also carried four arrows.

---

[3] Edible plants also used in medicines.

Finally, they put the wristbands on its arms. These bands, made of coyote skin, were fringed with paper cut into little strips.

The Beginning of the Fiesta

Early the next morning, the statue's face was uncovered by those who had been chosen for that ceremony. They gathered in front of the idol in single file and offered it gifts of food, such as round seedcakes or perhaps human flesh. But they did not carry it up to its temple on top of the pyramid.

All the young warriors were eager for the fiesta to begin. They had sworn to dance and sing with all their hearts, so that the Spaniards would marvel at the beauty of the rituals.

The procession began, and the celebrants filed into the temple patio to dance the Dance of the Serpent. When they were all together in the patio, the songs and the dance began. Those who had fasted for twenty days and those who had fasted for a year were in command of the others; they kept the dancers in file with their pine wands. (If anyone wished to urinate, he did not stop dancing, but simply opened his clothing at the hips and separated his clusters of heron feathers.)

If anyone disobeyed the leaders or was not in his proper place they struck him on the hips and shoulders. Then they drove him out of the patio, beating him and shoving him from behind. They pushed him so hard that he sprawled to the ground, and they dragged him outside by the ears. No one dared to say a word about this punishment, for those who had fasted during the year were feared and venerated; they had earned the exclusive title "Brothers of Huitzilopochtli."

The great captains, the bravest warriors, danced at the head of the files to guide the others. The youths followed at a slight distance. Some of the youths wore their hair gathered into large locks, a sign that they had never taken any captives. Others carried their headdresses on their shoulders; they had taken captives, but only with help.

Then came the recruits, who were called "the young warriors." They had each captured an enemy or two. The others called to them: "Come, comrades, show us how brave you are! Dance with all your hearts!"

The Spaniards Attack the Celebrants

At this moment in the fiesta, when the dance was loveliest and when song was linked to song, the Spaniards were seized with an urge to kill the celebrants. They all ran forward, armed as if for battle. They closed the entrances and passageways, all the gates of the patio: the Eagle Gate in the lesser palace, the Gate of the Canestalk and the Gate of the

Serpent of Mirrors. They posted guards so that no one could escape, and then rushed into the Sacred Patio to slaughter the celebrants. They came on foot, carrying their swords and their wooden or metal shields.

They ran in among the dancers, forcing their way to the place where the drums were played. They attacked the man who was drumming and cut off his arms. Then they cut off his head, and it rolled across the floor.

They attacked all the celebrants, stabbing them, spearing them, striking them with their swords. They attacked some of them from behind, and these fell instantly to the ground with their entrails hanging out. Others they beheaded: they cut off their heads, or split their heads to pieces.

They struck others in the shoulders, and their arms were torn from their bodies. They wounded some in the thigh and some in the calf. They slashed others in the abdomen, and their entrails all spilled to the ground. Some attempted to run away, but their intestines dragged as they ran; they seemed to tangle their feet in their own entrails. No matter how they tried to save themselves, they could find no escape.

Some attempted to force their way out, but the Spaniards murdered them at the gates. Others climbed the walls, but they could not save themselves. Those who ran into the communal houses were safe there for a while; so were those who lay down among the victims and pretended to be dead. But if they stood up again, the Spaniards saw them and killed them.

The blood of the warriors flowed like water and gathered into pools. The pools widened, and the stench of blood and entrails filled the air. The Spaniards ran into the communal houses to kill those who were hiding. They ran everywhere and searched everywhere; they invaded every room, hunting and killing.

DAVID PIETERZEN DeVRIES

A Dutch Massacre of the Algonquins

David Pieterzen DeVries was a ship's captain who became a landlord or "patroonship" holder in the Dutch colony of New Amsterdam (now New York). After a disastrous venture to establish a farming and whaling colony, Swanendael on the Delaware River (near modern Philadelphia), he was granted the first patroonship on Staten Island. There he had frequent contact with the Algonquin and Raritan Indians. He was a member of the Board of Directors (the Twelve Men), responsible to the Dutch West India Company for the governance of New Amsterdam. When in 1642, a new governor, Dutch merchant Willem Kieft, urged increased settlement and Indian removal, DeVries urged caution. He described what happened in February 1643 in his book, *Voyages from Holland to America.*

Why did DeVries oppose the governor's plan to attack the Algonquins? What does his story suggest about Dutch-Indian relations before 1643? What were the consequences of the massacre?

Thinking Historically

How is the Dutch treatment of the Algonquins different from the Spanish treatment of the Mexicans? What accounts for these differences?

Do you think an Algonquin account of this encounter would be significantly different from that of DeVries? How might it differ?

The 24th of February, sitting at a table with the Governor, he began to state his intentions, that he had a mind to *wipe the mouths* of the savages; that he had been dining at the house of Jan Claesen Damen, where Maryn Adriaensen and Jan Claesen Damen, together with Jacob Planck, had presented a petition to him to begin this work. I answered him that they were not wise to request this; that such work could not be done without the approbation of the Twelve Men; that it could not take place without my assent, who was one of the Twelve Men; that moreover I was the first patroon, and no one else hitherto had risked

David Pieterzen DeVries, *Voyages from Holland to America, A.D. 1632–1644,* trans. H. C. Murphy (New York: Billing Brothers, 1853), 114–17.

there so many thousands, and also his person, as I was the first to come from Holland or Zeeland to plant a colony; and that he should consider what profit he could derive from this business, as he well knew that on account of trifling with the Indians we had lost our colony in the South River at Swanendael, in the Hoere-kil, with thirty-two men, who were murdered in the year 1630; and that in the year 1640, the cause of my people being murdered on Staten Island was a difficulty which he had brought on with the Raritan Indians, where his soldiers had for some trifling thing killed some savages. . . . But it appeared that my speaking was of no avail. He had, with his comurderers, determined to commit the murder, deeming it a Roman deed, and to do it without warning the inhabitants in the open lands that each one might take care of himself against the retaliation of the savages, for he could not kill all the Indians. When I had expressed all these things in full, sitting at the table, and the meal was over, he told me he wished me to go to the large hall, which he had been lately adding to his house. Coming to it, there stood all his soldiers ready to cross the river to Pavonia to commit the murder. Then spoke I again to Governor Willem Kieft: "Let this work alone; you wish to break the mouths of the Indians, but you will also murder our own nation, for there are none of the settlers in the open country who are aware of it. My own dwelling, my people, cattle, corn, and tobacco will be lost." He answered me, assuring me that there would be no danger; that some soldiers should go to my house to protect it. But that was not done. So was this business begun between the 25th and 26th of February in the year 1643. I remained that night at the Governor's, sitting up. I went and sat by the kitchen fire, when about midnight I heard a great shrieking, and I ran to the ramparts of the fort, and looked over to Pavonia. Saw nothing but firing, and heard the shrieks of the savages murdered in their sleep. I returned again to the house by the fire. Having sat there awhile, there came an Indian with his squaw, whom I knew well, and who lived about an hour's walk from my house, and told me that they two had fled in a small skiff, which they had taken from the shore at Pavonia; that the Indians from Fort Orange had surprised them; and that they had come to conceal themselves in the fort. I told them that they must go away immediately; that this was no time for them to come to the fort to conceal themselves; that they who had killed their people at Pavonia were not Indians, but the Swannekens, as they call the Dutch, had done it. They then asked me how they should get out of the fort. I took them to the door, and there was no sentry there, and so they betook themselves to the woods. When it was day the soldiers returned to the fort, having massacred or murdered eighty Indians, and considering they had done a deed of Roman valor, in murdering so many in their sleep; where infants were torn from their mothers' breasts, and hacked to pieces in the presence of the parents, and the pieces thrown into the fire and in the water, and other sucklings, being bound to small boards, were cut, stuck, and pierced, and miserably massacred in a manner to move a heart of stone. Some were thrown into the river, and when the fathers and mothers endeavored to save them, the soldiers would not let them come on land but made both parents and children drown — children from five to six years of age, and also some old and decrepit persons. Those who fled from this onslaught, and concealed themselves in the neighboring sedge, and when it was morning, came out to beg a piece of bread, and to be permitted to warm themselves, were murdered in cold blood and tossed into the fire or the water. Some came to our people in the country with their hands, some with their legs cut off, and some holding their entrails in their arms, and others had such horrible cuts and gashes, that worse than they were could never happen. And these poor simple creatures, as also many of our own people, did not know any better than that they had been attacked by a party of other Indians — the Maquas. After this exploit, the soldiers were rewarded for their services, and Director Kieft thanked them by taking them by the hand and congratulating them. At another place, on the same night, on Corler's Hook near Corler's plantation, forty Indians were in the same manner attacked in their sleep, and massacred there in the same manner. Did the Duke of Alva in the Netherlands ever do anything more cruel? This is indeed a disgrace to our nation, who have so generous a governor in our Fatherland as the Prince of Orange, who has always endeavored in his wars to spill as little blood as possible. As soon as the savages understood that the Swannekens had so treated them, all the men whom they could surprise on the farmlands, they killed; but we have never heard that they have ever permitted women or children to be killed. They burned all the houses, farms, barns, grain, haystacks, and destroyed everything they could get hold of. So there was an open destructive war begun. They also burnt my farm, cattle, corn, barn, tobacco-house, and all the tobacco. My people saved themselves in the house where I alone lived, which was made with embrasures, through which they defended themselves. Whilst my people were in alarm the savage whom I had aided to escape from the fort in the night came there, and told the other Indians that I was a good chief, that I had helped him out of the fort, and that the killing of the Indians took place contrary to my wish. Then they all cried out together to my people that they would not shoot them; that if they had not destroyed my cattle they would not do it, nor burn my house; that they would let my little brewery stand, though they wished to get the copper kettle, in order to make darts for their arrows; but hearing now that it had been done contrary to my wish, they all went away, and left my house unbesieged. When now the Indians had destroyed so many farms and men in revenge for their people, I went to Governor Willem Kieft, and asked him if it was not as I had said it would be, that he would only effect the spilling of Christian blood. Who would now compensate us for our losses? But he gave me no answer. He said he wondered that no Indians came to the fort. I told him that I did not wonder at it; "why should the Indians come here where you have so treated them?"

┌─────┐
│ 9 │
└─────┘

NZINGA MBEMBA

Appeal to the King of Portugal

Europeans were unable to conquer Africa as they did the Americas until the end of the nineteenth century. Rivers that fell steeply to the sea, military defenses, and diseases like malaria proved insurmountable to Europeans before the age of the steamship, the machine gun, and quinine pills. Before the last half of the nineteenth century, Europeans had to be content with alliances with African kings and rulers. The Portuguese had been the first to meet Africans in the towns and villages along the Atlantic coast, and they became the first European missionaries and trading partners.

Nzinga Mbemba, whose Christian name was Affonso, was king of the west African state of Congo (comprising what is today parts of Angola as well as the two Congo states) from about 1506 to 1543. He succeeded his father, King Nzinga a Kuwu who, shortly after their first Portuguese contact in 1483, sent officials to Lisbon to learn European ways. In 1491 father and son were baptized, and Portuguese priests, merchants, artisans, and soldiers were provided with a coastal settlement.

What exactly is the complaint of the King of Congo? What seems to be the impact of Portuguese traders (factors) in the Congo? What does King Affonso want the King of Portugal to do?

Thinking Historically

This selection offers an opportunity to compare European expansion in the Americas and Africa. Portuguese contact with Nzinga Mbemba

Basil Davidson, *The African Past* (Boston: Little, Brown, and Company, 1964), 191–94.

of the Congo was roughly contemporaneous with the Spanish expedition to Mexico. What differences do you see between these two cases of early European expansion? Can you think of any reasons that Congo kings converted to Christianity while Mexican kings did not?

Compare the European treatment of Africans with their treatment of Native Americans. Why did Europeans enslave Africans and not, for the most part, American Indians?

Sir, Your Highness [of Portugal] should know how our Kingdom is being lost in so many ways that it is convenient to provide for the necessary remedy, since this is caused by the excessive freedom given by your factors and officials to the men and merchants who are allowed to come to this Kingdom to set up shops with goods and many things which have been prohibited by us, and which they spread throughout our Kingdoms and Domains in such an abundance that many of our vassals, whom we had in obedience, do not comply because they have the things in greater abundance than we ourselves; and it was with these things that we had them content and subjected under our vassalage and jurisdiction, so it is doing a great harm not only to the service of God, but to the security and peace of our Kingdoms and State as well.

And we cannot reckon how great the damage is, since the mentioned merchants are taking every day our natives, sons of the land and the sons of our noblemen and vassals and our relatives, because the thieves and men of bad conscience grab them wishing to have the things and wares of this Kingdom which they are ambitious of; they grab them and get them to be sold; and so great, Sir, is the corruption and licentiousness that our country is being completely depopulated, and Your Highness should not agree with this nor accept it as in your service. And to avoid it we need from those [your] Kingdoms no more than some priests and a few people to teach in schools, and no other goods except wine and flour for the holy sacrament. That is why we beg of Your Highness to help and assist us in this matter, commanding your factors that they should not send here either merchants or wares, because it is *our will that in these Kingdoms there should not be any trade of slaves nor outlet for them.*[1] Concerning what is referred above, again we beg of Your Highness to agree with it, since otherwise we cannot remedy such an obvious damage. Pray Our Lord in His mercy to have Your Highness under His guard and let you do for ever the things of His service. I kiss your hands many times.

---

[1] Emphasis in the original.

At our town of Congo, written on the sixth day of July.
João Teixeira did it in 1526.
The King. Dom Affonso.
[On the back of this letter the following can be read:
To the most powerful and excellent prince Dom João, King our Brother.]

Moreover, Sir, in our Kingdoms there is another great inconvenience which is of little service to God, and this is that many of our people [*naturaes*], keenly desirous as they are of the wares and things of your Kingdoms, which are brought here by your people, and in order to satisfy their voracious appetite, seize many of our people, freed and exempt men; and very often it happens that they kidnap even noblemen and the sons of noblemen, and our relatives, and take them to be sold to the white men who are in our Kingdoms; and for this purpose they have concealed them; and others are brought during the night so that they might not be recognized.

And as soon as they are taken by the white men they are immediately ironed and branded with fire, and when they are carried to be embarked, if they are caught by our guards' men the whites allege that they have bought them but they cannot say from whom, so that it is our duty to do justice and to restore to the freemen their freedom, but it cannot be done if your subjects feel offended, as they claim to be.

And to avoid such a great evil we passed a law so that any white man living in our Kingdoms and wanting to purchase goods in any way should first inform three of our noblemen and officials of our court whom we rely upon in this matter, and these are Dom Pedro Manipanza and Dom Manuel Manissaba, our chief usher, and Gonçalo Pires our chief freighter, who should investigate if the mentioned goods are captives or free men, and if cleared by them there will be no further doubt nor embargo for them to be taken and embarked. But if the white men do not comply with it they will lose the aforementioned goods. And if we do them this favor and concession it is for the part Your Highness has in it, since we know that it is in your service too that these goods are taken from our Kingdom, otherwise we should not consent to this. . . .

Sir, Your Highness has been kind enough to write to us saying that we should ask in our letters for anything we need, and that we shall be provided with everything, and as the peace and the health of our Kingdom depend on us, and as there are among us old folks and people who have lived for many days, it happens that we have continuously many and different diseases which put us very often in such a weakness that we reach almost the last extreme; and the same happens to our children, relatives, and natives owing to the lack in this country of physicians and surgeons who might know how to cure properly such diseases. And as we have got neither dispensaries nor drugs which might help us in this forlornness, many of those who had been already confirmed and instructed in the holy faith of Our Lord Jesus Christ perish and die; and the rest of the people in their majority cure themselves with herbs and breads and other ancient methods, so that they put all their faith in the mentioned herbs and ceremonies if they live, and believe that they are saved if they die; and this is not much in the service of God.

And to avoid such a great error and inconvenience, since it is from God in the first place and then from your Kingdoms and from Your Highness that all the good and drugs and medicines have come to save us, we beg of you to be agreeable and kind enough to send us two physicians and two apothecaries and one surgeon, so that they may come with their drug-stores and all the necessary things to stay in our kingdoms, because we are in extreme need of them all and each of them. We shall do them all good and shall benefit them by all means, since they are sent by Your Highness, whom we thank for your work in their coming. We beg of Your Highness as a great favor to do this for us, because besides being good in itself it is in the service of God as we have said above.

$$10$$

WILLEM BOSMAN

Slave Trader

Willem Bosman was the chief agent of the Dutch West India Company on the African coast. Here, in a letter to a friend in Holland, he explains how slaves were bought to Whydah, an English fort on the coast of Dahomey (between the Gold Coast of Ghana and the slave coast of Nigeria). Bosman discusses various ways in which he received slaves. What were these ways? Which does he seem to prefer?

Willem Bosman, *A New and Accurate Description of the Coast of Guinea, Divided into the Gold, Slave, and the Ivory Coasts*, trans. from Dutch, 2nd ed. (London: 1721), 339–45.

Thinking Historically

Compare Bosman's description of the slave trade with that of Nzinga Mbemba in the preceding selection. How do you account for the differences? Are they due to Dutch and Portuguese practice, to policies of the Congo and Dahomey, or to the passage of time between 1526 and 1700?

The author, a Dutchman, makes certain comparisons between Dutch slave ships and those of other Europeans. Do you see any evidence for his claims?

The first business of one of our factors [agents] when he comes to Fida [Whydah], is to satisfy the customs of the king and the great men, which amounts to about a hundred pounds in Guinea value, as the goods must yield there. After which we have free license to trade, which is published throughout the whole land by the crier.

But yet before we can deal with any person, we are obliged to buy the king's whole stock of slaves at a set price, which is commonly one third or one fourth higher than ordinary; after which, we obtain free leave to deal with all his subjects, of what rank soever. But if there happen to be no stock of slaves, the factor must then resolve to run the risk of trusting the inhabitants with goods to the value of one or two hundred slaves; which commodities they send into the inland country, in order to buy with them slaves at all markets, and that sometimes two hundred miles deep in the country. For you ought to be informed, that markets of men are here kept in the same manner as those of beasts with us.

Not a few in our country fondly imagine that parents here sell their children, men their wives, and one brother the other. But those who think so, do deceive themselves; for this never happens on any other account but that of necessity, or some great crime; but most of the slaves that are offered to us, are prisoners of war, which are sold by the victors as their booty.

When these slaves come to Fida, they are put in prison all together; and when we treat concerning buying them, they are all brought out together in a large plain; where, by our surgeons, whose province it is, they are thoroughly examined, even to the smallest member, and that naked, both men and women, without the least distinction or modesty. Those that are approved as good, are set on one side; and the lame or faulty are set by as invalids, which are here called *mackrons*: these are such as are above five and thirty years old, or are maimed in the arms, legs, or feet; have lost a tooth, are grey-haired, or have films over their eyes; as well as all those which are affected with any venereal distemper, or several other diseases.

The invalids and the maimed being thrown out, as I have told you, the remainder are numbered, and it is entered who delivered them. In the meanwhile, a burning iron, with the arms or name of the companies, lies in the fire, with which ours are marked on the breast. This is done that we may distinguish them from the slaves of the English, French, or others (which are also marked with their mark), and to prevent the Negroes exchanging them for worse, at which they have a good hand. I doubt not but this trade seems very barbarous to you, but since it is followed by mere necessity, it must go on; but we yet take all possible care that they are not burned too hard, especially the women, who are more tender than the men.

We are seldom long detained in the buying of these slaves, because their price is established, the women being one fourth or fifth part cheaper than the men. The disputes which we generally have with the owners of these slaves are, that we will not give them such goods as they ask for them, especially the *boesies* [cowry shells] (as I have told you, the money of this country) of which they are very fond, though we generally make a division on this head, in order to make one part of the goods help off another; because those slaves which are paid for in *boesies,* cost the company one half more than those bought with other goods. . . .

When we have agreed with the owners of the slaves, they are returned to their prison; where, from that time forwards, they are kept at our charge, cost us two pence a day a slave; which serves to subsist them, like our criminals, on bread and water: so that to save charges, we send them on board our ships with the very first opportunity, before which their masters strip them of all they have on their backs; so that they come to us stark-naked, as well women as men: in which condition they are obliged to continue, if the master of the ship is not so charitable (which he commonly is) as to bestow something on them to cover their nakedness.

You would really wonder to see how these slaves live on board; for though their number sometimes amounts to six or seven hundred, yet by the careful management of our masters of ships, they are so [well] regulated, that it seems incredible. And in this particular our nation exceeds all other Europeans; for as the French, Portuguese, and English slave-ships are always foul and stinking; on the contrary, ours are for the most part clean and neat.

The slaves are fed three times a day with indifferent good victuals, and much better than they eat in their own country. Their lodging place is divided into two parts; one of which is appointed for the men, the other for the women, each sex being kept apart. Here they lie as close together as it is possible for them to be crowded.

We are sometimes sufficiently plagued with a parcel of slaves which come from a far inland country, who very innocently persuade one another, that we buy them only to fatten, and afterwards eat them as a delicacy. When we are so unhappy as to be pestered with many of this sort, they resolve and agree together (and bring over the rest of their party) to run away from the ship, kill the Europeans, and set the vessel ashore; by which means they design to free themselves from being our food.

I have twice met with this misfortune; and the first time proved very unlucky to me, I not in the least suspecting it; but the uproar was timely quashed by the master of the ship and myself, by causing the abettor to be shot through the head, after which all was quiet.

But the second time it fell heavier on another ship, and that chiefly by the carelessness of the master, who having fished up the anchor of a departed English ship, had laid it in the hold where the male slaves were lodged, who, unknown to any of the ship's crew, possessed themselves of a hammer, with which, in a short time they broke all their fetters in pieces upon the anchor: After this, they came above deck, and fell upon our men, some of whom they grievously wounded, and would certainly have mastered the ship, if a French and English ship had not very fortunately happened to lie by us; who perceiving by our firing a distressed-gun, that something was in disorder on board, immediately came to our assistance with shallops and men, and drove the slaves under deck: notwithstanding which, before all was appeased, about twenty of them were killed.

The Portuguese have been more unlucky in this particular than we; for in four years time they lost four ships in this manner.

11

OLAUDAH EQUIANO

Enslaved Captive

This selection is part of the autobiography of an enslaved African, Olaudah Equiano. He was born in 1745 in what is today Nigeria, sold to British slavers at the age of eleven, and shipped off to the British West Indies. In 1766 he was able to buy his freedom and became involved in the antislavery movement in England. What was slavery in Africa like, and how did it differ from slavery in the Americas? For

"Olaudah Equiano of the Niger Ibo," ed. G. I. Jones, in *Africa Remembered,* ed. Philip D. Curtin (Madison: University of Wisconsin Press, 1967), 60–98.

those, like Equiano, who survived, what were the worst aspects of the Atlantic slave trade? What do you think of Equiano's criticism of "nominal Christians"?

Thinking Historically

Compare Equiano's attitude toward slavery with one of the other authors' in this chapter. Is Equiano opposed to all forms of slavery or only to certain kinds of slavery? How does Equiano's attitude compare with others you have read in this chapter?

I hope the reader will not think I have trespassed on his patience in introducing myself to him with some account of the manners and customs of my country. They had been implanted in me with great care, and made an impression on my mind, which time could not erase, and which all the adversity and variety of fortune I have since experienced served only to rivet and record; for, whether the love of one's country be real or imaginary, or a lesson of reason, or an instinct of nature, I still look back with pleasure on the first scenes of my life, though that pleasure has been for the most part mingled with sorrow.

My father, besides many slaves, had a numerous family, of which seven lived to grow up, including myself and a sister, who was the only daughter. As I was the youngest of the sons, I became, of course, the greatest favourite with my mother, and was always with her; and she used to take particular pains to form my mind. I was trained up from my earliest years in the arts of agriculture and war: My daily exercise was shooting and throwing javelins; and my mother adorned me with emblems, after the manner of our greatest warriors. In this way I grew up till I was turned the age of eleven, when an end was put to my happiness in the following manner: — Generally, when the grown people in the neighbourhood were gone far in the fields to labour, the children assembled together in some of the neighbour's premises to play; and commonly some of us used to get up a tree to look out for any assailant, or kidnapper, that might come upon us; for they sometimes took those opportunities of our parents' absence, to attack and carry off as many as they could seize. One day, as I was watching at the top of a tree in our yard, I saw one of those people come into the yard of our next neighbour but one, to kidnap, there being many stout young people in it. Immediately, on this, I gave the alarm of the rogue, and he was surrounded by the stoutest of them, who entangled him with cords, so that he could not escape till some of the grown people came and secured him. But alas! ere long, it was my fate to be thus attacked, and to be carried off, when none of the grown people were nigh. One day, when all our people were gone out to their works as usual, and only I and my dear sister were left to mind the house, two men and a woman got over our walls, and in a moment seized us both; and, without giving us time to cry out, or make resistance, they stopped our mouths, and ran off with us into the nearest wood. Here they tied our hands, and continued to carry us as far as they could, till night came on, when we reached a small house, where the robbers halted for refreshment, and spent the night. We were then unbound; but were unable to take any food; and, being quite overpowered by fatigue and grief, our only relief was some sleep, which allayed our misfortune for a short time. The next morning we left the house, and continued travelling all the day. For a long time we had kept the woods, but at last we came into a road which I believed I knew. I had now some hopes of being delivered; for we had advanced but a little way before I discovered some people at a distance, on which I began to cry out for their assistance, but my cries had no other effect than to make them tie me faster and stop my mouth, and then they put me into a large sack. They also stopped my sister's mouth, and tied her hands; and in this manner we proceeded till we were out of sight of these people. When we went to rest the following night they offered us some victuals; but we refused them; and the only comfort we had was in being in one another's arms all that night, and bathing each other with our tears. But alas! We were soon deprived of even the smallest comfort of weeping together. The next day proved a day of greater sorrow than I had yet experienced; for my sister and I were then separated, while we lay clasped in each other's arms: it was in vain that we besought them not to part us: she was torn from me, and immediately carried away, while I was left in a state of distraction not to be described. I cried and grieved continually; and for several days did not eat any thing but what they forced into my mouth. At length, after many days travelling, during which I had often changed masters, I got into the hands of a chieftain, in a very pleasant country. This man had two wives and some children, and they all used me extremely well, and did all they could to comfort me; particularly the first wife, who was something like my mother. Although I was a great many days journey from my father's house, yet these people spoke exactly the same language with us. This first master of mine, as I may call him, was a smith; and my principal employment was working his bellows, which were the same kind as I had seen in my vicinity. They were in some respects not unlike the stoves here in gentlemen's kitchens; and were covered over with leather; and in the middle of that leather a stick was fixed, and a person stood up, and worked it, in the same manner as is done to pump water out of a cask with a hand pump. I believe it was gold he worked, for it was of a lovely bright yellow colour, and was worn by the women on their wrists and ankles. . . .

Soon after this my master's only daughter and child by his first wife sickened and died, which affected him so much that for some time he was almost frantic, and really would have killed himself, had he not been watched and prevented. However, in a small time afterwards he recovered; and I was again sold. I was now carried to the left of the sun's rising, through many dreary wastes and dismal woods, amidst the hideous roarings of wild beasts. The people I was sold to used to carry me very often, when I was tired, either on their shoulders or on their backs. I saw many convenient well-built sheds along the roads, at proper distances, to accommodate the merchants and travellers, who lay in those buildings along with their wives, who often accompany them; and they always go well armed.

From the time I left my own nation I always found somebody that understood me till I came to the sea coast. The languages of different nations did not totally differ, nor were they so copious as those of the Europeans, particularly the English. They were therefore easily learned; and, while I was journeying thus through Africa, I acquired two or three different tongues. . . .

I came to a town called Timnah, in the most beautiful country I had yet seen in Africa. It was extremely rich, and there were many rivulets which flowed through it, and supplied a large pond in the centre of the town, where the people washed. Here I first saw and tasted cocoa nuts, which I thought superior to any nuts I had ever tasted before; and the trees, which were loaded, were also interspersed amongst the houses, which had commodious shades adjoining, and were in the same manner as ours, the insides being neatly plastered and white-washed. Here I also saw and tasted for the first time sugar-cane. Their money consisted of little white shells, the size of the fingernail: they were known in this country by the name of core.[1] I was sold here for one hundred and seventy-two of them by a merchant who lived and brought me there. I had been about two or three days at his house, when a wealthy widow, a neighbour of his, came there one evening, and brought with her an only son, a young gentleman about my own age and size. Here they saw me: and, having taken a fancy to me, I was bought of the merchant, and went home with them. Her house and premises were situated close to one of those rivulets I have mentioned, and were the finest I ever saw in Africa: they were very extensive, and she had a number of slaves to attend her. The next day I was washed

---

[1] Cowrie, a seashell obtained from the Maldive Islands and used as currency in many parts of West Africa. [Ed.]

and perfumed, and when mealtime came, I was led into the presence of my mistress, and ate and drank before her with her son. This filled me with astonishment; and I could scarce help expressing my surprise that the young gentleman should suffer me, who was bound, to eat with him who was free; and not only so, but that he would not at any time either eat or drink till I had taken first, because I was the eldest, which was agreeable to our custom. Indeed every thing here, and all their treatment of me, made me forget that I was a slave. The language of these people resembled ours so nearly, that we understood each other perfectly. They had also the very same customs as we. There were likewise slaves daily to attend us, while my young master and I, with other boys, sported with our darts and bows and arrows, as I had been used to do at home. In this resemblance to my former happy state, I passed about two months, and I now began to think I was to be adopted into the family, and was beginning to be reconciled to my situation, and to forget by degrees my misfortunes, when all at once the delusion vanished; for, without the least previous knowledge, one morning early, while my dear master and companion was still asleep, I was awakened out of my reverie to fresh sorrow, and hurried away even amongst the uncircumcised.

Thus, at the very moment I dreamed of the greatest happiness, I found myself most miserable; and it seemed as if fortune wished to give me this taste of joy only to render the reverse more poignant. The change I now experienced was as painful as it was sudden and unexpected. It was a change indeed from a state of bliss to a scene which is inexpressible by me, as it discovered to me an element I had never before beheld, and till then had no idea of, and wherein such instances of hardship and fatigue continually occurred as I can never reflect on but with horror.

The first object which saluted my eyes when I arrived on the coast was the sea, and a slaveship, which was then riding at anchor, and waiting for its cargo. These filled me with astonishment, which was soon converted into terror, which I am yet at a loss to describe, nor the then feelings of my mind. When I was carried on board I was immediately handled, and tossed up, to see if I were sound, by some of the crew; and I was now persuaded that I had got into a world of bad spirits, and that they were going to kill me. Their complexions too differing so much from ours, their long hair, and the language they spoke, which was very different from any I had ever heard, united to confirm me in this belief. Indeed, such were the horrors of my views and fears at the moment, that, if ten thousand worlds had been my own, I would have freely parted with them all to have exchanged my condition with that of the meanest slave in my own country. When I looked round the ship too, and saw a large furnace of copper boiling, and a multitude of black people of every description chained together, every one of their countenances expressing dejection and sorrow, I no longer doubted of my fate; and, quite overpowered with horror and anguish, I fell motionless on the deck and fainted. When I recovered a little, I found some black people about me, who I believed were some of those who brought me on board, and had been receiving their pay; they talked to me in order to cheer me, but all in vain. I asked them if we were not to be eaten by those white men with horrible looks, red faces, and long hair. They told me I was not; and one of the crew brought me a small portion of spirituous liquor in a wine-glass; but, being afraid of him, I would not take it out of his hand. One of the blacks therefore took it from him, and gave it to me, and I took a little down my palate, which, instead of reviving me, as they thought it would, threw me into the greatest consternation at the strange feeling it produced having never tasted any such liquor before. Soon after this, the blacks who brought me on board went off, and left me abandoned to despair. I now saw myself deprived of all chance of returning to my native country, or even the least glimpse of hope of gaining the shore, which I now considered as friendly; and I even wished for my former slavery, in preference to my present situation, which was filled with horrors of every kind, still heightened by my ignorance of what I was to undergo. I was not long suffered to indulge my grief; I was soon put down under the decks, and there I received such a salutation in my nostrils as I had never experienced in my life; so that, with the loathsomeness of the stench, and crying together, I became so sick and low that I was not able to eat, nor had I the least desire to taste any thing. I now wished for the last friend, death, to relieve me; but soon, to my grief, two of the white men offered me eatables; and, on my refusing to eat, one of them held me fast by the hands, and laid me across, I think, the windlass, and tied my feet while the other flogged me severely. I had never experienced any thing of this kind before; and, although not being used to the water, I naturally feared that element the first time I saw it; yet, nevertheless, could I have got over the nettings, I would have jumped over the side; but I could not; and, besides, the crew used to watch us very closely who were not chained down to the decks, lest we should leap into the water: and I have seen some of these poor African prisoners most severely cut for attempting to do so, and hourly whipped for not eating. This indeed was often the case with myself. In a little time after, amongst the poor chained men, I found some of my own nation, which in a small degree gave ease to my mind. I inquired of them what was to be done with us? They gave me to understand we were to be carried to these white people's country to work for them. I then was a little revived, and thought, if it were no worse than working, my situation was not so desperate: but still I feared I should be put to death, the white people looked and acted, as I thought, in so savage a manner; for I had never seen among any people such instances of brutal cruelty; and this not only shown towards us blacks, but also to some of the whites themselves. One white man in particular I saw, when we were permitted to be on deck, flogged[2] so unmercifully with a large rope near the foremast, that he died in consequence of it; and they tossed him over the side as they would have done a brute. This made me fear these people the more; and I expected nothing less than to be treated in the same manner. I could not help expressing my fears and apprehensions to some of my countrymen: I asked them if these people had no country, but lived in this hollow place the ship? They told me they did not, but came from a distant one. "Then," said I, "how comes it in all our country we never heard of them?" They told me, because they lived so very far off. I then asked, where were their women? Had they any like themselves? I was told they had. "And why," said I, "do we not see them?" They answered, because they were left behind. I asked how the vessel could go? They told me they could not tell; but that there were cloth put upon the masts by the help of the ropes I saw, and then the vessel went on; and the white men had some spell or magic they put in the water when they liked in order to stop the vessel. I was exceedingly amazed at this account, and really thought they were spirits. I therefore wished much to be from amongst them, for I expected they would sacrifice me: but my wishes were vain; for we were so quartered that it was impossible for any of us to make our escape. While we stayed on the coast I was mostly on deck; and one day, to my great astonishment, I saw one of these vessels coming in with the sails up. As soon as the whites saw it, they gave a great shout, at which we were amazed; and the more so as the vessel appeared larger by approaching nearer. At last she came to an anchor in my sight, and when the anchor was let go, I and my countrymen who saw it were lost in astonishment to observe the vessel stop; and were now convinced it was done by magic. Soon after this the other ship got her boats out, and they came on board of us, and the people of both ships seemed very glad to see each other. Several of the strangers also shook hands with us black people, and made motions with their hands, signifying, I suppose, we were to go to their country; but we did not understand them. At last, when the ship we were in had got in all her cargo, they made ready with many fearful noises, and we were all put under deck, so that we could not see how they managed the vessel. But this disappointment was the least of my sorrow. The stench of the hold while we were on the coast was so intolerably loathsome, that it was dangerous to remain there for any time, and some of us had been permitted to stay on the deck for the fresh air; but now that the whole ship's cargo were confined together, it became absolutely pestilential. The closeness of the place, and the heat of the

---

[2] Such brutal floggings were at this time considered essential to the maintenance of discipline in the British navy and on ships engaged in the slave trade. [Ed.]

climate, added to the number in the ship, which was so crowded that each had scarcely room to turn himself, almost suffocated us. This produced copious perspirations, so that the air soon became unfit for respiration, from a variety of loathsome smells, and brought on a sickness amongst the slaves, of which many died, thus falling victims to the improvident avarice, as I may call it, of their purchasers. This wretched situation was again aggravated by the galling of the chains, now become insupportable; and the filth of the necessary tubs, into which the children often fell, and were almost suffocated. The shrieks of the women, and the groans of the dying, rendered the whole a scene of horror almost inconceivable. Happily perhaps for myself I was soon reduced so low here that it was thought necessary to keep me almost always on deck; and from my extreme youth I was not put in fetters. In this situation I expected every hour to share the fate of my companions, some of whom were almost daily brought upon deck at the point of death, which I began to hope would soon put an end to my miseries. Often did I think many of the inhabitants of the deep much more happy than myself; I envied them the freedom they enjoyed, and as often wished I could change my condition for theirs. Every circumstance I met with served only to render my state more painful, and heighten my apprehensions and my opinion of the cruelty of the whites. One day they had taken a number of fishes; and when they had killed and satisfied themselves with as many as they thought fit, to our astonishment who were on the deck, rather than give any of them to us to eat, as we expected, they tossed the remaining fish into the sea again, although we begged and prayed for some as well as we could, but in vain; and some of my countrymen, being pressed by hunger, took an opportunity, when they thought no one saw them, of trying to get a little privately; but they were discovered, and the attempt procured them some very severe floggings.

One day, when we had a smooth sea, and moderate wind, two of my wearied countrymen, who were chained together (I was near them at the time), preferring death to such a life of misery, somehow made through the nettings, and jumped into the sea; immediately another quite dejected fellow, who, on account of his illness, was suffered to be out of irons, also followed their example; and I believe many more would very soon have done the same, if they had not been prevented by the ship's crew, who were instantly alarmed. Those of us that were the most active were in a moment put down under the deck; and there was such a noise and confusion amongst the people of the ship as I never heard before, to stop her, and get the boat out to go after the slaves. However, two of the wretches were drowned, but they got the other, and afterwards flogged him unmercifully, for thus attempting to prefer death to slavery. In this manner we continued to undergo more hardships than I can now relate; hardships which are inseparable from this accursed trade. Many a time we were near suffocation, from the want of fresh air, which we were often without for whole days together. This, and the stench of the necessary tubs, carried off many. During our passage I first saw flying fishes, which surprised me very much: They used frequently to fly across the ship, and many of them fell on the deck. I also now first saw the use of the quadrant. I had often with astonishment seen the mariners make observations with it, and I could not think what it meant. They at last took notice of my surprise; and one of them, willing to increase it, as well as to gratify my curiosity, made me one day look through it. The clouds appeared to me to be land, which disappeared as they passed along. This heightened my wonder, and I was now more persuaded than ever that I was in another world, and that every thing about me was magic. At last, we came in sight of the island of Barbadoes, at which the whites on board gave a great shout, and made many signs of joy to us. We did not know what to think of this; but, as the vessel drew nearer, we plainly saw the harbour, and other ships of different kinds and sizes; and we soon anchored amongst them off Bridge Town. Many merchants and planters now come on board, though it was in the evening. They put us in separate parcels, and examined us attentively. They also made us jump, and pointed to the land, signifying we were to go there. We thought by this we should be eaten by these ugly men, as they appeared to us; and when, soon after we were all put down under the deck again, there was much dread and trembling among us, and nothing but bitter cries to be heard all the night from these apprehensions, insomuch that at last the white people got some old slaves from the land to pacify us. They told us we were not to be eaten, but to work, and were soon to go on land where we should see many of our country people. This report eased us much; and sure enough, soon after we landed, there came to us Africans of all languages. We were conducted immediately to the merchant's yard, where we were all pent up together like so many sheep in a fold, without regard to sex or age. As every object was new to me, everything I saw filled me with surprise. What struck me first was, that the houses were built with bricks, in stories, and in every other respect different from those I have seen in Africa; but I was still more astonished on seeing people on horseback. I did not know what this could mean; and indeed I thought these people were full of nothing but magical arts. While I was in this astonishment, one of my fellow prisoners spoke to a countryman of his about the horses, who said they were the same kind they had in their country. I understood them, though they were from a distant part of Africa, and I thought it odd I had not seen any horses there; but afterwards, when I came to converse with different Africans, I found they had many horses amongst them, and much larger than those I then saw. We were not many days in the merchant's custody, before we were sold after their usual manner, which is this:

On a signal given (as the beat of a drum), the buyers rush at once into the yard where the slaves are confined, and make choice of that parcel they like best. The noise and clamour with which this is attended, and the eagerness visible in the countenances of the buyers, serve not a little to increase the apprehension of the terrified Africans, who may well be supposed to consider them as the ministers of that destruction to which they think themselves devoted. In this manner, without scruple, are relations and friends separated, most of them never to see each other again. I remember in the vessel in which I was brought over, in the men's apartment, there were several brothers who, in the sale, were sold in different lots; and it was very moving on this occasion to see and hear their cries at parting. O, ye nominal Christians! Might not an African ask you, learned you this from your God? Who says unto you, Do unto all men as you would men should do unto you. Is it not enough that we are torn from our country and friends to toil for your luxury and lust of gain? Must every tender feeling be likewise sacrificed to your avarice? Are the dearest friends and relations, now rendered more dear by their separation from their kindred, still to be parted from each other, and thus preventing from cheering the gloom of slavery with the small comfort of being together, and mingling their sufferings and sorrows? Why are parents to love their children, brothers their sisters, or husbands their wives? Surely this is a new refinement in cruelty, which, while it has no advantage to atone for it, thus aggravates distress, and adds fresh horrors even to the wretchedness of slavery.

REFLECTIONS

This chapter asks you to compare European encounters with Native Americans and Africans. Why did Europeans enslave Africans and not, for the most part, American Indians? Because so many Africans were brought to the Americas to work on plantations, this topic is especially compelling.

Initially, of course, Indians *were* enslaved. Recall the letter of Columbus (selection 4). Part of the reason this enslavement did not continue was the high mortality of Native Americans exposed to smallpox and Old World diseases. In addition, Native Americans who survived the bacterial onslaught had the "local knowledge" and support needed to escape from slavery.

Above and beyond this were the humanitarian objections of Spanish priests like Bartolomeo de Las Casas and the concerns of the Spanish monarchy that slavery would increase the power of the conquistadors at the expense of the crown. In 1542, the enslavement of Indians was outlawed in Spanish dominions of the New World. Clearly, these

"New Laws" were not always obeyed by Spaniards in the Americas or by the Portuguese subjects of the unified Spanish-Portuguese crown between 1580 and 1640. Still, the different legal positions of Africans and Indians in the minds of Europeans require further explanation.

Some scholars have suggested that the difference in treatment lies in the differing needs of the main European powers involved in the encounter. The anthropologist Marvin Harris makes the argument this way:

> The most plausible explanation of the New Laws [of 1542] is that they represented the intersection of the interests of three power groups: the Church, the Crown, and the colonists. All three of these interests sought to maximize their respective control over the aboriginal populations. Outright enslavement of the Indians was the method preferred by the colonists. But neither the Crown nor the Church could permit this to happen without surrendering their own vested and potential interests in the greatest resource of the New World — its manpower.

Why then did they permit and even encourage the enslavement of Africans? In this matter all three power groups stood to gain. Africans who remained in Africa were of no use to anybody, since effective military and political domination of that continent by Europeans was not achieved until the middle of the nineteenth century. To make use of African manpower, Africans had to be removed from their homelands. The only way to accomplish this was to buy them as slaves from dealers on the coast. For both the Crown and the Church, it was better to have Africans under the control of the New World colonists than to have to have Africans under the control of nobody but Africans.[1]

What do you think of this argument? Does it work for Portugal as well as for Spain? Does it explain the behavior of the Protestant Dutch or English? Can you offer an alternative explanation?

Finally, let us return to the more global perspective of the first chapter. We have not explored Chinese expansion in the same detail as we did European expansion, but a few comparisons might be possible. First, was slavery unique to European expansion, or was it practiced in the course of Chinese expansion as well? Remember the distinction between China's northern neighbors (Mongols and Manchus) and its trading partners of the Southeast; how did China treat these two regions differently? Was the difference between Chinese treatment of the Mongols and Chinese treatment of the peoples of the Southeast (India, Hormuz, and East Africa) similar to the difference between European treatment of Africans and Native Americans?

[1] Marvin Harris, *Patterns of Race in the Americas* (New York: Norton, 1964), 17.

3

Asian Continental Empires and Maritime States

Malacca, China, and Muslim Empires, 1500–1700

HISTORICAL CONTEXT

From 1500 to 1700, there were two kinds of states in Asia — large inland empires and maritime states. Most of the Asian landmass was dominated by a few large inland empires: the Chinese, Turkish Ottoman, Persian Safavid, and Indian Mughal (see Map 3.1). In addition, there were a number of small coastal or island-based maritime states: Hormuz on the Persian Gulf, Calicut on the southwest coast of India, and Malacca on the Malay Peninsula, among others. These maritime states along important trade routes relied on trade more than agriculture for their livelihoods. In Hormuz, saline soil prevented any agriculture at all, but even those states that were self-sufficient agriculturally earned the bulk of their livelihoods from commerce, taxing and reshipping the goods that came through their ports.

In this chapter, we will try to determine how land empires were different from maritime states. Clearly, land empires were much larger in territory, but were there benefits or drawbacks to size?

How did the populations of these two types of states differ? As we might suspect, compared with maritime states, a smaller proportion of the inhabitants of continental empires were fishermen, sailors, shipbuilders, or fish eaters, though all of these could be found to some extent in land-based empires, and many inhabitants of the smallest island states were none of these. Agriculturalists and armies tended to be more influential in landed empires while both were also needed in maritime states, and long-distance merchants, foreigners, and traders were less of a force in inland empires, though they were

90

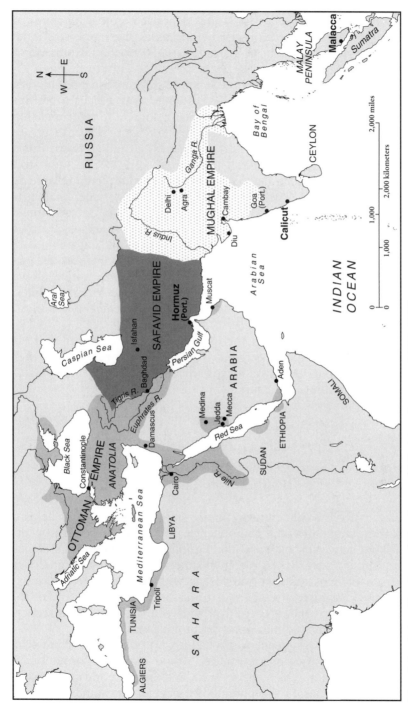

Map 3.1 Asian Continental Empires and Maritime States, c. 1500–1700.

also much in evidence. Maritime states depended more than continental empires on their merchant fleets and navies, but none was larger than the navy launched by China before 1450 or the Ottoman navy until 1571.

Historians have speculated on some of the consequences of these differences. They have argued, for instance, that because maritime states devoted a greater proportion of their resources to trade and shipping and a lesser proportion to farming, merchants played a greater role there than in landed states; trade goods and money were valued more than land; and such capitalist institutions as banking, joint stock companies, bills of credit, market pricing, and profit planning were developed more fully. Larger territorial states seemed richer than maritime states, but often their wealth came from tribute extracted from an unwilling peasantry and was frequently displayed in extravagant spectacles of power.

How important were such differences in size, occupation, defense, and homogeneity? Were territorial empires more conservative, slower to change? Did their greater size mean greater productivity than that of smaller, more capitalist states? Or were they more centralized, authoritarian, uniform, and inflexible?

In retrospect, we see that the modern world was shaped more by the innovative, capitalist merchant states; the territorial empires were the dinosaurs. But was this "obsolescence" inevitable? How viable, adaptable, and innovative could the territorial empires be?

THINKING HISTORICALLY
Sifting Evidence: Social, Economic, Political, and Cultural

In order to more easily compare entire states and empires, it helps to break them down into their component parts. Historians do this by distinguishing between society, economy, politics, and culture. Of course, none of these "parts" is completely distinct. Rather, they are analytical constructs or divisions that provide us with frames of reference and allow us to categorize a wide range of historical information. (For this chapter, you might find it useful to divide your notebook into sections for social, economic, political, and cultural material.)

For a frame of reference to be helpful, we must understand what the selected categories mean. *Society* would include information on family life, the roles of men and women, and of adults and children. Society also encompasses the community beyond the family: city and country, social class or caste, issues of status and prestige, and social customs regarding such things as marriage, child-rearing, and education. General information about the society is included as well: How many people are there? How dense is the population? Is it increasing or decreasing? What are the standards of health and well-being?

Some social issues are closely related to economics. But when we analyze economics, we think of finances, how people work, make, and spend (receive and distribute) the fruits of their labor; how they save and invest; and whether they are rich or poor, becoming richer or poorer, and to what extent. On a broader scale, we want to know about societal standards of living, the types of jobs people have, local and distant trade, and what products are produced. Though sometimes technology is considered separately, we include it here. What tools do people use? Is it an agrarian or industrial society? Is the society innovative? How does innovation occur?

Politics covers all areas of governance and power. Who makes decisions? With what advice or consultation are decisions made? Is power limited to a particular person, to particular groups of people, or to particular classes of people? Is power tyrannical, democratic, representative, competent, fair, just, efficient? How is power transferred from one leader to another? How knowledgeable are the decision makers? How heavy-handed is the government in its relations with the people?

Culture involves matters of the mind and spirit: art, music, literature, philosophy, religion, ethics, beliefs, goals. It also includes feelings, emotions, dreams, fears, anxieties, and hopes. Culture can be viewed in terms of the individual and in terms of society at large. It includes dance, ritual, custom, law, superstition, methods of learning, and methods of communication.

The overlap between these categories is clear: People can have ideas about anything. Notions of work are both cultural and economic; emotions can be cultural and social; education has cultural and social implications, not to mention its economic and political impact. You get the idea. As you begin recording "data" from each selection, do not concern yourself with overlap. Simply record information in the category that seems most appropriate. Later, you can examine and analyze, compare and contrast, your findings. Note that primary and secondary sources are used in this chapter.

12

SARNIA HAYES HOYT

From *Old Malacca*

We begin this chapter with one of the most important maritime states of the sixteenth century. Malacca was founded in 1402 by a Sumatran prince, Paramesvara, on the Malay Peninsula at one of its closest points to the island of Sumatra. The passage between Sumatra and the Malay Peninsula was the shortest distance between the Spice Islands or southern China and the Indian Ocean routes to Europe, the Middle East, and East Africa. Paramesvara's efforts to establish Malacca as a vital trade port were initially thwarted by Thailand, Chinese pirates, and the kingdom of Majapahit on neighboring Java, all of which enjoyed a percentage of the passing trade. With the help of the great Chinese expeditionary fleet under Admiral Zheng He, which eliminated the pirates and established a special relationship with Paramesvara, Malacca became a preeminent port, fostering trade between the China Sea and the Indian Ocean by 1500. The Portuguese arrived in 1509 and took the port by force.

The secondary source that follows is based in part on the primary account of Ma Huan, an Arabic-speaking Chinese Muslim who sailed with Zheng He. Ma Huan's account of Malacca is preserved in his *Ying-Yai Sheng-Lan,* or *General Account of the Shores of the Ocean* (see selection 2, "On Calicut, India," pp. 16–23).

In the selection, what signs do you see that the Malacca empire was primarily based on trade? How important were merchants in Malacca?

Thinking Historically

How would you distinguish between political and economic powers in Malacca? Did political or economic leaders have greater social status? How would you describe the culture of Malacca?

Ma Huan found a city surrounded by a palisade with four gates and watch-towers, and patrolled at night by watchmen ringing bells. Inside the city walls was a second fortress where godowns (warehouses),

Sarnia Hayes Hoyt, *Old Malacca* (Oxford and Kuala Lumpur: Oxford University Press, 1993), 15, 17–19, 21.

money, and provisions were kept. A city plan dividing the town into two parts separated by the river had been established, a pattern that endures today. The hill on the south side was maintained as a royal and aristocratic preserve where the sultan, his court, and bodyguards lived. Here also was the main mosque.

A bridge spanned the river, connecting the north and south banks with a market-place of twenty pavilions where commodities of all kinds were sold. North of the river lived the merchants, organized into separate ethnic communities — and trading centres — according to country of origin. These heterogeneous communities enjoyed considerable autonomy over their own affairs. Both Kampong Upeh (Tranquerah) and Bandar Hilir began as settlements of the Javanese, who controlled the rice trade. Especially numerous were the Klings (Hindus) and Bengalis from the east coast of India, the Tamils from south India, the Gujaratis (Muslims), the Chinese, and Japanese, but there were also Moors, Arabs, Jews, Filipinos, Burmese, Siamese, and Borneans.

Ma Huan reports that the king and his subjects revered the laws of Islam, observing its fasts and penances. The men got up at dawn and turned their faces toward heaven, invoking the name of Allah. Business deals were sealed with a handshake and a glance at heaven.

The Chinese visitor also took note of local fashions. Most men wore sarongs while the more distinguished wore short silk coats that hid their weapons. "The king wore a white turban of fine local cloth, a long floral robe of fine green calico, and leather shoes. . . ." Ordinary men also covered their heads in a square piece of cloth. Olive-skinned, dark-haired women wore their hair knotted at the back, but the wives of important people were never seen.

Well-to-do merchants were favoured by the trading system which required the stockpiling of a large inventory over several months. Rich traders did not hesitate to show off their wealth — besides offices in town they owned residences staffed with slaves and servants among orchards outside the town wall, and wore "robes of honour" for prestige.

Hwang Chung, author of the *Hai-Yu* ("Words About the Sea"), published in 1537 (quoted in Groeneveldt), commented that people in Malacca were well-mannered: "When people meet each other, they put their hands on each other's heart as a sign of politeness." They enjoyed music, ballads, and poetry. The men cultivated the arts of war, taking pride in their ability with the kris[1]; even a boy of two was allowed to carry a small dagger. People also took offence easily, reacting with fierce tempers, especially when someone put a hand on another's head or shoulder.

---

[1] A dagger used in fighting and ceremony in dance. [Ed.]

Hunting, fishing, and washing tin were important occupations among the lower classes. Malay *orang laut* (sea people) lived along the sea-shores or river banks. Their houses were built on piles about a metre off the ground, with floors made of split coconut trees fastened with rattan where people spread their mats. They sat, slept, and cooked in the same space.

Tomé Pires, a Portuguese apothecary, accountant, scholar, and diplomat came to Malacca in 1512, just after the Portuguese conquest, stayed for two years, and found 100,000 people speaking eighty-four languages living there. His *Suma Oriental,* intended as a reference for the Portuguese rulers, has been widely quoted even though Pires is bi- ased and his praises sound fulsome. As quoted in Cortesâo, he re- ported, for example, that Malacca was "a land of such freshness, of such fertility and of such good living . . . for it is certainly one of the outstanding things of the world, with beautiful orchards of trees and shades, many fruits, abundant fresh waters which come from the en- chanted hills."

Trade

Malacca was an international market-place, a capital, in Pires' words, "made for merchandise." He wrote that "no trading port as large as Malacca is known, nor any where they deal in such fine and highly prized merchandise. Goods from all over the east are found here; goods from all over the west are sold here." He goes on, "There is no doubt that the affairs of Malacca are of great importance, and of much profit and great honour. It is a land [that] cannot depreciate, on account of its position, but must always grow."

Today, spices are taken for granted, but in medieval Europe curries and peppers were in great demand to preserve and flavour meats, for it was too expensive to feed animals through the long winters. Pepper, for instance, was so scarce and so prized in England in 1607 that a single peppercorn could pay a nominal rent.

Malacca's location made it the most convenient place to receive goods like silk, camphor, and pottery from China, sugar from the Philippines, and cloves, nutmeg, and sandalwood from the Moluccas. April, the busiest trading month, was the time when Chinese traders de- parted after warehousing their goods in Malacca, leaving behind an agent to sell them to the Indians and Arabs.

These Western traders would soon arrive on the south-west mon- soon, bringing with them many kinds of printed cottons, copper weapons, seeds, grains, incense, tapestries, dyes, and opium.

Malacca's trade was complex. Traders had to know where to get the best spices at the best prices, how to get there, and what to barter in exchange for the greatest profits. Wooden ships had to be loaded with a small volume of high-value items, with the bulk of the cargo as ballast, for it would have ruined the richest merchant to lose a ship laden only with luxury goods. Most lucrative was the "blue water trade," collecting and distributing spices, silks, porcelain, and tea destined for Europe through the Middle East and Venice. Thus, Pires was able to write that "whoever is lord of Malacca has his hand on the throat of Venice."

China wanted little from Europe except silver bullion in exchange for its porcelain and silks, but it was still part of the "blue water trade." Certain products from South-East Asia, such as spices, birds' nests, and woods became highly prized.

Malacca also played a key role in the local distributive trade, bringing in goods such as pottery, arrack (liquor), pepper, rice, gold, musk, and tin from regional centres. As the sultanate expanded, Malacca offered goods in both the luxury and bulk trade, goods destined for distant ports as well as for local and regional consumption.

Despite the variety of its goods, Malacca's market-place still had curious anomalies. Gold was so ordinary that children played with it, but garlic and onions were valued, according to Piers, "more than musk, benzoin, and other precious things."

13

JONATHAN SPENCE

The Late Ming Empire

This is a secondary account of the Chinese Empire by a leading modern historian of China. Jonathan Spence provides us with a view of the Ming dynasty (1368–1644) at its height around 1600, but he also helps us understand some of the reasons that it fell to the Manchus from the northeast in 1644.

Jonathan D. Spence, *The Search for Modern China* (New York: W. W. Norton, 1990), 7–16.

Remember that Spence is describing the Ming Empire after China's great oceangoing expeditions had ceased in the 1430s. Those expeditions filled Ming treasuries with tribute payments and gifts, and they established trading relationships between China and ports as far-flung as East Africa. Do you see any signs here that Chinese trade has declined with the suspension of maritime trade?

How was China different from the rest of the world in 1600? How was it different from Malacca, as described in the previous selection?

Thinking Historically

As you read this selection, take notes under the four categories: social, economic, political, and cultural. This process will help you get a feel for what the different categories mean. Notice how Spence discusses each of these aspects separately, and how he relates one to the other. Specifically, how does Spence use examples of Chinese culture to illustrate aspects of Chinese society, economics, and politics?

Though Spence begins his survey in 1600 — the height of the Ming dynasty — he is most interested in understanding how Ming China changed and how it declined. What changes does he see in society, economics, politics, and culture? Does Spence argue that the causes of Ming decline were more social, economic, political, or cultural?

In the year A.D. 1600, the empire of China was the largest and most sophisticated of all the unified realms on earth. The extent of its territorial domains was unparalleled at a time when Russia was only just beginning to coalesce as a country, India was fragmented between Mughal and Hindu rulers, and a grim combination of infectious disease and Spanish conquerors had laid low the once great empires of Mexico and Peru. And China's population of some 120 million was far larger than that of all the European countries combined.

There was certainly pomp and stately ritual in capitals from Kyoto to Prague, from Delhi to Paris, but none of these cities could boast of a palace complex like that in Peking, where, nestled behind immense walls, the gleaming yellow roofs and spacious marble courts of the Forbidden City symbolized the majesty of the Chinese emperor. Laid out in a meticulous geometrical order, the grand stairways and mighty doors of each successive palace building and throne hall were precisely aligned with the arches leading out of Peking to the south, speaking to all comers of the connectedness of things personified in this man the Chinese termed the Son of Heaven.

Rulers in Europe, India, Japan, Russia, and the Ottoman Empire were all struggling to develop systematic bureaucracies that would expand their tax base and manage their swelling territories effectively, as well as draw to new royal power centers the resources of agriculture and trade. But China's massive bureaucracy was already firmly in place, harmonized by a millennium of tradition and bonded by an immense body of statutory laws and provisions that, in theory at least, could offer pertinent advice on any problem that might arise in the daily life of China's people.

One segment of this bureaucracy lived in Peking, serving the emperor in an elaborate hierarchy that divided the country's business among six ministries dealing respectively with finance and personnel, rituals and laws, military affairs and public works. Also in Peking were the senior scholars and academicians who advised the emperor on ritual matters, wrote the official histories, and supervised the education of the imperial children. This concourse of official functionaries worked in uneasy proximity with the enormous palace staff who attended to the emperor's more personal needs: the court women and their eunuch watchmen, the imperial children and their nurses, the elite bodyguards, the banquet-hall and kitchen staffs, the grooms, the sweepers, and the water carriers.

The other segment of the Chinese bureaucracy consisted of those assigned to posts in the fifteen major provinces into which China was divided during the Ming dynasty. These posts also were arranged in elaborate hierarchies, running from the provincial governor at the top, down through the prefects in major cities to the magistrates in the countries. Below the magistrates were the police, couriers, militiamen, and tax gatherers who extracted a regular flow of revenue from China's farmers. A group of officials known as censors kept watch over the integrity of the bureaucracy both in Peking and in the provinces.

The towns and cities of China did not, in most cases, display the imposing solidity in stone and brick of the larger urban centers in post-Renaissance Europe. Nor, with the exception of a few famous pagodas, were Chinese skylines pierced by towers as soaring as those of the greatest Christian cathedrals or the minarets of Muslim cities. But this low architectural profile did not signify an absence of wealth or religion. There were many prosperous Buddhist temples in China, just as there were Daoist temples dedicated to the natural forces of the cosmos, ancestral meeting halls, and shrines to Confucius, the founding father of China's ethical system who had lived in the fifth century B.C. A scattering of mosques dotted some eastern cities and the far western areas, where most of China's Muslims lived. There were also some synagogues, where descendants of early Jewish travelers still congregated, and dispersed small groups with hazy memories of the teachings of Nestorian Christianity, which had reached China a millenium earlier. The lesser grandeur of China's city architecture and religious centers represented not any absence of civic pride or disesteem of religion, but rather a political fact: The Chinese state was more effectively centralized than those elsewhere in the world; its religions were more effectively controlled; and the growth of powerful, independent cities was prevented by a watchful government that would not tolerate rival centers of authority.

With hindsight we can see that the Ming dynasty, whose emperors had ruled China since 1368, was past its political peak by the early seventeenth century; yet in the years around 1600, China's cultural life was in an ebullient condition that few, if any, other countries could match. If one points to the figures of exceptional brilliance or insight in late sixteenth-century European society, one will easily find their near equivalents in genius and imagination working away in China at just the same time. There was no Chinese dramatist with quite the range of Shakespeare, but in the 1590s Tang Xianzu was writing plays of thwarted, youthful love, of family drama and social dissonance, that were every bit as rich and complex as *A Midsummer Night's Dream* or *Romeo and Juliet.* And if there was no precise equal to Miguel de Cervantes, whose *Don Quixote* was to become a central work of Western culture, it was in the 1590s that China's most beloved novel of religious quest and picaresque adventure, the *Journey to the West,* was published. This novel's central hero, a mischievous monkey with human traits who accompanies the monk-hero on his action-filled travels to India in search of Buddhist scriptures, has remained a central part of Chinese folk culture to this day. Without pushing further for near parallels, within this same period in China, essayists, philosophers, nature poets, landscape painters, religious theorists, historians, and medical scholars all produced a profusion of significant works, many of which are now regarded as classics of the civilization.

Perhaps in all this outpouring, it is the works of the short-story writers and the popular novelists that make the most important commentary about the vitality of Ming society, for they point to a new readership in the towns, to new levels of literacy, and to a new focus on the details of daily life. In a society that was largely male-dominated, they also indicate a growing audience of literate women. The larger implications of expanding female literacy in China were suggested in the writings of late Ming social theorists, who argued that educating women would enhance the general life of society by bringing improvements in morals, child rearing, and household management.

These many themes run together in another of China's greatest novels, *Golden Lotus,* which was published anonymously in the early 1600s. In this socially elaborate and sexually explicit tale, the central character (who draws his income both from commerce and from his official connections) is analyzed through his relationships with his five consorts, each of whom speaks for a different facet of human nature. In many senses, *Golden Lotus* can be read as allegory, as a moral fable of the way greed and selfishness destroy those with the richest opportunities for happiness; yet it also has a deeply realistic side, and illuminates the tensions and cruelties within elite Chinese family life as few other works have ever done.

Novels, paintings, plays, along with the imperial compendia on court life and bureaucratic practice, all suggest the splendors — for the wealthy — of China in the late Ming. Living mainly in the larger commercial towns rather than out in the countryside, the wealthy were bonded together in elaborate clan or lineage organizations based on family descent through the male line. These lineages often held large amounts of land that provided income for support of their own schools, charity to those fallen on hard times, and the maintenance of ancestral halls in which family members offered sacrifices to the dead. The spacious compounds of the rich, protected by massive gates and high walls, were filled with the products of Chinese artisans, who were sometimes employed in state-directed manufactories but more often grouped in small, guild-controlled workshops. Embroidered silks that brought luster to the female form were always in demand by the rich, along with the exquisite blue and white porcelain that graced the elaborate dinner parties so beloved at the time. Glimmering lacquer, ornamental jade, feathery latticework, delicate ivory, cloisonné, and shining rosewood furniture made the homes of the rich places of beauty. And the elaborately carved brush holders of wood or stone, the luxurious paper, even the ink sticks and the stones on which they were rubbed and mixed with water to produce the best and blackest ink, all combined to make of every scholar's desk a ritual and an aesthetic world before he had even written a word.

Complementing the domestic decor, the food and drink of these wealthier Chinese would be a constant delight: pungent shrimp and bean curd, crisp duck and water chestnuts, sweetmeats, clear teas, smooth alcohol of grain or grape, fresh and preserved fruits and juices — all of these followed in stately sequence at parties during which literature, religion, and poetry were discussed over the courses. After the meal, as wine continued to flow, prize scroll paintings might be produced from the family collection, and new works of art, seeking to capture the essence of some old master, would be created by the skimming brushes of the inebriated guests.

At its upper social and economic levels, this was a highly educated society, held together intellectually by a common group of texts that reached back before the time of Confucius to the early days of the unification of a northern Chinese state in the second millennium B.C. While theorists debated its merits for women, education was rigorous and protracted for the boys of wealthy families, introducing them to the rhythms of classical Chinese around the age of six. They then kept at their studies in school or with private tutors every day, memorizing, translating, drilling until, in their late twenties or early thirties, they might be ready to tackle the state examinations. Success in these examinations, which rose in a hierarchy of difficulty from those held locally to those conducted in the capital of Peking, allegedly under the supervision of the emperor himself, brought access to lucrative bureaucratic office and immense social prestige. Women were barred by law from taking the state examinations; but those of good family often learned to write classical poetry from their parents or brothers, and courtesans in the city pleasure quarters were frequently well trained in poetry and song, skills that heightened their charms in the eyes of their educated male patrons. Since book printing with wooden blocks had been developing in China since the tenth century, the maintenance of extensive private libraries was feasible, and the wide distribution of works of philosophy, poetry, history, and moral exhortation was taken for granted.

Though frowned on by some purists, the dissemination of popular works of entertainment was also accelerating in the late sixteenth century, making for a rich and elaborate cultural mix. City dwellers could call on new images of tamed nature to contrast with their own noise and bustle, and find a sense of order in works of art that interpreted the world for them. The possibilities for this sense of contentment were caught to perfection by the dramatist Tang Xianzu in his play *The Peony Pavilion* of 1598. Tang puts his words into the mouth of a scholar and provincial bureaucrat named Du Bao. One side of Du Bao's happiness comes from the fact that administrative business is running smoothly:

> The mountains are at their loveliest
> and court cases dwindle,
> "The birds I saw off at dawn,
> at dusk I watch return,"
> petals from the vase cover my seal box,
> the curtains hang undisturbed.

This sense of peace and order, in turn, prompts a more direct response to nature, when official duties can be put aside altogether, the literary overlays forgotten, and nature and the simple pleasures enjoyed on their own terms:

> Pink of almond fully open,
> iris blades unsheathed,
> fields of spring warming to season's life.
> Over thatched hut by bamboo fence juts a tavern flag,
> rain clears, and the smoke spirals from kitchen stoves.

It was a fine vision, and for many these were indeed glorious days. As long as the country's borders remained quiet, as long as the bureaucracy worked smoothly, as long as the peasants who did the hard work in the fields and the artisans who made all the beautiful objects remained content with their lot — then perhaps the splendors of the Ming would endure.

Town and Farm

The towns and cities of Ming China, especially in the more heavily populated eastern part of the country, had a bustling and thriving air. Some were busy bureaucratic centers, where the local provincial officials had their offices and carried out their tax gathering and administrative tasks. Others were purely commercial centers, where trade and local markets dictated the patterns of daily life. Most were walled, closed their gates at night, and imposed some form of curfew.

As with towns and cities elsewhere in the world, those in China could be distinguished by their services and their levels of specialization. Local market towns, for instance, were the bases for coffin makers, ironworkers, tailors, and noodle makers. Their retail shops offered for sale such semispecial goods as tools, wine, headgear, and religious supplies, including incense, candles, and special paper money to burn at sacrifices. Such market towns also offered winehouses for customers to relax in. Larger market towns, which drew on a flow of traders and wealthy purchasers from a wider region, could support cloth-dyeing establishments, shoemakers, iron foundries, firecracker makers, and sellers of bamboo, fine cloth, and teas. Travelers here found bathhouses and inns, and could buy the services of local prostitutes. Rising up the hierarchy to the local cities that coordinated the trade of several regional market towns, there were shops selling expensive stationery, leather goods, ornamental lanterns, altar carvings, flour, and the services of tinsmiths, seal cutters, and lacquer-ware sellers. Here, too, visitors could find pawnshops and local "banks" to handle money exchanges, rent a sedan chair, and visit a comfortably appointed brothel. As the cities grew larger and their clientele richer, one found ever more specialized luxury goods and services, along with the kinds of ambience in which wealth edged — sometimes dramatically, sometimes unobtrusively — into the realms of decadence, snobbery, and exploitation.

At the base of the urban hierarchy, below the market towns, there were the small local townships where the population was too poor and scattered to support many shops and artisans, and where most goods were sold only by traveling peddlers at periodic markets. Such townships housed neither the wealthy nor any government officials; as a result, the simplest of teahouses, or perhaps a roadside stall, or an occasional temple fair would be the sole focus for relaxation. Nevertheless, such smaller townships performed a vast array of important functions, for they served as the bases for news and gossip, matchmaking, simple schooling, local religious festivals, traveling theater groups, tax collection, and the distribution of famine relief in times of emergency.

Just as the towns and cities of Ming China represented a whole spectrum of goods and services, architecture, levels of sophistication, and administrative staffing, making any simple generalization about them risky, so, too, was the countryside apparently endless in its variety. Indeed the distinction between town and country was blurred in China, for suburban areas of intensive farming lay just outside and sometimes even within the city walls, and artisans might work on farms in peak periods, or farmers work temporarily in towns during times of dearth.

It was south of the Huai River, which cuts across China between the Yellow River and the Yangzi, that the country was most prosperous, for here climate and soil combined to make intensive rice cultivation possible. The region was crisscrossed by myriad rivers, canals, and irrigation streams that fed lush market gardens and paddies in which the young rice shoots grew, or flowed into lakes and ponds where fish and ducks were raised. Here the seasonal flooding of the paddy fields returned needed nutrients to the soil. In the regions just south of the Yangzi River, farmers cultivated mulberry trees for the leaves on which silk worms fed, as well as tea bushes and a host of other products that created extra resources and allowed for a richly diversified rural economy. Farther to the south, sugarcane and citrus were added to the basic crops; and in the mountainous southwest, forests of bamboo and valuable hardwood lumber brought in extra revenue. Water transport was fast, easy, and cheap in south China. Its villages boasted strong lineage organizations that helped to bond communities together.

Although there were many prosperous farming villages north of the Huai River, life there was harsher. The cold in winter was extreme, as icy winds blew in from Mongolia, eroding the land, filling the rivers with silt, and swirling fine dust into the eyes and noses of those who could not afford to shelter behind closed doors. The main crops were wheat and millet, grown with much toil on overworked land, which the scattered farming communities painstakingly fertilized with every scrap of human and animal waste they could recycle. Fruit trees such as apple and pear grew well, as did soybeans and cotton; but by the end of the sixteenth century, much of the land was deforested, and the Yellow River was an unpredictable force as its silt-laden waters meandered across the wide plains to the sea. Unhindered by the dikes, paddies, and canals of the South, bandit armies could move men and equipment easily across the northern countryside, while cavalry forces could race ahead and to the flanks, returning to warn the slower foot soldiers of any danger from opposing forces or sorties from garrison towns. Lineage organizations were weaker here, villages more isolated, social life often more fragmented, and the tough-minded owner-cultivator, living not far above subsistence level, more common than either the prosperous landlord or the tenant farmer.

China's rural diversity meant that "landlords" could not be entirely distinguished from "peasants." For every wealthy absentee landlord living in one of the larger towns, for example, there might be scores of smaller-scale local landlords living in the countryside, perhaps renting out some of their land or hiring part-time labor to till it. Similarly, there were millions of peasant proprietors who owned a little more land than they needed for subsistence, and they might farm their own land with the help of some seasonal laborers. Others, owning a little *less* land than they needed for subsistence, might rent an extra fraction of an acre or hire themselves out as casual labor in the busy seasons. And in most peasant homes, there was some form of handicraft industry that connected the rural family to a commercial network.

The social structure was further complicated by the bewildering variety of land-sale agreements and rental contracts used in China. While the state sought extra revenue by levying a tax on each land deal, in return for which it granted an official contract with a red seal, many farmers — not surprisingly — tried to avoid these surcharges by drawing up their own unofficial contracts. The definition of a land sale, furthermore, was profoundly ambiguous. Most land sales were conducted on the general understanding that the seller might at some later date reclaim the land from the buyer at the original purchase price, or that the seller retained "subsurface" rights to the soil while the purchaser could till the land for a specified period. If land rose in price, went out of cultivation, became waterlogged, or was built upon, a maze of legal and financial problems resulted, leading often to family feuds and even to murder.

For centuries, whether in the north or the south, the peasantry of China had shown their ability to work hard and to survive even when sudden natural calamities brought extreme deprivation. In times of drought or flood, there were various forms of mutual aid, loans, or relief grain supplies that could help to tide them and their families over. Perhaps some sort of part-time labor could be secured, as a porter, an irrigation worker, or barge puller. Children could be indentured, on short- or long-term contracts, for domestic service with the rich. Female children could be sold in the cities; and even if they ended up in brothels, at least they were alive and the family freed of an extra mouth to feed. But if, on top of all the other hardships, the whole fabric of law and order within the society began to unravel, then the situation became hopeless indeed. If the market towns closed their gates, if bands of desperate men began to roam the countryside, seizing the few stores that the rural families had laid in against the coming winter's cold, or stealing the last seed grain carefully hoarded for the next spring's planting, then the poor farmers had no choice but to abandon their fields — whether the land was rented or privately owned — and to swell the armies of the homeless marchers.

In the early 1600s, despite the apparent prosperity of the wealthier elite, there were signs that this dangerous unraveling might be at hand. Without state-sponsored work or relief for their own needy inhabitants, then the very towns that barred their gates to the rural poor might erupt from within. Driven to desperation by high taxes and uncertain labor prospects, thousands of silk weavers in the Yangzi-delta city of Suzhou went on strike in 1601, burnt down houses, and lynched hated local tyrants. That same year, southwest of Suzhou, in the Jiangxi province porcelain-manufacturing city of Jingdezhen, thousands of workers rioted over low wages and the Ming court's demand that they meet heightened production quotas of the exquisite "dragon bowls" made for palace use. One potter threw himself into a blazing kiln and perished to underline his fellows' plight. A score of other cities and towns saw some kind of social and economic protest in the same period.

Instability in the urban world was matched by that in the countryside. There were incidents of rural protest in the late Ming, as in earlier periods, that can be seen as having elements of class struggle inherent in them. These incidents, often accompanied by violence, were of two main kinds: protests by indentured laborers or "bondservants" against their masters in attempts to regain their free status as farmers, and strikes by tenants who refused to pay their landlords what they regarded as unjust rents.

Even if they were not common, there were enough such incidents to offer a serious warning to the wealthier Chinese. In that same play, *The Peony Pavilion*, in which he speaks glowingly of the joys of the official's life, Tan Xianzu gently mocks the rustic yokels of China, putting into deliberately inelegant verse the rough-and-ready labor of their days:

Slippery mud,
sloppery thud,
short rake, long plough, clutch 'em as they slide.
After rainy night sow rice and hemp,
when sky clears fetch out the muck,
then a stink like long-pickled fish
floats on the breeze.

The verses sounded amusing. But Tang's audience had not yet begun to think through the implications of what might happen when those who labored under such conditions sought to overthrow their masters.

14

GHISLAIN DE BUSBECQ

The Ottoman Empire under Suleiman

Not all territorial states were the same. China's empire was vast and possessed such a long history that it must be viewed as unique. But how unique was China when compared with, say, the Ottoman Empire, the oldest of the three great Muslim territorial empires of the sixteenth and seventeenth centuries?

Far from China in Western Asia, the Ottoman Empire consisted of what is today Turkey, Greece, the Balkans, Syria, Iraq, Georgia, Ukraine, Palestine, Israel, Jordan, and parts of Saudi Arabia and Egypt. Turkish-speaking people from Central Asia invaded what is present-day Turkey in the 1300s, and between 1500 and 1700 the Ottoman Empire spanned from the Middle East to India. In 1453 the Ottoman Turks captured the city of Constantinople, which they renamed Istanbul, the successor to the thousand-year-old Byzantine Empire.

In this selection we use a primary source instead of a secondary one to enter the world of the Ottomans. Ghislain de Busbecq (1522–1590), a European diplomat, traveled to Istanbul in 1555. A Flemish nobleman, he had been sent on a diplomatic mission by the Hapsburg ruler Ferdinand I, Archduke of Austria and King of Hungary and Bohemia (later to become Holy Roman Emperor from 1556 to 1564). At the time, all of Europe — especially the Hapsburg Empire — was threatened by Ottoman expansion. In 1543 most of Ferdinand's Hungary had come under Ottoman domination, and the continual border wars between the Ottoman and Hapsburg

---

The Turkish Letters of Ogier Ghislain de Busbecq, Imperial Ambassador at Constantinople, 1534–1562, trans. Edward S. Foster (Oxford: Clarendon Press, 1927), 58–62, 65–66, 109–14.

Empires were to favor the Turks until as late as 1683. It is not surprising, then, that Busbecq finds much to admire and fear in Ottoman society. As well, he arrived in Istanbul in its heyday, during the reign of Suleiman I (r. 1520–1566), known as "Suleiman the Magnificent" and "Suleiman the Law Giver," one of the great Ottoman sultans.

What similarities do you see between the Ottoman sultan and his court and that of the emperor of China in the previous selection? What, according to Busbecq, are the main differences between the Ottoman system of government and that of European states like his own Hapsburg Empire? Do you think he exaggerates any of these differences? What advantages does Busbecq see in the Ottoman army? Do you see any disadvantages in the Ottoman army?

This chapter asks you to make comparisons on a number of different levels: continental empires versus maritime states; Ming China versus the Muslim empires; one Muslim empire with another. As you read this and the following two selections, consider how these large Muslim territorial empires are similar and different. Then compare the three Muslim empires with the Chinese empire.

Writing specifically of the great Muslim empires — Ottoman, Persian, and Indian — the historian Marshall Hodgson has classified them as "gunpowder empires" because gunpowder enabled their rulers to level the walls of rebellious cities and to control legions of nomadic cavalry and vast agricultural regions. If cannon and heavy artillery tipped the traditional balance from nomads and tribal federations to imperial industries and trained armies, older states like China and new non-Muslim ones like Russia might also be called gunpowder states. Indeed, the success of the maritime empires of Europe owed much to their ability to mount heavy cannons on wide-beamed ocean-going vessels as well as to employ field cannons in land wars.

The great Muslim empires also have been called "bureaucratic army states" due to the centralized bureaucracy that acted as a military arm and facilitated military rule. The founders of the great Muslim dynasties (that is, Ottoman, Safavid, and Mughal) owed their power to armed tribal leaders who, they feared, might always change allegiances. Thus, they had to find ways to undercut the power of these potentially dangerous rivals. Muslim leaders used the power of the state to confiscate and reward lands to a new military nobility. They also created armies of captured slaves, who, because they were foreign, had no loyalties to other clans or chieftains and provided a protective buffer against well-connected rivals.

The Ottoman Janissaries were such a Muslim "slave army," which explains, at least partially, Busbecq's remark that family, rank, and inheritance had no meaning for them. They were taken from their Christian families and raised as wards of the sultan, to whom they owed their lives and loyalties. Unable to marry or raise their own families (until 1572 when this practice changed), Janissaries were unlikely to develop their own dynastic ties or ambitions, so they were used by the sultan to counter the ambitions of other princes and other Turkish clan and tribal leaders. What evidence do you see here of the Ottoman's reliance on these slave soldiers? On what other soldiers did the empire rely? How effective was each of these armies? What social groups in Ottoman society had more status or prestige than soldiers? What social groups in China had more status or prestige than soldiers?

Thinking Historically

Organize Busbecq's description under the categories of economics, society, politics, and culture. Notice again how these categories overlap. What aspect of social organization does Busbecq think is the strength of Ottoman political power?

When Busbecq discusses the Ottoman army campaigns against Persia, he praises certain aspects of the Turkish force. What are these aspects, and would you term them social, economic, political, or cultural? What, according to Busbecq, is the source of Ottoman political strength? Is it social, economic, or cultural?

On reaching Amasya we were taken to pay our respects to Achmet, the Chief Vizier, and the other Pashas (for the Sultan himself was away), and we opened negotiations with them in accordance with the [King Ferdinand's] injunctions. The Pashas, anxious not to appear at this early stage prejudiced against our cause, displayed no opposition but postponed the matter until their master could express his wishes. On his return we were introduced into his presence; but neither in his attitude nor in his manner did he appear very well disposed to our address, or the arguments, which we used, or the instructions which we brought.

The Sultan was seated on a rather low sofa, not more than a foot from the ground and spread with many costly coverlets and cushions embroidered with exquisite work. Near him were his bow and arrows. His expression, as I have said, is anything but smiling, and has a sternness which, though sad, is full of majesty. On our arrival we were introduced into his presence by his chamberlains, who held our arms — a practice which has always been observed since a Croatian sought an interview and murdered the Sultan Amurath [Murad II] in revenge for the slaughter of his master, Marcus the Despot of Serbia. After going through the pretence of kissing his hand, we were led to the wall facing him backwards, so as not to turn our backs or any part of them towards him. He then listened to the recital of my message, but, as it did not correspond with his expectations (for the demands of my imperial master were full of dignity and independence, and, therefore, far from acceptable to one who thought that his slightest wishes ought to be obeyed), he assumed an expression of disdain, and merely answered "Giusel, Giusel," that is, "Well, Well." We were then dismissed to our lodging.

The Sultan's head-quarters were crowded by numerous attendants, including many high officials. All the cavalry of the guard were there . . . , and a large number of Janissaries. In all that great assembly no single man owed his dignity to anything but his personal merits and bravery; no one is distinguished from the rest by his birth, and honour is paid to each man according to the nature of the duty and offices which he discharges. Thus there is no struggle for precedence, every man having his place assigned to him in virtue of the function which he performs. The Sultan himself assigns to all their duties and offices, and in doing so pays no attention to wealth or the empty claims of rank, and takes no account of any influence or popularity which a candidate may possess; he only considers merit and scrutinizes the character, natural ability, and disposition of each. Thus each man is rewarded according to his deserts, and offices are filled by men capable of performing them. In Turkey every man has it in his power to make what he will of the position into which he is born and of his fortune in life. Those who hold the highest posts under the Sultan are very often the sons of shepherds and herdsmen, and, so far from being ashamed of their birth, they make it a subject of boasting, and the less they owe to their forefathers and to the accident of birth, the greater is the pride which they feel. They do not consider that good qualities can be conferred by birth or handed down by inheritance, but regard them partly as the gift of heaven and partly as the product of good training and constant toil and zeal. Just as they consider that an aptitude for the arts, such as music or mathematics or geometry, is not transmitted to a son and heir, so they hold that character is not hereditary, and that a son does not necessarily resemble his father, but his qualities are divinely infused into his bodily frame. Thus, among the Turks, dignities, offices, and administrative posts are the rewards of ability and merit; those who were dishonest, lazy, and slothful never attain to distinction, but remain in obscurity and contempt. This is why the Turks succeed in all that they attempt and are a dominating race and daily extend the bounds of their rule. Our method is very different; there is no room for merit, but everything depends on birth; considerations of which alone open the way to high official position. On this subject I shall perhaps say more in another place, and you must regard these remarks as intended for your ears only.

Now come with me and cast your eye over the immense crowd of turbaned heads, wrapped in countless folds of the whitest silk, and bright raiment of every kind and hue, and everywhere the brilliance of gold, silver, purple, silk, and satin. A detailed description would be a lengthy task, and no mere words could give an adequate idea of the novelty of the sight. A more beautiful spectacle was never presented to my gaze. Yet amid all this luxury there was a great simplicity and economy. The dress of all has the same form whatever the wearer's rank; and no edgings or useless trimmings are sewn on, as is the custom with us, costing a large sum of money and worn out in three days. Their most beautiful garments of silk or satin, even if they are embroidered, as they usually are, cost only a ducat to make. . . .

The Sultan, when he sets out on a campaign, takes as many as 40,000 camels with him, and almost as many baggage-mules, most of whom, if his destination is Persia, are loaded with cereals of every kind, especially rice. Mules and camels are also employed to carry tents and arms and warlike machines and implements of every kind. The territories called Persia which are ruled by the Sophi,[1] as we call him (the Turkish name being Kizilbash), are much less fertile than our country; and, further, it is the custom of the inhabitants, when their land is invaded, to lay waste and burn everything, and so force the enemy to retire through lack of food. The latter, therefore, are faced with serious peril, unless they bring an abundance of food with them. They are careful, however, to avoid touching the supplies which they carry with them as long as they are marching against their foes, but reserve them, as far as possible, for their return journey, when the moment for retirement comes and they are forced to retrace their steps through regions which the enemy has laid waste, or which the immense multitude of men and baggage animals has, as it were, scraped bare, like a swarm of locusts. It is only then that the Sultan's store of provisions is opened, and just enough food to sustain life is weighed out each day to the Janissaries and the other troops in attendance upon him. The other soldiers are badly off, if they have not provided food for their own use; most of them, having often experienced such difficulties during their campaigns — and this is particularly true of the cavalry — take a horse on a leading-rein loaded with many of the necessities of life.[2] These

---

[1] That is, Sûfi, Ismâ'îl II, Safavid Shâh. The Turks called the Safavids Kizilbash (red-headed or hatted) because of their distinctive red headgear. [Ed.]

[2] This refers to those irregular "feudal" troops called up during a general mobilization and responsible for their own supplies. [Ed.]

include a small piece of canvas to use as a tent, which may protect them from the sun or a shower of rain, also some clothing and bedding and a private store of provisions, consisting of a leather sack or two of the finest flour, a small jar of butter, and some spices and salt; on these they support life when they are reduced to the extremes of hunger. They take a few spoonfuls of flour and place them in water, adding a little butter, and then flavour the mixture with salt and spices. This, when it is put on the fire, boils and swells up so as to fill a large bowl. They eat of it once or twice a day, according to the quantity, without any bread, unless they have with them some toasted bread or biscuit. They thus contrive to live on short rations for a month or even longer, if necessary. Some soldiers take with them a little sack full of beef dried and reduced to a powder, which they employ in the same manner as the flour, and which is of great benefit as a more solid form of nourishment. Sometimes, too, they have recourse to horseflesh; for in a great army a large number of horses necessarily dies, and any that die in good condition furnish a welcome meal to men who are starving. I may add that men whose horses have died, when the Sultan moves his camp, stand in a long row on the road by which he is to pass with their harness or saddles on their heads, as a sign that they have lost their horses, and implore his help to purchase others. The Sultan then assists them with whatever gift he thinks fit.

All this will show you with what patience, sobriety, and economy the Turks struggle against the difficulties which beset them, and wait for better times. How different are our soldiers, who on campaign despise ordinary food and expect dainty dishes (such as thrushes and beccaficoes) and elaborate meals. If these are not supplied, they mutiny and cause their own ruin; and even if they are supplied, they ruin themselves just the same. For each man is his own worst enemy and has no more deadly foe than his own intemperance, which kills him if the enemy is slow to do so. I tremble when I think of what the future must bring when I compare the Turkish system with our own; one army must prevail and the other be destroyed, for certainly both cannot remain unscathed. On their side are the resources of a mighty empire, strength unimpaired, experience and practice in fighting, a veteran soldiery, habituation to victory, endurance of toil, unity, order, discipline, frugality, and watchfulness. On our side is public poverty, private luxury, impaired strength, broken spirit, lack of endurance and training; the soldiers are insubordinate, the officers avaricious; there is contempt for discipline; licence, recklessness, drunkenness, and debauchery are rife; and, worst of all, the enemy is accustomed to victory, and we to defeat. Can we doubt what the result will be? Persia alone interposes in our favour; for the enemy, as he hastens to attack, must keep an eye on this menace in his rear. But Persia is only delaying our fate; it cannot save us. When the Turks have settled with Persia, they will fly at our throats supported by the might of the whole East; how unprepared we are I dare not say!

But to return to the point from which I digressed. I mentioned that baggage animals are employed on campaign to carry the arms and tents, which mainly belong to the Janissaires. The Turks take the utmost care to keep their soldiers in good health and protected from the inclemency of the weather; against the foe they must protect themselves, but their health is a matter for which the State must provide. Hence one sees the Turk better clothed than armed. He is particularly afraid of the cold, against which, even in the summer, he guards himself by wearing three garments, of which the innermost — call it shirt or what you will — is woven of coarse thread and provides much warmth. As a further protection against cold and rain tents are always carried, in which each man is given just enough space to lie down, so that one tent holds twenty-five or thirty Janissaires. The material for the garments to which I have referred is provided at the public expense. To prevent any disputes or suspicion of favour, it is distributed in the following manner. The soldiers are summoned by companies in the darkness to a place chosen for the purpose — the balloting station or whatever name you like to give it — where are laid out ready as many portions of cloth as there are soldiers in the company; they enter and take whatever chance offers them in the darkness, and they can only ascribe it to chance whether they get a good or a bad piece of cloth. For the same reason their pay is not counted out to them but weighed, so that no one can complain that he has received light or chipped coins. Also their pay is given them not on the day on which it falls due but on the day previous.

The armour which is carried is chiefly for the use of the household cavalry, for the Janissaries are lightly armed and do not usually fight at close quarters, but use muskets. When the enemy is at hand and a battle is expected, the armour is brought out, but it consists mostly of old pieces picked up in various battlefields, the spoil of former victories. These are distributed to the household cavalry, who are otherwise protected by only a light shield. You can imagine how badly the armour, thus hurriedly given out, fits its wearers. One man's breastplate is too small, another's helmet is too large, another's coat of mail is too heavy for him to bear. There is something wrong everywhere; but they bear it with equanimity and think that only a coward finds fault with his arms, and vow to distinguish themselves in the fight, whatever their equipment may be; such is the confidence inspired by repeated victories and constant experience of warfare. Hence also they do not hesitate to re-enlist a veteran infantryman in the cavalry, though he has never fought on horseback, since they are convinced that one who has warlike experience and long service will acquit himself well in any kind of fighting. . . .

$\boxed{15}$

JOHN CHARDIN

From *Travels in Persia, 1673–1677*

John Chardin (1643–1713) was born into a wealthy Protestant family in Paris and was a jeweler like his father, but unlike his father he used his business to travel and learn about the world. In 1666 he traveled through the Ottoman Empire from Istanbul through the Black Sea to Persia, where he remained for eighteen months. After securing an order for jewelry from the ruler Shah Abbas II, who died in the fall of 1666, Chardin observed the succession and coronation of the Shah's son Sulayman (r. 1666–1694) and began his studies of Turkish and Persian language and culture. On his return to Paris, he wrote *The Coronation of Soleiman II*[1] and traveled throughout Europe to secure stones for the commissioned jewelry, now presumably destined for the new shah.

In 1672 Chardin returned to Persia with the finished jewelry and spent the next four years studying Persian culture and literature, "frequenting the most eminent and most Knowing Men of the Nation, the better to inform myself in all things that were Curious and New to us in Europe" and becoming — as he also put it — as fluent in Persian as in French and as knowledgeable of Isfahan, the Persian capital, as he was of Paris, where he was born and bred. After his return to Europe, characteristically by way of southern Africa to extend his travels, Chardin decided to settle in England, as Protestants were increasingly threatened in France. In addition to continuing his studies of Persia and writing an account of his travels from which this selection is

---

[1] Note the variety of spellings. Busbecq used Suleiman; modern scholars use Sulayman or Suleyman. [Ed.]

N. M. Penzer, *Sir John Chardin: Travels in Persia, 1673–1677* (1927; reprint, New York: Dover Publications, 1988), 6–9, 188–89, 192–95, 279–81, 282–83.

taken, Chardin served as court jeweler to King Charles II of England and agent of the East India Company of Holland.

The seventeenth-century English edition of Chardin's *Travels,* excerpted here, was published in two volumes: The first describes Chardin's activities in Persia; the second introduces the reader to various aspects of Persian life: its climate, food, customs, crafts, manufactures, and trade, among others. This selection includes parts from each volume.

The Persian Safavid Empire was somewhat smaller than the Ottoman Empire to the west and the Indian Mughal Empire to the east. It was founded later than the Ottoman, around 1500, about the same time as the Mughal. Its founder and namesake, Ismail Safavi, was a leader of a radical Shia sect of Turkish tribesmen; he was crowned shah by his own decree in 1502. In 1508 he conquered Baghdad and defeated the Uzbeks at Bokhara in Central Asia. The Ottoman army stopped Safavi's efforts at western expansion in 1514, but the two empires remained in an almost perpetual state of war for more than a hundred years. The conflict between Shia and Sunni Muslims was then and remains one of the great rifts in Islam, much like the rift between Protestants and Catholics in the Christian wars of the sixteenth century.

The power of the Safavi state reached its peak under Shah Abbas the Great (r. 1587–1629), who made Isfahan a great garden city and capital. In 1666, when Chardin was first at Isfahan, Persia was prosperous and at peace. Yet with peace may have come the decline of Persian military forces. The story is told that late in the reign of Abbas II, a parade of the dwindling Persian military forces had to be marched past the Shah several times. Abbas II died at the age of thirty-three, possibly of syphilis. Despite his distinctly un-Muslim life of dissipation, he was an effective ruler. His son inherited more of his vices than his leadership skills, however. He took the name Safi II in 1666, but rededicated his reign two years later, after a series of natural disasters, as Sulayman, his title when Chardin returned in 1672. The last years of his rule were more fortunate, owing to an absence of natural disasters and costly military campaigns, but Sulayman lessened the vitality of a dynasty that came to an abrupt end when his son and successor was defeated by an Afghan army in 1722.

Chardin writes in the beginning of this selection of the shah's drunkenness and rage. Persian kings thought themselves above such Muslim laws as the prohibition of alcohol, and they sometimes governed their subjects as if they were the captive slaves of armed conquest. Further, the fear of rivals to the throne lurking in their midst led to cruel punishments of those close to them. Often crown princes were blinded or murdered when the shah suspected they were being groomed by rival tribal chieftains, with the connivance of harem eunuchs. The absolute power of the king could be a source of great accomplishment, but in a weak king it also could herald instability and decline. Who are Chardin's closest associates in Isfahan? Why is he concerned about who will be prime minister?

The second section on the manners and customs of the Persians is Chardin's attempt to describe Persian behavior in general. What aspects of Persian behavior strike him? What do you make of his comparisons of Persian and European customs?

On the subject of the third section, trade, Chardin is more of an expert. After all, he is a merchant himself. What does Chardin think of the similarities and differences in trade practices between Persia and Europe? From these observations, would you judge Persia as more or less mercantile than Europe at the time? How would you compare the importance of trade in Persia with its importance in the Ottoman Empire and in China?

Thinking Historically

Take notes on the reading under four categories: politics, economy, society, and culture. As described by Chardin, what are the leading three or four characteristics of Persian society in each of these categories? Which of these characteristics are also found in Busbecq's description of the Ottoman Empire? Which do you find in Spence's history of Ming China?

I at the same time receiv'd a Piece of News, which confirm'd those Advices. This was, that the Day before, the King getting Drunk, as it had been his daily Custom almost for some Years, fell into a Rage against a Player on the Lute, who did not play well to his Taste, and commanded *Nesralibec,* his Favourite, Son to the Governour of *Irivan,* to cut his Hands off. The Prince in pronouncing that Sentence, threw himself on a Pile of Cushions to Sleep. The Favourite, who was not so Drunk, and knowing no Crime in the condemn'd Person, thought that the King had found none neither, and that this cruel Order was only a transport of Drunkenness, he therefore contented himself with Reprimanding the Player very severely, in that he did not study to please his Master better; the King wak'd in an Hours time, and seeing the Musician touch the Lute as before, he call'd to Mind the Orders he had given to his Favourite against the Musician, and flying into a great Passion with the young Lord, he commanded the Lord high Steward to cut off the Hands and Feet of them both; the Lord Steward threw himself at the King's Feet, to implore Mercy for the Favourite; the King, in the extream Violence of his Indignation and Fury, cry'd out to his Eunucks and his Guards, to execute his Sentence upon all three; *Cheic-ali-can,* that Grand Vizier who was out of his Post, happen'd to be there, as good Luck would have it, he flung himself at the King's Feet, and embracing them, he beseech'd him to show them Mercy; the King making a little Pause upon it, say'd to him, *thou art very bold to hope, that I should grant what thou desirest of me, I who can't obtain of thee to resume the Charge of Prime Minister. Sir,* reply'd the Suppliant, *I am your Slave, I will ever do what your Majesty shall command me.* The King being hereupon appeas'd, Pardon'd all the condemn'd Persons, and next Morning sent a *Calaat* to *Cheic-ali-can:* By that Name they call the Garments which the King presents great Men to do them Honour; he sent him besides the Garment, a Horse, with a Saddle, and Trappings of Gold, set with Diamonds, A Sword and Ponyard of the same kind, with the Inkhorn, Letters Patents, and other Marks, with denote the Post of the Prime Minister. . . .

Manners and Customs

. . . They walk gravely, make their Prayers and Purgations at set Times, and with the greatest Shew of Devotion; they hold the Wisest and Godliest Conversation possible, discoursing constantly of God's Glory, and of his Greatness, in the Nobelest Terms, and with all the outward Shew of the most fervent Faith. Altho' they be naturally dispos'd to good Nature, Hospitality, Pitty, Contempt of the World, and of its Riches, they affect them nevertheless, that they may appear to be possest of a larger Share of them than they really are. Whoever sees them only passing by, or in a Visit, will always give them the best Character in the World; but he that deals with them; and pries into their Affairs, will find that there is little Honesty in them; and that most of them are *Whited Sepulcres,* according to our Saviours Expression, which I think the more proper here, because the *Persians* study particularly a strict Observation of the Law. That is the Character of the Generality of the *Persians:* But there is without doubt, an Exception to that general Depravation; for among some of the *Persians,* there is as much Justice, Sincerity, Virtue and Piety to be found, as among those who profess the best Religions. But the more one Converses with that Nation, the fewer one finds included in the Exception, the Number of Truly, Honest and Courteous *Persians* being very small. . . .

The *Persians* neither love walking Abroad, nor Travelling. As to that of walking Abroad, they look upon that Custom of ours to be very Absurd; and they look upon the walking in the Alley, as Actions only proper for a Madman. They ask very gravely for what one goes to the End of the Alley, and why one does not stand still, if one has Business to go there. This proceeds no doubt from their living in a Climate that is more even than ours. They are not so Sanguine as we are *Northward,* nor so Fiery. The most Spirituous part of their Blood perspiring more than it does with us, which is the Reason that they are not so subject to the Motions of the Body, which look so like Lightness and Disquietude, and which go often to Extravagence, and even to Madness. They don't know such a Remedy in *Persia,* as that which we call *Exercise;* they are much better sitting or leaning, than walking. The *Women* and the *Eunuchs* generally Speaking, use no Exercise, and are always sitting or lying, without prejudicing the Health: For the Men, they ride on Horseback, but never walk, and their Exercises are only for Pleasure, and not for Health. The climate of each People is always, as I believe, the principal Effect of the Inclinations and Customs of the Men, which are no more different among them, than that of the Temper of the Air is different from one Place to another. As for what relates to travelling, those Journeys that are made out of pure Curiosity, are still more inconceivable to the *Persians,* than walking Abroad. They have no Taste of the Pleasure we enjoy in seeing different Manners from ours, and hearing of a Language which we do not Understand. . . . They ask'd me if it was possible that there should be such People amongst us, who would travel two or three thousand Leagues with so much Danger, and Inconveniency, only to see *how they were made, and what they did in Persia, and upon no other Design.* These people are of Opinion, as I have observ'd, that one cannot better attain to Virtue, nor have a fuller Taste of Pleasure than by resting and dwelling at Home, and that it is not good to Travel, but to acquire Riches. They believe likewise, that every Stranger is a Spy if he be not a Merchant, or a Handicrafts-Man, and the People of Quality look upon it to be a Crime against the State to receive 'em among them, or to Visit them. It is from this Spirit of theirs no doubt, that the *Persians* are so grosly Ignorant of the present State of other Nations of the World, and that they do not so much as understand *Geography,* and have no Maps; which comes from this, that having no Curiosity to see other Countries, they never mind the Distance, nor Roads, by which they might go thither. They have no such thing among 'em as Accounts of Foreign Countries, neither *Gazetts, News A-la-main,* nor *Offices* of *Intelligence.* This would seem very strange to People who pass their time in asking after News, and whose Health and Rest in a Manner, are Interested in it, as well as to those who apply themselves with so much care to the Study of the Maps and other Accounts; but this is however very true; and as I have represented the *Persians,* it is plain, that all that Knowledge is not requisite for the Pleasure and Tranquility of the Mind. The Ministers of State generally Speaking, know no more what passes in *Europe,* than in the World of the Moon. The greatest Part, even have but a confus'd Idea of *Europe,* which they look upon to be some little Island in the

North Seas, where there is nothing to be found that is either Good or Handsome; *from whence it comes,* say they, *that the Europeans go all over the World, in search of fine Things, and of those which are Necessary, as being destitute of them.*

Yet notwithstanding what I have been saying, it is certainly true, that there is not that Country in the World, which is less dangerous to travel in from the Security of the Roads, for which they provide with a great deal of Care; neither is it less Expensive any where, by Reason of the great Number of publick Buildings, which they keep for Travellers, in all Parts of the Empire, as well in the Cities, as in the Country. They lodge in those Houses without being put to any Charge; besides which, there are Bridges and Causways, in all the Places where the Roads are too bad, which are made for the Sake of the Caravans, and of all those who travel from a motive of Gain. . . .

Commerce or Trade

Trading is a very honourable Profession in the *East,* as being the best of those that have any Stability, and are not so liable to change. 'Tis not to be wonder'd at, for it cannot be otherwise in Kingdoms, where on the one hand there is no Title of Nobility, and therefore little Authority annexed to the Birth; and where on the other Hand, the form of Government being altogether Despotick and Arbitrary, the Authority annexed to Places and Employments cannot last longer than the Employments themselves, which are likewise precarious; for which Reason Trading is much set by in that part of the World, as a lasting and independent Station. Another Reason why it is valu'd is, because the Noblemen profess it, and the Kings also; they have their Deputies as the Merchants have, and under the same Denomination: They have most of them their Trading Ships, and their Store-Houses. The King of *Persia,* for Instance, sells and sends to the Neighbouring Kingdoms, Silk, Brocades, and other rich Goods, Carpets and Precious Stones. The Name of Merchant, is a Name much respected in the *East,* and is not allowed to Shop-keepers or Dealers in trifling Goods; nor to those who Trade not in foreign Countries: 'Tis allow'd only to such as employ Deputies or Factors in the remotest Countries: And those Men are sometimes rais'd to the highest Ranks, and are usually employed in Embassies. There are Merchants in *Persia* who have Deputies in all parts of the world: And when those Deputies are returned Home, they wait on their Master, under no better Denomination than that of a Servant, standing up always before them, and waiting at Table, tho' some of those Deputies are worth above threescore thousand Crowns. In the *Indies* the Laws are still more favourable to Traders, for tho' they are much more numerous than in *Persia,* they are nevertheless more set by. The Reason of this additional Respect, is, because in the *East,* Traders are Sacred Persons, who are never molested even in time of War; and are allowed a free Passage, they and their Effects, through the middle of Armies: 'Tis upon their account especially that the Roads are so safe all over *Asia,* and especially in *Persia.* The *Persians* call a Trader *Saudaguer, i. e.* Gain-Monger.

The Eastern Merchants affect Grandure in Trading, notwithstanding they send their Deputies into all Parts, and stay at Home themselves, as in the Center of their grand Concern; they make no Bargains themselves directly, there is no publick place of Exchange in their Towns; the Trade is carried on by Stock-jobbers, who are the subtilest, the cunningest, the slyest, the complaisantest, the patientest, and the most intriguing Men of the whole Society, having a valuable and insinuating Tongue beyond Expression: They are called *Delal,* which answers to Great Talkers, that Word being of a contrary Signification to *Lal, i. e.* Dumb. The *Mahometans* have a Proverb alluding to the Name of those Men, viz. That at the last Day, *Delal Lal,* the Stock-jobbers, or Talkers, will be Dumb; intimating that they will have nothing to say for themselves. 'Tis very curious to see them make Bargains: After they have Argued and Discoursed a while before the Seller, and commonly at his own House, they agree with their Fingers about the Price: They take hold of one another's right Hand under a Cloak or Handkerchief, and entertain one another in that manner; the strait Finger stands for Ten, the bent Finger for Five; the Finger end for One; the whole Hand for a Hundred; and the Fist for a Thousand. Thus they denote Pounds, Pence, and Farthings, with a Motion of their Fingers: While they bargain they put on such a grave and steady Countenance, that 'tis impossible to know in the least either what they think or say.

However, the *Mahometans* are not the greatest Traders in *Asia,* tho' they be dispers'd almost in every Part of it; and tho' their Religion bears sway in the larger part of it. Some of them are too Effeminate, and some too severe to apply themselves to Trade, especially foreign Trading. Wherefore in *Turky,* the *Christians* and *Jews* carry on the main foreign Trade: And in *Persia* the *Christians* and *Indian Gentiles.* As to the *Persians* they Trade with their own Countrymen, one Province with another, and most of them Trade with the *Indians.* The *Armenians* manage alone the whole European Trade; the Reason whereof is, because the *Mahometans* cannot strictly observe their Religion among the *Christians,* with relation to the outward Purity it requires of them; for Instance, Their Law forbids them to eat Flesh either Dress'd or Kill'd by a Man of a different Religion, and likewise to drink in the same Cup with such a one; it forbids to call upon God in a Place adorned with Figures; it even forbids in some Cases, the touching Persons of a contrary Opinion, which is a thing almost impossible to keep among the *Christians*. . . .

$$\boxed{16}$$

From *The Jahangirnama*

The Mughal Empire in India, the third of the great Muslim empires, was the largest, with a population between 100 and 150 million people and an area of 3.2 million square kilometers. Like the other Muslim empires, the Mughal Empire was founded by the descendants of Turkish and Mongol horsemen, and it replaced earlier dynasties that also had come out of the grasslands of Central Asia. Its founder, Babur (r. 1527–1530), a descendant of Timur and Chinghiz Khan, conquered northern India. He and his son, Humayun (r. 1530–1556), espoused the Shia faith (as did Ismail Safavi and his descendants), but Akbar the Great (r. 1556–1605) consolidated Muslim rule of India by adopting the more accommodating Sunni faith of Islam, marrying a Hindu princess, abolishing discriminatory practices against Hindus, and appointing Hindus to government positions. Akbar's son, Jahangir (r. 1605–1627), and his grandson, Shah Jahan (r. 1628–1657), continued these policies of religious toleration and inclusion.

Each of the Mughal rulers left an account of his reign, written in his native Persian and richly illustrated with miniature paintings. Jahangir's book, *The Jahangirnama*, is in many ways the most thorough and candid of these, and it reflects Mughal India at its height. Whereas his great grandfather's *Baburnama* was full of stories of military battles from the period of conquest, Jahangir wrote of the pleasures of the hunt, his constant travels, and his love of art. This selection is from the year 1618, his fiftieth year and the year his grandson was born. How did he celebrate these important events? How did the emperor occupy his time? What do you think were the strengths and weaknesses of a large continental empire like the Mughal?

The Jahangirnama: Memoirs of Jahangir, Emperor of India, ed. and trans. Wheeler M. Thackston (Oxford: Oxford University Press, 1999), 264, 265, 268, 273–76, 279–85.

Thinking Historically

Because this primary source is the work of a king, it is not surprising to find details about Mughal politics and government. What is surprising is how little attention Jahangir seems to have paid to the details of administration and war, the traditional concerns of a Mughal ruler. What inferences about the culture, economy, society, and politics of Mughal India might you draw from this selection? What do the miniature paintings included here tell you about Mughal civilization?

The Unattractiveness of Ahmadabad

I am perplexed at what beauty or goodness the builder of this city saw in this godforsaken land to have built a city here. Why have others after him spent their precious lives in this dust heap? The air is poisonous; the ground has little water and is sandy. The huge amount of dust has already been described. The water is particularly foul and tastes awful. The river bed next to the city is always dry except during the monsoon. The wells are mostly brackish and bitter. The reservoirs located on the outskirts of the city are milky with washermen's soap. The quality people who are rich enough have built cisterns in their houses and fill them with enough rainwater during the monsoon, and they drink it through to the next year. Of course, the unwholesomeness of water that is never exposed to the air and has no way to let off vapors is obvious. Outside the city in places with greenery, the plains are nothing but breeding grounds for thorns, and it is obvious how good a breeze that blows over thorns can be. "O thou paragon of all goodness, by what name shall I call thee?"

I have already called Ahmadabad "Gardabad" [Dustburg]. Now I don't know whether to call it Samumistan [land of the pestilential wind], Bimaristan [land of the ill], Zaqumzar [thorn patch], or Jahan-namabad [hell-ville] since it has qualities of all of them. Were it not for the monsoon, I wouldn't stay in this abode of tribulation for a single day but would get on my flying carpet like Solomon and fly away, delivering my men from this pain and tribulation.

Since the inhabitants of this city are extremely weak-hearted and feeble, as a precaution against any of the men from the camp entering private dwellings in aggression and tyranny or harassment of the poor and weak, and lest the cadi[1] and chief justice show partiality or not be

---

[1] The Supreme Judge of the Empire. [Ed.]

able to prevent oppression, from the date on which we settled in the city, I have sat every day after midday devotions, despite the severity of the heat, for two or three hours in the jharoka on the side of the river, where there is no sort of impediment like gates, walls, watchmen, or guards. There, as demanded by justice, I have attended to the cries of plaintiffs and ordered oppressors punished according to their crimes and offenses. Even while I was sick, despite the great pain and agony, I went to the jharoka[2] every day as usual, denying myself my needed rest.

In order to keep God's flock I do not let my eyes know sleep by night.

For the repose of others I suffer pain in my own body.

By God's grace I have accustomed myself not to have my time robbed by sleep for more than two hours in twenty-four. This has two benefits. One is awareness of what is going on in the realm, and the other is wakefulness of the heart to remembrance of God. It would be a pity for this short life to be wasted in negligence. Since we have a long sleep ahead of us, I try to make the most of this wakefulness, which we will not see again once we sleep, and not be unmindful of God for an instant. "Be awake, for there is a wonderful sleep ahead."...

My Enjoyment of Painting and My Expertise at Discrimination

I derive such enjoyment from painting and have such expertise in judging it that, even without the artist's name being mentioned, no work of past or present masters can be shown to me that I do not instantly recognize who did it. Even if it is a scene of several figures and each face is by a different master, I can tell who did which face. If in a single painting different persons have done the eyes and eyebrows, I can determine who drew the face and who made the eyes and eyebrows. . . . [See Figure 3.1.]

In the little garden in Khurram's place are a platform and a pool. On one side of the platform is a *maulsari* tree against which one can lean while sitting. Since one side of the trunk has a hole in it about a quarter of an ell wide, it looks ugly. I ordered a slab of marble carved to fit the hollow space so that one could sit and lead against it. At this time I composed a line of poetry extemporaneously and ordered the stone-carvers to engrave it on the stone as a remembrance for later

---

[2] Hindi for window. By tradition, the emperor sat at the window to be seen or to hear concerns of subjects. [Ed.]

Figure 3.1 The Court Welcoming Emperor Jahangir.

ages. The line is the following: "Seat of the king of the seven climes, Jahangir son of the King of Kings Akbar."

On the eve of Tuesday the nineteenth [August 31], a fair was held in the private palace. Prior to this it was customary for merchants and craftsmen of the city to set up shops upon command in the courtyard of the palace and bring to display for our view the jeweled implements, all sorts of trinkets, and brocades and textiles they sell in the marketplace. It occurred to me that if the market were to be held during the evening and many lanterns were to be placed before the shops, it would look wonderful. Without exaggeration, it turned out to be exceptionally splendid. I walked through all the shops and bought gems, jeweled items, and every sort of thing I liked. I gave Mulla Asiri something from every shop. He got so much stuff he was unable to keep track of it all.

Departure for Agra

On Thursday the [twenty]-first of Shahrivar [September 2] of the thirteenth regnal year, corresponding to the twenty-second of Ramadan 1027 of the Hegira, after the elapse of two and a half hours, the imperial banners were unfurled in the direction of the capital, Agra. As usual, I went from the palace as far as the Kankriya tank, where camp had been prepared, scattering coins.

Solar Weighing Ceremony

On this day the solar weighing ceremony was held. By solar reckoning the fiftieth year of my life began auspiciously, and, as usual, I was weighed against gold and other items. I scattered pearls and golden flowers. That night I watched an illumination and spent the evening pleasurably in the harem.

On Friday the twenty-second [September 3] I ordered all the shaykhs and religious figures who lived in the city to come and break the fast in my presence. This was done for three consecutive nights, and each night at the end of the gathering I stood and recited: "O Lord, thou art mighty. It is thou who nourishest the rich and the poor. / Neither am I a world conqueror nor a commander, but only one of the beggars at this court. / Help me to do good and be charitable, for otherwise what good could come from me? / I may be a master of slaves, but I am a dutiful slave to the Lord." According to their need I gave land and grants to all the poor who had not yet come into my presence and who had made requests for assistance. . . .

Sayyid Muhammad Is Given a Copy of the Koran Written by Yaqut

On Saturday the thirtieth [September 11] I ordered Sha-i-Alam's grand-son Sayyid Muhammad to request frankly anything he wanted, and I swore on the Koran I would give it to him. He said, "Since you swear on the Koran, I request a copy of the Koran to keep with me always, and when I recite from it the merit will accrue to Your Majesty." I therefore gave him a nice, small-sized copy of the Koran written by Yaqut, which was one of the treasures of the age.[3] On the back I wrote in my own hand that it had been given to Sayyid Muhammad on such-and-such a date in such-and-such a place.

This sayyid possesses an extremely fine disposition, and in addition to innate nobility and acquired learning, he is blessed with good char-acter and pleasing manners. He also has a cheerful disposition and an open countenance. Rarely have I seen anyone of this land to equal the mir in good character. I told him to translate the Koran word for word into Persian, without any consideration for explanation, interpretation, or the reason the verse was revealed, and not to add a single word to the literal text. After finishing it he was to send it to court with his son Sayyid Jalal. The mir's[4] son is also a young man adorned by external and internal skills, and his piety and auspiciousness are evident in his actions. The mir dotes on his son, and he is certainly a very nice young man worthy of his father's pride.

Although the shaykhs of Gujarat had been given many gifts, once again I awarded each of them cash and goods according to their merits and gave them leave to depart.

Since the climate of this land did not agree with me, and the physi-cians had advised me to decrease my usually amount of wine, I did as they suggested and took fewer bowls. Within a week I had decreased my in-take by one bowlful. I had been drinking six bowls at the beginning of each evening, each bowl being seven and a half tolas, a total of forty-five tolas,[5] and normally my wine was mixed. Now I have six bowls that hold six tolas and three mashas, a total of thirty-seven and a half tolas.

One of the marvels of the day is that sixteen or seventeen years ago in Allahabad I promised God that when I reached the age of fifty I would give up hunting with guns and not harm any animal with my own hand. Muqarrab Khan, who has been smiled upon by heaven,

---

[3] Yaqut Musta'simi, famed calligrapher of the Abassid period. [Ed.]

[4] Sayyid and mir both refer to descendants of the prophet Muhammad. [Ed.]

[5] A tola = .425 ounce.

knew of this intention. In short, now that I have reached the aforementioned age and begun my fiftieth year, one day I had such vapors that I could hardly breathe and was in great agony. While in that condition, by divine inspiration I remembered the oath I had sworn to my God, and my former resolve became firm in my mind. I swore to myself that when my fiftieth year came to an end and the term of my promise commenced, with God's help on a day I went to visit Arsh-Ashyani's shrine I would ask for his assistance in keeping my heart firm in this thing. As soon as this thought came to my mind the agony I was suffering disappeared and I found myself refreshed and happy. I thanked God for his blessing, and I hope he will grant me success.

> How well spake Firdawsi of pure lineage—may mercy descend upon his pure tomb: / "Harm not an ant dragging a crumb, for it has a soul, and life is precious."

• • •

The Death of Inayat Kahn

On this date news came of the death of Inayat Khan [see Figure 3.2]. He was one of my closest servants and subjects. In addition to eating opium he also drank wine when he had the chance. Little by little he became obsessed with wine, and since he had a weak frame, he drank more than his body could tolerate and was afflicted with diarrhea. While so weakened he was overcome two or three times by something like epileptic fits. By my order Hakim Rukna treated him, but no matter what he did it was to no avail. In addition, Inayat Khan developed a ravenous appetite, and although the doctor insisted that he not eat more than once a day, he couldn't restrain himself and raged like a madman. Finally he developed cachexia[6] and dropsy[7] and grew terribly thin and weak.

Several days prior to this he requested that he be taken ahead to Agra. I ordered him brought to me to be given leave to depart. He was put in palanquin[8] and brought. He looked incredibly weak and thin. "Skin stretched over bone." Even his bones had begun to disintegrate. Whereas painters employ great exaggeration when they depict skinny people, nothing remotely resembling him had ever been seen. Good God! how

---

[6] Literally, "bad condition." [Ed.]
[7] Fluids swelling the joints. [Ed.]
[8] Enclosed stretcher carried on the shoulders. [Ed.]

Figure 3.2   "Dying Inayat Khan" by Balacanda.

Source: Attributed to: Balacanda, "Dying Inayat Khan." Indian, Mughal, 1618–19. Object Place: Northern India. Ink and light wash on paper, 9.5 cm × 13.3 cm. Museum of Fine Arts, Boston, Francis Bartlett Donation of 1912 and Picture Fund; 14.679. Photograph © 2003 Museum of Fine Arts, Boston.

can a human being remain alive in this shape? The following two lines of poetry are appropriate to the situation: "If my shadow doesn't hold my leg, I won't be able to stand until Doomsday. / My sigh sees my heart so weak that it rests a while on my lip."

It was so strange I ordered the artists to draw his likeness. At any rate, I found him so changed that I said, "At this time you mustn't draw a single breath without remembrance of God, and don't despair of His graciousness. If death grants you quarter, it should be regarded as a reprieve and means for atonement. If your term of life is up, every breath taken with remembrance of Him is a golden opportunity. Do not occupy your mind or worry about those you leave behind, for with us the slightest claim through service is much." Since his distress had been reported to me, I gave him a thousand rupees for traveling expenses and gave him leave to depart. He died the second day. . . .

The Birth of Prince Awrangzeb

On the eve of Sunday the twelfth of Aban of the thirteenth regnal year, corresponding to the fifteenth of Dhu'l-Qa'da 1027 of the Hegira [October 24, 1618], under an ascendant in the nineteenth degree of Libra, the Divine bestowed upon my fortunate son Shahjahan by Asaf Khan's daughter a dear son. It is hoped that his advent will prove fortunate and auspicious to this eternal dynasty. . . .

A Birthday Celebration for Prince Awrangzeb

Since my son Shahjahan had not had a celebration for the birth of his son and Ujjain was one of his jagirs, he requested that the Thursday party on the thirtieth [November 11] be held in his quarters. Of course I granted his request and spent the day pleasurably and enjoyably in his quarters. Those special servants who are admitted to this kind of entertainment were made happy with brimful bowls. My son Shahjahan showed me the newborn child; presented trays of gems and jeweled items and fifty elephants, thirty male and twenty female; and requested a name for the child. God willing, he will be named at an auspicious hour. Seven of the elephants he presented were sent to the royal stable, and the rest were divided up among the garrison commanders. The total worth of what was accepted would be two lacs of rupees.

On this day Azududdawla came from his jagir[9] and paid homage. He presented eighty-one mohurs[10] as a vow and an elephant as a gift. I had summoned to court Qasim Khan, who had been replaced as governor of Bengal. He arrived at court and presented a thousand mohurs.

On Friday the first of Azar [November 12] I amused myself by going hunting with hawks and falcons. [See Figure 3.3.] While out riding I came across a field of *juwar* [Indian millet]. Although a stem usually gives only one spike, I spied three that had twelve spikes. This provoked my amazement, and at once I remembered the story of the king and the gardener.

[9] Administrative grant of land. [Ed.]
[10] Gold coin worth 165 grams of gold. [Ed.]

Figure 3.3   Shahjahan Firing a Matchlock.

The Story of the King and the Gardener

Once upon a time when it was hot a king came to the gate of an orchard. Seeing an old gardener standing at the gate, he asked, "Are there any pomegranates in this orchard?"

"There are," he replied. The king ordered him to bring a cup of pomegranate juice. The gardener had a daughter who was adorned both by beauty of form and by good conduct. He motioned to her to bring some pomegranate juice. The girl went and at once returned, bringing a cup full of pomegranate juice covered with several leaves. The king took it from her and drank it down. Then he asked the girl, "What was the reason for putting the leaves over the juice?"

The girl replied eloquently, "In such hot weather to come riding drenched in sweat and gulp down juice in an instant is contrary to wisdom. Therefore, as a precaution, I placed the leaves over the cup so that you would drink it slowly and carefully."

The king was highly pleased by this nice speech and thought to enter the girl among the servants in his harem. He asked the gardener, "What is your annual income from this orchard?"

"Three hundred dinars," he said.

"What do you give to the administration?" he asked.

"The king doesn't take anything for fruit," he replied, "but he takes a tenth on sown crops."

The king then thought to himself, saying, "There are many orchards and countless trees in my realm. If they were to give a tenth from the produce of orchards too, it would amount to a huge sum, and the peasants wouldn't have such an excess. I will order a tax to be taken on the produce of orchards too." Then he asked for another cup of pomegranate juice. The girl went, and after a long time she came back with a cup.

"The last time you went," said the king, "you came right back and brought more. This time it took you longer and you brought less."

"The other time I filled the cup brimful with the juice of one pomegranate," she said. "This time I had to squeeze five or six pomegranates, and still I didn't get as much juice."

The king was perplexed. Then the gardener said, "The prosperity of the crop is due to the good intention of the king. I think you must be the king. When you asked me what the income of my orchard was, your intention was otherwise than good. As a consequence the fruit lost its blessedness."

The king had a change of heart and put his new idea out of his mind. Then he said, "Bring me one more cup of pomegranate juice." The girl went and quickly brought out the cup overflowing and gave it to the king, smiling and happy. The king praised the gardener's perspicacity and told him the truth of the situation. Then he asked for the girl's hand in marriage. This story of the truth-perceiving king has remained on the pages of time.

In short, the appearance of such things are due to good intentions and the fruits of justice. Whenever a just and equitable monarch's mind and intention are focused upon the people's welfare and the peasants' prosperity, the blessings of good crops and produce are innumerable. Praise God that in this eternal empire it has never been and is still not customary to collect a tax on the produce of trees. Throughout this well-protected realm, not a dam or a grain enters the imperial treasury or the supreme administration by this means. Rather, it is ordered that anyone who builds an orchard on cultivated land be exempt from tax on the produce. It is hoped that God will keep this supplicant firm in his resolve to do good. "If my intention is charitable, thou givest me good."

Another Conversation with Jadrup

On Saturday the second [November 13] I had a great yearning to converse with Jadrup again. After performing my noontime devotions I got in a boat to go see him. Toward the end of the day I hastened into his corner of retirement and talked with him. I heard many lofty statements about gnostic truths, and he explained the fundamentals of mysticism without obfuscation. One can really enjoy his company. He is over sixty years old. He was twenty-two years old when he severed his ties to material things and set out on the highway of renunciation, and he has been in the "garb of garblessness" for thirty-eight years now. As I was leaving he said, "How can I express my gratitude for this God-given occasion? I have been occupied worshiping my deity with ease of mind and freedom from concern during the reign of such a just monarch, and never has any worry come to my doorstep."

On Sunday the third [November 14] we decamped from Kaliadeh and dismounted in the village of Qasimkhera. Along the way I occupied myself hunting with hawks and falcons. By change a *karwanak* crane took flight. I sent a white hawk of which I am extremely fond after it. The crane escaped its clutches, and the hawk rose into the air and went so high that it disappeared from view. No matter how hard or far the scouts and falconers searched, they found no trace. It seemed absurd to think that the hawk could be recovered in such a plain. Lashkar Mir Kashmiri, the chief of the Kashmiri falconers, was in charge of the said bird. He was searching for it frantically all over the plain when suddenly it appeared far away in a tree. When he approached, he found the hawk sitting on the end of a branch. He showed it a chicken and summoned it. Not three gharis[11] had passed before he had captured it and brought it to me. This was a gift from out of the blue that no one had expected, and it made me very happy. As a reward for this service I increased his rank and gave him a horse and a robe of honor.

REFLECTIONS

The land-based empires of Asia had vigorous systems of trade. Yet in none of these did the economy drive politics, as it did in Malacca. Rather, politics was driven by the emperor and imperial bureaucracy in

[11] A period of 24 minutes. [Ed.]

China and by the military alliances of tribal confederacies in the Muslim empires.

In the Muslim empires, to counter the influence of tribal confederacies, the shahs relied on two special social groups: (1) slaves in central state armies, imperial offices, and as bodyguards, and (2) eunuchs in the harem and palace. Neither of these social groups shared the institutional conservatism of Chinese officialdom. Their value was loyalty and effectiveness rather than tradition and wisdom. In India, the Mughal emperor relied less on slave armies, because he was better able to counterbalance the competing tribal interests of a diverse population that included other central Asian peoples as well as dependent Hindu princes.

The Confucian culture of China demeaned the military. Chinese political centralization had long since curbed the ambitions of internal feudal princes. There were no sources of competing military power within China, only without. When the Mongols conquered China and established the Yuan dynasty (1271–1368), they could not govern with armies from Mongolia. Even though they diminished the role of the Chinese civil service, they had to appoint Chinese and Mongol officials to a vast bureaucracy that had operated for centuries according to its own laws.

As China absorbed its Mongol conquerors, so did India absorb the Mughals. Yet the Mongol Yuan dynasty was overthrown by the nativist Chinese Ming. Perhaps, with an aggressive revival of Hinduism during the Mughal reign of Aurangzeb and without incursions of new foreigners from Europe, India would have encountered a similar fate.

In any case, the political systems of China and the Muslim empires were rooted in the field and pasture; the ruling classes were landed aristocrats and tribal chieftains, not merchants. Although trade, markets, and economic activity were very important in all territorial empires and a number of both Chinese and Indian cities were the largest in the world, merchants did not constitute a separate social class in any of these empires. Chardin reminds us of the role of Europeans like himself and of Armenians in Persia. The Ottomans used Jews and Armenians to build long-distance trading networks. The Mughals used Hindu merchants and manufacturers, and some Indians (especially Gujaratis) traded in Persia and throughout the Indian Ocean. Economic activity was strong throughout Eurasia in the sixteenth and seventeenth century, but as a social class merchants were always subservient to the state. The lords of the land dominated the state.

Tiny Malacca carved out a different political structure as early as the fifteenth century. There were numerous merchant communities in a maritime state that depended on trade to survive, yet the political ruler, the sultan, was not a merchant. (That would come at a later stage in the history of capitalism.) Rather, Malacca owed its existence to the most powerful monarch on earth in the 1430s — the Ming emperor. And it was precisely the smaller, more marginal states like Malacca that were able to free themselves of the kings of the land, from trade as tribute, and from the politics of armies and officials, to create the modern business state. What do these readings suggest about the relationship between political power and economic prosperity?

4

Gender and Family

China, Southeast Asia, Europe, and "New Spain," 1600–1750

HISTORICAL CONTEXT

Women are half of humanity. The family is the oldest and most important social institution. Marriage is one of the most important passages in one's life. Yet these subjects rarely register as important topics in world history. There are at least two reasons for this: One is the tendency to think of history as the story of public events only — the actions of political officials, governments, and their representatives — instead of the private and domestic sphere. The second is the assumption that the private or domestic sphere has no history, and that it has always been the same.

Since the urban revolution five thousand years ago most societies have been patriarchal. The laws, social codes, and dominant ideas have enshrined the power and prestige of men over women, husbands over wives, fathers over children, gods over goddesses, even brothers over sisters. Double standards for adultery, inheritance laws that favor sons, and laws that deny women property or political rights all attest to the power of patriarchal culture and norms. Almost everywhere patriarchies have limited women to the domestic sphere while granting men public and political power. It is no wonder that patriarchies have deemed domesticity dull and unchanging. But the evidence of centuries of diaries, letters, novels, gossip, and, more recently, telephone conversations and soap operas shows that most people find the personal and domestic anything but dull. And the constant attention people pay to the human dramas of home and family suggests the importance they attach to them. For historians, then, to assume otherwise would be foolish.

But how, then, to view the daily dramas that define so much of our lives? In this chapter, we peer through a couple of windows at particular moments in history. We have chosen to look at China, Southeast Asia, Mexico, and Europe so that our examples are varied enough to ensure that generalizations are not limited to a particular culture.

THINKING HISTORICALLY
Making Comparisons

We learn by making comparisons. Every new piece of knowledge we acquire leads to a comparison with what we already know. For example, we arrive in a new town and we are struck by something that we have not seen before. The town has odd street lamps, flowerpots on the sidewalks, or lots of trucks on the street. We start to formulate a theory about the differences between what we observe in the new town and what we already know about our old town. We think we're on to something, but our theory falls apart when we make more observations by staying in the new town another day, or traveling on to the next town, or going halfway across the world. As we gain more experience and make more observations, our original theory explaining an observed difference is supplanted by a much more complex theory about *types* of towns.

History is very much like travel. We learn by comparison, one step at a time, and the journey is never ending. On this trip we begin in China and then move on to other regions of the world. We begin with primary sources, but make comparisons based on secondary sources as well. In fact, we conclude with a secondary source that will allow us to draw upon our previous readings to make increasingly informed and complex comparisons. Welcome aboard. Next stop, China.

17

Family Instructions for the Miu Lineage

Chinese families in Ming times (1368–1644) often organized them-selves into groups by male lineage. These groups often shared com-mon land, built ancestral halls, published genealogies, honored their common ancestors, and ensured the success and well-being of future generations. To accomplish the last of these, lineage groups frequently compiled lists of family rules or instructions. This particular example, from the various lines of the Miu family of the Guangdong province in the south, shows how extensive these instructions could be. What values did these family instructions encourage? What activities did the Miu lineage regulate? What kind of families, and what kind of indi-viduals, were these rules intended to produce? How would these rules have had a different impact on women and men?

Thinking Historically

It is difficult to read this selection without thinking of one's own fam-ily and of families in one's own society. How many of the Miu lin-eage's concerns are concerns of families you know? Family instruc-tions and lineage organizations are not common features of modern American society, even among Chinese Americans who may have a sense of their lineage and family identity. What institutions in modern American society regulate the activities addressed by these family in-structions? Or are these activities allowed to regulate themselves or to go unregulated? From reading this document, what do you think are some of the differences between Ming-era Chinese families and mod-ern American families?

Work Hard at One of the Principal Occupations

1. To be filial to one's parents, to be loving to one's brothers, to be diligent and frugal — these are the first tenets of a person of good char-acter. They must be thoroughly understood and faithfully carried out.

One's conscience should be followed like a strict teacher and in-sight should be sought through introspection. One should study the words and deeds of the ancients to find out their ultimate meanings.

"Family Instructions for the Miu Lineage, Late Sixteenth Century," trans. Clara Yu, in *Chinese Civilization: A Sourcebook*, 2nd ed., ed. Patricia Ebrey (New York: Free Press, 1993), 238–40, 241–43.

One should always remember the principles followed by the ancients, and should not become overwhelmed by current customs. For if one gives in to cruelty, pride, or extravagance, all virtues will be undermined, and nothing will be achieved.

Parents have special responsibilities. The *Book of Changes* says: "The members of a family have strict sovereigns." The "sovereigns" are the parents. Their position in a family is one of unique authority, and they should utilize their authority to dictate matters to maintain order, and to inspire respect, so that the members of the family will all be obedient. If the parents are lenient and indulgent, there will be many troubles which in turn will give rise to even more troubles. Who is to blame for all this? The elders in a family must demand discipline of themselves, following all rules and regulations to the letter, so that the younger members emulate their good behavior and exhort each other to abide by the teachings of the ancient sages. Only in this way can the family hope to last for generations. If, however, the elders of a family should find it difficult to abide by these regulations, the virtuous youngsters of the family should help them along. Because the purpose of my work is to make such work easier, I am not afraid of giving many small details. . . .

2. Those youngsters who have taken Confucian scholarship as their hereditary occupation should be sincere and hard-working, and try to achieve learning naturally while studying under a teacher. Confucianism is the only thing to follow if they wish to bring glory to their family. Those who know how to keep what they have but do not study are as useless as puppets made of clay or wood. Those who study, even if they do not succeed in the examinations, can hope to become teachers or to gain personal benefit. However, there are people who study not for learning's sake, but as a vulgar means of gaining profit. These people are better off doing nothing.

Youngsters who are incapable of concentrating on studying should devote themselves to farming; they should personally grasp the ploughs and eat the fruit of their own labor. In this way they will be able to support their families. If they fold their hands and do nothing, they will soon have to worry about hunger and cold. If, however, they realize that their forefathers also worked hard and that farming is a difficult way of life, they will not be inferior to anyone. In earlier dynasties, officials were all selected because they were filial sons, loving brothers, and diligent farmers. This was to set an example for all people to devote themselves to their professions, and to ensure that the officials were familiar with the hardships of the common people, thereby preventing them from exploiting the commoners for their own profit.

3. Farmers should personally attend to the inspection, measurement, and management of the fields, noting the soil as well as the terrain. The early harvest as well as the grain taxes and the labor service

obligations should be carefully calculated. Anyone who indulges in indolence and entrusts these matters to others will not be able to distinguish one kind of crop from another and will certainly be cheated by others. I do not believe such a person could escape bankruptcy.

4. The usual occupations of the people are farming and commerce. If one tries by every possible means to make a great profit from these occupations, it usually leads to loss of capital. Therefore it is more profitable to put one's energy into farming the land; only when the fields are too far away to be tilled by oneself should they be leased to others. One should solicit advice from old farmers as to one's own capacity in farming.

Those who do not follow the usual occupations of farming or business should be taught a skill. Being an artisan is a good way of life and will also shelter a person from hunger and cold. All in all, it is important to remember that one should work hard when young, for when youth expires one can no longer achieve anything. Many people learn this lesson only after it is too late. We should guard against this mistake.

5. Fish can be raised in ponds by supplying them with grass and manure. Vegetables need water. In empty plots one can plant fruit trees such as the pear, persimmon, peach, prune, and plum, and also beans, wheat, hemp, peas, potatoes, and melons. When harvested, these vegetables and fruits can sustain life. During their growth, one should give them constant care, nourishing them and weeding them. In this way, no labor is wasted and no fertile land is left uncultivated. On the contrary, to purchase everything needed for the morning and evening meals means the members of the family will merely sit and eat. Is this the way things should be?

6. Housewives should take full charge of the kitchen. They should make sure that the store of firewood is sufficient, so that even if it rains several days in succession, they will not be forced to use silver or rice to pay for firewood, thereby impoverishing the family. Housewives should also closely calculate the daily grocery expenses, and make sure there is no undue extravagance. Those who simply sit and wait to be fed only are treating themselves like pigs and dogs, but also are leading their whole households to ruin. . . .

Exercise Restraint

1. Our young people should know their place and observe correct manners. They are not permitted to gamble, to fight, to engage in lawsuits, or to deal in salt privately. Such unlawful acts will only lead to their own downfall.

2. If land or property is not obtained by righteous means, descendants will not be able to enjoy it. When the ancients invented characters,

they put gold next to two spears to mean "money," indicating that the danger of plunder or robbery is associated with it. If money is not accumulated by good means, it will disperse like overflowing water; how could it be put to any good? The result is misfortune for oneself as well as for one's posterity. This is the meaning of the saying: "The way of Heaven detests fullness, and only the humble gain." Therefore, accumulation of great wealth inevitably leads to great loss. How true are the words of Laozi!

A person's fortune and rank are predestined. One can only do one's best according to propriety and one's own ability; the rest is up to Heaven. If one is easily contented, then a diet of vegetables and soups provides a lifetime of joy. If one does not know one's limitations and tries to accumulate wealth by immoral and dishonest means, how can one avoid disaster? To be able to support oneself through life and not leave one's sons and grandsons in hunger and cold is enough; why should one toil so much?

3. Pride is a dangerous trait. Those who pride themselves on wealth, rank, or learning are inviting evil consequences. Even if one's accomplishments are indeed unique, there is no need to press them on anyone else. "The way of Heaven detests fullness, and only the humble gain." I have seen the truth of this saying many times.

4. Taking concubines in order to beget heirs should be a last resort, for the sons of the legal wife and the sons of the concubine are never of one mind, causing innumerable conflicts between half brothers. If the parents are in the least partial, problems will multiply, creating misfortune in later generations. Since families have been ruined because of this, it should not be taken lightly.

5. Just as diseases are caused by what goes into one's mouth, misfortunes are caused by what comes out of one's mouth. Those who are immoderate in eating and unrestrained in speaking have no one else to blame for their own ruin.

6. Most men lack resolve and listen to what their women say. As a result, blood relatives become estranged and competitiveness, suspicion, and distance arise between them. Therefore, when a wife first comes into a family, it should be made clear to her that such things are prohibited. "Start teaching one's son when he is a baby; start teaching one's daughter-in-law when she first arrives." That is to say, preventive measures should be taken early.

7. "A family's fortune can be foretold from whether its members are early risers" is a maxim of our ancient sages. Everyone, male and female, should rise before dawn and should not go to bed until after the first drum. Never should they indulge themselves in a false sense of security and leisure, for such behavior will eventually lead them to poverty.

8. Young family members who deliberately violate family regulations should be taken to the family temple, have their offenses reported to the ancestors, and be severely punished. They should then be taught to improve themselves. Those who do not accept punishment or persist in their wrongdoings will bring harm to themselves.

9. As a preventive measure against the unpredictable, the gates should be closed at dusk, and no one should be allowed to go out. Even when there are visitors, dinner parties should end early, so that there will be no need for lighting lamps and candles. On very hot or very cold days, one should be especially considerate of the kitchen servants.

10. For generations this family had dwelt in the country, and everyone has had a set profession; therefore, our descendants should not be allowed to change their place of residence. After living in the city for three years, a person forgets everything about farming; after ten years, he does not even know his lineage. Extravagance and leisure transform people, and it is hard for anyone to remain unaffected. I once remarked that the only legitimate excuse to live in a city temporarily is to flee from bandits.

11. The inner and outer rooms, halls, doorways, and furniture should be swept and dusted every morning at dawn. Dirty doorways and courtyards and haphazardly placed furniture are sure signs of a declining family. Therefore, a schedule should be followed for cleaning them, with no excuses allowed.

12. Those in charge of cooking and kitchen work should make sure that breakfast is served before nine o'clock in the morning and dinner before five o'clock in the afternoon. Every evening the iron wok and other utensils should be washed and put away, so that the next morning, after rising at dawn, one can expect tea and breakfast to be prepared immediately and served on time. In the kitchen no lamps are allowed in the morning or at night. This is not only to save the expense, but also to avoid harmful contamination of food. Although this is a small matter, it has a great effect on health. Furthermore, since all members of the family have their regular work to do, letting them toil all day without giving them meals at regular hours is no way to provide comfort and relief for them. If these rules are deliberately violated, the person in charge will be punished as an example to the rest.

13. On the tenth and twenty-fifth days of every month, all the members of this branch, from the honored aged members to the youngsters, should gather at dusk for a meeting. Each will give an account of what he has learned, by either calling attention to examples of good and evil, or encouraging diligence, or expounding his obligations, or pointing out tasks to be completed. Each member will take turns presenting his own opinions and listening attentively to others. He should examine himself in the matters being discussed and make efforts to

improve himself. The purpose of these meetings is to encourage one another in virtue and to correct each other's mistakes.

The members of the family will take turns being the chairman of these meetings, according to schedule. If someone is unable to chair a meeting on a certain day, he should ask the next person in line to take his place. The chairman should provide tea, but never wine. The meetings may be canceled on days of ancestor worship, parties, or other such occasions, or if the weather is severe. Those who are absent from these meetings for no reason are only doing themselves harm.

There are no set rules for where the meeting should be held, but the place should be convenient for group discussions. The time of the meeting should always be early evening, for this is when people have free time. As a general precaution the meeting should never last until late at night.

14. Women from lower-class families who stop at our houses tend to gossip, create conflicts, peek into the kitchens, or induce our women to believe in prayer and fortune-telling, thereby cheating them out of their money and possessions. Consequently, one should question these women often and punish those who come for no reason, so as to put a stop to the traffic.

15. Blood relatives are as close as the branches of a tree, yet their relationships can still be differentiated according to importance and priority: Parents should be considered before brothers, and brothers should be considered before wives and children. Each person should fulfill his own duties and share with others profit and loss, joy and sorrow, life and death. In this way, the family will get along well and be blessed by Heaven. Should family members fight over property or end up treating each other like enemies, then when death or misfortune strikes they will be of even less use than strangers. If our ancestors have consciousness, they will not tolerate these unprincipled descendants who are but animals in man's clothing. Heaven responds to human vices with punishments as surely as an echo follows a sound. I hope my sons and grandsons take my words seriously.

16. To get along with patrilineal relatives, fellow villages, and relatives through marriage, one should be gentle in speech and mild in manners. When one is opposed by others, one may remonstrate with them; but when others fall short because of their limitations, one should be tolerant. If one's youngsters or servants get into fights with others, one should look into oneself to find the blame. It is better to be wronged than to wrong others. Those who take affront and become enraged, who conceal their own shortcomings and seek to defeat others, are courting immediate misfortune. Even if the other party is unbearably unreasonable, one should contemplate the fact that the ancient sages had to endure much more. If one remains tolerant and forgiving, one will be able to curb the other party's violence.

$$\boxed{18}$$

MAO XIANG

How Dong Xiaowan Became My Concubine

Mao Xiang (1611–1693) was one of the great poets, artists, and cal-
ligraphers of the late Ming dynasty and, after its demise in 1644, a
persistent critic of the succeeding Manchu or Quing dynasty. He was
also known for his love of beautiful women, especially three famous courtesans who were also talented artists: Dong Xiaowan
(1625–1651), Cai Han (1647–1686), and Qin Yue (c. 1660–1690).
(Note what these dates reveal.) Whether or not this is a reliable account of how Dong Xiaowan became his concubine, what does this
piece from Mao Xiang's memoir tell you about his society's attitudes
towards women, marriage, and family?

Thinking Historically

If comparisons originate in our recognition of institutions and ideas
that are foreign to our own, certainly the acceptance of concubines in
seventeenth-century Chinese society is a sharp contrast to modern
American family values. Concubines were mainly an indulgence of
upper-class Chinese men, but concubinage was an institution that
touched all classes of Chinese society. Poor peasants knew that they
could sell their daughters into the trade, if need be. And even middle-
class wives worried that a concubine might be waiting in the wings
should they prove to be infertile, unable to bear a son, or otherwise
displeasing to their husband or mother-in-law.

    We might also compare this selection with the previous one. How
does the blatant acceptance of concubinage in this selection compare
to the emphasis on family stability in the Miu lineage rules? Are these
documents from two different Chinas, or are they compatible? Does
this selection force you to modify the contrast you drew between
Ming China and modern America from the previous selection?

I was rather depressed that evening, so I got a boat and went with a
friend on an excursion to Tiger Hill. My plan was to send a messenger
to Xiangyang the next morning and then set out for home. As our boat

---

"How Dong Xiaowan Became My Concubine," in *Chinese Civilization: A Sourcebook*, 2nd
ed., ed. Patricia Ebrey (New York: Free Press, 1993), 246–49.

143

passed under a bridge, I saw a small building by the bank. When I asked who lived there, my friend told me that this was [the singing girl] Dong's home. I was wildly happy with memories of three years before. I insisted on the boat's stopping, wanting to see Xiaowan at once. My friend, however, restrained me, saying, "Xiaowan has been terrified by the threat of being kidnapped by a powerful man and has been seriously ill for eighteen days. Since her mother's death,[1] she is said to have locked her door and refrained from receiving any guests." I nevertheless insisted on going ashore.

Not until I had knocked two or three times did the door open. I found no light in the house and had to grope my way upstairs. There I discovered medicine all over the table and bed.

Xiaowan, moaning, asked where I had come from and I told her I was the man she once saw beside a winding balustrade, intoxicated.

"Well, Sir," she said, recalling the incident, "I remember years ago you called at my house several times. Even though she only saw you once, my mother often spoke highly of you and considered it a great pity that I never had the chance to wait on you. Three years have passed. Mother died recently, but on seeing you now, I can hear her words in my ears. Where are you coming from this time?"

With an effort, she rose to draw aside the curtains and inspected me closely. She moved the lamp and asked me to sit on her bed. After talking awhile, I said I would go, not wanting to tire her. She, however, begged me to remain, saying, "During the past eighteen days I have had no appetite for food, nor have I been able to sleep well. My soul has been restless, dreaming almost all the time. But on seeing you, I feel as if my spirit has revived and my vigor returned." She then had her servant serve wine and food at her bedside, and kept refilling my cup herself.

Several times I expressed my desire to leave, but each time she urged me to stay. . . . The following morning, I was eager to set off on the trip home, but my friend and my servant both asked me not to be ungrateful for Xiaowan's kindness as she had had only a brief chance to talk with me the previous night. Accordingly I went to say goodbye to her. I found her, fresh from her toilet, leaning against a window upstairs quite composed. On seeing my boat approaching the bank, she hurried aboard to greet me. I told her that I had to leave immediately, but she said that she had packed up her belongings and would accompany me. I felt unable to refuse her.

We went from Hushuguan to Wuxi, and from there to Changzhou, Yixing, and Jiangyin, finally arriving at Jinjiang. All this took twenty-

---

1 The "mother" here may well be the woman who managed her, rather than her natural mother.

seven days, and twenty-seven times I asked her to go back, but she was firm in her desire to follow me. On climbing Golden Hill, she pointed to the river and swore, "My body is as constant as the direction of the Yangzi River. I am determined never to go back to Suzhou!"

On hearing her words, I turned red and reiterated my refusal, "The provincial examination is coming up soon. Because my father's recent posts have been dangerous ones, I have failed to attend to family affairs and have not been able to look after my mother on a daily basis. This is my first chance to go back and take care of things. Moreover, you have so many creditors in Suzhou and it will take a lot to redeem your singing-girl's contract in Nanjing. So please go back to Suzhou for the time being. After I have taken the examination at the end of summer, I will send word and meet you in Nanjing. At any rate, I must await the result of the examination before I even think about these matters. Insisting on it now will do neither of us any good."

She, however, still hesitated. There were dice on the table, and one of my friends said to her jokingly, "If you are ever going to get your wish [to become his concubine], they will land with the same side up." She then bowed toward the window, said a prayer, and tossed the dice. They all landed on six. All on board expressed their amazement, and I said to her, "Should Heaven really be on our side, I'm afraid we might bungle the whole thing if we proceed too hurriedly. You had better leave me temporarily, and we'll see what we can do by and by." Thus against her wishes she said goodbye, concealing her tearstained face with her hands.

I had pity for her plight but at the same time once I was on my own felt relieved of a heavy burden. Upon arrival at Taizhou, I sat for the examination. When I got home in the sixth month, my wife said to me, "Xiaowan sent her father to bring word that since her return to Suzhou, she has kept to a vegetarian diet and confined herself to her home, waiting on tiptoe for you to bring her to Nanjing as you promised. I felt awkward and gave her father ten taels[2] of silver, asking him to tell her that I am in sympathy with her and consent to her request, but she must wait till you finish the examination."

I appreciated the way my wife had handled Xiaowan's request. I then directly proceeded to Nanjing without keeping my promise to send someone to fetch her, planning to write to her after I had finished the examination. However, scarcely, had I come out of the examination hall on the morning of the 15th of the eighth month when she suddenly called at my lodgings at Peach Leaf Ferry. It turned out that after waiting in vain for news from me, she had hired a boat, setting out from Suzhou and proceeding along the river with an old woman as her

---

[2]A tael is equivalent to about 1¼ ounce. [Ed.]

companion. She met with robbers on the way, and her boat had to hide among reeds and rushes. With the rudder broken, the boat could not proceed, and she had had practically nothing to eat for three days. She arrived at Sanshan Gate of Nanjing on the 8th, but not wanting to disturb my thoughts during the examination, she delayed entering the city for two days.

Though delighted to see me, she looked and sounded rather sad as she vividly described what had happened during the hundred days of our separation, including her confinement at home on vegetarian fare, her encounter with robbers on the river, and her other experiences of a voyage fraught with danger. Now she was more insistent than ever on getting her wish. The men in my literary society from Kashan, Sungjiang, Fujian, and Henan all admired her farsightedness and sincerity and encouraged her with their verses and paintings.

When the examination was over, I thought I might pass it, so hoped I would soon be able to settle my affairs and gratify her desire to become my concubine. Unexpectedly, on the 17th I was informed that my father had arrived by boat. . . . I had not seen him for two years and was overjoyed that he had returned alive from the battlefront. Without delaying to tell Xiaowan, I immediately went to meet him. . . . Before long she set out by boat in pursuit of me from the lodging house at Peach Leaf Ferry. A storm at Swallow's Ledge nearly cost her her life. At Shierhui she came on board and stayed with me again for seven days.

When the results of the examination were announced, I found my name on the list of the not quite successful candidates. I then traveled day and night to get home, while she followed weeping, unwilling to part. I was, however, well aware that I could not by myself settle her affairs in Suzhou and that her creditors would, on discovering her departure, increase their demands. Moreover, my father's recent return and my disappointment in the exams had made it all the more difficult to gratify her desire at once. On arrival at Puchao on the outskirts of my native city, I had to put on a cold face and turn ironhearted to part from her, telling her to go back to Suzhou to set her creditors at ease and thus pave the way for our future plans.

In the tenth month, while passing Jinjiang, I went to visit Mr. Zheng, the man who had been my examiner. At that time, Liu Daxing of Fujian had arrived from the capital. During a drinking party in his boat with General Chen, my friend Prefect Liu, and myself, my servant returned from seeing Xiaowan home. He reported that on arrival at Suzhou she did not change out of her autumn clothing, saying that she intended to die of cold if I did not see my way to settle her affairs promptly. On hearing this, Liu Daxing pointed to me and said, "Pijiang, you are well known as a man of honor. Could you really betray a girl like this?"

"Surely scholars are not capable of the gallant deeds of Huang Shanke and Gu Yaya," I replied.

The prefect raised his cup, and with a gesture of excitement exclaimed, "Well, if I were given a thousand taels of silver to pay my expenses, I'd start right away today!"

General Chen at once lent me several hundred taels, and Liu Daxing helped with a present of several catties[3] of ginseng. But how could it have been anticipated that the prefect, on arrival at Suzhou, failed to carry out his mission, and that when the creditors had kicked up a row and the matter had been brought to a deadlock, he fled to Wujiang? I had no chance to make further inquiries, as I returned home shortly afterwards.

Xiaowan was left in an awkward position, with little she could do. On hearing of her trouble, Qian Qianyi of Changshu went to Bantang himself and brought her to his boat. He approached her creditors, from the gentry to the townsmen, and within three days managed to clear every single debt of hers, the bills redeemed piling up a foot in height. This done, he arranged a farewell banquet on a pleasure boat and entertained her at the foot of Tiger Hill. He then hired a boat and sent someone to see her to Rugao.

On the evening of the 15th of the eleventh month when I was drinking wine with my father in our Zhuocun Hall, I was suddenly informed that Xiaowan had arrived at the jetty. After reading Qian's long interesting letter, I learned how she had gotten here. I also learned that Qian had written to a pupil of his, Zhang of the ministry of rites, asking him to redeem her singing's girl's contract at once. Her minor problems at Suzhou were later settled by Mr. Zhou of the bureau of ceremonies while Mr. Li, formerly attached to that bureau, had also rendered her great assistance in Nanjing.

Ten months thereafter, her desire was gratified [and she became my concubine]. After the endless tangle of troubles and emotional pain, we had what we wanted.

---

[3]One catty is equivalent to 16 taels, 20 ounces, or a British pound. [Ed.]

19

ANTHONY REID

Commerce and Gender in Southeast Asia

This selection is from a modern historian's study of Southeast Asia between 1450 and 1680. The cultures of Southeast Asia (modern
Burma, Thailand, Cambodia, Malaysia, Indonesia, and Vietnam)
were influenced by, but traditionally quite different from, neighboring
India and China. In addition to Indian and Chinese influences, these
traditional cultures withstood periodic waves of Buddhist, Christian,
and Muslim missionaries and merchants, all of which influenced and
shaped them to some extent. What was the traditional role of women
in Southeast Asia? How did foreign cultures affect women's lives?
Why was Vietnam's culture different from the cultures of other Southeast Asian countries?

Thinking Historically

Clearly, Asian societies, past and present, are not all alike. One striking comparison that we can make between this and the two previous
selections is the difference between gender relations in China and
Southeast Asia during the sixteenth and seventeenth centuries. How
were the lives of women in Southeast Asia different from the lives of
women in China? Was Southeast Asian society still a patriarchy?

Reid's discussion of Southeast Asian sexuality also elicits comparative questions. How, according to Reid, was Southeast Asian society
the opposite of contemporaneous European society? Is modern American sexuality closer to that of seventeenth-century Europe or Southeast Asia?

Sexual Relations

Relations between the sexes represented one aspect of the social system
in which a distinctive Southeast Asian pattern was especially evident.
Even the gradual strengthening of the influence of Islam, Christianity,
Buddhism, and Confucianism in their respective spheres over the last
four centuries has by no means eliminated a common pattern of rela-

Anthony Reid, "Commerce and Gender in Southeast Asia," in *Southeast Asia in the Age of
Commerce, vol. 1: The Land Below the Winds* (New Haven: Yale University Press, 1988),
146–50, 162–64.

tively high female autonomy and economic importance. In the sixteenth and seventeenth centuries the region probably represented one extreme of human experience on these issues. It would be wrong to say that women were *equal* to men — indeed, there were very few areas in which they competed directly. Women had different functions from men, but these included transplanting and harvesting rice, weaving, and marketing. Their reproductive role gave them magical and ritual powers which it was difficult for men to match. These factors may explain why the value of daughters was never questioned in Southeast Asia as it was in China, India, and the Middle East; on the contrary, [it was believed that] "the more daughters a man has, the richer he is."

Throughout Southeast Asia wealth passed from the male to the female side in marriage — the reverse of European dowry. Vietnam in modern times has been the exception to this pattern as to many others, because of the progressive imposition of the sternly patriarchal Confucian system beginning in the fifteenth century. Yet in southern Vietnam as late as the seventeenth century men continued what must have been an older Southeast Asian pattern, giving bride-wealth at marriage and even residing with the families of their brides.

To some early Christian missionaries the practice of paying bride-wealth was disapproved as a form of buying a wife. Although the terminology of the market was occasionally used in this as in other transactions, the practice of bride-wealth in fact demonstrated the high economic value of women and contributed to their autonomy. In contrast to the other major area of bride-price, Africa, where the wealth went to the bride's father and was eventually inherited through the male line, Southeast Asian women benefited directly from the system. Tomé Pires put it strongly for the Malays he knew [in 1515]: "The man must give the woman ten *tahil*[1] and six *mas*[2] of gold as dowry which must always be actually in her power." In other cases bride-wealth was paid to the bride's parents, who transferred some property to their daughter.

In sharp contrast to the Chinese pattern, the married couple more frequently resided in the wife's than in the husband's village. In Thailand, Burma, and Malaya that was the rule. Southeast Asian legal codes differed markedly from their supposed Indian or Chinese (in Vietnam) models in their common insistence that property be held jointly by the married couple and administered together. In inheritance all children had an equal claim regardless of sex, though favoured children or those caring for the aged might obtain a larger share. Islamic law, which required that sons receive double the inheritance of daughters, was never

[1]Equivalent to 580 grams of silver. [Ed.]
[2]Small gold coin. [Ed.]

effectively implemented. The stern Chinese legal principle that wives had no say in the disposal of family property found its way into some nineteenth-century Vietnamese law codes, but never into Vietnamese practice.

The relative autonomy enjoyed by women extended to sexual relations. Southeast Asian literature of the period leaves us in little doubt that women took a very active part in courtship and lovemaking, and demanded as much as they gave by way of sexual and emotional gratification. The literature describes the physical attractiveness of male heroes and their appeal to women as enthusiastically as it does the reverse. One of the themes of classical Malay and Javanese literature is the physical attraction of such heroes as Panji and Hang Tuah: "If Hang Tuah passed, married women tore themselves from the embraces of their husbands so that they could go out and see him. . . ."

As usual, Chou Ta-kuan [in the 1200s] had a colorful way of describing the expectations the Cambodian women of his day had of their men. "If the husband is called away for more than ten days, the wife is apt to say, 'I am not a spirit; how am I supposed to sleep alone?'" The idea of the ever faithful wife left behind during her husband's travels was upheld in the pages of Indian-derived epics, but not in everyday life. At Javanese marriages, according to [Stamford] Raffles [in 1815], the groom was solemnly warned, "If you should happen to be absent from her for the space of seven months on shore, or one year at sea, without giving her any subsistence . . . your marriage shall be dissolved, if your wife desires it, without any further form or process." Vietnamese law as promulgated in the fifteenth century (once again diverging sharply from Chinese practice) set a similar period of five months' absence, or twelve months if the marriage had produced children.

The most graphic demonstration of the strong position women enjoyed in sexual matters was the painful surgery men endured on their penis to increase the erotic pleasure of women. Once again, this is a phenomenon whose dispersion throughout Southeast Asia is very striking, though it appears to be absent in other parts of the world. Although it is the Indian *Kama Sutra* which makes the earliest reference to such surgery, this probably refers to Southeast Asian practice. A careful recent survey of the ethnographic evidence suggests that the phenomenon may best be understood as a symptom of the power and autonomy enjoyed by Southeast Asian women. . . .

The most draconian surgery was the insertion of a metal pin, complemented by a variety of wheels, spurs, or studs, in the central and southern Philippines and parts of Borneo. Pigafetta [in 1524] was the first of the astonished Europeans to describe the practice:

The males, large and small, have the penis pierced from one side to the other near the head with a gold or tin bolt as large as a goose quill. In both ends of the same bolt some have what resembles a spur, with points upon the ends; others are like the head of a cart nail. I very often asked many, both old and young, to see their penis, because I could not credit it. In the middle of the bolt is a hole, through which they urinate. . . . They say their women wish it so, and that if they did otherwise they would not have communication with them. When the men wish to have communication with their women, the latter themselves take the penis not in the regular way and commence very gently to introduce it, with the spur on top first, and then the other part. When it is inside it takes its regular position; and thus the penis always stays inside until it gets soft, for otherwise they could not pull it out.

The same phenomenon is described by many others, in different Visayan islands and in Mindanao, who agree that its purpose was always explained as enhancing sexual pleasure, especially for the women. Some peoples of northwest Borneo, notably the Iban and the Kayan, continued this practice until modern times, and their oral tradition attributes its origins to a legendary woman who found sexual intercourse without such an aid less satisfying than masturbation.

The same result was obtained in other parts of Southeast Asia by the less painful but probably more delicate operation of inserting small balls or bells under the loose skin of the penis. The earliest report is from the Chinese Muslim Ma Huan [in 1433]. He reported that in Siam,

when a man has attained his twentieth year, they take the skin which surrounds the *membrum virile,* and with a fine knife . . . they open it up and insert a dozen tin beads inside the skin; they close it up and protect it with medicinal herbs. . . . The beads look like a cluster of grapes. . . . If it is the king . . . or a great chief or a wealthy man, they use gold to make hollow beads, inside which a grain of sand is placed. . . . They make a tinkling sound, and this is regarded as beautiful.

Numerous European writers note the same phenomenon in Pegu during the fifteenth and sixteenth centuries, and Tomé Pires described it as a special feature of the Pegu men among all the varied traders visiting Melaka. "The Pegu lords wear as many as nine gold ones, with beautiful trebble, contralto and tenor tones, the size of the Alvares plums in our country; and those who are too poor . . . have them in lead." Pires adds, perhaps with tongue in cheek, "Our Malay women rejoice greatly when the Pegu men come to their country, and they are very fond of them. The reason for this must be their sweet harmony." The primary purpose seems again the pleasure of the female. When the Dutch admiral Jacob van Neck asked in some astonishment what purpose was served by the sweet-sounding little golden bells the wealthy Thais of Patani carried in their penises, they replied that "the women obtain inexpressible pleasure from it.". . .

That the majority Muslim population of Indonesia and Malaysia had divorce rates in excess of 50 percent as late as the 1960s is sometimes attributed to the influence of Islam in sanctioning easy divorce for men. Much more important, however, was the pan–Southeast-Asian pattern of female autonomy, which meant that divorce did not markedly reduce a woman's livelihood, status, or network of kin support. In noting the acceptance the Javanese gave to women of twenty-two or twenty-three living with their fourth or fifth husband, [G. W.] Earl attributed this attitude entirely to the freedom and economic independence enjoyed by women.

Christian Europe was until the eighteenth century a very "chaste" society in comparative terms, with an exceptionally late average age of marriage (in the twenties), with high proportions never marrying and with a low rate of extramarital conceptions by later standards. (In England this rate rose from only 12 percent of births in 1680 to 50 percent by 1800). Southeast Asia was in many respects the complete antithesis of that chaste pattern, and it seemed to European observers of the time that its inhabitants were preoccupied with sex. The Portuguese liked to say that the Malays were "fond of music and given to love," while Javanese, like Burmese, Thais, and Filipinos, were characterized as "very lasciviously given, both men and women." What this meant was that premarital sexual relations were regarded indulgently, and virginity at marriage was not expected of either party. If pregnancy resulted from these pre-marital activities, the couple were expected to marry, and failing that, resort might be had to abortion or (at least in the Philippines) to infanticide.

Female Roles

It is already clear that women had a relatively high degree of economic autonomy in premodern Southeast Asia. Nevertheless, it was taken for granted that the opposition of male and female characteristics was a fundamental part of the cosmic dualism. Perhaps for this very reason it was not thought necessary to create artificial markers of gender through dress, hairstyle, or speech patterns, none of which stressed the male-female distinction. A rash of recent studies on the anthropology of gender in Indonesia has uncovered a variety of expressions of the complementary opposition of male and female. Maleness is typically associated with white (semen), warmth, sky, form, control, and deliberate creativity; the female with red (blood), coolness, earth, substance, spontaneity, and natural creativity. The male feature is often seen (at least by males) as preferred, but both are necessary and the union of the two is a powerful ideal.

Such theoretical distinctions help explain the clear boundaries between male and female domains in the house, the fields, and the marketplace. Since everyday activities formed part of this cosmic dualism, especially when they affected plant and animal life, it was not a matter of indifference whether men or women performed them. Male work included all that pertained to metals and animals — ploughing, felling the jungle, hunting, metalworking, woodworking, and house building — as well as statecraft and formal (international) religion. The female domain included transplanting, harvesting, vegetable growing, food preparation, weaving, pottery making (in most areas), and marketing, as well as ancestor cults and mediation with the spirits.

At village level these dichotomies have not changed greatly in the last four centuries. The male domain has expanded enormously, however, through the greater role of statecraft and formal religion, and the ability of larger sections of the population to imitate aristocratic mores which portray women as dependent, decorous, and loyal. In the age of commerce, assumptions of male superiority already affected the courts and the urban elite, who listened to Indian epics of Rama and Sita, studied Chinese Confucian classics (in Vietnam), or were tutored by the theologians of Theravada Buddhism, Islam, or Christianity. In 1399, for example, the Thai queen of Sukhothai prayed that through her merit she might be "reborn as a male," thus moving up the Buddhist hierarchy.

That there was a discrepancy between courtly ideals and everyday reality there is no doubt. What requires examination is the extent to which women in that period were still able to extend their spheres of action into those larger events which are the normal subjects for historians. By examining successively trade, diplomacy, warfare, entertainment, literature, and statecraft we shall see that Southeast Asian women were playing an unusually influential role by comparison with later periods or with other parts of the world.

Since marketing was a female domain par excellence, this is the place to start. Even today Southeast Asian countries top the comparative statistics assembled by Ester Boserup for female participation in trade and marketing. Fifty-six percent of those so listed in Thailand were women, 51 percent in the Philippines, 47 percent in Burma, and 46 percent in Cambodia. Although Indonesia had a lower rate, 31 percent, this still contrasted sharply with other Muslim countries, particularly in the Middle East (1 to 5 percent). In Bangkok at the time of the 1947 census, three times as many Thai women as men were registered as owners or managers of businesses. A famous Minangkabau poem first written down in the 1820s exhorted mothers to teach their daughters "to judge the rise and fall of prices. "Southeast Asian women are still expected to show more commercially shrewd and thrifty attitudes than men, and male Chinese and European traders are apt to be derided for having the mean spirit of a woman on such matters.

Although the casual visitor to Southeast Asia today might not be aware of the female trading role, which is now restricted to rural and small-scale markets, this has not always been the case. Early European and Chinese traders were constantly surprised to find themselves dealing with women.

20

JOHN E. WILLS JR.
Sor Juana Inés de la Cruz

After the conquest of the Aztecs, the Spanish attempted to govern Mexico by converting the surviving Indians to Roman Catholicism and exploiting their labor. In addition, they encouraged fellow Spaniards to settle in the colony and imported African slaves, creating a mixed society of Europeans, Indians, and Africans. As in the rest of North America, the dividing line between slave and free was the most important social distinction. But unlike their English counterparts to the north, New Spain's colonists also distinguished between *Peninsulares*, colonists who were born in Spain, and Creoles, colonists who were born of Spanish parents in the Americas.

In the following selection a modern historian evokes the life of Sor Juana Inés de la Cruz (1651–1695), a poet, artist, and nun who lived in Mexico City in "New Spain." Sister Juana was a Creole woman and the author argues she was distinctly a product of Mexican Creole society. In what ways was she Spanish? In what ways was she Mexican? How do you think the life of a Creole woman, born and raised in the colony, would be different from that of a woman born in Spain?

Thinking Historically

In the previous selection, Anthony Reid suggested that Christianity, Islam, and Confucianism — three great patriarchal religious traditions — undermined the traditional autonomy of women in Southeast Asia. Do you think Christianity undermined the autonomy of native women in Mexico? Do you think Sor Juana found Christianity to be oppressive, neutral, or liberating? How was she able to use Christian culture to her advantage?

John E. Wills Jr., in "Sor Juana Inés de la Cruz," *1688: A Global History* (New York: W. W. Norton, 2001), 13–19.

On April 28, 1688, a long procession moved out of Mexico City, along the causeways that crossed the nearby lakes, and through the small towns and farms of the plateau, on its way toward the pass between the two volcanoes Iztaccihuatl and Popocatépetl, both more than sixteen thousand feet high, and down to the tropical port of Vera Cruz. The farmers in their villages and fields were used to a good deal of such coming and going, but this time they stopped their work to look and to call out to each other in Nahuatl, the main indigenous language, for this was no ordinary procession. Cavalry outriders and a huge coach were followed by many baggage wagons and a long line of fine coaches. The marquis of Laguna had served as viceroy of New Spain from 1680 to 1686. With their wealth, powerful connections in Madrid, and a taste for elegance and the arts, he and his wife had given the viceregal court a few years of splendor and sophistication comparable, if not to Madrid, certainly to many of the lesser courts of Europe. Now their wealthy Spanish friends were riding in their coaches as far as the Villa de Guadalupe, seeing the marquis and marchioness off on their voyage home to Spain.

> A child born of a slave shall be received,
> according to our Law, as property
> of the owner to whom fealty
> is rendered by the mother who conceived.
>   The harvest from a grateful land retrieved,
> the finest fruit, offered obediently,
> is for the lord, for its fecundity
> is owing to the care it has received.
>   So too, Lysis divine, these my poor lines:
> as children of my soul, born of my heart,
> they must in justice be to you returned;
>   Let not their defects cause them to be spurned,
> for of your rightful due they are a part,
> as concepts of a soul to yours consigned.

These lines were written sometime later in 1688 and sent off from Mexico to the marchioness of Laguna in Spain. They make use of metaphors and classical conceits to express and conceal the feelings of the author, who had lost, with the marchioness's departure, the object of the nearest thing she had ever known to true love and, with the marquis's departure, her ultimate protection from those who found her opinions and her way of life scandalous. The trouble was not that the author was lesbian — although her feelings toward men and women were unusually complicated and unconventional, anything approaching a physical relation or even passion is most unlikely — but that she was a cloistered Hieronymite nun, who read and studied a wide range of secular books, held long intellectual conversations with many friends, wrote constantly in a variety of religious and secular styles, and betrayed in her writings sympathy for Hermetic and Neoplatonic views that were on the edge of heresy if not beyond it. Her name in religion was Sor Juana Inés de la Cruz. She is recognized today as one of the great poets in the history of the Spanish language.

Mexico in the 1680s was a society of dramatic contradictions. The elegant viceregal court and the opulent ecclesiastical hierarchy looked toward Europe for style and ideas. The vast majority of the population sought to preserve as much as possible of the language, beliefs, and ways of life that had guided them before the coming of the Spaniards; the worship of the Virgin of Guadalupe, for example, owed much to the shrine of an Aztec goddess that had been the setting of the original appearance of the Virgin to a Mexican peasant. In between the "peninsular" elite and the "Indians," the native-born "creoles" of Spanish language and culture managed huge cattle ranches and sought constantly new veins of profitable silver ore and new techniques to exploit old ones. Neither "Spanish" nor "Indian," they experienced the full force of the contradictions of Mexican society and culture.

The literary world in which Sor Juana was such an anomalous eminence thrived on these contradictions of society and culture. This was a baroque culture. The word *baroque,* originating as a Portuguese term for the peculiar beauty of a deformed, uneven pearl, suggests a range of artistic styles in which the balance and harmony of the Renaissance styles are abandoned for imbalance, free elaboration of form, playful gesture, and surprising allusion, through which the most intense of emotions and the darkest of realities may be glimpsed, their power enhanced by the glittering surface that partially conceals them. Contradiction and its partial, playful reconciliation are the stuff of the baroque style. So is the layering of illusion on illusion, meaning upon meaning. And what more baroque conceit could be imagined than the literary eminence of a cloistered nun in a rough frontier society, with a church and state of the strongest and narrowest male supremacist prejudices? Look again at the poem quoted earlier: The chaste nun refers to her poem as her child or the harvest from a grateful land. She declares her love once again to the departed marchioness.

Sor Juana was a product of Mexican creole society, born on a ranch on the shoulder of the great volcano Popocatépetl. Her mother was illiterate and very probably had not been married to her father. But some of the family branches lived in the city, with good books and advantageous connections. As soon as she discovered the books in her grandfather's library, she was consumed with a thirst for solitude and reading. Her extraordinary talents for literature and learning were recognized. When she was fifteen, in 1664, she was taken into the household of a newly arrived viceroy, as his wife's favorite and constant companion. She must have enjoyed the attention, the luxury, the admiration of her cleverness. She no doubt participated in the highly stylized exchange of "gallantries" between young men and young women. But she had no dowry. Solitude was her natural habitat. As a wife and mother, what chance would she have to read, to write, to be alone? In 1668 she took her vows in the Hieronymite convent of an order named after Saint Jerome, cloistered and meditative by rule.

This was a big decision, but less drastic than one might think. Certainly she was a believing Catholic. Her new status did not require total devotion to prayer and extinction of self. It did not imply that she was abandoning all the friendships and secular learning that meant so much to her. The nuns had a daily round of collective devotions; but many rules were not fully honored, and the regimen left her much free time for reading and writing. Each of the nuns had comfortable private quarters, with a kitchen, room for a bathtub, and sleeping space for a servant and a dependent or two; Sor Juana usually had one slave and one or two nieces or other junior dependents living in her quarters. The nuns visited back and forth in their quarters to the point that Sor Juana complained of the interruptions to her reading and writing, but outsiders spoke to the nuns only in the locutory especially provided for that purpose. From the beginning she turned the locutory into an elegant salon, as the viceroy and his lady and other fashionable people came to visit her and they passed hours in learned debate, literary improvisation, and gossip.

One of Sor Juana's most constant friends and supporters was Carlos de Sigüenza y Góngora, professor of mathematics at the University of Mexico, an eminently learned creole scholar whose position was almost as anomalous as hers. He had been educated by the Jesuits and had longed to be one of them but had been expelled from their college. He had managed to obtain his position, without a university degree, by demonstrating his superior knowledge of his subject. He had added Góngora to his name to emphasize his distant kinship, through his mother's family, with the most famous of Spain's baroque poets. But he always felt insecure among the European-born professors, churchmen, and high officials. He wrote a great deal, much of it about the history of Mexico. He was in no way Sor Juana's equal as a writer, but he probably was responsible for most of her smattering of knowledge of modern science and recent philosophy.

There was a rule of poverty among the Hieronymites, but it was generally ignored. Sor Juana received many gifts, some of them substantial enough to enable the former dowerless girl to invest money at interest. By gift and purchase she built up a library of about four thousand volumes and a small collection of scientific instruments, probably provided by Sigüenza. Her reading was broad but not very systematic, contributing to the stock of ideas and allusions she drew on constantly in her writings but giving her little sense of the intellectual tensions and transformations that were building up in Europe. She wrote constantly, in a wide variety of complex and exacting forms. Voluntarily or upon commission or request, she wrote occasional poems of all kinds for her friends and patrons. A celebration might call for a *loa,* a brief theatrical piece in praise of a dignitary. In one of hers, for example, a character "clad in sunrays" declares:

> I am a reflection
> of that blazing sun
> who, among shining rays
> numbers brilliant sons:
> when his illustrious rays
> strike a speculum,
> on it is portrayed
> the likeness of his form.

Sor Juana's standing in society reached a new height with the arrival in 1680 of the marquis and marchioness of Laguana. Even in the public festivities celebrating their arrival, she outdid herself in baroque elaborations of texts and conceits for a temporary triumphal arch erected at the cathedral. It was an allegory on Neptune, in which the deeds of the Greek god were compared to the real or imaginary deeds of the marquis. Much was made of the echoes among the marquis's title of Laguna, meaning *lake,* Neptune's reign over the oceans, and the origins of Mexico City as the Aztec city of Tenochtitlán in the middle of its great lake: an elaborate union of sycophancy to a ruler, somewhat strained classical allusion, and a creole quest for a Mexican identity. In parts of the text the author even drew in Isis as an ancestor of Neptune, and in others of her works from this time she showed a great interest in Egyptian antiquity as it was then understood, including the belief that the god Hermes Trismegistus had revealed the most ancient and purest wisdom and anticipated the Mosaic and Christian revelations. These ideas, the accompanying quasi-Platonic separation of soul and body, and her use of them to imply that a female or androgynous condition was closer to the divine wisdom than the male took her to the edge of heresy or beyond and was turned against her in later years.

Sor Juana soon established a close friendship with the marchioness of Laguna. Some of the poems she sent her are among her very finest, and they are unmistakably love poems. Some of them accompanied a portrait of the author. Several portraits in which a very handsome woman gazes boldly at us, her black-and-white habit simply setting off her own strength and elegance, have come down to us. [See Figure 4.1.]

Figure 4.1   Portrait of Sor Juana Inés de la Cruz.

Source: Mexican, unknown artist. "Portrait of Sister Juana Inés de la Cruz." Philadelphia Museum of Art; The Robert H. Lamborn Collection, 1903.

And if it is that you should rue
the absence of a soul in me [the portrait],
you can confer one, easily,
from the many rendered you:
and as my soul I [Sor Juana] tendered you,
and though my being yours obeyed,
and though you look on me amazed
in this insentient apathy,
you are the soul of this body,
and are the body of this shade.

The marquis of Laguna stepped down as viceroy in 1686 but remained in Mexico until 1688. In that year Sor Juana was very busy. The marchioness was taking texts of her poems back to Spain, where they soon would be published. She added to them a play, *The Divine Narcissus,* interweaving the legend of Narcissus and the life of Jesus, which probably was performed in Madrid in 1689 or 1690. Her niece took her vows in the convent in 1688. Late in the year, after her noble friends had left, she wrote the poem quoted earlier as well as a romantic comedy, *Love Is the Greater Labyrinth,* which was performed in Mexico City early in 1689.

A large collection of her poetry was published in Madrid in 1689. The next year in Mexico she published a letter taking abstruse issue with a sermon preached decades before by the famous Portuguese Jesuit Antonio Vieira. Her casual way with the rules of the religious life, her flirtings with heresy, her many writings in secular forms with intimations of understanding of love inappropriate to her profession had made her many enemies, but they could do nothing while the marquis of Laguna and his lady were on hand to protect her. Now they closed in. In 1694 she was forced formally to renounce all writing and humane studies and to relinquish her library and collection of scientific instruments. In 1695 she devotedly cared for her sisters in the convent during an epidemic, caught the disease, and died.

21

MARY JO MAYNES AND ANN WALTNER

Women and Marriage in Europe and China

This article is the product of a rich collaboration between historians of China and Europe who show us how a study of women and marriage is anything but peripheral to a study of these areas. Rather it can help us answer a major historical question: How do we explain the dramatic rise of Western Europe after 1500, especially in the wake of prodigious Chinese growth that continued into the sixteenth century?

The authors begin by comparing the role of religion, the state, and the family in setting marriage patterns in both China and Europe. Did Christianity allow European women more independence than Confucianism allowed women in China? In which society was the patriarchal family more powerful, and what was the relative impact of patriarchy on women in both societies? How did the age and rate at which people married in each society compare? What was the importance of Chinese concubinage and Christian ideals of chastity?

Thinking Historically

The authors' questions about marriage in Europe and China lead finally to a consideration of one of the most frequently asked comparative questions: Why did Europe industrialize before China? Do the different European and Chinese marriage patterns answer this question? What other comparative questions would we have to ask to arrive at a full answer?

Comparing Marriage Cross-Culturally

A number of years ago, we were involved in organizing a comparative historical conference on gender and kinship (our areas of specialization are Chinese and European family and women's history). Conversations that began at the conference resulted in a collection of coedited articles, but they also spurred the two of us to collaboratively teach a world history course in which family and women's history play key roles. We introduce students in that course to historical comparison by talking about marriage. In particular, we begin with a pointed comparison

Mary Jo Maynes and Ann Waltner, "Childhood, Youth, and the Female Life Cycle: Women's Life-Cycle Transitions in a World-Historical Perspective: Comparing Marriage in China and Europe," *Journal of Women's History*, 12, no. 4. (Winter 2001), 11–19.

between the history of marriage in China and Europe based on research presented at the kinship conference.

Beginning in the late 1500s, women in northern Italy began to appeal to legal courts run by the Catholic Church when they got into disputes with their families over arranged marriages. Within the early modern Italy family system the father held a great deal of authority over his children and it was usual for the parents to determine when and whom sons and daughters married. Women and children held little power in comparison with adult men. But the Catholic Church's insistence that both parties enter into the marriage willingly gave some women an out — namely, an appeal to the Church court, claiming that the marriage their family wanted was being forced upon them without their consent. Surprisingly, these young women often won their cases against their fathers. In early modern China, by way of contrast, state, religion, and family were bound together under the veil of Confucianism. Paternal authority echoed and reinforced the political and the moral order. Religious institutions could rarely be called upon to intervene in family disputes. Therefore, young women (or young men, for that matter) had no clearly established institutional recourse in situations of unwanted marriage. So, despite the fact that paternal power was very strong in both early modern Italy and early modern China, specific institutional differences put young women at the moment of marriage in somewhat different positions.

We began with the presumption that however different the institution of "marriage" was in Italy and China, it nevertheless offered enough similarities that it made sense to speak comparatively about a category called "marriage." Parallels in the two cultures between the institution of marriage and the moment in the woman's life course that it represented make comparison useful. Nevertheless, this particular comparison also isolates some of the variable features of marriage systems that are especially significant in addressing gender relations in a world-historical context. In China, the rules of family formation and family governance were generally enforced within the bounds of each extended family group. State and religious influences were felt only indirectly through family leaders as mediators or enforcers of state and religious law. Throughout Europe, beginning in the Middle Ages, the institution of marriage was altered first by the effort of the Catholic Church to wrest some control over marriage from the family by defining it as a sacrament, and then eventually by the struggle between churches and state authorities to regulate families.

This contest among church, state, and family authorities over marriage decisions turns out to have been a particular feature of European history that had consequences for many aspects of social life. A focus on the moment of marriage presents special opportunities for understanding connections between the operation of gender relations in everyday life and in the realm of broader political developments. Marriage is a familial institution, of course, but, to varying degrees, political authorities also have a stake in it because of its implications for property transfer, reproduction, religion, and morality — in short, significant aspects of the social order. In this essay, we compare one dimension of marriage — its timing in a woman's life cycle — in two contexts, Europe and China. We argue that variations in marriage timing have world-historical implications. We examine how a woman's status and situation shifted at marriage and then suggest some implications of comparative differences in the timing and circumstances of this change of status.

The Moment of Marriage in European History

One striking peculiarity of Central and Western European history between 1600 and 1850 was the relatively late age at first marriage for men and women compared with other regions of the world. The so-called "Western European marriage pattern" was marked by relatively late marriage — that is, relative to other regions of the world where some form of marriage usually occurred around the time of puberty. In much of Europe, in contrast, men did not typically marry until their late twenties and women their mid-twenties. This practice of relatively late marriage was closely connected with the custom of delaying marriage until the couple commanded sufficient resources to raise a family. For artisans this traditionally meant having a shop and master status. For merchants it entailed saving capital to begin a business. In the case of peasant couples, this meant having a house and land and basic farming equipment. It was the responsibility of the family and the community to oversee courtship, betrothal, and marriage to assure that these conditions were met. This phenomenon was also rooted in the common practice of neolocality — the expectation that a bride and groom would set up their own household at or soon after marriage. This "delayed" marriage has attracted the attention of European historical demographers. The delay of marriage meant, quite significantly, that most European women did not begin to have children until their twenties. But this marriage pattern also has significance in other realms as well. In particular, young people of both sexes experienced a relatively long hiatus between puberty and marriage.

Unmarried European youth played a distinctive role in economic, social, cultural, and political life through such institutions as guilds, village youth groups, and universities. For the most part, historians' attention to European youth has centered on young men. Major works on the history of youth in Europe, like theories of adolescent development, tend to center on the male experience as normative. Only when gender differences in youth are recognized and the history of young women is written will the broad historical significance of the European marriage pattern become clear. Contrast between European demographic history and that of other world regions suggests a comparative pattern of particular significance for girls: Delayed marriage and childbearing meant that teenage girls were available for employment outside the familial household (either natal or marital) to a degree uncommon elsewhere. Household divisions of labor according to age and gender created constant demand for servants on larger farms; typically, unmarried youth who could be hired in from neighboring farms as servants filled this role. A period of service in a farm household, as an apprentice, or as a domestic servant in an urban household characterized male and female European youth in the lifecycle phase preceding marriage. Historians have noted but never fully explored the role young women played in European economic development, and in particular their role in the early industrial labor force.

Late marriage had gender-specific cultural ramifications as well. Whereas it was considered normal and even appropriate for teenage men to be initiated into heterosexual intercourse at brothels, in most regions of Europe, young women were expected to remain chaste until marriage. Delay of marriage heightened anxiety over unmarried women's sexuality, especially the dangers to which young women were increasingly exposed as the locus of their labor shifted from home and village to factory and city. Premarital or extramarital sexuality was uncommon, and was rigorously policed especially in the period following the religious upheavals of the Reformation in the sixteenth century. In rural areas, church and community, in addition to the family, exerted control over sexuality. Moreover, the unmarried male youth cohort of many village communities often served, in effect, as "morals police," enforcing local customs. These young men regulated courtship rituals, organized dances that young people went to, and oversaw the formation of couples. Sometimes, judging and public shaming by the youth group was the fate of couples who were mismatched by age or wealth or who violated sexual taboos. Some customs, at least symbolically, punished young men from far away who married local women, removing them from the marriage pool. Often, such a bridegroom had to pay for drinks in each village that the bridal couple passed through as they moved from the bride's parish church to their new abode — the longer the distance, the more expensive his bill.

Once married, a couple would usually begin having children immediately. Demographic evidence suggests that for most of Central and Western Europe there was virtually no practice of contraception among lower classes prior to the middle of the nineteenth century. Women had babies about every two years (more or less frequently according to region and depending on such local customs as breast-feeding length and intercourse taboos). Even though completed family sizes could be large by modern standards, the number of children most women bore was still less than if they had married in their teens. And prevailing high mortality rates further reduced the number of children who survived to adulthood.

The Moment of Marriage in Chinese History

The Chinese marriage system was traditionally characterized by early age at marriage, nearly universal marriage for women, virilocal residence (a newly married couple resided with the groom's parents), concubinage for elite men, and norms that discouraged widow remarriage. From the sixteenth through twentieth centuries, Chinese men and women married much younger on average than did their European counterparts — late teens or early twenties for women and a bit later for men. A bride typically moved to her husband's family home, which was often in a different village from her own. The moment of marriage not only meant that a girl would leave her parents but that she would also leave her network of kin and friends, all that was familiar. Families chose marriage partners, and a matchmaker negotiated the arrangements. Nothing resembling courtship existed; the bride and groom would often first meet on their wedding day.

Because a newly married Chinese couple would typically reside in an already-existing household, it was not necessary for an artisan to become established, a merchant to accumulate capital, or a peasant to own a farm before marrying. Newly married couples participated in ongoing domestic and economic enterprises that already supported the groom's family. New households were eventually established by a process of household division, which typically happened at the death of the father rather than the moment of marriage (although it could happen at other points in the family cycle as well).

Daughters were groomed from birth for marriage. They were taught skills appropriate to their social class or the social class into which their parents aspired to marry them. (In the ideal Chinese marriage, the groom was in fact supposed to be of slightly higher social status than the bride.) The feet of upper-class girls (and some who were not upper class) were bound, since Chinese men found this erotic. Bound feet also symbolically, if not actually, restricted upper-class women's movement. Thus bound feet simultaneously enhanced the sexual desirability of upper-class women and served to contain their sexuality within domestic bounds.

Virtually all Chinese girls became brides, though not all of them married as principal wives. (This contrasts with the European pattern where a substantial minority of women in most regions never married.)

Upper-class men might take one or more concubines in addition to a principal wife. The relationship between a man and his concubine was recognized legally and ritually, and children born of these unions were legitimate. A wife had very secure status: divorce was almost nonexistent. A concubine's status, in contrast, was much more tenuous. She could be expelled at the whim of her "husband"; her only real protection was community sentiment. Although only a small percentage of Chinese marriages (no more than 5 percent) involved concubines, the practice remained an important structural feature of the Chinese marriage system until the twentieth century. Concubinage also provides a partial explanation of why, despite the fact that marriage was nearly universal for women, a substantial proportion of men (perhaps as high as 10 percent) never married. Also contributing to this apparent anomaly was the practice of sex-selective infanticide, a common practice that discriminated against girl babies and, ultimately, reduced the number of potential brides.

Once married, Chinese couples began to have children almost immediately, generally spacing births at longer intervals than did European couples. The reasons for this are not yet completely understood, although infanticide, extended breast-feeding, and the fairly large number of days on which sexual intercourse was forbidden all seem to have played a role in lowering Chinese family size.

Early marriage in China meant that the category of "youth," which has been so significant for European social and economic history, has no precise counterpart in Chinese history. Young Chinese women labored, to be sure, but the location of their work was domestic — either in the household of their father or husband. Female servants existed in China, but their servitude was normally of longer duration than the life-cycle servitude common in Europe. The domestic location of young women's labor in the Chinese context also had implications for the particular ways in which Chinese industries were organized, as we suggest below.

Patterns of Marriage in Europe and China

To sum up, then, there are differences of both timing of and residency before and after marriage that are particularly germane to the comparative history of young women. As demographic historians James Z. Lee and Wang Feng also have argued, "in China, females have always married universally and early . . . in contrast to female marriage in Western Europe, which occurred late or not at all." Whereas, in the nineteenth century, all but 20 percent of young Chinese women were married by age twenty, among European populations, between 60 and 80 percent of young women remained single at this age. In traditional China, only

1 or 2 percent of women remained unmarried at age thirty, whereas between 15 and 25 percent of thirty-year-old Western European women were still single. (For men, the differences though in the same direction are far less stark.) As for residence, in the Western European neolocal pattern, norms and practices in many regions resulted in a pattern whereby newly married couples moved into a separate household at marriage; but concomitant with this was their delaying marriage until they could afford a new household. In China, newly married couples generally resided in the groom's father's household. In Western Europe, the majority of postpubescent young men and many young women left home in their teenage years for a period of employment. In the early modern era, such employment was often as a servant or apprentice in either a craft or a farm household, but, over time, that employment was increasingly likely to be in a nondomestic work setting, such as a factory, store, or other urban enterprise. "Youth" was a distinctive phase in the life course of young men and increasingly of young women in Europe, although there were important gender distinctions. Such a period of postpubescent semiautonomy from parental households did not exist for Chinese youth, especially not for young women in traditional China. Young men more typically remained in their father's household and young women moved at marriage in their late teens from their own father's household to that of their husband's father.

Comparing the Moment of Marriage: Implications and Cautions

We would now like to discuss some of the world-historical implications of this important (if crude) comparison in the marriage systems of China and Western Europe. There are obviously many possible realms for investigation. For example, these patterns imply differences in young women's education, intergenerational relationships among women (especially between mothers and daughters and mothers-in-law and daughters-in-law), and household power relations. Here, we restrict our discussion to two areas of undoubted world-historical significance, namely economic development, on the one hand, and sexuality and reproduction, on the other.

The question of why the Industrial Revolution, or, alternatively, the emergence of industrial capitalism, occurred first in Europe, has been and remains salient for both European and world historians. R. Bin Wong explores this question in his innovative comparative study of economic development in Europe and China. Wong argues that there were rough parallels in the dynamics linking demographic expansion and economic growth in China and Europe until the nineteenth century. Both economies were expanding on the basis of growth of rural industrial enterprises in which peasant families supplemented agricultural work and income with part-time industrial production. What the Chinese case demonstrates, Wong argues, is that this so-called protoindustrial form of development may be viewed as an alternative route to industrialization rather than merely a precursor of factory production. Indeed, Charles Tilly has suggested that a prescient contemporary observer of the European economy in 1750 would likely have predicted such a future — that is "a countryside with a growing proletariat working in both agriculture and manufacturing."

While Wong's study is devoted to comparative examination of the economic roots and implications of varying paths to industrial development, he also connects economic and demographic growth. In particular, Wong mentions the link between marriage and economic opportunity: "in both China and Europe, rural industry supported lower age at marriage and higher proportions of ever married than would have been plausible in its absence. This does not mean that ages at marriage dropped in Europe when rural industry appeared, but the possibility was present. For China, the development of rural industry may not have lowered ages at marriage or raised proportions married as much as it allowed previous practices of relatively low ages at marriage and high proportions of women ever married to continue." What Wong does not explore is the way in which these "previous practices" that connected the low age at marriage with both virilocality and a relatively high commitment to the domestic containment of daughters and wives also had implications for patterns of economic development. In a comparative account of why Chinese industrial development relied heavily on domestic production, the fact that the young female labor force in China was to an extent far greater than that of Europe both married and "tied" to the male-headed household needs to be part of the story. This pattern of female marriage and residency held implications for entrepreneurial choice that helped to determine the different paths toward industrialization in Europe and China. World-historical comparison, taking into account aspects of gender relations and marriage and kinship systems, highlights their possible significance for economic development, a significance that has not been given proper attention by economic historians. Indeed, it is arguable that the family and marital status of the young women who played so significant a role in the workforce (especially those employed in the textile industry, which was key to early industrial development in both Europe and China) were major factors in the varying paths to development followed in China and Europe in the centuries of protoindustrial growth and industrialization.

A second set of implications concerns sexuality and reproduction. Again, we are aided by another recent study, which, in a fashion parallel to Wong's, uses Chinese historical evidence to call into question generalizations about historical development based on a European model. In their book on Chinese demographic history, Lee and Wang argue against the hegemonic Malthusian (mis)understandings according to which the family and population history to China has been seen as an example of a society's failure to curb population growth by any means other than recurrent disaster (by "positive" rather than "preventive" checks in Malthusian terms). They note the important difference in marriage systems that we have just described, but they dispute conclusions too often drawn from the Chinese historical pattern concerning overpopulation. Instead, according to Lee and Wang "persistently high nuptiality . . . did not inflate Chinese fertility, because of . . . the low level of fertility within marriage."

This second example points to another important realm for which the age at which women marry has great consequences. But the findings reported by Lee and Wang also caution scholars against leaping to comparative conclusions about one society on the basis of models established in another, even while their claims still suggest the value of comparison. We should not presume that since Chinese women were married universally and young, they therefore had more children or devoted a greater proportion of their time and energy to childbearing and child rearing than did their later married counterparts in Europe. Although the evidence is far from definitive, it nevertheless indicates that total marital fertility may have been somewhat lower in China than in Europe until the late nineteenth or early twentieth centuries. The factors in China that produced this pattern included relatively high rates of infanticide, especially of female infants, as well as different beliefs and practices about child care and sexuality. For example, babies were apparently breast-fed longer in China than in Europe (a pattern in turn related to the domestic location of women's work), which would have both increased infants' chances of survival and also lengthened the intervals between births. In the realm of sexuality, pertinent factors include both prescriptions for men against overly frequent intercourse, and coresidence with a parental generation whose vigilance included policing young couples' sexual behavior.

These two examples are meant to suggest how looking at women's life cycles comparatively both enhances our understanding of the implications of varying patterns for women's history and also suggests the very broad ramifications, indeed world-historical significance, of different ways of institutionalizing the female life cycle.

REFLECTIONS

It is impossible to predict exactly what comparisons or generalizations one will draw from reading particular selections. So much of what we learn depends on who we are, what we already know, and the inimitable ways in which our imaginations are engaged by what we read or experience. Nevertheless, the first selection in this chapter is likely to evoke some kind of comparison between traditional Chinese and modern American family life, as we compare what we know with what we are encountering for the first time. Building on the first reading, we might compare Mao Xiang's story of Chinese concubines with the picture of ideal family life presented in the Miu lineage selection. This comparison raises a number of questions: Was concubinage completely antithetical to traditional Chinese family values, or was it accepted as an unavoidable reality? Instead of undermining the lineage system, might concubinage have been incorporated into it to strengthen it? What might have been the significance of this?

The first two selections reinforce the perception that all traditional family-based societies were patriarchal, and that all traditional family systems have thrived at the expense of women. But the third selection undermines this assumption. Reid's piece on Southeast Asia, which underscores women's economic autonomy and strong sexual identity, suggests that the traditional world was more varied. The view that traditional families were all patriarchal comes into question.

As we move through the chapter it becomes increasingly difficult to generalize about gender and family in "traditional" societies. For more clues we turn to European-American society with the piece on Sor Juana Inés de la Cruz. Her biography raises questions about the power of individual women to challenge patriarchy and encourages us to compare women's roles in different cultures. Did some cultures offer women more opportunity than others? How did individual women shape their lives within these cultures? In trying to answer these questions our understanding of gender becomes more complex, and we recognize the diversity and variation in women's history around the globe and throughout the ages.

The chapter concludes with a sophisticated comparison of Chinese and European marriages and societies and an attempt to explain Europe's rapid industrialization. What evidence do the authors present to explain the industrialization of Europe before China? Is their argument plausible? How does it build on what we've learned from the previous selections? What does it say about the overall importance of the history of gender and the family?

5

The Scientific Revolution

Europe, Ottoman Empire, China, and Japan, 1600–1800

HISTORICAL CONTEXT

Modern life is unthinkable apart from science. We surround ourselves with its products, from cars and computers to telephones and televisions; we are dependent on its institutions — its hospitals, universities, and research laboratories; and we have internalized the methods and procedures of science in every aspect of our daily lives, from balancing checkbooks to counting calories. Even on social and humanitarian questions, the scientific method has become almost the exclusive model of knowledge in modern society.

We can trace the scientific focus of modern society to the "scientific revolution" of the seventeenth century. The seventeenth-century scientific revolution was a European phenomenon, with such notables as Copernicus in Poland, Galileo in Tuscany, and Newton in England. But it was also a global event, prompted initially by Europe's new knowledge of Asia, Africa, and the Americas, and ultimately spread as a universal method for understanding and manipulating the world.

What was the scientific revolution? How revolutionary was it? How similar, or different, was European science from that practiced elsewhere in the world? And how much did the European revolution affect scientific traditions elsewhere? These are some of the issues we will study in this chapter.

THINKING HISTORICALLY
Sifting Evidence: "Before" and "After"

This chapter's documents and essays concern intellectual or cultural history because they describe how people think. But it is obvious that scientific ideas, at least when put into practice, have an enormous impact on how people behave. Indeed, the idea of a scientific revolution implies not just a vast change of ideas but also transformation of the material world.

In order to evaluate the extent of the scientific revolution, in this chapter we will try to determine exactly what changed, by how much, and with what impact. Understanding change is a basic goal of historical study — some might say *the* basic goal of historical study. To understand change, then, we must be very precise about describing the "before" and "after."

In this chapter we will study both secondary articles in which a historian argues that a particular set of changes occurred and primary sources that we must critique to determine what is new and what is not. As we progress, we can use each source in conjunction with the others to answer larger questions about the scientific revolution.

$$\boxed{22}$$

FRANKLIN LE VAN BAUMER

The Scientific Revolution in the West

In this selection, an intellectual historian of Europe summarizes the scientific revolution. Without enumerating the achievements of European science in the seventeenth century, Baumer finds evidence of the "revolutionary" nature of the transformation by referring to the popularity of scientific societies and the powerful appeal of the new scientific mentality. How does he define the scientific revolution? How does he date it? Why does he believe that it was a revolution?

Thinking Historically

What intellectual or cultural changes did the scientific revolution bring about, according to Baumer? What ideas did Europeans have about nature before the scientific revolution? Baumer suggests that we can see the scientific revolution in new intellectual institutions, educational reforms, and new careers. What were these changes? Would you call them cultural or social changes?

Franklin Le Van Baumer, "The Scientific Revolution in the West," in *Main Currents of Western Thought,* ed. F. Le Van Baumer (New Haven: Yale University Press, 1978).

What were the causes of the scientific revolution? What political and economic events of the period before the seventeenth century helped to bring it about?

In his book *The Origins of Modern Science* Professor [Herbert] Butterfield of Cambridge writes that the "scientific revolution" of the sixteenth and seventeenth centuries "outshines everything since the rise of Christianity and reduces the Renaissance and Reformation to the rank of mere episodes, mere internal displacements, within the system of medieval Christendom." "It looms so large as the real origin both of the modern world and of the modern mentality that our customary periodisation of European history has become an anachronism and an encumbrance." This view can no longer be seriously questioned. The scientific achievements of the century and a half between the publication of Copernicus's *De Revolutionibus Orbium Celestium* (1543) and Newton's *Principia* (1687) marked the opening of a new period of intellectual and cultural life in the West, which I shall call the Age of Science. What chiefly distinguished this age from its predecessor was that science — meaning by science a body of knowledge, a method, an attitude of mind, a metaphysic (to be described below) — became the directive force of Western civilization, displacing theology and antique letters. Science made the world of the spirit, of Platonic Ideas, seem unreliable and dim by comparison with the material world. In the seventeenth century it drove revealed Christianity out of the physical universe into the region of history and private morals; to an ever growing number of people in the two succeeding centuries it made religion seem outmoded even there. Science invaded the schools, imposed literary canons, altered the world-picture of the philosophers, suggested new techniques to the social theorists. It changed profoundly man's attitude toward custom and tradition, enabling him to declare his independence of the past, to look down condescendingly upon the "ancients," and to envisage a rosy future. The Age of Science made the intoxicating discovery that melioration depends, not upon "change from within" (St. Paul's birth of the new man), but upon "change from without" (scientific and social mechanics).

1

Some people will perhaps object that there was no such thing as "scientific revolution" in the sixteenth and seventeenth centuries. They will say that history does not work that way, that the new science was not "revolutionary," but the cumulative effect of centuries of trial and error among scientists. But if by "scientific revolution" is meant the occasion when science became a real intellectual and cultural force in the West, this objection must surely evaporate. The evidence is rather overwhelming that sometime between 1543 and 1687, certainly by the late seventeenth century, science captured the interest of the intellectuals and upper classes. Francis Bacon's ringing of a bell to call the wits of Europe together to advance scientific learning did not go unheeded. Note the creation of new intellectual institutions to provide a home for science — the *Academia del Cimento* at Florence (1661), the Royal Society at London (1662), the *Académie des Sciences* at Paris (1666), the Berlin Academy (1700), to mention only the most important. These scientific academies signified the advent of science as an organized activity. Note the appearance of a literature of popular science, of which Fontenelle's *Plurality of Worlds* is only one example, and of popular lectures on scientific subjects. Note the movement for educational reform sponsored by Bacon and the Czech John Amos Comenius, who denounced the traditional education for its exclusive emphasis upon "words rather than things" (literature rather than nature itself). Evidently, by the end of the seventeenth century the prejudice against "mechanical" studies as belonging to practical rather than high mental life had all but disappeared. Bacon complained in 1605 that "matters mechanical" were esteemed "a kind of dishonour unto learning to descend to inquiry or meditation upon." But the Royal Society included in its roster a number of ecclesiastics and men of fashion. The second marquis of Worcester maintained a laboratory and published a book of inventions in 1663. Not a few men appear to have been "converted" from an ecclesiastical to a scientific career, and, as Butterfield notes, to have carried the gospel into the byways, with all the zest of the early Christian missionaries.

To account historically for the scientific revolution is no easy task. The problem becomes somewhat more manageable, however, if we exclude from the discussion the specific discoveries of the scientists. Only the internal history of science can explain how Harvey, for example, discovered the circulation of the blood, or Newton the universal law of gravitation.

But certain extrascientific factors were plainly instrumental in causing so many people to be simultaneously interested in "nature," and, moreover, to think about nature in the way they did. Professor [Alfred North] Whitehead reminds us that one of these factors was medieval Christianity itself and medieval scholasticism. Medieval Christianity sponsored the Greek, as opposed to the primitive, idea of a rationally ordered universe which made the orderly investigation of nature seem possible. Scholasticism trained western intellectuals in exact thinking. The Renaissance and the Protestant Reformation also prepared the ground for the scientific revolution — not by design, but as an indirect consequence of their thinking. . . . [H]umanism and Protestantism represented a movement toward the concrete. Erasmus preferred ethics to the metaphysical debates of the philosophers and theologians. The Protestants reduced the miraculous element in institutional Christianity and emphasized labor in a worldly calling. Furthermore, by attacking scholastic theology with which Aristotle was bound up, they made it easier for scientists to think about physics and astronomy in un-Aristotelian terms. As [philosopher] E. A. Burtt has noted of Copernicus, these men lived in a mental climate in which people generally were seeking new centers of reference. Copernicus, the architect of the heliocentric theory of the universe, was a contemporary of Luther and Archbishop Cranmer, who moved the religious center from Rome to Wittenberg and Canterbury. In the sixteenth century the economic center of gravity was similarly shifting from the Mediterranean to the English Channel and the Atlantic Ocean. The revival of ancient philosophies and ancient texts at the Renaissance also sharpened the scientific appetite. The Platonic and Phythagorean revival in fifteenth-century Italy undoubtedly did a good deal to accustom scientists to think of the universe in mathematical, quantitative terms. The translation of Galen and Archimedes worked the last rich vein of ancient science, and made it abundantly clear that the ancients had frequently disagreed on fundamentals, thus necessitating independent investigation. By their enthusiasm for natural beauty, the humanists helped to remove from nature the medieval stigma of sin, and thus to make possible the confident pronouncement of the scientific movement that God's Word could be read not only in the Bible but in the great book of nature.

But no one of these factors, nor all of them together, could have produced the scientific revolution. One is instantly reminded of Bacon's statement that "by the distant voyages and travels which have become frequent in our times, many things in nature have been laid open and discovered which may let in new light upon philosophy." The expansion of Europe, and increased travel in Europe itself, not only stimulated interest in nature but opened up to the West the vision of a "Kingdom of Man" upon earth. Much of Bacon's imagery was borrowed from the geographical discoveries: He aspired to be the Columbus of a new intellectual world, to sail through the Pillars of Hercules (symbol of the old knowledge) into the Atlantic Ocean in search of new and more useful knowledge. Bacon, however, failed to detect the coincidence of the scientific revolution with commercial prosperity and the rise of the middle class. Doubtless, the Marxist Professor Hessen greatly oversimplified when he wrote that "Newton was the typical representative of the rising bourgeoisie, and in his philosophy he embodies the characteristic features of his class." The theoretical scientists had mixed motives. Along with a concern for technology, they pursued truth for its own sake, and they sought God in his great creation. All the same, it is not stretching the imagination too far to see a rough correspondence between the mechanical universe of the seventeenth-century philosophers and the bourgeois desire for rational, predictable order. Science and business were a two-way street. If science affected business, so did business affect science — by its businesslike temper and its quantitative thinking, by its interest in "matter" and the rational control of matter.

2

The scientific revolution gave birth to a new conception of knowledge, a new methodology, and a new worldview substantially different from the old Aristotelian-Christian worldview. . . .

Knowledge now meant exact knowledge: what you know for certain, and not what may possibly or even probably be. Knowledge is what can be clearly apprehended by the mind, or measured by mathematics, or demonstrated by experiment. Galileo came close to saying this when he declared that without mathematics "it is impossible to comprehend a single word of (the great book of the universe);" likewise Descartes when he wrote that "we ought never to allow ourselves to be persuaded of the truth of anything unless on the evidence of our Reason." The distinction between "primary" and "secondary qualities" in seventeenth-century metaphysics carried the same implication. To Galileo, Descartes, and Robert Boyle those mathematical qualities that inhered in objects (size, weight, position, etc.) were "primary," i.e., matters of real knowledge; whereas all the other qualities that our senses tell us are in objects (color, odor, taste, etc.) were "secondary," less real because less amenable to measurement. The inference of all this is plain: Knowledge pertains to "natural philosophy" and possibly social theory, but not to theology or the older philosophy or poetry which involve opinion, belief, faith, but not knowledge. The Royal Society actually undertook to renovate the English language, by excluding from it metaphors and pulpit eloquence which conveyed no precise meaning. The "enthusiasm" of the religious man became suspect as did the "sixth sense" of the poet who could convey pleasure but not knowledge.

The odd thing about the scientific revolution is that for all its avowed distrust of hypotheses and systems, it created its own system of nature, or worldview. "I perceive," says the "Countess" in Fontenelle's popular dialogue of 1686, "Philosophy is now become very Mechanical." "I value (this universe) the more since I know it resembles a Watch, and the whole order of Nature the more plain and easy it is, to me it appears the more admirable." Descartes and other philosophers of science in the seventeenth century constructed a mechanical universe which resembled the machines — watches, pendulum clocks, steam engines — currently being built by scientists and artisans. However, it was not the observation of actual machines but the new astronomy and physics that made it possible to picture the universe in this way. The "Copernican revolution" destroyed Aristotle's "celestial world" of planets and stars which, because they were formed of a subtle substance having no weight, behaved differently from bodies on earth and in the "sublunary world." The new laws of motion formulated by a succession of physicists from Kepler to Newton explained the movement of bodies, both celestial and terrestrial, entirely on mechanical and mathematical principles. According to the law of inertia, the "natural" motion of bodies was in a straight line out into Euclidean space. The planets were pulled into their curvilinear orbits by gravitation which could operate at tremendous distances, and which varied inversely as the square of the distance.

Thus, the universe pictured by Fontenelle's Countess was very different from that of Dante in the thirteenth, or Richard Hooker in the sixteenth century. Gone was the Aristotelian-Christian universe of purposes, forms, and final causes. Gone were the spirits and intelligences which had been required to push the skies daily around the earth. The fundamental features of the new universe were numbers (mathematical quantities) and invariable laws. It was an economical universe in which nature did nothing in vain and performed its daily tasks without waste. In such a universe the scientist could delight and the bourgeois could live happily ever after — or at least up to the time of Darwin. The fact that nature appeared to have no spiritual purpose — Descartes said that it would continue to exist regardless of whether there were any human beings to think it — was more than compensated for by its dependability. Philosophy had indeed become very mechanical. Descartes kept God to start his machine going, and Newton did what he could to save the doctrine of providence. But for all practical purposes, God had become the First Cause, "very well skilled in mechanics and geometry." And the rage for mechanical explanation soon spread beyond the confines of physics to encompass the biological and social sciences. Thus did Descartes regard animals as a piece of clockwork, Robert Boyle the human body as a "matchless engine."

Under the circumstances, one would logically expect there to have been warfare between science and religion in the seventeenth century. But such was not the case. To be sure, some theologians expressed dismay at the downfall of Aristotelianism, and the Roman Church took steps to suppress Copernicanism when Giordano Bruno interpreted it to mean an infinite universe and a plurality of worlds. But the majority of the scientists and popularizers of science were sincerely religious men — not a few were actually ecclesiastics — who either saw no conflict or else went to some lengths to resolve it. Science itself was commonly regarded as a religious enterprise. . . .

In the final analysis, however, the new thing in seventeenth-century thought was the dethronement of theology from its proud position as the sun of the intellectual universe. Bacon and Descartes and Newton lived in an age that was finding it increasingly difficult to reconcile science and religion. To save the best features of both they effected a shaky compromise. For all practical purposes they eliminated religious purpose from nature — thus allowing science to get on with its work, while leaving religion in control of private belief and morals. By their insistence that religious truth itself must pass the tests of reason and reliable evidence, John Locke and the rationalists further reduced theology's prerogatives. Bacon was prepared to believe the word of God "though our reason be shocked at it." But not Locke: "'I believe because it is impossible,' might," he says, "in a good man, pass for a sally of zeal, but would prove a very ill rule for men to choose their opinions or religion by." Good Christian though Locke might be, his teaching had the effect of playing down the supernatural aspects of religion, of equating religion with simple ethics. . . .

23

BONNIE S. ANDERSON
AND JUDITH P. ZINSSER

Women and Science

This selection from a history of European women shows how some women, especially the better educated, could participate in the scientific revolution of the seventeenth and eighteenth centuries. But Anderson and Zinsser also demonstrate how much of the scientific revolution endowed male prejudices with false scientific respectability. What factors seem to have enabled women to participate in the scientific revolution? In what ways was the scientific revolution a new bondage for women?

Bonnie S. Anderson and Judith P. Zinsser, *A History of Their Own: Women in Europe from Prehistory to the Present,* vol. II (New York: Harper & Row, 1988) 87–89, 96–99.

Thinking Historically

What do the authors mean when they say that for women "there was no scientific revolution"? In what ways were women's lives different after the scientific revolution? In what ways were they the same? Were the differences caused by the scientific revolution?

Women Scientists

In the same way that women responded to and participated in Humanism,[1] so they were drawn to the intellectual movement known as the Scientific Revolution. The excitement of the new discoveries of the seventeenth and eighteenth centuries, in particular, inspired a few gifted women scientists to formulate their own theories about the natural world, to perform their own experiments, and to publish their findings. In contrast to those educated strictly and formally according to Humanist precepts, these women had little formal training, and chose for themselves what they read and studied. Rather than encouraging them, their families at best left them to their excitement with the wonders of the "Scientific Revolution"; at worst, parents criticized their daughters' absorption in such inappropriate, inelegant, and unfeminine endeavors.

All across Europe from the sixteenth to the eighteenth centuries these women found fascination in the natural sciences. They corresponded and studied with the male scientists of their day. They observed, and they formulated practical applications from their new knowledge of botany, horticulture, and chemistry. The Countess of Chinchon, wife of the Viceroy to Peru, brought quinine bark to Spain from Latin America because it had cured her malaria. Some noblewomen, like the German Anna of Saxony (1532–1582), found medical uses for the plants they studied. The most gifted of these early naturalists is remembered not as a scientist but as an artist. Maria Sibylla Merian (1647–1717) learned drawing and probably acquired her interest in plants and insects from her stepfather, a Flemish still-life artist. As a little girl she went with him into the fields to collect specimens. Though she married, bore two daughters, and ran a household, between 1679 and her death in 1717 she also managed to complete and have published six collections of engravings of European flowers and insects. These were more than artist's renderings. For example, her study of caterpillars was unique for the day. Unlike the still life done by her contemporaries, the drawings show the insect at every stage of development as observed

---

[1] A faith in the capacities of humans that reached religious dimensions in the sixteenth century. [Ed.]

from the specimens that she collected and nursed to maturity. She explained:

> From my youth I have been interested in insects, first I started with silkworms in my native Frankfurt-am-Main. After that . . . I started to collect all the caterpillars I could find to observe their changes.

Merian's enthusiasm, patience, and skill brought her to the attention of the director of the Amsterdam Botanical Gardens and other male collectors. When her daughter married and moved to the Dutch colony of Surinam, their support was important when she wanted to raise the money for a new scientific project. In 1699, at the age of fifty-two, Maria Sibylla Merian set off on what became a two-year expedition into the interior of South America. She collected, made notations and sketches. Only yellow fever finally forced her to return to Amsterdam in 1701. The resulting book of sixty engravings established her contemporary reputation as a naturalist.

Mathematics, astronomy, and studies of the universe also interested these self-taught women scientists. In 1566 in Paris Marie de Coste Blanche published *The Nature of the Sun and Earth*. Margaret Cavendish (1617–1673), the seventeenth-century Duchess of Newcastle, though haphazard in her approach to science, produced fourteen books on everything from natural history to atomic physics.

Even more exceptional in the eighteenth century was the French noblewoman and courtier, Emilie du Châtelet (1706–1749). She gained admission to the discussions of the foremost mathematicians and scientists of Paris, earned a reputation as a physicist and as an interpreter of the theories of Leibnitz and Newton. Emilie du Châtelet showed unusual intellectual abilities even as a child. By the age of ten she had read Cicero, studied mathematics and metaphysics. At twelve she could speak English, Italian, Spanish, and German and translated Greek and Latin texts like Aristotle and Virgil. Presentation at court and life as a courtier changed none of her scientific interests and hardly modified her studious habits. She seemed to need no sleep, read incredibly fast, and was said to appear in public with ink stains on her fingers from her notetaking and writing. When she took up the study of Descartes, her father complained to her uncle: "I argued with her in vain; she would not understand that no great lord will marry a woman who is seen reading every day." Her mother despaired of a proper future for such a daughter who "flaunts her mind, and frightens away the suitors her other excesses have not driven off." It was her lover and lifelong friend, the Duke de Richelieu, who encouraged her to continue and to formalize her studies by hiring professors in mathematics and physics from the Sorbonne to tutor her. In 1733 she stormed her way into the Café Gradot, the Parisian coffee-house where the scientists, mathematicians, and philosophers regularly met. Barred because she was a woman, she simply had a suit of men's clothes made for herself and reappeared, her long legs now in breeches and hose, to the delight of cheering colleagues and the consternation of the management.

From the early 1730s until the late 1740s her affair with the *philosophe* Voltaire made possible over ten years of study and writing. He paid for the renovation of her husband's country château in Champagne where they established a life filled with their work and time with each other. They had the windows draped so that shifts from day to night would not distract them. They collected a library of ten thousand volumes, more than the number at most universities. He had his duty; she hers.

Emilie du Châtelet usually rose at dawn, breakfasted on fish, bread, stew, and wine, then wrote letters, made the household arrangements for the day, and saw her children. Then she studied. She set up her experiments in the great hall of the château — pipes, rods, and wooden balls hung from the rafters as she set about duplicating the English physicist Newton's experiments. She and Voltaire broke the day with a meal together. Then more study and more writing. When she had trouble staying awake she put her hands in ice water until they were numb, then paced and beat them against her arms to restore the circulation.

Châtelet made her reputation as a scientist with her three-volume work on the German mathematician and philosopher Leibnitz, *The Institutions of Physics,* published in 1740. Contemporaries also knew of her work from her translation of Newton's *Principles of Mathematics,* her book on algebra, and her collaboration with Voltaire on his treatise about Newton.

From the fifteenth to the eighteenth centuries privileged women participated in the new intellectual movements. Like the men of their class, they became humanist scholars, naturalists, and scientists. Unfortunately, many of these women found themselves in conflict with their families and their society. A life devoted to scholarship conflicted with the roles that women, however learned, were still expected to fulfill.

Science Affirms Tradition

In the sixteenth and seventeenth centuries Europe's learned men questioned, altered, and dismissed some of the most hallowed precepts of Europe's inherited wisdom. The intellectual upheaval of the Scientific Revolution caused them to examine and describe anew the nature of the universe and its forces, the nature of the human body and its functions. Men used telescopes and rejected the traditional insistence on the smooth surface of the moon. Galileo, Leibnitz, and Newton studied and charted the movement of the planets, discovered gravity and the true relationship between the earth and the sun. Fallopio dissected the human body, Harvey discovered the circulation of the blood, and Leeuwenhoek found spermatozoa with his microscope.

For women, however, there was no Scientific Revolution. When men studied female anatomy, when they spoke of female physiology, of women's reproductive organs, of the female role in procreation, they ceased to be scientific. They suspended reason and did not accept the evidence of their senses. Tradition, prejudice, and imagination, not scientific observation, governed their conclusions about women. The writings of the classical authors like Aristotle and Galen continued to carry the same authority as they had when first written, long after they had been discarded in other areas. Men spoke in the name of the new "science" but mouthed words and phrases from the old misogyny. In the name of "science" they gave a supposed physiological basis to the traditional views of women's nature, function, and role. Science affirmed what men had always known, what custom, law, and religion had postulated and justified. With the authority of their "objective," "rational" inquiry they restated ancient premises and arrived at the same traditional conclusions: the innate superiority of the male and the justifiable subordination of the female.

In the face of such certainty, the challenges of women like Lucrezia Marinella and María de Zayas had little effect. As Marie de Gournay, the French essayist, had discovered at the beginning of the seventeenth century, those engaged in the scientific study of humanity viewed the female as if she were of a different species — less than human, at best; nature's mistake, fit only to "play the fool and serve [the male]."

The standard medical reference work, *Gynaecea,* reprinted throughout the last decades of the sixteenth century, included the old authorities like Aristotle and Galen, and thus the old premises about women's innate physical inferiority. A seventeenth-century examination for a doctor in Paris asked the rhetorical question "Is woman an imperfect work of nature?" All of the Aristotelian ideals about the different "humors" of the female and male survived in the popular press even after they had been rejected by the medical elite. The colder and moister humors of the female meant that women had a passive nature and thus took longer to develop in the womb. Once grown to maturity, they were better able to withstand the pain of childbirth.

Even without reference to the humors, medical and scientific texts supported the limited domestic role for women. Malebranche, a French seventeenth-century philosopher, noted that the delicate fibers of the woman's brain made her overly sensitive to all that came to it; thus she could not deal with ideas or form abstractions. Her body and mind were so relatively weak that she must stay within the protective confines of the home to be safe.

No amount of anatomical dissection dispelled old bits of misinformation or changed the old misconceptions about women's reproductive organs. Illustrations continued to show the uterus shaped like a flask with two horns, and guides for midwives gave the principal role in labor to the fetus. As in Greek and Roman medical texts these new "scientific" works assumed that women's bodies dictated their principal function, procreation. Yet even this role was devalued. All of the evidence of dissection and deductive reasoning reaffirmed the superiority of the male's role in reproduction. Men discovered the spermatazoon, but not the ovum. They believed that semen was the single active agent. Much as Aristotle had done almost two millennia earlier, seventeenth-century scientific study hypothesized that the female supplied the "matter," while the life and essence of the embryo came from the sperm alone.

These denigrating and erroneous conclusions were reaffirmed by the work of the seventeenth-century English scientist William Harvey. Having discovered the circulation of the blood, Harvey turned his considerable talents to the study of human reproduction and published his conclusions in 1651. He dissected female deer at all stages of their cycle, when pregnant and when not. He studied chickens and roosters. With all of this dissection and all of this observation he hypothesized an explanation for procreation and a rhapsody to male semen far more extreme than anything Aristotle had reasoned. The woman, like the hen with her unfertilized egg, supplies the matter, the man gives it form and life. The semen, he explained, had almost magical power to "elaborate, concoct"; it was "vivifying". . . . endowed with force and spirit and generative influence," coming as it did from "vessels so elaborate, and endowed with such vital energy." So powerful was this fluid that it did not even have to reach the woman's uterus or remain in the vagina. Rather he believed it gave off a "fecundating power," leaving the woman's body to play a passive, or secondary, role. Simple contact with this magical elixir of life worked like lightning, or — drawing on another set of his experiments — "in the same way as iron touched by the magnet is endowed with its powers and can attract other iron to it." The woman was but the receiver and the receptacle.

Anatomy and physiology confirmed the innate inferiority of woman and her limited reproductive function. They also proved as "scientific truth" all of the traditional negative images of the female nature. A sixteenth-century Italian anatomist accepted Galen's view and believed the ovaries to be internal testicles. He explained their strange placement so "as to keep her from perceiving and ascertaining her sufficient perfection," and to humble her "continual desire to dominate." An early-seventeenth-century French book on childbirth instructed the midwife to tie the umbilical cord far from the body to assure a long penis and a well-spoken young man for a male child and close to the body to give the female a straighter form and to ensure that she would talk less.

No one questioned the equally ancient and traditional connection between physiology and nature: the role of the uterus in determining a woman's behavior. The organ's potential influence confirmed the female's irrationality and her need to accept a subordinate role to the male. The sixteenth-century Italian anatomist Fallopio repeated Aristotle's idea that the womb lusted for the male in its desire to procreate. The French sixteenth-century doctor and writer Rabelais took Plato's view of the womb as insatiable, like an animal out of control when denied sexual intercourse, the cause of that singularly female ailment, "hysteria." Other sixteenth- and seventeenth-century writers on women and their health adopted all of the most misogynistic explanations of the traditional Greek and Roman authorities. No menstruation meant a diseased womb, an organ suffocating in a kind of female excrement. Only intercourse with a man could prevent or cure the condition. Left untreated the uterus would put pressure on other organs, cause convulsions, or drive the woman crazy. Thus, the male remained the key agent in the woman's life. She was innately inferior, potentially irrational, and lost to ill-health and madness without his timely intervention.

So much changed from the fifteenth to the eighteenth centuries in the ways in which women and men perceived their world, its institutions and attitudes. The Renaissance offered the exhilaration of a society in which the individual could be freed from traditional limitations. In the spirit of Humanistic and scientific inquiry men questioned and reformulated assumptions about the mind's capabilities and the description of the natural universe. New methods of reasoning and discourse, of observation and experimentation, evolved and led to the reorientation of the natural universe and more accurate descriptions of the physical world, including man's own body. Yet when it came to questions and assumptions about women's function and role and to descriptions of her nature and her body, no new answers were formulated. Instead, inspired by the intellectual excitement of the times and the increasing confidence in their own perceptions of the spiritual and material world, men argued even more strongly from traditional premises, embellishing and revitalizing the ancient beliefs. Instead of breaking with tradition, descriptions of the female accumulated traditions: the classical, the religious, the literary, the customary, and the legal — all stated afresh in the secular language of the new age. Instead of being freed, women were ringed with yet more binding and seemingly incontrovertible versions of the traditional attitudes about their inferior nature, their proper function and role, and their subordinate relationship to men.

With the advent of printing, men were able to disseminate these negative conclusions about women as they never could before. From the sixteenth century on the printing presses brought the new tracts, pamphlets, treatises, broadsides, and engravings to increasing numbers of Europeans: pictures of the sperm as a tiny, fully formed infant; works by scholars and jurists explaining the female's "natural" physical and legal incapacity; romances and ballads telling of unchaste damsels and vengeful wives set to plague man.

Although these misogynistic attitudes about women flourished and spread, the defense of women had also begun. In her *Book of the City of Ladies* Christine de Pizan, the fifteenth-century writer, asks why no one had spoken on their behalf before, why the "accusations and slanders" had gone uncontradicted for so long? Her allegorical mentor, "Rectitude," replies, "Let me tell you that in the long run, everything comes to a head at the right time."

The world of the courts had widened the perimeters of women's expectations and given some women increased opportunities. However, for the vast majority of women, still not conscious of their disadvantaged and subordinate status, changes in material circumstances had a far greater impact. From the seventeenth to the twentieth centuries more women were able to live the life restricted in previous ages to the few. In Europe's salons and parlors they found increased comfort, greater security, and new ways to value their traditional roles and functions. For these women, "the right time" — the moment for questioning and rejecting the ancient premises of European society — lay in the future.

24

LADY MARY WORTLEY MONTAGUE

Letter on Turkish Smallpox Inoculation

Lady Mary Wortley Montague, an English aristocrat, came down with smallpox in 1715. She survived, but was badly scarred by the rash that accompanied the often-fatal disease. Her younger brother died from smallpox, one of the tens of thousands who succumbed in epidemics across Europe and around the world in the eighteenth and nineteenth centuries. Two years after her recovery Montague traveled

---

Letters of Lady Mary Wortley Montague, written during her travels in Europe, Asia, and Africa, to which are added poems by the same author (Bordeaux, J. Pinard, 1805). The UCLA Louis M. Darling Biomedical Library, History and Special Collections Division.

to Istanbul with her husband, who was the British ambassador to the Ottoman Empire. There, she witnessed a new approach to warding off smallpox infections, as she described in the following letter to a friend in England. What process does Montague describe in her letter? What was her response to the events she witnessed in Turkey?

Thinking Historically

This letter provides a clear example of how scientific observation can change the material world in which we live. After observing the Turkish smallpox inoculation Montague had her son and daughter inoculated. In fact, she became an advocate for smallpox inoculation in England and played an important role in persuading the English medical profession to support the innovative procedure. Montague paved the way for a safer vaccine, developed by Edward Jenner in 1796, that would eventually eradicate the disease from the planet.

Despite her admirable efforts, it was difficult to convince Europeans to embrace smallpox inoculation, which had been practiced in Asia for centuries. Even though the effectiveness of inoculation came to be recognized in England during Montague's lifetime, the French and other Europeans, according to Voltaire, thought that the English were "fools and madmen" for experimenting with inoculation. What does this suggest about the nature of scientific discovery? Besides lack of knowledge, what other obstacles need to be overcome?

To Mrs. S. C., Adrianople, April I, O.S.

A Propos of distempers, I am going to tell you a thing, that will make you wish yourself here. The small pox, so fatal, and so general amongst us, is here entirely harmless, by the invention of ingrafting, which is the term they give it. There is a set of old women, who make it their business to perform the operation, every autumn, in the month of september, when the great heat is abated. People send to one another to know if any of their family has a mind to have the small-pox; they make parties for this purpose, and when they are met (commonly fifteen or sixteen together) the old woman comes with a nut-shell full of the matter of the best sort of small pox, and asks what vein you please to have opened. She immediately rips open that you offer to her, with a large needle (which gives you no more pain that a common scratch), and puts into the vein as much matter as can lie upon the head of her needle, and after that, binds up the little wound with a hollow bit of shell, and in this manner opens four of five veins. The Grecians have commonly the superstition of opening one in the middle of the forehead, one in each arm, and one in the breast, to mark the sign of the cross; but this has a very ill effect, all these wounds leaving little scars, and is not done by those that are not superstitious, who choose to have them in the legs, or that part of the arm that is concealed. The children or young patients play together all the rest of the day, and are in perfect health to the eighth.

Then the fever begins to seize them, and they keep their beds two days, very seldom three. They have very rarely above twenty or thirty in their faces, which never mark, and in eight days time they are as well as before their illness. Where they are wounded, there remains running sores during the distemper, which I don't doubt is a great relief to it. Every year thousands undergo this operation, and the French ambassador says pleasantly that they take the small-pox here by way of diversion, as they take the waters in other countries. There is no example of any one that has died in it, and you may believe I am well satisfied of the safety of this experiment, since I intend to try it on my dear little son. I am patriot enough to take pains to bring this useful invention into fashion in England, and I should not fail to write to some of our doctors very particularly about it, if I knew any one of them that I thought had virtue enough to destroy such a considerable branch of their revenue, for the good of mankind. But that distemper is too beneficial to them, not to expose to all their resentment the hardy wight that should undertake to put an end to it. Perhaps if I live to return, I may, however have the courage to war with them. Upon this occasion, admire the heroism in the heart of

Your friend, etc. etc.

$$25$$

BERNARD LE BOVIER DE FONTENELLE

From *Conversations on the Plurality of Worlds*

In the first selection of this chapter, Baumer points out that the seventeenth-century scientific revolution was not only a change in scientific method and discovery, but it was also the popularization of science. Fontenelle (1657–1757), a French dramatist and philosopher, was one of the first European writers to interpret the new science of

Bernard le Bovier de Fontenelle, *Conversations on the Plurality of Worlds,* trans. H. A. Hargreaves (Berkeley: University of California Press, 1990), 8–12, 18–20, 62–64.

Copernicus and Descartes for a wide popular audience. His brief book, *Conversations on the Plurality of Worlds* (1686), was an instant best-seller. In an imagined conversation between a charming philosopher and his hostess, the Marquise, Fontenelle explores the meaning and implications of the new science. Notice how Fontenelle moves the conversation from the common, even romantic, idea of the heavens, to the findings of the new astronomy. What are the new ideas about the heavens that Fontenelle's philosopher reveals? Some historians of science have argued that the scientific revolution was spurred not by dramatic new innovations or observations, but by the ability to reconfigure existing evidence, theories, and paradigms in innovative ways. Can you see any evidence for this interpretation in this selection?

Thinking Historically

In 1543 Nicholas Copernicus argued that the earth, far from being the center of the universe, actually revolved around the sun. In 1600, Giordano Bruno was burned at the stake for supporting the Copernican theory and suggesting the possibility of life on other worlds. In 1632 Galileo wrote *Dialogue Concerning the Two Chief World Systems* to popularize the new astronomy and was placed under house arrest and forced to recant. That Fontenelle took up a similar challenge only fifty years later is a mark of courage, but his book's great success is also an indicator of how rapidly things were changing. Judging from the Marquise's responses to each of the philosopher's revelations, what seem to have been the most threatening elements of the new astronomy in 1686? Considering the time it took these ideas to be accepted, would you call this development a scientific revolution or a gradual change?

One evening after supper we went to walk in the garden. There was a delicious breeze, which made up for the extremely hot day we had had to bear. The Moon had risen about an hour before, and shining through the trees it made a pleasant mixture of bright white against the dark greenery that appeared black. There was no cloud to hide even the smallest star; they were all pure and shining gold and stood out clearly against their blue background. The spectacle set me to musing, and I might have gone on like that for some time if it had not been for the Marquise, but in the company of such a lovely woman I could hardly give myself up to the Moon and stars.

"Don't you find," I asked her, "that the day is less beautiful than a beautiful night?"

"Yes," she answered, "day's beauty is blond and dazzling, but the night's beauty is brunette, which is more moving."

"You're very generous," I replied, "to defer to the brunettes when you're not one yourself, but it's certainly true that the day is the most beautiful thing in nature, and that the most beautiful things in the imagination, the heroines of Romances, are nearly always blonds too."

"Beauty is nothing," said she, "if it doesn't move us. Admit it—no day has ever thrown you into such a sweet reverie as the one you were about to fall into just now, at the sight of this beautiful evening."

"No doubt," I answered. "Nevertheless, a blond such as you would make me dream more sweetly than the most beautiful dark night in the world."

"Even if that were true," she laughed, "I shouldn't be satisfied unless the day, which is the counterpart of blonds, had the same effect. Why do you suppose lovers, who are the best judges of what stirs our emotions, address all their songs and poems to the night?"

"It's the night, of course," I said, "that deserves their thanks."

"The night hears all their complaints as well," she replied. "Why is it they don't tell their secrets to the day?"

"Apparently," said I, "the day doesn't inspire sadness and passion like the night, when everything seems to be at rest. We imagine that the stars move more quietly than the sun; everything is softer in starlight; we can fix our eyes more comfortably on the heavens; our thoughts are freer because we're so foolish as to imagine ourselves the only ones abroad to dream. Besides, in daylight we see nothing but sun and blue sky, but the night gives us all the profusion of stars in a thousand different random designs, stirring as many pleasantly confused thoughts in us."

"I've always felt that," she said. "I love the stars, and I'm almost angry with the Sun overpowering them."

"I can never forgive it," I cried, "for making me lose sight of all those worlds."

"What do you mean, worlds?" she asked, turning to me.

"Excuse me," I answered. "You've set me onto my weakness, and my imagination is getting the best of me."

"What is this weakness?" she asked, not to be deterred.

"I'm ashamed to admit it," I said, "but I have a peculiar notion that every star could well be a world. I wouldn't swear that it's true, but I think so because it pleases me to think so. The idea sticks in my mind in a most delightful way. As I see it, this pleasure is an integral part of truth itself."

"Well," said the Marquise, "if your idea is so pleasing, share it with me. I'll believe that the stars are anything you say, if I enjoy it."

"Ah, Madame," I answered, "this isn't enjoyment such as you'd find in a Molière comedy; it's enjoyment that involves our reasoning powers. It only delights the mind."

"What?" she cried. "Do you think I'm capable of enjoying intellectual pleasures? I'll show you otherwise right now. Tell me about your stars!"

"No!" I answered. "It will never be said of me that in an arbor, at ten o'clock in the evening, I talked of philosophy to the most beautiful woman I know. Look elsewhere for the philosophers."

Although I excused myself in this manner several times, I had to give in, but at least, for the preservation of my honor, I made her promise to keep it a secret. Then when I finally had no excuses left and decided to speak, I didn't know where to begin. To someone like the Marquise, who knew nothing of Natural Philosophy, I would have to go a long way to prove that the Earth might be a planet, the other planets Earths, and all the stars solar systems. I told her several times that it would be better to talk about trifles, as all reasonable people would in our place. Finally, however, to give her a general idea of philosophy, here is the proposal into which I threw myself.

"All philosophy," I told her, "is based on two things only: curiosity and poor eyesight; if you had better eyesight you could see perfectly well whether or not these stars are solar systems, and if you were less curious you wouldn't care about knowing, which amounts to the same thing. The trouble is, we want to know more than we can see. Again, if we could really see things as they are, we would really know something, but we see things other than as they are. So true philosophers spend a lifetime not believing what they do see, and theorizing on what they don't see, and it's not, to my way of thinking, a very enviable situation. On this subject I have always thought that nature is very much like an opera house. From where you are at the opera you don't see the stages exactly as they are; they're arranged to give the most pleasing effect from a distance, and the wheels and counter-weights that make everything move are hidden out of sight. You don't worry, either, about how they work. Only some engineer in the pit, perhaps, may be struck by some extraordinary effect and be determined to figure out for himself how it was done. That engineer is like the philosophers. But what makes it harder for the philosophers is that, in the machinery that Nature shows us, the wires are better hidden — so well, in fact, that they've been guessing for a long time at what causes the movements of the universe.

"Imagine all the Sages at an opera — the Pythagorases, Platos, Aristotles, and all those whose names nowadays are dinned into our ears. Suppose that they watched Phaeton lifted by the winds, but they couldn't discover the wires and didn't know how the backstage area was arranged. One of them would say: 'Phaeton has a certain hidden property that makes him lighter.' Another: 'Phaeton is composed of certain numbers that make him rise.' Another: 'Phaeton has a peculiar attraction to the top of the theater, and he is uneasy if he's not up there.' Still another: 'Phaeton wasn't made for flying, but he would rather fly than leave a vacuum in the upper part of the stage.' And there are a hundred other notions which I'm astonished haven't destroyed the reputation of the whole of Antiquity. Finally, Descartes and some other moderns would come along, and they would say: 'Phaeton rises because he's pulled by wires, and because a weight heavier than he is descends.' Nowadays we no longer believe that a body will move if it's not affected by another body and in some fashion pulled by wires; we don't believe that it will rise or fall except when it has a spring or a counter-weight. Whoever sees nature as it truly is simply sees the back-stage area of the theater."

"In that case," said the Marquise, "nature has become very mechanical."

"So mechanical," I replied, "that I fear we'll soon grow ashamed of it. They want the world to be merely, on a large scale, what a watch is on a small scale, so that everything goes by regular movements based on the organization of its parts. Admit it! Didn't you have a more grandiose concept of the universe, and didn't you give it more respect than it deserved? Most men esteem it less since they've come to know it."

"Well I hold it in much higher regard," she answered, "now that I know it's like a watch; it's superb that, wonderful as it is, the whole order of nature is based upon such simple things." . . .

"Have you noticed," I asked her, "that a ball that rolls on the ground has two motions? It goes toward the target at which it's aimed, and at the same time turns a great number of times upon itself, so that the parts on top go to the bottom and those on the bottom come to the top. The Earth does the same thing. In the time that it advances on the circle it describes in one year around the Sun, it turns on itself each twenty-four hours, so that in twenty-four hours each part of the Earth loses the Sun and recovers it. Whenever we turn toward the place where the Sun is, it seems to rise; when we begin to move away, it seems to set."

"It really amuses me," she replied, "that the Earth is taking everything upon itself, while the Sun does nothing. And when the Moon and the other planets and the fixed stars appear to turn over our heads in twenty-four hours, is this also imagined?"

"Pure imagination," I answered, "which comes from the same cause. Simply that the planets make their circles around the Sun in those unequal times corresponding to their unequal distances, and the one which we see today corresponding to a certain point of the Zodiac, or the sphere of fixed stars, we see tomorrow corresponding to a different point, partly because it has progressed on its circle and partly because we've advanced on ours. We move and so do the other planets; this places us at different viewpoints from them, and makes it appear to us that there are irregularities in their courses, of which I need not speak. It's enough for you to know that what looks irregular among the planets comes only from the diverse means by which our movements make us encounter one another, and that basically they're all quite regular."

"I consent that they shall be so," said the Marquise, "but I really wish that their regularity demanded less of the Earth; it's not good management, and for so heavy and solid a mass as it has, a lot of agility is required."

"But," I asked her, "would you rather that the Sun and all the other stars, which are such huge bodies, made an immense turn of an infinite number of leagues around the Earth every day in twenty-four hours? Because they would have to if the Earth doesn't turn on itself in twenty-four hours."

"Oh," she replied, "the Sun and the stars are all fire, movement costs them nothing; but the Earth scarcely seems portable."

"And would you believe," said I, "if you hadn't any experience, that a great ship loaded with a hundred and fifteen mounted cannon and three thousand men, plus a very large number of supplies, was a very portable thing? Yet it takes only a little puff of wind to make it travel on the water, because water is liquid, yielding easily and offering little resistance to the movement of the ship. And so the Earth, as massive as it is, is easily carried in the celestial matter, which is a thousand times more fluid than water, and which fills all this great space where the planets swim. And where could the Earth be moored to resist the movement of this celestial matter and not be carried away? It's as if a little ball of wood were able to resist the current of a river."

"But," she asked again, "how does the Earth, with all its weight, support itself on your celestial matter, which must be very light since it's so fluid?"

"It doesn't follow," I answered, "that what is fluid is necessarily light. What have you to say about our great ship which with all its weight is still much lighter than water, since it floats on it?"

"As long as you have your great ship," she said as if in anger, "I don't want to say anything more to you. But can you reassure me that there's nothing to fear on a spinning top such as you make the Earth?"

"Oh well," I told her, "let's have the Earth supported by four elephants, as the Indians do."

"So here's another system," she cried. "At least I like those people for having seen to their own security by making good foundations; instead of which we Copernicans are so imprudent as to want to swim off haphazardly in this celestial matter. I'll wager that if the Indians thought the Earth were in the least danger of moving they'd double their elephants."

"That's very good," said I, laughing at her thought. "Don't spare the elephants when it's a question of sleeping securely. If you need some tonight, we'll add as many as you please to our system, then we'll take them away little by little as your confidence grows."

"Seriously," she answered, "I don't think they'll be necessary from now on, and I feel I have enough courage to dare the turning." . . .

The Marquise was really impatient to know what might happen with the fixed stars. "Will they be inhabited like the planets," she asked me, "or not? What will we make of them?"

"You could probably guess if you really wanted to," I said. "The fixed stars can't be less distant from the Earth than fifty million leagues or so, and if you were to anger an astronomer he's put them still farther away. The distance from the Sun to the farthest planet is nothing in comparison with the distance from the Sun or the Earth to the fixed stars, and one doesn't take the trouble to compute it. Their light, as you see, is bright and sparkling enough. If they received it from the Sun, it would have to be a very feeble light after a trip of fifty million leagues, and they would have to send it back across this time distance by reflection, which would weaken it that much more. It would be impossible for a light that had to suffer reflection, and go twice fifty million leagues, to have the strength and brightness of the fixed stars' light. So they must be self-illuminated and all of them, in a word, so many Suns."

"Would I be tricking myself," the Marquise cried, "or do I see where you want to lead me? Are you going to tell me 'The fixed stars are suns, too; our Sun is the center of a vortex which rotates around it; why shouldn't each fixed star also be the center of a vortex which moves about it? Our Sun has planets which it lights; why shouldn't each fixed star have some which it lights, too?"

"I can only answer," I told her, "what Phaedra said to Oenone: 'You said it!'"

"But," she replied, "here's a universe so large that I'm lost, I no longer know where I am, I'm nothing. What, is everything to be divided into vortices, thrown together in confusion? Each star will be the center of a vortex, perhaps as large as ours? All this immense space which holds our Sun and our planets will be merely a small piece of the universe? As many spaces as there are fixed stars? This confounds me — troubles me — terrifies me."

"And as for me," I answered, "this puts me at my ease. When the sky was only this blue vault, with the stars nailed to it, the universe seemed small and narrow to me; I felt oppressed by it. Now that they've given infinitely greater breadth and depth to this vault by dividing it into thousands and thousands of vortices, it seems to me that I breathe more freely, that I'm in a larger air, and certainly the universe has a completely different magnificence. Nature has held back nothing to produce it; she's made a profusion of riches altogether worthy of her. Nothing is so beautiful to visualize as this prodigious number of vortices, each with a sun at its center making planets rotate around it. The inhabitants of a planet in one of these infinite vortices see on all sides the lighted centers of the vortices surrounding them, but aren't able to see their planets which, having only a feeble light borrowed from their sun, don't send it beyond their own world."

"You offer me," she said, "a kind of perspective so long that my eyes can't reach the end of it. I see the Earth's inhabitants clearly; next you make me see those of the Moon and the other planets of our vortex clearly enough, it's true, though less clearly than those of Earth. After them come the inhabitants of the planets of the other vortices who are, I must confess, completely in the dark. Whatever effort I make to see them, I can hardly perceive them at all. And in effect, aren't they nearly annihilated by the phrase you have to use in speaking of them? You're forced to call them 'inhabitants of one of the planets of one of these infinite vortices.' We ourselves, to whom the same phrase applies — admit that you'd scarcely know how to pick us out in the middle of so many worlds. As for me, I'm beginning to see the Earth so frighteningly small that I believe hereafter I'll never be impressed by another thing. Assuredly, if people have such a love of acquisition, if they make up plan after plan, if they go to so much trouble, it's because they don't know about vortices. I can claim that my new enlightenment justifies my laziness, and when anyone reproaches me for my indolence I'll answer: 'Ah, if you knew what the fixed stars are!'"

$$26$$

LYNDA NORENE SHAFFER

China, Technology, and Change

In this essay an important contemporary world historian asks us to compare the revolutionary consequences of scientific and technological changes that occurred in China and Europe before the seventeenth century. What is Shaffer's argument? In what ways was the European scientific revolution different from the changes in China she describes here?

Thinking Historically

What exactly was the impact of printing, the compass, and gunpowder in Europe? What was the "before" and "after" for each of these innovations? What, according to Shaffer, was the situation in China before and after each of these innovations? Which of these six causal

Lynda Norene Shaffer, "China, Technology and Change," World History Bulletin, 4, no. 1 (Fall/Winter, 1986–87), 1–6.

explanations do you find most convincing? Were these innovations as revolutionary in China as they were in Europe?

Francis Bacon (1561–1626), an early advocate of the empirical method, upon which the scientific revolution was based, attributed Western Europe's early modern take-off to three things in particular: printing, the compass, and gunpowder. Bacon had no idea where these things had come from, but historians now know that all three were invented in China. Since, unlike Europe, China did not take off onto a path leading from the scientific to the Industrial Revolution, some historians are now asking why these inventions were so revolutionary in Western Europe and, apparently, so unrevolutionary in China.

In fact, the question has been posed by none other than Joseph Needham, the foremost English-language scholar of Chinese science and technology. It is only because of Needham's work that the Western academic community has become aware that until Europe's take-off, China was the unrivaled world leader in technological development. That is why it is so disturbing that Needham himself has posed this apparent puzzle. The English-speaking academic world relies upon him and repeats him; soon this question and the vision of China that it implies will become dogma. Traditional China will take on supersociety qualities — able to contain the power of printing, to rein in the potential of the compass, even to muffle the blast of gunpowder.

The impact of these inventions on Western Europe is well known. Printing not only eliminated much of the opportunity for human copying errors, it also encouraged the production of more copies of old books and an increasing number of new books. As written material became both cheaper and more easily available, intellectual activity increased. Printing would eventually be held responsible, at least in part, for the spread of classical humanism and other ideas from the Renaissance. It is also said to have stimulated the Protestant Reformation, which urged a return to the Bible as the primary religious authority.

The introduction of gunpowder in Europe made castles and other medieval fortifications obsolete (since it could be used to blow holes in their walls) and thus helped to liberate Western Europe from feudal aristocratic power. As an aid to navigation the compass facilitated the Portuguese- and Spanish-sponsored voyages that led to Atlantic Europe's sole possession of the Western Hemisphere, as well as the Portuguese circumnavigation of Africa, which opened up the first all-sea route from Western Europe to the long-established ports of East Africa and Asia.

Needham's question can thus be understood to mean, Why didn't China use gunpowder to destroy feudal walls? Why didn't China use the compass to cross the Pacific and discover America, or to find an all-sea route to Western Europe? Why didn't China undergo a Renaissance or Reformation? The implication is that even though China possessed these technologies, it did not change much. Essentially Needham's question is asking, What was wrong with China?

Actually, there was nothing wrong with China. China was changed fundamentally by these inventions. But in order to see the changes, one must abandon the search for peculiarly European events in Chinese history, and look instead at China itself before and after these breakthroughs.

To begin, one should note that China possessed all three of these technologies by the latter part of the Tang dynasty (618–906) — between four and six hundred years before they appeared in Europe. And it was during just that time, from about 850, when the Tang dynasty began to falter, until 960, when the Song dynasty (960–1279) was established, that China underwent fundamental changes in all spheres. In fact, historians are now beginning to use the term *revolution* when referring to technological and commercial changes that culminated in the Song dynasty, in the same way that they refer to the changes in eighteenth- and nineteenth-century England as the Industrial Revolution. And the word might well be applied to other sorts of changes in China during this period.

For example, the Tang dynasty elite was aristocratic, but that of the Song was not. No one has ever considered whether the invention of gunpowder contributed to the demise of China's aristocrats, which occurred between 750 and 960, shortly after its invention. Gunpowder may, indeed, have been a factor although it is unlikely that its importance lay in blowing up feudal walls. Tang China enjoyed such internal peace that its aristocratic lineages did not engage in castle-building of the sort typical in Europe. Thus, China did not have many feudal fortifications to blow up.

The only wall of significance in this respect was the Great Wall, which was designed to keep steppe nomads from invading China. In fact, gunpowder may have played a role in blowing holes in this wall, for the Chinese could not monopolize the terrible new weapon, and their nomadic enemies to the north soon learned to use it against them. The Song dynasty ultimately fell to the Mongols, the most formidable force ever to emerge from the Eurasian steppe. Gunpowder may have had a profound effect on China — exposing a united empire to foreign invasion and terrible devastation — but an effect quite opposite to the one it had on Western Europe.

On the other hand, the impact of printing on China was in some ways very similar to its later impact on Europe. For example, printing contributed to a rebirth of classical (that is, preceding the third century A.D.) Confucian learning, helping to revive a fundamentally humanistic outlook that had been pushed aside for several centuries.

After the fall of the Han dynasty (206 B.C.–A.D. 220), Confucianism had lost much of its credibility as a world view, and it eventually lost its central place in the scholarly world. It was replaced by Buddhism, which had come from India. Buddhists believed that much human pain and confusion resulted from the pursuit of illusory pleasures and dubious ambitions: Enlightenment and, ultimately, salvation would come from a progressive disengagement from the real world, which they also believed to be illusory. This point of view dominated Chinese intellectual life until the ninth century. Thus the academic and intellectual comeback of classical Confucianism was in essence a return to a more optimistic literature that affirmed the world as humans had made it.

The resurgence of Confucianism within the scholarly community was due to many factors, but printing was certainly one of the most important. Although it was invented by Buddhist monks in China, and at first benefited Buddhism, by the middle of the tenth century, printers were turning out innumerable copies of the classical Confucian corpus. This return of scholars to classical learning was part of a more general movement that shared not only its humanistic features with the later Western European Renaissance, but certain artistic trends as well.

Furthermore, the Protestant Reformation in Western Europe was in some ways reminiscent of the emergence and eventual triumph of Neo-Confucian philosophy. Although the roots of Neo-Confucianism can be found in the ninth century, the man who created what would become its most orthodox synthesis was Zhu Xi (Chu Hsi, 1130–1200). Neo-Confucianism was significantly different from classical Confucianism, for it had undergone an intellectual (and political) confrontation with Buddhism and had emerged profoundly changed. It is of the utmost importance to understand that not only was Neo-Confucianism new, it was also heresy, even during Zhu Xi's lifetime. It did not triumph until the thirteenth century, and it was not until 1313 (when Mongol conquerors ruled China) that Zhu Xi's commentaries on the classics became the single authoritative text against which all academic opinion was judged.

In the same way that Protestantism emerged out of a confrontation with the Roman Catholic establishment and asserted the individual Christian's autonomy, Neo-Confucianism emerged as a critique of Buddhist ideas that had taken hold in China, and it asserted an individual moral capacity totally unrelated to the ascetic practices and prayers of the Buddhist priesthood. In the twelfth century Neo-Confucianists lifted the work of Mencius (Meng Zi, 370–290 B.C.) out of obscurity and assigned it a place in the corpus second only to that of the *Analects of Confucius*. Many facets of Mencius appealed to the Neo-Confucianists, but one of the most important was his argument that humans by nature are fundamentally good. Within the context of the Song dynasty, this was an assertion that morally could be pursued through an engagement in human affairs, and that the Buddhist monk's withdrawal from life's mainstream did not bestow upon them any special virtue.

The importance of these philosophical developments notwithstanding, printing probably had its greatest impact on the Chinese political system. The origin of the civil service examination system in China can be traced back to the Han dynasty, but in the Song dynasty government-administered examinations became the most important route to political power in China. For almost a thousand years (except the early period of Mongol rule), China was governed by men who had come to power simply because they had done exceedingly well in examinations on the Neo-Confucian canon. At any one time thousands of students were studying for the exams, and thousands of inexpensive books were required. Without printing such a system would not have been possible.

The development of this alternative to aristocratic rule was one of the most radical changes in world history. Since the examinations were ultimately open to 98 percent of all males (actors were one of the few groups excluded), it was the most democratic system in the world prior to the development of representative democracy and popular suffrage in Western Europe in the eighteenth and nineteenth centuries. (There were some small-scale systems, such as the classical Greek city-states, which might be considered more democratic, but nothing comparable in size to Song China or even the modern nation-states of Europe.)

Finally we come to the compass. Suffice it to say that during the Song dynasty, China developed the world's largest and most technologically sophisticated merchant marine and navy. By the fifteenth century its ships were sailing from the north Pacific to the east coast of Africa. They could have made the arduous journey around the tip of Africa and on into Portuguese ports; however, they had no reason to do so. Although the Western European economy was prospering, it offered nothing that China could not acquire much closer to home at much less cost. In particular, wool, Western Europe's most important export, could easily be obtained along China's northern frontier.

Certainly, the Portuguese and the Spanish did not make their unprecedented voyages out of idle curiosity. They were trying to go to the Spice Islands, in what is now Indonesia, in order to acquire the most valuable commercial items of the time. In the fifteenth century these islands were the world's sole suppliers of the fine spices, such as cloves, nutmeg, and mace, as well as a source for the more generally available pepper. It was this spice market that lured Columbus westward from Spain and drew Vasco Da Gama around Africa and across the Indian Ocean.

After the invention of the compass, China also wanted to go to the Spice Islands and, in fact, did go, regularly — but Chinese ships did not have to go around the world to get there. The Atlantic nations of Western Europe, on the other hand, had to buy spices from Venice (which controlled the Mediterranean trade routes) or from other Italian city-states; or they had to find a new way to the Spice Islands. It was necessity that mothered those revolutionary routes that ultimately changed the world.

Gunpowder, printing, the compass — clearly these three inventions changed China as much as they changed Europe. And it should come as no surprise that changes wrought in China between the eighth and tenth centuries were different from changes wrought in Western Europe between the thirteenth and fifteenth centuries. It would, of course, be unfair and ahistorical to imply that something was wrong with Western Europe because the technologies appeared there later. It is equally unfair to ask why the Chinese did not accidentally bump into the Western Hemisphere while sailing east across the Pacific to find the wool markets of Spain.

27

SUGITA GEMPAKU

A Dutch Anatomy Lesson in Japan

Sugita Gempaku (1733–1817) was a Japanese physician who, as he tells us here, suddenly discovered the value of Western medical science when he chanced to witness a dissection shortly after he obtained a Dutch anatomy book.

What was it that Sugita Gempaku learned on that day in 1771? What were the differences between the treatments of anatomy in the Chinese *Book of Medicine* and the Dutch medical book? What accounts for these differences?

Thinking Historically

How did the Dutch book change the way the author practiced medicine? How did it change his knowledge of the human body? How did it change the relevance of his knowledge of the human body to the medicine he practiced?

Sugita Gempaku, "A Dutch Anatomy Lesson in Japan," in *Sources of Japanese History,* ed. David John Lu, vol. 1 (New York: McGraw-Hill, 1974), 253–55.

Somehow, miraculously I obtained a book on anatomy written in [The Netherlands]. . . . It was a strange and even miraculous happening that I was able to obtain that book in that particular spring of 1771. Then at the night of the third day of the third month, I received a letter from a man by the name of Tokuno, who was in the service of the Town Commissioner. Tokuno stated in his letter that "A post-mortem examination of the body of a condemned criminal by a resident physician will be held tomorrow at Senjukotsugahara. You are welcome to witness it if you so desire."

The next day, when we arrived at the location . . . Ryotaku reached under his kimono to produce a Dutch book and showed it to us. "This is a Dutch book of anatomy called *Tabulae Anatomicae*. I bought this a few years ago when I went to Nagasaki, and kept it." As I examined it, it was the same book I had and was of the same edition. We held each other's hands and exclaimed: "What a coincidence!" Ryotaku continued by saying: "When I went to Nagasaki, I learned and heard," and opened this book. "These are called *long* in Dutch, they are lungs," he taught us. "This is *hart,* or the heart. When it says *maag* it is the stomach, and when it says *milt* it is the spleen." However, they did not look like the heart given in the Chinese medical books, and none of us were sure until we could actually see the dissection.

Thereafter we went together to the place which was especially set for us to observe the dissection. . . . That day, the old butcher pointed to this and that organ. After the heart, liver, gall bladder, and stomach were identified, he pointed to other parts for which there were no names. "I don't know their names. But I have dissected quite a few bodies from my youthful days. Inside of everyone's abdomen there were these parts and those parts." . . . The old butcher again said, "Every time I had a dissection, I pointed out to those physicians many of these parts, but not a single one of them questioned 'What was this?' or 'What was that?'" We compared the body as dissected against the charts both Ryotaku and I had, and could not find a single variance from the charts. The Chinese *Book of Medicine* says that the lungs are like the eight petals of the lotus flower, with three petals hanging in front, three in back, and two petals forming like two ears and that the liver has three petals to the left and four petals to the right. There were no such divisions, and the positions and shapes of intestines and gastric organs were all different from those taught by the old theories. The official physicians . . . had witnessed dissection seven or eight times. Whenever they witnessed the dissection, they found that the old theories contradicted reality. Each time they were perplexed and could not resolve their doubts. Every time they wrote down what they thought was strange. They wrote in their books, "The more we think of it, there must be fundamental differences in the bodies of Chinese and of the eastern barbarians." I could see why they wrote this way.

That day, after the dissection was over, we decided that we also should examine the shape of the skeletons left exposed on the execution ground. We collected the bones, and examined a number of them. Again, we were struck by the fact that they all differed from the old theories while conforming to the Dutch charts.

The three of us, Ryotaku, Junan, and I went home together. On the way home we spoke to each other and felt the same way. "How marvelous was our actual experience today. It is a shame that we were ignorant of these things until now. As physicians who serve their masters through medicine, we performed our duties in complete ignorance of the true form of the human body. How disgraceful it is. Somehow, through this experience, let us investigate further the truth about the human body. If we practice medicine with this knowledge behind us, we can make contributions for people under heaven and on this earth." Ryotaku spoke to us. "Indeed, I agree with you wholeheartedly." Then I spoke to my companion. "Somehow if we can translate anew this book called *Tabulae Anatomicae,* we can get a clear notion of the human body inside out. It will have great benefit in the treatment of our patients. Let us do our best to read it and understand it without the help of translators." . . .

The next day, we assembled at the house of Ryotaku and recalled the happenings of the previous day. When we faced that *Tabulae Anatomicae,* we felt as if we were setting sail on a great ocean in a ship without oars or a rudder. With the magnitude of the work before us, we were dumbfounded by our own ignorance. However, Ryotaku had been thinking of this for some time, and he had been in Nagasaki. He knew some Dutch through studying and hearing, and knew some sentence patterns and words. He was also ten years older than I, and we decided to make him head of our group and our teacher. At that time I did not know the twenty-five letters of the Dutch alphabet. I decided to study the language with firm determination, but I had to acquaint myself with letters and words gradually.

REFLECTIONS

It is important to emphasize the revolutionary impact of the European scientific revolution of the seventeenth century without slighting the scientific and technological achievements of other civilizations. The scientific developments in Europe sprang from foreign innovations, and in some fields Europe was not as advanced as other societies. Yet the scientific revolution's unique combination of observation and generalization, experimentation and mathematics, induction and deduction established a body of knowledge and a method for research that proved lasting and irreversible.

Why was it that China, so scientifically and technologically adept during the Sung dynasty, pictured hearts and lungs as flower petals in the late-Ming and early-Ch'ing seventeenth century? Was it that Chinese science lost momentum or changed direction? Or does such a question, as Lynda Shaffer warns, judge China unfairly by Western standards? Do the petal hearts reflect a different set of interests rather than a failure of Chinese science?

Chinese scientists excelled in acupuncture, massage, and herbal medicine, while European scientists excelled in surgery. It turned out that the inner workings of the human body were better revealed in surgical dissection than in muscle manipulation or in oral remedies. And, as Sugita Gempaku reminds us, the Europeans not only cut and removed, they also named what they found and tried to understand how it worked. Perhaps the major difference between science in Europe and that in India, China, and Japan in the seventeenth century was one of perspective: Europeans were beginning to imagine the human body as a machine and asking how it worked. In some respects, the metaphor of man as a machine proved more fruitful than organic metaphors of humans as plants or animals.

Probing questions also changed our understanding of the heavens. In Bertold Brecht's play *Galileo,* the great astronomer chides the cardinals of the church to look through a telescope so they can see the features of the moon and those revolving around Jupiter. Brecht opposes scientific observation with the church's reliance on biblical and Aristotelian authority, but this simple antithesis misses the mark. Galileo was a mathematician and an astronomer. Mathematics is not a matter of observation; it is quantifiable, an unbending authority. If mathematical calculations indicated that a star would appear at a particular spot in the heavens and it did not, Galileo might just as soon have questioned the observation as the math. From the seventeenth century on, scientists would check one or the other on the assumption that observation and mathematics could be brought together to understand the same event, that they would have to be in agreement, and that such agreement could lead to laws that could then be tested and proved or disproved.

It is this method of inquiry, not the discoveries, that was new. Astrology could lead to knowledge of astronomy, but they are not the same. The knowledge of the astrologer is metaphorical rather than scientific. The idea that a person born under Gemini, a stellar configuration that looks like twins, will be pulled in two directions is a psychological metaphor, not a matter of physics. It cannot be tested, validated, or built upon. On the other hand, physics and astronomy can. To the extent to which we combine astrology with astronomy, we lose the precision, quantifiability, and the reliability and certainty of science.

The scientific method is a systematic means of inquiry based on agreed-upon rules of hypothesis, experimentation, theory testing, law, and dissemination. Scientific inquiry is a social process in two important ways: First, any scientific discovery must be reproducible and recognized by other scientists to gain credence. Second, a community of scientists is needed to question, dismiss, or validate the work of its members.

Finally, we return to Baumer's emphasis on the societies of seventeenth-century science. The numerous organizations in Europe are testaments not only to a popular interest in science but to a continuing public conversation. Steven Shapin, a historian of science, has written of the importance of a class of "honorable gentlemen" with like interests who could trust each other's work and conclusions: "Truth flowed along the same personal channels as civil conversation. Knowledge was secured by trusting people with whom one was familiar, and familiarity could be used to gauge the truth of what they said."[1]

Ultimately, the difference between European science and that of India or China in the seventeenth century may have had more to do with society than with culture. The development of modern scientific methods relied on the numerous debates and discussions of a self-conscious class of gentlemen scientists in a Europe where news traveled quickly and ideas could be translated and tested with confidence across numerous borders. To what extent does science everywhere today demonstrate the hallmarks of the seventeenth-century scientific revolution? How does the spread of science make human behavior more uniform?

---

[1] Steven Shapin, *A Social History of Truth: Civility and Science in Seventeenth Century England* (Chicage: University of Chicago Press, 1994), 410.

6

Enlightenment and Revolution

Europe and the Americas, 1650–1850

HISTORICAL CONTEXT

The modern world puts its faith in science, reason, and democracy. The seventeenth-century scientific revolution established reason as the key to understanding nature, and its application directed thought, organized society, and measured governments during the eighteenth-century Enlightenment. Most — though, as we shall see, not all — people believed that reason would eventually lead to freedom. Freedom of thought, religion, and association, and political liberties and representative governments were hailed as hallmarks of the Age of Enlightenment.

For some, enlightened society meant a more controlled rather than a more democratic society. Philosophers like Immanuel Kant and Jean-Jacques Rousseau wanted people to become free but thought most people were incapable of achieving such a state. Rulers who were called "enlightened despots" believed that the application of reason to society would make people happier, not necessarily freer.

Ultimately, however, the Enlightenment's faith in reason led to calls for political revolution as well as for schemes of order. In England in the seventeenth century, in America and France at the end of the eighteenth century, and in Latin America shortly thereafter, revolutionary governments were created according to rational principles of liberty and equality that dispatched monarchs and enshrined the rule of the people. In this chapter we will concentrate on the heritage of the Enlightenment, examining competing tendencies toward order and revolution, stability and liberty, equality and freedom. We will also compare the American and the French Revolutions, and these with the later revolutions in Latin America. Finally, in reflection, we will briefly compare these distinctly European and American developments with processes in other parts of the world.

THINKING HISTORICALLY
Close Reading and
Interpretation of Texts

At the core of the Enlightenment was a trust in reasoned discussion, a belief that people could understand each other, even if they were not in agreement. Such understanding demanded clear and concise communication in a world where the masses were often swayed by fiery sermons and flamboyant rhetoric. But the Enlightenment also put its faith in the written word and a literate public. Ideas were debated face to face in the salons and coffeehouses of Europe and in the meeting halls of America, but it was through letters, diaries, the new world of newspapers, and the burgeoning spread of printed books that the people of the Enlightenment learned what they and their neighbors thought.

It is appropriate then for us to read the selections in this chapter — all primary sources — in the spirit in which they were written. We will pay special attention to the words and language that the authors use and will attempt to understand exactly what they meant, even why they chose the words they did. Such explication is a twofold process; we must understand the words first and foremost; then we must strive to understand the words in their proper context, as they were intended by the author. To achieve our first goal, we will paraphrase, a difficult task because the eighteenth-century writing style differs greatly from our own: Sentences are longer and arguments are often complex. Vocabularies were broad during this period, and we may encounter words that are used in ways unknown to us. As to our latter goal, we must try to make the vocabulary and perspective of the authors our own. Grappling with what makes the least sense to us and trying to understand why it was said is the challenge.

28

DAVID HUME

On Miracles

The European Enlightenment of the eighteenth century was the expression of a new class of intellectuals, independent of the clergy but allied with the rising middle class. Their favorite words were *reason, nature,* and *progress.* They applied the systematic doubt of René Descartes (1596–1650) and the reasoning method of the scientific revolution to human affairs, including religion and politics. With caustic wit and good humor, they asked new questions and popularized new points of view that would eventually revolutionize Western politics and culture. While the French *philosophes* and Voltaire (1694–1778) may be the best known, the Scottish philosopher David Hume (1711–1776) may have been the most brilliant. What does Hume argue in this selection? Does he prove his point to your satisfaction? How does he use reason and nature to make his case? Is reason incompatible with religion?

Thinking Historically

The first step in understanding what Hume means in this essay must come from a careful reading — a sentence-by-sentence exploration. Try to paraphrase each sentence, putting it into your own words. For example, you might paraphrase the first sentence like this: "I've found a way to disprove superstition; this method should be useful as long as superstition exists, which may be forever." Notice the content of such words as *just* and *check.* What does Hume mean by these words and by *prodigies?*

The second sentence is a concise definition of the scientific method. How would you paraphrase it? The second and third sentences summarize the method Hume has discovered to counter superstition. What is the meaning of the third sentence?

In the rest of the essay, Hume offers four proofs, or reasons, why miracles do not exist. How would you paraphrase each of these? Do you find these more or less convincing than his more general opening and closing arguments? What does Hume mean by *miracles?*

The Philosophical Works of David Hume (Edinburgh: A. Black and W. Tait, 1826).

I flatter myself that I have discovered an argument . . . , which, if just, will, with the wise and learned, be an everlasting check to all kinds of superstitious delusion, and consequently will be useful as long as the world endures; for so long, I presume, will the accounts of miracles and prodigies be found in all history, sacred and profane. . . .

A wise man proportions his belief to the evidence. . . .

A miracle is a violation of the laws of nature; and as a firm and unalterable experience has established these laws, the proof against a miracle, from the very nature of the fact, is as entire as any argument from experience can possibly be imagined. . . . Nothing is esteemed a miracle, if it ever happens in the common course of nature. It is no miracle that a man, seemingly in good health, should die on a sudden; because such a kind of death, though more unusual than any other, has yet been frequently observed to happen. But it is a miracle that a dead man should come to life; because that has never been observed in any age or country. There must, therefore, be an uniform experience against every miraculous event, otherwise the event would not merit that appellation. And as an uniform experience amounts to a proof, there is here a direct and full *proof,* from the nature of the fact, against the existence of any miracle. . . .

(Further) there is not to be found, in all history, any miracle attested by a sufficient number of men, of such unquestioned good sense, education, and learning, as to secure us against all delusion in themselves; of such undoubted integrity, as to place them beyond all suspicion of any design to deceive others; of such credit and reputation in the eyes of mankind, as to have a great deal to lose in case of their being detected in any falsehood. . . .

Secondly, We may observe in human nature a principle which, if strictly examined, will be found to diminish extremely the assurance, which we might, from human testimony, have in any kind of prodigy. . . . The passion of *surprise* and *wonder,* arising from miracles, being an agreeable emotion, gives a sensible tendency towards the belief of those events from which it is derived. . . .

With what greediness are the miraculous accounts of travellers received, their descriptions of sea and land monsters, their relations of wonderful adventures, strange men, and uncouth manners? But if the spirit of religion join itself to the love of wonder, there is an end of common sense; and human testimony, in these circumstances, loses all pretensions to authority. A religionist may be an enthusiast, and imagine he sees what has no reality: He may know his narrative to be false, and yet persevere in it, with the best intentions in the world, for the sake of promoting so holy a cause: Or even where this delusion has not place, vanity, excited by so strong a temptation, operates on him more powerfully than on the rest of mankind in any other circumstances; and self-interest with equal force. . . .

The many instances of forged miracles and prophecies and supernatural events, which, in all ages, have either been detected by contrary evidence, or which detect themselves by their absurdity, prove sufficiently the strong propensity of mankind to the extraordinary and marvellous, and ought reasonably to beget a suspicion against all relations of this kind. . . .

Thirdly, It forms a strong presumption against all supernatural and miraculous relations, that they are observed chiefly to abound among ignorant and barbarous nations; or if a civilized people has ever given admission to any of them, that people will be found to have received them from ignorant and barbarous ancestors, who transmitted them with that inviolable sanction and authority which always attend received opinions. . . .

I may add, as a *fourth* reason, which diminishes the authority of prodigies, that there is no testimony for any, even those which have not been expressly detected, that is not opposed by any infinite number of witnesses; so that not only the miracle destroys the credit of testimony, but the testimony destroys itself. To make this the better understood, let us consider, that in matters of religion, whatever is different is contrary; and that it is impossible the religions of ancient Rome, of Turkey, of Siam, and of China, should all of them be established on any solid foundation. Every miracle, therefore, pretended to have been wrought in any of these religions (and all of them abound in miracles), as its direct scope is to establish the particular system to which it is attributed; so has it the same force, though more indirectly, to overthrow every other system. In destroying a rival system, it likewise destroys the credit of those miracles on which that system was established, so that all the prodigies of different religions are to be regarded as contrary facts, and the evidences of these prodigies, whether weak or strong, as opposite to each other. . . .

Upon the whole, then, it appears, that no testimony for any kind of miracle has ever amounted to a probability, much less to a proof; and that, even supposing it amounted to proof, it would be opposed by another proof, derived from the very nature of the fact which it would endeavour to establish. It is experience only which gives authority to human testimony; and it is the same experience which assures us of the laws of nature. When, therefore, these two kinds of experience are contrary, we have nothing to do but to subtract the one from the other, and embrace an opinion either on one side or the other, with that assurance which arises from the remainder. But according to the principle here explained, this subtraction with regard to all popular religions amounts to an entire annihilation; and therefore we may establish it as a maxim, that no human testimony can have such force as to prove a miracle, and make it a just foundation for any such system of religion.

29

VOLTAIRE

On Patriotism, and On Tolerance

François Marie Arouet, known to the world by his pen name, Voltaire, came to personify the Enlightenment during his long life (1694–1778), which spanned most of the eighteenth century. As a philosopher, wit, playwright, and cultural critic, he dedicated himself to confronting power and prejudice with skepticism and reason. Partly as a consequence of his biting wit, he was imprisoned in the Bastille and exiled from his native France to England and Prussia. After his return to France, however, Voltaire's country house near Switzerland attracted so many visiting intellectuals from all over Europe that it became a kind of cultural capital of the continent.

At the core of the Enlightenment was the idea that people could use reason to overcome the bias and self-interest of their own region, nation, religion, group, or tribe and empathize with a larger group. With what group did Voltaire urge people to empathize and identify in these selections? Why might he have done so?

Thinking Historically

In the selection on patriotism, notice how Voltaire makes the reader gradually question the ostensibly harmless idea of loving one's country. What exactly are his arguments against loving one's country? How would you paraphrase Voltaire's argument for tolerance? In what ways is his argument for tolerance similar to his argument against patriotism?

Patrie (Country) in The Philosophical Dictionary (1752)

A young journeyman pastry cook who had been to school, and who still knew a few of Cicero's phrases, boasted one day of loving his country. "What do you mean by your 'country'?" a neighbor asked him. "Is it your oven? Is it the village where you were born and which you have never seen since? Is it the street where dwelled your father and mother who have been ruined and have reduced you to baking

---

Voltaire, on patriotism, from "Patrie" in *The Philosophical Dictionary*, 1752, H. I. Woolf, ed., *Voltaire's Philosophical Dictionary* (London, 1923), 131–32. Adapted by the editor.
On tolerance, from *Traite sur la Tolerance* (1763), Institut et Musée Voltaire, Genève, trans. by the editor.

little pies for a living? Is it the town hall where you will never be a police superintendent's clerk? Is it the Church of Our Lady where you
have not been able to become a choirboy, while an absurd man is archbishop and duke with an income of twenty thousand golden louis?"

The journeyman pastry cook did not know what to answer. A
thinker who was listening to this conversation, concluded that in a
large country there were often many thousand men who had no country at all.

You, pleasure-loving Parisian, who have never made any great journey save that to Dieppe to eat fresh fish; who know nothing but your var-
nished town house, your pretty country house, and your box at that
Opera where the rest of Europe persists in feeling bored; who speak your
own language agreeably enough because you know no other, you love all
that, and you love further the girls you keep, the champagne which comes
to you from Rheims, the dividends which the Hôtel de Ville pays you
every six months, and you say you love your country!

In all conscience, does a financier cordially love his country? The
officer and the soldier who will pillage their winter quarters, if one lets
them, have they a very warm love for the peasants they ruin? . . . Where
was the country of Attila and of a hundred heroes of this type? I would
like someone to tell me which was Abraham's country. The first man to
write that the country is wherever one feels comfortable was, I believe,
Euripides in his *Phaeton*. But the first man who left his birthplace to
seek his comfort elsewhere has said it before him.

Where then is the country? Is it not a good field, whose owner,
lodged in a well-kept house, can say: "This field that I till, this house
that I have built, are mine; I live there protected by laws which no
tyrant can infringe. When those who, like me, possess fields and
houses, meet in their common interest, I have my voice in the assembly;
I am a part of everything, a part of the community, a part of the dominion; there is my country"?

Well, now, is it better for your country to be a monarchy or a republic? For four thousand years has this question been debated. Ask
the rich for an answer, they all prefer aristocracy; question the people,
they want democracy; only kings prefer royalty. How then is it that
nearly the whole world is governed by monarchs? . . . It is sad that
often in order to be a good patriot one is the enemy of the rest of
mankind. To be a good patriot is to wish that one's city may be en-
riched by trade, and be powerful by arms. It is clear that one country
cannot gain without another losing, and that it cannot conquer without
making misery. Such then is the human state that to wish for one's
country's greatness is to wish harm to one's neighbors. He who should
wish his country might never be greater, smaller, richer, poorer, would
be the citizen of the world.

On Universal Tolerance

It does not require great art, or magnificently trained eloquence, to prove that Christians should tolerate each other. I, however, am going further: I say that we should regard all men as our brothers. What? The Turk my brother? The Chinaman my brother? The Jew? The Siam? Yes, without doubt; are we not all children of the same father and creatures of the same God?

But these people despise us; they treat us as idolaters! Very well! I will tell them that they are grievously wrong. It seems to me that I would at least astonish the proud, dogmatic Islam imam or Buddhist priest, if I spoke to them as follows:

"This little globe, which is but a point, rolls through space, as do many other globes; we are lost in the immensity of the universe. Man, only five feet high, is assuredly only a small thing in creation." One of these imperceptible beings says to another one of his neighbors, in Arabia or South Africa: "Listen to me, because God of all these worlds has enlightened me: there are nine hundred million little ants like us on the earth, but my ant-hole is the only one dear to God; all the other are cast off by Him for eternity; mine alone will be happy, and all the others will be eternally damned."

They would then interrupt me, and ask which fool blabbed all this nonsense. I would be obliged to answer, "You, yourselves."

30

The American Declaration of Independence

If anyone had taken a poll of American colonials in the thirteen lower colonies (and certainly the colony of Canada to the north) as late as 1775, independence would not have won a majority vote anywhere. Massachusetts might have come close, perhaps, but nowhere in the land was there a definitive urge to separate from the British empire. Still, tensions between the colonies and Britain were inevitable. Three thousand miles was a long way for news, views, appointees, and peti-

A Documentary History of the United States, ed. Richard D. Heffner (New York: Penguin Books, 1991), 15–18.

tions to travel. While the colonists respected the king, George III, they found his ministers inadequately informed about events in their homeland. Royal governors were generally judged to be inept and punitive. And none of the colonies participated in the election of members of the British Parliament.

Of course, each side looked at the cost of colonial administration differently. The British believed that they had carried a large part of the costs of migration, administration of trade, and control of the sea, while the colonists found they had borne the costs and the humiliation resulting from the lack of political representation. Each effort at taxation — the Stamp Act of 1765, the Townshend Act of 1767, the Tea Act of 1773 — provoked violent responses from colonists, stiffened the resolve of both sides, and led to militant retribution by the parliament and the king. The Coercive Acts or, as the colonists called them, the "Intolerable Acts" (1774) intended to punish them — especially in Massachusetts after the Boston Tea Party — by closing the port of Boston, reducing colonial political authority, and imposing the quartering of British troops. In response, the first Continental Congress was called in the fall of 1774 and a second the following May. By the spring of 1775, events were rapidly pushing the colonies toward independence. In April, British troops engaged colonial forces at Lexington and Concord, instigating a land war that was to last until 1781.

In the midst of other urgent business, most notably raising an army, the Congress asked a committee that included Thomas Jefferson, Benjamin Franklin, and John Adams to compose a statement outlining the reasons for separation from Britain. Jefferson wrote the first draft, most of which became the final version approved by the committee and accepted by the Continental Congress on July 4, 1776.

The Declaration of Independence was preeminently a document of the Enlightenment. Its principal author, Thomas Jefferson, exemplified the Enlightenment intellectual. Conversant in European literature, law, and political thought, he made significant contributions to eighteenth-century knowledge in natural science and architecture. Likewise, Benjamin Franklin, a printer by profession, was a leading scientist, writer, and wit. Both men founded universities — the Universities of Virginia and Pennsylvania, respectively. Both were at home in France, where they served the new government of the United States as diplomats after the war. Other delegates to the Congress in Philadelphia were similarly accomplished.

It is no wonder, then, that the Declaration and the establishment of an independent United States of America should strike the world as the realization of the Enlightenment's basic tenets: That a new country could be created afresh by people with intelligence and foresight, according to principles of reason, and to realize human liberty seemed a fitting capstone to the eighteenth-century mind. Images of America as a virgin land ("In the beginning there was America," John Locke had declared) ignored the presence of native inhabitants. Declarations of freedom overlooked human slavery. But notions of the Enlightenment and the ideal of man, governing himself, rationally and for the common good, was a heady brew.

What were the goals of the authors of this document? In what ways was the Declaration a call for democracy? In what ways was it not?

Thinking Historically

Before interpreting any document, we must read it carefully and put it into context — that is, determine the what, where, and why. Some of this information may be available in the text itself. For instance, whom is the Declaration addressed to? What is the reason given for writing it?

We interpret or extract meaning from documents by asking questions that emerge from the reading. These questions may arise from passages we do not understand, from lack of clarity in the text, or from an incongruence between the text and our expectations. It may surprise some readers, for example, that the Declaration criticizes the king so sharply. To question this might lead us to explore the need for American colonists to defend their actions in terms of British legal tradition. For years, the American colonists blamed the king's ministers for their difficulties; in July 1776 they blamed the king — a traditional sign of revolutionary intent in England, which meant efforts toward independence were imminent. Yet while they cast blame upon the king, the colonists also sought the approval from the court of British opinion.

What about the disparity between the lofty sentiments of liberty and independence and the existence of slavery in the Americas? How is it possible, we ask ourselves, that Jefferson and some of the signers of the Declaration could own slaves while declaring it "self-evident that all men are created equal"? Did it not occur to them to think of slaves as men? Did they mean some abstract equality between "men" (or women) in Britain and America rather than between individuals?

In Congress, July 4, 1776, the Unanimous Declaration of the Thirteen United States of America

When in the course of human events, it becomes necessary for one people to dissolve the political bands which have connected them with another, and to assume among the powers of the earth, the separate and equal station to which the Laws of Nature and of Nature's God entitle them, a decent respect to the opinions of mankind requires that they should declare the causes which impel them to the separation.

We hold these truths to be self-evident, that all men are created equal, that they are endowed by their Creator with certain unalienable rights, that among these are life, liberty, and the pursuit of happiness. That to secure these rights, governments are instituted among men, deriving their just powers from the consent of the governed. That whenever any form of government becomes destructive of these ends, it is the right of the people to alter or to abolish it, and to institute new government, laying its foundation on such principles and organizing its powers in such form, as to them shall seem most likely to effect their safety and happiness. Prudence, indeed, will dictate that governments long established should not be changed for light and transient causes; and accordingly all experience hath shown, that mankind are more disposed to suffer, while evils are sufferable, than to right themselves by abolishing the forms to which they are accustomed. But when a long train of abuses and usurpations, pursuing invariably the same object evinces a design to reduce them under absolute despotism, it is their right, it is their duty, to throw off such government, and to provide new guards for their future security. Such has been the patient sufferance of these Colonies; and such is now the necessity which constrains them to alter their former systems of government. The history of the present King of Great Britain is a history of repeated injuries and usurpations, all having in direct object the establishment of an absolute tyranny over these States. To prove this, let facts be submitted to a candid world.

He has refused his assent to laws, the most wholesome and necessary for the public good.

He has forbidden his Governors to pass laws of immediate and pressing importance, unless suspended in their operation till his assent should be obtained; and when so suspended, he has utterly neglected to attend to them.

He has refused to pass other laws for the accommodation of large districts of people, unless those people would relinquish the right of representation in the Legislature, a right inestimable to them and formidable to tyrants only.

He has called together legislative bodies at places unusual, uncomfortable, and distant from the depository of their public records, for the sole purpose of fatiguing them into compliance with his measures.

He has dissolved representative houses repeatedly, for opposing with manly firmness his invasions on the rights of the people.

He has refused for a long time, after such dissolutions, to cause others to be elected; whereby the legislative powers, incapable of annihilation, have returned to the people at large for their exercise; the State remaining in the meantime exposed to all the dangers of invasion from without and convulsions within.

He has endeavoured to prevent the population of these states; for that purpose obstructing the laws of naturalization of foreigners; refusing to pass others to encourage their migration hither, and raising the conditions of new appropriations of lands.

He has obstructed the administration of justice, by refusing his assent to laws for establishing judiciary powers.

He has made judges dependent on his will alone, for the tenure of their offices, and the amount and payment of their salaries.

He has erected a multitude of new offices, and sent hither swarms of officers to harass our people, and eat out their substance.

He has kept among us, in times of peace, standing armies without the consent of our legislatures.

He has affected to render the military independent of and superior to the civil power.

He has combined with others to subject us to a jurisdiction foreign to our constitution, and unacknowledged by our laws; giving his assent to their acts of pretended legislation:

For quartering large bodies of armed troops among us:

For protecting them, by a mock trial, from punishment for any murders which they should commit on the inhabitants of these States:

For cutting off our trade with all parts of the world:

For imposing taxes on us without our consent:

For depriving us in many cases, of the benefits of trial by jury:

For transporting us beyond seas to be tried for pretended offences:

For abolishing the free system of English laws in a neighbouring Province, establishing therein an arbitrary government, and enlarging its boundaries so as to render it at once an example and fit instrument for introducing the same absolute rule into these Colonies:

For taking away our Charters, abolishing our most valuable laws, and altering fundamentally the forms of our governments:

For suspending our own Legislatures, and declaring themselves invested with power to legislate for us in all cases whatsoever.

He has abdicated government here, by declaring us out of his protection and waging war against us.

He has plundered our seas, ravaged our coasts, burnt our towns, and destroyed the lives of our people.

He is at this time transporting large armies of foreign mercenaries to complete the works of death, desolation, and tyranny, already begun with circumstances of cruelty and perfidy scarcely paralleled in the most barbarous ages, and totally unworthy the head of a civilized nation.

He has constrained our fellow citizens taken captive on the high seas to bear arms against their country, to become the executioners of their friends and brethren, or to fall themselves by their hands.

He has excited domestic insurrections amongst us, and has endeavoured to bring on the inhabitants of our frontiers, the merciless Indian savages, whose known rule of warfare, is an undistinguished destruction of all ages, sexes, and conditions.

In every state of these oppressions we have petitioned for redress in the most humble terms: our repeated petitions have been answered only by repeated injury. A prince whose character is thus marked by every act which may define a tyrant is unfit to be the ruler of a free people.

Nor have we been wanting in attention to our British brethren. We have warned them from time to time of attempts by their legislature to extend an unwarrantable jurisdiction over us. We have reminded them of the circumstances of our emigration and settlement here. We have appealed to their native justice and magnanimity, and we have conjured them by the ties of our common kindred to disavow these usurpations, which would inevitably interrupt our connections and correspondence. They too have been deaf to the voice of justice and of consanguinity. We must, therefore, acquiesce in the necessity, which denounces our separation, and hold them, as we hold the rest of mankind, enemies in war, in peace friends.

We, therefore, the Representatives of the United States of America, in General Congress assembled, appealing to the Supreme Judge of the world for the rectitude of our intentions, do, in the name, and by authority of the good people of these Colonies, solemnly publish and declare, That these United Colonies are, and of right ought to be Free and Independent States; that they are absolved from all allegiance to the British Crown, and that all political connection between them and the State of Great Britain, is and ought to be totally dissolved; and that as Free and Independent States, they have full power to levy war, conclude peace, contract alliances, establish commerce, and to do all other acts and things which Independent States may of right do. And for the support of this declaration, with a firm reliance on the protection of Divine Province, we mutually pledge to each other our lives, our fortunes, and our sacred honor.

31

ABIGAIL ADAMS AND JOHN ADAMS
Remember the Ladies

As a delegate to the Second Continental Congress, future American president John Adams was in Philadelphia in the spring of 1776, collaborating on writing the Declaration of Independence. In the meantime his wife, Abigail, assumed the role of the head of the household, caring for their children and managing the family farm in Braintree, Massachusetts. Their relationship had always been characterized by robust intellectual debate, and John even referred to his wife as "Sister Delegate." In their famous correspondence during this period, Abigail urged her husband to "remember the ladies" as he and his fellow revolutionaries constructed the basis for the new American government. What did she mean by this? How did her husband respond? What did she think of his response?

Thinking Historically

Enlightenment thinkers often employed grand abstractions like "all men are created equal" for both their rational simplicity and their dramatic revolutionary claim. As a consequence, such abstractions were often more sweeping in their implications than even the revolutionaries of the era intended. For example, John and Abigail Adams, both of whom opposed slavery, did not intend for "all men" to include blacks, either enslaved or free. But men like Adams might not have seriously considered how women would respond to the proclamation of universal equality. What in Adams's response to his wife reveals that he did not intend to extend universal equality to women? Does his response somehow undermine the Declaration of Independence?

Letters from Abigail Adams to John Adams, 31 March – 5 April 1776, John Adams to Abigail Adams, 14 April 1776, Abigail Adams to John Adams, 7 – 9 May 1776 [electronic editions]. *Adams Family Papers: An Electronic Archive* (Boston: Massachusetts Historical Society, 2002), http://www.masshist.org/digitaladams/.

Letter from Abigail Adams to John Adams, 31 March–5 April 1776

. . . I long to hear that you have declared an independency — and by the way in the new Code of Laws which I suppose it will be necessary for you to make I desire you would Remember the Ladies, and be more generous and favourable to them than your ancestors. Do not put such unlimited power into the hands of the Husbands. Remember all Men would be tyrants if they could. If perticuliar care and attention is not paid to the Ladies we are determined to foment a Rebellion, and will not hold ourselves bound by any Laws in which we have no voice, or Representation.

That your Sex are Naturally Tyrannical is a Truth so thoroughly established as to admit of no dispute, but such of you as wish to be happy willingly give up the harsh title of Master for the more tender and endearing one of Friend. Why then, not put it out of the power of the vicious and the Lawless to use us with cruelty and indignity [with impunity]. Men of Sense in all Ages abhor those customs which treat us only as the vassals of your Sex. Regard us then as Beings placed by providence under your protection and in imitation of the Supreme Being make use of that power only for our happiness.

Letter from John Adams to Abigail Adams, 14 April 1776

. . . As to Declarations of Independency, be patient. Read our Privateering Laws, and our Commercial Laws. What signifies a Word.

As to your extraordinary Code of Laws, I cannot but laugh. We have been told that our Struggle has loosened the bands of Government every where. That Children and Apprentices were disobedient — that schools and Colleges were grown turbulent — that Indians slighted their Guardians and Negroes grew insolent to their Masters.

But your Letter was the first Intimation that another Tribe more numerous and powerfull than all the rest were grown discontented. — This is rather too coarse a Compliment but you are so saucy, I wont blot it out.

Depend upon it, We know better than to repeal our Masculine systems. Altho they are in full Force, you know they are little more than Theory. We dare not exert our Power in its full Latitude. We are obliged to go fair, and softly, and in Practice you know We are the subjects. We have only the Name of Masters, and rather than give up this, which would compleatly subject Us to the Despotism of the Peticoat, I hope General Washington, and all our brave Heroes would fight. I am sure every good Politician would plot, as long as he would against Despotism, Empire, Monarchy, Aristocracy, Oligarchy, or Ochlocracy. . . .

Letter from Abigail Adams to John Adams, 7–9 May 1776

. . . I can not say that I think you very generous to the Ladies, for whilst you are proclaiming peace and good will to Men, Emancipating all Nations, you insist upon retaining an absolute power over Wives. But you must remember that Arbitary power is like most other things which are very hard, very liable to be broken — and notwithstanding all your wise Laws and Maxims we have it in our power not only to free ourselves but to subdue our Masters, and without violence throw both your natural and legal authority at our feet. . . .

32

The French Declaration of the Rights of Man and Citizen

The American Revolution began as a movement for independence and ended in the formation of a new government of the people — a republic without a king, without even a hereditary nobility like the British House of Lords. At that time, there were few historical republics to serve as models — ancient Greek and Italian Renaissance city-states and England under the revolutionary government of Oliver Cromwell (1599–1658) — and most did not last.

The founding of the Republic of the United States of America provided another model to emulate. Not suprisingly then, when the French movement to end political injustices turned to revolution in 1789 and the revolutionaries convened at the National Assembly, the Marquis de Lafayette (1757–1834), hero of the American Revolution,

---

A Documentary History of the French Revolution, ed. John Hall Stewart (London: Macmillan, 1979).

proposed a Declaration of the Rights of Man and Citizen. Lafayette had the American Declaration in mind, and he had the assistance of Thomas Jefferson, present in Paris as the first United States ambassador to France, America's earliest ally.

While the resulting document appealed to a party of French revolutionaries who believed in natural and inalienable rights, the French were not able to start afresh as the Americans had done. The Americans established a republic because they had no king. In 1789 Louis XVI was still king of France: He could not be made to leave by a turn of phrase. Nor were men created equal in France in 1789. Those born into the nobility led lives different from those born into the Third Estate (the 99 percent of the population who were not nobility or clergy), and they had different legal rights as well. This disparity was precisely what the revolutionaries and the Declaration sought to change. Inevitably, though, such change would prove to be a more violent and revolutionary proposition than it had been in the American colonies. The American experience showed that it was rational and possible to create a society of citizens whose rights were protected by their own laws, but only French radicals believed that the American model could work in France.

In what ways did the Declaration of the Rights of Man and Citizen resemble the American Declaration of Independence? In what ways was it different? Which was more democratic?

Thinking Historically

As we have noted, the French Declaration is full of abstract, universal principles. But notice how such abstractions can claim our consent by their rationality without informing us as to how they will be implemented. What is meant by the first right, for instance? What does it mean to say that men are "born free"? Why is it necessary to distinguish between "born" and "remain"? What is meant by the phrase "general usefulness"? Do statements like these increase people's liberties, or are they intentionally vague so they can be interpreted at will?

The slogan of the French Revolution was "Liberty, Equality, Fraternity." Which of the rights in the French Declaration emphasize liberty, which equality? Can these two goals be opposed to each other? Was the French declaration more likely to create equality than the American Declaration of Independence?

The representatives of the French people, organized in National Assembly, considering that ignorance, forgetfulness, or contempt of the rights of man are the sole causes of public misfortunes and of the corruption of governments, have resolved to set forth in a solemn declaration the natural, inalienable, and sacred rights of man, in order that such declaration, continually before all members of the social body, may be a perpetual reminder of their rights and duties; in order that the acts of the legislative power and those of the executive power may constantly be compared with the aim of every political institution and may accordingly be more respected; in order that the demands of the citizens, founded henceforth upon simple and incontestable principles, may always be directed towards the maintenance of the Constitution and the welfare of all.

Accordingly, the National Assembly recognizes and proclaims, in the presence and under the auspices of the Supreme Being, the following rights of man and citizen.

1. Men are born and remain free and equal in rights; social distinctions may be based only upon general usefulness.

2. The aim of every political association is the preservation of the natural and inalienable rights of man; these rights are liberty, property, security, and resistance to oppression.

3. The source of all sovereignty resides essentially in the nation; no group, no individual may exercise authority not emanating expressly therefrom.

4. Liberty consists of the power to do whatever is not injurious to others; thus the enjoyment of the natural rights of every man has for its limits only those that assure other members of society the enjoyment of those same rights; such limits may be determined only by law.

5. The law has the right to forbid only actions which are injurious to society. Whatever is not forbidden by law may not be prevented, and no one may be constrained to do what it does not prescribe.

6. Law is the expression of the general will; all citizens have the right to concur personally, or through their representatives, in its formation; it must be the same for all, whether it protects or punishes. All citizens, being equal before it, are equally admissible to all public offices, positions, and employments, according to their capacity, and without other distinction than that of virtues and talents.

7. No man may be accused, arrested, or detained except in the cases determined by law, and according to the forms prescribed thereby. Whoever solicit, expedite, or execute arbitrary orders, or have them executed, must be punished; but every citizen summoned or apprehended in pursuance of the law must obey immediately; he renders himself culpable by resistance.

8. The law is to establish only penalties that are absolutely and obviously necessary; and no one may be punished except by virtue of a law established and promulgated prior to the offence and legally applied.

9. Since every man is presumed innocent until declared guilty, if arrest be deemed indispensable, all unnecessary severity for securing the person of the accused must be severely repressed by law.

10. No one is to be disquieted because of his opinions, even religious, provided their manifestation does not disturb the public order established by law.

11. Free communication of ideas and opinions is one of the most precious of the rights of man. Consequently, every citizen may speak, write, and print freely, subject to responsibility for the abuse of such liberty in the cases determined by law.

12. The guarantee of the rights of man and citizen necessitates a public force; therefore, is instituted for the advantage of all and not for the particular benefit of those to whom it is entrusted.

13. For the maintenance of the public force and for the expenses of administration a common tax is indispensable; it must be assessed equally on all citizens in proportion to their means.

14. Citizens have the right to ascertain, by themselves or through their representatives, the necessity of the public tax, to consent to it freely, to supervise its use, and to determine its quota, assessment, payment, and duration.

15. Society has the right to require of every public agent an accounting of his administration.

16. Every society in which the guarantee of rights is not assured or the separation of powers not determined has no constitution at all.

17. Since property is a sacred and inviolate right, no one may be deprived thereof unless a legally established public necessity obviously requires it, and upon condition of a just and previous indemnity.

33

TOUSSAINT L'OUVERTURE

Letter to the Directory

When the French revolutionaries proclaimed the Declaration of the Rights of Man and Citizen in 1789, the French colony of San Domingo (now Haiti) contained a half million African slaves, most of whom worked on the sugar plantations that made France one of the richest countries in the world. Thus, the French were confronted with

---

Toussaint L'Ouverture, "Letter to the Directory, November 5, 1797," in *The Black Jacobins,* ed. C. R. James (New York: Vintage Books, 1989), 195–97.

the difficult problem of reconciling their enlightened principles with the extremely profitable, but fundamentally unequal, institution of slavery.

French revolutionaries remained locked in debate about this issue when in 1791, the slaves of San Domingo organized a revolt that culminated in establishing Haiti's national independence twelve years later. Toussaint L'Ouverture, a self-educated Haitian slave, led the revolt and the subsequent battles against the French planter class and French armies, as well as the Spanish forces of neighboring Santo Domingo and the antirevolutionary forces of Britain, all of whom vied for control of the island at the end of the eighteenth century.

At first L'Ouverture enjoyed the support of the revolutionary government in Paris; in the decree of 16 Pluviôse (1794) the National Convention abolished slavery in the colonies. But after 1795, the revolution turned on itself and L'Ouverture feared the new conservative government, called the Directory, might send troops to restore slavery on the island.

In 1797 he wrote the Directory the letter that follows. Notice how L'Ouverture negotiated a difficult situation. How did he try to reassure the government of his allegiance to France? At the same time, how did he attempt to convince the Directory that a return to slavery was unthinkable?

Thinking Historically

Notice how the idea of "patriotism," which Voltaire dismissed in favor of internationalism, became a necessary component of the French revolutionary ideology after 1789. Where did L'Ouverture's true loyalty lie? At the time he wrote this letter events had not yet forced him to declare the independence of San Domingo (Haiti); this would not happen until January 1, 1804. But, according to the letter, how and why did L'Ouverture regard the principles of the French Revolution as more important than his loyalty to France?

. . . "The impolitic and incendiary discourse of Vaublanc has not affected the blacks nearly so much as their certainty of the projects which the proprietors of San Domingo are planning: insidious declarations should not have any effect in the eyes of wise legislators who have decreed liberty for the nations. But the attempts on that liberty which the colonists propose are all the more to be feared because it is with the veil of patriotism that they cover their detestable plans. We know that they seek to impose some of them on you by illusory and specious promises, in order to see renewed in this colony its former scenes of horror.

Already perfidious emissaries have stepped in among us to ferment the destructive leaven prepared by the hands of liberticides. But they will not succeed. I swear it by all that liberty holds most sacred. My attachment to France, my knowledge of the blacks, make it my duty not to leave you ignorant either of the crimes which they meditate or the oath that we renew, to bury ourselves under the ruins of a country revived by liberty rather than suffer the return of slavery.

"It is for you, Citizens Directors, to turn from over our heads the storm which the eternal enemies of our liberty are preparing in the shades of silence. It is for you to enlighten the legislature, it is for you to prevent the enemies of the present system from spreading themselves on our unfortunate shores to sully it with new crimes. Do not allow our brothers, our friends, to be sacrificed to men who wish to reign over the ruins of the human species. But no, your wisdom will enable you to avoid the dangerous snares which our common enemies hold out for you. . . .

"I send you with this letter a declaration which will acquaint you with the unity that exists between the proprietors of San Domingo who are in France, those in the United States, and those who serve under the English banner. You will see there a resolution, unequivocal and carefully constructed, for the restoration of slavery; you will see there that their determination to succeed has led them to envelop themselves in the mantle of liberty in order to strike it more deadly blows. You will see that they are counting heavily on my complacency in lending myself to their perfidious views by my fear for my children. It is not astonishing that these men who sacrifice their country to their interests are unable to conceive how many sacrifices a true love of country can support in a better father than they, since I unhesitatingly base the happiness of my children on that of my country, which they and they alone wish to destroy.

"I shall never hesitate between the safety of San Domingo and my personal happiness; but I have nothing to fear. It is to the solicitude of the French Government that I have confided my children. . . . I would tremble with horror if it was into the hands of the colonists that I had sent them as hostages; but even if it were so, let them know that in punishing them for the fidelity of their father, they would only add one degree more to their barbarism, without any hope of ever making me fail in my duty. . . . Blind as they are! They cannot see how this odious conduct on their part can become the signal of new disasters and irreparable misfortunes, and that far from making them regain what in their eyes liberty for all has made them lose, they expose themselves to a total ruin and the colony to its inevitable destruction. Do they think that men who have been able to enjoy the blessing of liberty will calmly see it snatched away? They supported their chains only so long as they did not know any condition of life more happy than that of slavery. But to-day when they have left it, if they had a thousand lives they would sacrifice them all rather than be forced into slavery again. But no, the same hand which has broken our chains will not enslave us anew. France will not revoke her principles, she will not withdraw from us the greatest of her benefits. She will protect us against all our enemies; she will not permit her sublime morality to be perverted, those principles which do her most honour to be destroyed, her most beautiful achievement to be degraded, and her Decree of 16 Pluviôse which so honours humanity to be revoked. *But if, to re-establish slavery in San Domingo, this was done, then I declare to you it would be to attempt the impossible: we have known how to face dangers to obtain our liberty, we shall know how to brave death to maintain it.*

"This, Citizens Directors, is the morale of the people of San Domingo, those are the principles that they transmit to you by me.

"My own you know. It is sufficient to renew, my hand in yours, the oath that I have made, to cease to live before gratitude dies in my heart, before I cease to be faithful to France and to my duty, before the god of liberty is profaned and sullied by the liberticides, before they can snatch from my hands that sword, those arms, which France confided to me for the defence of its rights and those of humanity, for the triumph of liberty and equality."

34

SIMÓN BOLÍVAR

A Constitution for Venezuela

The Enlightenment principles of reason, human rights, and equality ignited revolutions on both sides of the Atlantic. In Europe, these revolutions overturned kings and tyrannies, marshaling national citizen armies and creating parliamentary democracies. In the American colonies, the revolutions took shape as anticolonial struggles for independence. Sometimes the effort to create both an independent nation *and* a democracy proved overwhelming.

Selected Writings of Bolívar, comp. Vincent Lecuna, ed. Harold A. Bierck Jr., 2 vols. (New York: Colonial Press, 1951), 175–91.

Simón Bolívar (1783–1830), called "the Liberator," successfully led the Latin American revolution for independence from Spain between 1810 and 1824. In 1819, he became president of Venezuela and of what is today Colombia, Ecuador, and Panama, and he gave the speech on the Constitution of Venezuela that follows.

What does Bolívar see as the difference between the independence of Spanish-American colonies and that of the American colonies? What does he mean when he says that Latin Americans have been denied "domestic tyranny"? Would you call Bolívar a "democrat"? Is he more or less democratic than the French or North American revolutionaries? What kind of society do you think would result from the constitution he envisions?

Thinking Historically

How does Bolívar characterize the revolutionary population of South America? How does this subjective characterization differ from that of North American revolutionaries? What do you think accounts for this difference?

In what ways did the revolutionaries of South America, North America, and France see their problems and needs differently? How did Bolívar propose to solve what he perceived to be the unique problems of South America? What do you think of his solution?

Let us review the past to discover the base upon which the Republic of Venezuela is founded.

America, in separating from the Spanish monarchy, found herself in a situation similar to that of the Roman Empire when its enormous framework fell to pieces in the midst of the ancient world. Each Roman division then formed an independent nation in keeping with its location or interests; but this situation differed from America's in that those members proceeded to reestablish their former associations. We, on the contrary, do not even retain the vestiges of our original being. We are not Europeans; we are not Indians; we are but a mixed species of aborigines and Spaniards. Americans by birth and Europeans by law, we find ourselves engaged in a dual conflict: We are disputing with the natives for titles of ownership, and at the same time we are struggling to maintain ourselves in the country that gave us birth against the opposition of the invaders. Thus our position is most extraordinary and complicated. But there is more. As our role has always been strictly passive and political existence nil, we find that our quest for liberty is now even more difficult of accomplishment; for we, having been placed in a state lower than slavery, had been robbed not only of our freedom but also of the right to exercise an active domestic tyranny. Permit me to explain this paradox.

In absolute systems, the central power is unlimited. The will of the despot is the supreme law, arbitrarily enforced by subordinates who take part in the organized oppression in proportion to the authority that they wield. They are charged with civil, political, military, and religious functions; but, in the final analysis, the satraps of Persia are Persian, the pashas of the Grand Turk are Turks, and the sultans of Tartary are Tartars. China does not seek her mandarins in the homeland of Genghis Khan, her conqueror. America, on the contrary, received everything from Spain, who, in effect, deprived her of the experience that she would have gained from the exercise of an active tyranny by not allowing her to take part in her own domestic affairs and administration. This exclusion made it impossible for us to acquaint ourselves with the management of public affairs; nor did we enjoy that personal consideration, of such great value in major revolutions, that the brilliance of power inspires in the eyes of the multitude. In brief, Gentlemen, we were deliberately kept in ignorance and cut off from the world in all matters relating to the science of government.

Subject to the three-fold yoke of ignorance, tyranny, and vice, the American people have been unable to acquire knowledge, power, or [civic] virtue. The lessons we received and the models we studied, as pupils of such pernicious teachers, were most destructive. We have been ruled more by deceit than by force, and we have been degraded more by vice than by superstition. Slavery is the daughter of darkness: An ignorant people is a blind instrument of its own destruction. Ambition and intrigue abuse the credulity and experience of men lacking all political, economic, and civic knowledge; they adopt pure illusion as reality; they take license for liberty, treachery for patriotism, and vengeance for justice. This situation is similar to that of the robust blind man who, beguiled by his strength, strides forward with all the assurance of one who can see, but, upon hitting every variety of obstacle, finds himself unable to retrace his steps.

If a people, perverted by their training, succeed in achieving their liberty, they will soon lose it, for it would be of no avail to endeavor to explain to them that happiness consists in the practice of virtue; that the rule of law is more powerful than the rule of tyrants, because, as the laws are more inflexible, every one should submit to their beneficent austerity; that proper morals, and not force, are the bases of law; and that to practice justice is to practice liberty. Therefore, Legislators, your work is so much the more arduous, inasmuch as you have to reeducate men who have been corrupted by erroneous illusions and false incentives. Liberty, says Rousseau, is a succulent morsel, but one difficult to digest. Our weak fellow-citizens will have to strengthen their spirit greatly before they can digest the wholesome nutriment of freedom. Their limbs benumbed by chains, their sight dimmed by the darkness of dungeons, and their strength sapped by the pestilence of servitude, are they capable of marching toward the august temple of Liberty without faltering? Can they come near enough to bask in its brilliant rays and to breathe freely the pure air which reigns therein? . . . .

The more I admire the excellence of the federal Constitution of Venezuela, the more I am convinced of the impossibility of its application to our state. And to my way of thinking, it is a marvel that its prototype in North America endures so successfully and has not been overthrown at the first sign of adversity or danger. Although the people of North America are a singular model of political virtue and moral rectitude; although the nation was cradled in liberty, reared on freedom, and maintained by liberty alone; and — I must reveal everything — although those people, so lacking in many respects, are unique in the history of mankind, it is a marvel, I repeat, that so weak and complicated a government as the federal system has managed to govern them in the difficult and trying circumstances of their past. But, regardless of the effectiveness of this form of government with respect to North America, I must say that it has never for a moment entered my mind to compare the position and character of two states as dissimilar as the English-American and the Spanish-American. Would it not be most difficult to apply to Spain the English system of political, civil, and religious liberty? Hence, it would be even more difficult to adapt to Venezuela the laws of North America. Does not *L'Esprit des Lois* state that laws should be suited to the people for whom they are made; that it would be a major coincidence if those of one nation could be adapted to another; that laws must take into account the physical conditions of the country, climate, character of the land, location, size, and mode of living of the people; that they should be in keeping with the degree of liberty that the Constitution can sanction respecting the religion of the inhabitants, their inclinations, resources, number, commerce, habits, and customs? This is the code we must consult, not the code of Washington! . . .

Venezuela had, has, and should have a republican government. Its principles should be the sovereignty of the people, division of powers, civil liberty, proscription of slavery, and the abolition of monarchy and privileges. We need equality to recast, so to speak, into a unified nation, the classes of men, political opinions, and public customs.

Among the ancient and modern nations, Rome and Great Britain are the most outstanding. Both were born to govern and to be free and both were built not on ostentatious forms of freedom, but upon solid institutions. Thus I recommend to you, Representatives, the study of the British Constitution, for that body of laws appears destined to bring about the greatest possible good for the peoples that adopt it; but, however perfect it may be, I am by no means proposing that you imitate it slavishly. When I speak of the British government, I only refer to its republican features; and, indeed, can a political system be labelled a monarchy when it recognizes popular sovereignty, division and balance of powers, civil liberty, freedom of conscience and of press, and all that is politically sublime? Can there be more liberty in any other type of republic? Can more be asked of any society? I commend this Constitution to you as that most worthy of serving as model for those who aspire to the enjoyment of the rights of man and who seek all the political happiness which is compatible with the frailty of human nature.

Nothing in our fundamental laws would have to be altered were we to adopt a legislative power similar to that held by the British Parliament. Like the North Americans, we have divided national representation into two chambers; that of Representatives and the Senate. The first is very wisely constituted. It enjoys all its proper functions, and it requires no essential revision, because the Constitution, in creating it, gave it the form and powers which the people deemed necessary in order that they might be legally and properly represented. If the Senate were hereditary rather than elective, it would, in my opinion, be the basis, the tie, the very soul of our republic. In political storms this body would arrest the thunderbolts of the government and would repel any violent popular reaction. Devoted to the government because of a natural interest in its own preservation, a hereditary senate would always oppose any attempt on the part of the people to infringe upon the jurisdiction and authority of their magistrates. It must be confessed that most men are unaware of their best interests, and that they constantly endeavor to assail them in the hands of their custodians — the individual clashes with the mass, and the mass with authority. It is necessary, therefore, that in all governments there be a neutral body to protect the injured and disarm the offender. To be neutral, this body must not owe its origin to appointment by the government or to election by the people, if it is to enjoy a full measure of independence which neither fears nor expects anything from these two sources of authority. The hereditary senate, as a part of the people, shares its interests, its sentiments, and its spirit. For this reason it should not be presumed that a hereditary senate would ignore the interests of the people or forget its legislative duties. The senators in Rome and in the House of Lords in London have been the strongest pillars upon which the edifice of political and civil liberty has rested.

At the outset, these senators should be elected by Congress. The successors to this Senate must command the initial attention of the government, which should educate them in a *colegio* designed especially to train these guardians and future legislators of the nation. They ought to learn the arts, sciences, and letters that enrich the mind of a public figure. From childhood they should understand the career for which they have been destined by Providence, and from earliest youth they should prepare their minds for the dignity that awaits them.

The creation of a hereditary senate would in no way be a violation of political equality. I do not solicit the establishment of a nobility, for as a celebrated republican has said, that would simultaneously destroy equality and liberty. What I propose is an office for which the candidates must prepare themselves, an office that demands great knowledge and the ability to acquire such knowledge. All should not be left to chance and the outcome of elections. The people are more easily deceived than is Nature perfected by art; and, although these senators, it is true, would not be bred in an environment that is all virtue, it is equally true that they would be raised in an atmosphere of enlightened education. Furthermore, the liberators of Venezuela are entitled to occupy forever a high rank in the Republic that they have brought into existence. I believe that posterity would view with regret the effacement of the illustrious names of its first benefactors. I say, moreover, that it is a matter of public interest and national honor, of gratitude on Venezuela's part, to honor gloriously, until the end of time, a race of virtuous, prudent, and persevering men who, overcoming every obstacle, have founded the Republic at the price of the most heroic sacrifices. And if the people of Venezuela do not applaud the elevation of their benefactors, then they are unworthy to be free, and they will never be free.

A hereditary senate, I repeat, will be the fundamental basis of the legislative power, and therefore the foundation of the entire government. It will also serve as a counterweight to both government and people; and as a neutral power it will weaken the mutual attacks of these two eternally rival powers. In all conflicts the calm reasoning of a third party will serve as the means of reconciliation. Thus the Venezuelan senate will give strength to this delicate political structure, so sensitive to violent repercussions; it will be the mediator that will lull the storms and it will maintain harmony between the head and the other parts of the political body.

35

A. E. ROZEN

Memoir of the Russian Decembrist Movement

The call for national democratic revolutions inspired by Enlightenment ideas did not end with the independence of Latin American states by 1824. In some respects it continues even today. But we close the chapter with one more example, from Russia in 1825, to show how revolutionary ideas spread globally. Ironically, this memoir by A. E. Rozen illustrates how Russian soldiers imbibed the wine of "civic consciousness, freedom, and constitutional rights" while in France fighting *against* Napoleon's soldiers, who thought they were the heirs of the French revolution. Inspired by Enlightenment ideals, these Russians sought to bring constitutional reform to czarist rule in their own country.

According to Rozen (1788–1884), who was exiled to Siberia for his involvement in the movement, what were the goals of the Decembrists? Were they democratic? Why did the movement fail?

Thinking Historically

Rozen's memoir inadvertently raises questions about the possibilities of constitutional revolution in Russia in 1825. Consider, for instance, the number of princes involved in the movement, the role of secret societies and the church, and the absence of leadership at critical times. One is reminded of V. I. Lenin's argument almost a hundred years later that in czarist Russia democracy could not be established democratically. Yet Rozen argues that success seemed possible, and he seems perplexed that the czarist regime did not make fine liberal distinctions between thought and action in the later investigation and punishment.

Memoirs are a special kind of text. Often, they are written like this one, many years after the events described. Thus, there is the problem of memory as well as personal interest. In trying to determine Rozen's reliability consider the following: Which of these events did he likely witness? Can any of his own views be drawn from the memoir? What did he lose or gain from the events described? Do you think his retelling of the events was obscured by idealism, or is it realistic and accurate?

Glynn R. Barratt, *The Rebel on the Bridge: A Life of the Decembrist Baron Andrey Rozen, 1800–1884* (Athens: Ohio University Press, 1976).

The question of self-interest brings us full circle to the legacy of the Enlightenment, especially its core belief that people can empathize with others and reason together. Today we live in an age when every motive is dissected, and every claim to truth or sincerity questioned. The thinkers and revolutionaries of the Enlightenment proclaimed ideals that were often beyond their capacity to realize, sometimes even to understand. Does this mean that they were naive, or ahead of their time?

For the young Russian nobles serving in the Guards regiments, the campaigns [of 1813–1815] in Germany and France were like an entrance into a new cultural world which heretofore only single individuals or private persons had had any conception of. . . . The struggle of the numerous political parties then existing in France found its most avid and intelligent spectators and listeners among the young foreigners.

It was precisely the most talented and active of the young Russian guardsmen who enthusiastically imbibed the ideas of civic consciousness, freedom, and constitutional rights and attentively and admiringly entered into the life of the nation they had come from the remote east to pacify. Many began to consider the possibility of transmitting to their homeland the best of the constructive reforms, and with the fiery enthusiasm of youth they leaped across the wide chasm separating the levels of Russian and French cultural development.

When the final hour of their sojourn in France had struck, the flower of the Guards officer corps returned home with the intention of transplanting France in Russia. Thus in most of the best regiments Masonic lodges of a purely political cast were formed. When these lodges were closed and abolished, their members came together in secret societies which had the goal of obtaining a constitutional regime for Russia. They all knew that the emperor Alexander had himself formed this intention, and they thought they would be acting in his spirit by undertaking preparatory measures. But Alexander, frightened by the liberal movements in Germany, changed the course of his policy, and the young nobles in the regiments were left in a position clearly at variance with the dominant system. Various restraining measures proved fruitless, since some of the soldiers had been infected with the French poison and desired the same sort of treatment to which they had become accustomed in France. The most ardent of the conspirators finally turned to a republican ideal.

On the evening of December 12 [1825], I was invited to the homes of Ryleev and Prince Obolenskii for conferences; there I found the chief participants in [the events of] December 14. It was decided to gather in

Senate Square on the day appointed for taking the new oath of allegiance, to lead there as many of the troops as possible under the pretense of supporting the rights of Constantine, [and] to entrust command to Prince Trubetskoi, unless [General] M. F. Orlov should arrive from Moscow by that time. If our side should be stronger, we would proclaim the abolition of the monarchy and immediately establish a provisional government consisting of five persons, chosen by the members of the State Council and Senate. Among the five, the names of I. S. Mordvinov, M. M. Speranskii, and P. I. Pestel were proposed in advance. The provisional government would direct all affairs of state with the assistance of the Council and Senate, until such time as elected representatives from the entire Russian land could gather and lay the foundation for a new government. . . . The measures adopted for the uprising were unclear and indefinite, and thus to certain of my objections and remarks Prince Obolenskii and Bulatov replied ironically: "After all, we can't very well stage rehearsals!"

There were altogether more than two thousand soldiers in Senate Square taking part in the uprising. Under the command of a single leader this strength, in view of the thousands of people gathered around and ready to give help, might have been decisive, the more so since in the event of an attack many battalions would have joined the rebels, who stood without their overcoats in a cold of −10 degrees [Centigrade], in newly fallen snow and with a sharp wind from the east, remained passive, and kept warm only by continual shouts of "Hurrah!" The dictator [Prince S. P. Trubetskoi] was nowhere to be seen, nor were his assistants on the spot. Command was offered to Bulatov: he refused; then to N. A. Bestuzhev: he refused on the grounds that he was a naval officer; finally command was thrust upon Prince E. P. Obolenskii, not as a tactician but as an officer whom the soldiers knew and liked. There was anarchy in the full meaning of the word; in the absence of any instructions everyone could give commands, everyone was waiting for something, and while waiting they jointly repelled attacks, stubbornly refused to surrender, and proudly rejected any offer of Pardon.

But the success of the intended venture was possible, taking all factors into consideration. Two thousand soldiers, and ten times that many onlookers, were ready for anything at a leader's beckoning. . . . Meanwhile time was passing; there was no unity of command: thus instead of acting our forces remained purely passive. The troops of the Moscow [Guards] Regiment stood firm and repelled five attacks by the Horse Guards. The soldiers yielded neither to threats nor to inducements. They did not waver in the presence of the metropolitan [Serafim of Saint Petersburg], who came out in full vestments and with a cross, imploring them in the name of the Lord. This force stood motionless in the cold and without overcoats for several hours, at a time when it could have seized the cannon loaded against it. The cannon stood nearby under cover of a platoon of the Chevalier Guards, commanded by a member of the secret society, I. A. Annenkov.

The investigating committee did not wish to understand the difference between an actual uprising, on one hand, and, on the other, an intention of staging an uprising or an intention of assassinating the tsar; it not only condemned the rebels for their actions but also viewed as crimes their criminal words and phrases which had nothing to do with the uprising or even opposed an uprising. The investigating committee imposed shameful sentences of death and exile not only upon the participants in the uprising but also upon those who had desired an uprising or had merely discussed an uprising without taking any actual part in it. It found equally guilty those who had rebelled and those who had merely discussed rebellion.

REFLECTIONS

The Enlightenment and its legacies — secular order and revolutionary republicanism — were European in origin but global in impact. In this chapter, we have touched on just a few of the crosscurrents of what some historians call an "Atlantic Revolution." A tide of revolutionary fervor swept through France, the United States, and Latin America, found sympathy in Russia in 1825, and echoed in the Muslim heartland, resulting in secular, modernizing regimes in Turkey and Egypt in the next century.

The Age of Revolution also marked the beginning of an age of mass migration, the earliest examples prompted by recruitment of soldiers for foreign wars. King George III of Britain shipped German Hessian troops across the Atlantic to suppress the American Revolution. The American revolutionaries moved quickly toward a Declaration of Independence in 1776 so that, as an independent nation, they could request military assistance from France, which they felt might be hesitant to meddle in British colonial affairs. Simón Bolívar owed a great deal of his success to Irish volunteers who saw the Liberator's struggle against Spain as comparable with their own against England.

The appeal of the Enlightenment, of rationally ordered society, and of democratic government continues. Elements of this eighteenth-century revolution — the rule of law; regular, popular elections of representatives; the separation of church and state, of government and politics, and of civil and military authority — are widely recognized ideals and emerging global realities. Like science, the principles of the Enlightenment are universal in their claims and often seem universal in their appeal. Nothing is simpler, more rational, or easier to follow than a call to reason, law, liberty, justice, or equality. And yet every society has evolved its own guidelines under different circumstances, often with lasting results. France had its king and still has a relatively centralized state. The United States began with slavery and still suffers from racism. South American states became free of Europe only to dominate Native Americans, and they continue to do so. One democratic society has a king, another a House of Lords, another a national church. Are these different adaptations of the Enlightenment ideal? Or are these examples of incomplete revolution, cases of special interests allowing their governments to fall short of principle?

The debate continues today as more societies seek to realize responsive, representative government and the rule of law while oftentimes respecting conflicting traditions. Muslim countries and Israel struggle with the competing demands of secular law and religion, citizenship and communalism. Former communist countries adopt market economies and struggle with traditions of collective support and the appeal of individual liberty.

Perhaps these are conflicts within the Enlightenment tradition itself. How is it possible to have both liberty and equality? How can we claim inalienable rights on the basis of a secular, scientific creed? How does a faith in human reason lead to revolution? And how can ideas of order or justice avoid the consequences of history and human nature?

7

Capitalism and the
Industrial Revolution

Europe and the World, 1750–1900

HISTORICAL CONTEXT

Two principal forces have shaped the modern world: capitalism and the industrial revolution. As influential as the transformations discussed in Chapters 5 and 6 (the rise of science and the democratic revolution), these two forces are sometimes considered to be one and the same, because the industrial revolution occurred first in capitalist countries such as England, Holland, and the United States. In fact, the rise of capitalism preceded the industrial revolution by centuries.

Capitalism denotes a particular economic organization of a society, whereas *industrial revolution* refers to a particular transformation of technology. Specifically, in capitalism market forces (supply and demand) set money prices that determine how goods are distributed. Markets for products and services are found in virtually all city societies, but throughout much of history these markets have played only minor roles in people's lives. Most economic behavior was regulated by family, religion, tradition, and political authority rather than by markets. Increasingly after 1500 in Europe, feudal dues were converted into money rents, periodic fairs became institutionalized, banks were established, modern book-keeping procedures were developed, and older systems of inherited economic status were loosened. After 1800, new populations of urban workers had to work for money to buy food and shelter; after 1850 even clothing had to be purchased in the new "department stores." By 1900, the market had become the operating metaphor of society: One sold oneself; everything had its price. Viewed positively, a capitalist society is one in which buyers and sellers, who together compose the market, make most decisions about the production and distribution of resources. Viewed less favorably, it is the capitalists — those who own the resources of the society — who make the decisions about production and distribution. The democratic process of one person, one vote is supplanted by one dollar, one vote.

The industrial revolution made mass production possible with the use of power-driven machines. Mills driven by waterwheels existed in ancient times, but the construction of identical, replaceable machinery — the machine production of machines — revolutionized industry and enabled the coordination of production on a vast scale, occurring first in England's cotton textile mills at the end of the eighteenth century. The market for such textiles was capitalist, though the demand for many early mass-produced goods, such as muskets and uniforms, was government-driven.

The origins of capitalism are hotly debated among historians. Because the world's first cities, five thousand years ago, created markets, merchants, money, and private ownership of capital, some historians refer to an ancient capitalism. In this text, *capitalism* refers to those societies whose markets, merchants, money, and private ownership became central to the way society operated. As such, ancient Mesopotamia, Rome, and Sung dynasty China, which had extensive markets and paper money a thousand years ago, were not among the first capitalist societies. Smaller societies in which commercial interests and merchant classes took hold to direct political and economic matters were the capitalist forerunners. Malacca, Venice, Florence, Holland, and England, the mercantile states of the fifteenth to seventeenth centuries, exemplify *commercial capitalism* or mercantile capitalism. Thus, the shift to industrial capitalism was more than a change in scale; it was also a transition from a trade-based economy to a manufacturing-based economy, a difference that meant an enormous increase in productivity, profits, and prosperity.

THINKING HISTORICALLY
Distinguishing Causes of Change

Because industry and capitalism are so closely associated, it is difficult to distinguish the effects of one from the other. Still, such a distinction is necessary if we are to understand historical change.

Try to make an analytical distinction between capitalism and industrialization, even when the sources in this chapter do not. By determining what changes can be attributed to each, you will come to understand the changes that capitalism and industrialization might bring to other societies and the impact they may have had in other time periods.

36

ARNOLD PACEY

Asia and the Industrial Revolution

Here a modern historian of technology demonstrates how Indian manufacturing techniques were assimilated by Europeans, particularly by the English successors of the Mughal Empire, providing a boost to the industrial revolution in Britain. In what ways was Indian technology considered superior prior to the industrial revolution? How did European products gain greater markets than those of India?

Thinking Historically

Notice how the author distinguishes between capitalism and the industrial revolution. Was India more industrially advanced than capitalistic? Did the British conquest of India benefit more from capitalism, industry, or something else?

Deindustrialization

During the eighteenth century, India participated in the European industrial revolution through the influence of its textile trade, and through the investments in shipping made by Indian bankers and merchants. Developments in textiles and shipbuilding constituted a significant industrial movement, but it would be wrong to suggest that India was on the verge of its own industrial revolution. There was no steam engine in India, no coal mines, and few machines. . . . [E]xpanding industries were mostly in coastal areas. Much of the interior was in economic decline, with irrigation works damaged and neglected as a result of the breakup of the Mughal Empire and the disruption of war. Though political weakness in the empire had been evident since 1707, and a Persian army heavily defeated Mughal forces at Delhi in 1739, it was the British who most fully took advantage of the collapse of the empire. Between 1757 and 1803, they took control of most of India except the Northwest. The result was that the East India Company now administered major sectors of the economy, and quickly reduced the role of the big Indian bankers by changes in taxes and methods of collecting them.

Arnold Pacey, *Technology in World Civilization* (Cambridge: MIT Press, 1990), 128–35.

Meanwhile, India's markets in Europe were being eroded by competition from machine-spun yarns and printed calicoes made in Lancashire, and high customs duties were directed against Indian imports into Britain. Restrictions were also placed on the use of Indian-built ships for voyages to England. From 1812, there were extra duties on any imports they delivered, and that must be one factor in the decline in shipbuilding. A few Indian ships continued to make the voyage to Britain, however, and there was one in Liverpool Docks in 1839 when Herman Melville arrived from America. It was the *Irrawaddy* from Bombay and Melville commented: "Forty years ago, these merchantmen were nearly the largest in the world; and they still exceed the generality." They were "wholly built by the native shipwrights of India, who . . . surpassed the European artisans." Melville further commented on a point which an Indian historian confirms, that the coconut fibre rope used for rigging on most Indian ships was too elastic and needed constant attention. Thus the rigging on the *Irrawaddy* was being changed for hemp rope while it was in Liverpool. Sisal rope was an alternative in India, used with advantage on some ships based at Calcutta.

Attitudes to India changed markedly after the subcontinent had fallen into British hands. Before this, travellers found much to admire in technologies ranging from agriculture to metallurgy. After 1803, however, the arrogance of conquest was reinforced by the rapid development of British industry. This meant that Indian techniques which a few years earlier seemed remarkable could now be equalled at much lower cost by British factories. India was then made to appear rather primitive, and the idea grew that its proper role was to provide raw materials for western industry, including raw cotton and indigo dye, and to function as a market for British goods. This policy was reflected in 1813 by a relaxation of the East India Company's monopoly of trade so that other British companies could now bring in manufactured goods freely for sale in India. Thus the textile industry, iron production, and shipbuilding were all eroded by cheap imports from Britain, and by handicaps placed on Indian merchants.

By 1830, the situation had become so bad that even some of the British in India began to protest. One exclaimed, "We have destroyed the manufactures of India," pleading that there should be some protection for silk weaving, "the last of the expiring manufactures of India." Another observer was alarmed by a "commercial revolution" which produced "so much present suffering to numerous classes in India."

The question that remains is the speculative one of what might have happened if a strong Mughal government had survived. Fernand Braudel argues that although there was no lack of "capitalism" in India, the economy was not moving in the direction of home-grown industrialization. The historian of technology inevitably notes the lack of development of machines, even though there had been some increase in the use of water-wheels during the eighteenth century both in the iron industry and at gunpowder mills. However, it is impossible not to be struck by the achievements of the shipbuilding industry, which produced skilled carpenters and a model of large-scale organizations. It also trained up draughtsmen and people with mechanical interests. It is striking that one of the Wadia shipbuilders installed gas lighting in his home in 1834 and built a small foundry in which he made parts for steam engines. Given an independent and more prosperous India, it is difficult not to believe that a response to British industrialization might well have taken the form of a spread of skill and innovation from the shipyards into other industries.

As it was, such developments were delayed until the 1850s and later, when the first mechanized cotton mill opened. It is significant that some of the entrepreneurs who backed the development of this industry were from the same Parsi families as had built ships in Bombay and invested in overseas trade in the eighteenth century.

Guns and Rails: Asia, Britain, and America

Asian Stimulus

Britain's "conquest" of India cannot be attributed to superior armaments. Indian armies were also well equipped. More significant was the prior breakdown of Mughal government and the collaboration of many Indians. Some victories were also the result of good discipline and bold strategy, especially when Arthur Wellesley, the future Duke of Wellington, was in command. Wellesley's contribution also illustrates the distinctive western approach to the organizational aspect of technology. Indian armies might have had good armament, but because their guns were made in a great variety of different sizes, precise weapons drill was impossible and the supply of shot to the battlefield was unnecessarily complicated. By contrast, Wellesley's forces standardized on just three sizes of field gun, and the commander himself paid close attention to the design of gun carriages and to the bullocks which hauled them, so that his artillery could move as fast as his infantry, and without delays due to wheel breakages.

Significantly, the one major criticism regularly made of Indian artillery concerned the poor design of gun carriages. Many, particularly before 1760, were little better than four-wheeled trolleys. But the guns themselves were often of excellent design and workmanship. Whilst some were imported and others were made with the assistance of foreign craftworkers, there was many a brass cannon and mortar of Indian design, as well as heavy muskets for camel-mounted troops. Captured field guns were often taken over for use by the British, and after capturing ninety guns in one crucial battle, Wellesley wrote that seventy were "the finest brass ordnance I have ever seen." They were probably made in northern India, perhaps at the great Mughal arsenal at Agra.

Whilst Indians had been making guns from brass since the sixteenth century, Europeans could at first only produce this alloy in relatively small quantities because they had no technique for smelting zinc. By the eighteenth century, however, brass was being produced in large quantities in Europe, and brass cannon were being cast at Woolwich Arsenal near London. Several European countries were importing metallic zinc from China for this purpose. However, from 1743 there was a smelter near Bristol in England producing zinc, using coke[1] as fuel, and zinc smelters were also developed in Germany. At the end of the century, Britain's imports of zinc from the Far East were only about forty tons per year. Nevertheless, a British party which visited China in 1797 took particular note of zinc smelting methods. These were similar to the process used in India, which involved vaporizing the metal and then condensing it. There is a suspicion that the Bristol smelting works of 1743 was based on Indian practice, although the possibility of independent invention cannot be excluded.

A much clearer example of the transfer of technology from India occurred when British armies on the subcontinent encountered rockets, a type of weapon of which they had no previous experience. The basic technology had come from the Ottoman Turks or from Syria before 1500, although the Chinese had invented rockets even earlier. In the 1790s, some Indian armies included very large infantry units equipped with rockets. French mercenaries in Mysore had learned to make them, and the British Ordnance Office was enquiring for somebody with expertise on the subject. In response, William Congreve, whose father was head of the laboratory at Woolwich Arsenal, undertook to design a rocket on Indian lines. After a successful demonstration, about two hundred of his rockets were used by the British in an attack on Boulogne in 1806. Fired from over a kilometre away, they set fire to the town. After this success, rockets were adopted quite widely by European armies, though some commanders, notably the Duke of Wellington, frowned on such imprecise weapons, and they tended to drop out of use later in the century. What happened next, however, was typical of the whole British relationship with India. William Congreve set up a factory to manufacture the weapons in 1817, and part of its output was exported to India to equip rocket troops operating there under British command.

Yet another aspect of Asian technology in which eighteenth-century Europeans were interested was the design of farm implements. Reports on seed drills and ploughs were sent to the British Board of Agriculture from India in 1795. A century earlier the Dutch had found much of

---

[1] Fuel from soft coal. [Ed.]

interest in ploughs and winnowing machines of a Chinese type which they saw in Java. Then a Swedish party visiting Guangzhou (Canton) took a winnowing machine back home with them. Indeed, several of these machines were imported into different parts of Europe, and similar devices for cleaning threshed grain were soon being made there. The inventor of one of them, Jonas Norberg, admitted that he got "the initial idea" from three machines "brought here from China," but had to create a new type because the Chinese machines "do not suit our kinds of grain." Similarly, the Dutch saw that the Chinese plough did not suit their type of soil, but it stimulated them to produce new designs with curved metal mould-boards in contrast to the less efficient flat wooden boards used in Europe hitherto.

In most of these cases, and especially with zinc smelting, rockets, and winnowing machines, we have clear evidence of Europeans studying Asian technology in detail. With rockets and winnowers, though perhaps not with zinc, there was an element of imitation in the European inventions which followed. In other instances, however, the more usual course of technological dialogue between Europe and Asia was that European innovation was challenged by the quality or scale of Asian output, but took a different direction, as we have seen in many aspects of the textile industry. Sometimes, the dialogue was even more limited, and served mainly to give confidence in a technique that was already known. Such was the case with occasional references to China in the writings of engineers designing suspension bridges in Britain. The Chinese had a reputation for bridge construction, and before 1700 Peter the Great had asked for bridge-builders to be sent from China to work in Russia. Later, several books published in Europe described a variety of Chinese bridges, notably a long-span suspension bridge made with iron chains.

Among those who developed the suspension bridge in the West were James Finley in America, beginning in 1801, and Samuel Brown and Thomas Telford in Britain. About 1814, Brown devised a flat, wrought-iron chain link which Telford later used to form the main structural chains in his suspension bridges. But beyond borrowing this specific technique, what Telford needed was evidence that the suspension principle was applicable to the problem he was then tackling. Finley's two longest bridges had spanned seventy-four and ninety-three metres, over the Merrimac and Schuylkill Rivers in the eastern United States. Telford was aiming to span almost twice the larger distance with his 176-metre Menai Bridge. Experiments at a Shropshire ironworks gave confidence in the strength of the chains. But Telford may have looked for reassurance even further afield. One of his notebooks contains the reminder, "Examine Chinese bridges." It is clear from the wording which follows that he had seen a recent booklet advocating a "bridge of chains," partly based on a Chinese example, to cross the Firth of Forth in Scotland.

ADAM SMITH

From *The Wealth of Nations*

An Inquiry into the Nature and Causes of the Wealth of Nations might justly be called the bible of free-market capitalism. Written in 1776 in the context of the British (and European) debate over the proper role of government in the economy, Smith's work takes aim at *mercantilism,* or government supervision of the economy. Mercantilists believed that because there was a finite amount of wealth in the world, one country's gain would result in another country's loss. Therefore, the national economy required government assistance and direction to prosper. For example, after 1660 England imposed a series of acts on British colonies, requiring that they purchase British products and use British shipping — policies that were not well received in America.

Smith argues that free trade will produce greater wealth than mercantilist trade and that free markets allocate resources more efficiently than the government. At the time, Smith's ideas were not entirely new. His notion of *laissez-faire* (literally "let do") capitalism was advocated by the Physiocrat (economic) philosophers in France, although they believed wealth was only in land. Smith does not believe that capitalists are virtuous or that governments should absent themselves entirely from the economy. However, he does believe that the greed of capitalists generally negates itself and produces results that are advantageous to, but unimagined by, the individual. "It is not from the benevolence of the butcher, the brewer, or the baker, that we expect our dinner," Smith wrote, "but from their regard of their own interest. We address ourselves not to their humanity, but to their self-love, and never talk to them of our own necessities, but of their advantage."[1] Each person seeks to maximize his or her own gain, thereby creating an efficient market in which the cost of goods is instantly adjusted to exploit changes in supply and demand, while the market provides what is needed at the price people are willing to pay "as if by an invisible hand."

What would Smith say to a farmer or manufacturer who wanted to institute tariffs or quotas to limit the number of cheaper imports entering the country and to minimize competition? What would he say

---

[1] Book I, chapter 2.

Adam Smith, *The Wealth of Nations* (London: Everyman's Library, M. Dent & Sons, Ltd., 1910).

to a government official who wanted to protect an important domestic industry? What would he say to a worker who complained about low wages or boring work?

Thinking Historically

The Wealth of Nations was written in defense of free capitalism at a moment when the industrial revolution was just beginning. Some elements of Smith's writing suggest a preindustrial world, as in the quotation about the butcher, brewer, and baker mentioned earlier. Still, Smith was aware how new industrial methods were transforming age-old labor relations and manufacturing processes. In some respects, Smith recognized that capitalism could create wealth, not just redistribute it, because he appreciated the potential of industrial technology.

As you read this selection, note when Smith is discussing capitalism, the economic system, and the power of the new industrial technology. In his discussion of the division of labor, what relationship does Smith see between the development of a capitalistic market and the rise of industrial technology? According to Smith, what is the relationship between money and industry, and which is more important? What would Smith think about a "postindustrial" or "service" economy in which few workers actually make products? What would he think of a prosperous country that imported more than it exported?

Book I: Of the Causes of Improvement in the Productive Powers of Labour, and of the Order According to Which Its Produce Is Naturally Distributed among the Different Ranks of the People

Chapter 1: Of the Division of Labour

The greatest improvement in the productive powers of labour, and the greater part of the skill, dexterity, and judgment with which it is anywhere directed, or applied, seem to have been the effects of the division of labour.

The effects of the division of labour, in the general business of society, will be more easily understood by considering in what manner it operates in some particular manufactures. It is commonly supposed to be carried furthest in some very trifling ones; not perhaps that it really is carried further in them than in others of more importance: but in those trifling manufactures which are destined to supply the small wants of but a small number of people, the whole number of workmen must necessarily be small; and those employed in every different branch of the work can often be collected into the same workhouse, and placed at once under the view of the spectator. In those great manufactures, on the contrary, which are destined to supply the great wants of the great body of the people, every different branch of the work employs so great a number of workmen that it is impossible to collect them all into the same workhouse. We can seldom see more, at one time, than those employed in one single branch. Though in such manufactures, therefore, the work may really be divided into a much greater number of parts than in those of a more trifling nature, the division is not near so obvious, and has accordingly been much less observed.

To take an example, therefore, from a very trifling manufacture; but one in which the division of labour has been very often taken notice of, the trade of the pin-maker; a workman not educated to this business (which the division of labour has rendered a distinct trade), nor acquainted with the use of the machinery employed in it (to the invention of which the same division of labour has probably given occasion), could scarce, perhaps, with his utmost industry, make one pin in a day, and certainly could not make twenty. But in the way in which this business is now carried on, not only the whole work is a peculiar trade, but it is divided into a number of branches, of which the greater part are likewise peculiar trades. One man draws out the wire, another straights it, a third cuts it, a fourth points it, a fifth grinds it at the top for receiving the head; to make the head requires two or three distinct operations; to put it on is a peculiar business, to whiten the pins is another; it is even a trade by itself to put them into the paper; and the important business of making a pin is, in this manner, divided into about eighteen distinct operations, which, in some manufactories, are all performed by distinct hands, though in others the same man will sometimes perform two or three of them. I have seen a small manufactory of this kind where ten men only were employed, and where some of them consequently performed two or three distinct operations. But though they were very poor, and therefore but indifferently accommodated with the necessary machinery, they could, when they exerted themselves, make among them about twelve pounds of pins in a day. There are in a pound upwards of four thousand pins of a middling size. Those ten persons, therefore, could make among them upwards of forty-eight thousand pins in a day. Each person, therefore, making a tenth part of forty-eight thousand pins, might be considered as making four thousand eight hundred pins in a day. But if they had all wrought separately and independently, and without any of them having been educated to this peculiar business, they certainly could not each of them have made twenty, perhaps not one pin in a day; that is, certainly, not the two hundred and fortieth, perhaps not the four thousand eight hundredth part of what they are at present capable of performing, in consequence of a proper division and combination of their different operations.

In every other art and manufacture, the effects of the division of labour are similar to what they are in this very trifling one; though, in many of them, the labour can neither be so much subdivided, nor reduced to so great a simplicity of operation. . . .

Chapter 3: That the Division of Labour Is Limited by the Extent of the Market

As it is the power of exchanging that gives occasion to the division of labour, so the extent of this division must always be limited by the extent of that power, or, in other words, by the extent of the market. When the market is very small, no person can have any encouragement to dedicate himself entirely to one employment, for want of the power to exchange all that surplus part of the produce of his own labour, which is over and above his own consumption, for such parts of the produce of other men's labour as he has occasion for.

There are some sorts of industry, even of the lowest kind, which can be carried on nowhere but in a great town. A porter, for example, can find employment and subsistence in no other place. A village is by much too narrow a sphere for him. . . .

Chapter 5: Of the Real and Nominal Price of Commodities, or Their Price in Labour, and Their Price in Money

Every man is rich or poor according to the degree in which he can afford to enjoy the necessaries, conveniences, and amusements of human life. But after the division of labour has once thoroughly taken place, it is but a very small part of these with which a man's own labour can supply him. The far greater part of them he must derive from the labour of other people, and he must be rich or poor according to the quantity of that labour which he can command, or which he can afford to purchase. The value of any commodity, therefore, to the person who possesses it, and who means not to use or consume it himself, but to exchange it for other commodities, is equal to the quantity of labour which it enables him to purchase or command. Labour, therefore, is the real measure of the exchangeable value of all commodities. . . .

Chapter 7: Of the Natural and Market Price of Commodities

. . . When the quantity of any commodity which is brought to market falls short of the effectual demand, all those who are willing to pay the whole value of the rent, wages, and profit, which must be paid in order to bring it thither, cannot be supplied with the quantity which they want. Rather than want it altogether, some of them will be willing to give more. A competition will immediately begin among them, and the market price will rise more or less above the natural price, according as either the greatness of the deficiency, or the wealth and wanton luxury of the competitors, happen to animate more or less the eagerness of the competition. Among competitors of equal wealth and luxury the same deficiency will generally occasion a more or less eager competition, according as the acquisition of the commodity happens to be of more or less importance to them. Hence the exorbitant price of the necessaries of life during the blockade of a town or in a famine.

When the quantity brought to market exceeds the effectual demand, it cannot be all sold to those who are willing to pay the whole value of the rent, wages, and profit, which must be paid in order to bring it thither. Some part must be sold to those who are willing to pay less, and the low price which they give for it must reduce the price of the whole. The market price will sink more or less below the natural price, according as the greatness of the excess increases more or less the competition of the sellers, or according as it happens to be more or less important to them to get immediately rid of the commodity. The same excess in the importation of perishables will occasion a much greater competition than in that of durable commodities; in the importation of oranges, for example, than in that of old iron.

When the quantity brought to market is just sufficient to supply the effectual demand, and no more, the market price naturally comes to be either exactly, or as nearly as can be judged of, the same with the natural price. The whole quantity upon hand can be disposed of for this price, and cannot be disposed of for more. The competition of the different dealers obliges them all to accept of this price, but does not oblige them to accept of less.

The quantity of every commodity brought to market naturally suits itself to the effectual demand. It is the interest of all those who employ their land, labour, or stock, in bringing any commodity to market, that the quantity never should exceed the effectual demand; and it is the interest of all other people that it never should fall short of that demand.

Book II: On the Nature, Accumulation, and Employment of Stock

Chapter 3: Of the Accumulation of Capital, or of Productive and Unproductive Labour

There is one sort of labour which adds to the value of the subject upon which it is bestowed: There is another which has no such effect. The former, as it produces a value, may be called productive; the latter, unproductive labour. Thus the labour of a manufacturer adds, generally, to the value of the materials which he works upon, that of his own maintenance, and of his master's profit. The labour of a menial servant, on the contrary, adds to the value of nothing. Though the manufacturer has his wages advanced to him by his master, he, in reality, costs him no expence, the value of those wages being generally restored, together with a profit, in the improved value of the subject upon which his labour is bestowed. But the maintenance of a menial servant never is restored. A man grows rich by employing a multitude of manufacturers: He grows poor, by maintaining a multitude of menial servants. The labour of the latter, however, has its value, and deserves its reward as well as that of the former. But the labour of the manufacturer fixes and realizes itself in some particular subject or vendible commodity, which lasts for some time at least after that labour is past. . . .

The labour of some of the most respectable orders in the society is, like that of menial servants, unproductive of any value, and does not fix or realize itself in any permanent subject, or vendible commodity, which endures after that labour is past, and for which an equal quantity of labour could afterwards be procured. The sovereign, for example, with all the officers both of justice and war who serve under him, the whole army and navy, are unproductive labourers. They are the servants of the publick, and are maintained by a part of the annual produce of the industry of other people. Their service, how honourable, how useful, or how necessary soever, produces nothing for which an equal quantity of service can afterwards be procured. The protection, security, and defence of the commonwealth, the effect of their labour this year, will not purchase its protection, security, and defence, for the year to come. In the same class must be ranked, some both of the gravest and most important, and some of the most frivolous professions: churchmen, lawyers, physicians, men of letters of all kinds; players, buffoons, musicians, opera-singers, opera-dancers, and so forth. The labour of the meanest of these has a certain value, regulated by the very same principles which regulate that of every other sort of labour; and that of the noblest and most useful, produces nothing which could afterwards purchase or procure an equal quantity of labour. Like the declamation of the actor, the harangue of the orator, or the tune of the musician, the work of all of them perishes in the very instant of its production. . . .

Book IV: Of Systems of Political Economy

Chapter 1: Of the Principle of the Commercial or Mercantile System

I thought it necessary, though at the hazard of being tedious, to examine at full length this popular notion that wealth consists in money, or in gold and silver. Money in common language, as I have already observed, frequently signifies wealth, and this ambiguity of expression has rendered this popular notion so familiar to us that even they who are convinced of its absurdity are very apt to forget their own principles, and in the course of their reasonings to take it for granted as a certain and undeniable truth. Some of the best English writers upon commerce set out with observing that the wealth of a country consists, not in its gold and silver only, but in its lands, houses, and consumable goods of all different kinds. In the course of their reasonings, however, the lands, houses, and consumable goods seem to slip out of their memory, and the strain of their argument frequently supposes that all wealth consists in gold and silver, and that to multiply those metals is the great object of national industry and commerce. . . .

Chapter 2: Of Restraints upon the Importation from Foreign Countries of Such Goods as Can Be Produced at Home

. . . The produce of industry is what it adds to the subject or materials upon which it is employed. In proportion as the value of this produce is great or small, so will likewise be the profits of the employer. But it is only for the sake of profit that any man employs a capital in the support of industry; and he will always, therefore, endeavour to employ it in the support of that industry of which the produce is likely to be of the greatest value, or to exchange for the greatest quantity either of money or of other goods.

But the annual revenue of every society is always precisely equal to the exchangeable value of the whole annual produce of its industry, or rather is precisely the same thing with that exchangeable value. As every individual, therefore, endeavours as much as he can both to employ his capital in the support of domestic industry, and so to direct that industry that its produce may be of the greatest value; every individual necessarily labours to render the annual revenue of the society as great as he can. He generally, indeed, neither intends to promote the public interest, nor knows how much he is promoting it. By preferring the support of domestic to that of foreign industry, he intends only his own security; and by directing that industry in such a manner as its produce may be of the greatest value, he intends only his own gain, and he is in this, as in many other cases, led by an invisible hand to promote an end which was no part of his intention. Nor is it always the worse for the society that it was no part of it. By pursuing his own interest he frequently promotes that of the society more effectually than when he really intends to promote it. I have never known much good done by those who affected to trade for the public good. It is an affectation, indeed, not very common among merchants, and very few words need be employed in dissuading them from it.

What is the species of domestic industry which his capital can employ, and of which the produce is likely to be of the greatest value, every individual, it is evident, can, in his local situation, judge much better than any statesman or lawgiver can do for him. The statesman who should attempt to direct private people in what manner they ought to employ their capitals would not only load himself with a most unnecessary attention, but assume an authority which could safely be trusted, not only to no single person, but to no council or senate whatever, and which would nowhere be so dangerous as in the hands of a man who had folly and presumption enough to fancy himself fit to exercise it.

To give the monopoly of the home market to the produce of domestic industry, in any particular art or manufacture, is in some measure to direct private people in what manner they ought to employ their capitals, and must, in almost all cases, be either a useless or a hurtful regulation. If the produce of domestic can be brought there as cheap as that of foreign industry, the regulation is evidently useless. If it cannot, it must generally be hurtful. It is the maxim of every prudent master of a family never to attempt to make at home what it will cost him more to make than to buy. The tailor does not attempt to make his own shoes, but buys them of the shoemaker. The shoemaker does not attempt to make his own clothes, but employs a tailor. The farmer attempts to make neither the one nor the other, but employs those different artificers. All of them find it for their interest to employ their whole industry in a way in which they have some advantage over their neighbours, and to purchase with a part of its produce, or what is the same thing, with the price of a part of it, whatever else they have occasion for.

What is prudence in the conduct of every private family can scarce be folly in that of a great kingdom. If a foreign country can supply us with a commodity cheaper than we ourselves can make it, better buy it of them with some part of the produce of our own industry employed in a way in which we have some advantage. The general industry of the country, being always in proportion to the capital which employs it, will not thereby be diminished, no more than that of the above-mentioned artificers; but only left to find out the way in which it can be employed with the greatest advantage. It is certainly not employed to the greatest advantage when it is thus directed towards an object which it can buy cheaper than it can make. . . .

38

From *The Sadler Report of the House of Commons*

Although children were among the ideal workers in the factories of the industrial revolution, according to many factory owners, increasingly their exploitation became a concern of the British Parliament. One important parliamentary investigation, chaired by Michael Sadler, took volumes of testimony from child workers and older people who had worked as children in the mines and factories. The following is only a brief, representative sample of the testimony gathered in the Sadler Report. The report led to child-labor reform in the Factory Act of 1833.

What seem to be the causes of Crabtree's distress? How could they have been alleviated?

Thinking Historically

To what extent are the problems faced by Matthew Crabtree the inevitable results of machine production? To what extent are his problems caused by capitalism? How might the owner of this factory have addressed these issues?

If you asked the owner why he didn't pay more, shorten the workday, provide more time for meals, or provide medical assistance when it was needed, how do you think he would have responded? Do you think Matthew would have been in favor of reduced hours if it meant reduced wages?

Friday, 18 May 1832 — Michael Thomas Sadler, Esquire, in the Chair

Mr. Matthew Crabtree, *called in; and Examined.*
　　What age are you? — Twenty-two.
　　What is your occupation? — A blanket manufacturer.
　　Have you ever been employed in a factory? — Yes.
　　At what age did you first go to work in one? — Eight.
　　How long did you continue in that occupation? — Four years.

From *The Sadler Report: Report from the Committee on the Bill to Regulate the Labour of Children in the Mills and Factories of the United Kingdom.* London: The House of Commons, 1832.

Will you state the hours of labour at the period when you first went to the factory, in ordinary times? — From 6 in the morning to 8 at night.

Fourteen hours? — Yes.

With what intervals for refreshment and rest? — An hour at noon.

Then you had no resting time allowed in which to take your breakfast, or what is in Yorkshire called your "drinking"? — No.

When trade was brisk what were your hours? — From 5 in the morning to 9 in the evening.

Sixteen hours? — Yes.

With what intervals at dinner? — An hour.

How far did you live from the mill? — About two miles.

Was there any time allowed for you to get your breakfast in the mill? — No.

Did you take it before you left your home? — Generally.

During those long hours of labour could you be punctual; how did you awake? — I seldom did awake spontaneously; I was most generally awoke or lifted out of bed, sometimes asleep, by my parents.

Were you always in time? — No.

What was the consequence if you had been too late? — I was most commonly beaten.

Severely? — Very severely, I thought.

In whose factory was this? — Messrs. Hague & Cook's, of Dewsbury.

Will you state the effect that those long hours had upon the state of your health and feelings? — I was, when working those long hours, commonly very much fatigued at night, when I left my work; so much so that I sometimes should have slept as I walked if I had not stumbled and started awake again; and so sick often that I could not eat, and what I did eat I vomited.

Did this labour destroy your appetite? — It did.

In what situation were you in that mill? — I was a piecener.

Will you state to this Committee whether piecening is a very laborious employment for children, or not? — It is a very laborious employment. Pieceners are continually running to and fro, and on their feet the whole day.

The duty of the piecener is to take the cardings from one part of the machinery, and to place them on another? — Yes.

So that the labour is not only continual, but it is unabated to the last? — It is unabated to the last.

Do you not think, from your own experience, that the speed of the machinery is so calculated as to demand the utmost exertions of a child supposing the hours were moderate? — It is as much as they could do at the best; they are always upon the stretch, and it is commonly very difficult to keep up with their work.

State the condition of the children toward the latter part of the day, who have thus to keep up with the machinery. — It is as much as they can do when they are not very much fatigued to keep up with their work, and toward the close of the day, when they come to be more fatigued, they cannot keep up with it very well, and the consequence is that they are beaten to spur them on.

Were you beaten under those circumstances? — Yes.

Frequently? — Very frequently.

And principally at the latter end of the day? — Yes.

And is it your belief that if you had not been so beaten, you should not have got through the work? — I should not if I had not been kept up to it by some means.

Does beating then principally occur at the latter end of the day, when the children are exceedingly fatigued? — It does at the latter end of the day, and in the morning sometimes, when they are very drowsy, and have not got rid of the fatigue of the day before.

What were you beaten with principally? — A strap.

Anything else? — Yes, a stick sometimes; and there is a kind of roller which runs on the top of the machine called a billy, perhaps two or three yards in length, and perhaps an inch and a half, or more in diameter; the circumference would be four or five inches; I cannot speak exactly.

Were you beaten with that instrument? — Yes.

Have you yourself been beaten, and have you seen other children struck severely with that roller? — I have been struck very severely with it myself, so much so as to knock me down, and I have seen other children have their heads broken with it.

You think that it is a general practice to beat the children with the roller? — It is.

You do not think then that you were worse treated than other children in the mill? — No, I was not, perhaps not so bad as some were.

In those mills is chastisement towards the latter part of the day going on perpetually? — Perpetually.

So that you can hardly be in a mill without hearing constant crying? — Never an hour, I believe.

Do you think that if the overlooker were naturally a humane person it would be still found necessary for him to beat the children, in order to keep up their attention and vigilance at the termination of those extraordinary days of labour? — Yes, the machine turns off a regular quantity of cardings, and of course they must keep as regularly to their work the whole of the day; they must keep with the machine, and therefore however humane the slubber may be, as he must keep up with the machine or be found fault with, he spurs the children to keep up also by various means but that which he commonly resorts to is to strap them when they become drowsy.

At the time when you were beaten for not keeping up with your work, were you anxious to have done it if you possibly could? — Yes; the dread of being beaten if we could not keep up with our work was a sufficient impulse to keep us to it if we could.

When you got home at night after this labour, did you feel much fatigued? — Very much so.

Had you any time to be with your parents, and to receive instruction from them? — No.

What did you do? — All that we did when we got home was to get the little bit of supper that was provided for us and go to bed immediately. If the supper had not been ready directly, we should have gone to sleep while it was preparing.

Did you not, as a child, feel it a very grievous hardship to be roused so soon in the morning? — I did.

Were the rest of the children similarly circumstanced? — Yes, all of them; but they were not all of them so far from their work as I was.

And if you had been too late you were under the apprehension of being cruelly beaten? — I generally was beaten when I happened to be too late; and when I got up in the morning the apprehension of that was so great, that I used to run, and cry all the way as I went to the mill.

That was the way by which your punctual attendance was secured? — Yes.

And you do not think it could have been secured by any other means? — No.

Then it is your impression from what you have seen, and from your own experience, that those long hours of labour have the effect of rendering young persons who are subject to them exceedingly unhappy? — Yes.

You have already said it had a considerable effect upon your health? — Yes.

Do you conceive that it diminished your growth? — I did not pay much attention to that; but I have been examined by some persons who said they thought I was rather stunted, and that I should have been taller if I had not worked at the mill.

What were your wages at that time? — Three shillings (per week).

And how much a day had you for overwork when you were worked so exceedingly long? — A halfpenny a day.

Did you frequently forfeit that if you were not always there to a moment? — Yes; I most frequently forfeited what was allowed for those long hours.

You took your food to the mill; was it in your mill, as is the case in cotton mills, much spoiled by being laid aside? — It was very frequently covered by flues from the wool; and in that case they had to be blown off with the mouth, and picked off with the fingers before it could be eaten.

So that not giving you a little leisure for eating your food, but obliging you to take it at the mill, spoiled your food when you did get it? — Yes, very commonly.

And that at the same time that this over-labour injured your appetite? — Yes.

Could you eat when you got home? — Not always.

What is the effect of this piecening upon the hands? — It makes them bleed; the skin is completely rubbed off, and in that case they bleed in perhaps a dozen parts.

The prominent parts of the hand? — Yes, all the prominent parts of the hand are rubbed down till they bleed; every day they are rubbed in that way.

All the time you continue at work? — All the time we are working. The hands never can be hardened in that work, for the grease keeps them soft in the first instance, and long and continual rubbing is always wearing them down, so that if they were hard they would be sure to bleed.

It is attended with much pain? — Very much.

Do they allow you to make use of the back of the hand? — No; the work cannot be so well done with the back of the hand, or I should have made use of that.

39

KARL MARX AND FRIEDRICH ENGELS

From *The Communist Manifesto*

The Communist Manifesto was written in 1848 in the midst of European upheaval, a time when capitalist industrialization had spread from England to France and Germany. Marx and Engels were Germans who studied and worked in France and England. In the *Manifesto,* they imagine a revolution that will transform all of Europe. What do they see as the inevitable causes of this revolution? How, according to their analysis, is the crisis of "modern" society different from previous crises? Were Marx and Engels correct?

Karl Marx and Friedrich Engels, *Manifesto of the Communist Party* (Arlington Heights, IL: Harlan Davidson, 1955). Reprinted in the Crofts Classics Series.

Thinking Historically

Notice how Marx and Engels describe the notions of capitalism and industrialization without using those words. The term *capitalism* developed later from Marx's classic *Das Kapital* (1859), but the term *bourgeoisie,* as Engels notes in this selection, stands for the capitalist class. For Marx and Engels, the industrial revolution (another, later phrase) is the product of a particular stage of capitalist development. Thus, if Marx and Engels were asked whether capitalism or industry was the principal force that created the modern world, what would their answer be?

The Communist Manifesto is widely known as the classic critique of capitalism, but a careful reading reveals a list of achievements of capitalist or "bourgeois civilization." What are these achievements? Did Marx and Engels consider them to be achievements? How could Marx and Engels both praise and criticize capitalism?

Bourgeois and Proletarians[1]

The history of all hitherto existing society is the history of class struggles.

Freeman and slave, patrician and plebeian, lord and serf, guildmaster and journeyman, in a word, oppressor and oppressed, stood in constant opposition to one another, carried on an uninterrupted, now hidden, now open fight, a fight that each time ended, either in a revolutionary reconstitution of society at large, or in the common ruin of the contending classes.

In the earlier epochs of history, we find almost everywhere a complicated arrangement of society into various orders, a manifold gradation of social rank. In ancient Rome we have patricians, knights, plebeians, slaves; in the Middle Ages, feudal lords, vassals, guildmasters, journeymen, apprentices, serfs; in almost all of these classes, again, subordinate gradations.

The modern bourgeois society that has sprouted from the ruins of feudal society, has not done away with class antagonisms. It has but established new classes, new conditions of oppression, new forms of struggle in place of the old ones.

---

[1] In French *bourgeois* means a town-dweller. *Proletarian* comes from the Latin, *proletarius,* which meant a person whose sole wealth was his offspring (*proles*). [Ed.]

[Note by Engels] By "bourgeoisie" is meant the class of modern capitalists, owners of the means of social production and employers of wage-labor; by "proletariat," the class of modern wage-laborers who, having no means of production of their own, are reduced to selling their labor power in order to live.

Our epoch, the epoch of the bourgeoisie, possesses, however, this distinctive feature: It has simplified the class antagonisms. Society as a whole is more and more splitting up into the two great hostile camps, into two great classes directly facing each other — bourgeoisie and proletariat.

From the serfs of the Middle Ages sprang the chartered burghers of the earliest towns. From these burgesses the first elements of the bourgeoisie were developed.

The discovery of America, the rounding of the Cape, opened up fresh ground for the rising bourgeoisie. The East-Indian and Chinese markets, the colonization of America, trade with the colonies, the increase in the means of exchange and in commodities generally, gave to commerce, to navigation, to industry, an impulse never before known, and thereby, to the revolutionary element in the tottering feudal society, a rapid development.

The feudal system of industry, in which industrial production was monopolized by closed guilds, now no longer sufficed for the growing wants of the new markets. The manufacturing system took its place. The guildmasters were pushed aside by the manufacturing middle class; division of labor between the different corporate guilds vanished in the face of division of labor in each single workshop.

Meantime the markets kept ever growing, the demand ever rising. Even manufacture[2] no longer sufficed. Thereupon, steam and machinery revolutionized industrial production. The place of manufacture was taken by the giant, modern industry, the place of the industrial middle class, by industrial millionaires — the leaders of whole industrial armies, the modern bourgeois.

Modern industry has established the world market, for which the discovery of America paved the way. This market has given an immense development to commerce, to navigation, to communication by land. This development has, in its turn, reacted on the extension of industry; and in proportion as industry, commerce, navigation, railways extended, in the same proportion the bourgeoisie developed, increased its capital, and pushed into the background every class handed down from the Middle Ages.

We see, therefore, how the modern bourgeoisie is itself the product of a long course of development, of a series of revolutions in the modes of production and of exchange.

Each step in the development of the bourgeoisie was accompanied by a corresponding political advance of that class. An oppressed class

---

[2] By *manufacture* Marx meant the system of production which succeeded the guild system but which still relied mainly upon direct human labor for power. He distinguished it from modern industry which arose when machinery driven by water and steam was introduced. [Ed.]

under the sway of the feudal nobility, it became an armed and self-governing association in the medieval commune; here independent urban republic (as in Italy and Germany), there taxable "third estate" of the monarchy (as in France); afterwards, in the period of manufacture proper, serving either the semifeudal or the absolute monarchy as a counterpoise against the nobility, and, in fact, cornerstone of the great monarchies in general — the bourgeoisie has at last, since the establishment of modern industry and of the world market, conquered for itself, in the modern representative state, exclusive political sway. The executive of the modern state is but a committee for managing the common affairs of the whole bourgeoisie.

The bourgeoisie has played a most revolutionary role in history.

The bourgeoisie, wherever it has got the upper hand, has put an end to all feudal, patriarchal, idyllic relations. It has pitilessly torn asunder the motley feudal ties that bound man to his "natural superiors," and has left no other bond between man and man than naked self-interest, than callous "cash payment." It has drowned the most heavenly ecstasies of religious fervor, of chivalrous enthusiasm, of philistine sentimentalism, in the icy water of egotistical calculation. It has resolved personal worth into exchange value, and in place of the numberless indefeasible chartered freedoms, has set up that single, unconscionable freedom — Free Trade. In one word, for exploitation, veiled by religious and political illusions, it has substituted naked, shameless, direct, brutal exploitation.

The bourgeoisie has stripped of its halo every occupation hitherto honored and looked up to with reverent awe. It has converted the physician, the lawyer, the priest, the poet, the man of science, into its paid wage-laborers.

The bourgeoisie has torn away from the family its sentimental veil, and has reduced the family relation to a mere money relation.

The bourgeoisie has disclosed how it came to pass that the brutal display of vigor in the Middle Ages, which reactionaries so much admire, found its fitting complement in the most slothful indolence. It has been the first to show what man's activity can bring about. It has accomplished wonders far surpassing Egyptian pyramids, Roman aqueducts, and Gothic cathedrals; it has conducted expeditions that put in the shade all former migrations of nations and crusades.

The bourgeoisie cannot exist without constantly revolutionizing the instruments of production, and thereby the relations of production, and with them the whole relations of society. Conservation of the old modes of production in unaltered form, was, on the contrary, the first condition of existence for all earlier industrial classes. Constant revolutionizing of production, uninterrupted disturbance of all social conditions, everlasting uncertainty and agitation distinguished the bourgeois epoch from all earlier ones. All fixed, fast-frozen relations, with their train of ancient and venerable prejudices and opinions, are swept away, all new-formed ones become antiquated before they can ossify. All that is solid melts into air, all that is holy is profaned, and man is at last compelled to face with sober senses his real conditions of life and his relations with his kind.

The need of a constantly expanding market for its products chases the bourgeoisie over the whole surface of the globe. It must nestle everywhere, settle everywhere, establish connections everywhere.

The bourgeoisie has through its exploitation of the world market given a cosmopolitan character to production and consumption in every country. To the great chagrin of reactionaries, it has drawn from under the feet of industry the national ground on which it stood. All old-established national industries have been destroyed or are daily being destroyed. They are dislodged by new industries, whose introduction becomes a life and death question for all civilized nations, by industries that no longer work up indigenous raw material, but raw material drawn from the remotest zones; industries whose products are consumed, not only at home, but in every quarter of the globe. In place of the old wants, satisfied by the production of the country, we find new wants, requiring for their satisfaction the products of distant lands and climes. In place of the old local and national seclusion and self-sufficiency, we have intercourse in every direction, universal interdependence of nations. And as in material, so also in intellectual production. The intellectual creations of individual nations become common property. National one-sidedness and narrow-mindedness become more and more impossible, and from the numerous national and local literatures there arises a world literature.

The bourgeoisie, by the rapid improvement of all instruments of production, by the immensely facilitated means of communication, draws all nations, even the most barbarian, into civilization. The cheap prices of its commodities are the heavy artillery with which it batters down all Chinese walls, with which it forces the barbarians' intensely obstinate hatred for foreigners to capitulate. It compels all nations, on pain of extinction, to adopt the bourgeois mode of production; it compels them to introduce what it calls civilization into their midst, i.e., to become bourgeois themselves. In a word, it creates a world after its own image.

The bourgeoisie has subjected the country to the rule of the towns. It has created enormous cities, has greatly increased the urban population as compared with the rural, and has thus rescued a considerable part of the population from the idiocy of rural life. Just as it has made the country dependent on the towns, so it has made barbarian and semi-barbarian countries dependent on the civilized ones, nations of peasants on nations of bourgeois, the East on the West.

More and more the bourgeoisie keeps doing away with the scattered state of the population, of the means of production, and of property. It has agglomerated population, centralized means of production, and has concentrated property in a few hands. The necessary consequence of this was political centralization. Independent, or but loosely connected provinces, with separate interests, laws, governments and systems of taxation, became lumped together into one nation, with one government, one code of laws, one national class interest, one frontier and one customs tariff.

The bourgeoisie, during its rule of scarce one hundred years, has created more massive and more colossal productive forces than have all preceding generations together. Subjection of nature's forces to man, machinery, application of chemistry to industry and agriculture, steam-navigation, railways, electric telegraphs, clearing of whole continents for cultivation, canalization of rivers, whole populations conjured out of the ground — what earlier century had even a presentiment that such productive forces slumbered in the lap of social labor?

We see then that the means of production and of exchange, which served as the foundation for the growth of the bourgeoisie, were generated in feudal society. At a certain stage in the development of these means of production and of exchange, the conditions under which feudal society produced and exchanged, the feudal organization of agriculture and manufacturing industry, in a word, the feudal relations of property became no longer compatible with the already developed productive forces; they became so many fetters. They had to be burst asunder; they were burst asunder.

Into their place stepped free competition, accompanied by a social and political constitution adapted to it, and by the economic and political sway of the bourgeois class.

A similar movement is going on before our own eyes. Modern bourgeois society with its relations of production, of exchange and of property, a society that has conjured up such gigantic means of production and exchange, is like the sorcerer who is no longer able to control the powers of the nether world whom he has called up by his spells. For many a decade past the history of industry and commerce is but the history of the revolt of modern productive forces against modern conditions of production, against the property relations that are the conditions for the existence of the bourgeoisie and of its rule. It is enough to mention the commercial crises that by their periodical return put the existence of the entire bourgeoisie society on trial, each time more threateningly. In these crises a great part not only of the existing products, but also of the previously created productive forces, are periodically destroyed. In these crises there breaks out an epidemic that, in all earlier epochs, would have seemed an absurdity — the epidemic of overproduction. Society suddenly finds itself put back into a state of momentary barbarism; it appears as if a famine, a universal war of devastation had cut off the supply of every means of subsistence; industry and commerce seem to be destroyed. And why? Because there is too much civilization, too much means of subsistence, too much industry, too much commerce. The productive forces at the disposal of society no longer tend to further the development of the conditions of bourgeois property; on the contrary, they have become too powerful for these conditions, by which they are fettered, and no sooner do they overcome these fetters than they bring disorder into the whole of bourgeois society, endanger the existence of bourgeois property. The conditions of bourgeois society are too narrow to comprise the wealth created by them. And how does the bourgeoisie get over these crises? On the one hand by enforced destruction of a mass of productive forces; on the other, by the conquest of new markets, and by the more thorough exploitation of the old ones. That is to say, by paving the way for more extensive and more destructive crises, and by diminishing the means whereby crises are prevented.

The weapons with which the bourgeoisie felled feudalism to the ground are now turned against the bourgeoisie itself.

But not only has the bourgeoisie forged the weapons that bring death to itself; it has also called into existence the men who are to wield those weapons — the modern working class — the proletarians.

In proportion as the bourgeoisie, i.e., capital, is developed, in the same proportion is the proletariat, the modern working class, developed — a class of labourers, who live only so long as they find work, and who find work only so long as their labour increases capital. These labourers, who must sell themselves piece-meal, are a commodity, like every other article of commerce, and are consequently exposed to all the vicissitudes of competition, to all the fluctuations of the market.

Owing to the extensive use of machinery and to division of labour, the work of the proletarians has lost all individual character, and consequently, all charm for the workman. He becomes an appendage of the machine, and it is only the most simple, most monotonous, and most easily acquired knack, that is required of him. Hence, the cost of production of a workman is restricted, almost entirely, to the means of subsistence that he requires for his maintenance, and for the propagation of his race. But the price of a commodity, and therefore also of labour, is equal to its cost of production. In proportion therefore, as the repulsiveness of the work increases, the wage decreases. Nay more, in proportion as the use of machinery and division of labour increases, in the same proportion the burden of toil also increases, whether by prolongation of the working hours, by increase of the work exacted in a given time or by increased speed of the machinery, etc.

Modern industry has converted the little workshop of the patriarchal master into the great factory of the industrial capitalist. Masses of labourers, crowded into the factory, are organised like soldiers. As privates of the industrial army they are placed under the command of a perfect hierarchy of officers and sergeants. Not only are they slaves of the bourgeois class, and of the bourgeois State; they are daily and hourly enslaved by the machine, by the over-looker, and, above all, by the individual bourgeois manufacturer himself. The more openly this despotism proclaims gain to be its end and aim, the more petty, the more hateful and the more embittering it is.

The less the skill and exertion of strength implied in manual labour, in other words, the more modern industry becomes developed, the more is the labour of men superseded by that of women. Differences of age and sex have no longer any distinctive social validity for the working class. All are instruments of labour, more or less expensive to use, according to their age and sex.

No sooner is the exploitation of the labourer by the manufacturer, so far, at an end, that he receives his wages in cash, than he is set upon by the other portions of the bourgeoisie, the landlord, the shopkeeper, the pawnbroker, etc.

The lower strata of the middle class — the small tradespeople, shopkeepers, retired tradesmen generally, the handicraftsmen and peasants — all these sink gradually into the proletariat, partly because their diminutive capital does not suffice for the scale on which Modern Industry is carried on, and is swamped in the competition with the large capitalists, partly because their specialized skill is rendered worthless by the new methods of production. Thus the proletariat is recruited from all classes of the population.

The proletariat goes through various stages of development. With its birth begins its struggle with the bourgeoisie. At first the contest is carried on by individual labourers, then by the workpeople of a factory, then by the operatives of one trade, in one locality, against the individual bourgeois who directly exploits them. They direct their attacks not against the bourgeois conditions of production, but against the instruments of production themselves; they destroy imported wares that compete with their labour, they smash to pieces machinery, they set factories ablaze, they seek to restore by force the vanished status of the workman of the Middle Ages.

At this stage the labourers still form an incoherent mass scattered over the whole country, and broken up by their mutual competition. If anywhere they united to form more compact bodies, this is not yet the consequence of their own active union, but of the union of the bourgeoisie, which class, in order to attain its own political ends, is compelled to set the whole proletariat in motion, and is moreover yet, for a time, able to do so. At this stage, therefore, the proletarians do not fight their enemies, but the enemies of their enemies, the remnants of absolute monarchy, the landowners, the non-industrial bourgeois, the petty bourgeoisie. Thus the whole historical movement is concentrated in the hands of the bourgeoisie, every victory so obtained is a victory for the bourgeoisie.

But with the development of industry the proletariat not only increases in number; it becomes concentrated in greater masses, its strength grows, and it feels that strength more. The various interests and conditions of life within the ranks of the proletariat are more and more equalised, in proportion as machinery obliterates all distinctions of labour, and nearly everywhere reduces wages to the same low level. The growing competition among the bourgeois, and the resulting commercial crises, make the wages of the workers ever more fluctuating. The unceasing improvement of machinery, ever more rapidly developing, makes their livelihood more and more precarious; the collisions between individual workmen and individual bourgeois take more and more the character of collisions between two classes. Thereupon the workers begin to form combinations (Trades Unions) against the bourgeois; they club together in order to keep up the rate of wages; they found permanent associations in order to make provision beforehand for these occasional revolts. Here and there the contest breaks out into riots.

Now and then the workers are victorious, but only for a time. The real fruit of their battles lies, not in the immediate result, but in the ever-expanding union of the workers. This union is helped on by the improved means of communication that are created by modern industry and that place the workers of different localities in contact with one another. It was just this contact that was needed to centralise the numerous local struggles, all of the same character, into one national struggle between classes. But every class struggle is a political struggle. And that union, to attain which the burghers of the Middle Ages, with their miserable highways, required centuries, the modern proletarians, thanks to railways, achieve in a few years.

This organisation of the proletarians into a class, and consequently into a political party, is continually being upset again by the competition between the workers themselves. But it ever rises up again, stronger, firmer, mightier. It compels legislative recognition of particular interests of the workers, by taking advantage of the divisions among the bourgeoisie itself. Thus the ten-hours' bill in England was carried.

Altogether collisions between the classes of the old society further, in many ways, the course of development of the proletariat. The bourgeoisie finds itself involved in a constant battle. At first with the aristocracy; later on, with those portions of the bourgeoisie itself, whose interests have become antagonistic to the progress of industry; at all times, with the bourgeoisie of foreign countries. In all these battles it sees itself compelled to appeal to the proletariat, to ask for its help, and thus, to drag it into the political arena. The bourgeoisie itself, therefore, supplies the proletariat with its own instruments of political and general education, in other words, it furnishes the proletariat with weapons for fighting the bourgeoisie.

Further, as we have already seen, entire sections of the ruling classes are, by the advance of industry, precipitated into the proletariat, or are at least threatened in their conditions of existence. These also supply the proletariat with fresh elements of enlightenment and progress.

Finally, in times when the class struggle nears the decisive hour, the process of dissolution going on within the ruling class, in fact within the whole range of society, assumes such a violent, glaring character, that a small section of the ruling class cuts itself adrift, and joins the revolutionary class, the class that holds the future in its hands. Just as, therefore, at an earlier period, a section of the nobility went over to the bourgeoisie, so now a portion of the bourgeoisie goes over to the proletariat, and in particular, a portion of the bourgeois ideologists, who have raised themselves to the level of comprehending theoretically the historical movement as a whole.

40

SUSAN B. HANLEY

From *Everyday Things in Premodern Japan*

When American Commodore Matthew Perry arrived in Japan in 1854 he encountered a society that was far behind the United States and Europe in its economic and industrial development. This has led many to conclude that the Japanese quality of life must have been poorer than its Western counterparts. Historian Susan Hanley asks us to rethink this assumption. It is true that Perry came from a part of the world that was undergoing an industrial revolution, a striking symbol of which was the large gunship that he brought into Yokohama harbor. In fact, the shock of Western maritime and industrial power hastened the end of the feudal Tokugawa regime in 1868. The succeeding Meiji government quickly resolved to catch up with the West and sent numerous officials, educators, and students to study the technology and institutions of Western Europe and the United States. In this selection, Hanley recalls one Japanese commission's

Susan B. Hanley, *Everyday Things in Premodern Japan* (Berkeley: University of California Press, 1997), 176–84.

conclusion that Japan would be able to catch up to the West in just forty years. What, according to the author, were the real differences between Japan and the West in 1871?

Thinking Historically

Hanley does not dispute the visible impact of the industrial revolution, but she raises questions about its significance for people's health and quality of life. Hanley argues that Japanese development in the Tokugawa period (1600–1868) was different rather than inferior to Western industrialization and that, in many ways, Japanese society was healthier than Western industrial society. What do you think of her argument and evidence?

The official report of the Iwakura Mission, which visited various countries in the West from 1871 to 1873, concluded that the Europe of the 1870s was very different from the Europe of only forty years earlier when there had been no trains, steamships, or telegraph, when horse-drawn carriages provided transportation on land and letter carriers ran between stations. The tone of the Mission's report was one of optimism, for if Europe could change so much in only forty years, then Japan could expect to do so too. But how could the Japanese perceive themselves as being only forty years behind a part of the world that had been industrializing for a century? The answer, lies in the developments that took place in Japan during the two and a half centuries of the Tokugawa period [1600–1848]. Despite a widespread view of the Tokugawa lifestyle as largely unchanging, most aspects of life improved significantly from the early-seventeenth century to the nineteenth. The aspects of the mid-nineteenth century lifestyle viewed as backward were for the most part only superficially so, and other differences have been, I suspect, the result of upper-class Westerners in the nineteenth century looking at all income groups in a society vastly different from their own.

The reasons for the lingering perception that Japan was not anywhere near the Western level also lie in the effects of the industrial revolution on life in the West. The new technology brought dramatically visible changes to the observer: trains, telegraph, electricity, and factories using steam or other inanimate power. What was less noticeable and still argued today is the effect of these changes on the quality of life for most people in the early decades of industrialization. And just as the effects of the new technology on the level of physical well-being in the West were more difficult to discern than the effects of the new technology on the economy and on the landscape, so too were the changes in the level of physical well-being that occurred in Tokugawa Japan. These changes came slowly and quietly, not unnoticed entirely, but they have certainly been neglected by twentieth-century historians. The few who have studied aspects of the material culture have done so in terms of Japan's cultural history, and thus for the economic historian, the material culture is a forgotten legacy.

In Japan, on average, all aspects of the material culture that affected the level of physical well-being improved during the course of the Tokugawa period, . . . Housing developed from rather crudely built dwellings with earthen floors and no foundation stones in the seventeenth century to carpenter-crafted houses of sawn lumber with wooden floors in most and tatami in many, though earthen floors could certainly still be found in poor areas. Whereas people commonly slept in straw mats around the fire or in an inner corner in the early-sixteenth century, most houses had an enclosed room for sleeping by the mid-nineteenth century, and bedding made of cotton batting could be found all over Japan. Houses were no longer primarily for protection from the elements, wild animals, and intruders, and with few and tiny windows. By the nineteenth century houses became more comfortable with sliding doors that opened up to let in the sun and let the air circulate. People now wore clothes made of cotton as ordinary everyday dress, took baths regularly, and warmed themselves with portable heaters. Indigenous technological improvements allowed the Japanese to cook and heat themselves using less fuel and less iron, substituting charcoal and enclosed stoves for open hearths and firewood, and iron rings with clay pots for iron cookware. The changes improved energy efficiency, sanitation, health, and comfort, and caused a rise in the level of physical well-being.

These improvements were first enjoyed by the well-to-do in Japan but over time were diffused among the general population. Many of the new elements in the material culture originated in the Muromachi and Sengoku periods; these included tatami in place of wooden floors, cotton clothing, more open styles of housing with sliding doors (*shoin* style), tempura and other new foods, and baths. As the economy grew in the Tokugawa period, an increasing percentage of Japanese could enjoy these amenities, and this resulted in samurai such as Ogyū Sorai complaining about commoners using mosquito netting, eating miso, drinking sake, and wearing store-bought clothes instead of wearing homemade hemp garments, "eating inferior grains such as barley, millet, and barnyard grass," and using brushwood for fuel. The growing economy meant a rising living standard, which resulted in many commoners, first city dwellers and then villages, enjoying what previously only the elite among the samurai had consumed. What occurred was a "samurai-zation" of Japanese material culture, which created a very different national culture by the nineteenth century than existed in the Western industrializing world.

In contrast, life in the industrializing West by the mid-nineteenth century was dominated, at least to outward appearances, by the new technology. Most apparent were the new forms of communication and transportation, including the telegraph, steamships, and trains. By 1860 the United States had over thirty thousand miles of railroad, and by 1871 Germany had over twelve thousand and France three-quarters of that. In 1854, there were over one hundred million passengers on British trains, and since they took people to their destinations not only faster but more cheaply than horses, people began to travel for leisure and to move out of the center of the city into what became the suburbs. The modern postal system combined with the telegraph speeded up personal and business communications. And the factories and mills that made all of this possible caused tremendous urban growth and a transformation of previous rural centers into noisy, polluted industrial cities.

But did new technology improve the level of physical well-being in the West? It is clear that industrialization affected the mass of people only slowly and that many of the effects of industrial technology did little to improve the health and physical well-being of the people. As incomes rose, especially for those already well-to-do and the new middle classes, people could afford armchairs, sofas, curtains, carpets, and numerous decorative articles for their homes, but at the same time that homes became more comfortable for sitting, the drapes and the numerous furnishings made them darker and dustier as well as warmer. It is not clear how having more furniture and other material objects would have improved health, any more than faster communication and travel would.

The new developments that would eventually transform the level of physical well-being in the West only began to appear in the mid-nineteenth century. Inexpensive soap became available for the first time, along with new ideas about the importance of cleanliness, and as a consequence bathing became more frequent. By the 1860s a daily bath had become the custom for the upper classes in England, whereas the middle classes were satisfied with one a week. But bathrooms did not become common until the turn of the century, which meant that people were bathing in tubs they filled with water heated on the stove. The poor continued to bathe infrequently, if at all. In France in the 1830s, daily washings were limited to the face; soap was used only once a week. Public baths did not exist in the countryside. In contrast, bathing was common in both urban and rural Japan by the nineteenth century.

The industrial magnates in the West built splendid mansions and the affluent middle classes multistory houses, but the industrial revolution also produced notorious slums. "The misery and desperation that Friedrich Engels observed on the banks of the River Irk in Manchester, Jacob Riis found in the tenements of Cherry Street in New York City,

Andrew Mearns and George Sims uncovered in central London, and Gustav Schmoller detected in Berlin. . . . Social critics in the late-nineteenth century were almost universal in their condemnation of cities and the life-styles of their inhabitants." The industrialization of the Ruhr Basin in the second half of the nineteenth century transformed the rural towns into industrial cities, and the strain on housing produced slums that became the subject of special study in 1886. Dortmund, Essen, and Bochum were the focus of this report on the housing crisis. The nearby city of Duisburg prohibited the building of large tenements but still ended up with what one contemporary observer considered "some of the worst living conditions in all of Germany." Crowding in French cities led to notoriously poor living conditions as well; in the heart of Toulouse in the nineteenth century, inhabitants continued to raise poultry, goats, or pigs in their houses, and the roads were regularly piled high with various forms of excrement. In Toulon at mid-century an average of thirty to forty people lived in each house in the center of town, compared to an average of ten to twelve in the well-off districts. It wasn't until the 1860s that there was any general effort to provide cities with a regular supply of drinking water.

Examples of dubious practices in hygiene and sanitation in nineteenth-century Western countries are numerous. For instance, in 1832, it was found that in Manchester's cotton factories, workers ate their meals out of a communal dish with spoons. The water closet was diffused widely only after 1850, and collection of night soil tended to be left to private means and was often inadequate. Human waste fouled rural areas as well as urban. In France, farmers persisted in keeping dunghills just outside their doors, and rag-and-bone men in Paris in 1832 rioted against the decisions of the police to remove the rubbish heaps from which they made their living. Where the poor lived in the same room as animals, the floors tended to be filthy, but even where people had very high standards of cleanliness with respect to floors, bedbugs and other vermin were a problem. Thus the problems foreigners coped with in Japan in the late-nineteenth century were the same as those they had to cope with in their own countries, except that the streets were far cleaner.

How well people ate in the West is inextricably tied to the debate over whether the standard of living rose or fell during the early decades of the industrial revolution. Although the well-to-do in England began to enjoy an even greater abundance of foods than they had previously, in the 1860s an English woman noted that migrants to New Zealand soon begin to look "well-fed" and "healthy" instead of "half-starved" and "depressed." What we know as the English breakfast and afternoon tea were Victorian innovations, first for the upper and then the middle classes, but both meals can be starchy and full of fat. The daily food intake for the working classes certainly improved after the mid-nineteenth century, but among the items whose consumption rose were sugar, beer, and tobacco. An analysis of diets reveals that even in the 1890s, many people in England were "inadequately nourished"; bread and potatoes were still the staple foods in these families' diets. It now appears that in the United States, incomes, and hence standard of living, rose in the first half of the nineteenth century, while at the same time health, or the level of physical well-being, worsened. The same has been argued for England using a variety of sources.

Though it is impossible to determine exactly who was eating what in the nineteenth century, diets in the industrializing countries improved by mid-century. In France, for example, the last serious crisis in the supply of bread occurred in the 1840s, and during the second half of the century milk, sugar, fruit, and fresh vegetables came into reach of working-class budgets, starting the shift away from the traditional reliance on starch-based foods. However, not all changes were immediately beneficial; there is evidence that the diseases transmitted by contaminated milk out-weighed the nutritional benefits of increased consumption. In any case, in the West significant improvement in the level of physical well-being came well after the onset of industrialization, not until the time of the Meiji Restoration and the beginning of Japan's move to industrialize.

Despite the differences in culture and the economy that affected the material lifestyles for the elites of Japan and the West in the nineteenth century, elements of the lifestyle of the poor were surprisingly similar. If we compare Japan and England, not only were there earthen floors in houses and a lack of furniture, but even the methods of preparing meals were similar. One-pot meals were cooked in a pot hung over the fire, porridge in the British Isles and boiled grains with vegetables added in Japan. In England, even more elaborate meals could be boiled in just one pot, using bacon and water as a base for cooking various vegetables and a pudding, and this method, common in the late-nineteenth century, could still be found in England in the 1920s. In fact, the English had stew stoves that looked almost exactly like *kamado*.[1] As England industrialized, those with money enjoyed an increasing number of consumer goods, but even in the nineteenth century, bedding continued to be the most valuable object in the households of the poor.

These examples of the level of physical well-being in the West do not prove that on average people in the Western industrializing nations in the nineteenth century were worse off or better off than the Japanese in the same century. But the number of problems pointed out by contemporary observers of the West, the government reports and policies dealing with them, and the amount of evidence that exists showing that

---

[1] Traditional Japanese stove of stone, brick, on earth. [Ed.]

major portions of the population were worse off as a result of industrial development are confirmation that many groups in all industrializing nations were not physically well-off. Although their living standard, that is income, may not have fallen, the content of their diet, crowded and unsanitary living conditions, and urban pollution lowered the quality of life and level of physical well-being as measured by mortality for urban slum dwellers and factory workers, and conditions in the countryside were often as appalling.

In contrast, in Japan in the mid-nineteenth century, city dwellers did not live in multistory tenements, one or more families plus lodgers in the same room. Edo's water supply was as good as or better than London's, and the sewage system far superior though technologically more primitive, and this could be said of the sanitation in the rest of the country as well. There is no evidence that the diet and housing were less adequate than those in the West. Not only could the Japanese rely on their premodern social infrastructure during the process of industrialization, but they could rely on social customs as well. By the late Tokugawa period, bathing was a well-entrenched habit, the most popular drink was tea, clothing could be readily laundered, and footgear was removed before entering buildings to keep out the dirt. Japanese social customs led to a clean and tidy, and what might even be characterized in some cases as a hygienic, environment.

Convincing proof that the level of physical well-being in Japan was similar to that in the West in the mid-nineteenth century is that life expectancy was similar. Life expectancy for males in Western Europe is estimated at 39.6 in 1840 and 41.1 in 1860; life expectancy in the U.S. in 1850 is estimated at 37 for males and 39 for females. This is very similar to many of the village samples in Japan in the same period. We must be careful about our comparisons when we make assessments about how good or bad life expectancy was. Ann Jannetta and Samuel Preston found deathrates "high" in the temple records of the Ogen-ji. At age one in the period 1816–1835, life expectancy was 46.1 for males and 42.2 for females. For Fujito, I found life expectancy at age one in 1830–1835 to be 43.6 for males and 40.9 for females, and I came to the opposite conclusion. We have similar findings, and yet the deathrates for either Ogen-ji or Fujito are high only in comparison with contemporary Japan and not for a premodern society or the nineteenth century. I think it can be argued that in crucial respects Japan by the mid-nineteenth century was more nearly at the level of the West than at first glance it appears, and that the Iwakura Mission's optimism that Japan was no more than forty years behind the West is justified. . . .

41

IWASAKI YATARO

Mitsubishi Letter to Employees

Japan was the first country outside the West to undergo an industrial revolution. After 1854 when American Commodore Perry forced Japan to open its ports to the West, Japanese society underwent a wide range of changes. In 1868, the previously ceremonial emperor restored imperial power, moved the court to Edo (Tokyo), and undercut the power of aristocrats. This Meiji (Enlightened) Restoration government proceeded to mobilize the population to learn Western methods of industrial production and many other facets of Western culture and society. Many Japanese were educated in the United States and Europe, especially in Germany. Japanese industry was organized along the German model, with considerable government direction and power vested in leading families. Politics was not democratic, and the economy was not capitalist. In 1870, for example, the Meiji government launched a major railroad construction plan. It hoped to raise capital from private sources, but when none was offered, the government went ahead on its own. Gradually, with the help of foreign loans and Japanese capitalists, a mixed public and private economy developed.

One of the entrepreneurs who directed Japanese industrialization was Iwasaki Yataro, a clerk for a feudal lord, who used his ability and connections to create a steamship company that put the government Nippon line out of business and then went on to challenge the American and British lines. His company, Mitsubishi, was well on the way to becoming one of the great conglomerates of modern Japan.

In 1876, however, the British Peninsular and Oriental Steam Navigation Company challenged Mitsubishi's dominance in Japanese coastal trade. Mitsubishi responded by halving its coastal fares and cutting employee wages by one-third. In this letter to his employees, Iwasaki asks for their support.

Notice Iwasaki's appeal to national security and pride. Does the appeal strike you as genuine or contrived? Would it have been an unreasonable request to control Japanese coastal traffic, Japanese ports, and traffic from Japan to China? What would Adam Smith or Karl Marx have said about this request?

David John Lu, *Sources of Japanese History*, vol. 2 (New York: McGraw-Hill, 1974), 80–82.

Thinking Historically

Iwasaki Yataro was both a capitalist and an industrialist. While Japanese industrialization enjoyed greater state sponsorship than did British or American industrialization, entrepreneurs like Yataro played a crucial role. In this letter, does Iwasaki speak more as a capitalist or industrialist? Is there any disparity between these two roles, or are they woven together inextricably?

Many people have expressed differing opinions concerning the principles to be followed and advantages to be obtained in engaging foreigners or Japanese in the task of coastal trade. Granted, we may permit a dissenting voice, which suggests that in principle both foreigners and Japanese must be permitted to engage in coastal trade, but once we look into the question of advantages, we know that coastal trade is too important a matter to be given over to the control of foreigners. If we allow the right of coastal navigation to fall into the hands of foreigners in peacetime, it means a loss of business and employment opportunities for our own people, and in wartime it means yielding the vital right of gathering information to foreigners. In fact, this is not too different from abandoning the rights of our country as an independent nation.

Looking back into the past, at the time when we abandoned the policy of seclusion and entered into an era of friendly intercourse and commerce with foreign nations, we should have been prepared for this very task. However, due to the fact that our people lack knowledge and wealth, we have yet to assemble a fleet sufficient to engage in coastal navigation. Furthermore, we have neither the necessary skills for navigation nor a plan for developing a maritime transportation industry. This condition has attracted foreign shipping companies to occupy our maritime transport lines. Yet our people show not a sense of surprise at it. Some people say that our treaties with foreign powers contain an express provision allowing foreign ships to proceed from Harbor A to Harbor B, and others claim that such a provision must not be regarded as granting foreign ships the right to coastal navigation inasmuch as it is intended not to impose unduly heavy taxes on them. I am not qualified to discuss its legal merit, but the issue remains an important one.

I now propose to do my utmost, and along with my 35 million compatriots, perform my duty as a citizen of this country. That is to recover the right of coastal trade in our hands and not to delegate that task to foreigners. Unless we propose to do so, it is useless for our government to revise the unequal treaties[1] or to change our entrenched customs. We need people who can respond, otherwise all the endeavors of the government will come to naught. This is the reason why the government protects our company, and I know that our responsibilities are even greater than the full weight of Mt. Fuji thrust upon our shoulders. There have been many who wish to hinder our progress in fulfilling our obligations. However, we have been able to eliminate one of our worst enemies, the Pacific Mail Company of the United States, from contention by applying appropriate means available to us. Now another rival has emerged. It is the Peninsula & Oriental Team Navigation Company of Great Britain, which is setting up a new line between Yokohama and Shanghai and is attempting to claim its rights over the ports of Nagasaki, Kobe, and Yokohama. The P & O Company is backed by its massive capital, its large fleet of ships, and by its experiences of operating in Oriental countries. In competing against this giant, what methods can we employ?

I have thought about this problem very carefully and have come to one conclusion. There is no other alternative but to eliminate unnecessary positions and unnecessary expenditures. This is a time-worn solution and no new wisdom is involved. Even though it is a familiar saying, it is much easier said than done, and this indeed has been the root cause of difficulties in the past and present times. Therefore, starting immediately, I propose that we engage in this task. By eliminating unnecessary personnel from the payroll, eliminating unnecessary expenditures, and engaging in hard and arduous tasks, we shall be able to solidify the foundation of our company. If there is a will, there is a way. Through our own efforts, we shall be able to repay the government for its protection and answer our nation for its confidence shown in us. Let us work together in discharging our obligations and let us not be ashamed of ourselves. Whether we succeed or fail, whether we can gain profit or sustain loss, we cannot anticipate at this time. Hopefully, all of you will join me in a singleness of heart to attain this cherished goal, forbearing and undaunted by setbacks, to restore to our own hands the right to our own coastal trade. If we succeed it will not only be an accomplishment for our company but also a glorious event for our Japanese Empire, which shall let its light shine to all four corners of the earth. We may succeed and we may

[1] *Unequal treaties* was a term the Chinese used to designate the treaties that were forced upon them by the opium wars; they were "unequal" in the sense that the superior power of the British forced the defeated Chinese to comply with British demands. Here the term refers to the commercial agreements that Japan was made to sign after Admiral Perry's arrival. [Ed.]

fail, and it depends on your effort or lack of it. Do your utmost in this endeavor!

REFLECTIONS

After 1900 the industrial revolution spread throughout the world, but its pace was not always revolutionary. Even today some societies are still largely rural with a majority of workers engaged in subsistence farming or small-scale manufacturing by hand. But over the long course of history people have always tried to replace human labor with machines and increase the production of machine-made goods. In some cases, the transformation has been dramatic. Malaysia, once a languid land of tropical tea and rubber plantations, sprouted enough microchip and electronics factories after 1950 to account for 60 percent of its exports by the year 2000. By the 1990s an already highly industrialized country like Japan could produce luxury cars in factories that needed only a handful of humans to monitor the work of computer-driven robots. Despite occasional announcements of the arrival of a "postindustrial" society, the pressure to mechanize continues unabated in the twenty-first century.

The fate of capitalism in the twentieth century was more varied. The second wave of industrial revolutions — beginning with Germany after 1850 and Japan after 1880 — was directed by governments as much as capitalists. Socialist parties won large support in industrial countries in the first half of the twentieth century, creating welfare states in some after World War II. In Russia after 1917, the Communist party pioneered a model of state-controlled industrialization that attracted imitators from China to Chile and funded anticapitalist movements throughout the world.

The Cold War (1947–1991) between the United States and the Soviet Union, though largely a power struggle between two superpowers, was widely seen as an ideological contest between capitalism and socialism. Thus, the demise of the Soviet Union and its Communist party in 1991 was widely heralded as the defeat of socialism and the victory of capitalism. As Russia, China, and other previously communist states embraced market economies, socialism was declared dead.

But could proclaiming the death of socialism be as premature as heralding the end of industrial society? *The Communist Manifesto* of 1848 long predates the Russian revolution of 1917. Karl Marx died in 1883. Socialists like Rosa Luxembourg criticized Lenin and the Russian communists for misinterpreting Marxism in their impatience to transform Russian society. Socialists, even Marxists, continue to write, advise, and govern today, often urging restraints on the spread of global capital markets and the threat of unregulated capitalism on the global environment.

One of the principal concerns of the twenty-first century will surely be the need for sustainable economic development. Susan B. Hanley showed us how economic well-being was possible in Japan without industrialization. But it was not satisfactory for the Japanese of the nineteenth century, nor, one suspects, is it satisfactory for the people of the world today. The first industrialists controlled far more than their share of the world's resources to benefit their sparse populations. No one imagines that the world can sustain the economic development of its other billions of people with the same level of resource exploitation and pollution. Some wonder if global industrialization on the scale of U.S. industrialization is possible at all. What would sustainable development look like, and how could it be accomplished? Does it mean scaling back the level of industrialization? Or does it require different economic priorities and decision processes?

8

Colonized and Colonizers

Europeans in Africa and Asia, 1850–1930

HISTORICAL CONTEXT

The first stage of European colonialism, beginning with Columbus, was a period in which Europeans — led by the Spanish and Portuguese — settled in the Western Hemisphere and created plantations with African labor. From 1492 to 1776, European settlement in Asia was limited to a few coastal port cities where merchants and missionaries operated. The second stage — the years between 1776, when Britain lost most of its American colonies, and 1880, when the European scramble for African territory began — has sometimes been called a period of *free-trade imperialism*. This term refers to the desire by European countries in general and by Britain in particular to expand their zones of free-trade. It also refers to a widespread opposition to the expense of colonization, a conviction held especially among the British, who garnered all of the advantages of political empire without the costs of occupation and outright ownership.

The British used to say that their second global empire was created in the nineteenth century "in a fit of absentmindedness." But colonial policy in Britain and the rest of Europe was more planned and continuous than that schema might suggest. British control of India (including Burma) increased throughout the nineteenth century, as did British control of South Africa, Australia, the Pacific, and parts of the Americas. At the same time, France, having lost most of India to the British, began building an empire that included parts of North Africa, Southeast Asia, and the Pacific.

This new age of colonialism, beginning in the mid-nineteenth century, reached a fever pitch with the partition of Africa at the end of the century. The period spawned renewed settlement and massive population transfers,

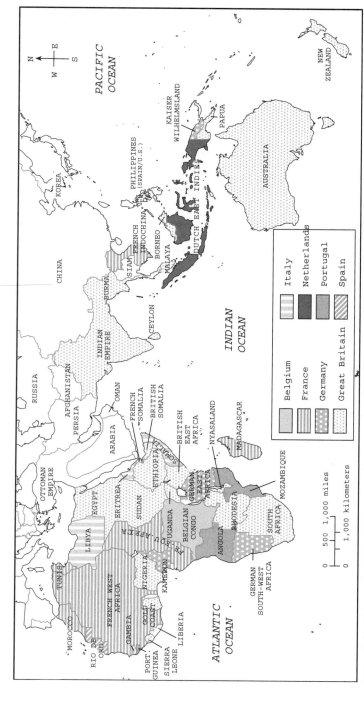

Map 8.1 European Colonialism in Africa and Asia, 1880–1914.

277

with most European migrants settling in the older colonies of the Americas (as well as in South Africa and Australia), where indigenous populations had been reduced. Even where settlement remained light, however, Europeans took political control of large areas of the Earth's surface (see Map 8.1).

In the first reading in this chapter, a historian offers a brief history of this second stage of European colonialism and describes what the renewed era of colonization meant, both for the colonizers and the colonized. Subsequent readings examine aspects of colonial society — in British Burma, French Africa, and the Spanish Philippines.

THINKING HISTORICALLY
Using Literature in History

This chapter also explores whether literature can and should be used in the quest to better understand history. Beginning with some basic questions about the differences between literary and historical approaches, we examine a number of fictional accounts of colonialism, some written by the colonizers, others by the colonized or their descendants. How do these literary accounts add to, or detract from, a historical understanding of colonialism? The rich, evocative literature of the colonial period, both well informed and insightful, aids us in determining how we separate fact from fiction, construct historical knowledge, and appreciate the past in all its dimensions.

42

JURGEN OSTERHAMMEL
From *Colonialism*

In this selection, modern historian Jurgen Osterhammel provides us with an overview of European colonialism. In the first part, "Colonial Epochs," the author discusses ways in which European colonialism changed from the late eighteenth to the early twentieth century. In the second section, "Colonial Societies," he discusses the special character of the colonial social order throughout this period.

Jurgen Osterhammel, *Colonialism*, trans. Shelly Frisch (Princeton: Markus Wiener, 1997), 32–34, 86–89.

How, according to Osterhammel, did colonialism change between 1760 and 1930? How were these changes reflected in the evolution of "colonial society"?

Thinking Historically

Unlike philosophy, which tends to deal with general principles, history studies specific details. Yet as this general overview of colonialism shows, history can include summaries of long-term change and generalizations about different parts of the world over entire centuries as well as specific names and dates. What sort of generalizations are made in this excerpt?

History, like fiction, is a form of storytelling. Fictional storytelling tends to be far more specific than history, usually documenting minutes or hours in the amount of space that it takes many historians to cover years and Osterhammel to cover centuries. Does this selection tell you a story in any sense, or is it too general to do that?

Colonial Epochs

The most important colonial advance of the period [1760–1830] was the extension of the British position in *India*. The British East India Company (EIC) originally conducted trade from port cities. Later on, it becomes increasingly involved in Indian domestic politics, which were determined by the antagonisms of regional powers in the declining phase of the Mughal empire. Unlike the Spanish in Central America, the British in India at first pursued no plans to conquer and certainly no plans to proselytize. They were far from possessing military advantages over the Indian states until about the middle of the century. In Bengal, where British trade interests were increasingly concentrated, a mutually advantageous agreement was reached with the regional prince, the Nabob. Only when a collapse of this "collaboration" was brought about by a concatenation of causes did the idea of territorial rule originate. In 1755, Robert Clive, the future conqueror of Bengal, expressed a hitherto unthinkable idea: "We must indeed become the Nabobs ourselves." From then on the British pursued a strategy of subjugation within a polycentric Indian state system, interrupted repeatedly by phases of deadlock and consolidation. Until the end of the colonial period in 1947, hundreds of seemingly autonomous principalities continued to exist, but after 1818 the British could consider themselves the "paramount power" on the subcontinent.

The East India Company continued to play its double role as business enterprise and state organization. Under constant supervision of the government in London it accompanied the military expansion of its sphere of power with the gradual establishment of colonial structures, which, in rough schematic terms, passed through a characteristic sequences of steps: (1) securing an effective trade monopoly, (2) securing military dominance and disarmament of any subjugated indigenous powers, (3) achieving a tax collection system, (4) stabilizing government by comprehensive legal regulations and the establishment of a bureaucratic administration, and (5) intervening in the indigenous society for purposes of social and humanitarian reform. This fifth stage was reached in the early 1830s. Not only did the age of European rule over highly civilized Asian societies begin in India, but India also became the prototype of an exploitation colony without settlers, a model for British expansion in other parts of Asia and Africa.

The period between 1830 and 1880 was certainly not a calm interlude in the history of European expansion. Only the Caribbean, once so rich, became a "forgotten derelict corner of the world." In an age of "free trade imperialism," China, Japan, Siam (Thailand) and, to a greater extent than was previously the case, the Ottoman Empire as well as Egypt, now de facto independent from it, were forced to open their economies. Sovereignty limitations characteristic of "informal empires" were imposed on them. Latin America, which was *no longer* colonial, and West Africa, which was rid of the slave trade but *not yet* colonized, were integrated into the world economy more closely than ever. On Java, the major island of the Netherlands East Indies, direct colonial intervention in the utilization of land began after 1830; the outer Indonesian islands were gradually subjugated in the period to follow. Foreign encroachment on continental Southeast Asia began after about 1820. First the lowlands near the coast fell into foreign hands: in 1852–1853 Lower Burma, and in 1857 Cochin China. By 1870, the later colonial borders could be distinguished clearly. During the entire period, the Tsarist Empire advanced in the Caucasus and Central Asia with military force, and shortly thereafter in the Far East with somewhat more diplomatic means, thereby intensifying the so-called "Great Game," a sustained cold war between the two Asiatic Great Powers Russia and Great Britain.

Despite these continuities of European world conquest and of ties between classic European diplomacy and "high imperialism," there is something to be said for marking a new epoch around 1870–1880. Most of the reasons can be found in the broader imperialist environment of colonialism, that is, in the structural changes of the world economy and international system. In terms of *colonial* history, the chief development over the last two decades of the nineteenth century was the European occupation of Africa, a singularly condensed expropriation of an entire continent termed the "partition of Africa." On the eve of this process, only South Africa and Algeria had been regions of European colonization, South Africa since 1652 and Algeria since

1830. Elsewhere the Portuguese (Angola, Mozambique), French (Senegal), and British (Sierra Leone, Lagos) made their presence felt in a more limited way. After all, by 1870 over 270,000 white people were already living in Algeria and about 245,000 in South Africa (including the two Boer Republics). The further expansion of these early cores of colonization was also an impetus for the occupation of Africa in the last quarter of the century. The discovery of diamond deposits in 1867 and of gold in 1886 unleashed a development that changed South Africa into a capitalist center of growth and a magnet for international capital. At the same time, it strengthened white supremacy. In Algeria the same result was achieved simultaneously under almost purely agrarian conditions by extensive land transfers from the Arabs to a rapidly growing settlement population.

The actual "partition" of Africa in the years between the occupation of Tunis by the French in 1881 and of Egypt by the British in 1882 on the one hand and the Boer War of the years 1899–1902 on the other was initially a somewhat symbolic process. With treaties *amongst themselves*, the European Great Powers committed themselves to mutual recognition of colonies, protectorates, and spheres of influence. "Paper partition" was only slowly and incompletely transformed into effective occupation, "partition on the ground." However, the borders that were drawn endured with the later establishment of independent African national states. For Africans, the so-called partition of their continent often meant the brutal disruption of bonds and established ways of life. However, partition could also result in the exact opposite: "a ruthless act of political amalgamation, whereby something of the order of ten thousand units was reduced to a mere forty." Particularly in Islamic North Africa (Egypt, Morocco, Tunesia, and Algeria) as well as in parts of Asia (Vietnam, Korea, and Burma), colonialism encountered fairly complex proto-nation-states. Colonial rule in these countries was considered even less legitimate than elsewhere.

Colonial Societies

. . . Characteristic of the social and cultural history of modern colonialism, especially in Asia, was the increasing alienation between two societies that had shared the bond of a colonial relationship since the late eighteenth century. While the status scale in Iberian America was rapidly refined, thereby placing renewed emphasis on racial criteria, the dualization of the colonial social landscape intensified in Asia and Africa. Only in Portuguese Asia was there significant progress in societal interaction, especially where native clergy were concerned, owing to the enlightened politics of the crown under the Marquis de Pombal in the 1760s and 1770s. The sealing off of the European communities from the indigenous environment had many causes, which were manifested in varying combinations: (1) Although Portugal and the Netherlands in particular had officially encouraged marriage between European men and Asian women at first, and the other colonial powers had tolerated it tacitly, immigration of European women raised the sexual autarky of the colonial societies. (2) The transition from trade to rule and often to direct production with dependent workers transformed the "age of partnership" into an age of subordination. (3) Violent resistance by the natives, such as the Native American massacre of colonists in Virginia in 1622 and the Indian rebellion of 1857–1858, strengthened the resolve of white minorities to shield themselves for self-protection. (4) A European attitude of superiority over the rest of the world, stemming from the Christian Eurocentrism of early encounters, made it appear increasingly "unreasonable" to Europeans to maintain close egalitarian relationships with non-Europeans and to make cultural accommodations to them. (5) After the gradual abolition of slave trade and slavery, racist thought lived in the less blatant, but now "scientifically" legitimated forms. It bears pointing out, however, that racism is often not the *cause* of segregation, but the *effect*. Racism has often been used to justify segregation after the fact.

Ethnosocial distancing was an outgrowth of societal interaction and was not always based on discriminatory laws. A telling example was Batavia, the most populous and resplendent city in Asia that was governed by Europe. In the first half of the seventeenth century, a mixed society was formed based on house slavery and the expansion of "Creole" family and patronage networks with relatively high tolerance for interracial family relationships. This society resembled its counterpart in Mexico and was even more akin to Portuguese colonization in Asia (Goa). In the manner of living of its upper class, the mixed society of Batavia conformed almost as closely to its Javanese surroundings as it did to Holland. A distinct demarcation between the European and Asian spheres commenced with the British interregnum of 1811–1816. In the eyes of the British, the Batavian Dutch were appallingly infected by their contact with Asians. Cultural decontamination was decreed. The whites in the city and their mestizo relatives were told to develop an identity as civilized Europeans and clearly display it in their appearances before the Javanese public.

The English in India had always been somewhat more detached from the indigenous environment than the Dutch in Indonesia. After the 1780s, their isolation gradually intensified and became obvious with the decline in status of Eurasian Anglo-Indians, even though some influential Indian politicians in 1830 were still dreaming of a racially mixed India modelled on Mexico. The club became the center of British social life in India and the other Asian colonies during the Victorian era. In clubs, one could feel like a gentleman among other gentlemen while being served by a native staff. In Kuala Lumpur, very few non-

Europeans were admitted before 1940; in Singapore no non-Europeans were allowed in at all. The large clubs of Calcutta remained closed to Indians until 1946. This type of color bar was especially disturbing because it excluded from social recognition the very people who had carried their self-Anglicizing the furthest and loyally supported British rule. Even Indian members of the Indian Civil Service were excluded.

In most regions of Africa, the colonial period began at a time when exclusionist thought and action were most pronounced. In Africa there was virtually no history of intercultural proximity and therefore no need for policies enforcing detachment. The Europeans saw themselves as foreign rulers separated from the African cultures by an abyss. This absolute aloofness extended even to Islam, which they certainly did not consider "primitive," but rather historically obsolete. Color bars in Africa varied in height; they were lowest in West Africa and highest in the settlement colonies of the far north and the deep south. A process of great symptomatic significance was the rejection of the highly educated West Africans who had worked with the early mission. They had envisioned the colonial takeover as an opportunity for a joint European-African effort to modernize and civilize Africa. Instead, they were now, as "white Negroes," despised by all.

$$43$$

GEORGE ORWELL

From *Burmese Days*

This selection, from one of the great novels on colonialism, captures the life of the British colonial class in a remote "upcountry" town in Burma in the 1920s. The chapter is set in the European club. Flory, the principal character, is the only Englishman at all sympathetic to the Burmese. Though he has befriended the Indian physician, Dr. Veraswami, Flory is too weak to propose him as the first "native" member of the club. The other main characters are Westfield, District Superintendent of Police; Ellis, local company manager and the most racist of the group; Lackersteen, local manager of a timber company

George Orwell, *Burmese Days* (1934; reprint, San Diego: Harcourt Brace, 1962), 17–27.

who is usually drunk; Maxwell, a forest officer; and Macgregor, Deputy Commissioner and secretary of the club.

Why does the club loom so large in the lives of these Englishmen? If they complain so much, why are they in Burma? How do you account for the virulent racism of these men? Why does Ellis "correct" the butler's English? What does this story suggest about women in the colonial world?

Thinking Historically

As different as this selection is from Osterhammel's historical overview, both touch on the subjects of dual society, the European club, and colonial racism. How does this selection from Orwell support some of Osterhammel's generalizations? How does it deepen your understanding of these subjects?

The structure of a novel like this one bears certain similarities to history — a description of a place, proper names and biographies, descriptions of human interactions, an accounting of change, and a story. There are also structural differences in a novel — a lot of dialogue, greater attention to physical appearance and character, and a more prominent narrative. Do the fictional constructs in this selection detract from our historical understanding? Can such elements add to our understanding of what actually happened?

Of course, the problem with structural elements such as dialogue and story is that they are fiction. The author of a novel makes no pretense of telling the truth. Nevertheless, an author draws on what he or she knows to create a plausible scenario that is recognizable and consistent. Interestingly, Orwell knew Burma quite well. He was born in India in 1903. His father worked in the Opium Department of the Indian Civil Service. After attending school at Eton in England, Orwell returned to Burma, where he spent five years as a member of the Indian Imperial Police. Orwell, therefore, had a broad knowledge of Burma on which to base his story. Is there any way to determine what Orwell invented and what he merely described in this account?

Orwell was politically engaged throughout his life. Would political ideas make him better or worse as a historian or novelist? How so?

Flory's house was at the top of the maidan,[1] close to the edge of the jungle. From the gate the maidan sloped sharply down, scorched and khaki-coloured, with half a dozen dazzling white bungalows scattered round it. All quaked, shivered in the hot air. There was an English

[1] Parade-ground. [Ed.]

cemetery within a white wall half-way down the hill, and nearby a tiny tin-roofed church. Beyond that was the European Club, and when one looked at the Club — a dumpy one-storey wooden building — one looked at the real centre of the town. In any town in India the European Club is the spiritual citadel, the real seat of the British power, the Nirvana for which native officials and millionaires pine in vain. It was doubly so in this case, for it was the proud boast of Kyauktada Club that, almost alone of Clubs in Burma, it had never admitted an Oriental to membership. Beyond the Club, the Irrawaddy flowed huge and ochreous, glittering like diamonds in the patches that caught the sun; and beyond the river stretched great wastes of paddy fields, ending at the horizon in a range of blackish hills.

The native town, and the courts and the jail, were over to the right, mostly hidden in green groves of peepul trees. The spire of the pagoda rose from the trees like a slender spear tipped with gold. Kyauktada was a fairly typical Upper Burma town, that had not changed greatly between the days of Marco Polo and 1910, and might have slept in the Middle Ages for a century more if it had not proved a convenient spot for a railway terminus. In 1910 the Government made it the headquarters of a district and a seat of Progress — interpretable as a block of law courts, with their army of fat but ravenous pleaders, a hospital, a school, and one of those huge, durable jails which the English have built everywhere between Gibraltar and Hong Kong. The population was about four thousand, including a couple of hundred Indians, a few score Chinese and seven Europeans. There were also two Eurasians named Mr. Francis and Mr. Samuel, the sons of an American Baptist missionary and a Roman Catholic missionary respectively. The town contained no curiosities of any kind, except an Indian fakir who had lived for twenty years in a tree near the bazaar, drawing his food up in a basket every morning.

Flory yawned as he came out of the gate. He had been half drunk the night before, and the glare made him feel liverish. "Bloody, bloody hole!" he thought, looking down the hill. And, no one except the dog being near, he began to sing aloud, "Bloody, bloody, bloody, oh, how thou art bloody" to the tune of "Holy, holy, holy, oh how Thou art holy," as he walked down the hot red road, switching at the dried-up grasses with his stick. It was nearly nine o'clock and the sun was fiercer every minute. The heat throbbed down on one's head with a steady, rhythmic thumping, like blows from an enormous bolster. Flory stopped at the Club gate, wondering whether to go in or to go farther down the road and see Dr. Veraswami. Then he remembered that it was "English mail day" and the newspapers would have arrived. He went in, past the big tennis screen, which was overgrown by a creeper with starlike mauve flowers.

In the borders beside the path swathes of English flowers, phlox and larkspur, hollyhock and petunia, not yet slain by the sun, rioted in vast size and richness. The petunias were huge, like trees almost. There was no lawn, but instead a shrubbery of native trees and bushes — gold mohur trees like vast umbrellas of blood-red bloom, frangipanis with creamy, stalkless flowers, purple bougainvillea, scarlet hibiscus, and the pink, Chinese rose, bilious-green crotons, feathery fronds of tamarind. The clash of colours hurt one's eyes in the glare. A nearly naked *mali,*[2] watering-can in hand, was moving in the jungle of flowers like some large nectar-sucking bird.

On the Club steps a sandy-haired Englishman, with a prickly moustache, pale grey eyes too far apart, and abnormally thin calves to his legs, was standing with his hands in the pockets of his shorts. This was Mr. Westfield, the District Superintendent of Police. With a very bored air he was rocking himself backwards and forwards on his heels and pouting his upper lip so that his moustache tickled his nose. He greeted Flory with a slight sideways movement of his head. His way of speaking was clipped and soldierly, missing out every word that well could be missed out. Nearly everything he said was intended for a joke, but the tone of his voice was hollow and melancholy.

"Hullo, Flory me lad. Bloody awful morning, what?"

"We must expect it at this time of year, I suppose," Flory said. He had turned himself a little sideways, so that his birthmarked cheek was away from Westfield.

"Yes, dammit. Couple of months of this coming. Last year we didn't have a spot of rain till June. Look at that bloody sky, not a cloud in it. Like one of those damned great blue enamel saucepans. God! What'd you give to be in Piccadilly now, eh?"

"Have the English papers come?"

"Yes. Dear old *Punch, Pink'un,* and *Vie Parisienne.* Makes you homesick to read 'em, what? Let's come in and have a drink before the ice all goes. Old Lackersteen's been fairly bathing in it. Half pickled already."

They went in, Westfield remarking in his gloomy voice, "Lead on, Macduff." Inside, the Club was a teak-walled place smelling of earthoil, and consisting of only four rooms, one of which contained a forlorn "library" of five hundred mildewed novels, and another an old and mangy billiard-table — this, however, seldom used, for during most of the year hordes of flying beetles came buzzing round the lamps and littered themselves over the cloth. There were also a card-room and a "lounge" which looked towards the river, over a wide veranda; but at this time of day all the verandas were curtained with green bamboo

2 Gardener. [Ed.]

chicks. The lounge was an unhomelike room, with coco-nut matting on the floor, and wicker chairs and tables which were littered with shiny illustrated papers. For ornament there were a number of "Bonzo" pictures, and the dusty skulls of sambhur. A punkah, lazily flapping, shook dust into the tepid air.

There were three men in the room. Under the punkah a florid, fine-looking, slightly bloated man of forty was sprawling across the table with his head in his hands, groaning in pain. This was Mr. Lackersteen, the local manager of a timber firm. He had been badly drunk the night before, and he was suffering for it. Ellis, local manager of yet another company, was standing before the notice board studying some notice with a look of bitter concentration. He was a tiny wiry-haired fellow with a pale, sharp-featured face and restless movements. Maxwell, the acting Divisional Forest Officer, was lying in one of the long chairs reading the *Field,* and invisible except for two large-boned legs and thick downy forearms.

"Look at this naughty old man," said Westfield, taking Mr. Lackersteen half affectionately by the shoulders and shaking him. "Example to the young, what? There, but for the grace of God and all that. Gives you an idea what you'll be like at forty."

Mr. Lackersteen gave a groan which sounded like "brandy."

"Poor old chap," said Westfield; "regular martyr to booze, eh? Look at it oozing out of his pores. Reminds me of the old colonel who used to sleep without a mosquito net. They asked his servant why and the servant said: 'At night, master too drunk to notice mosquitoes; in the morning, mosquitoes too drunk to notice master.' Look at him — boozed last night and then asking for more. Got a little niece coming to stay with him, too. Due tonight, isn't she, Lackersteen?"

"Oh, leave that drunken sot alone," said Ellis without turning round. He had a spiteful cockney voice. Mr. Lackersteen groaned again, " ——the niece! Get me some brandy, for Christ's sake."

"Good education for the niece, eh? Seeing uncle under the table seven times a week. — Hey, butler! Bringing brandy for Lackersteen master!"

The butler, a dark, stout Dravidian with liquid, yellow-irised eyes like those of a dog, brought the brandy on a brass tray. Flory and Westfield ordered gin. Mr. Lackersteen swallowed a few spoonfuls of brandy and sat back in his chair, groaning in a more resigned way. He had a beefy, ingenuous face, with a toothbrush moustache. He was really a very simple-minded man, with no ambitions beyond having what he called "a good time." His wife governed him by the only possible method, namely, by never letting him out of her sight for more than an hour or two. Only once, a year after they were married, she had left him for a fortnight, and had returned unexpectedly a day before her time, to find Mr. Lackersteen, drunk, supported on either side by a naked Burmese girl, while a third up-ended a whisky bottle into his mouth. Since then she had watched him, as he used to complain, "like a cat over a bloody mousehole." However, he managed to enjoy quite a number of "good times," though they were usually rather hurried ones.

"My Christ, what a head I've got on me this morning," he said. "Call that butler again, Westfield. I've got to have another brandy before my missus gets here. She says she's going to cut my booze down to four pegs a day when our niece gets here. God rot them both!" he added gloomily.

"Stop playing the fool, all of you, and listen to this," said Ellis sourly. He had a queer wounding way of speaking, hardly ever opening his mouth without insulting somebody. He deliberately exaggerated his cockney accent, because of the sardonic tone it gave to his words. "Have you seen this notice of old Macgregor's? A little nosegay for everyone. Maxwell, wake up and listen!"

Maxwell lowered the *Field*. He was a fresh-coloured blond youth of not more than twenty-five or six — very young for the post he held. With his heavy limbs and thick white eyelashes he reminded one of a carthorse colt. Ellis nipped the notice from the board with a neat, spiteful little movement and began reading it aloud. It had been posted by Mr. Macgregor, who, besides being Deputy Commissioner, was secretary of the Club.

"Just listen to this. 'It has been suggested that as there are as yet no Oriental members of this club, and as it is now usual to admit officials of gazetted rank, whether native or European, to membership of most European Clubs, we should consider the question of following this practice in Kyauktada. The matter will be open for discussion at the next general meeting. On the one hand it may be pointed out' — oh, well, no need to wade through the rest of it. He can't even write out a notice without an attack of literary diarrhœa. Anyway, the point's this. He's asking us to break all our rules and take a dear little nigger-boy into this Club. *Dear* Dr. Veraswami, for instance. Dr. Very-slimy, I call him. That *would* be a treat, wouldn't it? Little pot-bellied niggers breathing garlic in your face over the bridge-table. Christ, to think of it! We've got to hang together and put our foot down on this at once. What do you say, Westfield? Flory?"

Westfield shrugged his thin shoulders philosophically. He had sat down at the table and lighted a black, stinking Burma cheroot.

"Got to put up with it, I suppose," he said. "B———s of natives are getting into all the Clubs nowadays. Even the Pegu Club, I'm told. Way this country's going, you know. We're about the last Club in Burma to hold out against 'em."

"We are; and what's more, we're damn well going to go on holding out. I'll die in the ditch before I'll see a nigger in here." Ellis had produced a stump of pencil. With the curious air of spite that some men can put into their tiniest action, he re-pinned the notice on the board and pencilled a tiny, neat "B. F." against Mr. Macgregor's signature — "There, that's what I think of his idea. I'll tell him so when he comes down. What do *you* say, Flory?"

Flory had not spoken all this time. Though by nature anything but a silent man, he seldom found much to say in Club conversations. He had sat down at the table and was reading G. K. Chesterton's article in the *London News,* at the same time caressing Flo's head with his left hand. Ellis, however, was one of those people who constantly nag others to echo their own opinions. He repeated his question, and Flory looked up, and their eyes met. The skin round Ellis's nose suddenly turned so pale that it was almost grey. In him it was a sign of anger. Without any prelude he burst into a stream of abuse that would have been startling, if the others had not been used to hearing something like it every morning.

"My God, I should have thought in a case like this, when it's a question of keeping those black, stinking swine out of the only place where we can enjoy ourselves, you'd have the decency to back me up. Even if that pot-bellied, greasy little sod of a nigger doctor *is* your best pal. *I* don't care if you choose to pal up with the scum of the bazaar. If it pleases you to go to Veraswami's house and drink whisky with all his nigger pals, that's your look-out. Do what you like outside the Club. But, by God, it's a different matter when you talk of bringing niggers in here. I suppose you'd like little Veraswami for a Club member, eh? Chipping into our conversation and pawing everyone with his sweaty hands and breathing his filthy garlic breath in our faces. By God, he'd go out with my boot behind him if ever I saw his black snout inside that door. Greasy, pot-bellied little————!" etc.

This went on for several minutes. It was curiously impressive, because it was so completely sincere. Ellis really did hate Orientals — hated them with a bitter, restless loathing as of something evil or unclean. Living and working, as the assistant of a timber firm must, in perpetual contact with the Burmese, he had never grown used to the sight of a black face. Any hint of friendly feeling towards an Oriental seemed to him a horrible perversity. He was an intelligent man and an able servant of his firm, but he was one of those Englishmen — common, unfortunately — who should never be allowed to set foot in the East.

Flory sat nursing Flo's head in his lap, unable to meet Ellis's eyes. At the best of times his birthmark made it difficult for him to look people straight in the face. And when he made ready to speak, he could feel his voice trembling — for it had a way of trembling when it should have been firm; his features, too, sometimes twitched uncontrollably.

"Steady on," he said at last, sullenly and rather feebly. "Steady on. There's no need to get so excited. *I* never suggested having any native members in here."

"Oh, didn't you? We all know bloody well you'd like to, though. Why else do you go to that oily little babu's house every morning, then? Sitting down at table with him as though he was a white man, and drinking out of glasses his filthy black lips have slobbered over — it makes me spew to think of it."

"Sit down, old chap, sit down," Westfield said. "Forget it. Have a drink on it. Not worth while quarrelling. Too hot."

"My God," said Ellis a little more calmly, taking a pace or two up and down, "my God, I don't understand you chaps. I simply don't. Here's that old fool Macgregor wanting to bring a nigger into this Club for no reason whatever, and you all sit down under it without a word. Good God, what are we supposed to be doing in this country? If we aren't going to rule, why the devil don't we clear out? Here we are, supposed to be governing a set of damn black swine who've been slaves since the beginning of history, and instead of ruling them in the only way they understand, we go and treat them as equals. And all you silly b———s take it for granted. There's Flory, makes his best pal of a black babu who calls himself a doctor because he's done two years at an Indian so-called university. And you, Westfield, proud as Punch of your knock-kneed, bribe-taking cowards of policemen. And there's Maxwell, spends his time running after Eurasian tarts. Yes, you do, Maxwell; I heard about your goings-on in Mandalay with some smelly little bitch called Molly Pereira. I supposed you'd have gone and married her if they hadn't transferred you up here? You all seem to *like* the dirty black brutes. Christ, I don't know what's come over us all. I really don't."

"Come on, have another drink," said Westfield. "Hey, butler! Spot of beer before the ice goes, eh? Beer, butler!"

The butler brought some bottles of Munich beer. Ellis presently sat down at the table with the others, and he nursed one of the cool bottles between his small hands. His forehead was sweating. He was sulky, but not in a rage any longer. At all times he was spiteful and perverse, but his violent fits of rage were soon over, and were never apologised for. Quarrels were a regular part of the routine of Club life. Mr. Lackersteen was feeling better and was studying the illustrations in *La Vie Parisienne*. It was after nine now, and the room, scented with the acrid smoke of Westfield's cheroot, was stifling hot. Everyone's shirt stuck to his back with the first sweat of the day. The invisible *chokra*[3] who pulled the punkah rope outside was falling asleep in the glare.

"Butler!" yelled Ellis, and as the butler appeared, "go and wake that bloody *chokra* up!"

"Yes, master."

---

[3] Person who pulls the punkah rope that moves a large panel to let in a breeze.

"And butler!"

"Yes, master?"

"How much ice have we got left?"

"'Bout twenty pounds, master. Will only last to-day, I think. I find it very difficult to keep ice cool now."

"Don't talk like that, damn you — 'I find it very difficult!' Have you swallowed a dictionary? 'Please, master, can't keeping ice cool' — that's how you ought to talk. We shall have to sack this fellow if he gets to talk English too well. I can't stick servants who talk English. D'you hear, butler?"

"Yes, master," said the butler, and retired.

"God! No ice till Monday," Westfield said. "You going back to the jungle, Flory?"

"Yes. I ought to be there now. I only came in because of the English mail."

"Go on tour myself, I think. Knock up a spot of Travelling Allowance. I can't stick my bloody office at this time of year. Sitting there under the damned punkah, signing one chit after another. Paper-chewing. God, how I wish the war was on again!"

"I'm going out the day after to-morrow," Ellis said. "Isn't that damned padre coming to hold his service this Sunday? I'll take care not to be in for that, anyway. Bloody knee-drill."

"Next Sunday," said Westfield. "Promised to be in for it myself. So's Macgregor. Bit hard on the poor devil of a padre, I must say. Only gets here once in six weeks. Might as well get up a congregation when he does come."

"Oh, hell! I'd snivel psalms to oblige the padre, but I can't stick the way these damned native Christians come shoving into our church. A pack of Madrassi servants and Karen school-teachers. And then those two yellow-bellies, Francis and Samuel — they call themselves Christians too. Last time the padre was here they had the nerve to come up and sit on the front pews with the white men. Someone ought to speak to the padre about that. What bloody fools we were ever to let those missionaries loose in this country! Teaching bazaar sweepers they're as good as we are. 'Please, sir, me Christian same like master.' Damned cheek."

CHINUA ACHEBE

From *Things Fall Apart*

Missionaries, as the previous selection reminds us, were among the
earliest European colonialists. The first missionaries went to the
Americas with the Spanish conquistadors in the decades after Columbus. But long after the conquistadors were replaced by professional
soldiers, administrators, policemen, mining engineers, company
agents, and other representatives of a more bureaucratic and industrial age, the missionaries continued to seek out souls to save beyond
the frontiers of colonial settlement.

In this selection from his novel, *Things Fall Apart*, Chinua Achebe
imagines the arrival and impact of some of the first Anglican missionaries among the Ibo people of Nigeria — his own ancestors — after
1857. What, according to Achebe, were the principal obstacles faced
by the missionaries? What elements in Christianity attracted some
Africans? What elements repelled others? Judging from this selection,
how would you characterize the overall impact of Christianity in
Africa?

Thinking Historically

Unlike Orwell, Achebe is not describing historical events he witnessed, since he is writing about a period before he was born. And yet,
he has a firsthand experience of Ibo culture. How does that experience
make his fiction different from that of Multatuli and Orwell? What
does Achebe's fiction add to a historical understanding of missionaries
in Africa?

The arrival of the missionaries had caused a considerable stir in the village of Mbanta. There were six of them and one was a white man.
Every man and woman came out to see the white man. Stories about
these strange men had grown since one of them had been killed in
Abame and his iron horse tied to the sacred silk-cotton tree. And so
everybody came to see the white man. It was the time of the year when
everybody was at home. The harvest was over.

When they had all gathered, the white man began to speak to them.
He spoke through an interpreter who was an Ibo man, though his di-

Chinua Achebe, *Things Fall Apart* (Oxford: Heinemann, 1958), 101–109.

alect was different and harsh to the ears of Mbanta. Many people laughed at his dialect and the way he used words strangely. Instead of saying "myself" he always said "my buttocks." But he was a man of commanding presence and the clansmen listened to him. He said he was one of them, as they could see from his colour and his language. The other four black men were also their brothers, although one of them did not speak Ibo. The white man was also their brother because they were all sons of God. And he told them about this new God, the Creator of all the world and all the men and women. He told them that they worshipped false gods, gods of wood and stone. A deep murmur went through the crowd when he said this. He told them that the true God lived on high and that all men when they died went before Him for judgment. Evil men and all the heathen who in their blindness bowed to wood and stone were thrown into a fire that burned like palm-oil. But good men who worshipped the true God lived for ever in His happy kingdom. "We have been sent by this great God to ask you to leave your wicked ways and false gods and turn to Him so that you may be saved when you die," he said.

"Your buttocks understand our language," said someone light-heartedly and the crowd laughed.

"What did he say?" the white man asked his interpreter. But before he could answer, another man asked a question: "Where is the white man's horse?" he asked. The Ibo evangelists consulted among themselves and decided that the man probably meant bicycle. They told the white man and he smiled benevolently.

"Tell them," he said, "that I shall bring many iron horses when we have settled down among them. Some of them will even ride the iron horse themselves." This was interpreted to them but very few of them heard. They were talking excitedly among themselves because the white man had said he was going to live among them. They had not thought about that.

At this point an old man said he had a question. "Which is this god of yours," he asked, "the goddess of the earth, the god of the sky, Amadiora of the thunderbolt, or what?"

The interpreter spoke to the white man and he immediately gave his answer. "All the gods you have named are not gods at all. They are gods of deceit who tell you to kill your fellows and destroy innocent children. There is only one true God and He has the earth, the sky, you and me, and all of us."

"If we leave our gods and follow your god," asked another man, "who will protect us from the anger of our neglected gods and ancestors?"

"Your gods are not alive and cannot do you any harm," replied the white man. "They are pieces of wood and stone."

When this was interpreted to the men of Mbanta they broke into derisive laughter. These men must be mad, they said to themselves.

How else could they say that Ani and Amadiora were harmless? And Idemili and Ogwugwu too? And some of them began to go away.

Then the missionaries burst into song. It was one of those gay and rollicking tunes of evangelism which had the power of plucking at silent and dusty chords in the heart of an Ibo man. The interpreter explained each verse to the audience, some of whom now stood enthralled. It was a story of brothers who lived in darkness and in fear, ignorant of the love of God. It told of one sheep out on the hills, away from the gates of God and from the tender shepherd's care.

After the singing the interpreter spoke about the Son of God whose name was Jesu Kristi. Okonkwo, who only stayed in the hope that it might come to chasing the men out of the village or whipping them, now said:

"You told us with your own mouth that there was only one god. Now you talk about his son. He must have a wife, then." The crowd agreed.

"I did not say He had a wife," said the interpreter, somewhat lamely.

"Your buttocks said he had a son," said the joker. "So he must have a wife and all of them must have buttocks."

The missionary ignored him and went on to talk about the Holy Trinity. At the end of it Okonkwo was fully convinced that the man was mad. He shrugged his shoulders and went away to tap his afternoon palm-wine.

But there was a young lad who had been captivated. His name was Nwoye, Okonkwo's first son. It was not the mad logic of the Trinity that captivated him. He did not understand it. It was the poetry of the new religion, something felt in the marrow. The hymn about brothers who sat in darkness and in fear seemed to answer a vague and persistent question that haunted his young soul — the question of the twins crying in the bush and the question of Ikemefuna who was killed. He felt a relief within as the hymn poured into his parched soul. The words of the hymn were like the drops of frozen rain melting on the dry plate of the panting earth. Nwoye's callow mind was greatly puzzled.

The missionaries spent their first four or five nights in the marketplace, and went into the village in the morning to preach the gospel. They asked who the king of the village was, but the villagers told them that there was no king. "We have men of high title and the chief priests and the elders," they said.

It was not very easy getting the men of high title and the elders together after the excitement of the first day. But the missionaries persevered, and in the end they were received by the rulers of Mbanta. They asked for a plot of land to build their church.

Every clan and village had its "evil forest." In it were buried all those who died of the really evil diseases, like leprosy and smallpox. It was also the dumping ground for the potent fetishes of great medicine-men when they died. An "evil forest" was, therefore, alive with sinister forces and powers of darkness. It was such a forest that the rulers of Mbanta gave to the missionaries. They did not really want them in their clan, and so they made them that offer which nobody in his right senses would accept.

"They want a piece of land to build their shrine," said Uchendu to his peers when they consulted among themselves. "We shall give them a piece of land." He paused, and there was a murmur of surprise and disagreement. "Let us give them a portion of the Evil Forest. They boast about victory over death. Let us give them a real battlefield in which to show their victory." They laughed and agreed, and sent for the missionaries, whom they had asked to leave them for a while so that they might "whisper together." They offered them as much of the Evil Forest as they cared to take. And to their greatest amazement the missionaries thanked them and burst into song.

"They do not understand," said some of the elders. "But they will understand when they go to their plot of land tomorrow morning." And they dispersed.

The next morning the crazy men actually began to clear a part of the forest and to build their house. The inhabitants of Mbanta expected them all to be dead within four days. The first day passed and the second and third and fourth, and none of them died. Everyone was puzzled. And then it became known that the white man's fetish had unbelievable power. It was said that he wore glasses on his eyes so that he could see and talk to evil spirits. Not long after, he won his first three converts.

Although Nwoye had been attracted to the new faith from the very first day, he kept it secret. He dared not go too near the missionaries for fear of his father. But whenever they came to preach in the open market-place or the village playground, Nwoye was there. And he was already beginning to know some of the simple stories they told.

"We have now built a church," said Mr Kiaga, the interpreter, who was now in charge of the infant congregation. The white man had gone back to Umuofia, where he built his headquarters and from where he paid regular visits to Mr Kiaga's congregation at Mbanta.

"We have now built a church," said Mr Kiaga, "and we want you all to come in every seventh day to worship the true God."

On the following Sunday, Nwoye passed and re-passed the little red-earth and thatch building without summoning enough courage to enter. He heard the voice of singing and although it came from a handful of men it was loud and confident. Their church stood on a circular clearing that looked like the open mouth of the Evil Forest. Was it waiting to snap its teeth together? After passing and re-passing by the church, Nwoye returned home.

It was well known among the people of Mbanta that their gods and ancestors were sometimes long-suffering and would deliberately allow a man to go on defying them. But even in such cases they set their limit at seven market weeks or twenty-eight days. Beyond that limit no man was suffered to go. And so excitement mounted in the village as the seventh week approached since the impudent missionaries built their church in the Evil Forest. The villagers were so certain about the doom that awaited these men that one or two converts thought it wise to suspend their allegiance to the new faith.

At last the day came by which all the missionaries should have died. But they were still alive, building a new red-earth and thatch house for their teacher, Mr Kiaga. That week they won a handful more converts. And for the first time they had a woman. Her name was Nneka, the wife of Amadi, who was a prosperous farmer. She was very heavy with child.

Nneka had had four previous pregnancies and childbirths. But each time she had borne twins, and they had been immediately thrown away. Her husband and his family were already becoming highly critical of such a woman and were not unduly perturbed when they found she had fled to join the Christians. It was a good riddance.

One morning Okonkwo's cousin, Amikwu, was passing by the church on his way from the neighbouring village, when he saw Nwoye among the Christians. He was greatly surprised, and when he got home he went straight to Okonkwo's hut and told him what he had seen. The women began to talk excitedly, but Okonkwo sat unmoved.

It was late afternoon before Nwoye returned. He went into the *obi* and saluted his father, but he did not answer. Nwoye turned round to walk into the inner compound when his father, suddenly overcome with fury, sprang to his feet and gripped him by the neck.

"Where have you been?" he stammered.

Nwoye struggled to free himself from the choking grip.

"Answer me," roared Okonkwo, "before I kill you!" He seized a heavy stick that lay on the dwarf wall and hit him two or three savage blows.

"Answer me!" he roared again. Nwoye stood looking at him and did not say a word. The women were screaming outside, afraid to go in.

"Leave that boy at once!" said a voice in the outer compound. It was Okonkwo's uncle Uchendu. "Are you mad?"

Okonkwo did not answer. But he left hold of Nwoye, who walked away and never returned.

He went back to the church and told Mr Kiaga that he had decided to go to Umuofia, where the white missionary had set up a school to teach young Christians to read and write.

Mr Kiaga's joy was very great. "Blessed is he who forsakes his father and his mother for my sake," he intoned. "Those that hear my words are my father and my mother."

Nwoye did not fully understand. But he was happy to leave his father. He would return later to his mother and his brothers and sisters and convert them to the new faith.

As Okonkwo sat in his hut that night, gazing into a log fire, he thought over the matter. A sudden fury rose within him and he felt a strong desire to take up his matchet, go to the church, and wipe out the entire vile and miscreant gang. But on further thought he told himself that Nwoye was not worth fighting for. Why, he cried in his heart, should he, Okonkwo, of all people, be cursed with such a son? He saw clearly in it the finger of his personal god or *chi*. For how else could he explain his great misfortune and exile and now his despicable son's behaviour? Now that he had time to think of it, his son's crime stood out in its stark enormity. To abandon the gods of one's father and go about with a lot of effeminate men clucking like old hens was the very depth of abomination. Suppose when he died all his male children decided to follow Nwoye's steps and abandon their ancestors? Okonkwo felt a cold shudder run through him at the terrible prospect, like the prospect of annihilation. He saw himself and his father crowding round their ancestral shrine waiting in vain for worship and sacrifice and finding nothing but ashes of bygone days, and his children the while praying to the white man's god. If such a thing were ever to happen, he, Okonkwo, would wipe them off the face of the earth.

Okonkwo was popularly called the "Roaring Flame." As he looked into the log fire he recalled the name. He was a flaming fire. How then could he have begotten a son like Nwoye, degenerate and effeminate? Perhaps he was not his son. No! He could not be. His wife had played him false. He would teach her! But Nwoye resembled his grandfather, Unoka, who was Okonkwo's father. He pushed the thought out of his mind. He, Okonkwo, was called a flaming fire. How could he have begotten a woman for a son? At Nwoye's age Okonkwo had already become famous throughout Umuofia for his wrestling and his fearlessness.

He sighed heavily, and as if in sympathy the smouldering log also sighed. And immediately Okonkwo's eyes were opened and he saw the whole matter clearly. Living fire begets cold, impotent ash. He sighed again, deeply.

45

RUDYARD KIPLING

The White Man's Burden

This poem, written by Rudyard Kipling (1865–1936), is often presented as the epitome of colonialist sentiment, though some readers see in it a critical, satirical attitude toward colonialism. Do you find the poem to be for or against colonialism? Can it be both?

Thinking Historically

"The White Man's Burden" is a phrase normally associated with European colonialism in Africa. In fact, however, Kipling wrote the poem in response to the annexation of the Philippines by the United States. How does this historical context change the meaning of the poem for you? Does the meaning of a literary work depend on the motives of the writer, the historical context in which it is written, or both?

Take up the White Man's burden —
    Send forth the best ye breed —
Go, bind your sons to exile
    To serve your captives' need;
To wait, in heavy harness,
    On fluttered folk and wild —
Your new-caught sullen peoples,
    Half devil and half child.

Take up the White Man's burden —
    In patience to abide,
To veil the threat of terror
    And check the show of pride;
By open speech and simple,
    An hundred times made plain,
To seek another's profit
    And work another's gain.

Take up the White Man's burden —
    The savage wars of peace —

Rudyard Kipling, "The White Man's Burden," *McClure's Magazine* 12, no. 4 (February 1899): 290–91.

Fill full the mouth of Famine,
    And bid the sickness cease;
And when your goal is nearest
    (The end for others sought)
Watch sloth and heathen folly
    Bring all your hope to nought.

Take up the White Man's burden —
    No iron rule of kings,
But toil of serf and sweeper —
    The tale of common things.
The ports ye shall not enter,
    The roads ye shall not tread,
Go, make them with your living
    And mark them with your dead.

Take up the White Man's burden,
    And reap his own reward —
The blame of those ye better
    The hate of those ye guard —
The cry of hosts ye humour
    (Ah, slowly!) toward the light: —
"Why brought ye us from bondage,
    Our loved Egyptian night?"

Take up the White Man's burden —
    Ye dare not stoop to less —
Nor call too loud on Freedom
    To cloke your weariness.
By all ye will or whisper,
    By all ye leave or do,
The silent sullen peoples
    Shall weigh your God and you.

Take up the White Man's burden!
    Have done with childish days —
The lightly-proffered laurel,
    The easy ungrudged praise:
Comes now, to search your manhood
    Through all the thankless years,
Cold, edged with dear-bought wisdom,
    The judgment of your peers.

46

JOSÉ RIZAL

From *Noli Me Tangere*

Widely regarded as the great national Filipino novel, *Noli Me Tangere* (Latin for "touch me not") was published in 1887. It introduces the reader to a broad spectrum of life in colonial Manila just before the outbreak of the revolution against Spanish colonialism in 1896.

The selection begins with the opening scene of the novel: a party thrown by Don Santiago de los Santos. Notice the distinctions that are made between the Spanish and the Filipino "natives." Like other colonial worlds, the Philippines was a dual world, at least in the minds of those from Spain. But here we are reminded that not all natives are poor or powerless.

In the second part of the selection, the hero Ibarra, who has just left the dinner party given in his honor after a seven-year absence in Europe, learns how his father died. What does this reading suggest about the meaning of *Spaniard* and *native* in a colony approaching rebellion? How is it possible that a wealthy, well-connected Spaniard can be thought more subversive than a poor native?

Thinking Historically

Noli Me Tangere uniquely prefigured, reflected, and made history. When it was published in 1887, it was condemned as "heretical" and "subversive" by the Catholic Church and banned by the government, but it gave rise to a nationalist movement, and revolution in 1896 echoed the novel. For his prescience and presumed subversion, Rizal was arrested and executed in 1896.

Rizal's novel helped shape a Philippine national identity. When he formed the national organization called Filipino League in 1892, the Philippines (named after the Spanish King Philip) comprised thousands of islands of "Indios" in what was called "overseas Spain." Different indigenous peoples were identified by their particular island, region, dialect, or language. Rizal's novel helped to give people a sense of nationhood.

In one important respect, Rizal's fictional revolution was not the one that occurred. Instead of the national movement of middle-class intellectuals that Rizal envisioned, the revolution of 1896, led by Emilio Aguinaldo, galvanized the poor. And yet when Aguinaldo pro-

José Rizal, *Noli Me Tangere*, trans. Leon Ma Guerrero (New York: Norton, 1961), 1–8.

claimed the independence of the Philippines in 1898, creating the first republic in Asia, and became president in 1899, his support cut across all social classes and ethnic groups. How was this national unity a predictable consequence of the Manila that Rizal described in the novel? How does a work of fiction become a blueprint for history? To what extent do people use fictional characters or situations as models of behavior?

The United States did not accept Philippine independence. In its own imperial quest at the end of the century, the United States demanded the transfer of the Philippines from the defeated Spanish at the end of the Spanish-American War of 1898. U.S. troops captured President Aguinaldo in 1901 and brought an end to the ensuing guerrilla resistance the following year. How does Kipling's poem, "The White Man's Burden," apply to the U.S. seizure of the Philippines?

A Party

Don Santiago de los Santos was giving a dinner party one evening towards the end of October in the 1880's. Although, contrary to his usual practice, he had let it be known only on the afternoon of the same day, it was soon the topic of conversation in Binondo, where he lived, in other districts of Manila, and even in the Spanish walled city of Intramuros. Don Santiago was better known as Capitan Tiago — the rank was not military but political, and indicated that he had once been the native mayor of a town. In those days he had a reputation for lavishness. It was well known that his house, like his country, never closed its doors — except, of course, to trade and any idea that was new or daring.

So the news of his dinner party ran like an electric shock through the community of spongers, hangers-on, and gate-crashers whom God, in His infinite wisdom, had created and so fondly multiplied in Manila. Some of these set out to hunt polish for their boots; others, collar-buttons and cravats; but one and all gave the gravest thought to the manner in which they might greet their host with the assumed intimacy of long-standing friendship, or, if the occasion should arise, make a graceful apology for not having arrived earlier where presumably their presence was so eagerly awaited.

The dinner was being given in a house on Anloague Street which may still be recognised unless it has tumbled down in some earthquake. Certainly it will not have been pulled down by its owner; in the Philippines, that is usually left to God and Nature. In fact, one often thinks that they are under contract to the Government for just that purpose. The house was large enough, in a style common to those parts. It was situated in that section of the city which is crossed by a branch of the Pasig river, called by some the creek of Binondo, which, like all rivers of Manila at that time, combined the functions of public bath, sewer, laundry, fishery, waterway, and, should the Chinese water-pedlar find it convenient, even a source of drinking water. For a stretch of almost a kilometre this vital artery, with its bustling traffic and bewildering activity, hardly counted with one wooden bridge, and this one was under repair at one end for six months, and closed to traffic at the other end for the rest of the year. Indeed, in the hot season, carriage horses had been known to avail themselves of the situation and to jump into the water at this point, to the discomfiture of any day-dreamer in their vehicles who had dozed off while pondering the achievements of the century.

On the evening in question a visitor would have judged the house to be rather squat; its lines, not quite correct, although he would have hesitated to say whether this was due to the defective eyesight of its architect or to earthquake and typhoon. A wide staircase, green-banistered and partly carpeted, rose from the tiled court at the entrance. It led to the main floor along a double line of potted plants and flower vases set on stands of Chinese porcelain, remarkable for their fantastical colours and designs.

No porter or footman would have asked the visitor for his invitation card; he would have gone up freely, attracted by the strains of orchestra music and the suggestive tinkle of silver and china, and perhaps, if a foreigner, curious about the kind of dinner parties that were given in what was called the Pearl of the Orient.

Men are like turtles; they are classified and valued according to their shells. In this, and indeed in other respects, the inhabitants of the Philippines at that time were turtles, so that a description of Capitan Tiago's house is of some importance. At the head of the stairs the visitor would have found himself in a spacious entrance hall, serving for the occasion as a combination of music- and dining-room. The large table in the centre, richly and profusely decorated, would have been winking delectable promises to the uninvited guest at the same time that it threatened the timid and naïve young girl with two distressing hours in close company with strangers whose language and topics of conversation were apt to take the most extraordinary lines. In contrast with these earthly concerns would have been the paintings crowded on the walls, depicting such religious themes as *Purgatory, Hell, The Last Judgment, The Death of the Just Man,* and *The Death of the Sinner,* and, in the place of honour, set off by an elegant and splendid frame carved in the Renaissance style by the most renowned woodworker of the day, a strange canvas of formidable dimensions in which were to be seen two old crones, with the inscription: *Our Lady of Peace and Happy Voyage, Venerated in Antipolo, Visits in the Guise of a Beggar the Pious and Celebrated Capitana Inés, Who Lies Gravely Ill.* This composition made up for its lack of taste and artistry with a realism that some might have considered extreme; the blue and yellow tints of the patient's face suggested a corpse in an advanced state of decomposition, and the tumblers and other receptacles which were about her, the cortège of long illnesses, were reproduced so painstakingly as to make their contents almost identifiable. The sight of these paintings, so stimulating to the appetite, and so evocative of carefree ease, might have led the visitor to think that his cynical host had formed a very shrewd opinion of the character of his guests; and that indeed it was only to disguise his judgment that he had hung the room about with charming Chinese lanterns, empty bird-cages, silvered crystal balls in red, green, and blue, slightly withered air-plants, stuffed fishes, and other such decorations, the whole coming to a point in fanciful wooden arches, half Chinese, half European, which framed the side of the room overlooking the river, and gave a glimpse of a porch with trellises and kiosks dimly lighted by multi-coloured paper lanterns.

The dinner guests were gathered in the main reception room which had great mirrors and sparkling chandeliers. On a pinewood platform stood enthroned a magnificent grand piano, for which an exorbitant price had been paid, and which this night seemed more precious still because nobody was presumptuous enough to play on it. There was also a large portrait in oils of a good-looking man in a frock coat, stiff and straight, as well-balanced as the tasselled cane of office between his rigid ring-covered fingers, who seemed to be saying: "See what a lot of clothes I have on, and how dignified I look!"

The furniture was elegant; uncomfortable, perhaps, and not quite suited to the climate, but then the owner of the house would have been thinking of self-display rather than the health of his guests, and would have told them: "Shocking thing, this dysentery, I know, but after all you are now seated in armchairs come straight from Europe, and you can't always do that, can you?"

The salon was almost full, the men segregated from the women as in Catholic churches and in synagogues. The few ladies were mostly young girls, some Filipinas, Spaniards the others, hastily covering their mouths with their fans when they felt a yawn coming on, and scarcely saying a word. If someone ventured to start a conversation it died out in monosyllables, not unlike the night-noises of mice and lizards. Did the images of Our Lady in her various appellations, which hung from the walls in between the mirrors, oblige them to keep this curious silence and devout demeanour, or were women in the Philippines in those times simply an exception?

Only one took the trouble of making the lady guests welcome; she was a kindly-faced old woman, a cousin of Capitan Tiago, who spoke Spanish rather badly. Her hospitality and good manners did not extend beyond offering the Spanish ladies cigars and betel-nut chew on a tray, and giving her hand to be kissed by her compatriots, exactly like a friar. The poor old woman ended up by becoming thoroughly bored, and, hearing the crash of a broken plate, hurriedly seized the excuse to leave the room, muttering:

"*Jesús!* Just you wait, you wretches!"

She never came back.

The men, however, were already in higher spirits. In one corner a number of cadets were vivaciously whispering to one another, sharing scarcely muffled laughs as they glanced about the room, sometimes pointing openly to this or that person. On the other hand two foreigners, dressed in white, went striding up and down the salon, their hands clasped behind them, and without exchanging a single word, exactly like bored passengers pacing the deck of a ship. The centre of interest and liveliness seemed to be a group composed of two priests, two laymen, and an officer, who were at a small table with wine and English biscuits.

The officer was an ageing lieutenant, Guevara by name, tall, stern, with the air of a Duke of Alba left stranded in the lower ranks of the Constabulary roster. He said little, but what he said was heard to be sharp and brief. One of the friars was a young Dominican, Father Sibyla, handsome, well-groomed, and as bright as his gold-rimmed glasses. He had an air of premature gravity. Parish priest of Binondo, and formerly a professor at the Dominican College of San Juan de Letrán, he had the reputation of being a consummate casuist, so much so that in other times, when members of his Order still dared to match subtleties with laymen, the most skilful debater among the latter had never succeeded in trapping or confusing him; the agile distinctions of Father Sibyla had made his antagonist look like a fisherman trying to catch eels with a piece of string. The Dominican seemed to weigh his words and they were few.

By way of contrast, the other friar, a Franciscan, was a man of many words and even more numerous gestures. Although his hair was greying, his robust constitution seemed well preserved. His classic features, penetrating look, heavy jaws, and herculean build, gave him the appearance of a Roman patrician in disguise, and recalled one of those three monks in the German story who in the September equinox would cross a Tyrolean lake at midnight, and each time place in the hand of the terror-stricken boatman a silver coin, cold as ice. However, Father Dámaso was not so mysterious as that; he was a jovial man, and if the tone of his voice was rough, like that of a man who has never held his tongue and who thinks that what he says is dogma and beyond question, his frank and jolly laugh erased this disagreeable impression; one could even forgive him when he thrust out toward the company a naked pair of hairy legs that would have made a fortune at the freak-show of any suburban fair.

One of the civilians, Mr Laruja, was a small man with a black beard whose only notable feature was a nose so large that it seemed to belong to an entirely different person. The other was a fair-haired young man, apparently a newcomer to the country, who was just then engaged in an excited discussion with the Franciscan.

"You'll see," said the latter. "A few more months in this country, and you'll be agreeing with me; it's one thing to govern from Madrid, and quite another to make-do in the Philippines."

"But . . ."

"Take me, for example," Father Dámaso continued, raising his voice to keep the floor, "I've had twenty-three years of rice and bananas, and I can speak with authority on the matter. Don't come to me with theories and rhetoric; I know the natives. Listen, when I first arrived, I was assigned to a town, small it's true, but very hard-working in the fields. At that time I didn't know much Tagalog, but I was already hearing the women's Confessions; we understood one another, if you see what I mean. Well, sir, they came to like me so much that three years later, when I was transferred to a larger parish, left vacant by the death of a native priest, you should have seen all those women! They broke down and cried, they loaded me with presents, they saw me off with brass bands!"

"But that only goes to show . . ."

"Just a moment, one moment! Hold your horses! Now, my successor served a shorter time, and when he left, why, sir, he had an even greater escort, more tears were shed, more music played, and that in spite of the fact that he used to flog them more and had doubled the parish fees!"

"Permit me . . ."

"And that isn't all. Some time after, I served in the town of San Diego for twenty years; it's only a few months since I . . . left it." The recollection seemed to depress and anger him. "Well, twenty years! Nobody will deny that's time enough to know *any* town. There were six thousand souls in San Diego, and I couldn't have known each and every one of them better if I had given them birth and suck myself. I knew in which foot this little fellow limped, or where the shoe pinched that other little fellow, who was making love to that other dusky lady, and how many love affairs still another one had, and with whom, mind you, and who was the real father of this or that little urchin; all that sort of thing — after all, I was hearing the Confessions of each and every one of those rascals; they knew they had better be careful about fulfilling their religious duties, believe me. Santiago, our host, can tell you I'm speaking the honest truth; he has a lot of property there; in fact that is where we got to be friends. Well, sir, just to show you what the native is really like: When I left, there was scarcely a handful of old crones and lay members of our Order to see me off! That, after twenty years!"

"But I don't see the connection between this and the abolition of the tobacco monopoly," complained the new arrival when the Franciscan paused to refresh himself with a glass of sherry.

Father Dámaso was so taken aback that he almost dropped the glass. He glared at the young man for some time, and then exclaimed with unfeigned shock:

"What? How's that? But is it possible that you can't see what's clearer than daylight? Don't you see, my dear boy, that all this is tangible proof that the reforms proposed by the Ministers in Madrid are mad?"

It was the young man's turn to be puzzled. Beside him Lieutenant Guevara deepened his frown, while Mr Laruja moved his head ambiguously, uncertain whether to nod approval or shake disapproval of Father Dámaso. The Dominican, Father Sibyla, for his part, merely turned away from them.

"You believe . . ." the young Spaniard finally managed to blurt out, his face grave and inquiring.

"Believe it? Just as I believe in Holy Gospel! The native is so lazy!"

"Excuse me," said the new arrival, lowering his voice and drawing his chair closer. "What you have just said interests me very much indeed. Are the natives really *born* lazy? Or was that foreign traveller right who said that we Spaniards use this charge of laziness to excuse our own, as well as to explain the lack of progress and policy in our colonies? He was, of course, speaking of other colonies of ours, but I think the inhabitants there belong to the same race as these people."

"Rubbish! Pure envy! Mr Laruja here knows the country as well as I do; ask him, go on, ask him if the ignorance and laziness of these fellows can be matched."

"Quite right," Mr Laruja agreed promptly, "there is nobody lazier anywhere in the whole wide world than the native of these parts."

"None more vicious, or more ungrateful!"

"Or so ill-bred!"

The fair-haired young man looked uneasily around him.

"Gentlemen," he whispered, "I believe we are in the house of a native. Those young ladies . . ."

A Subversive Heretic

After leaving the dinner party Ibarra hesitated at the threshold of Capitan Tiago's house. The night air, already chilly at that time of year in Manila, seemed to clear his head. He bared his brow to the breeze, sighed, and went off toward the square of Binondo, looking searchingly about him.

Private carriages dashed past hansom cabs, their horses at a walk while waiting for a fare, and pedestrians of all nationalities. The streets looked exactly the same as when he had seen them last, with the same white-washed stucco-faced houses trimmed with blue. The lighted clock on the church tower, the Chinese corner-stores with their grimy curtains and iron railings, were all the same — even to the rail he himself had twisted out of shape one night as a prank.

"We go slow," he said to himself, turning down De la Sacristía Street.

Ice-cream pedlars were crying out their wares as of old, and the same kerosene lamps lighted the old fruit and vegetable stalls.

"Amazing," he thought, "why, that's the same Chinaman I saw there seven years ago, and that old woman . . . still there! It might've been last night, and I could have dreamed those seven years in Europe. And, good God, there's that cobblestone, just as I left it."

There it was indeed, dislodged from the sidewalk at the corner of San Jacinto and De la Sacristía.

He was thus pondering the phenomenon of an unchanging city in a country of uncertainties, when he felt the gentle touch of a hand on his shoulder. He turned and found himself face to face with Lieutenant Guevara, whose habitually hard frown had now softened almost into amiability.

"Watch your step, young fellow," he said. "Learn from your father."

"I beg your pardon, but you seem to have thought a lot of my father; could you tell me how and where he died?" asked Ibarra.

"What!" exclaimed the officer. "Don't you know?"

"I asked Don Santiago, but he put off telling me until tomorrow. Do you yourself happen to know?"

"Of course. Like everybody else. He died in prison."

The young man fell back a step, and stared astonished at the lieutenant.

"In prison? Who died in prison?"

"My dear sir, your father, of course." The officer seemed puzzled.

"My father in prison? What are you saying? Do you realise who my father was?" The young man was so distraught that he had seized the officer by the arm.

"I think I know," he replied. "Don Rafael Ibarra. You told me so yourself earlier this evening."

"Yes, Don Rafael Ibarra."

"But I thought you knew," Guevara protested pityingly, conscious of the turmoil in Ibarra's mind. "I supposed that . . . But come now, face it! In this country it's an honour to have gone to prison."

"You cannot be joking; I suppose I must believe you," said Ibarra in a strangled tone after a short silence. "Can you tell me why he was in prison?"

The old man reflected.

"Odd you should know so little about your family affairs."

"In his last letter, a year ago, my father asked me not to worry if I didn't hear from him; he said he expected to be very busy. He commended me to my studies, and sent his blessing."

"Then he must have written to you shortly before he died. It will be a year since he was buried in your home town."

"But why was my father imprisoned?"

"For a very honourable cause. But I'm due at the barracks. Come with me, take my arm, and I'll tell you as we go along."

This was the story he told.

"As you know yourself, your father was the richest man in your province, and, although he was loved and honoured by many, others hated or envied him. Unfortunately, those of us Spaniards who come to the Philippines aren't always what we should be. I mean not only your father's enemies, but one of your own grandparents, as you shall see. The continual changes in the administration, demoralisation in high places, favouritism, combined with the cheaper fares and shorter trip out here since the Suez Canal was opened, are to blame for everything; the worst elements of the Peninsula come here, and if a good man comes, he is soon corrupted by the present conditions of the country. It was among these Spaniards, including the friars, that your father had his enemies, and they were many.

"Some months after your departure your father began to have trouble with Father Dámaso; I don't really know why. The parish priest accused him of not going to Confession; but then, he hadn't gone to Confession before that, and it hadn't stopped them from being friends, as you yourself will remember. Anyway, Don Rafael was honest and just, more so than many who go to Confession, or hear Confessions, for that matter. He had his own strict code of ethics. When, for instance, we talked about his disagreements with Father Dámaso, he would ask me: "Mr Guevara, do you believe that God forgives a crime, say, a murder, merely upon Confession to a priest, a man who, after all, is bound to secrecy? And what do you say to a confession made in fear of hell, which is an act of mere attrition rather than contrition? Does one win forgiveness by being a coward and shamelessly playing it safe? I have a different idea of God. For myself I think that one wrong does not right another, and forgiveness cannot be won with useless tears or alms to the Church. I put it to you: If I had murdered the father of a family, if I had widowed some unhappy woman and turned happy children into destitute orphans, would I have satisfied divine justice by allowing myself to be hanged, or perhaps by confiding my secret to one sworn never to reveal it, by giving alms to priests who needed it least, by making a cash settlement of any penances imposed, or even by weeping night and day? What good would this have done the widow and the orphans? My conscience tells me that I should have taken in every possible way the place of my victim, dedicating myself, for the whole of my life, to the good of that family for whose misfortunes I was responsible, and even then, even then, who could make amends for the loss of a loving husband and father?" That was the way your father reasoned. He always acted in accordance with these exacting principles. One can truly say he never did anyone a conscious injury; on the contrary, he tried to atone with good deeds for certain injustices which, he said, had been committed by his grandparents. But to return to his troubles with the parish priest; things were beginning to look ugly; Father Dámaso was making allusions to your father from the very pulpit, and, considering that anything might be expected from a man like him, it was a miracle that he didn't name your father outright. I could see that sooner or later things were going to end badly.

"At that time there was a former artillery-man going the rounds in your province. He was so gross and stupid that he had been dismissed from the service, and, since he had to make a living and could not be allowed to do manual work, which would have hurt our prestige, someone gave him the job of collecting the tax on vehicles. This oaf had no schooling at all, and the natives soon found out. To them a Spaniard who didn't know how to read and write was a freak. So they all took to making fun of the poor wretch, who had to pay with humiliations for the taxes he collected. He knew he was the butt of their jokes, which further soured his already rough and evil temper. They would give him papers upside down; he would pretend to read them, and then would sign on the most likely blank space — and when I say sign, I mean he would make a series of clumsy squiggles. The natives paid their taxes, but they had their fun; he swallowed his pride, but collected. In this frame of mind he was in no mood to give anyone his due of respect, and he even had very harsh exchanges with your father.

"One day he was given an official paper in a shop, and he was turning it over and over trying to put it straight, when a schoolboy burst out laughing, pointing him out to his mates. Our man heard them laugh, and looking round him, he saw that people were trying hard to keep a straight face. He lost his temper and turned on the schoolboys. They ran away, mockingly reciting the alphabet as he chased them. He was blind with rage and, when he could not catch them up, he hurled his stick at them. It hit one of the boys on the head and knocked him down. The wretched tax-collector promptly ran up to him, and started kicking him; none of those who had been having such fun now dared to step in. Unfortunately, your father happened to be passing by. He was shocked and, seizing the tax-collector by the arm, was remonstrating

with him when the latter, still in a rage, started a wild swing. Your father did not give him time to finish it and, with the strength of a true
descendant of Basques . . . well, some say that he hit him, others, that
he did no more than give him a push. In any case the tax-collector staggered and fell a few feet away, hitting his head against a stone. Don
Rafael calmly lifted the hurt child in his arms and took him to the
town-hall. The tax-collector was throwing up blood; he never recovered consciousness and died a few minutes later. Naturally, the police
intervened, your father was imprisoned, and all his hidden enemies
showed their heads. All sorts of lies began to pour in; he was accused of
heresy and sedition. Heresy is always a very serious charge; more so in
this case, because the governor of the province at that time was a man
who made a great show of piety, even saying the Rosary in church in a
loud voice and with his servants for a chorus, perhaps so everyone
hearing him would start praying too. But subversion of the established
order is even worse than heresy, or the murder of *three* tax-collectors
capable of reading, writing, and making philosophical distinctions.
Your father was deserted by all; his papers and books were confiscated.
He was accused of subscribing to the *Overseas Mail* and other newspapers from Madrid, of having sent you to the German — and therefore
Protestant — part of Switzerland, of having in his possession a photograph and even letters from a native priest executed for complicity in
rebellion — and I don't know what else. Everything they could think of
was charged against him: even the fact that, being of Spanish blood, he
dressed like a native. Perhaps, if your father had been someone else,
he would have been released in a short time. One physician attributed
the tax-collector's death to apoplexy. But your father's great wealth, his
faith in justice, and his hatred of the illegal and the unjust, ruined him.
I did all I could; I hate begging favours, but I went to see the Governor
General himself, the predecessor of the present one, and submitted to
him that a man like your father, who took into his own house and fed
every Spaniard who was poor or homeless, and in whose veins there
ran good Spanish blood, could not be guilty of subversion. I offered to
stand surety for him. I swore to his innocence by my poverty and my
military honour. But all I got was a cold reception, an even colder dis-
missal, and the reputation of being a crank.

"Your father asked me to take charge of his case. I first applied to a
young but already famous Filipino lawyer. He refused to undertake
your father's defence. "I would be ruined," he told me. "If I took the
case, that very fact could be made into a new charge against him, and
perhaps against myself." He suggested that I engage a Spanish lawyer,
and named one who was a fluent and forceful orator and enjoyed an
immense prestige. I did so, and renowned counsel accepted the defence,
which he carried out masterfully, brilliantly. But your father's enemies
were many, some of them hidden and unknown. There were plenty of

false witnesses, and their lies, which in other cases would have been exploded with a jibe from counsel, were now given credit for solidity and consistency. If counsel succeeded in discrediting them by showing their contradictions not only with each other, but even in themselves, new charges soon took the place of the old ones. He was accused of illegal and inequitable usurpation of many of his properties; indemnities and damages were demanded; he was said to have connections with bandits to buy protection for his fields and his herds. In short, the case became so complicated that after a year nobody could make head or tail of it. The governor left his post; his successor had a reputation for justice, but, alas, did not stay in office for more than a few months; and his successor, in turn, was too fond of fast horses.

"Your father's sufferings and disappointments, the rigours of prison, or perhaps grief at such ingratitude, broke his iron constitution, and he fell ill, of such an illness as only death can heal. He died in prison, with nobody by his side, just when everything was coming to an end, when he was about to be acquitted both of sedition and of murder. I arrived in time to see him die."

The old man fell silent. Ibarra had not said a word. They had reached the barracks gate. The officer paused and put out his hand.

"Ask Capitan Tiago for the details, my boy. And now, good-night. I must go in and see what's new."

Silently but with emotion, Ibarra gripped the withered old hand, and followed him with his eyes until he was lost from sight.

He turned slowly and hailed a passing carriage.

"Hotel Lala," he ordered, in an almost unintelligible voice.

"This chap must be just out of gaol," thought the coachman, whipping up his horses.

REFLECTIONS

All the novels excerpted in this chapter are well worth reading in their entirety, and many other excellent colonial novels can be chosen from this period as well as from the 1930s and 1940s. E. M. Forster's *A Passage to India* and Paul Scott's *The Raj Quartet* stand out as fictional introductions to British colonialism in India. (Both have also received excellent adaptations to film, the latter as the series for television called *The Jewel in the Crown*.) In addition to Chinua Achebe, Amos Tutuola and Wole Soyinka have written extensively on Nigeria; as well, Francis Bebey, Ferdinand Oyono, and Mongo Beti address French colonialism in Africa. On South Africa, the work of Alan Payton, Andre Brink, J. M. Coetzee, Peter Abrams, and James McClure, among many others, stands out.

The advantage of becoming engrossed in a novel is that we feel part of the story and have a sense that we are learning something firsthand. Of course, we are reading a work of fiction, not gaining firsthand experience or reading an accurate historical account of events. A well-made film poses an even greater problem. Its visual and aural impact imparts a psychological reality that becomes part of our experience. If it is about a subject of which we know little, the film quickly becomes our "knowledge" of the subject, and this knowledge may be incomplete or inaccurate.

On the other hand, a well-written novel or film can whet our appetite and inspire us to learn more. Choose and read a novel about colonialism or some other historical subject. Then, read a biography of the author or research his or her background to determine how much the author knew about the subject. Next, read a historical account of the subject. How much attention does the historian give to the novelist's subject? How does the novel add depth to the historical account? How does the historical account place the novel in perspective? Finally how does the author's background place the novel in historical context?

9

Nationalism and Westernization

The Philippines, Japan, India, and China, 1880–1930

HISTORICAL CONTEXT

As the peoples of Asia and Africa adapted to Western colonialism or struggled to free themselves from it, they inevitably faced the issue of Westernization. To become Westernized was to accept and adopt the ways of the powerful colonial powers of the West: Western Europe and its more distant western offshoot, the United States. All colonized peoples were exposed to some degree of Western education, indoctrination, or control. As they sought their independence and worked to create their own national identities, they frequently revived older indigenous traditions, languages, and religions — ideas that had fallen into disuse or had been replaced by Western culture. This rebirth of traditional culture often meant a specific and determined rejection of Western ways.

This chapter explores a number of Asian responses to Westernization at the end of the nineteenth and the beginning of the twentieth century. The first selection gives an overall picture of how these societies came to grips with the West, culturally as well as politically. In every case, a people who sought its own national identity had to determine the degree of Westernization, if any, it desired to retain. Selection 48 explores the challenges of forming a national identity in a colonial environment by examining the life and work of one man, José Rizal of the Philippines.

Selections 49 and 50 examine Westernization in Japan, a country that was never colonized but that experienced cultural discord as it strove to "catch up" with the West. Japan's economic and industrial

313

Westernization was so successful that Japan was deemed a Western power. What was the range of attitudes toward the West in Japan, and how strong was the impact of Westernization on its people?

We next turn to India for comparison. While Japan adopted Western ways in its successful effort to escape Western colonization, India's colonization by the British led to various forms of Westernization. However, the Westernization of India was not a monolithic process, as selections 51–53 illustrate. There were both English colonials who opposed it and Indians who favored it. India was more fully Westernized than Japan, but its opposition to Westernization was more intense and eventually provided a foundation for rejecting British rule.

Finally, we compare China with India and Japan, as the degree of China's colonization fell somewhere between the two. China also had an ancient cultural tradition and a long imperial political history. Borrowing from non-Chinese cultures seemed a far-fetched proposition. And yet, rather suddenly, in the beginning of the twentieth century, Chinese intellectuals jettisoned age-old elements of Confucian and imperial traditions to embark on a new history, largely modeled on Western political ideas (first Franco-American and then Russian) and staffed and financed by overseas Chinese in Europe and the United States.

What accounted for the appeal of the West in these different settings? Consider the label "the West." It can include the United States as well as Europe (Eastern Europe as well as Western Europe) and possibly even Japan. Did the intellectuals of Japan, China, and India mean the same thing by the West? Did the Westernizers seek to imitate different aspects of the West? And what motivated those who rejected the West? Did they have similar or different agendas?

THINKING HISTORICALLY
Appreciating Contradictions

The process of Westernization, like the experience of conquest and colonization that often preceded it, was wrought with conflict and led to frequent contradictions. Often, the struggle for national independence meant the borrowing of Western practices, words, even languages. In India, for instance, English was the only common language of all educated Indians. Therefore, it is not surprising that contradictory behavior and ambivalent relationships were endemic in the postcolonial world, just as they had been under colonialism. These contradictions usually manifested themselves in an individual's cultural identity. How do colonized persons adopt Western ways, embrace traditional culture, and not feel as though their identity has been divided between the two? Such individuals do not fit entirely into either world and so cannot help but be torn between who they were and who they have become. The somewhat anguished experiences of these colonized people are difficult to understand. We typically want to accept one view or another, to praise or to blame. But as we have learned, the history of peoples and nations is rarely that clear. In examining some of the fundamental contradictions in the history of Westernization, we might better understand how people were variously affected.

There is a tradition of historical thought, associated with the philosophies of G. W. F. Hegel and Karl Marx, which maintains that contradictions are the driving force of history. Contradictions are products of the historical process, results of social and cultural forces. Hegel and Marx would call this attention to how contradictions emerge, compete, and lead both to new levels of understanding and to new contradictions "thinking dialectically." We will content ourselves with identifying and appreciating contradictions in the following selections.

47

THEODORE VON LAUE

From *The World Revolution of Westernization*

Western colonialism, according to von Laue, a modern historian, brought about a "world revolution of Westernization," the victory of Western culture that accompanied Western political domination. What, according to von Laue, are these Western ideas that spread throughout the world during the nineteenth century? Did these ideas spread peacefully or were they forced on non-Western peoples? What groups of people were most attracted to Western ideas? Why did some non-Western people prefer Western culture to their own?

Does von Laue believe that this "world revolution" was a good thing? Does he believe it is over? What, according to von Laue, must still be done?

Theodore von Laue, *The World Revolution of Westernization* (New York: Oxford University Press, 1987), 27–34.

Thinking Historically

Von Laue is particularly interested in the plight of what he calls the "Westernized non-Western intelligentsia." Who are these people? What is their problem? What does von Laue mean when he says that "as a result of their Westernization they became anti-Western nationalists"? How could Westernization make people anti-Western?

Throughout this selection, von Laue discusses paradoxical or ironic behavior. He writes of people learning lessons that were not formally taught and of psychological conflicts or love-hate attitudes. At one point he generalizes this phenomenon of seemingly contradictory behavior by quoting an eighteenth-century maxim that states, "To do just the opposite is also a form of imitation." Is von Laue describing some paradoxical aspect of human nature, or are these conflicts a particular product of colonialism?

While the world revolution of Westernization created a political world order radically above the horizons of all past human experience, it also unhinged, in the revolutionary manner sensed by Lord Lytton,[1] the depths of non-Western societies constituting the bulk of humanity. As he had said, "The application of the most refined principles of European government and some of the most artificial institutions of European society to a . . . vast population in whose history, habits, and traditions they have had no previous existence" was a risky enterprise, perhaps more than he had anticipated.

Examining the history of colonial expansion, one can discern a rough but generally applicable pattern for the revolutionary subversion of non-Western societies. Subversion began at the apex, with the defeat, humiliation, or even overthrow of traditional rulers. The key guarantee of law, order, and security from external interference was thus removed. With it went the continuity of tradition, whether of governance or of all other social institutions down to the subtle customs regulating the individual psyche. Thus ended not only political but also cultural self-determination. Henceforth, the initiatives shaping collective existence came from without, "mysterious formulas of a foreign and more or less uncongenial system" not only of administration but also of every aspect of life.

Once the authority of the ruler (who often was the semi-divine intermediary between Heaven and Earth) was subverted, the Western attack on the other props of society intensified. Missionaries, their se-

---

[1] British viceroy of India from 1876 to 1880.

curity guaranteed by Western arms, discredited the local gods and their guardians, weakening the spiritual foundations of society. At the same time, colonial administrators interfered directly in indigenous affairs by suppressing hallowed practices repulsive to them, including human sacrifice, slavery, and physical cruelty in its many forms. Meanwhile, Western businessmen and their local agents redirected the channels of trade and economic life, making local producers and consumers dependent on a world market beyond their comprehension and control. In a thousand ways the colonial administration and its allies, though not necessarily in agreement with each other, introduced a new set of rewards and punishments, of prestige and authority. The changeover was obvious even in the externals of dress. Africans became ashamed of their nudity, women covered their breasts; Chinese men cut off their queues and adopted Western clothes. The boldest even tried to become like Westerners "in taste, in opinion, in morals, and intellect."

The pathways of subversion here outlined indicate the general pattern and the directions which it followed over time. Its speed depended on Western policy and the resilience of local society. Things seemingly fell apart quickly in the case of the most vulnerable small-scale societies of Africa and much more slowly in India or China, if at all in Japan. Often the colonial administration itself, under the policy of "indirect rule," slowed the Western impact for fear of causing cultural chaos and making trouble for itself. In all cases, tradition (however subverted) persisted in a thousand forms, merely retreating from the external world into the subliminally conditioned responses of the human psyche, its last refuge. It is still lurking in the promptings of "soul" today.

And did things really fall apart? The world revolution of Westernization prevailed by the arts of both war and peace. Certain aspects of Western power possessed an intrinsic appeal which, even by indigenous judgment, enhanced life. New crops often brought ampler food; European rule often secured peace. Through their command of the seas and of worldwide trade Europeans and Americans opened access to survival and opportunity in foreign lands to countless millions of people in China and India. Or take even the persuasion of raw power: Once convinced of the superiority of European weapons, who would not crave possession of them too? And more generally, being associated with European power also carried weight; it patently held the keys to the future. More directly perhaps, doing business with Westerners promised profit. If they played it right, compradors would get rich.

More subtly, certain categories of the local population eagerly took to foreign ways. Missionaries sheltered outcasts: slaves held for sacrifice, girls to be sold into prostitution or abandoned, or married women feeling abused and oppressed. The struggle for sexual equality is still raging in our midst, yet by comparison even Victorian England offered hope to women in Africa or East Asia. Regarding Japan, Fukuzawa[2] related the story of a highborn dowager lady who "had had some unhappy trials in earlier days." She was told of "the most remarkable of all the Western customs . . . the relations between men and women," where "men and women had equal rights, and monogamy was the strict rule in any class of people. . . ." It was, Fukuzawa reported, "as if her eyes were suddenly opened to something new. . . ." As a messenger of women's rights he certainly had Japanese women, "especially the ladies of the higher society," on his side. In China liberated women rushed to unbind their feet.

In addition, the Westerners introduced hospitals and medicines that relieved pain and saved lives, a fact not unappreciated. Besides, whose greed was not aroused by the plethora of Western goods, all fancier than local products: stronger liquor, gaudier textiles, faster transport? Simple minds soon preferred Western goods merely because they were Western. Given the comparative helplessness of local society, was it surprising that everything Western tended to be judged superior?

The Westerners with their sense of mission also introduced their education. It was perhaps not enough, according to anti-Western nationalist suspicious of European desires, to keep the natives down, yet it offered access to Western skills at some sacrifice on the part of teachers willing to forgo the easier life in their own culture. Privileged non-Westerners even attended schools and universities in the West. Thus, as part of the general pattern of Westernization, a new category of cultural half-breeds was created, the Westernized non-Western intelligentsia. It differed somewhat according to cultural origins, but shared a common predicament. Product of one culture, educated in another, it was caught in invidious comparison. As [philosopher] Thomas Hobbes observed "Man, whose Joy consisteth in comparing himselfe with other men, can relish nothing but what is eminent." Riveted to Western pre-eminence, this intelligentsia struggled for purpose, identity, and recognition in the treacherous no-man's-land in between — and most furiously in lands where skin color added to its disabilities. Talented and industrious, these intellectuals threw themselves heroically into the study of Western society and thought so alien to their own.

Along the way they soon acquired a taste for the dominant ideals of the West, foremost the liberal plea for equality, freedom, and self-determination and the socialists' cry of social justice for all exploited and oppressed peoples and classes. They were delighted by the bitter self-criticism they discovered among Westerners — Western society produced many doubters, especially among its fringes in central and eastern Europe. At the same time, non-Western intellectuals quickly

2 See selection 49. [Ed.]

perceived the pride that lurked behind Western humanitarianism. They might be treated as equals in London or Paris, but "east of Aden" on the Indian circuit or anywhere in the colonies, they were "natives" — natives hypersensitive to the hypocrisy behind the Western mission of exporting high ideals without the congenital ingredient of equality. Thus they learned the lessons of power not formally taught by their masters. They needed power — state power — not only to carry the Western vision into practice on their own but also to make equality real.

Inevitably, the non-Western intellectuals turned their lessons to their own use. The ideals of freedom and self-determination justified giving free rein not only to the promptings of their own minds and souls, but also to protests over the humiliation of their countries and cultures. As a result of their Westernization they became anti-Western nationalists, outwardly curtailing, in themselves and their compatriots, the abject imitation of the West. Yet, as an 18th-century German wag had said, "To do just the opposite is also a form of imitation." Anti-Western self-assertion was a form of Westernization copying the cultural self-assertion of the West. Moreover, limiting western influence in fact undercut any chance of matching Western power (and the issue of power was never far from their minds). Thus anti-Western intellectuals were caught in a love-hate attitude toward the West, anti-Western purveyors of further Westernization.

Take Mohandas Gandhi,[3] perhaps the greatest among the Westernized non-Western intellectuals. Born into a prominent tradition-oriented Hindu family and of a lively, ambitious mind, he broke with Hindu taboo and studied English law in London, fashionably dressed and accepted in the best society, though by preference consorting with vegetarians and students of Eastern religion. After his return he confessed that "next to India, [he] would rather live in London than in any other place in the world." From 1892 to 1914, however, he lived in South Africa, using his legal training for defending the local Indian community against white discrimination. There he put together from Indian and Western sources a philosophy as well as a practice of non-violent resistance, strengthening the self-confidence and civil status of his clients. . . .

One of Gandhi's precursors, Narendranath Datta, better known as Swami Vivekananda, had gone even further. At a lecture in Madras he exhorted his audience: "This is the great ideal before us, and everyone must be ready for it — the conquest of the whole world by India — nothing less than that. . . . Up India and conquer the world with your spirituality." Western globalized nationalism, obviously, was working its way around the world, escalating political ambition and cultural messianism to novel intensity. . . .

[3] See selection 52. [Ed.]

. . . [T]he run of Westernized non-Western intellectuals led awkward lives — "in a free state," as [Indian novelist] V. S. Naipaul has put it — forever in search of roots, and certitude; inwardly split, part backward, part Western, camouflaging their imitation of the West by gestures of rejection; forever aspiring to build lofty halfway houses that bridged the disparate cultural universes, often in all-embracing designs, never admitting the fissures and cracks in their lives and opinions; and always covering up their unease with a compensating presumption of moral superiority based on the recognition that the promptings of heart and soul are superior to the dictates of reason. Knowing their own traditions and at least some of the essentials of the West, they sensed that they had a more elevated grasp of human reality; the future belonged to them rather than to the "decadent" West. Out of that existential misery of "heightened consciousness" (as [Russian novelist] Dostoyevsky called it) have come some of the most seminal contributions to the intellectual and political developments of the 20th century, including the anti-Western counterrevolutions.

. . . Let it be said first that the relations between the colonized and the colonizer are exceedingly subtle and complex, subject to keen controversy among all observers, all of them partisans, all of them now judging not by indigenous but by Westernized standards. Western ideals and practices have shaped and intensified the protests of Westernized non-Western intellectuals taking full advantage of the opportunities offered by Western society. Their protests, incidentally, were hardly ever turned against past inhumanities committed by their own kind (because traditionally they were not considered as such).

Next, having already surveyed the not inconsiderable side benefits of Western domination, let us ask: Did the Westerners in their expansion behave toward the non-Westerners worse than they behaved toward themselves? While they never treated their colonial subjects as equals, they never killed as many people in all their colonial campaigns as they did in their own wars at home (the brutality of Europe's cultural evolution has been carefully rinsed out of all current historical accounts). And in their peaceful intercourse with non-Westerners we find the whole range of emotions common in Western society. It was darkness at heart on one extreme and saintliness on the other, and every mix in between, with the balance perhaps tending toward darkness. As one colonial officer in East Africa confided to his diary: "It is but a small percentage of white men whose characters do not in one way or another undergo a subtle process of deterioration when they are compelled to live for any length of time among savage races and under conditions as exist in tropical climates." The colonial district commissioner, isolated among people whose ways sharply contradicted his own upbringing, often suffering from tropical sickness, and scared at heart, found himself perhaps in a worse dilemma than the Westernized non-Western intellectuals. Some of them, no doubt, were unscrupulous opportunists seeking escape from the trammels of civic conformity at home; they turned domineering sadists in the colonies. On the other hand, missionaries often sacrificed their lives, generally among uncomprehending local folk. It was perhaps a credit to the Westerners that the victims of imperialism found considerable sympathy in their own midst. The evils stood out while the good intentions were taken for granted.

Yet — to take a longer view — even compassionate Western observers generally overlook the fact that among all the gifts of the West the two most crucial boons were missing: cultural equality as the basis for political equality and reasonable harmony in the body politic. The world revolution of Westernization perpetuated inequality and ruinous cultural subversion while at the same time improving the material conditions of life. More people survived, forever subject to the agonies of inequality and disorientation resulting from enforced change originating beyond their ken. Collectively and individually, they straddled the border between West and non-West, on the one side enjoying the benefits of Western culture, on the other feeling exploited as victims of imperialism. Indigenous populations always remained backward and dependent, unable to match the resources and skills of a fast-advancing West.

What we should weigh, then, in any assessment of Western colonial expansion before World War I is perhaps not only the actions, good or evil, of the colonial powers, but also the long-run consequences thereafter. The victims of Western colonialism do not include only the casualties of colonial wars but also the far greater multitudes killed or brutalized in the civil commotions in the emerging modern nation-states. Whatever the mitigating circumstances, the anti-Western fury has its justifications indeed.

And yet, in the all-inclusive global perspective, is it morally justified? Was the outreach with all its outrages planned by the Westerners? Was it based on a deliberate design of conquest? Or was it the accidental result of stark imbalances in the resources of power for both war and peace which had come about through circumstances beyond human control? Why were the Westerners so powerful? Their stock answer has been: because of their ideals embedded in their religion, culture, and political institutions, adding up to their overwhelming material superiority. That answer, however, will not suffice for the overview appropriate to this age. In the enlarged contexts of global interaction human beings appear far more helpless than in their smaller settings, where they may claim a measure of control. As argued above, it was merely by historical and geographic accident that the Europeans were enabled to create the cultural hothouse that made them uniquely powerful in the world.

. . . As we now see the grand connections more clearly, we also understand that the burden of responsibility for bringing about cultural equality falls more heavily on those who have been so privileged, so spoiled, by circumstances beyond their control. They have furnished the energies behind the world revolution of Westernization; they carry the obligation to complete it according to their ideals of freedom, equality, and human dignity and in a manner beneficial to all humanity.

48

BENEDICT ANDERSON

The First Filipino

In the following essay Benedict Anderson does more than celebrate José Rizal (1861–1896), the author of the great Filipino novel *Noli Me Tangere*, excerpted in the previous chapter. By calling Rizal "the first Filipino," Anderson explores national identity as a human construct rather than a fact of nature. In any society national identity can be constructed out of strange and contradictory qualities. Why is this especially true in the case of colonial societies? According to Anderson, what were the particular contradictions that shaped José Rizal's identity? In what ways was he "the first Filipino"?

Thinking Historically

Anderson refers to Rizal's phrase "the spectre of comparisons," a haunting inability to see one's own society as it is, but instead to compare it constantly with other societies. Why might a colonial view the world this way? Why might a writer like Rizal be especially vulnerable to the spectre, or ghost, of comparisons in a Spanish colony like the Philippines? Although Rizal described the spectre of comparisons as a kind of handicap, Anderson argues that this double consciousness is the origin of nationalism. What does Anderson mean by this? What is the effect of Anderson's use of comparison in his own writing?

Benedict Anderson, "The First Filipino," in *The Spectre of Comparisons: Nationalism, Southeast Asia and the World* (London: Verso, 1998), 227–30, 232–33.

Few countries give the observer a deeper feeling of historical vertigo than the Philippines. Seen from Asia, the armed uprising against Spanish rule of 1896, which triumphed temporarily with the establishment of an independent republic in 1898, makes it the visionary forerunner of all the other anticolonial movements in the region. Seen from Latin America, it is, with Cuba, the last of the Spanish imperial possessions to have thrown off the yoke, seventy-five years after the rest. Profoundly marked, after three and a half centuries of Spanish rule, by Counter-Reformation Catholicism, it was the only colony in the Empire where the Spanish language never became widely understood. But it was also the only colony in Asia to have had a university in the nineteenth century. In the 1890s barely 3 percent of the population knew "Castilian," but it was Spanish-readers and -writers who managed to turn movements of resistance to colonial rule from hopeless peasant uprisings into a revolution. Today, thanks to American imperialism, and the Philippines' new self-identification as "Asian," almost no one other than a few scholars understands the language in which the revolutionary heroes communicated among themselves and with the outside world — to say nothing of the written archive of pre-twentieth-century Philippine history. A virtual lobotomy has been performed.

The central figure in the revolutionary generation was José Rizal, poet, novelist, ophthalmologist, historian, doctor, polemical essayist, moralist, and political dreamer. He was born in 1861 into a well-to-do family of mixed Chinese, Japanese, Spanish, and Tagalog descent: five years after Freud, four years after Conrad, one year after Chekhov; the same year as Tagore, three years before Max Weber, five before Sun Yat-sen, eight before Gandhi, and nine before Lenin. Thirty-five years later he was arrested on false charges of inciting Andrés Bonifacio's uprising of August 1896, and executed by a firing squad composed of native soldiers led by Spanish officers. The execution was carried out in what is now the beautiful Luneta Park, which fronts the shore line of Manila Bay. (On the other side of the Spanish world, José Marti, the hero of Cuban nationalism, had died in action the previous year.) At the time of Rizal's death, Lenin had just been sentenced to exile in Siberia, Sun Yat-sen had begun organizing for Chinese nationalism outside China, and Gandhi was conducting his early experiments in anticolonial resistance in South Africa.

Rizal had the best education then available in the colony, provided exclusively by the religious Orders, notably the Dominicans and Jesuits. It was an education that he later satirized mercilessly, but it gave him a command of Latin (and some Hebrew), a solid knowledge of classical antiquity, and an introduction to western philosophy and even to medical science. It is again vertiginous to compare what benighted Spain offered with what the enlightened, advanced imperial powers provided in the same Southeast Asian region: no real universities in French

Indochina, the Dutch East Indies, or British Malaya and Singapore till after World War II. From very early on, Rizal exhibited remarkable literary abilities. At the age of nineteen he entered an open literary competition, and won first prize, defeating Spanish rivals writing in their native tongue.

He was growing up at a time when modern politics had begun to arrive in the colony. More than any other imperial power, nineteenth-century Spain was wracked by deep internal conflicts, not merely the endless Carlist wars over the succession, but also between secular liberalism and the old aristocratic-clerical order. The brief liberal triumph in the Glorious Revolution of 1868, which drove the licentious Isabella II from Madrid, had immediate repercussions for the remote Pacific colony. The revolutionaries promptly announced that the benefits of their victory would be extended to the colonies. The renewed ban on the Jesuits and the closure of monastic institutions seemed to promise the end of the reactionary power of the Orders overseas. In 1869, the first "liberal" Captain-General, Carlos María de la Torre, arrived in Manila, it is said to popular cries of "Viva la Libertad!" (How unimaginable is a scene of this kind in British India or French Algeria.) During his two-year rule, de la Torre enraged the old-guard colonial elite, not merely by instituting moves to give equal legal rights to natives, mestizos, and peninsulars, but also by going walkabout in Manila in everyday clothes and without armed guards. The collapse of the Glorious Revolution brought about a ferocious reaction in Manila, however, culminating in 1872 in the public garroting of three secular (i.e. non-Order) priests (one creole, two mestizo), framed for masterminding a brief mutiny in the arsenal of Cavite.

The Rizal family was an immediate victim of the reaction. In 1871, when José was ten years old, his mother was accused of poisoning a neighbour, forced to walk twenty miles to prison, and held there for over two years before being released. His elder brother Paciano, a favourite pupil of Father Burgos, the leader of the garroted priests, narrowly escaped arrest and was forced to discontinue his education. Under these circumstances, in 1882, with his brother's support, José left quietly for the relative freedom of Spain to continue his medical studies.

He spent the next five years in Europe, studying on and off, but also traveling widely — to Bismarck's Germany and Gladstone's England, as well as Austro-Hungary, Italy, and France — and picking up French, German, and English with the ease of an obsessive and gifted polyglot. Europe affected him decisively, in two related ways. Most immediately, he came quickly to understand the backwardness of Spain itself, something which his liberal Spanish friends frequently bemoaned. This put him in a position generally not available to colonial Indians and Vietnamese, or, after the Americans arrived in Manila, to his younger countrymen: that of being able to ridicule the metropolis from the same high ground from which, for generations, the metropolis had ridiculed the natives. More profoundly, he encountered what he later described as *"el demonio de las comparaciones,"* a memorable phrase that could be translated as "the spectre of comparisons." What he meant by this was a new, restless double-consciousness which made it impossible ever after to experience Berlin without at once thinking of Manila, or Manila without thinking of Berlin. Here indeed is the origin of nationalism, which lives by making comparisons.

It was this spectre that, after some frustrating years writing for *La Solidaridad,* the organ of the small group of committed "natives" fighting in the metropole for political reform, led him to write *Noli Me Tangere,* the first of the two great novels for which Rizal will always be remembered. He finished it in Berlin just before midnight on February 21, 1887 — eight months after Gladstone's first Home Rule Bill was defeated, and eight years before *Almayer's Folly* was published. He was twenty-six.

The two most astonishing features of *Noli Me Tangere* are its scale and its style. Its characters come from every stratum of late colonial society, from the liberal-minded peninsular Captain-General down through the racial tiers of colonial society — creoles, mestizos, *chinos* ("pure" Chinese) to the illiterate *indio* masses. Its pages are crowded with Dominicans, shady lawyers, abused acolytes, corrupt policemen, Jesuits, small-town caciques, mestiza schoolgirls, ignorant peninsular carpetbaggers, hired thugs, despairing intellectuals, social-climbing *dévotes,* dishonest journalists, actresses, nuns, gravediggers, artisans, gamblers, peasants, market-women, and so on. (Rizal never fails to give even his most sinister villains their moments of tenderness and anguish.) Yet the geographical space of the novel is strictly confined to the immediate environs of the colonial capital, Manila. The Spain from which so many of the characters have at one time or another arrived is always off stage. This restriction made it clear to Rizal's first readers that "The Philippines" was a society in itself, even though those who lived in it had as yet no common name. That he was the first to imagine this social whole explains why he is remembered today as the First Filipino. . . .

. . . The mother tongue of Rizal was Tagalog, a minority language spoken by perhaps two million people in the multilingual Philippine archipelago, with no tradition of prose writing, and readable by perhaps only a few thousand. He tells us why he wrote in Spanish, a language understood by only 3 percent of his countrymen, when he invokes, *"tú, que me lees, amigo o enemigo"* — "you who read me, friend or enemy." He wrote as much for the enemy as the friend, something that did not happen with the Raj until the work, a century later, of Salman Rushdie.

Rizal could not know it, but there were to be huge costs involved in choosing to write in Spanish. Five years after his martyrdom, a greedy and barbarous American imperialism destroyed the independent Republic of the Philippines, and reduced the inhabitants once again to the status of colonial subjects. American was introduced as the new language of truth and international status, and promoted through an expanding school system. By the eve of World War II, it had (narrowly) become the most widely understood language in the archipelago. Spanish gradually disappeared, so that by the time a quasi-independence was bestowed in 1946, it had become unreadable. Not merely the novels, essays, poetry, and political articles of Rizal himself, but the writings of the whole nation-imagining generation of the 1880s and 1890s had become inaccessible. Today, most of the work of the brilliant anti-colonial propagandist Marcelo del Pilar, of the Revolution's architect Apolinario Mabini, and of the Republic's tragically assassinated general of genius Antonio Luna remain sepulchred in Spanish.

Hence the eerie situation which obliges Filipinos to read the work of the most revered hero of the nation in translation — into local vernaculars, and into American.

49

FUKUZAWA YUKICHI

Good-bye Asia

Fukuzawa Yukichi (1835–1901) was one of the most important Japanese Westernizers during Japan's late-nineteenth-century rush to catch up with the West. The son of a lower samurai (military) family, Fukuzawa left home in 1854 to learn gunnery in the Dutch settlement of Nagasaki. His pursuit of Western knowledge took him to a Dutch school in Osaka, where he studied everything from the Dutch language to chemistry, physics, and anatomy, and to Yedo where he studied English. Due to his privileged background and Western schooling, he was naturally included in the first Japanese mission to the United States in 1860 as well as in the first diplomatic mission

Fukuzawa Yukichi, "Datsu-a Ron" ("On Saying Good-bye to Asia"), in *Japan: A Documentary History,* vol. II, ed. David J. Lu (Armonk, NY: M. E. Sharpe, 1997), 351–53. From Takeuchi Yoshimi, ed. *Azia Shugi (Asianism) Gendai Nihon Shisō Taikei (Great Compilation of Modern Japanese Thought)*, vol. 8 (Tokyo: Chikuma Shobō, 1963), 38–40.

to Europe in 1862. When Fukuzawa returned to Japan, he found him-self to be the target of Japanese assassins who attacked foreigners and Japanese suspected of being sympathizers with foreign ways.

Afraid to go out at night, Fukuzawa spent many years teaching in his school and writing the books that would make him famous. The best known of these was *Seiyo Jijo (Things Western)*, which in 1866 introduced more than two hundred fifty thousand Japanese to the daily life and typical institutions of Western society. For Fukuzawa, the elements of Western success that Japan needed to imitate were sci-entific advancement and independence. According to Fukuzawa, the main obstacle that prevented Japanese society from developing these traits was a long heritage of Chinese Confucianism. Fukuzawa thought that Confucian emphasis on respect and order stifled educa-tional independence.

In the years after the Meiji Restoration of 1868, in which feudalism was abolished and power was restored to the emperor, Fukuzawa be-came the most popular spokesman for the Westernizing policies of the new government. In this essay, "Good-bye Asia," written in 1885, Fukuzawa describes the spread of Western civilization in Japan. Does he believe that it is both inevitable and desirable? Why? What do you make of Fukuzawa's attitude toward Chinese and Korean civiliza-tions? Do you think he is fair in the way he dismisses their potential?

Thinking Historically

Does this selection from Fukuzawa display any of the contradictions, ambivalence, or love-hate feelings that von Laue describes as common among Westernized non-Western intellectuals? Were such conflicts in-evitable? How might someone like Fukuzawa avoid this conflict, am-bivalence, or uncertainty? (A reading of *The Autobiography of Yu-kichi Fukuzawa* is recommended for deeper insight.)

Transportation has become so convenient these days that once the wind of Western civilization blows to the East, every blade of grass and every tree in the East follow what the Western wind brings. Ancient Westerners and present-day Westerners are from the same stock and are not much different from one another. The ancient ones moved slowly, but their contemporary counterparts move vivaciously at a fast pace. This is possible because present-day Westerners take advantage of the means of transportation available to them. For those of us who live in the Orient, unless we want to prevent the coming of Western civiliza-tion with a firm resolve, it is best that we cast our lot with them. If one observes carefully what is going on in today's world, one knows the fu-tility of trying to prevent the onslaught of Western civilization. Why not float with them in the same ocean of civilization, sail the same waves, and enjoy the fruits and endeavors of civilization?

The movement of a civilization is like the spread of measles. Measles in Tokyo start in Nagasaki and come eastward with the spring thaw. We may hate the spread of this communicable disease, but is there any effective way of preventing it? I can prove that it is not possible. In a communicable disease, people receive only damages. In a civilization, damages may accompany benefits, but benefits always far outweigh them, and their force cannot be stopped. This being the case, there is no point in trying to prevent their spread. A wise man encourages the spread and allows our people to get used to its ways.

The opening to the modern civilization of the West began in the reign of Kaei (1848–58). Our people began to discover its utility and gradually and yet actively moved toward its acceptance. However, there was an old-fashioned and bloated government that stood in the way of progress. It was a problem impossible to solve. If the government were allowed to continue, the new civilization could not enter. The modern civilization and Japan's old conventions were mutually exclusive. If we were to discard our old conventions, that government also had to be abolished. We could have prevented the entry of this civilization, but it would have meant loss of our national independence. The struggles taking place in the world civilization were such that they would not allow an Eastern island nation to slumber in isolation. At that point, dedicated men (*shijin*) recognized the principle of "the country is more important than the government," relied on the dignity of the Imperial Household, and toppled the old government to establish a new one. With this, public and the private sectors alike, everyone in our country accepted the modern Western civilization. Not only were we able to cast aside Japan's old conventions, but we also succeeded in creating a new axle toward progress in Asia. Our basic assumptions could be summarized in two words: "Good-bye Asia (*Datsu-a*)."

Japan is located in the eastern extremities of Asia, but the spirit of her people have already moved away from the old conventions of Asia to the Western civilization. Unfortunately for Japan, there are two neighboring countries. One is called China and another Korea. These two peoples, like the Japanese people, have been nurtured by Asiatic political thoughts and mores. It may be that we are different races of people, or it may be due to the differences in our heredity or education; significant differences mark the three peoples. The Chinese and Koreans are more like each other and together they do not show as much similarity to the Japanese. These two peoples do not know how to progress either personally or as a nation. In this day and age with transportation becoming so convenient, they cannot be blind to the manifestations of Western civilization. But they say that what is seen or heard cannot influence the disposition of their minds. Their love affairs with ancient ways and old customs remain as strong as they were centuries ago. In this new and vibrant theater of civilization when we speak of education, they only refer back to Confucianism. As for school education, they can only cite [Chinese philosopher Mencius's] precepts of humanity, righteousness, decorum, and knowledge. While professing their abhorrence to ostentation, in reality they show their ignorance of truth and principles. As for their morality, one only has to observe their unspeakable acts of cruelty and shamelessness. Yet they remain arrogant and show no sign of self-examination.

In my view, these two countries cannot survive as independent nations with the onslaught of Western civilization to the East. Their concerned citizens might yet find a way to engage in a massive reform, on the scale of our Meiji Restoration, and they could change their governments and bring about a renewal of spirit among their peoples. If that could happen they would indeed be fortunate. However, it is more likely that would never happen, and within a few short years they will be wiped out from the world with their lands divided among the civilized nations. Why is this so? Simply at a time when the spread of civilization and enlightenment (*bummei kaika*) has a force akin to that of measles, China and Korea violate the natural law of its spread. They forcibly try to avoid it by shutting off air from their rooms. Without air, they suffocate to death. It is said that neighbors must extend helping hands to one another because their relations are inseparable. Today's China and Korea have not done a thing for Japan. From the perspectives of civilized Westerners, they may see what is happening in China and Korea and judge Japan accordingly, because of the three countries' geographical proximity. The governments of China and Korea still retain their autocratic manners and do not abide by the rule of law. Westerners may consider Japan likewise a lawless society. Natives of China and Korea are deep in their hocus pocus of nonscientific behavior. Western scholars may think that Japan still remains a country dedicated to the *yin* and *yang* and five elements.[1] Chinese are mean-spirited and shameless, and the chivalry of the Japanese people is lost to the Westerners. Koreans punish their convicts in an atrocious manner, and that is imputed to the Japanese as heartless people. There are many more examples I can cite. It is not different from the case of a righteous man living in a neighborhood of a town known for foolishness, lawlessness, atrocity, and heartlessness. His action is so rare that it is always buried under the ugliness of his neighbors' activities. When these

---

[1] *Yin* and *yang* is a traditional Chinese duality (hot/cold, active/passive, male/female) illustrated by a circle divided by an "s" to show unity within duality. The five elements suggest another traditional, prescientific idea that everything is made of five basic ingredients.

incidents are multiplied, that can affect our normal conduct of diplomatic affairs. How unfortunate it is for Japan.

What must we do today? We do not have time to wait for the enlightenment of our neighbors so that we can work together toward the development of Asia. It is better for us to leave the ranks of Asian nations and cast our lot with civilized nations of the West. As for the way of dealing with China and Korea, no special treatment is necessary just because they happen to be our neighbors. We simply follow the manner of the Westerners in knowing how to treat them. Any person who cherishes a bad friend cannot escape his bad notoriety. We simply erase from our minds our bad friends in Asia.

50

Images from Japan: Views of Westernization

This selection consists of three prints by Japanese artists. The first print, Figure 9.1, called *Beef Eater,* illustrates a character in Kanagaki Robun's *Aguranabe* (1871). The author, a popular newspaper humorist, parodies a new class of urban Westernized Japanese who carry watches and umbrellas and eat beef (banned by Buddhist law for centuries but added to the Japanese diet by Westerners).

The second piece, Figure 9.2, called *Monkey Show Dressing Room* (1879), by Honda Kinkachiro, shows monkeys dressing in a European style to "ape" the foreigners. Notice how much more Westernized the targets of this print are, just eight years after Figure 9.1 was created. What is this print's message? What is the artist's attitude toward Westernization?

The third piece, Figure 9.3, *The Exotic White Man,* shows a child born to a Western man and a Japanese woman. What is the artist's message? Does the artist favor such unions? What does the artist think of Westerners?

Beef Eater, from Kanagaki Robun, *Aguranabe* (1871) in G. B. Sansom, *The Western World and Japan* (Tokyo: Charles E. Tuttle Co., 1977). Honda Kinkachiro, *Monkey Show Dressing Room,* in Julia Meech-Pekarik, *The World of the Meiji Print* (New York: John Weatherhill, 1986). Japanese color print, late 19th c., Dutch private collection, in C. A. Burland, *The Exotic White Man* (New York: McGraw Hill, 1969), fig. 38.

Thinking Historically

Prints, like cartoons, are a shorthand that must capture an easily recognizable trait. What, evidently, were the widely understood Japanese images of the West? Where do you think these stereotypes of the West came from? Do you see any signs in these prints of ambivalence on the part of the artist?

Figure 9.1 Beef Eater.

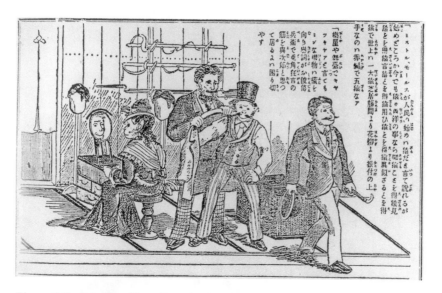

Figure 9.2   Monkey Show Dressing Room.

Figure 9.3   The Exotic White Man.

51

RAMMOHUN ROY

Letter on Indian Education

India's Westernization was less voluntary than Japan's. While Japan successfully limited European colonialism to a few seaports in the seventeenth century and was not forced to deal with the West again until after Admiral Perry's steam-age arrival in 1853, India became increasingly colonized by England throughout the eighteenth and nineteenth centuries. Because of India's long history as a British colony, aspects of Westernization there were deeper and more complex, the most obvious being use of the English language.

A colonial and foreign tongue, English had the advantage of uniting a country with dozens of regional languages (some of which were also imposed by foreign conquerors), while at the same time providing access to universities and a body of knowledge and literature as advanced as any in the world. English instruction — rather than ancient Sanskrit or Hindi or another Indian regional language — was championed by Britons who thought it would make Indians loyal and by Indians who thought it would unite them as a nation. The Indian use of English had its detractors, too: Britons who thought it dangerous or unseemly, and Britons and Indians who thought it patronizing and demeaning.

The debate over teaching English or Indian languages was part of a larger debate about the relative value of Western and Indian culture. Increasingly, toward the end of the nineteenth century as science took center stage in English culture, Indians found themselves torn between the claim of science and the appeal of traditional Indian religious knowledge.

Rammohun Roy (1772–1833) was an Indian social and religious reformer, as well as one of the earliest proponents of English education. Roy was an accomplished linguist who knew Latin, Greek, Hebrew, Arabic, Persian, and ancient Indian Sanskrit as well as his native Bengali. Yet when the British proposed to build a new Sanskrit school in Calcutta, Roy fired off the following letter to the British prime minister. Why did Roy object to a school that taught Sanskrit, the sacred

Rammohun Roy, letter on Indian Education, in H. Sharp, ed., *Selections from Educational Records, Part I, 1781–1839* (Calcutta: Superintendent Government Printing, 1920; reprint, Delhi: National Archives of India, 1965), 98–101.

language of ancient Hindu culture? What were his reasons for preferring English education for Indians?

Thinking Historically

To effectively communicate his ideas on Indian education, Roy had to strike a delicate balance in expressing deference to the British government while asserting enough authority to be taken seriously. How did he accomplish this dual task? How did he suggest that he knew more about the issue than his superiors in the English government, without seeming arrogant or ungrateful? How does his letter show that he was an Indian who benefited from an English education but did not pose a threat to British rule? What does his letter reveal about the inherent tensions in colonial India, within individuals and the society as a whole?

To His Excellency the Right Hon'ble William Pitt, Lord Amherst
My Lord,

Humbly reluctant as the natives of India are to obtrude upon the notice of Government the sentiments they entertain on any public measure there are circumstances when silence would be carrying this respectful feeling to culpable excess. The present Rulers of India, coming from a distance of many thousand miles to govern a people whose language, literature, manners, customs, and ideas are almost entirely new and strange to them, cannot easily become so intimately acquainted with their real circumstances, as the natives of the country are themselves. We should therefore be guilty of a gross dereliction of duty to ourselves, and afford our Rulers just ground of complaint at our apathy, did we omit on occasions of importance like the present to supply them with such accurate information as might enable them to devise and adopt measures calculated to be beneficial to the country, and thus second by our local knowledge and experience their declared benevolent intentions for its improvement.

The establishment of a new Sanskrit School in Calcutta evinces the laudable desire of Government to improve the Natives of India by Education, a blessing for which they must ever be grateful; and every well wisher of the human race must be desirous that the efforts made to promote it should be guided by the most enlightened principles, so that the stream of intelligence may flow into the most useful channels.

When this Seminary of learning was proposed, we understood that the Government in England had ordered a considerable sum of money to be annually devoted to the instruction of its Indian Subjects. We were filled with sanguine hopes that this sum would be laid out in employing European Gentlemen of talents and education to instruct the natives of India in Mathematics, Natural Philosophy, Chemistry, Anatomy and other useful Sciences, which the Nations of Europe have carried to a degree of perfection that has raised them above the inhabitants of other parts of the world.

While we looked forward with pleasing hope to the dawn of knowledge thus promised to the rising generation, our hearts were filled with mingled feelings of delight and gratitude; we already offered up thanks to Providence for inspiring the most generous and enlightened of the Nations of the West with the glorious ambitions of planting in Asia the Arts and Sciences of modern Europe.

We now find that the Government are establishing a Sanskrit school under Hindu Pundits to impart such knowledge as is already current in India. This Seminary (similar in character to those which existed in Europe before the time of Lord Bacon[1]) can only be expected to load the minds of youth with grammatical niceties and metaphysical distinctions of little or no practicable use to the possessors or to society. The pupils will there acquire what was known two thousand years ago, with the addition of vain and empty subtilties [*sic*] since produced by speculative men, such as is already commonly taught in all parts of India.

The Sanskrit language, so difficult that almost a life time is necessary for its perfect acquisition, is well known to have been for ages a lamentable check on the diffusion of knowledge; and the learning concealed under this almost impervious veil is far from sufficient to reward the labour of acquiring it. But if it were thought necessary to perpetuate this language for the sake of the portion of the valuable information it contains, this might be much more easily accomplished by other means than the establishment of a new Sanskrit College; for there have been always and are now numerous professors of Sanskrit in the different parts of the country, engaged in teaching this language as well as the other branches of literature which are to be the object of the new Seminary. Therefore their more diligent cultivation, if desirable, would be effectually promoted by holding out premiums and granting certain allowances to those most eminent Professors, who have already undertaken on their own account to teach them, and would by such rewards be stimulated to still greater exertions.

From these considerations, as the sum set apart for the instruction of the Natives of India was intended by the Government in England, for the improvement of its Indian subjects, I beg leave to state, with due

---

[1] Francis Bacon, English philosopher often credited with developing the scientific method. See selections 22 and 26 in Chapter 5. [Ed.]

deference to your Lordship's exalted situation, that if the plan now
adopted be followed, it will completely defeat the object proposed;
since no improvement can be expected from inducing young men to
consume a dozen of years of the most valuable period of their lives in
acquiring the niceties of the Byakurun or Sanskrit Grammar. For instance, in learning to discuss such points as the following: *Khad* signifying to eat, *khaduti*, he or she or it eats. Query, whether does the word
khaduti, taken as a whole, convey the meaning *he, she,* or *it eats*, or are
separate parts of this meaning conveyed by distinct portions of the
word? As if in the English language it were asked, how much meaning
is there in the *eat,* how much in the *s?* and is the whole meaning of the
word conveyed by those two portions of it distinctly, or by them taken
jointly?

Neither can much improvement arise from such speculations as the
following, which are the themes suggested by the Vedanta: In what
manner is the soul absorbed into the deity? What relation does it bear
to the divine essence? Nor will youths be fitted to be better members of
society by the Vedantic doctrines, which teach them to believe that all
visible things have no real existence; that as father, brother, etc., have
no actual entirety, they consequently deserve no real affection, and
therefore the sooner we escape from them and leave the world the better. Again, no essential benefit can be derived by the student of the
Meemangsa from knowing what it is that makes the killer of a goat sin-
less on pronouncing certain passages of the Vedas, and what is the real
nature and operative influence of passages of the Veda, etc.

Again the student of the Nyaya Shastra cannot be said to have improved his mind after he has learned from it into how many ideal
classes the objects in the Universe are divided, and what speculative relation the soul bears to the body, the body to the soul, the eye to the
ear, etc.

In order to enable your Lordship to appreciate the utility of encouraging such imaginary learning as above characterised, I beg your Lordship will be pleased to compare the state of science and literature in Europe before the time of Lord Bacon, with the progress of knowledge
made since he wrote.

If it had been intended to keep the British nation in ignorance of
real knowledge the Baconian philosophy would not have been allowed to
displace the system of the schoolmen, which was the best calculated
to perpetuate ignorance. In the same manner the [Sanskrit] system of
education would be the best calculated to keep this country in darkness, if such had been the policy of the British Legislature. But as the
improvement of the native population is the object of the Government,
it will consequently promote a more liberal and enlightened system of
instruction, embracing mathematics, natural philosophy, chemistry and
anatomy, with other useful sciences which may be accomplished with

the sum proposed by employing a few gentlemen of talents and learning educated in Europe, and providing a college furnished with the necessary books, instruments, and other apparatus.

In representing this subject to your Lordship I conceive myself discharging a solemn duty which I owe to my countrymen and also to that enlightened Sovereign and Legislature which have extended their benevolent cares to this distant land actuated by a desire to improve its inhabitants and I therefore humbly trust you will excuse the liberty I have taken in thus expressing my sentiments to your Lordship.

I have, etc.,

Rammohun Roy
Calcutta;
The 11th December 1823

52

MOHANDAS K. GANDHI

From *Hind Swaraj*

Mohandas K. Gandhi (1869–1948), the father of Indian independence, combined the education of an English lawyer with the temperament of an Indian ascetic to lead a national resistance movement against the British. In the century after Rammohun Roy helped reform the Indian education system, British rule had become far more pervasive and increasingly hostile toward Indian culture. Unlike Roy, who had embraced Western culture as a means to uplift Indians, Gandhi was extremely critical of Western culture as he witnessed the havoc British rule wreaked on his country.

Gandhi began to develop his ideas of *Hind Swaraj*, or Indian Home Rule, after he sailed from England to South Africa in 1908. An early version of this essay, published then, was reissued in its present form in 1921, two years after he returned to his birthplace, India, and again in 1938, in the last years of struggle against British rule.

M. K. Gandhi, *Hind Swaraj* (Ahmedabad, India: Navajivan, 1938), 15–16, 26–27, 28, 30–31, 32–33, 58–60, 69–71, 82–85.

After Gandhi's introduction, the essay takes the form of questions and answers. The questions are posed by a presumed "reader" of Gandhi's paper. As "editor," Gandhi explains what he means. How does Gandhi compare life in Europe and India? What does he think of the possibility of Hindus and Muslims living together? What does he mean by passive resistance or soul-force (Satyagraha)? Why does he think it is preferable to violence, or body-force? What kind of India would Gandhi have tried to create had he lived?

Thinking Historically

Some historians have argued that Gandhi's contradictory roles — Hindu philosopher espousing secular nationalism and anti-modernist revolutionary — were ultimately unbridgeable. Notice how Gandhi makes a lawyer's case for traditional Indian values. How does he combine both religious and secular goals for India? How does he combine Hindu religious ideas with respect for Muslims? Were Gandhi's contradictions a fatal flaw, or could they have been his strength?

Civilization

READER: Now you will have to explain what you mean by civilization.

EDITOR: Let us first consider what state of things is described by the word "civilization." Its true test lies in the fact that people living in it make bodily welfare the object of life. We will take some examples. The people of Europe today live in better-built houses than they did a hundred years ago. This is considered an emblem of civilization, and this is also a matter to promote bodily happiness. Formerly, they wore skins, and used spears as their weapons. Now, they wear long trousers, and, for embellishing their bodies, they wear a variety of clothing, and, instead of spears, they carry with them revolvers containing five or more chambers. If people of a certain country, who have hitherto not been in the habit of wearing much clothing, boots, etc., adopt European clothing, they are supposed to have become civilized out of savagery. Formerly, in Europe, people ploughed their lands mainly by manual labour. Now, one man can plough a vast tract by means of steam engines and can thus amass great wealth. This is called a sign of civilization. Formerly, only a few men wrote valuable books. Now, anybody writes and prints anything he likes and poisons people's minds. Formerly, men travelled in waggons. Now, they fly through the air in trains at the rate of four hundred and more miles per day. This is considered the height of civilization. It has been stated that, as men progress, they shall be able to travel in airship and reach any part of the world in a few hours. Men will not need the use of their hands and feet.

They will press a button, and they will have their clothing at their side. They will press another button, and they will have their newspaper. A third, and motor-car will be in waiting for them. They will have a variety of delicately dished up food. Everything will be done by machinery. Formerly, when people wanted to fight with one another, they measured between them their bodily strength; now it is possible to take away thousands of lives by one man working behind a gun from a hill. This is civilization. Formerly, men worked in the open air only as much as they liked. Now thousands of workmen meet together and for the sake of maintenance work in factories or mines. Their condition is worse than that of beasts. They are obliged to work, at the risk of their lives, at most dangerous occupations, for the sake of millionaires. Formerly, men were made slaves under physical compulsion. Now they are enslaved by temptation of money and of the luxuries that money can buy. There are now diseases of which people never dreamt before, and an army of doctors is engaged in finding out their cures, and so hospitals have increased. This is a test of civilization. Formerly, special messengers were required and much expense was incurred in order to send letters; today, anyone can abuse his fellow by means of a letter for one penny. True, at the same cost, one can send one's thanks also. Formerly, people had two or three meals consisting of home-made bread and vegetables; now, they require something to eat every two hours so that they have hardly leisure for anything else. What more need I say? All this you can ascertain from several authoritative books. These are all true tests of civilization. And if anyone speaks to the contrary, know that he is ignorant. This civilization takes note neither of morality nor of religion. Its votaries calmly state that their business is not to teach religion. Some even consider it to be a superstitious growth. Others put on the cloak of religion, and prate about morality. But, after twenty years' experience, I have come to the conclusion that immorality is often taught in the name of morality. Even a child can understand that in all I have described above there can be no inducement to morality. Civilization seeks to increase bodily comforts, and it fails miserably even in doing so. . . .

The Hindus and the Mahomedans

READER: Has the introduction to Mahomedanism [Islam] not unmade the nation?

EDITOR: India cannot cease to be one nation because people belonging to different religions live in it. The introduction of foreigners does not necessarily destroy the nation; they merge in it. A country is one nation only when such a condition obtains in it. That country must have a faculty for assimilation. India has ever been such a country. In reality there are as many religions as there are individuals; but those who are conscious of the spirit of nationality do not interfere with one another's religion. If they do, they are not fit to be considered a nation. If the Hindus believe that India should be peopled only by Hindus, they are living in dreamland. The Hindus, the Mahomedans, the Parsis and the Christians who have made India their country are fellow-countrymen, and they will have to live in unity, if only for their own interest. In no part of the world are one nationality and one religion synonymous terms; nor has it ever been so in India.

READER: But what about the inborn enmity between Hindus and Mahomedans?

EDITOR: That phrase has been invented by our mutual enemy. When the Hindus and Mahomedans fought against one another, they certainly spoke in that strain. They have long since ceased to fight. How, then, can there be any inborn enmity? Pray remember this too, that we did not cease to fight only after British occupation. The Hindus flourished under Moslem sovereigns and Moslems under the Hindu. Each party recognized that mutual fighting was suicidal, and that neither party would abandon its religion by force of arms. Both parties, therefore, decided to live in peace. With the English advent quarrels recommenced.

The proverbs you have quoted were coined when both were fighting; to quote them now is obviously harmful. Should we not remember that many Hindus and Mahomedans own the same ancestors and the same blood runs through their veins? Do people become enemies because they change their religion? Is the God of the Mahomedan different from the God of the Hindu? Religions are different roads converging to the same point. What does it matter that we take different roads so long as we reach the same goal? Wherein is the cause for quarrelling?

Moreover, there are deadly proverbs as between the followers of Siva and those of Vishnu, yet nobody suggests that these two do not belong to the same nation. It is said that the Vedic religion is different from Jainism, but the followers of the respective faiths are not different nations. The fact is that we have become enslaved and, therefore, quarrel and like to have our quarrels decided by a third party. There are Hindu iconoclasts as there are Mahomedan. The more we advance in true knowledge, the better we shall understand that we need not be at war with those whose religion we may not follow. . . .

How Can India Become Free?

READER: If Indian civilization is, as you say, the best of all, how do you account for India's slavery?

EDITOR: This civilization is unquestionably the best, but it is to be observed that all civilizations have been on their trial. That civilization which is permanent outlives it. Because the sons of India were found wanting, its civilization has been placed in jeopardy. But its strength is to be seen in its ability to survive the shock. Moreover, the whole of India is not touched. Those alone who have been affected by Western civilization have become enslaved. We measure the universe by our own miserable foot-rule. When we are slaves, we think that the whole universe is enslaved. Because we are in an abject condition, we think that the whole of India is in that condition. As a matter of fact, it is not so, yet it is as well to impute our slavery to the whole of India. But if we bear in mind the above fact, we can see that if we become free, India is free. And in this thought you have a definition of Swaraj. It is Swaraj when we learn to rule ourselves. It is, therefore, in the palm of our hands. Do not consider this Swaraj to be like a dream. There is no idea of sitting still. The Swaraj that I wish to picture is such that, after we have once realized it, we shall endeavour to the end of our life-time to persuade others to do likewise. But such Swaraj has to be experienced, by each one for himself. One drowning man will never save another. Slaves ourselves, it would be a mere pretension to think of freeing others. Now you will have seen that it is not necessary for us to have as our goal the expulsion of the English. If the English become Indianized, we can accommodate them. If they wish to remain in India along with their civilization, there is no room for them. It lies with us to bring about such a state of things.

READER: It is impossible that Englishmen should ever become Indianized.

EDITOR: To say that is equivalent to saying that the English have no humanity in them. And it is really beside the point whether they become so or not. If we keep our own house in order, only those who are fit to live in it will remain. Others will leave of their own accord. Such things occur within the experience of all of us. . . .

Passive Resistance

READER: Is there any historical evidence as to the success of what you have called soul-force or truth-force? No instance seems to have happened of any nation having risen through soul-force. I still think that the evil-doers will not cease doing evil without physical punishment.

EDITOR: The [Hindu] poet Tulsidas [1532–1623] has said: "Of religion, pity, or love, is the root, as egotism of the body. Therefore, we should not abandon pity so long as we are alive." This appears to me to be a scientific truth. We have evidence of its working at every step. The universe would disappear without the existence of that force. . . .

The fact that there are so many men still alive in the world shows that it is based not on the force of arms but on the force of truth or love. Therefore, the greatest and most unimpeachable evidence of the success of this force is to be found in the fact that, in spite of the wars of the world, it still lives on.

Thousands, indeed tens of thousands, depend for their existence on a very active working of this force. Little quarrels of millions of families in their daily lives disappear before the exercise of this force. Hundreds of nations live in peace. History does not and cannot take note of this fact. History is really a record of every interruption of the even working of the force of love or of the soul. Two brothers quarrel; one of them repents and re-awakens the love that was lying dormant in him; the two again begin to live in peace; nobody takes note of this. But if the two brothers, through the intervention of solicitors or some other reason take up arms or go to law — which is another form of the exhibition of brute force, — their doings would be immediately noticed in the press, they would be the talk of their neighbours and would probably go down to history. And what is true of families and communities is true of nations. There is no reason to believe that there is one law for families and another for nations. History, then, is a record of an interruption of the course of nature. Soul-force, being natural, is not noted in history.

READER: According to what you say, it is plain that instances of this kind of passive resistance are not to be found in history. It is necessary to understand this passive resistance more fully. It will be better, therefore, if you enlarge upon it.

EDITOR: Passive resistance is a method of securing rights by personal suffering; it is the reverse of resistance by arms. When I refuse to do a thing that is repugnant to my conscience, I use soul-force. For instance, the Government of the day has passed a law which is applicable to me. I do not like it. If by using violence I force the Government to repeal the law, I am employing what may be termed body-force. If I do not obey the law and accept the penalty for its breach, I use soul-force. It involves sacrifice of self.

Everybody admits that sacrifice of self is infinitely superior to sacrifice of others. Moreover, if this kind of force is used in a cause that is unjust, only the person using it suffers. He does not make others suffer for his mistakes. Men have before now done many things which were subsequently found to have been wrong. No man can claim that he is absolutely in the right or that a particular thing is wrong because he thinks so, but it is wrong for him so long as that is his deliberate judgment. It is therefore meet that he should not do that which he knows to be wrong, and suffer the consequence whatever it may be. This is the key to the use of soul-force.

53

JAWAHARLAL NEHRU

Gandhi

Mohandas K. Gandhi and Jawaharlal Nehru were the two most important leaders of India's national independence movement. Though they worked together and Nehru was Gandhi's choice as the first Indian prime minister, they expressed in their personalities and ideas two very different Indias. How would you describe these two Indias? Was it Gandhi's or Nehru's vision of the future that was realized? Who do you think was a better guide for India?

Thinking Historically

Think of Gandhi and Nehru as the two sides of the Indian struggle for independence. Did India benefit from having both of these sides represented? What would have happened if there had been only Gandhi's view or only Nehru's?

How was the debate in India about the influence of the West different from the debate in Japan?

I imagine that Gandhiji is not so vague about the objective as he sometimes appears to be. He is passionately desirous of going in a certain direction, but this is wholly at variance with modern ideas and conditions, and he has so far been unable to fit the two, or to chalk out all the intermediate steps leading to his goal. Hence the appearance of vagueness and avoidance of clarity. But his general inclination has been clear enough for a quarter of a century, ever since he started formulating his philosophy in South Africa. I do not know if those early writings still represent his views. I doubt if they do so in their entirety, but they do help us to understand the background of his thought.

"India's salvation consists," he wrote in 1909, "in unlearning what she has learned during the last fifty years. The railways, telegraphs, hospitals, lawyers, doctors, and suchlike have all to go; and the

J. Nehru, *Toward Freedom: The Autobiography of Jawaharlal Nehru* (New York: John Day Company, 1942).

so-called upper classes have to learn consciously, religiously, and deliberately the simple peasant life, knowing it to be a life giving true happiness." And again: "Every time I get into a railway car or use a motor bus I know that I am doing violence to my sense of what is right"; "to attempt to reform the world by means of highly artificial and speedy locomotion is to attempt the impossible."

All this seems to me utterly wrong and harmful doctrine, and impossible of achievement. Behind it lies Gandhiji's love and praise of poverty and suffering and the ascetic life. For him progress and civilization consist not in the multiplication of wants, of higher standards of living, "but in the deliberate and voluntary restriction of wants, which promotes real happiness and contentment, and increases the capacity for service." If these premises are once accepted, it becomes easy to follow the rest of Gandhiji's thought and to have a better understanding of his activities. But most of us do not accept those premises, and yet we complain later on when we find that his activities are not to our liking.

Personally I dislike the praise of poverty and suffering. I do not think they are at all desirable, and they ought to be abolished. Nor do I appreciate the ascetic life as a social ideal, though it may suit individuals. I understand and appreciate simplicity, equality, self-control; but not the mortification of the flesh. Just as an athlete requires to train his body, I believe that the mind and habits have also to be trained and brought under control. It would be absurd to expect that a person who is given to too much self-indulgence can endure much suffering or show unusual self-control or behave like a hero when the crisis comes. To be in good moral condition requires at least as much training as to be in good physical condition. But that certainly does not mean asceticism or self-mortification.

Nor do I appreciate in the least the idealization of the "simple peasant life." I have almost a horror of it, and instead of submitting to it myself I want to drag out even the peasantry from it, not to urbanization, but to the spread of urban cultural facilities to rural areas. Far from his life's giving me true happiness, it would be almost as bad as imprisonment for me. What is there in "The Man with the Hoe" to idealize over? Crushed and exploited for innumerable generations, he is only little removed from the animals who keep him company.

> Who made him dead to rapture and despair,
> A thing that grieves not and that never hopes,
> Stolid and stunned, a brother to the ox?

This desire to get away from the mind of man to primitive conditions where mind does not count, seems to me quite incomprehensible. The very thing that is the glory and triumph of man is decried and discouraged, and a physical environment which will oppress the mind and prevent its growth is considered desirable. Present-day civilization is full of evils, but it is also full of good; and it has the capacity in it to rid itself of those evils. To destroy it root and branch is to remove that capacity from it and revert to a dull, sunless, and miserable existence. But even if that were desirable it is an impossible undertaking. We cannot stop the river of change or cut ourselves adrift from it, and psychologically we who have eaten of the apple of Eden cannot forget that taste and go back to primitiveness.

It is difficult to argue this, for the two standpoints are utterly different. Gandhiji is always thinking in terms of personal salvation and of sin, while most of us have society's welfare uppermost in our minds. I find it difficult to grasp the idea of sin, and perhaps it is because of this that I cannot appreciate Gandhiji's general outlook.

54

DENG YINGCHAO

The Spirit of the May Fourth Movement

On May 4, 1919, university students in Peking, China, gathered to protest a provision in the Versailles Peace Treaty that awarded parts of China to Japan in compensation for Japan's alliance with the victors of World War I. The local warlord government arrested the students and suppressed the demonstration, but it sparked sympathetic protests throughout China that came to be known as the May Fourth Movement and symbolized the Chinese nationalist struggle.

This memoir of the movement was written by Deng Yingchao (1904–1992), who was a young girl at the time and later married the Chinese communist party leader Zhou Enlai (1898–1976). Because of the role of students, the May Fourth Movement has often been pictured as a generational conflict, which it certainly was. But perhaps more significantly, the May Fourth Movement was a nationalist movement that embraced Western ideals to effect change. Which ideas presented below were Chinese? Which ideas seem to have come from

Deng Yingchao, "The Spirit of the May Fourth Movement," trans. Liu Xiaochong, in *Women of China*, reprinted from Patricia Ebrey, ed., *Chinese Civilization: A Sourcebook*, 2nd ed., (New York: Free Press, 1993), 360–63.

the West? Notice also how the movement embraced women's rights. Was this due to Chinese or Western influence?

Thinking Historically

Notice how Chinese nationalism was stimulated by Western ideas. Did this pose a contradiction for Deng Yingchao? Notice also how the Western ideas espoused by the May Fourth Movement came from two diametrically opposed sources. Was the Chinese nationalism born of the May Fourth Movement more or less Western than Gandhi's nationalism?

When the May Fourth Movement took place in 1919, I was only sixteen years old, a student at the Tianjin Women's Normal College. . . . On May 4, 1919, students in Beijing held a demonstration asking the government to refuse to sign the Versailles Peace Treaty and to punish the traitors at home. In their indignation, they burned the house at Zhaojialou and beat up Lu Zhongxiang, then Chinese envoy to Japan. The following day, when the news reached Tianjin, it aroused the indignation of students there who staged their own demonstration on May 7th. They began by organizing such patriotic societies as the Tianjin Student Union, the Tianjin Women's Patriotic Society, and the Tianjin Association of National Salvation. We had no political theory to guide us at that time, only our strong patriotic enthusiasm. In addition to the Beijing students' requests, we demanded, "Abrogate the Twenty-One Demands!" "Boycott Japanese Goods!" and "Buy Chinese-made goods!" Furthermore, we emphatically refused to become slaves to foreign powers!

Despite the fact that it was a patriotic students' demonstration, the Northern warlord government of China resorted to force to quell the protest. The police dispersed the march with rifles fixed with bayonets and with hoses; later they resorted to rifle butts and to even arrest. However, our political awareness awakened a new spirit in us during our struggle with the government. New European ideas and culture had poured into China after World War I, and the success of the 1917 October Revolution in Russia introduced Marxism-Leninism to China. . . . We did not yet know that to achieve our revolutionary goal, we intellectuals should unite with workers and peasants. We just had some vague idea that Lenin, the leader of the Russian revolution, wanted to liberate the oppressed workers and peasants.

What we did know intuitively was that alone we students did not have enough strength to save China from foreign powers. To awaken our compatriots, we organized many speakers' committees to spread propaganda among the people. I became the head of the speakers' group in the Tianjin Women's Patriotic Society and in the Tianjin Student Union. Frequently we gave speeches off campus. At first, we women did not dare give speeches on the street due to the feudal attitudes that then existed in China. So the female students went instead to places where people had gathered for an exhibition or a show, while the male students gave speeches in the street to passersby. There were always a lot of listeners. We told them why we should be united to save our country; that traitors in the government must be punished; and that people should have the right to freedom of assembly and association. We talked about the suffering of the Korean people after their country was conquered; and we publicly lodged our protests against the Northern warlord government that persecutes progressive students. Usually tears streamed down our cheeks when we gave our speeches and our listeners were often visibly moved.

In addition to making speeches we also visited homes in out-of-the-way places and slum areas. We went door to door to make our pleas, and some families gave us a warm welcome while others just slammed the door on us. However, nothing could discourage us. One day during summer vacation, we went to the suburbs to give speeches. On our way back to the city, we got caught in a downpour. Everybody was soaking wet, just like a drowned chicken! The next day, however, everyone was ready to go again.

We delivered handbills and published newspapers to spread our patriotic enthusiasm even further. The Student Union newspaper, for example, was run by the Tianjin Student Union and each issue sold more than twenty thousand copies — a considerable number at that time! It was originally published every three days; however, later it was increased to every day. Its editor-in-chief was Zhou Enlai. The Women's Patriotic Society also published a weekly. Both papers reported foreign and national current events, student movements across the country, student editorials, progressive articles, and cultural and art news.

The reactionary Northern warlord government, however, turned a deaf ear to us. They ultimately bowed to Japanese powers, shielded the traitors, and tried to suppress the student movement. At that time people were denied expressing their patriotic views. So what we then struggled most urgently for was freedom of assembly and association; the right to express one's political views; and freedom of the press. United under these common goals, we struggled bravely.

Various associations for national salvation in Tianjin decided to organize a general mass meeting of the residents of Tianjin on October 10, 1919. The purpose was to demand that the officials who betrayed China be punished and to call on local residents to boycott all Japanese goods. A march was scheduled at the conclusion of the meeting. Prior to the meeting, however, news spread that Yang Yide, the chief of the police department, was going to disband the meeting and if necessary use force to stop the march. We were not frightened, but got ready to fight back if fighting broke out. During the meeting, female students stood at the periphery of the group so that we could be the first to escape if the meeting were broken up by the police. We chose strong bamboo poles to carry our banners since they could be used as weapons if needed.

Shortly after we began the meeting, a group of policemen arrived, surrounded the group, and instantly pointed their rifles at us. Our meeting continued as if nothing had happened. It was not until it was time to assemble for the march that conflict occurred. The police refused to let us pass. So finally we just charged at them, shouting, "Policemen should be patriotic, too!" "Don't strike patriotic students!" The police hit with their rifle butts and many students were beaten. Some even broke their glasses. We fought back with our bamboo poles. Then some students knocked off the policemen's hats so that when they bend down to retrieve them, it gave us a means of escape.

Just at that moment, the speakers from the Tianjin Student Union arrived in the back of a truck. With them helping on the outside, we broke through the encirclement and the march began! We marched around the city until daybreak the next day. It was not until we had lodged protests against Yang Yide for his savage treatment of the students that we finally ended the demonstration. Yang's ruthlessness had so aroused our indignation, that we women broke with tradition and the next day appeared on the streets proclaiming Yang Yide's cruelty towards students to all who passed by.

After the October 10th incident, the situation worsened. In November, the Tianjin Association for National Salvation was closed down and twenty-four leaders were arrested. Soon the Tianjin Student Union was also disbanded. But we continued our progressive activities secretly and found a room in a student's home in the concession area to use as our office. A concession area was a track of land in a Chinese port or city leased to an imperialist power and put under its colonial rule.

In December of that year another confrontation occurred. That day the students gathered around the office building of the provincial government to present a petition to Governor Cao Rui, asking for the release of the arrested students and for the various national salvation associations to be allowed to resume operation. However, not only did he refuse to receive us, but he had the gates locked and posted armed guards. Our representatives, Zhou Enlai, Guo Longzhen (a woman), and Yu Fangzhou, managed to get in from a hole under the door. They were beaten once they were inside. The students became more indignant and refused to leave. At midnight, the armed guards drove the students away by brutal force, hitting students with bayonets and rifle butts and spraying them with columns of water. Many students were wounded and some had to be sent to the hospital. In this we saw clearly the ferocious face of the reactionary government and that freedom and democratic rights could not be gained without a fierce struggle.

In the following year, we shifted our priority to rescuing the arrested students. We struggled to win over public sentiment, fought against illegal arrests, and asked for public trial of our representatives. It was not until that summer, however, that all twenty-eight of those who had been arrested were finally released.

During the movement, not only were we suppressed by the reactionary government, but were suppressed by the college authorities as well. They ordered students not to leave the campus to take part in any progressive activities. On May 7, 1920, a group of us from the Women's Normal College planned to attend a meeting commemorating the May 7th Incident, the day the Japanese government sent an ultimatum to the Chinese government urging it to sign the Twenty-One Demands. When we were ready to leave, we discovered college authorities were refusing to let us. A confrontation ensued and resulted in our eventually forcing open the gate and attending the meeting.

When we returned, much to our surprise, a notice had been posted that all the students who had attended the meeting — a total of two hundred — were expelled! How enraged we were! We decided to leave the college as soon as possible. Our dedication to our patriotic duty was so strong that we were ready to sacrifice anything for the goal of national independence! Without any rest or supper we spent the night packing our luggage. When we were ready to leave en masse, luggage in hand we again discovered that the gate had been locked. In addition to this, they had cut off our communication with the outside world by locking up the telephone room. This time the confrontation lasted through the night and into the morning of the next day when all two hundred of us left the college. One week later, public pressure forced them to reinstate us, and we immediately returned to school.

The women's liberation movement was greatly enhanced by the May Fourth Movement; this became an important part of the movement. And slogans such as "sexual equality," "freedom of marriage," "coeducational universities," "social contracts for women," and "job opportunity for women," were all put forward. In Tianjin we merged the men's students union with the women's. Fearing that public opinion would be against it, some of the women were hesitant at first. However, the male and female activists among us took the lead and we worked together bravely to overcome all obstacles. In our work, we were equal and we respected each other. Everyone worked wholeheartedly for the goal of saving China, and we competed with each other in our efforts. Women students, particularly the more progressive ones, worked especially hard for we knew we were pioneers among Chinese women to show that women are not inferior to men. Inspired by the new ideals, the progressive men students broke down the tradition of sexual discrimination and treated us with respect. For example, each department of the student union had one male and one female in charge. In addition, women had equal say in decision making. The men and women's student union in Beijing admired us for our brilliant work and merged afterwards.

At this time cultural movements were developing rapidly and students were receptive to publications which promoted new ideas. In Beijing, for example, there were *New Youth, Young China*, and *New Tide* magazines. In Tianjin, the Student Union every week would invite a progressive professor (such as Li Dazhao) to give us an academic lecture on new literary ideas such as how to write in vernacular Chinese rather than in classical stereotyped writings. Today these things are commonplace, but then it was very new and important. As more scientific subjects and new ideas poured into China, we felt an urgency to learn, discuss, study, and understand them. Thus by the end of that summer, a small well-organized group — the Awakening Society — was established by twenty of the more progressive student activists. I was the youngest in the Society. Although I often heard other members talking about such things as socialism or anarchism, I was too young to understand them. At that time we did not have definite political convictions, nor did we know much about Communism. We just had a vague idea that the principle of distribution in the most advantageous society was "from each according to his ability, to each according to his needs." We knew only that a revolution led by Lenin in Russia had been successful, and that the aim of that revolution was to emancipate the majority of the people who were oppressed, and to establish a classless society. How we longed for such a society! But at that time we could not learn about such a society because we could scarcely find any copy of Lenin's ideas or information about the October Revolution.

The Awakening Society existed for only a few months. We lost some members when they were arrested in the incident over the petition to the governor. Others graduated and left Tianjin. Eventually the Society ceased to exist. However, the majority of us eventually joined the Chinese Socialist Youth League established in 1920, or the Communist party established in 1921. . . .

REFLECTIONS

The earliest phase of Westernization occurred in Russia under the direction of Czar Peter the Great. Before and after Peter's efforts to import Western European institutions and values in order to "modernize" Russia, his country was riven by conflict between "Westernizers" and "Slavophiles," the latter determined to preserve an older Russian identity as ethnic Slavs in tradition, language, and religion. In some ways, the Russians were the first "non-Europeans" to struggle with the question of how much to borrow from the West. But due to Peter's reforms, the construction of a Western capital at St. Petersburg, and the encouragement of Western education, military organization, and culture, Russia chose to align herself with Europe rather than with Asia. After the Russian Revolution of 1917, the Soviet Union became the "West of choice" for many Chinese revolutionaries. The Soviet Union (and Communist China) was Western in its commitment to German Marxism, economic modernization, social and economic equality, and its cosmopolitan opposition to religious or ethnic tribalism. Still, Slavophilism never completely disappeared.

With the end of communism, after 1989, anti-Western forces revived in Russia. When Russian capitalism floundered in the 1990s, the voices of religious orthodoxy, proponents of military might, and revivers of Slavic culture grew louder. In the new world of global markets, contradictions abounded. In 1999, Nikita Mikhakov, a Slavophile and internationally respected film director, built an international reputation and campaign chest to run for president of Russia, promising a return to the Russian values of the czars, one of whom, Alexander III, he played in his film, *Barber of Siberia*. This cinematic celebration of pre-Western Russia was filmed by a genius in Western marketing techniques, with 70 percent of the dialogue in English so that it might qualify for a "Best Picture" Oscar outside the foreign film category.

Our brief summary of Westernization in Asia recalls many stories like this. Why do so many nationalist leaders emerge from outside their native countries? Did Gandhi become more Indian in England or South Africa? Were the Chinese and Indians who lived overseas more free to express themselves, better able to contribute financially, or more optimistic about changing societies? We cannot overlook the international aspects of nationalist movements in the twentieth century. Westernizers and anti-Westernizers seem to have been profoundly influenced by their foreign travel experiences. Is the history of Westernization, and of the opposition to Westernization, ultimately a global story? And are the global processes such that the story eventually becomes irrelevant?

At the beginning of the twenty-first century, it is difficult to distinguish Westernization from globalization, as the forces that threaten the national economies or cultures of Asia, Africa, and Latin America tend to come from every direction. Perhaps future generations will see Westernization as only the initial stage of a larger process of economic and cultural integration which we now call globalization.

World War and
Its Consequences

*Europe, the Soviet Union, and the Middle
East, 1914–1920*

HISTORICAL CONTEXT

The Europe that so many Asian intellectuals sought to imitate or reject
between 1880 and 1920 came very close to self-destructing between
1914 and 1918, and bringing many of the world's peoples from Asia,
Africa, and the Americas down with it. The orgy of bloodletting, then
known as the "Great War," put seventy million men in uniform, of
whom ten million were killed and twenty million were wounded. Most
of the soldiers were Europeans, though Russia contributed more soldiers than France or Germany, while Japan enlisted as many as the
Austro-Hungarian empire that began the war. Enlisted men also came
from the United States, Canada, Australia, New Zealand, South Africa,
and the colonies: India, French West Africa, German East Africa,
among others. The majority of soldiers were killed in Europe, especially
along the German Western front — four hundred miles of trenches that
spanned from Switzerland to the English Channel, across northeastern
France. But battles were also fought along the borders of German,
French, and English colonies in Africa, and there were high Australian
casualties on the coast of Gallipoli in Ottoman Turkey.

The readings in this chapter focus on the lives and deaths of the
soldiers, as well as the efforts of some of their political leaders to rede-
fine the world around them. We examine the experiences of soldiers
and how the war changed the lives of those who survived its devastating toll. We compare the accounts of those who fought on both sides
of the great divide. Germany and the Austro-Hungarian empire, joined
by the Ottomon Empire, formed an alliance called the Central Powers
(see Map 10.1). In opposition, England, France, and Russia, the Allied

354

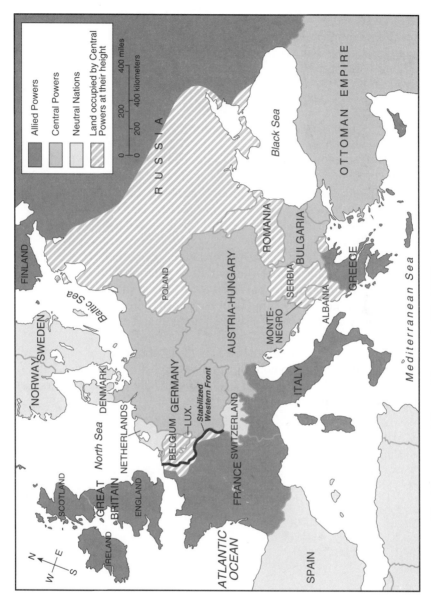

Map 10.1 Allied Powers and Central Powers in World War I.

Legend:
- Allied Powers
- Central Powers
- Neutral Nations
- Land occupied by Central Powers at their height

400 miles
400 kilometers
200
200
0
0

RUSSIA

FINLAND

NORWAY

SWEDEN

DENMARK

Baltic Sea

NETHERLANDS

GREAT BRITAIN

SCOTLAND

ENGLAND

IRELAND

North Sea

ATLANTIC OCEAN

BELGIUM

LUX.

GERMANY

Stabilized Western Front

FRANCE

SWITZERLAND

POLAND

AUSTRIA-HUNGARY

ITALY

SPAIN

Mediterranean Sea

MONTE-NEGRO

SERBIA

ALBANIA

ROMANIA

BULGARIA

GREECE

Black Sea

OTTOMAN EMPIRE

N
E
W
S

Powers, were later joined by Italy, Greece, Japan, and the United States. We compare views across the generational divide as well as the trenches and government offices.

THINKING HISTORICALLY
Understanding Causes and Consequences

From 1914 to 1920, the greatest divide was the war itself. It marked the end of one era and the beginning of another. Few events have left the participants with such a profound sense of fundamental change. And so our study of the war is an appropriate place to ask two of the universal questions of major historical change: What caused it? and, What were the consequences?

The *causes* are those events or forces that came before; the *consequences* are the results, what the war itself prompted to occur. Thus, causes and consequences are part of the same continuum. Still, we must remember that not everything that happened before the war was a cause of the war. Similarly, not everything that happened afterward was a result of the war.

In this chapter we explore specific ideas about cause and consequence. Our goal is not to compile a definitive list of either but, rather, to explore some of the ways that historians and thoughtful readers can make sense of the past.

55

SALLY MARKS

The Coming of the First World War

Sally Marks, a modern scholar, begins the following selection by declaring that, after much debate, historians have recently come to agree
that Germany was the country primarily responsible for causing the
First World War. Other countries were not blameless, however, and
waging war in the twentieth century required willing recruits and popular support on all sides. Further, as Marks notes, there were secondary or background causes that precipitated the outbreak of war.
What were these secondary causes? How important were they?

Thinking Historically

In studying the causes of major historical events, historians distinguish
between structural or long-term causes, direct or immediate causes,
and contingent events or accidents. Which events and circumstances
leading up to the First World War would you place in each of these
categories? Marks writes mainly of political decisions made by governments, which are often the most immediate causes of war. She also
writes of long-term historic developments, however, such as competition for colonies, the difference between "young" and "old" states,
the balance of power in international politics, the development of nationalism, as well as more personal factors such as leaders' fears and
miscalculations. Were any of these long-term developments "causes"
of war? How important does Marks think they were? Why does she
think German political decisions were more important?

There is little that historians debate more endlessly than causation,
and certainly much ink has been expended in arguing the origins of
World War I. In recent years, however, a degree of consensus has
emerged, even among German scholars, that primary responsibility
should be assigned to the Second Reich, though debate continues about
German motives and intentions. It now seems clear that Germany's

Sally Marks, *The Ebbing of European Ascendancy: An International History of the World,
1914–1945* (New York: Oxford University Press, 2002), 19–22, 25, 26, 31–36.

power, policies, actions, and diplomatic style provided a continual factor between its creation in 1870–1871 and the great collision of 1914.

Germany's unification, coupled with its industrial and demographic growth, brought a young but very strong power to the center of the European stage, hitherto a comparatively weak area. The power balance was at once implicitly altered. But Prince Otto von Bismarck, Chancellor of the new Germany until 1890, chose not to make this explicit in Europe or elsewhere. Preferring to build the Reich's institutions and industry, he restored the Concert of Europe, used it to settle quarrels threatening the peace and his new empire, and eschewed colonies.

Bismarck also tended to Germany's defences to protect its future. He had firm grasp of the inescapable geographic fact that it occupied the centre of the continent without defensible natural boundaries and had three great power neighbours. He knew his Reich was unlikely to triumph in a war against two of them. Hence the central task of Bismarck's diplomacy was to ensure that no two of these great powers combined against Germany. As France was unlikely to forgive its humiliating defeat in the Franco-Prussian war of 1870, this meant ensuring that Russia and Austria-Hungary remained at Germany's side despite their clashing interests in the Balkans. Through increasingly convoluted diplomacy, Bismarck managed this tricky task throughout his tenure, also adding Italy to Germany's allies.

By Bismarck's last years, however, keeping Russia and Austria in the same camp was becoming difficult and pressures were growing within the Reich to join the imperial race. Further, in a move predictive of future Berlin diplomacy, Bismarck tried to pressure Russia by refusing to list its bonds on the Berlin stock exchange. Like later German efforts to browbeat great powers, this had the opposite effect from that intended. Financial necessity and the decision of Bismarck's successors not to renew the Russian alliance sent St Petersburg into the arms of France. The latter, now in its Third Republic, had capital to export; Russia had the population for cannon fodder which France lacked; and both feared Germany's growing power. Austria and Italy remained tied to Germany by formal defensive treaties in the Triple Alliance or Triplice.

France and Russia also signed a defensive treaty in 1894. The impetus to further alliance-building came when Germany began to flex its new muscles and develop more. In 1897, the irrepressible young German Emperor (or Kaiser), Wilhelm II, announced that Germany was embarking on *Weltpolitik* or a world policy. Though initially aimed at China and colonies, this was always amorphous and undefined, and unfocused expansionism, but it often meant that when another power gained something, Germany demanded compensation. Then in 1898 in Damascus, Wilhelm declared himself the protector of the world's Muslims, most of whom were subjects of other European powers. Also in

1898, Germany, already the possessor of Europe's finest army, launched a major naval building programme, which alarmed London, and in 1899 it signed a contract with the Turkish government to build a railway from Berlin to Baghdad. Since railway construction offered many opportunities to acquire political and military as well as economic influence, the possibility now arose that Germany might displace Britain and France in the Ottoman Empire and thus in the Middle East.

Though Germany, chronically short of capital, offered financial participation in the railway to foreign powers, these moves were potentially or directly threatening to Britain, France, and Russia. Britain, offended by Berlin's vociferous support to South Africa's Boers as tension built toward the Boer war of 1899–1902, viewed Germany's *Weltpolitik* and naval programme as threats to its Empire and import-driven economy. Thus it reacted quickly in 1898 with the first of several overtures to Germany, all of which failed because Berlin was confident that Britain would never join its traditional enemies, France and Russia, and so Germany could wait to attain fully its steep terms for an arrangement and perhaps even an alliance against France and Russia.

After the initial failure to reach agreement, and with vital interests at stake, Britain hastened to solve its problems elsewhere so as to be free to face the new challenge. "Splendid isolation" no longer seemed so attractive. In 1990, it conceded the future Panama Canal to the United States, moving toward a rapprochement of the English-speaking nations, and in 1902 it signed an alliance with Japan, which was initially directed partly against Russia. It also began to modernize the Royal Navy, which led to a naval race with Germany. Meanwhile, Britain's effort to acquire a north-south line of African colonies from Cairo to Capetown clashed with France's reach for an east-west string from the Red Sea to the Atlantic and had led in 1898 to a tense confrontation at Fashoda in the southern Sudan. Mindful of her own limited power and her burgeoning neighbour, France backed down. The confrontation cleared the air and led in time to the Anglo-French Entente Cordiale of 1904. This was not a formal treaty but rather merely the settlement of a series of colonial disputes, notably in North Africa, and an informal but historic willingness to be friends after five hundred years of hostility. Clearly, both states were responding to perceived threats from the new great power.

The Entente Cordiale had been negotiated but not yet signed when the Russo-Japanese war broke out, raising the possibility that Britain and France could be forced into war with each other by their respective allies. That did not happen, but the prospect occasioned further diplomacy, especially as France was eager to bring her two friends together. In addition, the destruction of the Russian fleet at Tshushima and the transfer of Russian attention after its defeat from east Asia to the Balkans made Russia seem less threatening to Britain whereas Berlin continued its blustering, browbeating diplomacy, notably during the first Moroccan crisis of 1904–1905. Germany seemed to seek both domination of the European continent and parity with Britain elsewhere in the world and on the seas, thereby ensuring German preeminence, endangering British imperial lifelines, and negating London's long-standing policy of resisting the continental ascendance of any power. As a consequence, Germany now seemed the greater danger to Britain, who accordingly came to terms with Russia in 1907, ending long hostility and signing agreements about Tibet (Xi Zang), Persia, and Afghanistan. There now developed the Triple Entente (with Japan attached), an informal grouping of Britain, France, and Russia.

Although the old Concert was not quite moribund, all European powers of consequence were thus aligned in the two blocs, the Triple Alliance down the center of Europe, and the Triple Entente on the edges. Germany saw the Entente policy of containment as encirclement, and its fears in this respect only increased 'the amalgam of insecurity and self-assertion in her make-up. . .'. Thus its diplomacy became more bullying, which had the effect of driving Britain and France together, causing the Triple Entente to solidify. Both Germany's insistent claims and Russia's return from East Asia to compete with Austria in the Balkans contributed to growing conflict and tension between the two alignments.

Most of the conflicts concerned imperial matters although a European power struggle underlay them all. Part of the trouble was that the days when there were plenty of colonies available for everybody had passed, and as the powers bumped into each other, the latecomers were dissatisfied. Timing proved crucial to the imperial race; those who did not seize the moment encountered difficulties in doing later what other powers had done earlier. The latecomers were Germany, Japan, and Italy, impatient youngsters who remained dissatisfied, always seeking more until they went down to decisive defeat in World War II. But in the decade before the First World War, the collisions were not only in Africa and Asia, but also in the Balkans, as Russia turned to Austria's sole remaining sphere. Wherever confrontations occurred they brought with them the risk of a major conflagration, not merely a local conflict between two states, but a global struggle between two alignments of powers.

War among the major powers was avoided for a decade despite a series of crises, but only at the price of exhausting options and reducing flexibility, thus rendering resolution more difficult for the future. Great powers, especially the more precarious ones, could not repeatedly accept defeat and humiliation and still remain great powers. Another option which several states exhausted was that of not supporting an ally. With Europe divided into two camps, both of which were arming briskly, retaining one's allies was vital. However, one can desert an ally only so often and still keep it as an ally. Equally, the need for allies meant that both crises and atonements for desertion tended to solidify the two rival alignments, further reducing flexibility.

During the decade before 1914 the Anglo-German naval competition continued, despite British efforts to come to terms, and crises, often entailing lack of support from allies or diplomatic defeat, were too numerous to recount briefly. Though all depleted the reservoirs of good will and elasticity, only a few were so serious that they brought the risk of a pan-European war. Nonetheless, the fact that Europe came to the brink of a great war five or six times in ten short years is indicative of the instability and tension which were mounting.

Part of the problem was that Europe's power system was increasingly out of balance. The Habsburg Empire was no longer really a great power, while France was fading in comparative terms. Russia's vast size did not fully compensate for technological and organizational weakness, especially after the regime was shaken by defeat and revolution in 1905, while at the other end of the continent, Britain's economic lead was less commanding than before. In the middle of Europe Germany was becoming comparatively something of a superpower, already dominant economically, especially in relation to its neighbours, and aspiring to a comparable political and world position. And this young, thrustingly ambitious Reich pursued a high-risk policy of confrontation which created or aggravated crises, contributing to ten years of international tension. . . .

In the chanceries of Europe, a major war was anticipated before long. Some leaders thought that sooner rather than later would be more advantageous for their countries. All assumed that a pan-European war would be short — for economic and technological reasons. But despite the decade of crises and mounting tension, the situation seemed more serene in 1914. In particular, Anglo-German relations appeared improved. The two countries had worked together at the conference of ambassadors in London in 1913 to prevent an Austro-Serbian war, though the German calculations and hope was that if war came, Russia would be blamed and Britain would remain neutral. But that was not public knowledge. However, the citizenry did know that there had not been a major European war for a hundred years; collisions between the great powers had been short and snappy, especially since mid-century, and the last one had occurred nearly 45 years before. A widespread assumption had developed that wars were something which occurred only overseas or in the backward Balkans among quarrelsome infant states. Even Anglo-German naval relations were now less tense, and in July of 1914 the two countries reached an agreement about the Berlin to Baghdad railway. For these and other reasons, the prospects for peace looked better than in the recent past as the spectacularly beautiful summer of 1914 opened.

The sunny calm was shattered on 28 June 1914 by the assassination of the heir to the Austrian throne and his wife in Sarajevo, the capital of Bosnia, by young Bosnian nationalists backed by Unification or Death,[1] a secret Serbian society in which key Serbian army officers were dominant. Their complicity is clear; members of the Serbian cabinet may have had partial foreknowledge as well. The chanceries of Europe anticipated an Austrian reaction directed against Serbia, whose involvement was widely assumed, but not a major war. However, the assassination led to the July crisis of 1914, culminating in World War I. . . .

Austria's actions played a substantial contributory role, and the Habsburg monarchy is usually assigned secondary responsibility for causing World War I, but only secondary, because Austria's actions were obviously contingent. It is beyond serious doubt that it would not have acted against Serbia or risked war with Russia without solid German support. Berlin not only gave that support and repeatedly urged Austria on but also decided upon war now and declared it against Russia and France without any direct provocation from either. A leading German scholar of the July crisis has concluded that "the German Government opened Pandora's box in an act of sheer political and ideological despair."

One must ask what brought the European continent's strongest power to such despair and created a situation where it almost desperately opted to set off a continental war with the risk of world war. Some of the answers lie within German domestic politics and the psychological frame of reference of its leaders. Additional answers lie, as do the contributory errors from other powers, in broader aspects of the European scene in 1914.

For example, there were both men and nations which could ill afford to back down. Too often in the past, the Russian foreign minister, his Austrian counterpart, and the German Kaiser had all displayed timidity, hesitation, and reluctance to commit themselves to firm action. Kaiser Wilhelm in particular was determined to prove that he was not a coward, and, like the Russian foreign minister, he was rather unstable. Similarly, it was doubtful whether the Austrian and Russian regimes could survive major diplomatic defeats. Austria was internally so precarious and Russia had sustained so many recent humiliations that disintegration of the one and revolution in the other were real possibilities. This factor loomed large in the calculations of leaders in Vienna, St Petersburg, and Berlin. Paris concentrated more on retaining its Russian ally. Moreover, the intensity of public opinion in most countries made backing down almost impossible for weak regimes and politicians who wished to retain office. Under the circumstances, it was

[1] Popularly known as the Black Hand.

easy to hope that a strong stand would deter others and solve the problem.

The stronger great powers feared that their allies would cease to be great powers and, to varying degrees, felt a need to bolster them. There was also a widespread fear of losing an ally altogether. Both Britain and France had worried in past crises about losing Russia: France because she compensated for her own deficiencies with the Russian tie, Britain from fear of adding Russia to its enemies. Austria and Germany feared losing each other: Austria because its need was great, Germany from a sense of isolation. Both France and Germany worried that Russia and Austria would fight only if their own interests were involved. Each concluded that it was better for war to come on an issue where the ally's concerns were directly engaged.

Most states feared losing prestige and great power status. This was of intense concern to Austria and Russia, and in both instances was focused primarily on the Balkans, which impacted on domestic concerns and where the situation had changed so rapidly with the removal of Turkey. Yet dread of the results of backing down was widespread and extended even to Britain, master of the seas and of the world's greatest empire. On 31 July 1914, a senior British official argued for action by saying, "The theory that England cannot engage in a big war means her abdiction as an independent state. . . . A balance of power cannot be maintained by a State that is incapable of fighting and consequently carries no weight."

Threats to prestige, authority, and vital interests were almost universally perceived. Britain had long recognized a German challenge on and beyond the seas; the invasion of Belgium seemed to be striking at the British heartland. France, aside from other considerations, could hardly hand over her border forts without becoming a defenceless laughing stock. Russia felt its future in the Balkans and among the Slavs was at stake. Austria saw Serbia as a danger to its very existence, whereas Germany perceived a Russian threat and perhaps was as obsessed by Russia as Britain had been in the mid-nineteenth century and the United States would be in the mid-twentieth century. Clearly, some threats were more real and immediate than others, but leaders acted upon their perceptions, even if erroneous.

Nationalism, whether unifying or divisive, and imperialism contributed to the crises and tensions of the pre-war years, if they did not themselves directly cause the war. And certainly Austria-Hungary's ageing, archaic multinational empire, trying to maintain itself against mounting nationalist pressures, was a major contributing factor, as was the Austro-Russian rivalry among the infant national states of the Balkans. The pre-war arms race contributed to the international tension of the era but of itself was not a direct causal factor, despite the beliefs of a later generation, particularly of Americans.

More important, probably, was a widespread pseudo-Darwinian view of international politics, an assumption that it was a question of dog eat dog with the strongest and speediest dog surviving. Furthermore, crises had become the norm, so much so that some leaders expected war before long. Especially in Germany, there was a belief that war and Darwinian struggle were unavoidable, which perhaps explains the preoccupation with an assumed Russian threat and a fatalistic view that a Russo-German war was inevitable soon. Nowhere was there any awareness of what a war would be like; as a result there was scant caution about the dangers war would bring. The short war illusion was widespread and had contributed to the arms race on the assumption that the war would be fought with what equipment one had at the outset. The businessmen would see to it that the war was brief (if they did not prevent it altogether, as some believed, but not those determining national policies). Few in power had much appreciation of what the industrialization, nationalization, and democratization of war signified. Indeed, it was widely held that war was good and glorious and cleansing.

In some countries, military men and military plans played a considerable role. The military plans were rigid, too few in number, and had tight timetables; the military men were wedded to them. The generals tended to be more eager for war than the civilian leaders; even where they were not, there was a fear that any delay in mobilization would be catastrophic. Initially there was often lack of co-ordination between civilian and military leaders, thanks to administrative inadequacy at the top, especially in Germany and Russia, and then tugs-of-war ensued, particularly to sway the autocrat. At a more fundamental level, appreciations in various countries of the military balance of power, then and as it would be in the future, clearly contributed to the pressures toward war.

The alliance system did not of itself cause any war, local, continental, or world. But it constituted a substantial reason why a local crisis became a world war, and partially explains why a murder in Bosnia caused Germany to invade Belgium and why that event in turn led to a world war, with Japan occupying Germany's Asian colonies. This is particularly true in view of the suddenness and speed of the crisis. Peace movements collapsed, and little time was left for diplomacy. Furthermore, previous crises had made the alliances more rigid. Europe had managed to edge past the abyss repeatedly in recent years, but only at the price of expending options and losing flexibility. Now governments felt they had few choices left. . . .

In the end, the debate always comes back to Germany. Clearly, Austria intended to start nothing without Germany at its side, and none of the Entente powers actively wanted a war in 1914. There was no Entente equivalent to Wilhelm's "Now or never." Thus, one must ask whether Germany wanted war in 1914, if so why, and what its reasons and motives were. Why did it encourage local war, accept continental war, and risk world war? The answers are contradictory, thanks to il-logic, conflicts, and differing perceptions within Berlin's upper eche-lons, where policy-making was disorganized. . . .

War came when it did primarily because Germany opted for a war, if not necessarily for the war which eventuated. There has been a good deal of debate about why Germany did so and to what end. Was it largely a matter of miscalculation? Had there been a systematic two-year German plan for world conquest? Was Germany running a calcu-lated risk, hoping to get its way without intent of war? Was the goal a preventive war, to deter future Russian aggression, or was Germany it-self engaging in an opportunistic war of aggression?

The answers to these questions are a matter of opinion and the ob-ject of heated historical debate. Certainly there was miscalculation aplenty, and repeated gambles constituted calculated or miscalculated risks. It is perhaps begging the question to say that little German policy formulation was systematic, but, despite conferences debating war in December 1912 and thereafter, evidence for a conscious systematic two-year drive toward a world war depends heavily on interpretation and is hotly disputed. Clearly, Germany seized the opportunity for a war of aggression, but the question is why it thought it should.

Perhaps it is best to let German leaders speak for themselves. In February 1918 Bethmann Hollweg, who had been Chancellor in 1914, explained privately, "Yes, my god, in a certain sense it was a preventive war. But when war was hanging above us, when it had to come in two years even more dangerously and more inescapably, and when the gen-erals said, now it is still possible, without defeat, but not in two years time." And in August 1916, Bethmann's close aide and confidante, who himself propounded the theory of the calculated risk, explained that the purpose of the war was "defence against present-day France, preventive war against the Russia of the future, struggle with Britain for world domination."

56

ERICH MARIA REMARQUE

From *All Quiet on the Western Front*

In this selection, the beginning of possibly the most famous war novel ever written, we are introduced to the main characters and to the daily routines of the German army on "the Western Front," the long line of trenches that stretched across northern France from Switzerland to the English Channel for most of the war between 1914 and 1918. What does this selection suggest about the types of people recruited to serve in the army? How does Remarque view friendship, authority, and discipline in the army? Do you imagine these German soldiers behaved very differently from French or English soldiers?

Thinking Historically

Remarque's novel is not intended as an explanation of the causes of war, but this excerpt offers an explanation of how young men were recruited to fight and gives us some idea of their mental state. How might you use material from this novel, assuming that it is factual, to propose at least one cause of World War I?

In this brief selection, the author also suggests something about the consequences of the war. What, according to Remarque, are the war's likely outcomes? The consequences described here are arrived at very early in the war. Is it likely that they will change significantly as the war continues?

Kantorek had been our schoolmaster, a stern little man in a grey tail-coat, with a face like a shrew mouse. He was about the same size as Corporal Himmelstoss, the "terror of Klosterberg." It is very queer that the unhappiness of the world is so often brought on by small men. They are so much more energetic and uncompromising than the big fellows. I have always taken good care to keep out of sections with small company commanders. They are mostly confounded little martinets.

During drill-time Kantorek gave us long lectures until the whole of our class went, under his shepherding, to the District Commandant and

Erich Maria Remarque, *All Quiet on the Western Front*, trans. A. W. Wheen (New York: Fawcett Books, 1929), 1–18.

volunteered. I can see him now, as he used to glare at us through his spectacles and say in a moving voice: "Won't you join up, Comrades?"

These teachers always carry their feelings ready in their waistcoat pockets, and trot them out by the hour. But we didn't think of that then.

There was, indeed, one of us who hesitated and did not want to fall into line. That was Joseph Behm, a plump, homely fellow. But he did allow himself to be persuaded, otherwise he would have been ostracized. And perhaps more of us thought as he did, but no one could very well stand out, because at that time even one's parents were ready with the word "coward"; no one had the vaguest idea what we were in for. The wisest were just the poor and simple people. They knew the war to be a misfortune, whereas those who were better off, and should have been able to see more clearly what the consequences would be, were beside themselves with joy.

Katczinsky said that was a result of their upbringing. It made them stupid. And what Kat said, he had thought about.

Strange to say, Behm was one of the first to fall. He got hit in the eye during an attack, and we left him lying for dead. We couldn't bring him with us, because we had to come back helter-skelter. In the afternoon suddenly we heard him call, and saw him crawling about in No Man's Land. He had only been knocked unconscious. Because he could not see, and was mad with pain, he failed to keep under cover, and so was shot down before anyone could go and fetch him in.

Naturally we couldn't blame Kantorek for this. Where would the world be if one brought every man to book? There were thousands of Kantoreks, all of whom were convinced that they were acting for the best — in a way that cost them nothing.

And that is why they let us down so badly.

For us lads of eighteen they ought to have been mediators and guides to the world of maturity, the world of work, of duty, of culture, of progress — to the future. We often made fun of them and played jokes on them, but in our hearts we trusted them. The idea of authority, which they represented, was associated in our minds with a greater insight and a more humane wisdom. But the first death we saw shattered this belief. We had to recognize that our generation was more to be trusted than theirs. They surpassed us only in phrases and in cleverness. The first bombardment showed us our mistake, and under it the world as they had taught it to us broke in pieces.

While they continued to write and talk, we saw the wounded and dying. While they taught that duty to one's country is the greatest thing, we already knew that death-throes are stronger. But for all that we were no mutineers, no deserters, no cowards — they were very free with all these expressions. We loved our country as much as they; we went courageously into every action; but also we distinguished the false from true, we had suddenly learned to see. And we saw that there was nothing of their world left. We were all at once terribly alone; and alone we must see it through.

Before going over to see Kemmerich we pack up his things: He will need them on the way back.

In the dressing station there is great activity: It reeks as ever of carbolic, pus, and sweat. We are accustomed to a good deal in the billets, but this makes us feel faint. We ask for Kemmerich. He lies in a large room and receives us with feeble expressions of joy and helpless agitation. While he was unconscious someone had stolen his watch.

Müller shakes his head: "I always told you that nobody should carry as good a watch as that."

Müller is rather crude and tactless, otherwise he would hold his tongue, for anybody can see that Kemmerich will never come out of this place again. Whether he finds his watch or not will make no difference, at the most one will only be able to send it to his people.

"How goes it, Franz?" asks Kropp.

Kemmerich's head sinks.

"Not so bad . . . but I have such a damned pain in my foot."

We look at his bed covering. His leg lies under a wire basket. The bed covering arches over it. I kick Müller on the shin, for he is just about to tell Kemmerich what the orderlies told us outside: that Kemmerich has lost his foot. The leg is amputated. He looks ghastly, yellow and wan. In his face there are already the strained lines that we know so well, we have seen them now hundreds of times. They are not so much lines as marks. Under the skin the life no longer pulses, it has already pressed out the boundaries of the body. Death is working through from within. It already has command in the eyes. Here lies our comrade, Kemmerich, who a little while ago was roasting horse flesh with us and squatting in the shell-holes. He it is still and yet it is not he any longer. His features have become uncertain and faint, like a photographic plate from which two pictures have been taken. Even his voice sounds like ashes.

I think of the time when we went away. His mother, a good plump matron, brought him to the station. She wept continually, her face was bloated and swollen. Kemmerich felt embarrassed, for she was the least composed of all; she simply dissolved into fat and water. Then she caught sight of me and took hold of my arm again and again, and implored me to look after Franz out there. Indeed he did have a face like a child, and such frail bones that after four weeks' pack-carrying he already had flat feet. But how can a man look after anyone in the field!

"Now you will soon be going home," says Kropp. "You would have had to wait at least three or four months for your leave."

Kemmerich nods. I cannot bear to look at his hands, they are like wax. Under the nails is the dirt of the trenches, it shows through blue-black like poison. It strikes me that these nails will continue to grow like lean fantastic cellar-plants long after Kemmerich breathes no more.

I see the picture before me. They twist themselves into corkscrews and grow and grow, and with them the hair on the decaying skull, just like grass in a good soil, just like grass, how can it be possible ———

Müller leans over. "We have brought your things, Franz."

Kemmerich signs with his hands. "Put them under the bed."

Müller does so. Kemmerich starts on again about the watch. How can one calm him without making him suspicious?

Müller reappears with a pair of airman's boots. They are fine English boots of soft, yellow leather which reach to the knees and lace up all the way — they are things to be coveted.

Müller is delighted at the sight of them. He matches their soles against his own clumsy boots and says: "Will you be taking them with you then, Franz?"

We all three have the same thought; even if he should get better, he would be able to use only one — they are no use to him. But as things are now it is a pity that they should stay here; the orderlies will of course grab them as soon as he is dead.

"Won't you leave them with us?" Müller repeats.

Kemmerich doesn't want to. They are his most prized possessions.

"Well, we could exchange," suggests Müller again. "Out here one can make some use of them." Still Kemmerich is not to be moved.

I tread on Müller's foot; reluctantly he puts the fine boots back again under the bed.

We talk a little more and then take our leave.

"Cheerio, Franz."

I promise him to come back in the morning. Müller talks of doing so, too. He is thinking of the lace-up boots and means to be on the spot.

Kemmerich groans. He is feverish. We get hold of an orderly outside and ask him to give Kemmerich a dose of morphia.

He refuses. "If we were to give morphia to everyone we would have to have tubs full ———"

"You only attend to officers properly," says Kropp viciously.

I hastily intervene and give him a cigarette. He takes it.

"Are you usually allowed to give it, then?" I ask him.

He is annoyed. "If you don't think so, then why do you ask?"

I press a few more cigarettes into his hand. "Do us the favour ———"

"Well, all right," he says.

Kropp goes in with him. He doesn't trust him and wants to see. We wait outside.

Müller returns to the subject of the boots. "They would fit me perfectly. In these boots I get blister after blister. Do you think he will last till tomorrow after drill?" If he passes out in the night, we know where the boots ———"

Kropp returns. "Do you think ———?" he asks.

"Done for," said Müller emphatically.

We go back to the huts. I think of the letter that I must write to-morrow to Kemmerich's mother. I am freezing. I could do with a tot of rum. Müller pulls up some grass and chews it. Suddenly little Kropp throws his cigarette away, stamps on it savagely, and looking around him with a broken and distracted face, stammers "Damned shit, the damned shit!"

We walk on for a long time. Kropp has calmed himself; we understand, he saw red; out there every man gets like that sometime.

"What has Kantorek written to you?" Müller asks him.

He laughs. "We are the Iron Youth."

We all three smile bitterly, Kropp rails: He is glad that he can speak.

Yes, that's the way they think, these hundred thousand Kantoreks! Iron Youth! Youth! We are none of us more than twenty years old. But young? Youth? That is long ago. We are old folk.

57

Government Posters:
Enlistment and War Bonds

Posters were the communication medium of the First World War. In an age when governments had still not taught most people how to read but increasingly needed their consent or compliance, images spoke louder than words.

The American poster from 1917 and the German poster from 1915–1916 implored men to enlist in the army; the Italian poster from 1917 encouraged people to buy war bonds (see Figure 10.1). What do you think accounts for the similar graphic style used in all three posters? How effective do you think the pointed finger of responsibility was? Some people have suggested that these images are the sign of a mass society where the individual can become anonymous but must be reached and motivated anyway. What do you think?

James Montgomery Flagg, Recruiting poster for U.S. Army, 1917. Museum of Modern Art, New York. Achille Luciano Mauzan, Italian poster for national war loan, 1917. Museo Civico Luigi Bailo, Salce Collection, Treviso. German poster Anonymous, Recruiting poster for German Army, 1915–1916. Stuttgart Staatsgalerie. Max Gallo, *The Poster in History* (New York: American Heritage, McGraw-Hill, 1972), 132–33.

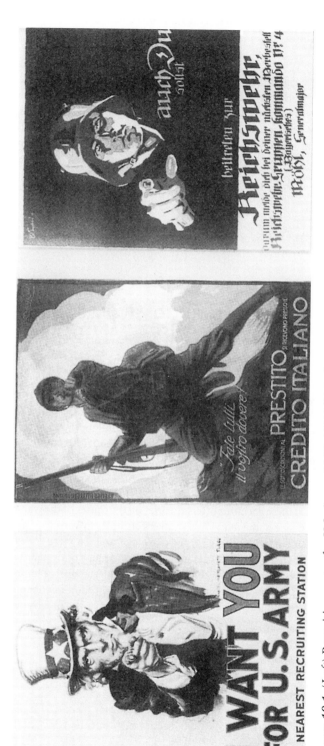

Figure 10.1 (*Left*) Recruiting poster for U.S. Army, 1917; (*Middle*) Italian poster for national war loan, 1917; (*Right*) Recruiting poster for German Army, 1915–1916.

Thinking Historically

The rise of nationalism is often cited as one of the causes for the outbreak of the First World War. Do you see any hallmarks of separate national identity in these posters? Is the similarity of these posters an indication of the merging national identities of countries at war? Is it possible that one of the consequences of the war was such a convergence of identities, perhaps due to the similar experiences of each country in wartime?

58

S. V. BRITTEN, HUGO MULLER, BILL BLAND, AND KANDE KAMARA

Witness of Soldiers

These four soldiers came from different backgrounds and different parts of the world, but they all dug into the trenches on the Western Front in France. How were their experiences alike? How were they different? What do their experiences tell you about the daily lives of soldiers on the front?

Thinking Historically

While none of these accounts offers theories on the causes of the war, each provides evidence of the individual soldier's attitudes toward war and the enemy. If these individuals are representative of their country and social class, what do their comments suggest about the origins of the war?

The consequences of war for millions was death. Both Bland and Muller were killed in 1916 on the Western Front, Bland in June in the battle of the Somme River and Muller in October in the nearby Ancre

Sergeant S. V. Britten, The Royal Highlanders of Canada, "Diary of a Canadian" (1915), in *Voices and Images of the Great War* (Lyn Macdonald, 1988). Hugo Muller, German Army (1915 letter), in *German Students' War Letters* (Philip Witkopp, 1929). Captain Bill Bland, 22nd Battalion, The Manchester Regiment, 7th Manchester Pais (1916 letter), Imperial War Museum. Kande Kamara, Oral Testimony recorded Sept. 22–24, 1976, from Joe Harris Lunn, "Kande Kamara Speaks: An Oral History of the West African Experience in France, 1914–1918," in *Africa and the First World War*, ed. Melvin E. Page (London: Macmillan, 1987), 44–45, 48.

Valley. We can only imagine the consequences for those they left behind. Judging from these accounts, however, what do you imagine were the consequences of the war for those who fought and survived? What impact might these veterans have had on their countries domestically and internationally? Would their common experiences in war have prompted common consequences after the war, or would these people simply go back to their different lives?

Diary of a Canadian
[S. V. Britten]

Diary: 17 April 1915

Rose at 8.30, went down to Ypres with Capt. Morrisey & Rae, & spent day there, saw over the ruins of the Cathedral & Cloth Hall etc. Stopped all the afternoon, bought a handkerchief of Flemish Lace (& sending it to Vera as a souvenir), brought back a quantity of stuff for ourselves, including two bottles of wine. Witnessed an exciting battle between a British & a German biplane. The latter was brought down about 7 p.m. Terrific artillery fire started about 6 p.m., & lasted all night.

22 April

Left at 6.30 p.m. for reserve trenches and reached our reserve dugouts via St Julien. Just rat holes! One hell of accommodation! Got to the trenches as a fatigue party with stake & sandbags, and thought they were reserve trenches, they were so rotten. No trenches at all in parts, just isolated mounds. Found German's feet sticking up through the ground. The Gurkhas[1] had actually used human bodies instead of sandbags.

Right beside the stream where we were working were the bodies of two dead, since November last, one face downwards in full marching order, with his kit on his back. He died game! Stench something awful and dead all round. Water rats had made a home of their decomposed bodies. Visited the barbed wire with Rae — ordinary wire strung across. Quit about 1 a.m., came back to our dugouts and found them on fire. Had to march out to St Julien, & put up in a roofless house — not a roof left on anything in the whole place. Found our sack of food had been stolen and we were famished. Certainly a most unlucky day, for I lost my cherished pipe in the evening also. Bed at 4 a.m.

23 April

Up about noon and had no breakfast. Had a good view of the village of the dead, everything in a most heartbreaking state. We found a piano and

---

[1] Soldiers from Nepal.

had music. Furious shelling started about 4.30 p.m., and we took to the dugouts. Almost suffocated by the poisonous fumes! Got into marching order (without packs) & lined for action outside the village. Got to No. 7 station & found Captain Morrisey there, almost suffocated. Brought Lieutenant Molson out to St Jean, & we came to St Julien, getting a lift in an ambulance. Village a mess of dead horses, limbers, and men. Went on ration fatigue & tried to get up to the trenches but failed. Scouted the road, waited under heavy shell fire for about two hours, then moved off, & made a circumference up to the trenches via 48th communication trench. Getting there at almost daybreak.

23 April

Terrible day, no food or water, dead & dying all around.

Letter from a Former German Law Student
[Hugo Muller]

At Agny, near Arras,
17 October 1915

I am enclosing a French field-postcard, which I want you to put with my war-souvenirs. It came out of the letter-case of a dead French soldier. It has been extremely interesting to study the contents of the letter-cases of French killed and prisoners. The question frequently recurs, just as it does with us: "When will it all end?"

To my astonishment I practically never found any expression of hatred or abuse of Germany or German soldiers. On the other hand, many letters from relations revealed an absolute conviction of the justice of their cause, and sometimes also of confidence in victory. In every letter mother, fiancée, children, friends, whose photographs were often enclosed, spoke of a joyful return and a speedy meeting — and now they are all lying dead and hardly even buried between the trenches, while over them bullets and shells sing their gruesome dirge.

Letter from a Former
English University Lecturer
[Bill Bland]

18 February 1916
[France]

Darling, I can't bear you to be unhappy about me. Don't be grey and old, my darling. Think of the *cause,* the cause. It is England, England, England, always and all the time. The individual counts as nothing, the common cause everything. Have faith, my dear. If only you will have faith in the ultimate victory of the good, the true, and the beautiful, you will not be unhappy even if I never return to you. Dear, if one's number is up, one will go under. I am here, and I shall either survive or not survive. In the meantime, I have never been truly happier.

P.S. Hardship be damned! It's all one long blaze of glory.

Memories of a West African in France
[Kande Kamara]

. . . One of my younger brothers . . . was shot in the thigh . . . and he cried out . . . "Brother, they've shot me." But I didn't look at him — I didn't help him — because during wartime, even if your friend is shot dead, you would continue facing the enemy to save your own life. Because [officers] were watching you, and if you were afraid to shoot the enemy . . . your own people would shoot you down. . . . I didn't say anything; I kept quiet. I wasn't looking at him, but tears were running down my face.

Soon the doctor came with the ambulance to look in the gutters [trenches]. And they found my brother there, and . . . they picked him up, and my brother said, "I'm not going back in the vehicle." And he asked, "Why did I come here?" And they answered, "You came to fight." And he said, "I'm going to, just come tie my wound." And the doctor came and tied his leg and gave him some medicine. . . . Then my brother said, "Let me go . . . that's my brother down there, and wherever he dies, I will die there too." And that's when they said to him, "You have a really strong heart." . . . And because he wasn't going to stop fighting, and he was already wounded, and he was going to stay with me, he was promoted to sergeant for his bravery.

At the beginning, the white people were always in the front line. . . . But when we got to understand them . . . and when they started trusting us . . . that changed. . . . At the very end we were all mixed, because by then everyone knew that mind and their heart and no one was afraid of color except for innocents.

[When] you see a black sergeant . . . and a white corporal comes . . . and he doesn't salute the black sergeant, and the black sergeant would arrest him . . . [then you know you have] equality with the white man.

If we hadn't fought, if we — the black people — hadn't fought in western wars, and been taken overseas, and demonstrated some ability of human dignity, we wouldn't have been regarded today as anything.

59

WILFRED OWEN
Dulce et Decorum Est

Wilfred Owen enlisted in the British Army in 1915, was wounded in 1917, and was hospitalized, released, and sent back to the front, where he died on November 4, 1918, one week before the end of the war. In this poem, he describes a poison gas attack. Like the machine gun and the airplane, gas was a common element of the new mechanized mass warfare. Owen describes how physically debilitating the effects of gas were. Why was gas such an effective and deadly weapon? How, according to Owen, had the nature of war changed?

Thinking Historically

The concluding phrase, which means "Sweet and proper it is to die for one's country," was a Latin declaration of patriotic duty that English students repeated as a lesson, not only in Latin classes but, more important, in their political education as subjects of the British empire. How does Owen portray this lesson as a cause of the war? What does he imagine to be the consequences of fighting a war with such patriotic slogans in mind?

Dulce et Decorum Est

Bent double, like old beggars under sacks,
Knock-kneed, coughing like hags, we cursed
    through sludge,
Till on the haunting flares we turned our backs
And towards our distant rest began the trudge.
Men marched asleep. Many had lost their boots
But limped on, blood-shod. All went lame; all
    blind;
Drunk with fatigue; deaf even to the hoots
Of tired, outstripped Five-Nines[1] that dropped
    behind.

Gas! GAS! Quick, boys! — An ecstasy of
    fumbling,

---

[1] German artillery shells.

Wilfred Owen, *Poems,* ed. Siegfried Sassoon (London: Chatto and Windus, 1920).

Fitting the clumsy helmets just in time;
But someone still was yelling out and stumbling,
And flound'ring like a man in fire or lime. . . .
Dim, through the misty panes and thick green
 light,
As under a green sea, I saw him drowning.

In all my dreams, before my helpless sight,
He plunges at me, guttering, choking,
 drowning.

If in some smothering dreams you too could
 pace
Behind the wagon that we flung him in,
And watch the white eyes writhing in his face,
His hanging face, like a devil's sick of sin;
If you could hear, at every jolt, the blood
Come gargling from the froth-corrupted lungs,
Obscene as cancer, bitter as the cud
Of vile, incurable sores on innocent tongues,
My friend, you would not tell with such high
 zest,
To children ardent for some desperate glory.
The old Lie: Dulce et decorum est
Pro patria mori.

60

V. I. LENIN

From *War and Revolution*

One of the great casualties of the First World War was the Russian
empire, including the czar, his family, many of the members of their
class, and its centuries-old autocratic system. The burden of war was
simply too much for Russian society to bear. The disillusionment in
the army and civilian society, along with the overwhelming costs of

V. I. Lenin, *Collected Works,* vol. 24, 4th English ed. (Moscow: Progress Publishers, 1964), 398–421.

war, fueled uprisings among civilians and the army. Czar Nicholas II was forced to abdicate in February of 1917 and to turn power over to a group of nobles and the Russian parliament. The government that emerged, under Alexander Kerensky, proved unable to satisfy the growing demands of peasants, veterans, and urban workers for "land, peace, and bread," a slogan that V. I. Lenin and the communists exploited, successfully seizing power from the moderate parliamentarians in October of that year.

As a Marxist, Lenin believed that he could establish a socialist society in Russia, but he argued that Russian conditions (e.g., economic underdevelopment; the devastation of war; the opposition of Europe, the United States, and Russian nobles to the revolution) made a democratic transition impossible. According to Lenin, a self-appointed government acting in the interests of the working class was the only way to a socialist Soviet Union. Lenin called this government "the dictatorship of the proletariat." And just as the government had to be protected from "counter-revolutionary" enemies who would take advantage of democratic procedures, so too did the governing party have to be administered tightly by a "vanguard" of professionals who would act secretly and ruthlessly to secure the interests of the proletariat. Thus, Lenin insisted, to secure socialism in a country at war with capitalism internally and externally, a highly motivated, tightly controlled Bolshevik party was needed to enforce the dictatorship of the proletariat.

Lenin delivered his "War and Revolution" address in May of 1917, during the fateful summer that followed the liberal February revolution and preceded the Bolshevik revolution in October. How did Lenin view the First World War and Russia's continued participation in it? What did he hope to accomplish in the summer of 1917? How did he hope to accomplish it? The most important news for Russia's allies, England and France, in the summer of 1917 was the United States' entry into the war on their behalf. What was Lenin's reaction to this development?

Thinking Historically

According to Lenin, what were the causes of the First World War? What did he believe to be the main cause of the Russian revolution that occurred in February? What were the consequences of that revolution? What did he think would be the causes of a new revolution in Russia?

What we have at present is primarily two leagues, two groups of capitalist powers. We have before us all the world's greatest capitalist powers —

Britain, France, America, and Germany — who for decades have doggedly pursued a policy of incessant economic rivalry aimed at achieving world supremacy, subjugating the small nations, and making threefold and tenfold profits on banking capital, which has caught the whole world in the net of its influence. That is what Britain's and Germany's policies really amount to. . . .

These policies show us just one thing — continuous economic rivalry between the world's two greatest giants, capitalist economies. On the one hand we have Britain, a country which owns the greater part of the globe, a country which ranks first in wealth, which has created this wealth not so much by the labour of its workers as by the exploitation of innumerable colonies, by the vast power of its banks which have developed at the head of all the others into an insignificantly small group of some four or five super-banks handling billions of rubles, and handling them in such a way that it can be said without exaggeration that there is not a patch of land in the world today on which this capital has not laid its heavy hand, not a patch of land which British capital has not enmeshed by a thousand threads. This capital grew to such dimensions by the turn of the century that its activities extended far beyond the borders of individual states and formed a group of giant banks possessed of fabulous wealth. Having begotten this tiny group of banks, it has caught the whole world in the net of its billions. . . .

On the other hand, opposed to this, mainly Anglo-French group, we have another group of capitalists, an even more rapacious, even more predatory one, a group who came to the capitalist banqueting table when all the seats were occupied, but who introduced into the struggle new methods for developing capitalist production, improved techniques, and superior organization, which turned the old capitalism, the capitalism of the free-competition age, into the capitalism of giant trusts, syndicates, and cartels. This group introduced the beginnings of state-controlled capitalist production, combining the colossal power of capitalism with the colossal power of the state into a single mechanism and bringing tens of millions of people within the single organization of state capitalism. Here is economic history, here is diplomatic history, covering several decades, from which no one can get away. It is the one and only guide-post to a proper solution of the problem of war; it leads you to the conclusion that the present war, too, is the outcome of the policies of the classes who have come to grips in it, of the two supreme giants, who, long before the war, had caught the whole world, all countries, in the net of financial exploitation and economically divided the globe up among themselves. They were bound to clash, because a redivision of this supremacy, from the point of view of capitalism, had become inevitable. . . .

The present war is a continuation of the policy of conquest, of the shooting down of whole nationalities, of unbelievable atrocities

committed by the Germans and the British in Africa, and by the British
and the Russians in Persia — which of them committed most it is difficult to say. It was for this reason that the German capitalists looked
upon them as their enemies. Ah, they said, you are strong because you
are rich? But we are stronger, therefore we have the same "sacred"
right to plunder. That is what the real history of British and German finance capital in the course of several decades preceding the war
amounts to. That is what the history of Russo-German, Russo-British,
and German-British relations amounts to. There you have the clue to
an understanding of what the war is about. That is why the story that
is current about the cause of the war is sheer duplicity and humbug.
Forgetting the history of finance capital, the history of how this war
had been brewing over the issue of redivision, they present the matter
like this: Two nations were living at peace, then one attacked the other,
and the other fought back. All science, all banks are forgotten, and the
peoples are told to take up arms, and so are the peasants, who know
nothing about politics. . . .

. . . What revolution did we make? We overthrew Nicholas. The
revolution was not so very difficult compared with one that would have
overthrown the whole class of landowners and capitalists. Who did the
revolution put in power? The landowners and capitalists — the very
same classes who have long been in power in Europe. Revolutions like
this occurred there a hundred years ago. . . . The [February] Russian
revolution has not altered the war, but it has created organizations
which exist in no other country and were seldom found in revolutions
in the West. Most of the revolutions were confined to the emergence of
governments of our Tereshchenko and Konovalov, type, while the
country remained passive and disorganized. The Russian revolution has
gone further than that. In this we have the germ of hope that it may
overcome the war. Besides the government of "near-socialist" ministers, the government of imperialist war, the government of offensive, a
government tied up with Anglo-French capital — besides this government and independent of it we have all over Russia a network of Soviets of Workers', Soldiers', and Peasants' Deputies. Here is a revolution
which has not said its last word yet. Here is a revolution which Western Europe, under similar conditions, has not known. Here are organizations of those classes which really have no need for annexations,
which have not put millions in the banks, and which are probably not
interested in whether the Russian Colonel Lyakhov and the British Liberal ambassador divided Persia properly or not. . . .

. . . In the two months following the revolution the industrialists
have robbed the whole of Russia. Capitalists have made staggering
profits; every financial report tells you that. And when the workers,
two months after the revolution, had the "audacity" to say they wanted

to live like human beings, the whole capitalist press throughout the country set up a howl.

On the question of America entering the war I shall say this. People argue that America is a democracy, America has the White House. I say: Slavery was abolished there half a century ago. The anti-slave war ended in 1865. Since then multimillionaires have mushroomed. They have the whole of America in their financial grip. They are making ready to subdue Mexico and will inevitably come to war with Japan over a carve-up of the Pacific. This war has been brewing for several decades. All literature speaks about it. America's real aim in entering the war is to prepare for this future war with Japan. The American people do enjoy considerable freedom and it is difficult to conceive them standing for compulsory military service, for the setting up of an army pursuing any aims of conquest — a struggle with Japan, for instance. The Americans have the example of Europe to show them what this leads to. The American capitalists have stepped into this war in order to have an excuse, behind a smoke-screen of lofty ideals championing the rights of small nations, for building up a strong standing army. . . .

. . . Tens of millions of people are facing disaster and death; safeguarding the interests of the capitalists is the last thing that should bother us. The only way out is for all power to be transferred to the Soviets, which represent the majority of the population. Possibly mistakes may be made in the process. No one claims that such a difficult task can be disposed of offhand. We do not say anything of the sort. We are told that we want the power to be in the hands of the Soviets, but they don't want it. We say that life's experience will suggest this solution to them, and the whole nation will see that there is no other way out. We do not want a "seizure" of power, because the entire experience of past revolutions teaches us that the only stable power is the one that has the backing of the majority of the population. "Seizure" of power, therefore, would be adventurism, and our Party will not have it. . . .

Nothing but a workers' revolution in several countries can defeat this war. The war is not a game, it is an appalling thing taking a toll of millions of lives, and it is not to be ended easily.

The soldiers at the front cannot tear the front away from the rest of the state and settle things their own way. The soldiers at the front are a part of the country. So long as the country is at war the front will suffer along with the rest. Nothing can be done about it. The war has been brought about by the ruling classes and only a revolution of the working class can end it. Whether you will get a speedy peace or not depends on how the revolution will develop.

Whatever sentimental things may be said, however much we may be told: Let us end the war immediately — this cannot be done without the development of the revolution. When power passes to the Soviets the capitalists will come out against us. Japan, France, Britain — the governments of all countries will be against us. The capitalists will be against, but the workers will be for us. That will be the end of the war which the capitalists started. There you have the answer to the question of how to end the war.

$$61$$

ROSA LUXEMBURG

From *The Russian Revolution*

Events moved very quickly in Russia in 1917. In May, Lenin insisted that the February revolution was incomplete. Remaking Russian society could not be achieved by a seizure of the state alone, but would also require mobilizing the support of a majority of the country's workers. The new Soviets, or workers' organizations, were to provide the foundation for this grassroots revolution. Futher, Lenin believed that workers throughout Europe needed to be liberated through revolution before peace and stability could be attained. The realities of the October revolution, however, obscured many of these original ideas. By the fall, Lenin and his Bolshevik party seized power without majority support while civil war still raged in Russia. The success of the Bolshevik revolution in October required a new revolutionary ideology.

Rosa Luxemburg (1870–1919) was born in Russian Poland, but at the age of nineteen fled to Switzerland, where she earned a doctorate in law and political science. At twenty-five she migrated to Germany where, as a journalist and theorist, she became an impassioned and influential voice in the German democratic socialist movement. She criticized its bureaucratic leadership and excoriated its submission to war hysteria. Her opposition to the war led to frequent imprisonment. While Luxemburg was imprisoned, Lenin seized power, and she composed her thoughts on the Russian Revolution in 1918.

As a cofounder of the German Spartacus League (which later became the German Communist Party), Luxemburg believed that the

Rosa Luxemburg, "The Russian Revolution," in *The Russian Revolution and Leninism or Marxism?* trans. Workers Age (Ann Arbor: University of Michingan Press, 1961), 69–72, 78–80.

Bolshevik Revolution could mean the liberation of working people throughout Russia, then Germany and the rest of Europe. But since 1904 she disagreed with Lenin's ideas of centralized control and party discipline. What objections does she make to Lenin's revolution? What do you think of her arguments?

Ironically, the apparent success of Lenin's strategy in Russia led many in the German Spartacus League to agitate for a similar seizure of power in Germany at the end of the war. Rosa Luxemburg tried to dissuade them, believing it to be suicidal. Outvoted, she joined their uprising in Berlin in January 1919, and was subsequently arrested and murdered by the police.

Thinking Historically

Causes and consequences are often different sides of the same event. We might say that the First World War was a cause of the Russian Revolution or, conversely, that the Russian Revolution was a consequence of the First World War. Lenin argued that one of the consequences of the First World War was the particular sort of revolution he advocated, on the grounds that a democratic revolution was impossible under the circumstances. What do you think of that argument? Rosa Luxemburg disagreed that such draconian measures were necessary, and she argued that Lenin's revolutionary strategy would have its own consequences. What were the consequences she envisioned? Was she right?

Lenin says: The bourgeois state is an instrument of oppression of the working class; the socialist state, of the bourgeoisie. To a certain extent, he says, it is only the capitalist state stood on its head. This simplified view misses the most essential thing: Bourgeois class rule has no need of the political training and education of the entire mass of the people, at least not beyond certain narrow limits. But for the proletarian dictatorship, that is the life element, the very air without which it is not able to exist. . . .

Freedom only for the supporters of the government, only for the members of one party — however numerous they may be — is no freedom at all. Freedom is always and exclusively freedom for the one who thinks differently. Not because of any fanatical concept of "justice" but because all that is instructive, wholesome, and purifying in political freedom depends on this essential characteristic, and its effectiveness vanishes when "freedom" becomes a special privilege.

The Bolsheviks themselves will not want, with hand on heart, to deny that, step by step, they have to feel out the ground, try out, experiment, test now one way now another, and that a good many of their measures do not represent priceless pearls of wisdom. Thus it must and will be with all of us when we get to the same point — even if the same difficult circumstances may not prevail everywhere.

The tacit assumption underlying the Lenin-Trotsky[1] theory of the dictatorship is this: that the socialist transformation is something for which a ready-made formula lies completed in the pocket of the revolutionary party, which needs only to be carried out energetically in practise. This is, unfortunately — or perhaps fortunately — not the case. Far from being a sum of ready-made prescriptions which have only to be applied, the practical realization of socialism as an economic, social, and juridical system is something which lies completely hidden in the mists of the future. What we possess in our program is nothing but a few main signposts which indicate the general direction in which to look for the necessary measures, and the indications are mainly negative in character at that. Thus we know more or less what we must eliminate at the outset in order to free the road for a socialist economy. But when it comes to the nature of the thousand concrete, practical measures, large and small, necessary to introduce socialist principles into economy, law, and all social relationships, there is no key in any socialist party program or textbook. That is not a shortcoming but rather the very thing that makes scientific socialism superior to the utopian varieties. The socialist system of society should only be, and can only be, an historical product, born out of the school of its own experiences, born in the course of its realization, as a result of the developments of living history, which — just like organic nature of which, in the last analysis, it forms a part — has the fine habit of always producing along with any real social need the means to its satisfaction, along with the task simultaneously the solution. However, if such is the case, then it is clear that socialism by its very nature cannot be decreed or introduced by *ukase*.[2] It has as its prerequisite a number of measures of force — against property, etc. The negative, the tearing down, can be decreed; the building up, the positive, cannot. New territory. A thousand problems. Only experience is capable of correcting and opening new ways. Only unobstructed, effervescing life falls into a thousand new forms and improvisations, brings to light creative force, itself corrects all mistaken attempts. The public life of countries with limited freedom is so poverty-stricken, so miserable, so rigid, so unfruitful, precisely because, through the exclusion of democracy, it cuts off the living sources of all spiritual riches and progress. (Proof: the year 1905 and

---

[1] Leon Trotsky (1899–1940) played a major role in the revolution in 1917, was appointed foreign minister in 1918, organized the Red Army in 1918–1920, and was exiled by Stalin in 1929. [Ed.]

[2] Order.

the months from February to October 1917.)[3] There it was political in character; the same thing applies to economic and social life also. The whole mass of the people must take part in it. Otherwise, socialism will be decreed from behind a few official desks by a dozen intellectuals.

Public control is indispensably necessary. Otherwise the exchange of experiences remains only with the closed circle of the officials of the new regime. Corruption becomes inevitable. (Lenin's words, Bulletin No. 29) Socialism in life demands a complete spiritual transformation in the masses degraded by centuries of bourgeois class rule. Social instincts in place of egotistical ones, mass initiative in place of inertia, idealism which conquers all suffering, etc., etc. No one knows this better, describes it more penetratingly; repeats it more stubbornly than Lenin. But he is completely mistaken in the means he employs. Decree, dictatorial force of the factory overseer, draconic penalties, rule by terror — all these things are but palliatives. The only way to a rebirth is the school of public life itself, the most unlimited, the broadest democracy, and public opinion. It is rule by terror which demoralizes.

When all this is eliminated, what really remains? In place of the representative bodies created by general, popular elections, Lenin and Trotsky have laid down the soviets as the only true representation of the laboring masses. But with the repression of political life in the land as a whole, life in the soviets must also become more and more crippled. Without general elections, without unrestricted freedom of press and assembly, without a free struggle of opinion, life dies out in every public institution, becomes a mere semblance of life, in which only the bureaucracy remains as the active element. Public life gradually falls asleep, a few dozen party leaders of inexhaustible energy and boundless experience direct and rule. Among them, in reality only a dozen outstanding heads do the leading and an elite of the working class is invited from time to time to meetings where they are to applaud the speeches of the leaders, and to approve proposed resolutions unanimously — at bottom, then, a clique affair — a dictatorship, to be sure, not the dictatorship of the proletariat, however, but only the dictatorship of a handful of politicians, that is a dictatorship in the bourgeois sense, in the sense of the rule of the Jacobins[4] (the postponement of the Soviet Congress from three-month periods to six-month period!). Yes, we can go even further: Such conditions must inevitably cause a brutalization of public life: attempted assassinations, shooting of hostages, etc. (Lenin's speech on discipline and corruption.)

. . . Everything that happens in Russia is comprehensible and represents an inevitable chain of causes and effects, the starting point and

---

[3] Periods of unsuccessful or limited revolution in Russia. [Ed.]
[4] Radicals in the French Revolution.

end term of which are: the failure of the German proletariat and the occupation of Russia by German imperialism. It would be demanding something superhuman from Lenin and his comrades if we should expect of them that under such circumstances they should conjure forth the finest democracy, the most exemplary dictatorship of the proletariat, and a flourishing socialist economy. By their determined revolutionary stand, their exemplary strength in action, and their unbreakable loyalty to international socialism, they have contributed whatever could possibly be contributed under such devilishly hard conditions. The danger begins only when they make a virtue of necessity and want to freeze into a complete theoretical system all the tactics forced upon them by these fatal circumstances, and want to recommend them to the international proletariat as a model of socialist tactics. When they get in their own light in this way, and hide their genuine, unquestionable historical service under the bushel of false steps forced upon them by necessity, they render a poor service to international socialism for the sake of which they have fought and suffered; for they want to place in its storehouse as new discoveries all the distortions prescribed in Russia by necessity and compulsion — in the last analysis only by-products of the bankruptcy of international socialism in the present world war.

Let the German Government Socialists cry that the rule of the Bolsheviks in Russia is a distorted expression of the dictatorship of the proletariat. If it was or is such, that is only because it is a product of the behavior of the German proletariat, in itself a distorted expression of the socialist class struggle. All of us are subject to the laws of history, and it is only internationally that the socialist order of society can be realized. The Bolsheviks have shown that they are capable of everything that a genuine revolutionary party can contribute within the limits of the historical possibilities. They are not supposed to perform miracles. For a model and faultless proletarian revolution in an isolated land, exhausted by world war, strangled by imperialism, betrayed by the international proletariat, would be a miracle.

What is in order is to distinguish the essential from the nonessential, the kernel from the accidental excrescences in the policies of the Bolsheviks. In the present period, when we face decisive final struggles in all the world, the most important problem of socialism was and is the burning question of our time. It is not a matter of this or that secondary question of tactics, but of the capacity for action of the proletariat, the strength to act, the will to power of socialism as such. In this, Lenin and Trotsky and their friends were the *first*, those who went ahead as an example to the proletariat of the world; they are still the *only ones* up to now who can cry with [sixteenth-century reformer Urlich von] Hutten: "I have dared!"

This is the essential and *enduring* in Bolshevik policy. In *this* sense theirs is the immortal historical service of having marched at the head of the international proletariat with the conquest of political power and the practical placing of the problem of the realization of socialism, and of having advanced mightily the settlement of the score between capital and labor in the entire world. In Russia the problem could only be posed. It could not be solved in Russia. And in *this* sense, the future everywhere belongs to "Bolshevism."

62

WOODROW WILSON

Fourteen Points

Woodrow Wilson (1856–1924) was president of the United States during the First World War. He presented these "Fourteen Points" to Congress in January 1918 as a basis for a just peace treaty to end the war.

You may wish to compare these proposals with the actual peace settlement. Only points VII, VIII, X, and XIV were realized. Point IV was applied only to the defeated nations. The Versailles Treaty, which the defeated Germans were forced to sign on June 28, 1919, contained much harsher terms, including the famous "war guilt" clause (Article 231):

> The Allied and Associated Governments affirm and Germany accepts the responsibility of Germany and her allies for causing all the loss and damage to which the Allied and Associated Governments and their nationals have been subjected as a consequence of the war imposed upon them by the aggression of Germany and her allies.

Why do you think there was such a gap between Wilson's ideals and the actual treaty? How might Wilson have improved on these Fourteen Points? Could he reasonably expect all of them to be accepted?

Woodrow Wilson, *War and Peace: Presidential Messages, Addresses, and Public Papers (1917–1924),* vol. 1, ed. Ray Stannard Baker and William E. Dodd (New York: Harper Brothers, 1927).

Thinking Historically

What does the first paragraph suggest Wilson thought was one cause of the war? What does the beginning of the second paragraph suggest about the cause for U.S. entry into the war? What would have been the consequences of a peace fashioned along the lines Wilson envisioned in his Fourteen Points?

It will be our wish and purpose that the processes of peace, when they are begun, shall be absolutely open, and that they shall involve and permit henceforth no secret understandings of any kind. The day of conquest and aggrandizement is gone by; so is also the day of secret covenants entered into in the interest of particular Governments and likely at some unlooked-for moment to upset the peace of the world. It is this happy fact, now clear to the view of every public man whose thoughts do not still linger in an age that is dead and gone, which makes it possible for every nation whose purposes are consistent with justice and the peace of the world to avow now or at any other time the objects it has in view.

We entered this war because violations of right had occurred which touched us to the quick and made the life of our own people impossible unless they were corrected and the world secured once for all against their recurrence. What we demand in this war, therefore, is nothing peculiar to ourselves. It is that the world be made fit and safe to live in; and particularly that it be made safe for every peace-loving nation which, like our own, wishes to live its own life, determine its own institutions, be assured of justice and fair dealing by the other peoples of the world as against force and selfish aggression. All the peoples of the world are in effect partners in this interest, and for our own part we see very clearly that unless justice be done to others it will not be done to us. The program of the world's peace, therefore, is our program; and that program, the only possible program, as we see it, is this:

I. Open covenants of peace, openly arrived at, after which there shall be no private international understandings of any kind but diplomacy shall proceed always frankly and in the public view.

II. Absolute freedom of navigation upon the seas, outside territorial waters, alike in peace and in war, except as the seas may be closed in whole or in part by international action. . . .

III. The removal, so far as possible, of all economic barriers and the establishment of an equality of trade conditions among all the nations consenting to the peace and associating themselves for its maintenance.

IV. Adequate guarantees given and taken that national armaments will be reduced to the lowest point consistent with domestic safety.

V. A free, open-minded, and absolutely impartial adjustment of all colonial claims, based upon a strict observance of the principle that in determining all such questions of sovereignty the interests of the populations concerned must have equal weight with the equitable claims of the government whose title is to be determined.

VI. The Evacuation of all Russian territory and such a settlement of all questions affecting Russia as will secure the best and freest cooperation of the other nations of the world in obtaining for her an unhampered and unembarrassed opportunity for the independent determination of her own political development and national policy and assure her of a sincere welcome into the society of free nations under institutions of her own choosing; and, more than a welcome, assistance also of every kind that she may need and may herself desire. The treatment accorded Russia by her sister nations in the months to come will be the acid test of their good will, of their comprehension of her needs as distinguished from their own interests, and of their intelligent and unselfish sympathy.

VII. Belgium, the whole world will agree, must be evacuated and restored, without any attempt to limit the sovereignty which she enjoys in common with all other free nations. No other single act will serve to restore confidence among the nations in the laws which they have themselves set and determined for the government of their relations with one another. Without this healing act the whole structure and validity of international law is forever impaired.

VIII. All French territory should be freed and the invaded portions restored, and the wrong done to France by Prussia in 1871 in the matter of Alsace-Lorraine, which has unsettled the peace of the world for nearly fifty years, should be righted, in order that peace may once more be made secure in the interest of all.

IX. A readjustment of the frontiers of Italy should be effected along clearly recognizable lines of nationality.

X. The peoples of Austria-Hungary, whose place among the nations we wish to see safeguarded and assured, should be accorded the freest opportunity of autonomous development.

XI. Rumania, Serbia, and Montenegro should be evacuated; occupied territories restored; Serbia accorded free and secure access to the sea; and the relations of the several Balkan states to one another determined by friendly counsel along historically established lines of allegiance and nationality; and international guarantees of the political and economic independence and territorial integrity of the several Balkan states should be entered into.

XII. The Turkish portions of the present Ottoman Empire should be assured a secure sovereignty, but the other nationalities which are now under Turkish rule should be assured an undoubted security of life and an absolutely unmolested opportunity of autonomous development, and the Dardanelles should be permanently opened as a free passage to the ships and commerce of all nations under international guarantees.

XIII. An independent Polish state should be erected which should include the territories inhabited by indisputably Polish populations, which should be assured a free and secure access to the sea, and whose political and economic independence and territorial integrity should be guaranteed by international covenant.

XIV. A general association of nations must be formed under specific covenants for the purpose of affording mutual guarantees of political independence and territorial integrity to great and small states alike.

In regard to these essential rectifications of wrong and assertions of right we feel ourselves to be intimate partners of all the governments and peoples associated together against the Imperialists. We cannot be separated in interest or divided in purpose. We stand together until the end.

For such arrangements and covenants we are willing to fight and to continue to fight until they are achieved; but only because we wish the right to prevail and desire a just and stable peace such as can be secured only by removing the chief provocations to war, which this program does remove. We have no jealousy of German greatness, and there is nothing in this program that impairs it. We grudge her no achievement or distinction of learning or of pacific enterprise such as have made her record very bright and very enviable. We do not wish to injure her or to block in any way her legitimate influence or power. We do not wish to fight her either with arms or with hostile arrangements of trade if she is willing to associate herself with us and the other peace-loving nations of the world in covenants of justice and law and fair dealing. We wish her only to accept a place of equality among the peoples of the world, — the new world in which we now live — instead of a place of mastery.

Neither do we presume to suggest to her any alteration or modification of her institutions. But it is necessary, we must frankly say, and necessary as a preliminary to any intelligent dealings with her on our part, that we should know whom her spokesmen speak for when they speak to us, whether for the Reichstag majority or for the military party and the men whose creed is imperial domination. We have spoken now, surely in terms too concrete to admit of any further doubt or question. An evident principle runs through the whole program I have outlined. It is the principle of justice to all peoples and nationalities, and their right to live on equal terms of liberty and safety with one another, whether they be strong or weak. Unless this principle be made its foundation no part of the structure of international justice can stand. The people of the United States could act upon no other principle; and to the vindication of this principle they are ready to devote their lives, their honor, and everything that they possess. The moral climax of this the culminating and final war for human liberty has come, and they are ready to put their own strength, their own highest purpose, their own integrity and devotion to the test.

63

Syrian Congress Memorandum

Article 22 of the League of Nations Covenant, which established a system of mandates to rule the colonies and territories of the defeated powers, came as a shock to the peoples of the defeated Ottoman Empire who had fought with the English and French during the war and expected their independence. This selection is the Syrian statement of such expectations, sent as a memorandum to the King-Crane Commission, the body responsible for overseeing the transfer of Ottoman territory. What specifically was the Syrian Congress asking for? Who did it represent? Why did it ask the United States for aid? In what ways did European powers try to block Syrian independence?

Thinking Historically

Do you think this conflict could have been an expected consequence of the First World War? Do you think Wilson's Fourteen Points made the Syrian demands more likely? Do you think the European powers expected this response to the League Covenant?

We the undersigned members of the General Syrian Congress, meeting in Damascus on Wednesday, July 2nd 1919, . . . provided with credentials

---

The King-Crane Commission Report, in *Papers Relating to the Foreign Relations of the United States: Paris Peace Conference, 1919* (Washington, D.C., 1942–1947), vol. 12, 780–81.

and authorizations by the inhabitants of our various districts, Muslims, Christians, and Jews, have agreed upon the following statement of the desires of the people of the country who have elected us to present them to the American Section of the International Commission; the fifth article was passed by a very large majority; all the other articles were accepted unanimously.

1. We ask absolutely complete political independence for Syria within these boundaries. The Taurus System on the North; Rafah and a line running from Al Jauf to the south of the Syrian and the Hejazian line to Akaba on the south; the Euphrates and Khabur Rivers and a line extending east of Abu Kamal to the east of Al Jauf on the east; and the Mediterranean on the west.

2. We ask that the Government of this Syrian country should be a democratic civil constitutional Monarchy on broad decentralization principles, safeguarding the rights of minorities, and that the King be the Emir Feisal, who carried on a glorious struggle in the cause of our liberation and merited our full confidence and entire reliance.

3. Considering the fact that the Arabs inhabiting the Syrian area are not naturally less than other more advanced races and that they are by no means less developed than the Bulgarians, Serbians, Greeks, and Romanians at the beginning of their independence, we protest against Article 22 of the Covenant of the League of Nations, placing us among the nations in their middle stage of development which stand in need of a mandatory power.

4. In the event of the rejection by the Peace Conference of this just protest for certain considerations that we may not understand, we, relying on the declarations of President Wilson that his object in waging war was to put an end to the ambition of conquest and colonization, can only regard the mandate mentioned in the Covenant of the League of Nations as equivalent to the rendering of economical and technical assistance that does not prejudice our complete independence. And desiring that our country should not fall a prey to colonization and believing that the American Nation is furthest from any thought of colonization and has no political ambition in our country, we will seek the technical and economical assistance from the United States of America, provided that such assistance does not exceed 20 years.

5. In the event of America not finding herself in a position to accept our desire for assistance, we will seek this assistance from Great Britain, also provided that such assistance does not infringe the complete independence and unity of our country and that the duration of such assistance does not exceed that mentioned in the previous article.

6. We do not acknowledge any right claimed by the French Government in any part whatever of our Syrian country and refuse that she should assist us or have a hand in our country under any circumstances and in any place.

7. We oppose the pretensions of the Zionists to create a Jewish commonwealth in the southern part of Syria, known as Palestine, and oppose Zionist migration to any part of our country; for we do not acknowledge their title but consider them a grave peril to our people from the national, economical, and political points of view. Our Jewish compatriots shall enjoy our common rights and assume the common responsibilities.

8. We ask that there should be no separation of the southern part of Syria, known as Palestine, nor of the littoral western zone, which includes Lebanon, from the Syrian country. We desire that the unity of the country should be guaranteed against partition under whatever circumstances.

9. We ask complete independence for emancipated Mesopotamia and that there should be no economic barriers between the two countries.

10. The fundamental principles laid down by President Wilson in condemnation of secret treaties impel us to protest most emphatically against any treaty that stipulates the partition of our Syrian country and against any private engagement aiming at the establishment of Zionism in the southern part of Syria; therefore we ask the complete annulment of these conventions and agreements.

The noble principles enunciated by President Wilson strengthen our confidence that our desires emanating from the depths of our hearts, shall be the decisive factor in determining our future; and that President Wilson and the free American people will be our supporters for the realization of our hopes, thereby proving their sincerity and noble sympathy with the aspiration of the weaker nations in general and our Arab people in particular.

We also have the fullest confidence that the Peace Conference will realize that we would not have risen against the Turks, with whom we had participated in all civil, political, and representative privileges, but for their violation of our national rights, and so will grant us our desires in full in order that our political rights may not be less after the war than they were before, since we have shed so much blood in the cause of our liberty and independence.

We request to be allowed to send a delegation to represent us at the Peace Conference to defend our rights and secure the realization of our aspirations.

REFLECTIONS

By studying causes and consequences of world events, we learn how things change but more important we learn how to avoid repeating past mistakes. History is full of lessons that breed humility as well as confidence. In *The Origins of the First World War*,[1] historian James Joll points out how unprepared people were for the war as late as the summer of 1914. Even after the Austrian ultimatum to Serbia was issued on July 23 (almost a month after the assassination of the Archduke Franz Ferdinand on June 28), diplomats across Europe left for their summer holidays. By August, all of Europe was at war, though the expectation was that it would be over in a month.

We could make a good case for diplomatic blundering as an important cause of the First World War. It is safe to say that few statesmen had any inkling of the consequences of their actions in 1914. And yet, if we concentrate on the daily decisions of diplomats that summer, we may pay attention only to the tossing of lit matches by people sitting on powder kegs rather than on the origins of the powder kegs themselves....

President Wilson blamed secret diplomacy, the international system of alliances, and imperialism as the chief causes of the war. The idea that countries could be forced into war by secret treaties must have lost some of its cogency when the U.S. Congress refused to ratify Wilson's own negotiations, and neither alliances nor imperialism were regarded as un-American or likely to end in 1919. But Wilson's radical moral aversion to reviving Old World empires might have prevented a new stage of imperialism in the League of Nations mandate system. One of the consequences of a Wilsonian peace might have been the creation of independent states in the Middle East and Africa a generation earlier.

The principle of the "self-determination of nations" that Wilson espoused, however, was a double-edged sword. The fact that the war had been "caused" by a Bosnian Serb nationalist assassin in 1914 might have been a warning that national self-determination could become an infinite regress in which smaller and smaller units sought to separate themselves from "foreign" domination. On the issue of nationalism versus internationalism, Wilson might have benefited from listening to Rosa Luxemburg. When asked about anti-Semitism, Luxemburg, a Jew from Russian Poland answered:

What do you want with this particular suffering of the Jews? The poor victims of the rubber plantations of Putumayo, the Negroes of Africa with whose bodies the Europeans play a game of catch are just as near to me.... I have no special corner of my heart reserved for the ghetto: I am at home wherever in the world there are clouds, birds, and human tears.[2]

---

1 James Joll, *The Origins of the First World War* (London: Longman, 1992), 200.
2 Jay Winter and Blaine Baggett, *The Great War* (New York: Penguin, 1996), 248, quoting Rosa Luxemburg.

Woodrow Wilson was a historian and president of Princeton University before he became president of the United States. Rosa Luxemburg was a professional revolutionary — perhaps the leading socialist theorist in Europe. Both were trained to think historically. Which of the two better understood the causes and consequences of the First World War? Which of the two had a better appreciation of the problems of nationalism that were to continue to haunt the twentieth century?

The rise of nationalist movements and international organizations were only two consequences of the First World War. Historians have attributed many other aspects of the twentieth century to the war. In an engaging account of his own search for the evidence of war along the Western Front, Stephen O'Shea writes:

> It is generally accepted that the Great War and its fifty-two months of senseless slaughter encouraged, or amplified, among other things: the loss of a belief in progress, a mistrust of technology, the loss of religious faith, the loss of a belief in Western cultural superiority, the rejection of class distinctions, the rejection of traditional sexual roles, the birth of the Modern [in art], the rejection of the past, the elevation of irony to a standard mode of apprehending the world, the unbuttoning of moral codes, and the conscious embrace of the irrational.[3]

What evidence can you find of any of these consequences in the participant accounts of this chapter?

---

[3] Stephen O'Shea, *Back to the Front: An Accidental Historian Walks the Trenches of World War I* (New York: Avon Books, 1996), 9.

Fascism, World War II, and Genocide

Germany, Poland, France, Japan, and China, 1931–1945

HISTORICAL CONTEXT

It is easier to understand the causes of the Second World War than of the First World War. In 1914, we might have pointed to Serbia or Austria, Germany or England, even the bellicosity of Russia and France. But in 1939, it was Hitler's invasion of Poland that led to war with France (which was defeated along with most of Europe in 1940), England, and the nations of the British Commonwealth, followed by the Soviet Union after 1940 and the United States after 1941. As in 1914, Germany was allied with Austria (a remnant of the former empire annexed by Germany after 1937) and the new Axis alliance of Japan and Italy (until 1943).

World War II was even more of a global conflict than World War I. It began with the Japanese invasion of Manchuria in 1931, continuing with Japan's conquest of most of China in 1937 and of Southeast Asia and the Pacific in 1941. For Africans, the war began with the Italian invasion of Ethiopia in 1935. After 1940, North Africa became an increasingly important battleground. As in World War I, soldiers were drawn from all over the world, from Africa and India, the Caribbean and Middle East, but especially in the end, from the United States, Canada, Australia, and New Zealand.

The death toll from World War II may have approached one hundred million, soldiers and civilians combined. Russian deaths alone have been estimated to be between ten and forty million, an indication of the imprecision of such estimates. A common figure of fifty million deaths for all of Europe includes twenty million Russians. Asian casualties number around ten million in China alone. Civilian casualties in an age of lightning tank attacks, military occupation of cities, and aerial bombing were enormous. World War I blurred the distinction between soldiers

396

and civilians; World War II ended it. Millions of civilians died in Eastern Europe — along the paths of invading armies — in the great cities of China, and in the bombed-out cities of Germany and Japan. The numbers of wounded, mentally or physically, cannot be counted. The destruction of property, the disruption of normal lives, the hunger, famine, disease, and deprivation continued long after the end of the war in 1945.

Death tolls offer a crude glimpse of war, and clearly World War II was one of the worst. This chapter focuses on a terrifying aspect of the conflict: the war within the war. Worse than the international struggles of armies, worse than the millions of collaborative casualties of civilians caught in harm's way was the mass murder of civilians, for which the war was no excuse. Hitler's attempt to rid the world of Jews was genocide. The systematic roundup and murder of gypsies, homosexuals, and psychiatric patients, among others, was part of his larger attempt at racial "cleansing" and "Aryan" domination for which the war was little more than a pretext (see Map 11.1). In addition, Hitler undertook the mass slaughter of all leaders and educated civilians in occupied Poland and Russia for the express purpose of turning those nations into docile armies of brute labor for German industry.

The Nazi racist agenda of genocide brought a particularly horrific dimension to war. The level of bestiality, of gross indifference to human life, of sadistic killing of defenseless civilians — among them women and children, the helpless, infirm, and aged — reached unimagined heights. Whether this was due to factors that distinguish the twentieth century from earlier eras (e.g., the anonymity of mass society, a global mix of populations, the rise of racist ideas, economic depression, the rise of fascist political parties and movements, the militarization of political life) we do not know. We do know that the Nazi experience was not singular. Imperial Japan, run by a militaristic fascist government in the 1930s, encouraged similar racist and inhumane behavior in its troops in Manchuria, China, and Southeast Asia. Both Germany and Japan gave scientists and common soldiers motive and approval for killing helpless wards in the most painful ways, without remorse or concern. Were such barbarities limited to these two countries? Certainly not. To a certain extent the encouragement of inhumanity was a product of dictatorship — the eclipse of individual will or power in fascist regimes and in Stalinist Russia as well.

THINKING HISTORICALLY
Understanding the Unforgivable

Occasionally when we learn of something horrendous, we simply say, "I don't believe it." Our disbelief harbors two feelings: first, our sense of outrage and anger, a rejection of what was done; second, our unwillingness

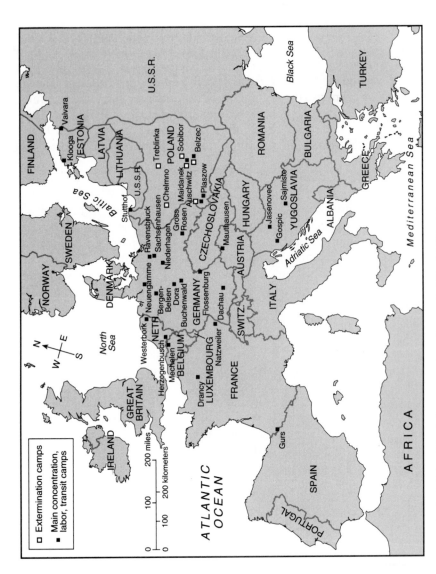

Map 11.1 Major Nazi Concentration Camps in World War II.

to believe that such a thing could happen or did happen. Our choice of words expresses the difficulty we have making sense of the senseless.

We must try, however, to understand such catastrophes so that we can help to prevent similar horrors in the future. Understanding requires a level of empathy that is often difficult to arouse when we find someone's actions reprehensible. As you read these selections, you will be encouraged to understand, not to forgive.

$$\boxed{64}$$

JOACHIM C. FEST

The Rise of Hitler

World War II had its origins in World War I. The peace terms imposed by the victors demanded the removal of the kaiser, the demilitarization of Germany, the transfer of Germany's industrial heartland to France, and the payment of enormous sums in reparation for the war. In addition, the revolutionary establishment of a republic by the German socialist party was followed by the unsuccessful uprising by the far more radical Spartacus League, which had raised the specter of a Bolshevik coup that would later turn Germany into a communist state.

In this essay, historian Joachim Fest explores the response of German conservative, nationalist, and middle-class groups to these developments. The National Socialists (the Nazi party) was just one of many fascist groups in Germany. Initiated by Mussolini in Italy in 1922, fascism was a movement that spread throughout Europe. As defined by Mussolini, in fascism the state dominates everything else:

> For the Fascist the state is all-embracing; outside it no human or spiritual values exist, much less have worth. In this sense Fascism is totalitarian, and the Fascist State — a synthesis and a unity of all values — interprets, develops, and gives power to the whole life of the people.[1]

---

[1] *Enciclopedia Italiana*, vol. xiv, s.v. "fascism," signed by Mussolini but actually written by the philosopher Giovanni Gentile (1932), 847.

Joachim C. Fest, *Hitler*, trans. Clara and Richard Winston (New York: Harcourt Brace and Co., 1974), 89–91, 92–93, 99–102, 104–105.

Why did fascism appeal more to the middle class than to the working class? Was Hitler typical of those who were attracted to fascism?
Was Hitler out of touch with reality, or was he tuned in to the feelings
of many?

Thinking Historically

Fest helps us understand some of the appeal of fascism by putting it
into the context of Germany's defeat in World War I and the real or
imagined threat of a Bolshevik revolution. Can you imagine empathiz-
ing with antirevolutionary fears if you lived then? Imagine how you
might have responded to some of the other fascist appeals: fewer
politicians, more police? The nobility of sacrificing for higher purposes; challenging the gray ordinariness of modern life; following instinct rather than reason; and war as authentic experience.

Are there mainstream Americans today who respond favorably to
the idea of "revolt on behalf of order," who desire "authority, guidance, and order," or who are disgusted with liberalism?

At the end of the First World War the victory of the democratic idea
seemed beyond question. Whatever its weaknesses might be, it rose
above the turmoil of the times, the uprisings, the dislocations, and the
continual quarrels among nations as the unifying principle of the new
age. For the war had not only decided a claim to power. It had at the
same time altered a conception of government. After the collapse of virtually all the governmental structures of Central and Eastern Europe,
many new political entities had emerged out of turmoil and revolution.
And these for the most part were organized on democratic principles.
In 1914 there had been only three republics alongside of seventeen
monarchies in Europe. Four years later there were as many republics as
monarchies. The spirit of the age seemed to be pointing unequivocally
toward various forms of popular rule.

Only Germany seemed to be opposing this mood of the times, after
having been temporarily gripped and carried along by it. Those who
would not acknowledge the reality created by the war organized into a
fantastic swarm of *völkisch* (racist-nationalist) parties, clubs, and free
corps. To these groups the revolution had been an act of treason; parliamentary democracy was something foreign and imposed from without, merely a synonym for "everything contrary to the German political
will," or else an "institution for pillaging created by Allied capitalism."

Germany's former enemies regarded the multifarious symptoms of
nationalistic protest as the response of an inveterately authoritarian
people to democracy and civic responsibility. To be sure, the Germans

were staggering beneath terrible political and psychological burdens: There was the shock of defeat, the moral censure of the Versailles Treaty, the loss of territory and the demand for reparations, the impoverishment and spiritual undermining of much of the population. Nevertheless, the conviction remained that a great moral gap existed between the Germans and most of their neighbours. Full of resentment, refusing to learn a lesson, this incomprehensible country had withdrawn into its reactionary doctrines, made of them a special virtue, abjured Western rationality and humanity, and in general set itself against the universal trend of the age. For decades this picture of Germany dominated the discussion of the reasons for the rise of National Socialism.

But the image of democracy victorious was also deceptive. The moment in which democracy seemed to be achieving historic fulfillment simultaneously marked the beginning of its crisis. Only a few years later the idea of democracy was challenged in principle as it had never been before. Only a few years after it had celebrated its triumph it was overwhelmed or at least direly threatened by a new movement that had sprung to life in almost all European countries.

This movement recorded its most lasting successes in countries in which the war had aroused considerable discontent or made it conscious of existing discontent, and especially in countries in which the war had been followed by leftist revolutionary uprisings. In some places these movements were conservative, harking back to better times when men were more honorable, the valleys more peaceable, and money had more worth; in others these movements were revolutionary and vied with one another in their contempt for the existing order of things. Some attracted chiefly the petty bourgeois elements, others the peasants, others portions of the working class. Whatever their strange compound of classes, interests, and principles, all seemed to be drawing their dynamic force from the less conscious and more vital lower strata of society. National Socialism was merely one variant of this widespread European movement of protest and opposition aimed at overturning the general order of things.

National Socialism rose from provincial beginnings, from philistine clubs, as Hitler scornfully described them, which met in Munich bars over a few rounds of beer to talk over national and family troubles. No one would have dreamed that they could ever challenge, let alone outdo, the powerful, highly organized Marxist parties. But the following years proved that in these clubs of nationalistic beer drinkers, soon swelled by disillusioned homecoming soldiers and proletarianized members of the middle class, a tremendous force was waiting to be awakened, consolidated, and applied.

In Munich alone there existed, in 1919, nearly fifty more or less political associations, whose membership consisted chiefly of confused remnants of the prewar parties that had been broken up by war and revolution.

They had such names as New Fatherland, Council of Intellectual Work, Siegfried Ring, Universal League, Nova Vaconia, League of Socialist Women, Free Union of Socialist Pupils, and Ostara League. The German Workers' Party was one such group. What united them all and drew them together theoretically and in reality was nothing but an overwhelming feeling of anxiety.

First of all, and most immediate, there was the fear of revolution, that *grande peur* which after the French Revolution had haunted the European-bourgeoisie throughout the nineteenth century. The notion that revolutions were like forces of nature, elemental mechanisms operating without reference to the will of the actors in them, following their own logic and leading perforce to reigns of terror, destruction, killing, and chaos — that notion was seared into the public mind. That was the unforgettable experience, not [German philosopher Immanuel] Kant's belief that the French Revolution had also shown the potentiality for betterment inherent in human nature. For generations, particularly in Germany, this fear stood in the way of any practical revolutionary strivings and produced a mania for keeping things quiet, with the result that every revolutionary proclamation up to 1918 was countered by the standard appeal to law and order.

This old fear was revived by the pseudorevolutionary events in Germany and by the menace of the October Revolution in Russia. Diabolical traits were ascribed to the Reds. The refugees pouring into Munich described bloodthirsty barbarians on a rampage of killing. Such imagery had instant appeal to the nationalists. . . .

This threat dominated Hitler's speeches of the early years. In garish colors he depicted the ravages of the "Red squads of butchers," the "murderous communists," the "bloody morass of Bolshevism." In Russia, he told his audiences, more than thirty million persons had been murdered, "partly on the scaffold, partly by machine guns and similar means, partly in veritable slaughterhouses, partly, millions upon millions, by hunger; and we all know that this wave of hunger is creeping on . . . and see that this scourge is approaching, that it is also coming upon Germany." The intelligentsia of the Soviet Union, he declared, had been exterminated by mass murder, the economy utterly smashed. Thousands of German prisoners-of-war had been drowned in the Neva or sold as slaves. Meanwhile, in Germany the enemy was boring away at the foundations of society "in unremitting, ever unchanging undermining work." The fate of Russia, he said again and again, would soon be ours! And years later, when he was already in power, he spoke again of "the horror of the Communist international hate dictatorship" that had preyed on his mind at the beginning of his career: "I tremble at the thought of what would become of our old, overcrowded continent if the chaos of the Bolshevik revolution were to be successful."

National Socialism owed a considerable part of its emotional appeal, its militancy, and its cohesion to this defensive attitude toward the threat of Marxist revolution. The aim of the National Socialist Party, Hitler repeatedly declared, "is very brief: Annihilation and extermination of the Marxist world view." This was to be accomplished by an "incomparable, brilliantly orchestrated propaganda and information organization" side by side with a movement "of the most ruthless force and most brutal resolution, prepared to oppose all terrorism on the part of the Marxists with tenfold greater terrorism." At about the same time, for similar reasons, Mussolini was founding his Fasci di combattimento [battle group]. Henceforth, the new movements were to be identified by the general name of "Fascism."

But the fear of revolution would not have been enough to endow the movement with that fierce energy, which for a time seemed to stem the universal trend toward democracy. After all, for many people revolution meant hope. A stronger and more elemental motivation had to be added. And in fact Marxism was feared as the precursor of a far more comprehensive assault upon all traditional ideas. It was viewed as the contemporary political aspect of a metaphysical upheaval, as a "declaration of war upon the European . . . idea of culture." Marxism itself was only the metaphor for something dreaded that escaped definition. . . .

This first phase of the postwar era was characterized both by fear of revolution and anticivilizational resentments; these together, curiously intertwined and reciprocally stimulating each other, produced a syndrome of extraordinary force. Into the brew went the hate and defense complexes of a society shaken to its foundations. German society had lost its imperial glory, its civil order, its national confidence, its prosperity, and its familiar authorities. The whole system had been turned topsy-turvy, and now many Germans blindly and bitterly wanted back what they thought had been unjustly taken from them. These general feelings of unhappiness were intensified and further radicalized by a variety of unsatisfied group interests. The class of white-collar workers, continuing to grow apace, proved especially susceptible to the grand gesture of total criticism. For the industrial revolution had just begun to affect office workers and was reducing the former "noncommissioned officers of capitalism" to the status of last victims of "modern slavery." It was all the worse for them because unlike the proletarians they had never developed a class pride of their own or imagined that the breakdown of the existing order was going to lead to their own apotheosis. Small businessmen were equally susceptible because of their fear of being crushed by corporations, department stores, and rationalized competition. Another unhappy group consisted of farmers who, slow to change and lacking capital, were fettered to backward modes of production. Another group were the academics and formerly solid bourgeois who felt themselves caught in the tremendous suction of proletarianization. Without outside support you found yourself "at once despised, declassed; to be unemployed is the same as being a communist," one victim stated in a questionnaire of the period. No statistics, no figures on rates of inflation, bankruptcies, and suicides can describe the feelings of those threatened by unemployment or poverty, or can express the anxieties of those others who still possessed some property and feared the consequences of so much accumulated discontent. Public institutions in their persistent weakness offered no bulwark against the seething collective emotions. It was all the worse because the widespread anxiety no longer, as in the time of Lagarde and Langbehn, was limited to cries of woe and impotent prophecies. The war had given arms to the fearful.

The vigilante groups and the free corps that were being organized in great numbers, partly on private initiative, partly with covert government support, chiefly to meet the threat of Communist revolution, formed centers of bewildered but determined resistance to the *status quo*. The members of these paramilitary groups were vaguely looking around for someone to lead them into a new system. At first there was another reservoir of militant energies alongside the parliamentary groups: the mass of homecoming soldiers. Many of these stayed in the barracks dragging out a pointless military life, baffled and unable to say good-bye to the warrior dreams of their recent youth. In the front-line trenches they had glimpsed the outlines of a new meaning to life; in the sluggishly resuming normality of the postwar period they tried in vain to find that meaning again. They had not fought and suffered for years for the sake of this weakened regime with its borrowed ideals which, as they saw it, could be pushed around by the most contemptible of their former enemies. And they also feared, after the exalting sense of life the war had given them, the ignobility of the commonplace bourgeois world.

It remained for Hitler to bring together these feelings and to appoint himself their spearhead. Indeed, Hitler regarded as a phenomenon seems like the synthetic product of all the anxiety, pessimism, nostalgia, and defensiveness we have discussed. For him, too, the war had been education and liberation. If there is a "Fascistic" type, it was embodied in him. More than any of his followers he expressed the underlying psychological, social, and ideological motives of the movement. He was never just its leader; he was also its exponent.

His early years had contributed their share to that experience of overwhelming anxiety which dominated his intellectual and emotional constitution. That lurking anxiety can be seen at the root of almost all his statements and reactions. It had everyday as well as cosmic dimensions. Many who knew him in his youth have described his pallid, "timorous" nature, which provided the fertile soil for his lush fantasies. His "constant fear" of contact with strangers was another aspect of that anxiety, as was his extreme distrust and his compulsion to wash frequently, which became more and more pronounced in later life. The same complex is apparent in his oft-expressed fear of venereal disease and his fear of contagion in general. He knew that "microbes are rushing at me." He was ridden by the Austrian Pan-German's fear of being overwhelmed by alien races, by fear of the "locust-like immigration of Russian and Polish Jews," by fear of "the niggerizing of the Germans," by fear of the Germans' "expulsion from Germany," and finally by fear that the Germans would be "exterminated." He had the *Völkische Boebachter* print an alleged French soldier's song whose refrain was: "Germans, we will possess your daughters!" Among his phobias were American technology, the birth rate of the Slavs, big cities, "industrialization as unrestricted as it is harmful," the "economization of the nation," corporations, the "morass of metropolitan amusement culture," and modern art, which sought "to kill the soul of the people" by painting meadows blue and skies green. Wherever he looked he discovered the "signs of decay of a slowly ebbing world." Not an element of pessimistic anticivilizational criticism was missing from his imagination.

What linked Hitler with the leading Fascists of other countries was the resolve to halt this process of degeneration. What set him apart from them, however, was the manic single-mindedness with which he traced all the anxieties he had ever felt back to a single source. For at the heart of the towering structure of anxiety, black and hairy, stood the figure of the Jew: evil-smelling, smacking his lips, lusting after blonde girls, eternal contaminator of the blood, but "racially harder" than the Aryan, as Hitler uneasily declared as late as the summer of 1942. A prey to his psychosis, he saw Germany as the object of a worldwide conspiracy, pressed on all sides by Bolshevists, Freemasons, capitalists, Jesuits, all hand in glove with each other and directed in their nefarious projects by the "bloodthirsty and avaricious Jewish tyrant." *The* Jew had 75 per cent of world capital at his disposal. He dominated the stock exchanges and the Marxist parties, the Gold and Red Internationals. He was the "advocate of birth control and the idea of emigration." He undermined governments, bastardized races, glorified fratricide, fomented civil war, justified baseness, and poisoned nobility: "the wirepuller of the destinies of mankind." The whole world was in danger, Hitler cried imploringly; it had fallen "into the embrace of this octopus." He groped for images in which to make his horror tangible, saw "creeping venom," "belly-worms," and "adders devouring the nation's body." In formulating his anxiety he might equally hit on the maddest and most ludicrous phrases as on impressive or at least memorable ones. Thus he invented the "Jewification of our spiritual life," "the mammonization of our mating instinct," and "the resulting syphilization of our people." He could prophesy: "If, with the help of his Marxist creed, the Jew is victorious over the other peoples of the world, his crown will be the funeral wreath of humanity and the planet will, as it did millions of years ago, move through the ether devoid of men."

The appearance of Hitler signaled a union of those forces that in crisis conditions had great political potential. The Fascistic movements all centered on the charismatic appeal of a unique leader. The leader was to be the resolute voice of order controlling chaos. He would have looked further and thought deeper, would know the despairs but also the means of salvation. This looming giant had already been given established form in a prophetic literature that went back to German folklore. Like the mythology of many other nations unfortunate in their history, that of the Germans has its sleeping leaders dreaming away the centuries in the bowels of a mountain, but destined some day to return to rally their people and punish the guilty world. . . .

The success of Fascism in contrast to many of its rivals was in large part due to its perceiving the essence of the crisis, of which it was itself the symptom. All the other parties affirmed the process of industrialization and emancipation, whereas the Fascists, evidently sharing the universal anxiety, tried to deal with it by translating it into violent action and histrionics. . . .

Hitler's unshakable confidence, which often seemed sheer madness, was based on the conviction that he was the only real revolutionary, that he had broken free of the existing system by reinstating the rights of human instincts. In alliance with these interests, he believed, he was invincible, for the instincts always won out in the end "against economic motivation, against the pressure of public opinion, even against reason." No doubt the appeal to instinct brought out a good deal of human baseness. No doubt what fascism wanted to restore was often a grotesque parody of the tradition they purported to honor, and the order they hailed was a hollow sham. But when Trotsky contemptuously dismissed the adherents of Fascistic movements as "human dust," he was only revealing the Left's characteristic ineptness in dealing with people's needs and impulses. That ineptness led to a multitude of clever errors of judgment by those who purported to understand the spirit of the age better than anyone else. . . .

65

HEINRICH HIMMLER

Speech to the SS

Heinrich Himmler (1900–1945) was one of the most powerful leaders of Nazi Germany. He was the head of the SS, or *Schutzstaffel,* an elite army that was responsible for, among other things, running the many concentration camps. Hitler gave Himmler the task of implementing the "final solution of the Jewish question": killing the Jewish population of Germany and the other countries the Nazis occupied. The horror that resulted is today often referred to by the biblical word *holocaust.*

The following reading is an excerpt from a speech Himmler gave to SS leaders on October 4, 1943. What was Himmler's concern in this speech? What kind of general support for the extermination of the Jews does this excerpt suggest existed?

Thinking Historically

Psychiatrists say that people use various strategies to cope when they must do something distasteful. We might summarize these strategies as denial, distancing, compartmentalizing, ennobling, rationalizing, and scapegoating. *Denial* is pretending that something has not happened. *Distancing* removes the idea, memory, or reality from the mind, placing it at a distance. *Compartmentalizing* separates one action, memory, or idea from others, allowing one to "put away" certain feelings. *Ennobling* makes the distasteful act a matter of pride rather than guilt, nobility rather than disgrace. *Rationalizing* creates "good" reasons for doing something, while *scapegoating* puts blame on someone else.

What evidence do you see of these strategies in Himmler's speech? Judging from the speech, which of these strategies do you think his listeners used? To the extent that they rationalized their actions, what sorts of rationalizations or reasons do you think they offered?

I also want to make reference before you here, in complete frankness, to a really grave matter. Among ourselves, this once, it shall be uttered

---

Heinrich Himmler, "Secret Speech at Posen," *A Holocaust Reader,* ed. Lucy S. Dawidowicz (New York: Behrman House, 1976), 132–33.

quite frankly; but in public we will never speak of it. Just as we did not hesitate on June 30, 1934, to do our duty as ordered, to stand up against the wall comrades who had transgressed,[1] and shoot them, so we have never talked about this and never will. It was the tact which I am glad to say is a matter of course to us that made us never discuss it among ourselves, never talk about it. Each of us shuddered, and yet each one knew that he would do it again if it were ordered and if it were necessary.

I am referring to the evacuation of the Jews, the annihilation of the Jewish people. This is one of those things that are easily said. "The Jewish people is going to be annihilated," says every party member. "Sure, it's in our program, elimination of the Jews, annihilation — we'll take care of it." And then they all come trudging, 80 million worthy Germans, and each one has his one decent Jew. Sure, the others are swine, but this one is an A-1 Jew. Of all those who talk this way, not one has seen it happen, not one has been through it. Most of you must know what it means to see a hundred corpses lie side by side, or five hundred, or a thousand. To have stuck this out — excepting cases of human weakness — to have kept our integrity, that is what has made us hard. In our history, this is an unwritten and never-to-be-written page of glory, for we know how difficult we would have made it for ourselves if today — amid the bombing raids, the hardships, and the deprivations of war — we still had the Jews in every city as secret saboteurs, agitators, and demagogues. If the Jews were still ensconced in the body of the German nation, we probably would have reached the 1916–17 stage by now.[2]

The wealth they had we have taken from them. I have issued a strict order, carried out by SS-Obergruppenfuhrer Pohl, that this wealth in its entirety is to be turned over to the Reich as a matter of course. We have taken none of it for ourselves. Individuals who transgress will be punished in accordance with an order I issued at the beginning, threatening that whoever takes so much as a mark of it for himself is a dead man. A number of SS men — not very many — have transgressed, and they will die, without mercy. We had the moral right, we had the duty toward our people, to kill this people which wanted to kill us. But we do not have the right to enrich ourselves with so much as a fur, a watch, a mark, or a cigarette, or anything else. Having exterminated a germ, we do not want, in the end, to be infected by the germ, and die of it. I will not stand by and let even a small rotten spot develop or take

[1] A reference to the "Night of the Long Knives," when Hitler ordered the SS to murder the leaders of the SA, a Nazi group he wished to suppress. [Ed.]

[2] Here Himmler is apparently referring to the stalemate on Germany's western front in World War I. [Ed.]

hold. Wherever it may form, we together will cauterize it. All in all, however, we can say that we have carried out this heaviest of our tasks in a spirit of love for our people. And our inward being, our soul, our character has not suffered injury from it.

66

JEAN-FRANÇOIS STEINER

From *Treblinka*

Treblinka, in Poland, was one of several Nazi death camps. (Auschwitz was the largest camp.) In these "death factories," the Nazis murdered millions of Jews as well as many thousands of gypsies, socialists, Soviet prisoners of war, and other people. In this selection, Steiner, who lost his father at Treblinka, reveals how "rational" and "scientific" mass murder can be. How could this happen? Can it happen again?

Thinking Historically

Try to imagine what went through the mind of Lalka as he designed the extermination process at Treblinka. How did concerns for efficiency and humanity enter into his deliberations? Do you think he found his work distasteful? If so, which of the strategies mentioned in the previous selection did he adopt?

What would it have been like to be a sign-painter, guard, or haircutter at Treblinka?

Each poorly organized debarkation [of deportees from trains arriving at Treblinka] gave rise to unpleasant scenes — uncertainties and confusion for the deportees, who did not know where they were going and were sometimes seized with panic.

Jean-François Steiner, *Treblinka* (New York: Simon & Schuster, 1967), 153–54, 155–58, 159–60.

So, the first problem was to restore a minimum of hope. Lalka[1] had many faults, but he did not lack a certain creative imagination. After a few days of reflection he hit upon the idea of transforming the platform where the convoys [trains] arrived into a false station. He had the ground filled in to the level of the doors of the cars in order to give the appearance of a train platform and to make it easier to get off the trains. . . . On [a] wall Lalka had . . . doors and windows painted in gay and pleasing colors. The windows were decorated with cheerful curtains and framed by green blinds which were just as false as the rest. Each door was given a special name, stencilled at eye level: "Stationmaster," "Toilet," "Infirmary" (a red cross was painted on this door). Lalka carried his concern for detail so far as to have his men paint two doors leading to the waiting rooms, first and second class. The ticket window, which was barred with a horizontal sign reading, "Closed," was a little masterpiece with its ledge and false perspective and its grill, painted line for line. Next to the ticket window a large timetable announced the departure times of trains for Warsaw, Bialystok, Wolkowysk, etc. . . . Two doors were cut into the [wall]. The first led to the "hospital," bearing a wooden arrow on which "Wolkowysk" was painted. The second led to the place where the Jews were undressed; that arrow said "Bialystok." Lalka also had some flower beds designed, which gave the whole area a neat and cheery look. . . .

Lalka also decided that better organization could save much time in the operations of undressing and recovery of the [deportees'] baggage. To do this you had only to rationalize the different operations, that is, to organize the undressing like an assembly line. But the rhythm of this assembly line was at the mercy of the sick, the old, and the wounded, who, since they were unable to keep the pace, threatened to bog down the operation and make it proceed even more slowly than before. . . . Individuals of both sexes over the age of ten, and children under ten, at a maximum rate of two children per adult, were judged fit to follow the complete circuit,[2] as long as they did not show serious wounds or marked disability. Victims who did not correspond to the norms were to be conducted to the "hospital" by members of the blue commando and turned over to the Ukrainians [guards] for special treatment. A bench was built all around the ditch of the "hospital" so that the victims would fall of their own weight after receiving the bullet in the back of the head. This bench was to be used only

---

[1] Kurt Franz, whom the prisoners called Lalka, designed the highly efficient system of extermination at Treblinka. [Ed.]

[2] The "complete" circuit was getting off the train, walking along the platform through the door to the men's or women's barracks, undressing, and being led to the gas chamber "showers." [Ed.]

when Kurland[3] was swamped with work. On the platform, the door which these victims took was surmounted by the Wolkowysk arrow. In the Sibylline language of Treblinka, "Wolkowysk" meant the bullet in the back of the neck or the injection. "Bialystok" meant the gas chamber.

Beside the "Bialystok" door stood a tall Jew whose role was to shout endlessly, "Large bundles here, large bundles here!" He had been nicknamed "Groysse Pack." As soon as the victims had gone through, Groysse Pack and his men from the red commando carried the bundles at a run to the sorting square, where the sorting commandos immediately took possession of them. As soon as they had gone through the door came the order, "Women to the left, men to the right." This moment generally gave rise to painful scenes.

While the women were being led to the left-hand barracks to undress and go to the hairdresser, the men, who were lined up double file, slowly entered the production line. This production line included five stations. At each of these a group of "reds" shouted at the top of their lungs the name of the piece of clothing that it was in charge of receiving. At the first station the victim handed over his coat and hat. At the second, his jacket. (In exchange, he received a piece of string.) At the third he sat down, took off his shoes, and tied them together with the string he had just received.) Until then the shoes were not tied together in pairs, and since the yield was at least fifteen thousand pairs of shoes per day, they were all lost, since they could not be matched up again.) At the fourth station the victim left his trousers, and at the fifth his shirt and underwear.

After they had been stripped, the victims were conducted, as they came off the assembly line, to the right-hand barracks and penned in until the women had finished: ladies first. However, a small number, chosen from among the most able-bodied, were singled out at the door to carry the clothing to the sorting square. They did this while running naked between two rows of Ukrainian guards. Without stopping once they threw their bundles onto the pile, turned around, and went back for another.

Meanwhile the women had been conducted to the barracks on the left. This barracks was divided into two parts: a dressing room and a beauty salon. "Put your clothes in a pile so you will be able to find them after the shower," they were ordered in the first room. The "beauty salon" was a room furnished with six benches, each of which could seat twenty women at a time. Behind each bench twenty prisoners

---

[3] Kurland was a Jew assigned to the "hospital," where he gave injections of poison to those who were too ill or crippled to make the complete circuit. [Ed.]

of the red commando, wearing white tunics and armed with scissors, waited at attention until all the women were seated. Between hair-cutting sessions they sat down on the benches and, under the direction of a *kapo* [prisoner guard] who was transformed into a conductor, they had to sing old Yiddish melodies.

Lalka, who had insisted on taking personal responsibility for every detail, had perfected the technique of what he called the "Treblinka cut." With five well-placed slashes the whole head of hair was transferred to a sack placed beside each hairdresser for this purpose. It was simple and efficient. How many dramas did this "beauty salon" see? From the very beautiful young woman who wept when her hair was cut off, because she would be ugly, to the mother who grabbed a pair of scissors from one of the "hairdressers" and literally severed a Ukrainian's arm; from the sister who recognized one of the "hairdressers" as her brother to the young girl, Ruth Dorfman, who, suddenly understanding and fighting back her tears, asked whether it was difficult to die and admitted in a small brave voice that she was a little afraid and wished it were all over.

When they had been shorn the women left the "beauty salon" double file. Outside the door, they had to squat in a particular way also specified by Lalka, in order to be intimately searched. Up to this point, doubt had been carefully maintained. Of course, a discriminating eye might have observed that . . . the smell was the smell of rotting bodies. A thousand details proved that Treblinka was not a transient camp, and some realized this, but the majority had believed in the impossible for too long to begin to doubt at the last moment. The door of the barracks, which opened directly onto the "road to heaven," represented the turning point. Up to here the prisoners had been given a minimum of hope, from here on this policy was abandoned.

This was one of Lalka's great innovations. After what point was it no longer necessary to delude the victims? This detail had been the subject of rather heated controversy among the Technicians. At the Nuremberg trials, Rudolf Höss, Commandant of Auschwitz, criticized Treblinka where, according to him, the victims knew that they were going to be killed. Höss was an advocate of the towel distributed at the door to the gas chamber. He claimed that this system not only avoided disorder, but was more humane, and he was proud of it. But Höss did not invent this "towel technique"; it was in all the manuals, and it was utilized at Treblinka until Lalka's great reform.

Lalka's studies had led to what might be called the "principle of the cutoff." His reasoning was simple: Since sooner or later the victims must realize that they were going to be killed, to postpone this moment was only false humanity. The principle "the later the better" did not apply here. Lalka had been led to make an intensive study of this problem upon observing one day completely by chance, that winded victims died much more rapidly than the rest. The discovery had led him to make a clean sweep of accepted principles. Let us follow his industrialist's logic, keeping well in mind that his great preoccupation was the saving of time. A winded victim dies faster. Hence, a saving of time. The best way to wind a man is to make him run — another saving of time. Thus Lalka arrived at the conclusion that you must make the victims run. A new question had then arisen: At what point must you make the victims run and thus create panic (a further aid to breathlessness)? The question had answered itself: As soon as you have nothing more to make them do. Franz located the exact point, the point of no return: the door of the barracks.

The rest was merely a matter of working out the details. Along the "road to heaven" and in front of the gas chambers he stationed a cordon of guards armed with whips, whose function was to make the victims run, to make them rush into the gas chambers of their own accord in search of refuge. One can see that this system is more daring than the classic system, but one can also see the danger it represents. Suddenly abandoned to their despair, realizing that they no longer had anything to lose, the victims might attack the guards. Lalka was aware of this risk, but he maintained that everything depended on the pace. "It's close work," he said, "but if you maintain a very rapid pace and do not allow a single moment of hesitation, the method is absolutely without danger." There were still further elaborations later on, but from the first day, Lalka had only to pride himself on his innovation: It took no more than three quarters of an hour, by the clock, to put the victims through their last voyage, from the moment the doors of the cattle cars were unbolted to the moment the great trap doors of the gas chamber were opened to take out the bodies. Three quarters of an hour, door to door, compared to an hour and a quarter and sometimes even as much as two hours with the old system; it was a record. . . .

But let us return to the men. The timing was worked out so that by the time the last woman had emerged from the left-hand barracks, all the clothes had been transported to the sorting square. The men were immediately taken out of the right-hand barracks and driven after the women into the "road to heaven," which they reached by way of a special side path. By the time they arrived at the gas chambers the toughest, who had begun to run before the others to carry the bundles, were just as winded as the weakest. Everyone died in perfect unison for the greater satisfaction of that great Technician Kurt Franz, the Stakhanovite [model worker] of extermination.

67

SUSAN ZUCCOTTI

A Village in Vichy France

When the Germans took Paris in the blitzkrieg, or lightning strike, of 1940, they imposed direct rule on northern France and a puppet government on the southern part of the country, led by World War I hero Marshall Philippe Pétain. Pétain governed from the old city of Vichy, about two hundred miles south of Paris. After 1941, the Germans began to impose their policy of anti-Semitism on the Vichy regime, as they had done in the north, insisting that Vichy capture and imprison Jews for shipment to concentration camps. Although much of southern France complied with the order, in a high plateau just a few hours south of Vichy, an area of independent French, many of them Protestants who had long resisted Catholic Paris, refused to do the Nazis' work. In this selection, a modern historian tells how the inhabitants of Le Chambon-sur-Lignon risked their lives to save Jewish children in their schools and Jewish families in their homes. How did the people of Le Chambon save Jews? What gave them the courage to resist the orders of their government and the Nazis? How were they so successful?

Thinking Historically

To understand evil, we must first understand goodness. To condemn, we must first be able to praise. To understand how people could commit horrendous acts, we must have some sense of their range of choice. Stories like that of Le Chambon-sur-Lignon aid us in that understanding. What supports did the people of this village have to disobey Nazi orders? Imagine yourself as a villager. What would you have done? Other pressures being equal, would you have gained strength from "doing the right thing"?

In interviews after the war, many of those — in France and throughout Europe — who had sheltered Jews at their own peril dismissed praise. In virtually every case, these protectors rejected the idea that they had done anything out of the ordinary. What did these people have that the Nazis had obviously taken away from so many others? How did the Nazis do it?

Susan Zuccotti, *The Holocaust, the French and the Jews* (New York: Basic Books, 1993), 227–31.

"Roughly fifty kilometers from Puy-en-Velay and about forty kilometers from Saint-Étienne, there is a little town, Le Chambon-sur-Lignon, the tiny capital of the plateau of the same name, an ancient Protestant village. There you can still find the caves where the Protestants gathered to practice their religion as well as to escape the king's dragoons." Thus begins Joseph Bass's postwar report on a remote village on a pine-studded plateau, about 960 meters above sea level, in the Massif Central west of Valence and the Rhône River. Léon Poliakov, who helped Bass hide Jews there, later described the department of Haute-Loire where Le Chambon is located as "one of the poorest and wildest regions of the Cévennes." Its Protestant inhabitants, he added, "distrust all authority, listening only to their conscience — or their pastors."

Long before Bass and Poliakov arrived there, hundreds of Jewish and non-Jewish refugees had already found their way to Le Chambon. Some had wandered into town as early as the winter of 1940–41. Most came independently at first, advised by friends or casual acquaintances of an isolated village of about one thousand people, reputedly sympathetic. Newcomers found shelter with village families or with the roughly two thousand peasants, most of them also Protestant, in the surrounding countryside. Others took rooms in one of more than a dozen hotels and boardinghouses in this popular summer resort area of pine forests, clear streams, and bracing air. Most were trying to escape internment, and most, needless to say, were not legally registered.

During the late spring and early summer of 1942, many foreign Jews and non-Jews released from internment camps to the care of charitable agencies also came to Le Chambon. Local institutions to care for them multiplied, openly and legally. Madeleine Barot and other young Protestant social workers of the CIMADE [a Protestant relief organization] established a family residence at the Hôtel Coteau Fleuri, outside of town. Quakers, with the help from Le Chambon's Pastor André Trocmé, funded a boardinghouse for young children. Older students joined two farm-schools operated by the Secours suisse, or moved into residences of the École Cévenol, a private Protestant secondary school slightly north of the village. Still others were welcomed at the École des roches in the village itself.

In August 1942, French police rounding up recent Jewish immigrants in the unoccupied zone did not overlook Le Chambon. They arrived in the village with three empty buses, demanding that Pastor Trocmé provide a list of resident Jews. Trocmé not only claimed ignorance, somewhat truthfully, of names and addresses but promptly sent his Protestant Boy Scouts to even the most distant farms to warn Jews to hide. Other local residents had undoubtedly already seen the approach of the police up the valley, along a road visible for miles from the Plateau. Then and later, that visibility was one secret to security in

Le Chambon. Police searched the region for two or three days and returned regularly for several weeks. They apparently netted only one victim, an Austrian who was later released because he was only half-Jewish.

Jews literally poured into Le Chambon after August 1942. By this point, their presence was totally unofficial. They came with the [Jewish resistance network] Service André — [its director Joseph] Bass later reported that the pastor never hesitated to help him — and with OSE [children's aid] and other clandestine networks. Some stayed in Le Chambon only long enough to find a guide to Switzerland, but many remained, hidden with families or in boardinghouses or schools. They kept coming until, as Poliakov observed, "in some hamlets, there was not a single farm which did not shelter a Jewish family." Roughly five thousand Jews are estimated to have been hidden among the three thousand native residents, all of whom knew about the refugees.

In his memoirs, Poliakov describes with touching detail his arrival at a local hotel with a group of Jewish children in 1943:

> Frightened, they hovered in a corner of the room. The first peasant couple enters: "We will take a little girl between eight and twelve years old," explains the woman. Little Myriam is called: "Will you go with this aunt and uncle?" Shy and frightened, Myriam does not answer. They muffle her up in blankets and carry her to the sleigh; she leaves for the farm where she will live a healthy and simple life with her temporary parents until the end of the war. . . . In a flash, all the children were similarly housed, under the benevolent eye of Pastor Trocmé.

Who was this pastor whose name appears in every account of Le Chambon-sur-Lignon during the war? Born in Saint-Quentin in Picardy in northern France in 1901, André Trocmé studied at the Union Theological Seminary in New York City, where he met his future wife, Italian-born Magda Grilli, in 1925. A pacifist and conscientious objector, Trocmé made no secret of his beliefs after his arrival in Le Chambon in 1934. Indeed, he and Pastor Édouard Theis, the director of the École Cévenol, were equally frank after 1940 about their dislike of the Vichy regime and the racial laws. Trocmé often spoke from the pulpit about the evils of racial persecution; Theis taught the same principles at the École Cévenol. On August 15, 1942, during a visit to the village by the Vichy youth minister, Georges Lamirand, and the departmental prefect and subprefect, several older students at the school presented the officials with a letter protesting the July 16 roundup [of Jews] in Paris and expressing local support of the Jews.

Trocmé, Theis, and Roger Darcissac, the director of the public school in Le Chambon, were arrested by French police in February 1943 and held for a month. At the end of the year, the two pastors went into hiding. During that period, Theis served as a guide for

CIMADE, escorting refugees to Switzerland. Magda Trocmé continued her husband's work during his absence; one scholar has judged that she was at least as important as he in saving lives. Mildred Theis kept the École Cévenol open and continued to shelter refugees. The two women had many aides. Bass remembered pastors named Poivre, Leenhardt, Jeannet, Curtet, Betrix, Vienney, and Besson from surrounding hamlets, as well as the Trocmés' good friend Simone Mairesse. Municipal officials also cooperated, if only by looking the other way. And the people of the plateau, often influenced by their outspoken pastors but guided as well by their own sense of justice, continued to protect their Jewish guests until the Liberation. Of them, Bass wrote after the war, "The conduct of the Protestant pastors and men of action of the plateau of Le Chambon deserves to be told to Jews throughout the entire world."

In considering the rescue of Jews in Le Chambon, two questions arise: Why was the local population so sympathetic, and why was it so successful? To answer the first, Madeleine Barot stresses the special status of Protestants in France as a minority persecuted by Catholics. Protestants in Le Chambon still told tales of persecution around their hearths on cold winter nights and visited caves where their ancestors had hidden. The memory of persecution made them suspicious of authority, sympathetic to other minorities, and comfortable with clandestine life. In addition, many French Protestants were skeptical about the Vichy regime, in part because authoritarianism often bodes ill for minorities, but especially because, according to Barot, "Pétain dedicated France to the Virgin, and made it an intensely Catholic state." Finally, Christian anti-Semitism notwithstanding, Bible-reading Protestants of the type living around Le Chambon sometimes articulate a special affinity for the Jews, based on a shared reverence for the Old Testament and a common acceptance of God's special compact with his chosen people.

These various factors certainly did not apply to all French Protestants. Many, especially those of the assimilated and highly educated urban classes who were more removed from their historical and cultural roots, were favorably inclined toward the Vichy regime for the same economic and social reasons as their Catholic neighbors, and held the same variety of attitudes toward Jews. But Protestants around Le Chambon cherished their historic memory. That love, combined with the sturdy individualism and independence of mountain people and the leadership of a group of exceptional pastors, made Le Chambon an equally exceptional place.

But why were the rescuers of Le Chambon so successful? Admittedly, even they had their tragedies and their victims. In the spring of 1943, the Gestapo raided the École des roches, seizing many students along with their dedicated director, Daniel Trocmé, Pastor Trocmé's second cousin. Nearly all, including Daniel, died in deportation. But the Germans did not return and thus failed as miserably as the French police to find most of the Jews they knew were there. Why?

Geographic factors were important. The isolation of the area was made even more extreme by the closing of access roads in winter. Any movement on those same approach roads could be seen from the plateau. Thick forests were good for hiding. The Gestapo and the French Milice [volunteer fascist corps], busy elsewhere, were reluctant or perhaps afraid to enter a hostile area that, however dedicated by its pastor to nonviolence, was surrounded by armed Resistance fighters. Why stir up a sleeping hornets' nest? French police and gendarmes not only shared that reluctance but were also affected by local sympathies for refugees.

Two witnesses tell amusing stories. Madeleine Barot later declared of her own experience, "When the *gendarmes* in Tence [the nearest town] received an order for an arrest, they made a habit of dragging themselves along the road very visibly, of calling a halt at the café before tackling the steep ascent to the Coteau, announcing loudly that they were about to arrest some of those 'dirty Jews.'" Poliakov confirms the description, explaining that when the gendarmes received an arrest order, "they went to the [local] Hotel May and ordered a glass of wine: Comfortably seated at their table, they took their papers from their satchels and spelled out 'Goldberg . . . it's about someone named Jacques Goldberg.' Unnecessary to add that when they arrived at Goldberg's domicile half an hour later, the latter was long gone." Poliakov adds that when a more serious danger approached in the form of the Gestapo or the Milice, a telephone call of warning usually preceded them from the valley.

Barot's and Poliakov's accounts both allude to the most important factor in the rescue success rate in Le Chambon — the determination of local residents to protect their guests. The people of Le Chambon lived in a state of constant alertness, with a warning system prepared. Their solidarity also made it difficult for potential informers to act. To whom could they safely leak information? Municipal authorities sympathized with the majority, as did, it appeared, many of the police. Even local censors of mail were likely to prevent a denunciation. In such a situation, a careless informer might even put himself in danger. In addition, it was psychologically more difficult for a solitary anti-Semite or opportunist to express his bile in a region where he was bucking an obvious majority. He could not so easily convince himself that he was acting as a "good and loyal Frenchman." And in any part of France — where so many individual arrests of Jews by preoccupied and understaffed local Gestapo units were prompted by denunciations — the reluctance of informers was decisive.

68

IRIS CHANG

From *The Rape of Nanking*

Nazi genocide was not the only systematic murder of civilian populations during World War II. The military government of Japan, a German ally during the war, engaged in some of the same tactics of brutal
and indiscriminate mass murder of civilians. In fact, atrocities in
Japan preceded those in Germany.

While for Europeans World War II began with the German invasion of Poland on September 1, 1939, and for Americans with the
Japanese attack at Pearl Harbor, Hawaii, on December 7, 1941, for
the Chinese it began ten years earlier with the Japanese invasion of
Manchuria in 1931. By 1937, Japanese troops occupied Peking and
Shanghai as well as the old imperial capital of Nanking. It is estimated
that more than twenty-five thousand civilians were killed by Japanese
soldiers in the months after the fall of Nanking on December 13,
1937. But it was the appalling brutality of Japanese troops that foreign residents remembered, even those who could recall the brutality
of the Chinese nationalist troops who captured the city in 1927. In the
Introduction to *The Rape of Nanking*, Iris Chang writes:

> The Rape of Nanking should be remembered not only for the
> number of people slaughtered but for the cruel manner in which
> many met their deaths. Chinese men were used for bayonet prac-
> tice and in decapitation contests. An estimated 20,000 to 80,000
> Chinese women were raped. Many soldiers went beyond rape to
> disembowel women, slice off their breasts, nail them alive to
> walls. Fathers were forced to rape their daughters, and sons their
> mothers, as other family members watched. Not only did live
> burials, castration, the carving of organs, and the roasting of
> people become routine, but more diabolical tortures were prac-
> ticed, such as hanging people by their tongues on iron hooks or
> burying people to their waist and watching them get torn apart by
> German shepherds. So sickening was the spectacle that even the
> Nazis in the city were horrified, one declaring the massacre to be
> the work of "bestial machinery." (p. 6)

In the selection that follows, the author asks how Japanese soldiers
were capable of such offenses. What is her answer?

Iris Chang, *The Rape of Nanking* (New York: Basic Books, 1997), 55–59.

Thinking Historically

What would have happened to these recruits if they had refused an order to kill a prisoner or noncombatant? Once they had killed one prisoner, why did they find it easier to kill another? Did they eventually enjoy it, feel pride, or think it insignificant? The last informant, Nagatomi, says he had been a "devil." Had he been possessed? By whom?

How then do we explain the raw brutality carried out day after day after day in the city of Nanking? Unlike their Nazi counterparts, who have mostly perished in prisons and before execution squads or, if alive, are spending their remaining days as fugitives from the law, many of the Japanese war criminals are still alive, living in peace and comfort, protected by the Japanese government. They are therefore some of the few people on this planet who, without concern for retaliation in a court of international law, can give authors and journalists a glimpse of their thoughts and feelings while committing World War II atrocities.

Here is what we learn. The Japanese soldier was not simply hardened for battle in China; he was hardened for the task of murdering Chinese combatants and noncombatants alike. Indeed, various games and exercises were set up by the Japanese military to numb its men to the human instinct against killing people who are not attacking.

For example, on their way to the capital, Japanese soldiers were made to participate in killing competitions, which were avidly covered by the Japanese media like sporting events. The most notorious one appeared in the December 7 issue of the *Japan Advertiser* under the headline "Sub-Lieutenants in Race to Fell 100 Chinese Running Close Contest."

> Sub-Lieutenant Mukai Toshiaki and Sub-Lieutenant Noda Takeshi, both of the Katagiri unit at Kuyung, in a friendly contest to see which of them will first fell 100 Chinese in individual sword combat before the Japanese forces completely occupy Nanking, are well in the final phase of their race, running almost neck to neck. On Sunday [December 5] . . . the "score," according to the Asahi, was: Sub-Lieutenant Mukai, 89, and Sub-Lieutenant Noda, 78.

A week later the paper reported that neither man could decide who had passed the 100 mark first, so they upped the goal to 150. "Mukai's blade was slightly damaged in the competition," the *Japan Advertiser* reported. "He explained that this was the result of cutting a Chinese in half, helmet and all. The contest was 'fun' he declared."

Such atrocities were not unique to the Nanking area. Rather, they were typical of the desensitization exercises practiced by the Japanese across China during the entire war. The following testimony by a Japanese private named Tajima is not unusual:

> One day Second Lieutenant Ono said to us, "You have never killed anyone yet, so today we shall have some killing practice. You must not consider the Chinese as a human being, but only as something of rather less value than a dog or cat. Be brave! Now, those who wish to volunteer for killing practice, step forward."
>
> No one moved. The lieutenant lost his temper.
>
> "You cowards!" he shouted. "Not one of you is fit to call himself a Japanese soldier. So no one will volunteer? Well then, I'll order you." And he began to call out names, "Otani — Furukawa — Ueno — Tajima!" (My God — me too!)
>
> I raised my bayoneted gun with trembling hands, and — directed by the lieutenant's almost hysterical cursing — I walked slowly towards the terror-stricken Chinese standing beside the pit — the grave he had helped to dig. In my heart, I begged his pardon, and — with my eyes shut and the lieutenant's curses in my ears — I plunged the bayonet into the petrified Chinese. When I opened my eyes again, he had slumped down into the pit. "Murderer! Criminal!" I called myself.

For new soldiers, horror was a natural impulse. One Japanese wartime memoir describes how a group of green Japanese recruits failed to conceal their shock when they witnessed seasoned soldiers torture a group of civilians to death. Their commander expected this reaction and wrote in his diary: "All new recruits are like this, but soon they will be doing the same things themselves."

But new officers also required desensitization. A veteran officer named Tominaga Shozo recalled vividly his own transformation from innocent youth to killing machine. Tominaga had been a fresh second lieutenant from a military academy when assigned to the 232nd Regiment of the 39th Division from Hiroshima. When he was introduced to the men under his command, Tominaga was stunned. "They had evil eyes," he remembered. "They weren't human eyes, but the eyes of leopards or tigers."

On the front Tominaga and other new candidate officers underwent intensive training to stiffen their endurance for war. In the program an instructor had pointed to a thin, emaciated Chinese in a detention center and told the officers: "These are the raw materials for your trial of courage." Day after day the instructor taught them how to cut off heads and bayonet living prisoners.

> On the final day, we were taken out to the site of our trial. Twenty-four prisoners were squatting there with their hands tied behind their backs. They were blindfolded. A big hole had been dug — ten meters long, two meters wide, and more than three meters deep. The

regimental commander, the battalion commanders, and the company commanders all took the seats arranged for them. Second Lieutenant Tanaka bowed to the regimental commander and reported, "We shall now begin." He ordered a soldier on fatigue duty to haul one of the prisoners to the edge of the pit; the prisoner was kicked when he resisted. The soldiers finally dragged him over and forced him to his knees. Tanaka turned toward us and looked into each of our faces in turn. "Heads should be cut off like this," he said, unsheathing his army sword. He scooped water from a bucket with a dipper, then poured it over both sides of the blade. Swishing off the water, he raised his sword in a long arc. Standing behind the prisoner, Tanaka steadied himself, legs spread apart, and cut off the man's head with a shout, "Yo!" The head flew more than a meter away. Blood spurted up in two fountains from the body and sprayed into the hole.

The scene was so appalling that I felt I couldn't breathe.

But gradually, Tominaga Shozo learned to kill. And as he grew more adept at it, he no longer felt that his men's eyes were evil. For him, atrocities became routine, almost banal. Looking back on his experience, he wrote: "We made them like this. Good sons, good daddies, good elder brothers at home were brought to the front to kill each other. Human beings turned into murdering demons. Everyone became a demon within three months."

Some Japanese soldiers admitted it was easy for them to kill because they had been taught that next to the emperor, all individual life — even their own — was valueless. Azuma Shiro, the Japanese soldier who witnessed a series of atrocities in Nanking, made an excellent point about his comrades' behavior in his letter to me. During his two years of military training in the 20th Infantry Regiment of Kyoto-fu Fukuchi-yama, he was taught that "loyalty is heavier than a mountain, and our life is lighter than a feather." He recalled that the highest honor a soldier could achieve during war was to come back dead: To die for the emperor was the greatest glory, to be caught alive by the enemy the greatest shame. "If my life was not important," Azuma wrote to me, "an enemy's life became inevitably much less important. . . . This philosophy led us to look down on the enemy and eventually to the mass murder and ill treatment of the captives."

In interview after interview, Japanese veterans from the Nanking massacre reported honestly that they experienced a complete lack of remorse or sense of wrongdoing, even when torturing helpless civilians. Nagatomi Hakudo spoke candidly about his emotions in the fallen capital:

I remember being driven in a truck along a path that had been cleared through piles of thousands and thousands of slaughtered bodies. Wild dogs were gnawing at the dead flesh as we stopped and pulled a group

of Chinese prisoners out of the back. Then the Japanese officer proposed a test of my courage. He unsheathed his sword, spat on it, and
with a sudden mighty swing he brought it down on the neck of a Chinese boy cowering before us. The head was cut clean off and tumbled
away on the group as the body slumped forward, blood spurting in
two great gushing fountains from the neck. The officer suggested I take
the head home as a souvenir. I remember smiling proudly as I took his
sword and began killing people.

After almost sixty years of soul-searching, Nagatomi is a changed
man. A doctor in Japan, he has built a shrine of remorse in his waiting
room. Patients can watch videotapes of his trial in Nanking and a full
confession of his crimes. The gentle and hospitable demeanor of the
doctor belies the horror of his past, making it almost impossible for one
to imagine that he had once been a ruthless murderer.

"Few know that soldiers impaled babies on bayonets and tossed
them still alive into pots of boiling water," Nagatomi said. "They gang-
raped women from the ages of twelve to eighty and then killed them
when they could no longer satisfy sexual requirements. I beheaded
people, starved them to death, burned them, and buried them alive,
over two hundred in all. It is terrible that I could turn into an animal
and do these things. There are really no words to explain what I was
doing. I was truly a devil."

69

RALPH BLUMENTHAL

Japanese Germ-Warfare Atrocities

**The Japanese concentration camps were not extermination camps,
though many prisoners of the Japanese died in them and many survivors were brutalized. But, as did the Nazis, some Japanese doctors
and scientists experimented on prisoners with deadly bacteria, chemi-
cal and biological agents, and surgical dismemberment without anes-
thesia and without any attempt to ease suffering or prevent death.**

Ralph Blumenthal with Judith Miller, "Japan Rebuffs Requests for Information About Its
Germ-Warfare Atrocities," *New York Times,* 4 March 1999, A12.

Some of these experiments were concentrated under the command of Unit 731 of the Japanese army.

How did this come about? Who was responsible? Why have the Japanese been reticent in releasing information about these activities almost seventy years after they began? What interest did the United States have in keeping these activities secret?

Thinking Historically

Try to imagine the mental framework of Shiro Ishii, the founder of Unit 731 and of Toshimi Mizobuchi, a member of the unit. How do you think each of them viewed what they were doing? How would you characterize their responsibility for what occurred? How would you compare their responsibility with that of the soldiers at Nanking in the previous selection? How would you compare their responsibility to that of the soldiers at Treblinka?

More than fifty years after the Japanese Army attacked China with germ weapons and conducted gruesome experiments on thousands of human beings, Japan is resisting demands that it compensate the victims or make records of the atrocities public.

The Japanese Government has declined to cooperate with efforts by the Justice Department to put the names of several hundred surviving veterans of the germ warfare operations on a list of suspected war criminals barred from entering the United States, American officials say.

It has also rebuffed researchers seeking access to a vast archive of military documents in Tokyo that detail the World War II activities of the Japanese Imperial Army, including its chief biological warfare arm, known as Unit 731. . . .

The Dead: The Numbers Remain in Dispute

The death toll from Japan's biological warfare remains in dispute. Some scholars assert that several hundred thousand people died, mostly in China. Others say the casualties were far lower. Scholars estimate that an additional ten thousand prisoners were killed in experiments, perhaps a dozen times the number who died at the hands of Dr. Josef Mengele and other Nazi scientists.

Eli M. Rosenbaum, director of the Office of Special Investigations in the Justice Department, said the dispute between Tokyo and Washington over suspected war criminals has been quietly building for three years.

The Justice Department's world-wide list of war crimes suspects now includes the names of about sixty thousand Germans and other

Europeans, including Kurt Waldheim, the former United Nations Secretary General, President of Austria, and wartime intelligence officer in Hitler's army.

By contrast, Mr. Rosenbaum said the United States had dates of birth and other identifying data on fewer than one hundred suspected Japanese war criminals. . . .

Little was publicly known about Japan's germ operations until the 1980s, when scholars published their first accounts. More recently, veterans of Unit 731 have been speaking publicly in Japan about their misdeeds, seeking expiation.

According to participants, victims, and records, the unit mounted widespread germ attacks with anthrax, typhoid, and other pathogens. Among other experiments, its doctors infected prisoners with disease germs, removed organs and blood, and withheld water to collect data on how the human body copes with illness and deprivation. Many victims were then dissected alive.

Only one former member of the unit was ever turned away from entering the United States: Yushio Shinozuka, who arrived last summer to join a forum and publicly express anguish over having prepared victims for vivisection.

Rather than fading with time, diplomats and scholars say, sensitivities over the issue are becoming sharper as new generations re-examine wartime events, as they have with the Holocaust in Europe.

Complicating the issue is the complicity of American officials in shielding from prosecution top Japanese scientists who turned over their data to the United States, which was developing its own germ warfare program.

Among the questions that remain unresolved is whether doctors working with Unit 731 experimented on American prisoners of war.

"The cover-up continues," said Sheldon H. Harris, emeritus professor of history at California State University in Northridge and the author of *Factories of Death* (Routledge, 1994), an account of the Japanese germ warfare program and the American hunger for its secrets. . . .

Mr. Harris said in an interview that while he had unearthed American translations of three Japanese autopsy reports comprising nearly a thousand pages recounting wartime medical experiments on dead and living prisoners, seventeen other reports were missing, along with some eight thousand photographic slides documenting the experiments.

The Campaign: Germ Bombs in the 1930s

The origins of Unit 731 go back to 1930 and the Tokyo laboratory of an ultranationalist surgeon and microbiologist, Shiro Ishii, who was later made a general. Within two years, after Japanese troops overran

Manchuria in northeast China, General Ishii, using the cover of a sanitation unit, set up the first of several large biological warfare and human research centers in Ping Fan and other areas around Harbin, a heavily Russian city near the Soviet border.

Over the next decade, scholars and researchers say, the Japanese attacked hundreds of heavily populated communities and remote regions with germ bombs. Evidence of the attacks continues to emerge.

"There appears to have been a massive germ war campaign in Yunnan Province bordering Burma," said Daniel Barenblatt, a graduate psychologist and New York City researcher who has been assembling material for five years for a documentary with the film director David Irving, chairman of the undergraduate film and television department at New York University.

"They seem to have been killing ethnic minorities in a jungle campaign," Mr. Barenblatt said.

Many questions remain unanswered.

It is still not established, for example, whether American prisoners of war were among those experimented on. Some Americans have said they were sickened by contaminated feathers in their food, and Japanese accounts tell of jars containing body parts labeled American among other nationalities.

Frank James, 77, a survivor of the Bataan Death March, ended up in 1942 at a Japanese prison camp in Mukden, Manchuria, where, he said, he became a seventy-pound living skeleton. "They gave us shots, sprays in the face," he recounted in a telephone interview from his home in Redwood City, California, where he is confined with diabetes and lung disease.

He said one of his jobs at Mukden was to retrieve for dissection frozen corpses that he was certain were American. "They opened them up so they could look into the lining of the stomach," he recalled. "The light pink icicles in the stomach weren't thawed."

A new [1999] hourlong documentary . . . *Unit 731: Nightmare in Manchuria,* features interviews with other surviving American war prisoners who say they were victimized by Japanese experiments.

But records of their debriefings by American officials remain unavailable. Mr. Harris, the author, said he applied for the records under the Freedom of Information Act several years ago and was told by the Veterans Administration that they had been destroyed in a fire in St. Louis.

After the war, American interest in prosecuting members of Unit 731 for war crimes faded fast. While Germany was split in a four-power occupation, the United States had a largely free hand in rebuilding Japan and was forging close ties to the new Government.

In addition, Mr. Harris said, American scientists were "salivating" over the chance to obtain the forbidden secrets of Japan's human experiments. The American authorities granted General Ishii and his associates immunity from prosecution and in exchange received detailed information.

The Allies did prosecute 5,570 Japanese, none for biological warfare. Nine Japanese medical school professionals were convicted, and some executed, for vivisecting eight captured American fliers in 1945.

Toshimi Mizobuchi makes no secret of his years with Unit 731. A vigorous 76-year-old real estate manager living outside the Japanese city of Kobe, Mr. Mizobuchi is organizing this year's reunion for the several hundred surviving veterans of Unit 731. He says he did not take part in experiments on humans, though he knew of them and argues that they were justifiable.

In an interview at home near Kobe with Rabbi Abraham Cooper of the Simon Wiesenthal Center that was recorded and transcribed through an interpreter, Mr. Mizobuchi said he still regarded the victims of the experiments as "maruta," or logs.

"They were logs to me," said Mr. Mizobuchi, a training officer with the unit. "Logs were not considered to be human. They were either spies or conspirators." As such, he said, "they were already dead. So now they die a second time. We just executed a death sentence."

He said that there were about thirty veterans of the unit living near him and that a reunion was held almost every year, drawing forty or fifty. Mr. Mizobuchi said he had never visited the American mainland but had been to Hawaii twice for sightseeing.

"It's a stain on history," said Rabbi Cooper, associate dean of the Wiesenthal Center, founded in 1977 in the name of the Viennese concentration camp survivor and Nazi-hunter.

Rabbi Cooper said he had interviewed former germ war soldiers and others last month in Japan and planned to present Congress and the White House with evidence he had gathered. "This blanket amnesty can't stand," he said.

70

ALLAN M. JALON

Meditating on War and Guilt, Zen Says It's Sorry

Genocide requires not only inhumane policies but also willing executioners. The fascist, militarized governments of Germany and Japan
were successful in indoctrinating ordinary citizens with racist hatred
and callous indifference to taking the lives of others. Both were able
to dehumanize the "enemy," but the Japanese went a step further by
also instilling soldiers with an indifference to their own lives. According to Jalon's article, what role did the ostensibly peaceful religion of
Zen Buddhism play in Japan during World War II?

Thinking Historically

The willingness of Japanese Zen Buddhist sects to confront and admit
their complicity in the atrocities of the Second World War stands in
marked contrast to the response of the Japanese government, as indicated in the previous selection. What accounts for the difference in the
Zen response? To what extent is the difference a result of historical
investigation, publications, and the distribution of knowledge? What
is the meaning and effect of apology?

To many Americans, Zen Buddhists primarily devote themselves to
discovering inner serenity and social peace. But Zen has had strong ties
to militarism — indeed so strong, that the leaders of one of the largest
denominations in Japan have remorsefully compared their former religious fanaticism during Japan's brutal expansionism in the 1930s and
40s to today's murderously militant Islamists.

The unexpected apology for wartime complicity by the leaders of
Myoshin-ji, the headquarters temple of one of Japan's main Zen sects,
was issued 16 days after 9/11, which gave it a particular resonance. But
the leaders of Myoshin-ji — as well as other Zen Buddhist leaders who
have also delivered apologies over the past two years — mainly credit a
disillusioned Westerner for their public regrets: Brian Victoria, a former
Methodist missionary, who is a Zen priest and historian.

Allan M. Jalon, "Meditating on War and Guilt, Zen Says It's Sorry," *New York Times* (January 11, 2003), p. B9.

Buddhist leaders in Japan and the United States said in recent interviews that Mr. Victoria had exerted a profound influence, especially in the West, by revealing in his 1997 book, *Zen at War,* a shockingly dark and unfamiliar picture of Zen during World War II to followers who had no idea about its history. Keiitsu Hosokawa, secretary general of Myoshin-ji, made a speech to the group's general assembly in September 2002 in which he said that the Japanese edition of *Zen at War* had been one of several factors that "provided the impetus" to issue the group's apology.

Now, in a new sequel called *Zen War Stories,* Mr. Victoria has dug more specifically into relationships between Zen leaders and the military during World War II.

From its beginnings in Japan, Zen has been associated with the warrior culture established by the early shoguns. But the extent of its involvement in World War II has stayed mostly submerged until recently. Many people in the United States and Europe know Zen's indirect traces through the poetry of the Beats or the quietist aura of contemporary architecture and clothing.

Even John Dower, a Pulitzer Prize–winning historian of modern Japan at MIT, whose early interest in Japan was kindled by Zen-inspired architecture, said that Mr. Victoria's works had opened his eyes to "how Zen violated Buddhism's teachings about compassion and nonviolence."

Ina Buitendijk, a Dutch Zen devotee, was so inspired by Mr. Victoria's work in 1999 that she mounted a letter-writing campaign pressing Zen leaders to confront their history. Mrs. Buitendijk's husband, along with other Dutch civilians, was interned by the Japanese in the Dutch East Indies during World War II. All this she put into the 28 letters she said she had written to Zen spiritual figures, educators, and administrative leaders in Japan. A number of leaders responded, sending her official apologies, some of which were published.

The Myoshin-ji statement, first issued on September 27, 2001, for example, was expanded in a major religious newspaper in Japan in September 2002. The initial statement said that the conflict between America and an anti-American jihad made it important to remember "that in the past our nation, under the banner of Holy War, initiated a conflict that led to great suffering."

The more detailed version apologized for helping to lend a religious purpose to invasions, colonization, and the former empire's destruction of "20 million precious lives." The self-critical account also described how Myoshin-ji members followed Japanese invaders across Asia, "established branch headquarters and missions" in conquered areas, even "conducted fund-raising drives to purchase military aircraft."

Two other Zen groups — the Tenryu-ji temple and the Sanbo-kyodan foundation — and several individual Zen leaders have also issued apologies after receiving Mrs. Buitendijk's letter for war-time complicity, which have appeared in Buddhist publications in Europe and the United States.

Mr. Victoria, 63, is a former Nebraskan who lives in Australia and teaches Japanese studies at the University of Adelaide. He embraced Zen in 1961, partly because he believed its history was free of the violent conflicts that had marked Western religion.

In 1964, ordained a Soto priest while living in Japan and increasingly active in opposing the Vietnam War, he was chastised by a religious superior for taking part in peace protests. He then discovered the writings of Ichikawa Hakugen, a Zen priest who had taken an early look at Zen's war-time role. It was buried, like that of Emperor Hirohito, by efforts to stabilize Japan during the cold war, Mr. Victoria said.

Mr. Victoria subsequently conducted numerous interviews with aging priests and plumbed Japanese military archives to detail how military figures and Zen leaders had jointly shaped Zen meditative practice into forms of military training.

"Zen was a large part of the spiritual training not only of the Japanese military but eventually of the whole Japanese people," he said in an interview. "It would have led them to commit national suicide if there had been an American invasion."

Zen War Stories quotes from manuals for battlefield behavior that Mr. Victoria says drew on Zen. It tells how the military modeled eating utensils on those in monasteries, how kamakazi pilots visited for spiritual preparation before their final missions.

Japanese Zen is a mosaic of different denominations, the two overarching groups being the Soto school, which emphasizes quiet sitting meditation, and the Rinzai school, which teaches a more aggressive practice based on solving spiritual riddles or koans. The Japanese tend to combine different kinds of Buddhist practice, including Zen and non-Zen forms.

Both of Mr. Victoria's books peel back layers of the career of D. T. Suzuki, who taught at Columbia University in the 1950s and remains the best-known Japanese advocate of Zen in the West. In 1938, however, Mr. Suzuki used his prestige as a scholar in Japan to assert that Zen's "ascetic tendency" teaches the Japanese soldier "that to go straight forward and crush the enemy is all that is necessary for him."

"What Brian Victoria has written is mostly right," said Jiun Kubota, the third patriarch of Sanbo-kyodan, a small Zen group outside Tokyo that has also issued an apology. "I dare say that Zen was used as the spiritual backbone of the military army and navies during the war."

Mr. Victoria's research has revealed that the founder of Sanbo-kyodan, Mr. Kubota's longtime teacher, was an outspoken militarist and anti-Semite during the war years. His name was Hakuun Yasutani, and he was one of the most significant figures in advancing the popularity of Zen Buddhism in the United States in the 1960s.

In 1999, the New York–based magazine *Tricycle* published excerpts of a 1943 book that Mr. Victoria had unearthed in which Yasutani expressed his hatred of "the scheming Jews." Actually, the Zen master probably knew few if any Jews, and Mr. Victoria believes he was using them as a stalking horse for liberalism.

Traditionally, Zen stresses an inward search for understanding and mental discipline. But Mr. Victoria said that imperial military trainers developed the self-denying egolessness Zen prizes into "a form of fascist mind-control." He said Suzuki and others helped by "romanticizing" the tie between Zen and the warrior ethos of the samurai. Worse, he charges, they stressed a connection between Buddhist compassion and the acceptance of death in a way that justified collective martyrdom and killing one's enemies.

"In Islam, as in the holy wars of Christianity, there is a promise of eternal life," Mr. Victoria said in an interview. "In Zen, there was the promise that there was no difference between life and death, so you really haven't lost anything."

Despite the apologies, some of the Zen leaders say that Mr. Victoria is too hard on Zen Buddhists. Thomas Kirchner, an American-born Myoshin-ji monk, who translated its World War II apology and those of other sects, argued that in the view of Japanese Zen leaders Mr. Victoria doesn't sufficiently explain "conformist pressures on all Japanese that were immense."

Masataka Toga, secretary general of Tenryu-ji, echoed that view. Mr. Kirchner also argued that Mr. Victoria doesn't offer a sufficiently textured picture of the religious landscape of wartime Japan. Other Buddhist sects and Japanese Christians also supported the war, along with the emperor-deifying religion of Shinto.

Herbert Bix, author of the Pulitzer Prize-winning *Hirohito and the Making of Modern Japan,* says it is important to see Mr. Victoria's work within the broad picture of Japanese religion and politics at the time.

Still, Mr. Bix, Mr. Kirchner, and others praise Mr. Victoria's work. Indeed, it's hard to find a scholar of authority who takes issue with the basic findings of *Zen at War,* which has chapter titles like "The Incorporation of Buddhism into the Japanese War Machine (1913–1930)."

Mr. Victoria sees hope for Buddhism in a Western-style "engaged Buddhism" that increasingly seeks to combine meditative practice with work for social progress and peace.

That moral growth, he believes, must come with a cold-eyed look at how basic Zen concepts were abused in the past: "I want my work to provide a model that it is possible to take an unflinching look at what

is really happening with a religion while remaining essentially committed to it."

REFLECTIONS

The massacre of civilians in times of war and the forced expulsion and
murder of people because of their race, religion, or ethnicity still go on
today. At the end of the twentieth century, the expulsion of over a million ethnic Albanian Kosovars by the Serbian police and military reminded many in the world of the events of the Nazi era.

Is the willingness to go to war to oppose genocide, ethnic cleansing,
state-sponsored mass-murder, and the abrogation of human rights a
sign of a new and welcome commitment in the world and in the United
States? The United States entered World War II, "the good fight"
against dictatorship, without knowledge of the holocaust and only after
Japan attacked Pearl Harbor and Germany declared war on the United
States. Oil, territory, or "national interest" more than principle has
often motivated much of American foreign policy. Wars fought for
principle are neither entirely new nor always salutary. In 1917 President Woodrow Wilson committed the United States to "a war to end
all wars," but this noble if paradoxical goal was combined with a
pledge to "make the world safe for democracy" and to ensure "the self-
determination of nations." We have lived with some of the darker implications of those principles ever since. Spreading democracy has
sometimes been viewed as a new form of Western imperialism, and the
seemingly innocent goal of national self-determination bears some responsibility for unleashing the ethnic hatreds witnessed in the former
Yugoslavia.

Short of war, the world community has adopted three other strategies to counter genocide and mass murder. The first is trial of war criminals. At the conclusion of World War II, war-crime trials of Nazis and
Japanese were conducted. The terms *war crimes* and *war criminals* are
unfortunate misnomers because they suggest a criminalization of military activities. In fact, the crimes recounted in this chapter were not
crimes of the battlefield but, rather, massive crimes against civilian populations.

Developing and refining international laws respecting human rights
is the second strategy. The "Declaration of Human Rights" passed by
the United Nations, itself a shaper and guardian of international law,
offers a recognized standard and continuing process for defining and
preventing genocide, mass murder, and "crimes against humanity."

The third strategy, one in which all of us can participate, is the dissemination of information and concerted efforts toward understanding.

To promote understanding, archives must be opened, and laws such as the Freedom of Information Act must be used aggressively. We must develop sensitivity to the plight of victims, knowledge of the victimizers' motives, and understanding about the ways that the horrendous can happen.

In recent years "truth and reconciliation" commissions have been formed in South Africa and El Salvador to enable those countries to get beyond years of government-sponsored terrorism. In cases like these, when such governments have relinquished power but their personnel are either too powerful or too numerous to be brought to justice, the new democratic governments and their truth and reconciliation commissions have asked for a complete and remorseful accounting of past crimes. Some say these commissions have been able to accept truth instead of revenge; others find it to be truth instead of justice. But truth can be an amazing restorative, especially when it is linked with genuine contrition. The price of amnesty can hardly be less. Forgiveness may be much more. Which, if any, of the crimes recalled in this chapter would you be willing to forgive? What should be necessary for acquittal or amnesty? How do we prevent such things from occurring again and again?

12

New States and
New Struggles

Middle East, South Africa,
China, and Vietnam, 1945–1975

HISTORICAL CONTEXT

World War II, like World War I before it, left in its wake the means and the motives for the creation of new states and new struggles throughout the world. Perhaps most significantly, the end of war in 1945 signaled that it was time to bring an end to colonies, to victors and vanquished — an agenda only dimly recognized in 1919. Even if both wars had not been caused by colonialism, the participation of colonized peoples on battlefields, in hospitals and factories, at home and in Europe made the pretenses of a League of Nations mandate seem to those in Africa and Asia to be colonialism under a different name. Further, the utter devastation of Germany and Japan and the sheer exhaustion of England and France made the continuation of colonialism a dubious proposition.

But the new reality dawned slowly. The sudden availability of former colonies of Germany and Japan tempted France, whose pride, more so than England's, had been shattered by the war. Although England released the Indian subcontinent in 1947, France held on to its former colony in Vietnam in 1945 and retained it until defeated in 1954.

The new state of Israel, carved out of the colonial British Mandate over Palestine by the United Nations in 1947, was the result of the success of the Jewish Zionist movement that had long campaigned for a Jewish state in the ancient home of Judaism (see Map 12.1). Even before the Nazi Holocaust, European governments thought a Jewish state would provide a Western outpost in the Arab world, but the virtual genocide of European Jewry by the Nazis gave the project renewed support. Ignored were the claims of resident Palestinian Arabs displaced by Jewish refugees from Europe and North Africa (see Map 12.2).

434

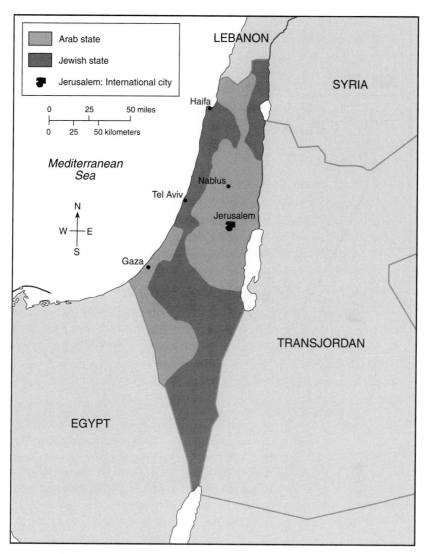

Legend:
- Arab state
- Jewish state
- Jerusalem: International city

0   25   50 miles
0   25   50 kilometers

LEBANON

SYRIA

Haifa

Mediterranean
Sea

Nablus

Tel Aviv

Jerusalem

N
W — E
S

Gaza

TRANSJORDAN

EGYPT

Map 12.1 UN Partition Plan for Palestine, 1947.

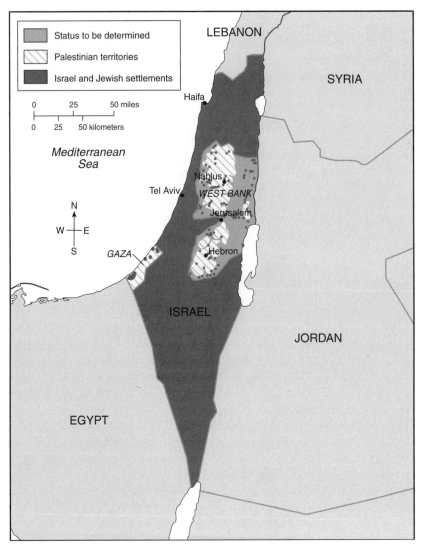

Map 12.2 Israel and the Palestinian Territories Today.

Not all new states after 1945 were products of decolonization. The communist victory in China in 1949 came at the end of Japanese colonization in 1945 but also after four more years of the unpopular Nationalist regime of Chiang Kai-shek, supported by the United States. The new People's Republic of China, established by Mao Zedong (Tsetung) in 1949, extended communism from the world's largest political territory, the Soviet Union and much of Eastern Europe, to the world's most populated country.

Even before Mao Zedong defeated Chiang Kai-shek's Nationalist army, Vietnamese socialists led by Ho Chi Minh declared their independence from defeated Japan and from France, their former occupier. With U.S. support, the French attempted to regain their colony, and when that effort failed in 1954, the United States replaced France for reasons that pertained to the communist victory in China and the politics of the Cold War between the United States and the Soviet Union.

South Africa was almost the only African state that was not newly founded between 1945 and 1975, but the victory of the Nationalist Party in 1948 brought about revolutionary changes for the country. For more than forty years, during this age of decolonization, a minority of white Europeans found ways to keep the majority Africans strangers in their own land.

In this chapter we examine examples of post–World War II politics to understand the forces of nationalism and division. While none of the struggles that developed in these societies was as destructive as World Wars I and II, many proved intractable, and some continue even today.

THINKING HISTORICALLY
Diagnosing Rifts and
Noting the Uses of History

The new struggles of the post–World War II period had roots in the war. The expectation of the imminent end to colonialism released the forces of nationalism. Some of these forces were religious and communal, as in the partitions of India and Pakistan and of Palestine and Israel. In the context of the developing Cold War between the United States and the Soviet Union, national movements had to define their relationship to the superpowers: capitalism or communism, freedom and democracy or international socialist solidarity. In all cases, there were also local, indigenous roots of conflict and the sort of economic, political, cultural, and social conflict that can be found in virtually any society.

As you read these selections, look for the rifts in these societies. *Rifts* are divides or fault lines along which tensions mount and conflicts arise. Every society has rifts — sometimes they are recognized; other times they are glossed over and denied. This chapter is partly an exercise in scrutinizing sources (all selections in the chapter are primary sources) to determine what is *not* said but implied. Note the disputes that the speech or document attempts to solve or ignore and the consensus that is assumed. In some cases, most obviously the racial divide in South Africa during the 1950s and 1960s, the rift is obvious and highlighted in the source. In others, the divisions are harder to pinpoint. We look for divisions for two reasons. First, understanding rifts tells us a great deal about a society. Recognizing a rift may not tell us how fragile a society is, but it does reveal what the society holds most important and where frictions are likely to develop. We might also be able to compare societies that have similar rifts (ethnic, racial, religious, political, economic, or social). Second, because rifts are the dynamic forces in a society, they show us how things are changing.

As you read these selections, you will be asked to think about the ways in which a people uses its history. Most of these sources, like so many others we could include, use historical accounts — explanations or stories of the past — to support their arguments. How can a historical account support a particular idea of the present or a vision of the future? What, after all, is the value of history?

71

Arab Opposition to a State of Israel

After the defeat of the Ottoman Empire in World War I, the League of Nations gave Great Britain a mandate to administer the region known as Palestine. British rule was beset by, on one hand, pressure from the Zionist movement to establish a Jewish homeland in Palestine and, on the other, pressure from Palestinian Arabs and neighboring Arab states to resist the Zionist demands. In the meantime, Zionist-inspired Jewish immigration to Palestine — mainly from Europe — continued and then increased with the rise of anti-Semitism

---

The Israel-Arab Reader: A Documentary History of the Middle East Conflict, ed. Walter Laquer and Barry Rubin (New York: Viking Penguin, 1995), 80, 82, 85, 88.

after Hitler's coming to power in Germany in 1933. As World War II ended, the situation in Palestine worsened: Both Zionist and Arab pressures intensified, with both sides resorting sometimes to violence. The horrendous experience of the Jewish people in Europe under Hitler's murderous rule naturally added to the difficulty of resolving the problem.

In November 1945 the United States and Great Britain established a commission to investigate the issue. This reading contains a portion of the Arab presentation to the commission. Why did Arabs oppose a Jewish state? What claims to Palestine did they make? Would they have accepted a nonreligious state that included Jews and Arabs? Was any compromise possible at this point? Why did the Arabs oppose the partition of Palestine?

Thinking Historically

What seems to have been the main conflict in Palestine at the time this document was written? Would you call it religious, economic, political, or something else? In what ways was this conflict likely to get worse, according to the Arab authors?

1. The whole Arab people is unalterably opposed to the attempt to impose Jewish immigration and settlement upon it, and ultimately to establish a Jewish State in Palestine. Its opposition is based primarily upon right. The Arabs of Palestine are descendants of the indigenous inhabitants of the country, who have been in occupation of it since the beginning of history; they cannot agree that it is right to subject an indigenous population against its will to alien immigrants, whose claim is based upon a historical connection which ceased effectively many centuries ago. Moreover they form the majority of the population; as such they cannot submit to a policy of immigration which if pursued for long will turn them from a majority into a minority in an alien state; and they claim the democratic right of a majority to make its own decisions in matters of urgent national concern.

2. The entry of incessant waves of immigrants prevents normal economic and social development and causes constant dislocation of the country's life; in so far as it reacts upon prices and values and makes the whole economy dependent upon the constant inflow of capital from abroad it may even in certain circumstances lead to economic disaster. It is bound moreover to arouse continuous political unrest and prevent the establishment of that political stability on which the prosperity and health of the country depend. This unrest is likely to increase in frequency and violence as the Jews come nearer to being the majority and the Arabs a minority.

Even if economic and social equilibrium is reestablished, it will be to the detriment of the Arabs. The superior capital resources at the disposal of the Jews, their greater experience of modern economic technique, and the existence of a deliberate policy of expansion and domination have already gone far toward giving them the economic mastery of Palestine. The biggest concessionary companies are in their hands; they possess a large proportion of the total cultivable land, and an even larger one of the land in the highest category of fertility; and the land they possess is mostly inalienable to non-Jews. The continuance of land-purchase and immigration, taken together with the refusal of Jews to employ Arabs on their lands or in their enterprises and the great increase in the Arab population, will create a situation in which the Arab population is pushed to the margin of cultivation and a landless proletariat, rural and urban, comes into existence. This evil can be palliated but not cured by attempts at increasing the absorptive capacity or the industrial production of Palestine; the possibility of such improvements is limited, they would take a long time to carry out, and would scarcely do more than keep pace with the rapid growth of the Arab population; moreover in present circumstances they would be used primarily for the benefit of the Jews and thus might increase the disparity between the two communities.

Nor is the evil economic only. Zionism is essentially a political movement, aiming at the creation of a state: immigration, land-purchase, and economic expansion are only aspects of a general political strategy. If Zionism succeeds in its aim, the Arabs will become a minority in their own country; a minority which can hope for no more than a minor share in the government, for the state is to be a Jewish state, and which will find itself not only deprived of that international status which the other Arab countries possess but cut off from living contact with the Arab world of which it is an integral part. . . .

8. In the Arab view, any solution of the problem created by Zionist aspirations must satisfy certain conditions:

(i) It must recognize the right of the indigenous inhabitants of Palestine to continue in occupation of the country and to preserve its traditional character.

(ii) It must recognize that questions like immigration, which affect the whole nature and destiny of the country, should be decided in accordance with democratic principles by the will of the population.

(iii) It must accept the principle that the only way by which the will of the population can be expressed is through the establishment of responsible representative Government. (The Arabs find something inconsistent in the attitude of Zionists who demand the establishment of a free democratic commonwealth in Palestine and then hasten to add that this should not take place until the Jews are in a majority.)

(iv) This representative Government should be based upon the principle of absolute equality of all citizens irrespective of race and religion.

(v) The form of Government should be such as to make possible the development of a spirit of loyalty and cohesion among all elements of the community, which will override all sectional attachments. In other words it should be a Government which the whole community could regard as their own, which should be rooted in their consent and have a moral claim upon their obedience.

(vi) The settlement should recognize the fact that by geography and history Palestine is inescapably part of the Arab world; that the only alternative to its being part of the Arab world and accepting the implications of its position is complete isolation, which would be disastrous from every point of view; and that whether they like it or not the Jews in Palestine are dependent upon the goodwill of the Arabs.

(vii) The settlement should be such as to make possible a satisfactory definition within the framework of U.N.O. of the relations between Palestine and the Western Powers who possess interests in the country.

(viii) The settlement should take into account that Zionism is essentially a political movement aiming at the creation of a Jewish state and should therefore avoid making any concession which might encourage Zionists in the hope that this aim can be achieved in any circumstances. . . .

The idea of partition and the establishment of a Jewish state in a part of Palestine is inadmissible for the same reasons of principle as the idea of establishing a Jewish state in the whole country. If it is unjust to the Arabs to impose a Jewish state on the whole of Palestine, it is equally unjust to impose it in any part of the country. Moreover, as the Woodhead Commission showed, there are grave practical difficulties in the way of partition; commerce would be strangled, communications dislocated, and the public finances upset. It would also be impossible to devise frontiers which did not leave a large Arab minority in the Jewish state. This minority would not willingly accept its subjection to the Zionists, and it would not allow itself to be transferred to the Arab state. Moreover, partition would not satisfy the Zionists. It cannot be too often repeated that Zionism is a political movement aiming at the domination at least of the whole of Palestine; to give it a foothold in part of Palestine would be to encourage it to press for more and to provide it with a base for its activities. Because of this, because of the pressure of population, and in order to escape from its isolation it would inevitably be thrown into enmity with the surrounding Arab states and this enmity would disturb the stability of the whole Middle East.

72

Israel's Proclamation of Independence

The Anglo-American Commission failed to resolve the problem of competing Zionist and Arab claims to Palestine. In 1947 Britain informed the United Nations, which had replaced the League of Nations, that it could not continue indefinitely to administer Palestine. The United Nations then called for the partition of Palestine into Jewish and Arab states. On May 14, 1948, the Jews of Palestine proclaimed the independent State of Israel. The next day — when British authority officially ended — armies from the Arab nations invaded Israel. But the Arabs were defeated. At the end of the war, Israel controlled 77 percent of the former Palestine rather than the 57 percent the United Nations had allotted to a Jewish state. In the course of the war, 900,000 of the 1,300,000 Arabs who had been living in the Israeli part of Palestine became refugees.

What reasons does this document give for the establishment of Israel? What provision does the new state seem ready to make for Palestinian Arabs? Do these differ from the rights of Jews?

Thinking Historically

Can you see signs of any potential future conflicts in this document? Does this proclamation minimize or resolve any of the conflicts you read about in the previous selection? Does it magnify the conflicts mentioned in selection 71? If so, how?

Notice how the authors of this document use their view of history to support their position. How might the Palestinian-Arab view of history differ?

The Land of Israel was the birthplace of the Jewish people. Here their spiritual, religious, and national identity was formed. Here they achieved independence and created a culture of national and universal significance. Here they wrote and gave the Bible to the world.

Exiled from the Land of Israel the Jewish people remained faithful to it in all the countries of their dispersion, never ceasing to pray and hope for their return and the restoration of their national freedom.

Impelled by this historical association, Jews strove throughout the

The Israel-Arab Reader: A Documentary History of the Middle East Conflict, ed. Walter Laquer and Barry Rubin (New York: Viking Penguin, 1995), 107–109.

centuries to go back to the land of their fathers and regain their state-hood. In recent decades they returned in their masses. They reclaimed the wilderness, revived their language, built cities and villages, and established a vigorous and ever-growing community, with its own economic and cultural life. They sought peace, yet were prepared to defend themselves. They brought the blessings of progress to all inhabitants of the country and looked forward to sovereign independence.

In the year 1897 the First Zionist Congress, inspired by Theodor Herzl's vision of the Jewish State, proclaimed the right of the Jewish people to national revival in their own country.

This right was acknowledged by the Balfour Declaration of November 2, 1917, and re-affirmed by the Mandate of the League of Nations, which gave explicit international recognition to the historic connection to the Jewish people with Palestine and their right to reconstitute their National Home.

The recent holocaust, which engulfed millions of Jews in Europe, proved anew the need to solve the problem of the homelessness and lack of independence of the Jewish people by means of the reestablishment of the Jewish State, which would open the gates to all Jews and endow the Jewish people with equality of status among the family of nations.

The survivors of the disastrous slaughter in Europe, and also Jews from other lands, have not desisted from their efforts to reach Eretz-Yisrael, in face of difficulties, obstacles, and perils; and have not ceased to urge their right to a life of dignity, freedom, and honest toil in their ancestral land.

In the second World War the Jewish people in Palestine made their full contribution to the struggle of the freedom-loving nations against the Nazi evil. The sacrifices of their soldiers and their war effort gained them the right to rank with the nations which founded the United Nations.

On November 29, 1947, the General Assembly of the United Nations adopted a Resolution requiring the establishment of a Jewish State in Palestine. The General Assembly called upon the inhabitants of the country to take all the necessary steps on their part to put the plan into effect. This recognition by the United Nations of the right of the Jewish people to establish their independent State is unassailable.

It is the natural right of the Jewish people to lead, as do all other nations, an independent existence in its sovereign State.

Accordingly we, the members of the National Council, representing the Jewish people in Palestine and the World Zionist Movement, are met together in solemn assembly today, the day of termination of the British Mandate for Palestine; and by virtue of the natural and historic right of the Jewish people and of the Resolution of the General Assembly of the United Nations.

We hereby proclaim the establishment of the Jewish State in Palestine, to be called Medinath Yisrael (The State of Israel).

The State of Israel will be open to the immigration of Jews from all countries of their dispersion; will promote the development of the country for the benefit of all its inhabitants; will be based on the principles of liberty, justice, and peace as conceived by the Prophets of Israel; will uphold the full social and political equality of all its citizens, without distinction of religion, race, or sex; will guarantee freedom of religion, conscience, education, and culture; will safeguard the Holy Places of all religions; and will loyally uphold the principles of the United Nations Charter.

The State of Israel will be ready to co-operate with the organs and representatives of the United Nations in the implementation of the Resolution of the Assembly of November 29, 1947, and will take steps to bring about the Economic Union over the whole of Palestine.

We appeal to the United Nations to assist the Jewish people in the building of its State and to admit Israel into the family of nations.

In the midst of wanton aggression [by Arab states], we yet call upon the Arab inhabitants of the State of Israel to preserve the ways of peace and play their part in the development of the State, on the basis of full and equal citizenship and due representation in all its bodies and institutions — provisional and permanent.

We extend our hand in peace, and neighbourliness to all the neighbouring states and their peoples, and invite them to cooperate with the independent Jewish nation for the common good of all. The State of Israel is prepared to make its contribution to the progress of the Middle East as a whole.

Our call goes out to the Jewish people all over the world to rally to our side in the task of immigration and development, and to stand by us in the great struggle for the fulfillment of the dream of generations for the redemption of Israel.

73

HENDRIK F. VERWOERD

On Apartheid

South Africa was settled by Europeans from Holland and England in the middle of the seventeenth century. From the beginning, Europeans had contact with the Khoikhoi indigenous people who were swiftly decimated by European diseases. As Europeans expanded inland from their original seacoast settlements, they farmed the interior with Khoikhoi labor and with slaves imported largely from Indonesia and Madagascar. By the end of the nineteenth century, European settlers engaged in frequent wars with the Xhosa and Zulu people (African Bantu speakers), who were ultimately subdued by machine guns. After the English defeated the Dutch in the Boer War at the turn of the century, the Republic of South Africa was declared in 1910. For most of the period before World War II, despite the English victory, moderate Dutch leaders ruled South Africa, restricting black African land ownership and civil rights. After the discovery of gold and diamonds in South Africa near the end of the nineteenth century, the need for workers from all races was great, and the friction between whites and blacks increased considerably.

During World War II, many white South Africans, some of whom had been educated in Germany, supported the Nazis. In 1948 a reconstituted Nationalist Party, backed by fascist and paramilitary movements, won a surprising electoral victory on the promise of a new, more segregationist policy called apartheid. In this selection, Hendrik F. Verwoerd explains the meaning of and rationale behind apartheid. Verwoerd, educated in Nazi Germany, was a key figure in the creation and execution of South African racial policy as the first "Native Minister" and later as prime minister (1958–1966).

The policy of apartheid was twofold: First, black "Bantu" speaking Africans (not the smaller and more absorbed populations of Khoikhoi and "people of mixed race"), who were needed for work but banned from "European cities," were declared to be no longer South African. Labeled instead "natives" of "independent homelands," this 70 percent of the population was moved to landlocked scrub, a paltry 13-percent share of former South African territory. Second, the needed black workers were allowed to commute weekly from these homelands to work in white South African mines and cities

A. N. Pelzer, ed., *Verwoerd Speaks: Speeches, 1948–1966* (Johannesburg: APB Publishers, 1966), 23–29.

if they carried appropriate passes and lived in designated dormitories while working. Of course, they were paid much less than their white counterparts who, it was thought, would then show greater appreciation for their privileges of race. Among the results of this policy were the effective elimination of what South African sociologists called "poor whiteism," the creation of a white middle class, clear color-coding of poverty, and increasing popularity for the Nationalist Party.

In the speech that follows, how does Verwoerd appeal to his white audience? How does he appeal to a black audience? Do you think he believed what he said? Did his audience?

In what ways does Verwoerd's policy toward black Africans resemble Israeli policy toward Palestinians or U.S. policy toward Native Americans? What are the differences?

Thinking Historically

Notice how Verwoerd argues that equality and intermingling will lead to conflict. What sort of conflict is he speaking about? Would you call it an economic conflict or an ethnic-racial conflict? How can ethnic-racial segregation minimize economic conflict? Is Verwoerd more interested in avoiding conflict or preserving privilege?

. . . Next, I wish to accede to the wish which, I understand, has long been felt by members of this council, namely that a member of the Government should explain the main features of what is implied by the policy of Apartheid. . . .

As a premise, the question may be put: Must Bantu and European in future develop as intermixed communities, or as communities separated from one another in so far as this is practically possible? If the reply is "intermingled communities," then the following must be understood. There will be competition and conflict everywhere. So long as the points of contact are still comparatively few, as is the case now, friction and conflict will be few and less evident. The more this intermixing develops, however, the stronger the conflict will become. In such conflict, the Europeans will, at least for a long time, hold the stronger position, and the Bantu be the defeated party in every phase of the struggle. This must cause to rise in him an increasing sense of resentment and revenge. Neither for the European, nor for the Bantu, can this, namely increasing tension and conflict, be an ideal future, because the intermixed development involves disadvantage to both.

Perhaps, in such an eventuality, it is best frankly to face the situation which must arise in the political sphere. In the event of an intermixed development, the Bantu will undoubtedly desire a share in the government of the intermixed country. He will, in due course, not be satisfied with a limited share in the form of communal representation, but will desire full participation in the country's government on the basis of an equal franchise. For the sake of simplicity, I shall not enlarge here on the fact that, simultaneously with the development of this demand, he will desire the same in the social, economic, and other spheres of life, involving in due course, intermixed residence, intermixed labour, intermixed living, and, eventually, a miscegenated population — in spite of the well-known pride of both the Bantu and the European in their respective purity of descent. It follows logically, therefore, that, in an intermixed country, the Bantu must, in the political sphere, have as their object equal franchise with the European.

Now examine the same question from the European's point of view. A section of the Europeans, consisting of both Afrikaans- and English-speaking peoples, says equally clearly that, in regard to the above standpoint, the European must continue to dominate what will be the European part of South Africa. It should be noted that, notwithstanding false representations, these Europeans do not demand domination over the whole of South Africa, that is to say, over the Native territories according as the Bantu outgrow the need for their trusteeship. Because that section of the European population states its case very clearly, it must not be accepted, however, that the other section of the European population will support the above possible future demand of the Bantu. That section of the European population (English as well as Afrikaans) which is prepared to grant representation to the Bantu in the country's government does not wish to grant anything beyond communal representation, and that on a strictly limited basis. They do not yet realize that a balance of power may thereby be given to the non-European with which an attempt may later be made to secure full and equal franchise on the same voters' roll. The moment they realize that, or the moment when the attempt is made, this latter section of the European population will also throw in its weight with the first section in the interests of European supremacy in the European portion of the country. This appears clearly from its proposition that, in its belief on the basis of an inherent superiority, or greater knowledge, or whatever it may be, the European must remain master and leader. The section is, therefore, also a protagonist of separate residential areas, and of what it calls separation.

My point is this that, if mixed development is to be the policy of the future in South Africa, it will lead to the most terrific clash of interests imaginable. The endeavours and desires of the Bantu and the endeavours and objectives of *all* Europeans will be antagonistic. Such a clash can only bring unhappiness and misery to both. Both Bantu and European must, therefore, consider in good time how this misery can be averted from themselves and from their descendants. They must find a plan to provide the two population groups with opportunities for the full development of their respective powers and ambitions without coming into conflict.

The only possible way out is the second alternative, namely, that both adopt a development divorced from each other. That is all that the word apartheid means. Any word can be poisoned by attaching a false meaning to it. That has happened to this word. The Bantu have been made to believe that it means oppression, or even that the Native territories are to be taken away from them. In reality, however, exactly the opposite is intended with the policy of apartheid. To avoid the above-mentioned unpleasant and dangerous future for both sections of the population, the present Government adopts the attitude that it concedes and wishes to give to others precisely what it demands for itself. It believes in the supremacy (baasskap) of the European in his sphere but, then, it also believes equally in the supremacy (baasskap) of the Bantu in his own sphere. For the European child it wishes to create all the possible opportunities for its own development, prosperity, and national service in its own sphere; but for the Bantu it also wishes to create all the opportunities for the realization of ambitions and the rendering of service to *their* own people. There is thus no policy of oppression here, but one of creating a situation which has never existed for the Bantu; namely, that, taking into consideration their languages, traditions, history, and different national communities, they may pass through a development of their own. That opportunity arises for them as soon as such a division is brought into being between them and the Europeans that they need not be the imitators and henchmen of the latter. . . .

I trust that every Bantu will forget the misunderstandings of the past and choose not the road leading to conflict, but that which leads to peace and happiness for both the separate communities. Are the present leaders of the Bantu, under the influence of Communist agitators, going to seek a form of equality which they will not get? For in the long run they will come up against the whole of the European community, as well as the large section of their own compatriots who prefer the many advantages of self-government within a community of their own. I cannot believe that they will. Nobody can reject a form of independence, obtainable with everybody's co-operation, in favour of a futile striving after that which promises to be not freedom but downfall. . . .

74

NELSON MANDELA

Rivonia Trial Statement

On May 1, 1994, Nelson Mandela was elected president of South Africa in the first general election in which all South Africans, black and white, were permitted to vote. Mandela, the leader of the African National Congress (A.N.C.), had spent twenty-seven years in jail when he was released by then-president F. W. de Klerk in 1990.

Mandela was born into a royal clan of the Thembu people in 1918 and, after his father's death, was prepared for the chieftainship by a cousin. He was educated at a British missionary school and Fort Harare University, experiences that broadened his identity as a South African so that he no longer "attached value to any kind of ethnicity." After earning a law degree, he joined the A.N.C., for which he rapidly became an important spokesman and organizer. As a political leader and attorney, Mandela worked peacefully and legally for the rights of black South Africans in the first decade of apartheid after 1948. But with mounting evidence of government oppression and, in 1961, the police killing of sixty-nine peaceful demonstrators in Sharpeville, Mandela led the A.N.C. to adopt tactics of armed resistance, becoming the first commander of the new guerilla army. Eight months later he was arrested.

Mandela was already in prison when a raid by South African police on the Rivonia farm hideout of the A.N.C. netted information implicating Mandela as organizer of the A.N.C.'s new military wing, Umkonto We Sizwe. At the trial he was given a life sentence. This selection is excerpted from the statement he made at his trial in 1964.

How was Mandela's vision for South Africa different from Verwoerd's? Was it inconsistent for Mandela to favor violence while claiming to be a democrat? Compare Mandela's nationalism with Gandhi's.

Thinking Historically

Notice how Mandela positioned himself as a modern force in the national struggle of South African blacks for full political participation. What, according to Mandela, were the tensions within the black community?

From Protest to Challenge: A Documentary History of African Politics in South Africa, 1882–1964, ed. Thomas Karis and Gwendolyn M. Carter, vol. III; *Challenge and Violence, 1953–1964,* ed. Thomas Karis and Gail M. Gerhart (Stanford: Hoover Institution Press, 1977), 771–77, 790–91, 795–96.

In the previous selection, Verwoerd defended racial and national division as a way of avoiding economic conflict. In this selection, Mandela defends the biracial policy of the A.N.C. and the establishment of a democracy without racial or national distinctions. Does such a society run the risk of increasing economic and social conflict? How did Mandela hope to curtail such conflict?

How does Mandela's telling of the history of the A.N.C. support his argument that violence against the state was nonracial and used only as a last resort?

I am the First Accused.

I hold a Bachelor's Degree in Arts and practised as an attorney in Johannesburg for a number of years in partnership with Oliver Tambo. I am a convicted prisoner serving five years for leaving the country without a permit and for inciting people to go on strike at the end of May, 1961.

At the outset, I want to say that the suggestion made by the State in its opening that the struggle in South Africa is under the influence of foreigners or communists is wholly incorrect. I have done whatever I did, both as an individual and as a leader of my people, because of my experience in South Africa and my own proudly-felt African background, and not because of what any outsider might have said.

In my youth in the Transkei I listened to the elders of my tribe telling stories of the old days. Amongst the tales they related to me were those of wars fought by our ancestors in defence of the fatherland. The names of Dingane and Bambata, Hintsa, and Makana, Squngthi and Dalasile, Moshoeshoe and Sekukhuni, were praised as the glory of the entire African nation. I hoped then that life might offer me the opportunity to serve my people and make my own humble contribution to their freedom struggle. This is what has motivated me in all that I have done in relation to the charges made against me in this case.

Having said this, I must deal immediately and at some length, with the question of violence. Some of the things so far told to the Court are true and some are untrue. I do not, however, deny that I planned sabotage. I did not plan it in a spirit of recklessness, nor because I have any love of violence. I planned it as the result of a calm and sober assessment of the political situation that had arisen after many years of tyranny, exploitation, and oppression of my people by the Whites. . . .

But the violence which we chose to adopt was not terrorism. We who formed Umkonto were all members of the African National Congress, and had behind us the A.N.C. tradition of non-violence and negotiation as a means of solving political disputes. We believe that South Africa belonged to all the people who lived in it, and not to one group, be it Black or White. We did not want an inter-racial war, and tried to avoid it to the last minute. If the Court is in doubt about this, it will be seen that the whole history of our organization bears out what I have said, and what I will subsequently say, when I describe the tactics which Umkonto decided to adopt. I want, therefore, to say something about the African National Congress.

The African National Congress was formed in 1912 to defend the rights of the African people which had been seriously curtailed by the South Africa Act, and which were then being threatened by the Native Land Act. For thirty-seven years — that is until 1949 — it adhered strictly to a constitutional struggle. It put forward demands and resolutions; it sent delegations to the Government in the belief that African grievances could be settled through peaceful discussion and that Africans could advance gradually to full political rights. But White Governments remained unmoved, and the rights of Africans became less instead of becoming greater. In the words of my leader, Chief Luthuli, who became President of the A.N.C. in 1952, and who was later awarded the Nobel Peace Prize:

> who will deny that thirty years of my life have been spent knocking in vain, patiently, moderately, and modestly at a closed and barred door? What have been the fruits of moderation? The past thirty years have seen the greatest number of laws restricting our rights and progress, until today we have reached a stage where we have almost no rights at all.

Even after 1949, the A.N.C. remained determined to avoid violence. At this time, however, there was a change from the strictly constitutional means of protest which had been employed in the past. The change was embodied in a decision which was taken to protest against apartheid legislation by peaceful, but unlawful, demonstrations against certain laws. Pursuant to this policy the A.N.C. launched the Defiance Campaign, in which I was placed in charge of volunteers. This campaign was based on the principles of passive resistance. More than 8,500 people defied apartheid laws and went to gaol. Yet there was not a single instance of violence in the course of this campaign on the part of any defier. I, and nineteen colleagues were convicted for the role we played in organizing the campaign, but our sentences were suspended mainly because the Judge found that discipline and nonviolence had been stressed throughout. This was the time when the volunteer section of the A.N.C. was established, and the word "Amadelakufa" was first used: This was the time when the volunteers were asked to take a pledge to uphold certain principles. Evidence dealing with volunteers and their pledges has been introduced into this case, but completely out of context. The volunteers were not, and are not, the soldiers of a Black Army pledged to fight a civil war against the Whites. They were, and are, the dedicated workers who are prepared to lead campaigns initiated by the A.N.C. to distribute leaflets; to organize strikes, or do whatever the particular campaign required. They are called volunteers because they volunteer to face the penalties of imprisonment and whipping which are now prescribed by the legislature for such acts.

During the Defiance Campaign, the Public Safety Act and the Criminal Law Amendment Act were passed. These Statutes provided harsher penalties for offences committed by way of protests against laws. Despite this, the protests continued and the A.N.C. adhered to its policy of non-violence. In 1956, one hundred and fifty-six leading members of the Congress Alliance, including myself, were arrested on a charge of High Treason and charged under the Suppression of Communism Act. The non-violent policy of the A.N.C. was put into issue by the State, but when the Court gave judgment some five years later, it found that the A.N.C. did not have a policy of violence. We were acquitted on all counts, which included a count that the A.N.C. sought to set up a Communist State in place of the existing regime. The Government has always sought to label all its opponents as communists. This allegation has been repeated in the present case, but as I will show, the A.N.C. is not, and never has been, a communist organization.

In 1960, there was the shooting at Sharpeville, which resulted in the proclamation of a State of Emergency and the declaration of the A.N.C. as an unlawful organization. My colleagues and I, after careful consideration, decided that we would not obey this decree. The African people were not part of the Government and did not make the laws by which they were governed. We believed in the words of the Universal Declaration of Human Rights, that "the will of the people shall be the basis of the authority of the Government," and for us to accept the banning was equivalent to accepting the silencing of the Africans for all time. The A.N.C. refused to dissolve, but instead went underground. We believed it was our duty to preserve this organization which had been built up with almost fifty years of unremitting toil. I have no doubt that no self-respecting White political organization would disband itself if declared illegal by a Government in which it had no say. . . .

The lack of human dignity experienced by Africans is the direct result of the policy of White supremacy. White supremacy implies Black inferiority. Legislation designed to preserve White supremacy entrenches this notion. Menial tasks in South Africa are invariably performed by Africans. When anything has to be carried or cleaned the White man will look around for an African to do it for him, whether the African is employed by him or not. Because of this sort of attitude, Whites tend to regard Africans as a separate breed. They do not look upon them as people with families of their own; they do not realise that they have emotions — that they fall in love like White people do; that they want to be with their wives and children like White people want to be with theirs; that they want to earn enough money to support their families properly, to feed and clothe them and send them to school. And what "house-boy" or "garden-boy" or labourer can ever hope to do this?

Pass Laws, which to the Africans are among the most hated bits of legislation of South Africa, render any African liable to police surveillance at any time. I doubt whether there is a single African male in South Africa who has not at some stage had a brush with the police over his pass. Hundreds and thousands of Africans are thrown into gaol every year under pass laws. Even worse than this is the fact that pass laws keep husband and wife apart and lead to the breakdown of family life.

Poverty and the breakdown of family life have secondary effects. Children wander about the streets of the Townships because they have no schools to go to, or no money to enable them to go to school, or no parents at home to see that they go to school, because both parents (if there be two) have to work to keep the family alive. This leads to a breakdown in moral standards, to an alarming rise in illegitimacy, and to growing violence which erupts, not only politically, but everywhere. Life in the townships is dangerous. There is not a day that goes by without somebody being stabbed or assaulted. And violence is carried out of the townships in the White living areas. People are afraid to walk the streets after dark. Housebreakings and robberies are increasing, despite the fact that the death sentence can now be imposed for such offences. Death sentences cannot cure the festering sore.

Africans want to be paid a living wage. Africans want to perform work which they are capable of doing, and not work which the Government declares them to be capable of. Africans want to be allowed to live where they obtain work, and not be endorsed out of an area because they were not born there. Africans want to be allowed to own land in places where they work, and not to be obliged to live in rented houses which they can never call their own. Africans want to be part of the general population, and not confined to living in their own ghettos. African men want to have their wives and children to live with them where they work, and not be forced into an unnatural existence in men's hostels. African women want to be with their men folk and not be left permanently widowed in the reserves. Africans want to be allowed out after 11 o'clock at night and not to be confined to their rooms like little children. Africans want to be allowed to travel in their own country and to seek work where they want to and not where the Labour Bureau tells them to. Africans want a just share in the whole of South Africa; they want security and a stake in society.

Above all, we want equal political rights, because without them our disabilities will be permanent. I know this sounds revolutionary to the

Whites in this country, because the majority of voters will be Africans. This makes the White man fear democracy.

But this fear cannot be allowed to stand in the way of the only solution which will guarantee racial harmony and freedom for all. It is not true that the enfranchisement of all will result in racial domination. Political division, based on colour, is entirely artificial and, when it disappears, so will the domination of one colour group by another. The A.N.C. has spent half a century fighting against racialism. When it triumphs it will not change that policy.

This then is what the A.N.C. is fighting. Their struggle is a truly national one. It is a struggle of the African people, inspired by their own suffering and their own experience. It is a struggle for the right to live.

During my lifetime I have dedicated myself to this struggle of the African people. I have fought against White domination, and I have fought against Black domination. I have cherished the ideal of a democratic and free society in which all persons live together in harmony and with equal opportunities. It is an ideal which I hope to live for and to achieve. But if needs be, it is an ideal for which I am prepared to die.

75

MAO ZEDONG

On Letting a Hundred Flowers Blossom

When Mao Zedong (Tse-tung) and the Chinese Communist party came to power in 1949, they were faced with the ruins of Japanese occupation and World War II, the abject political failure of the Chinese Republic, decades of economic hardship, and the bitterness and pain of the recently concluded civil war. The Communists intended to return China to its former prosperity and stature in the world and to transform it into a modern state, doing away with the gross injustices that had plagued the vast masses of poor rural peasants and urban workers.

Mao Tse-tung, "On Letting a Hundred Flowers Blossom," from *Mao Tse-tung on Art and Literature* (Peking: Foreign Language Press, 1960).

In rural areas, "people's courts" were set up. Landlords were tried, subjected to self-criticism, and then forced to give up their property. Many were executed, with estimates varying from hundreds of thousands to tens of millions killed. While some of those classified as "rich peasants" lost their livelihoods, the vast majority of Chinese peasants (a group that numbered around 600 million, one-fifth of the world's population) benefited from the land redistribution that followed.

The Communists had less experience in the cities than in the country. In 1927 they had been routed from the cities by a Nationalist purge. Forced to regroup in western rural China, they developed new roots among the peasantry, as Mao revised the traditional Marxist-Leninist vision of socialist transformation based on the revolutionary potential of the urban proletariat. But the Communists brought the same zeal to the cities that they had to the countryside. They arrested thieves, burglars, smugglers, prostitutes, and beggars, had them "re-educated" to Marxist social responsibility, and employed them in useful work.

Intellectuals were long a privileged class in China, perhaps the most privileged class. Those who had not joined the communist movement in the country, choosing instead to remain in the city, were suspected of supporting the defeated Nationalists. Still, many intellectuals were won over by Communist success in ridding urban politics of corruption, reducing inflation and unemployment, increasing literacy, and championing justice for women and the poor.

By 1957, Mao felt confident enough of the support of the intellectual class that he called on them to help the cause by constructively criticizing the party. This was the point of his speech on art and literature, "On Letting a Hundred Flowers Blossom," that is excerpted here.

How did Mao distinguish between acceptable and unacceptable criticism? Does he seem to be more interested in finding fragrant flowers or poisonous weeds?

Thinking Historically

Mao discusses a cultural rift in the country — a disagreement about ideas. How does he see the difference between Marxist and non-Marxist intellectuals? To what extent does Mao see this cultural divide as one primarily of social class?

"Let a hundred flowers blossom," and "let a hundred schools of thought contend," "long-term coexistence and mutual supervision" — how did these slogans come to be put forward?

They were put forward in the light of the specific conditions existing in China, on the basis of the recognition that various kinds of contradictions still exist in a socialist society, and in to the country's urgent
need to speed up its economic and cultural development.

The policy of letting a hundred flowers blossom and a hundred
schools of thought contend is designed to promote the flourishing of
the arts and the progress of science; it is designed to enable a socialist
culture to thrive in our land. Different forms and styles in art can develop freely and different schools in science can contend freely. We
think that it is harmful to the growth of art and science if administrative measures are used to impose one particular style of art or school of
thought and to ban another. Questions of right and wrong in the arts
and sciences should be settled through free discussion in artistic and scientific circles and in the course of practical work in the arts and sciences. They should not be settled in summary fashion. A period of trial
is often needed to determine whether something is right or wrong. In
the past, new and correct things often failed at the outset to win recognition from the majority of people and had to develop by twists and
turns in struggle. Correct and good things have often at first been
looked upon not as fragrant flowers but as poisonous weeds. Copernicus' theory of the solar system and Darwin's theory of evolution were
once dismissed as erroneous and had to win through over bitter opposition. Chinese history offers many similar examples. In socialist society,
conditions for the growth of new things are radically different from and
far superior to those in the old society. Nevertheless, it still often happens that new, rising forces are held back and reasonable suggestions
smothered.

The growth of new things can also be hindered, not because of deliberate suppression, but because of lack of discernment. That is why
we should take a cautious attitude in regard to questions of right and
wrong in the arts and sciences, encourage free discussion, and avoid
hasty conclusions. We believe that this attitude will facilitate the
growth of the arts and sciences.

Marxism has also developed through struggle. At the beginning,
Marxism was subjected to all kinds of attack and regarded as a poisonous weed. It is still being attacked and regarded as a poisonous
weed in many parts of the world. However, it enjoys a different position in the socialist countries. But even in these countries, there are
non-Marxist as well as anti-Marxist ideologies. It is true that in China,
socialist transformation, in so far as a change in the system of ownership is concerned, has in the main been completed, and the turbulent,
large-scale, mass class struggles characteristic of the revolutionary periods have in the main concluded. But remnants of the overthrown landlord and comprador classes still exist, the bourgeoisie still exists, and
the petty bourgeoisie has only just begun to remould itself. Class struggle is not yet over. The class struggle between the proletariat and the

bourgeoisie, the class struggle between various political forces, and the class struggle in the ideological field between the proletariat and the bourgeoisie will still be long and devious and at times may even become very acute. The proletariat seeks to transform the world according to its own world outlook, so does the bourgeoisie. In this respect, the question whether socialism or capitalism will win is still not really settled. Marxists are still a minority of the entire population as well as of the intellectuals. Marxism therefore must still develop through struggle. Marxism can only develop through struggle — this is true not only in the past and present, it is necessarily true in the future also. What is correct always develops in the course of struggle with what is wrong. The true, the good, and the beautiful always exist in comparison with the false, the evil and the ugly, and grow in struggle with the latter. As mankind in general rejects an untruth and accepts a truth, a new truth will begin struggling with new erroneous ideas. Such struggles will never end. This is the law of development of truth and it is certainly also the law of development of Marxism.

It will take a considerable time to decide the issue in the ideological struggle between socialism and capitalism in our country. This is because the influence of the bourgeoisie and of the intellectuals who come from the old society will remain in our country as the ideology of a class for a long time to come. Failure to grasp this, or still worse, failure to understand it at all, can lead to the gravest mistakes — to ignoring the necessity of waging the struggle in the ideological field. Ideological struggle is not like other forms of struggle. Crude, coercive methods should not be used in this struggle, but only the method of painstaking reasoning. Today, socialism enjoys favourable conditions in the ideological struggle. The main power of the state is in the hands of the working people led by the proletariat. The Communist Party is strong and its prestige stands high. Although there are defects and mistakes in our work, every fair-minded person can see that we are loyal to the people, that we are both determined and able to build up our country together with the people, and that we have achieved great successes and will achieve still greater ones. The vast majority of the bourgeoisie and intellectuals who come from the old society are patriotic; they are willing to serve their flourishing socialist motherland, and they know that if they turn away from the socialist cause and the working people led by the Communist Party, they will have no one to rely on and no bright future to look forward to.

People may ask: Since Marxism is accepted by the majority of the people in our country as the guiding ideology, can it be criticized? Certainly it can. As a scientific truth, Marxism fears no criticism. If it did, and could be defeated in arguments, it would be worthless. In fact, aren't the idealists criticizing Marxism every day and in all sorts of ways? As for those who harbour bourgeois and petty-bourgeois ideas and do not wish to change, aren't they also criticizing Marxism in all sorts of ways? Marxists should not be afraid of criticism from any quarter. Quite the contrary, they need to steel and improve themselves and win new positions in the teeth of criticism and the storm and stress of struggle. Fighting against wrong ideas is like being vaccinated — a man develops greater immunity from disease after the vaccine takes effect. Plants raised in hot-houses are not likely to be robust. Carrying out the policy of "letting a hundred flowers blossom and a hundred schools of thought contend" will not weaken but strengthen the leading position of Marxism in the ideological field.

What should our policy be towards non-Marxist ideas? As far as unmistakable counter-revolutionaries and wreckers of the socialist cause are concerned, the matter is easy: We simply deprive them of their freedom of speech. But it is quite a different matter when we are faced with incorrect ideas among the people. Will it do to ban such ideas and give them no opportunity to express themselves? Certainly not. It is not only futile but very harmful to use crude and summary methods to deal with ideological questions among the people, with questions relating to the spiritual life of man. You may ban the expression of wrong ideas, but the ideas will still be there. On the other hand, correct ideas, if pampered in hot-houses without being exposed to the elements or immunized from disease, will not win out against wrong ones. That is why it is only by employing methods of discussion, criticism, and reasoning that we can really foster correct ideas, overcome wrong ideas, and really settle issues. . . .

On the surface, these two slogans — "let a hundred flowers blossom" and "let a hundred schools of thought contend" — have no class character: The proletariat can turn them to account, so can the bourgeoisie and other people. But different classes, strata, and social groups each have their own views on what are fragrant flowers and what are poisonous weeds. So what, from the point of view of the broad masses of the people, should be the criteria today for distinguishing between fragrant flowers and poisonous weeds?

In the political life of our country, how are our people to determine what is right and what is wrong in our words and actions? Basing ourselves on the principles of our Constitution, the will of the overwhelming majority of our people, and the political programmes jointly proclaimed on various occasions by our political parties and groups, we believe that, broadly speaking, words and actions can be judged right if they:

1. Help to unite the people of our various nationalities, and do not divide them;
2. Are beneficial, not harmful, to socialist transformation and socialist construction;
3. Help to consolidate, not undermine or weaken, the people's democratic dictatorship;

4. Help to consolidate, not undermine or weaken, democratic centralism;
5. Tend to strengthen, not to cast off or weaken, the leadership of the Communist Party;
6. Are beneficial, not harmful, to international socialist solidarity and the solidarity of the peace-loving peoples of the world.

Of these six criteria, the most important are the socialist path and the leadership of the Party. These criteria are put forward in order to foster, and not hinder, the free discussion of various questions among the people. Those who do not approve of these criteria can still put forward their own views and argue their case. When the majority of the people have clear-cut criteria to go by, criticism and self-criticism can be conducted along proper lines, and these criteria can be applied to people's words and actions to determine whether they are fragrant flowers or poisonous weeds. These are political criteria. Naturally, in judging the truthfulness of scientific theories or assessing the aesthetic value of works of art, other pertinent criteria are needed, but these six political criteria are also applicable to all activities in the arts or sciences. In a socialist country like ours, can there possibly be any useful scientific or artistic activity which runs counter to these political criteria?

All that is set out above stems from the specific historical conditions in our country. Since conditions vary in different socialist countries and with different Communist Parties, we do not think that other countries and Parties must or need to follow the Chinese way.

| 76 |

HAN SUYIN

The Cultural Revolution

The "Hundred Flowers" period was short. Mao, evidently overwhelmed by the outpouring and severity of criticism, turned on the intellectuals, labeling them as rightist and antisocialist. Many, perhaps a half million, were sent into the countryside to better understand peasant life and problems. The purge of professionals left Mao dependent

Han Suyin, *Phoenix Harvest*, bk. V of *China: Autobiography, History* (Vol. II of *My House Has Two Doors*) (Reading, Engl.: Triad/Granada of Jonathan Cape, 1980), 9–12, 16–20.

on party zealots for his next effort, the "Great Leap Forward." Impatient with Soviet-style economic development, Mao decided in 1957 to "will" China into modernity by turning the countryside into giant communes run by ordinary people rather than experts. Swayed by Mao's utopian vision, loyal party workers promised the realization of impossible goals and then fabricated harvest and production figures to match the promises. The result was three years of famine conditions between 1959 and 1962.

In 1963, at seventy years old, Mao found himself stung by his errors. In danger of losing control of the party to more practical, moderate, and younger officials, he decided to fight back. In 1966 he took advantage of mass meetings of young people called "Red Guards" to urge a new campaign against moderates in the party, government, and universities. Mao probably intended the "Great Proletarian Cultural Revolution" as a safeguard, to make sure that the Communist bureaucracy lived up to the goals of the revolution. While many would agree that the party was in need of a renewal of revolutionary ideals, Mao's Red Guards created instead a personality cult, chanting slogans of "Mao Tse-tung thought" from his ubiquitous "Little Red Book," and brought the country close to civil war.

Han Suyin lived in China before the war, published her memoirs and a number of novels on prewar China in the United States, then returned to China twice in 1966 as the Cultural Revolution took hold. She describes what she saw in this selection. The Cultural Revolution broke out in the spring of 1966. The author's visit in January offered glimpses of what was about to occur. Notice how people expected "another rectification movement" in art and literature. What was the attitude of Han Suyin's friend Hualan and Hualan's sister? What was the appeal of a cultural revolution for some of those whom the author met in January? What were the author's apprehensions? How were those apprehensions verified during her later visit that summer?

Thinking Historically

Notice how cultural conflicts became political and political conflicts became cultural. Which conflict — political or cultural — do you think was primary? Was Mao, for instance, overly sensitive about a historical play in Shanghai, or was historical theater the way in which his opponents expressed their criticism? If historical interpretation and cultural criticism were more political and more important in Chinese society than they would be in our own, what does that tell us about the difference between the two societies?

We have called the rift that divided China political and cultural, not national or racial. In that way, the struggles of postwar China were different from those of Israel and South Africa. But is there any evidence in the previous readings on Israel or South Africa that cultural differences were also part of what defined the opposing sides and led to conflict in those communities?

In January 1966 I went to Peking for ten days, because I had been invited to a seminar to be held on China at Chicago University. At least five such seminars were taking place in mid-western cities of the United States that year. I wanted to glean the latest thinking in Peking.

I filled a notebook with interviews on China's policies, on economics, and became thoroughly confused. I was not able to see Chou Enlai.[1] Little did I then know that the most intense confrontation was occurring at the top, between Mao Tsetung and Liu Shaochi. . . .

Mao in his interview with [journalist] Edgar Snow had been non-committal. I had no opportunity to find out about the intense Party struggle that was going on; the pall of secrecy was clamped upon all hints. Hualan, not high enough in the cadre hierarchy to know, could only say that there would be another rectification movement "in art and literature and also in education." The Party establishment still envisaged the Cultural Revolution as merely another political campaign, of the style so customary in China.

Hualan's sister had returned from another stint in the rural areas, of "socialist education" and the "four cleans" in the countryside. The skin of her face was rough and her finger joints thickened with rheumatism. "My job was to try to break down feudal and capitalist ideas . . . I've had very little time to paint . . ." Many hundreds of thousands of cadres, intellectuals, and students had "gone down" in teams for this work. She was looking forward to teaching and painting again, "But at the moment we are having a great many political study classes on Mao Tsetung Thought." She added, "We are taking the army as a model." Hualan was full of enthusiasm. "It is very important: We are fighting revisionism in all its forms." The ballet, *The White-Haired Girl,* had been performed. It dated back to 1944 in Yenan, when it had been created (the music leaned heavily on Tchaikovsky). "Our workers–peasants–soldiers don't like Western ballet, they don't understand it. They want ballet, opera, with

---

[1] Zhou Enlai (Chou En-lai) and Liu Shaoqi (Liu Shao-chi) were leaders of the Communist party, along with Mao Zedong (Mao Tse-tung), from the 1920s. They were three of the five members of the "standing committee" that ran the politburo of the party when it took power in 1949; Mao was chairman. In the government structure, parallel to the party, Zhou Enlai was premier and foreign minister. Liu Shaoqi, assumed to be Mao's successor, replaced Mao as head of state in 1959, after the disastrous "Great Leap Forward" of the previous year. But in the Cultural Revolution, Liu fell out of Mao's favor. Vilified and broken, Liu died in 1969. Both Zhou and Mao died in 1976. [Ed.]

which they can identify, such as this one." A young man who was to dance the role of the Prince in *Swan Lake* came from a poor peasant family; he had rejected the role; he felt he was "throwing away the face" of his family by dancing as a prince ... "Only after the dancers have been to the villages can they put real emotion into the scenes of our new ballets and operas," said Hualan.

There was hushed talk among the writers of the criticism of a theatre piece by the Vice-Mayor of Peking, Wu Han. In November 1965 a literary critic from Shanghai, Yao Wenyuan, already known for his acerbic condemnations of rightists in 1957, had written a long and scathing attack against Peking Vice-Mayor Wu Han's theatre play *Hai Jui is Dismissed from Office*. Hai Jui, an honest Ming dynasty (1368 to 1644) official, had upbraided the Emperor for not listening to the people. Now it was rumoured that his "historical play," first shown in 1960, was a plea for the rehabilitation of Minister of Defence Peng Tehuai, who in August 1959 had openly criticized the Leap.

At dinner with some friends, the distinguished chief editor of the People's Literature Printing Press, Yen Wenching, asked me what I thought of *Hai Jui*. I replied truthfully that I had not seen the play. Historical subjects, articles about personages who had died many centuries ago, were vehicles for expressing present-day situations, events, and people. This had always been done in China, and it continued to be done. But now not only Vice-Mayor Wu Han, but many other historians were being attacked and criticized as "promoting a bourgeois line in history."

A foreign resident in China told me that Teng To, chief editor of the monthly *Frontline* (the magazine of Peking's Party Committee), was undergoing criticism. He had written: "Everyone must have some leisure and only eight hours of work." "The idea of leisure time and the idea of revolution don't go together," said this man. Young workers in the factories had been infected by the habit of looking at the clock.

The January air was not only freezing but turgid with unvoiced apprehensions and abstruse theoretical argument. I interviewed three philosophers, who were to give me the latest "thinking." (I had not reckoned that the word "thinking" would involve me in the high spheres of theoretical abstraction.) The three talked of the necessity of a cultural revolution. Only a change of thinking in the people could propel advance: a transformation of ideas and habits and behaviour *before* a change in the material conditions of living could occur. But could mankind really overleap itself in thought, overleap the environment in which it dealt? Certainly, they replied. Had not men dreamt of flying machines before the aeroplane was invented? ...

In May 1966 I went back to China. She was entirely *other* that May. Again that unpleasant throat clamp as the raucous loudspeakers assaulted my eardrums for hours ... how was it possible to remain sane with the perpetual noise, the blaring and the shouting and the screaming and the singing? All the posters had changed. Now furious-fisted young people squashed diminutive snakes and bull-headed figures (imperialists and revisionists). A thousand portly, rosy-faced Maos everywhere. The customs officials remained calm and courteous, relaxed, impervious to the cacophony.

At the railway station no lunch was available; the waitresses were holding a political meeting. I saw them practising a dance in front of a large panel painted to represent Mao. Their hands lifted imaginary hearts from their breasts towards his smile. I listened to the loudspeakers but there were too many of them and the sound waves interfered with each other so that the result was a hopeless quack.

In Hongkong the Kuomintang newspapers had predicted a rupture between Mao Tsetung and Liu Shaochi. There had been rumours of an assassination plot against Mao. Here there was much talk of a "black line" which had for the past seventeen years infected, infested, deviated, twisted, distorted culture and education and the arts and literature in order to promote "restoration of capitalism." I groaned inwardly. "That's it. The intelligentsia is going to catch it once again." But I continued, of course, to smile and to hold myself tightly in control. And to hope my Family would not suffer too much — and that I would not break down.

In Kuangchow the well-cut suits of 1965 had disappeared. Every one of the cadres greeting me wore unpressed shirts and baggy pants and plastic sandals. There was no brilliantine upon the hair of the men, and the women cadres all had straight short hair. No more perms.

In Peking, however, the admirable Hsing Chiang continued to wear a crisp neat blouse and skirt; until one day in July when Kung Peng would say quietly to her, "Your clothes look a bit bourgeois." A friendly warning.

Nowhere in China, in the next few months, was there any hint that Liu Shaochi was the target of the upheaval. In fact I would see him twice. He remained visible, making speeches, receiving guests, and the Hsinhua news agency would report on the mass rallies he held for Vietnam in July. And yet, in 1970, Edgar Snow would be told by Mao that in January 1965 Mao had already decided that Liu Shaochi must go . . .

"We shall be going to Manchuria, as you asked," said Hsing Chiang. We would be back in June in Peking.

Manchuria. Limitless flat plains, length to abolish the horizon; space and a clean sky that ran its blueness in echoless silence. The kind of land that makes one want to be on horseback, the sound of hooves to pound the silence into music.

I saw factories, and communes, in Shenyang and Changchun and Fushun and Anshan and Harbin; the Anshan steel works; the Fushun opencast mines (where, in 1947, nineteen years previously, Pao my husband had died). So many notes, so many people telling me of their lives. And in every factory the *tatzepao,* the wall posters, pasted upon all the walls, swinging like banners, strung across from machine to machine, almost swamping every workshop. All of them uttered dire threats against "black liners" and "freaks and monsters."

On May 8th an editorial against the "black anti-Party line" had come out. "All those who oppose Mao Tsetung Thought must be toppled, no matter how high or how famous," shrieked the posters. "Down with seventeen years of black anti-Party line" blared the radios. Occasionally I discerned names . . . names of experts, engineers, factory managers, not prominent political figures; names of educators in the universities. But obviously the Party was still firmly in control, "directing and leading" the Cultural Revolution. And so the search for "freaks and monsters" and for "bull-headed devils and snake spirits" was among the middle ranks, the technical experts, and professors and engineers. Not a single top leader in the Party, at the time, was mentioned. The highest in rank were Party secretaries at city level and some university chancellors.

The higher Party cadres receive me and entertain me lavishly. I eat bear paws, an expensive delicacy. I am given a marvellous ginseng root worth thousands of *yuan,* which I shall give to Wanchun when I return to Peking.

After a few days of reading accusatory editorials and slogans and listening to the radio my brain goes into a stupor. I am numbed; even by imprecations. I smile and nod and because there is too much repetition I begin to speak like the people round me, and so my trip is a success as I am outstandingly docile. I read now with practised, jaded eye the posters above the machinery: "Sung Chiming is enforcing a revisionist line in the screws and bolts third workshop!"; "Wang Ahmeng has countered Mao Tsetung Thought for many years by saying: Too much political verbiage, not enough scientific work." I do not know Sung and Wang; I only hope that things won't be too hard for them.

At the Shenyang machine tool plant I meet a worker who is a specialist at cutting tools through sheer application of Mao Tsetung Thought to knife-cutting edges. In almost every factory I am told how much harm the Russians have done, and of the enormous amount of meat, rare metals, oranges, textiles, and shoes paid out for equipment.

At Anshan, the great steel works and China's pride, I am shown innovations attributed to Mao Tsetung Thought. In one workshop the Party man in charge introduces me to a pretty young woman worker who writes poetry. She has written decadent, bourgeois love poetry because in school her teacher was following the decadent revisionist black line and corrupting her with feudal poems. But since the intense political studies started in January she has remoulded herself and written some excellent proletarian poetry for workers–peasants–soldiers. The pretty worker begins to recite one of her old poems so that I may judge her wickedness. Then she recites a new one. "I would like to have some of your poems," I say, hoping she will also give me the old one she has recited. But alas, the Party cadre has seen through my bland cunning. "Not these, not these," he says as she riffles through her loose-leaf notebook. I get, at last, three rather tedious slogany scribbles. "These are the latest," says the Party cadre, beaming. He is kind, but I turn back to look at the girl and she too is watching me, and picking meditatively at her thumb. I now wonder what will happen to my dearest friend Yeh, who has printed in *Chinese Literature,* his English monthly, some of my translations of decadent feudal song-poems of the Sung dynasty (AD 960–1279).

In March, Lin Piao,[2] designated as Mao's "close comrade-in-arms," has issued a directive to "put politics in command." And production has gone up by so much and so much per cent everywhere, owing to the "heightening of revolutionary consciousness" among the workers. Production increase is no longer ascribed to the heroic, the fantastic, the real work of the marvellous, incredibly patient, and stoic people of China, but solely to the study of Mao Tsetung Thought … Cadres frown when I say that pump stations, canals, fertilizer factories, increase production … And that here in Manchuria electrification of communes started in 1948 with the Leap Forward …

In one commune I am shown earth mounds terraced for cultivation. This brigade has distinguished itself learning from China's model, Tachai, proclaimed by Mao in 1964 as *the* example for all China. Tachai is sited in the cratered, fissured, gullied loess region of Shansi province. There are not twenty square metres of uniform flat land in these canyons of silt. Tachai terraced its promontories and filled its gullies by hand labour. But here in Manchuria the plains are flat … whence, then, these earth mounds? Eleven years later I shall learn the hilarious and pitiful story: The mounds I saw were artificial; they had been raised up and fields laddered upon them to resemble Tachai. That is how "In all things learn from Tachai" had been interpreted by the literal-minded cadres.

But the official taking me around in 1966 tells me that these terraced fields are the product of the young educated middle school students sent out to labour in the countryside. "They built these fields with one hand while their other hand was occupied by the precious book of Chairman Mao," he says. I write it all down.

---

[2] Lin Biao (Lin Piao) was an old Communist ally of Mao, minister of defense, and head of the People's Liberation Army, and he was chosen Mao's successor in 1969 after the eclipse and death of Liu Shaoqi. Lin helped Mao politicize the army and militarize society in the Cultural Revolution (1966–1969) but died in a plane crash in 1971, as he was branded a traitor — perhaps because Mao sought to reassert the authority of the party over the army.

77

HO CHI MINH

The Vietnamese Declaration of Independence

Colonized by France since 1858, Vietnam, like China, was occupied by Japan during World War II. With the defeat of Japanese forces, the Vietnamese declared their independence. This Declaration of Independence was written by Ho Chi Minh (1890–1969). Ho had been a student in France, where he became a poet, a socialist, and a Vietnamese nationalist. In 1919 while in Paris, he borrowed a suit and attended the Versailles peace conference, where he appealed to American president Woodrow Wilson to apply the principle of national self-determination to Vietnam, which had, after all, been an independent country for centuries before French occupation. When the victors merely dismantled the colonial empires of the defeated countries, Ho Chi Minh, like many other disappointed nationalists, found what he was looking for in Lenin's writings on nationalism and in the promise of support by the Congress of the Communist International in 1920. Ho Chi Minh became a founding member of both the French and the Indochinese Communist parties. For Ho Chi Minh, communism meant opposition to imperialism, to foreign control, and to "antipatriotic Vietnamese capitalists."

During the Japanese occupation in 1941, the broad-based nationalist organization, the Viet Minh, was formed and Ho was appointed its leader. On August 15, 1945, as news of the Japanese surrender reached Vietnam, the Viet Minh called for mass rallies. Thousands of peasants came to the cities of Saigon, Hanoi, and Hue to demonstrate against the emperor, Bao Dai, who had served as a Japanese puppet, as he had for the French and would again. On August 30, the emperor abdicated the throne.

On September 2, 1945, in front of half a million people in Hanoi, Ho Chi Minh read this Declaration of Independence. Notice the similarity between this document and the American Declaration of Independence. There was nothing inadvertent in the similarity. Ho had checked his translation of the opening phrases of the American Declaration with an American OSS (secret service) officer in Hanoi. After

Ho Chi Minh, Declaration of Independence of the Democratic Republic of Vietnam, in Nguyen Khac Vien and Hu Ngoc, *Vietnamese Literature* (Hanoi: Red River Foreign Languages Publishing House), 508–12.

Ho read the opening, he stopped, looked out over the crowd and asked, "Do you hear me distinctly, fellow countrymen?" They said they did, and Ho continued: "This immortal statement was made in the Declaration of Independence of the United States of America in 1776. In a broader sense, this means: All the people on earth are equal from birth, all the people have a right to live, to be happy and free."

In what other ways did the Vietnamese Declaration of Independence resemble that of the United States? Why do you think Ho Chi Minh wanted to take the U.S. Declaration as his model or make that connection? What were the grievances of the Vietnamese against the French?

Thinking Historically

A declaration of independence assumes a divide between the newly declared independent nation and the colonizing power, in this case France and Japan (but mainly France). Because declarations of independence are written at moments of unity against a foreigner, such documents rarely show internal rifts. Yet, we have noticed signs of internal differences in both the Israeli and American declarations of independence. What were they? Are there comparable signs of internal rifts in this document? If not, what might account for that? Was Vietnam more united in 1945 than Israel in 1947 or the United States in 1776?

"All men are created equal. They are endowed by their Creator with certain inalienable rights; among these are Life, Liberty, and the pursuit of Happiness."

This immortal statement was made in the Declaration of Independence of the United States of America in 1776. In a broader sense, this means: All the peoples on the earth are equal from birth, all the peoples have a right to live, to be happy and free.

The Declaration of the French Revolution made in 1791 on the Rights of Man and the Citizen also states: "All men are born free and with equal rights, and must always remain free and have equal rights."

Those are undeniable truths.

Nevertheless, for more than eighty years, the French imperialists, abusing the standard of Liberty, Equality, and Fraternity, have violated our Fatherland and oppressed our fellow-citizens. They have acted contrary to the ideals of humanity and justice.

In the field of politics, they have deprived our people of every democratic liberty.

They have enforced inhuman laws; they have set up three distinct political regimes in the North, the Center, and the South of Vietnam in order to wreck our national unity and prevent our people from being united.

They have built more prisons than schools. They have mercilessly slain our patriots; they have drowned our uprisings in rivers of blood.

They have fettered public opinion; they have practised obscurantism against our people.

To weaken our race they have forced us to use opium and alcohol.

In the field of economics, they have fleeced us to the backbone, impoverished our people, and devastated our land.

They have robbed us of our rice fields, our mines, our forests, and our raw materials. They have monopolized the issuing of bank-notes and the export trade. ·

They have invented numerous unjustifiable taxes and reduced our people, especially our peasantry, to a state of extreme poverty.

They have hampered the prospering of our national bourgeoisie; they have mercilessly exploited our workers.

In the autumn of 1940, when the Japanese Fascists violated Indochina's territory to establish new bases in their fight against the Allies, the French imperialists went down on their bended knees and handed over our country to them.

Thus, from that date, our people were subjected to the double yoke of the French and the Japanese. Their sufferings and miseries increased. The result was that towards the end of last year and the beginning of this year, from Quang Tri province to the North of Vietnam, more than two million of our fellow-citizens died from starvation. On March 9, the French troops were disarmed by the Japanese. The French colonialists either fled or surrendered, showing that not only were they incapable of "protecting" us, but that, in the span of five years, they had twice sold our country to the Japanese.

On several occasions before March 9, the Vietminh League urged the French to ally themselves with it against the Japanese. Instead of agreeing to this proposal, the French colonialists so intensified their terrorist activities against the Vietminh members that before fleeing they massacred a great number of our political prisoners detained at Yen Bay and Caobang.

Notwithstanding all this, our fellow-citizens have always manifested toward the French a tolerant and humane attitude. Even after the Japanese putsch of March 1945, the Vietminh League helped many Frenchmen to cross the frontier, rescued some of them from Japanese jails, and protected French lives and property.

From the autumn of 1940, our country had in fact ceased to be a French colony and had become a Japanese possession.

After the Japanese had surrendered to the Allies, our whole people rose to regain our national sovereignty and to found the Democratic Republic of Vietnam.

The truth is that we have wrested our independence from the Japanese and not from the French.

The French have fled, the Japanese have capitulated, Emperor Bao Dai has abdicated. Our people have broken the chains which for nearly a century have fettered them and have won independence for the Fatherland. Our people at the same time have overthrown the monarchic regime that has reigned supreme for dozens of centuries. In its place has been established the present Democratic Republic.

For these reasons, we, members of the Provisional Government, representing the whole Vietnamese people, declare that from now on we break off all relations of a colonial character with France; we repeal all the international obligation that France has so far subscribed to on behalf of Vietnam and we abolish all the special rights the French have unlawfully acquired in our Fatherland.

The whole Vietnamese people, animated by a common purpose, are determined to fight to the bitter end against any attempt by the French colonialists to reconquer their country.

We are convinced that the Allied nations which at Tehran and San Francisco have acknowledged the principles of self-determination and equality of nations, will not refuse to acknowledge the independence of Vietnam.

A people who have courageously opposed French domination for more than eight years, a people who have fought side by side with the Allies against the Fascists during these last years, such a people must be free and independent.

For these reasons, we, members of the Provisional Government of the Democratic Republic of Vietnam, solemnly declare to the world that Vietnam has the right to be a free and independent country — and in fact is so already. The entire Vietnamese people are determined to mobilize all their physical and mental strength, to sacrifice their lives and property in order to safeguard their independence and liberty.

78

ROBERT S. McNAMARA

From *In Retrospect:*
The Tragedy and Lessons of Vietnam

The Democratic Republic of Vietnam, established in September 1945, did not remain intact beyond October. In deference to the French government's insistence on regaining its lost colonies, both Britain and the United States did everything possible to assist France but fight, an option avoided due to the popular yearning to bring American and British troops home. In October 1945, the United States detoured twelve merchant marine ships engaged in returning American troops, instructing them instead to transport French troops to Vietnam. Already on September 13, the British general in charge of disarming Japanese troops in Saigon interrupted his efforts in order to arm French prisoners of war. He lent the French the use of his own Indian Gurkha troops for a coup against the Viet Minh executive committee administration of Saigon. While waiting for the arrival of the French troops on American carriers, the British general armed the Japanese and instructed them to prevent the Vietnamese from retaking control of the city.

American policy toward Vietnam after 1945 was initially support of France, America's oldest ally (without whom, ironically, the United States' Declaration of Independence would have been short-lived). Ho Chi Minh pleaded for an independent Vietnam to President Truman as he had with Wilson, but both turned out to be more loyal to allies than to principles. After 1949 and the Communist victory in China, the American attitude toward Vietnam became part of a larger policy of containing the spread of communism. In some cases, as when Eisenhower offered the French the use of nuclear weapons as they faced their ultimate defeat in 1954, it became an American war.

John F. Kennedy came to the presidency in 1961, a vigorous anticommunist with a "brain trust" of advisers that rivaled its famous predecessor under Franklin D. Roosevelt. Among "the best and the brightest" that came from American business and academia to serve the country with Kennedy was Robert S. McNamara, the new secretary of defense. Over the course of the buildup of the Vietnam War,

Robert S. McNamara, *In Retrospect: The Tragedy and Lessons of Vietnam* (New York: Vintage, 1995), 95–97, 101–102, 106–107.

perhaps no one but the president — Kennedy and then Lyndon Johnson after him — had more to do with expanding and defending the U.S. military role than McNamara. To many, it became known as "McNamara's war."

In this selection from his memoir, "the book I planned never to write," says McNamara, he tries to explain how he "got it wrong," "terribly wrong." What do you think of McNamara's argument for an eventual Kennedy withdrawal (if Kennedy had not been assassinated on November 22, 1963)? How, according to McNamara, did the United States become committed to the war in Vietnam in the beginning of the Johnson administration? What mistakes made by U.S. officials allowed this to happen?

Thinking Historically

The rifts in the United States during the 1960s are well known and are in good part attributable to the Vietnam War. The global reach of the United States peppered the period with global rifts as well. Pro-war and antiwar factions developed in Europe, Japan, Canada, Australia, New Zealand, among the U.S. allies asked to provide military or political support. Rifts between students and governments broke out throughout Europe as well as in the United States. Vietnamese relations with Russia and China were strained by fears that the United States would expand the war beyond Vietnam. Even the Chinese Cultural Revolution partially reflected Chinese fears of U.S. power in Asia. Rifts also divided Americans as "hawks" and "doves" and the Vietnamese as "communists" and "democrats," from the north and south, pro- and anti-American, although it was remarkable how often North Vietnamese leaders insisted that their quarrel was with the U.S. government, not the American people.

McNamara's memoir, published in 1995, reflects a different America, though the wounds of war have not completely healed some thirty years later. Readers who are struck by the author's sense of remorse and tragedy might want to ponder the other side of the question posed by Mao Zedong in the 1960s. Mao insisted that it was "better to be red than expert," better to have zeal than knowledge. In selection 76, we noted how this turned out to be a disastrous prescription for "the Great Leap Forward" and the cultural revolution. But even McNamara might warn us of the opposite problem — policy directed by brilliant experts who lack political sense. David Halberstam, whose book *The Best and the Brightest* defined the era and the problem, tells a story of how impressed Lyndon Johnson was with the Kennedy team of experts that he inherited on November 22, 1963. Johnson went reeling from his first meeting with McNamara and the others on November 24 to his mentor Sam Rayburn, the wily Texan, consummate legislator, and former Speaker of the House. Rayburn listened sympathetically to Johnson's praise, thought for a moment, and said: "Well Lyndon, you may be right and they may be every bit as intelligent as you say, but I'd feel a whole lot better about them if just one of them had run for sheriff once."[1]

Would a team of sheriffs and other elected representatives have moderated the zeal of the experts who had all the answers (as the Congress showed less enthusiasm for the war than the presidential appointees and advisers)? If a democracy requires experts to get things done, does it also require politicians to determine what to do?

History was used by both proponents and opponents of the Vietnam War. McNamara mentions Kennedy's lesson (from Barbara Tuchman's history of the First World War, *The Guns of August*) of how easy it is to "blunder" into war. One of the arguments made in the 1960s was that appeasement (like that of British prime minister Chamberlain to Hitler's demand for part of Czechoslovakia at Munich in 1938) encouraged Hitler and made war more, rather than less, likely. Keeping in mind that no two wars are ever exactly alike, what lessons does McNamara's history offer us?

What would John F. Kennedy have done about Vietnam had he lived? I have been asked that question countless times over the last thirty years. Thus far, I have refused to answer for two reasons: Apart from what I have related, the president did not tell me what he planned to do in the future. Moreover, whatever his thoughts may have been before Diem's death,[2] they might have changed as the effect of that event on the political dynamics in South Vietnam became more apparent. Also, I saw no gain to our nation from speculation by me — or others — about how the dead president might have acted.

But today I feel differently. Having reviewed the record in detail, and with the advantage of hindsight, I think it highly probable that, had President Kennedy lived, he would have pulled us out of Vietnam. He would have concluded that the South Vietnamese were incapable of defending themselves, and that Saigon's grave political weaknesses made it unwise to try to offset the limitations of South Vietnamese forces by sending U.S. combat troops on a large scale. I think he would have come to that conclusion even if he reasoned, as I believe he would have, that South Vietnam and, ultimately, Southeast Asia would then

---

[1] David Halberstam, *The Best and the Brightest* (New York: Random House, 1972), 53.
[2] Ngo Dinh Diem, U.S.-sponsored president of South Vietnam from 1954 until his assassination on November 2, 1963.

be lost to Communism. He would have viewed that loss as more costly than we see it now. But he would have accepted that cost because he would have sensed that the conditions he had laid down — i.e., it was a South Vietnamese war, that it could only be won by them, and to win it they needed a sound political base — could not be met. Kennedy would have agreed that withdrawal would cause a fall of the "dominoes" but that staying in would ultimately lead to the same result, while exacting a terrible price in blood.

Early in his administration, President Kennedy asked his cabinet officials and members of the National Security Council to read Barbara Tuchman's book *The Guns of August.* He said it graphically portrayed how Europe's leaders had bungled into the debacle of World War I. And he emphasized: "I don't ever want to be in that position." Kennedy told us after we had done our reading, "We are not going to bungle into war." . . .

So I conclude that John Kennedy would have eventually gotten out of Vietnam rather than move more deeply in. I express this judgment now because, in light of it, I must explain how and why we — including Lyndon Johnson — who continued in policy-making roles after President Kennedy's death made the decisions leading to the eventual deployment to Vietnam of half a million U.S. combat troops. Why did we do what we did, and what lessons can be learned from our actions?

. . . Johnson was left with a national security team that, although it remained intact, was deeply split over Vietnam. Its senior members had failed to face up to the basic questions that had confronted first Eisenhower and then Kennedy: Would the loss of South Vietnam pose a threat to U.S. security serious enough to warrant extreme action to prevent it? If so, what kind of action should we take? Should it include the introduction of U.S. air and ground forces? Launching attacks against North Vietnam? Risking war with China? What would be the ultimate cost of such a program in economic, military, political, and human terms? Could it succeed? If the chances of success were low and the costs high, were there other courses — such as neutralization or withdrawal — that deserved careful study and debate?

Lyndon Johnson inherited these questions (although they were not presented clearly to him), and he inherited them without answers. They remained unanswered throughout his presidency, and for many years thereafter. In short, Johnson inherited a god-awful mess eminently more dangerous than the one Kennedy had inherited from Eisenhower. One evening not long after he took office, Johnson confessed to his aide Bill Moyers that he felt like a catfish that had "just grabbed a big juicy worm with a right sharp hook in the middle of it."

Contrary to popular myth, however, Lyndon Johnson was not oblivious to Vietnam when he became president. Although he had visited the country only once — in May 1961 — and had attended few meetings on the subject during Kennedy's tenure, he was keenly aware of the problem and his responsibility to deal with it. Among his first acts as president was to schedule the November 24 meeting with his Vietnam advisers.

Some say he called this meeting for domestic political reasons. With an election coming within a year, the story goes, he feared that if he did not appear involved and firm he would face strident attacks from hardline, right-wing Republicans.

I disagree. Of course, domestic politics was always in the forefront of his mind, and, yes, he feared the domestic political consequences of appearing weak. He also feared the effect on our allies if the United States appeared unable or unwilling to meet our security obligations. But most of all Johnson was convinced that the Soviet Union and China were bent on achieving hegemony. He saw the takeover of South Vietnam as a step toward that objective — a break in our containment policy — and he was determined to prevent it. Johnson felt more certain than President Kennedy that the loss of South Vietnam had a higher cost than would the direct application of U.S. military force, and it was this view that shaped him and his policy decisions for the next five years. He failed to perceive the fundamentally political nature of the war. . . .

Shortly after my return to Washington, the president received a memorandum from Senate Majority Leader Mike Mansfield (D-Mont.), recommending that the United States try for a neutral Southeast Asia — neither dependent on U.S. military support nor subject to Chinese domination through some sort of truce or settlement. The president asked Dean, Mac, and me for our reactions.

All three of us felt Mansfield's path would lead to the loss of South Vietnam to Communist control with extremely serious consequences for the United States and the West. I stated the conventional wisdom among top U.S. civilian and military officials at the time:

> In Southeast Asia, Laos would almost certainly come under North Vietnamese domination, Cambodia might exhibit a façade of neutrality but would in fact accept Communist Chinese domination, Thailand would become very shaky, and Malaysia, already beset by Indonesia, the same; even Burma would see the developments as a clear sign that the whole of the area now had to accommodate completely to Communism (with serious consequences for the security of India as well).
>
> Basically, a truly "neutral" Southeast Asia is very unlikely to emerge from such a sequence of events, even if the U.S. itself tried to hold a firm position in Thailand, if Malaysia too tried to stand firm, and even

if remote and uninvolved powers such as France backed the concept of "neutrality."

In the eyes of the rest of Asia and of key areas threatened by Communism in other areas as well, South Vietnam is both a test of U.S. firmness and specifically a test of U.S. capacity to deal with "wars of national liberation." Within Asia, there is evidence — for example, from Japan — that U.S. disengagement and the acceptance of Communist domination would have a serious effect on confidence. More broadly, there can be little doubt that any country threatened in the future by Communist subversion would have reason to doubt whether we would really see the thing through. This would apply even in such theoretically remote areas as Latin America.

I have quoted extensively from my memo for two reasons: to show how limited and shallow our analysis and discussion of the alternatives to our existing policy in Vietnam — i.e., neutralization or withdrawal — had been; and to illustrate that the consequences of Southeast Asia's loss to U.S. and Western security were now being presented to President Johnson with greater force and in more detail than on previous occasions.

This memo hardened the president's preexisting attitude. As the likely failure of our training strategy became more apparent in the months ahead, we tilted gradually — almost imperceptibly — toward approving the direct application of U.S. military force. We did so because of our increasing fear — and hindsight makes it clear it was an exaggerated fear — of what would happen if we did not. But we never carefully debated what U.S. force would ultimately be required, what our chances of success would be, or what the political, military, financial, and human costs would be if we provided it. Indeed, these basic questions went unexamined.

We were at the beginning of a slide down a tragic and slippery slope.

REFLECTIONS

In this chapter we looked at different parts of the world, mainly but not exclusively new states, involved in important struggles in the thirty years after World War II. These struggles represent many others that divided new and old nations, then and now. We distinguished between various types of struggles and their accompanying fault lines: national and religious in Palestine and Israel, racial and national in South Africa, cultural and political in China.

In Vietnam, we observed the international struggle — against France, Japan, and then the United States — but no internal rift, at least none in evidence, in the Vietnamese Declaration of Independence. There have, of course, been internal divisions in Vietnam as in any society. Much of the American propaganda war in the 1960s was based on the differences between "communist" and "democratic" Vietnam, symbolized as north and south. In Vietnam there were also traditional differences between Chinese Confucian cultural influences in the north and Indian Buddhist cultural influences in the south, between Catholics and Buddhists, between Vietnamese and Chinese inhabitants, and between landlords and peasants. Some of these divides were ancient; still others, like those between Vietnamese capitalists and urban workers, fairly recent. It is important to note how the Vietnam War represents a pivotal conflict in the development of the Cold War, and how it fundamentally shaped the world between 1945 and 1975.

Of course, the Vietnam War was not the only globalizing rift during the decades of the Cold War. To what extent were the rifts in Palestine and Israel or those of South Africa deepened by a Cold War in which the United States and the Soviet Union sought influence and advantage? Were the rifts in China deepened, or were new divides created in Vietnam as a result of the international conflict? McNamara finds one American policy error: the failure to recognize that Vietnam was engaged in a civil war, rather than a foreign invasion from the north. To what extent was that civil war aided and encouraged, if not created, by American promises, threats, and expenditures? What was the impact of America's Cold War support for the governing white minority party in South Africa?

We study rifts or divides, as we study contradictions, to understand change. In some cases, a rift, like a geological fault line, suggests how things are likely to continue to change. Have we seen such continuous tension without resolution in Israel and Palestine during these last fifty years?

Sometimes a rift causes a conflict that results in something new. Would the new South Africa or contemporary China rightly be considered such a development?

Often, one side of a conflict overwhelms and transforms the other into its own image. Of course, that is precisely what occurred as colonial powers struggled to impose their wills on their colonies. Is it happening again with the popularity of American ideas of democracy and free markets? How does this American influence affect the new states of South Africa, Vietnam, and China today?

13

Women's World

1950–2000

HISTORICAL CONTEXT

Today, historians both male and female try not to restrict their work to
the activities or testimonies of men. Yet, because men dominated politics, war, and industry for many years, oftentimes important historical
studies have ignored women. Historians now attempt to research and
write more complete, balanced, historical accounts, addressing topics in
which women have played important roles. Such topics include the history of the family, sexuality, privacy, popular culture, domesticity, and
work, among others. In recent years, women's history and women's
studies have become vibrant fields of specialization and discovery.

This chapter offers readings that, taken together, constitute a history
of women during the latter half of the twentieth century. We will read
women's accounts from various parts of the world, as they describe aspects of their lives and those of other women. We begin, however, with
the Chinese Marriage Law of 1950 so we might consider the new legal
baseline for one-fifth of the world's population. (This law was replicated
in many other countries as well.) We then turn to the emerging women's
movement in the United States, spearheaded by a far-reaching book,
The Feminine Mystique (1963). Next, two African novelists — from
Algeria and Nigeria — reflect on youth, adolescence, and family. Then
two women from Latin America — an unemployed Brazilian and a revolutionary Guatemalan physician — talk about their lives. We conclude,
moving from the personal to the political, with letters from Aung San
Suu Kyi of Burma, recipient of the Nobel Peace Prize for her inspiring
leadership in her country's struggle to return to democracy.

All of the women featured in this chapter are articulate, literate,
self-conscious writers. Their eloquence allows us to reflect on the
power of words for women, as well as for men.

477

THINKING HISTORICALLY
Constructing Theory

The notion of "constructing theory" may seem much more demanding than it is. It is little more than bringing together ideas that explain phenomena in history. Stated in words, a theory offers a possible answer to a question or an explanation of a problem. Theories are not necessarily true; they are guesses, called hypotheses, and have to be tested and supported with evidence. Theories might come to us from reading either primary or secondary sources, but ultimately a theory must make sense of the primary sources, the raw experience of history. (For that reason, this chapter contains only primary sources.) A theory organizes experience in a way that makes it more comprehensible. It seeks patterns or an explanation of patterns: causes, consequences, connections, relationships, reasons.

Ultimately, of course, a theory must be tested with new evidence. A good theory will interpret or incorporate new evidence without need for much change in theory. In this chapter, you are asked only to focus on constructing theory. Occasionally, you will be reminded of the limitations of the primary sources included here, but our emphasis will be on conceiving and expressing theories that give meaning to the material at hand.

79

The Marriage Law of the People's Republic of China

Chinese revolutionaries in the twentieth century frequently called for women's rights and equality. The "women question" was at the forefront of the Nationalist revolution of 1911 and, again, of the Communist revolution of 1949. Women who had been active in the revolution of 1911 sought women's suffrage and an end to such patriarchal practices as foot-binding, the concubine system, child marriage, and prostitution. But the visions of Chinese revolutionaries often remained promises in word only.

The Marriage Law of the People's Republic of China (Peking: Foreign Languages Press, 1959).

The government of Chiang Kai-shek passed major resolutions in 1924 and 1926 to enact laws that would codify many of the aspirations of the women's movement: legal equality, right to own property, freely entered marriage, right to divorce, even equal pay for equal work. But in 1927, Chiang's Nationalist party broke its alliance with the communists and identified them with women's issues. In fact, many of the founders of the Communist party, including Mao Zedong, were proponents of family reform (free marriage and free love) before they were Marxists. Despite this, as they sought supporters and volunteers throughout China after 1927, especially in the more traditional and male-dominated countryside, they quickly dropped their calls for reform of the marriage and family laws.

When the Communists came to power in China in 1949, marriage reform again surfaced as a high-priority goal in constructing a new society. The 1950 Marriage Law, excerpted here, led to a widespread debate on the role of women in Chinese communist society. What practices did the Chinese Communists seek to curb with this law?

Thinking Historically

Construct a theory about how different groups of people in China might respond to this law. Among the groups you might consider are rich men, poor men, rich women, poor women, young and old, city and country people.

Chapter I. General Principles

Article 1. The arbitrary and compulsory feudal marriage system, which is based on the superiority of man over woman and which ignores the children's interests, shall be abolished.

The new democratic marriage system, which is based on free choice of partners, on monogamy, on equal rights for both sexes, and on protection of the lawful interests of women and children, shall be put into effect.

Article 2. Bigamy, concubinage, child betrothal, interference with the remarriage of widows, and the exaction of money or gifts in connection with marriage shall be prohibited. . . .

Chapter III. Rights and Duties of Husband and Wife

Article 7. Husband and wife are companions living together and shall enjoy equal status in the home.

Article 8. Husband and wife are in duty bound to love, respect, assist, and look after each other, to live in harmony, to engage in production, to care for the children, and to strive jointly for the welfare of the family and for the building up of a new society.

Article 9. Both husband and wife shall have the right to free choice of occupation and free participation in work or in social activities.

Article 10. Both husband and wife shall have equal right in the possession and management of family property.

80

BETTY FRIEDAN

From *The Feminine Mystique*

This book elicited an enormous response from women in the United States when it was published in 1963. What Friedan called "the problem that has no name" was immediately understood and widely discussed. What name would you give to the problem? What were its causes? Do women still feel it today?

Thinking Historically

In what ways were the needs of American women after World War II like those of Chinese women? In what ways were they different? Which do you find more striking, the similarities or the differences? What theories would explain why Chinese and American women had different problems in the 1950s and 1960s?

The problem lay buried, unspoken, for many years in the minds of American women. It was a strange stirring, a sense of dissatisfaction, a yearning that women suffered in the middle of the twentieth century in the United States. Each suburban wife struggled with it alone. As she made the beds, shopped for groceries, matched slipcover material, ate peanut butter sandwiches with her children, chauffeured Cub Scouts and Brownies, lay beside her husband at night — she was afraid to ask even of herself the silent question — "Is this all?"

Betty Friedan, *The Feminine Mystique* (New York: Dell, 1963), 11–12, 14, 15–16, 27.

For over fifteen years there was no word of this yearning in the millions of words written about women, for women, in all the columns, books, and articles by experts telling women their role was to seek fulfillment as wives and mothers. Over and over women heard in voices of tradition and of Freudian sophistication that they could desire no greater destiny than to glory in their own femininity. Experts told them how to catch a man and keep him, how to breastfeed children and handle their toilet training, how to cope with sibling rivalry and adolescent rebellion; how to buy a dishwasher, bake bread, cook gourmet snails, and build a swimming pool with their own hands; how to dress, look, and act more feminine and make marriage more exciting; how to keep their husbands from dying young and their sons from growing into delinquents. They were taught to pity the neurotic, unfeminine, unhappy women who wanted to be poets or physicists or presidents. They learned that truly feminine women do not want careers, higher education, political rights — the independence and the opportunities that the old-fashioned feminists fought for. Some women, in their forties and fifties, still remembered painfully giving up those dreams, but most of the younger women no longer even thought about them. A thousand expert voices applauded their femininity, their adjustment, their new maturity. All they had to do was devote their lives from earliest girlhood to finding a husband and bearing children. . . .

In the fifteen years after World War II, this mystique of feminine fulfillment became the cherished and self-perpetuating core of contemporary American culture. Millions of women lived their lives in the image of those pretty pictures of the American suburban housewife, kissing their husbands goodbye in front of the picture window, depositing their stationwagonsful of children at school, and smiling as they ran the new electric waxer over the spotless kitchen floor. They baked their own bread, sewed their own and their children's clothes, kept their new washing machines and dryers running all day. They changed the sheets on the beds twice a week instead of once, took the rug-hooking class in adult education, and pitied their poor frustrated mothers, who had dreamed of having a career. Their only dream was to be perfect wives and mothers; their highest ambition to have five children and a beautiful house, their only fight to get and keep their husbands. They had no thought for the unfeminine problems of the world outside the home; they wanted the men to make the major decisions. They gloried in their role as women, and wrote proudly on the census blank: "Occupation: housewife." . . .

If a woman had a problem in the 1950s and 1960s, she knew that something must be wrong with her marriage, or with herself. Other women were satisfied with their lives, she thought. What kind of a woman was she if she did not feel this mysterious fulfillment waxing the kitchen floor? She was so ashamed to admit her dissatisfaction that she never knew how many other women shared it. If she tried to tell her husband, he didn't understand what she was talking about. She did not really understand it herself. For over fifteen years women in America found it harder to talk about this problem than about sex. Even the psychoanalysts had no name for it. When a woman went to a psychiatrist for help, as many women did, she would say, "I'm so ashamed," or "I must be hopelessly neurotic." "I don't know what's wrong with women today," a suburban psychiatrist said uneasily. "I only know something is wrong because most of my patients happen to be women. And their problem isn't sexual." Most women with this problem did not go to see a psychoanalyst, however. "There's nothing wrong really," they kept telling themselves. "There isn't any problem."

But on an April morning in 1959, I heard a mother of four, having coffee with four other mothers in a suburban development fifteen miles from New York, say in a tone of quiet desperation, "the problem." And the others knew, without words, that she was not talking about a problem with her husband, or her children, or her home. Suddenly they realized they all shared the same problem, the problem that has no name. They began, hesitantly, to talk about it. Later, after they had picked up their children at nursery school and taken them home to nap, two of the women cried, in sheer relief, just to know they were not alone.

Gradually I came to realize that the problem that has no name was shared by countless women in America. As a magazine writer I often interviewed women about problems with their children, or their marriages, or their houses, or their communities. But after a while I began to recognize the telltale signs of this other problem. I saw the same signs in suburban ranch houses and split-levels on Long Island and in New Jersey and Westchester County; in colonial houses in a small Massachusetts town; on patios in Memphis; in suburban and city apartments; in living rooms in the Midwest. Sometimes I sensed the problem, not as a reporter, but as a suburban housewife, for during this time I was also bringing up my own three children in Rockland County, New York. I heard echoes of the problem in college dormitories and semi-private maternity wards, at PTA meetings and luncheons of the League of Women Voters, at suburban cocktail parties, in station wagons waiting for trains, and in snatches of conversation overheard at Schrafft's. The groping words I heard from other women, on quiet afternoons when children were at school or on quiet evenings when husbands worked late, I think I understood first as a woman long before I understood their larger social and psychological implications.

Just what was this problem that has no name? What were the words women used when they tried to express it? Sometimes a woman would say "I feel empty somehow . . . incomplete." Or she would say,

"I feel as if I don't exist." Sometimes she blotted out the feeling with a tranquilizer. Sometimes she thought the problem was with her husband, or her children, or that what she really needed was to redecorate her house, or move to a better neighborhood, or have an affair, or another baby. Sometimes, she went to a doctor with symptoms she could hardly describe: "A tired feeling . . . I get so angry with the children it scares me . . . I feel like crying without any reason." (A Cleveland doctor called it "the housewife's syndrome.") A number of women told me about great bleeding blisters that break out on their hands and arms. "I call it the housewife's blight," said a family doctor in Pennsylvania. "I see it so often lately in these young women with four, five, and six children who bury themselves in their dishpans. But it isn't caused by detergent and it isn't cured by cortisone." . . .

If I am right, the problem that has no name stirring in the minds of so many American women today is not a matter of loss of femininity or too much education, or the demands of domesticity. It is far more important than anyone recognizes. It is the key to these other new and old problems which have been torturing women and their husbands and children, and puzzling their doctors and educators for years. It may well be the key to our future as a nation and a culture. We can no longer ignore that voice within women that says: "I want something more than my husband and my children and my home."

┌─────┐
│ *81* │
└─────┘

ASSIA DJEBAR

Growing Up in Algeria

Excerpted from a novel by an Algerian author, this selection is about growing up in Algeria just before the revolution for independence from France, which began in 1954. To the extent to which her account is autobiographical, what do you think it was like to grow up in Algeria as a young teenage girl around 1950? How typical do you think this girl's life and concerns were?

Assia Djebar, "Growing Up in Algeria," in *Fantasia: An Algerian Cavalcade*, trans. Dorothy S. Blair (Portsmouth, NH: Heinemann, 1993), 179–85.

The author discusses how her experiences in the French and Koranic religious school pulled her in different directions. What were they? Writing and reading were very important to her, but they both meant different things in Arabic Muslim culture and French culture. "Read!" or "Recite!" was the injunction of the Archangel Gabriel to the illiterate Muhammad, the Prophet, who on these instructions recited the words of God that became the Koran in the seventh century. In the Koranic schools, young people learn the Koran by reciting and memorizing it (just as Mohammed did). What was the meaning of reading in French for the author? What were the different meanings of writing for her? Do you think this exposure to both languages was making her more Arabic or French? Which identity was more real for her?

In what ways were the needs and interests of this teenage girl similar to, or different from, those of an American teenage girl in the same period? Do you think their lives have become more alike since then?

Thinking Historically

Construct a theory that answers one of the questions posed above. Keep in mind that a theory is not an answer — it is a guiding principle for an answer. So, for instance, if you choose to consider the question, "Which identity was more real for her?", an answer might be "Arabic," and a theory could be that "a person's mother tongue determines who she is." A theory is a general principle supported by evidence. (For example, you could interview bilingual people to find out if their first language played a greater role than their second in shaping their identities.) Keep in mind many different theories are possible in answer to each question.

At the age when I should be veiled already, I can still move about freely thanks to the French school: Every Monday the village bus takes me to the boarding school in the nearby town, and brings me back on Saturday to my parents' home.

I have a friend who is half Italian and who goes home every weekend to a fishing port on the coast; we go together to catch our respective buses and are tempted by all sorts of escapades . . . With beating hearts we make our way into the centre of the town; to enter a smart cake-shop, wander along the edge of the park, stroll along the boulevard, which only runs alongside common barracks, seems the acme of freedom, after a week of boarding school! Excited by the proximity of forbidden pleasures, we eventually each catch our bus; the thrill lay in the risk of missing it!

As a young teenager I enjoy the exhilarating hours spent every Thursday in training on the sports field. I only have one worry: fear that my father might come to visit me! How can I tell him that it's compulsory for me to wear shorts, in other words, I have to show my legs? I keep this fear a secret, unable to confide in any of my schoolfriends; unlike me, they haven't got cousins who do not show their ankles or their arms, who do not even expose their faces. My panic is also compounded by an Arab woman's "shame." The French girls whirl around me; they do not suspect that my body is caught in invisible snares.

"Doesn't your daughter wear a veil yet?" asks one or other of the matrons, gazing questioningly at my mother with suspicious kohl-rimmed eyes, on the occasion of one of the summer weddings. I must be thirteen, or possibly fourteen.

"She reads!" my mother replies stiffly.

Everyone is swallowed up in the embarrassed silence that ensues. And in my own silence.

"She reads," that is to say in Arabic, "she studies." I think now that this command "to read" was not just casually included in the Quranic revelation made by the Angel Gabriel in the cave . . . "She reads" is tantamount to saying that writing to be read, including that of the unbelievers, is always a source of revelation: in my case of the mobility of my body, and so of my future freedom.

When I am growing up — shortly before my native land throws off the colonial yoke — while the man still has the right to four legitimate wives, we girls, big and little, have at our command four languages to express desire before all that is left for us is sighs and moans: French for secret missives; Arabic for our stifled aspirations towards God-the-Father, the God of the religions of the Book; Lybico-Berber which takes us back to the pagan idols — mother-gods — of pre-Islamic Mecca. The fourth language, for all females, young or old, cloistered or half-emancipated, remains that of the body: the body which male neighbours' and cousins' eyes require to be deaf and blind, since they cannot completely incarcerate it; the body which, in trances, dances or vociferations, in fits of hope or despair, rebels, and unable to read or write, seeks some unknown shore as destination for its message of love.

In our towns, the first woman-reality is the voice, a dart which flies off into space, an arrow which slowly falls to earth; next comes writing with the scratching pointed quill forming amorous snares with its liana letters. By way of compensation, the need is felt to blot out women's bodies and they must be muffled up, tightly swathed, swaddled like infants or shrouded like corpses. Exposed, a woman's body would offend every eye, be an assault on the dimmest of desires, emphasize every separation. The voice, on the other hand, acts like a perfume, a draft of fresh water for the dry throat; and when it is savoured, it can be enjoyed by several simultaneously; a secret, polygamous pleasure . . .

When the hand writes, slow positioning of the arm, carefully bending forward or leaning to one side, crouching, swaying to and fro, as in an act of love. When reading, the eyes take their time, delight in caressing the curves, while the calligraphy suggests the rhythm of the scansion: as if the writing marked the beginning and the end of possession.

Writing: Everywhere, a wealth of burnished gold and in its vicinity there is no place for other imagery from either animal or vegetable kingdom; it looks in the mirror of its scrolls and curlicues and sees itself as woman, not the reflection of a voice. It emphasizes by its presence alone where to begin and where to retreat; it suggests, by the song that smoulders in its heart, the dance floor for rejoicing and hair-shirt for the ascetic; I speak of the Arabic script; to be separated from it is to be separated from a great love. This script, which I mastered only to write the sacred words, I see now spread out before me cloaked in innocence and whispering arabesques — and ever since, all other scripts (French, English, Greek) seem only to babble, are never cathartic; they may contain truth, indeed, but a blemished truth.

Just as the pentathlon runner of old needed the starter, so, as soon as I learned the foreign script, my body began to move as if by instinct.

As if the French language suddenly had eyes, and lent them me to see into liberty; as if the French language blinded the peeping-toms of my clan and, at this price, I could move freely, run headlong down every street, annex the outdoors for my cloistered companions, for the matriarchs of my family who endured a living death. As if . . . Derision! I know that every language is a dark depository for piled-up corpses, refuse, sewage, but faced with the language of the former conquerer, which offers me its ornaments, its jewels, its flowers, I find they are the flowers of death — chrysanthemums on tombs!

Its script is a public unveiling in front of sniggering onlookers . . . A queen walks down the street, white, anonymous, draped, but when the shroud of rough wool is torn away and drops sudddenly at her feet, which a moment ago were hidden, she becomes a beggar again, squatting in the dust, to be spat at, the target of cruel comments.

In my earliest childhood — from the age of five to ten — I attended the French school in the village, and every day after lessons there I went on to the Quranic school.

Classes were held in a back room lent by a grocer, one of the village notables. I can recall the place, and its dim light: Was it because the time for the lessons was just before dark, or because the lighting of the room was so parsimonious? . . .

The master's image has remained singularly clear: delicate features, pale complexion, a scholar's sunken cheeks; about forty families supported him. I was struck by the elegance of his bearing and his traditional attire: A spotless light muslin was wrapped around his headdress and floated behind his neck; his serge tunic was dazzling white. I never saw this man except sitting.

In comparison, the horde of misbehaving little urchins squatting on straw mats — sons of *fellaheen* [peasants] for the most part — seemed crude riffraff, from whom I kept my distance.

We were only four or five little girls. I suppose that our sex kept us apart, rather than my supercilious amazement at their behaviour. In spite of his aristocratic bearing, the *taleb* [teacher] did not hesitate to lift his cane and bring it down on the fingers of a recalcitrant or slow-witted lad. (I can still hear it whistle through the air.) We girls were spared this regular punishment.

I can remember the little impromptu parties my mother devised in our flat when I brought home (as later my brother was to do) the walnut table decorated with arabesques. This was the master's reward when we had learnt a long *sura* by heart. My mother and our village nanny, who was a second mother to us, then let out that semi-barbaric "you-you." That prolonged, irregular, spasmodic cooing, which in our building reserved for teachers' families — all European except for ours — must have appeared incongruous, a truly primitive cry. My mother considered the circumstances (the study of the Quran undertaken by her children) sufficiently important for her to let out this ancestral cry of jubilation in the middle of the village where she nevertheless felt herself an exile.

At every prize-giving ceremony at the French school, every prize I obtained strengthened my solidarity with my own family; but I felt there was more glory in this ostentatious clamour. The Quranic school, that dim cavern in which the haughty figure of the Sheikh was enthroned above the poor village children, this school became, thanks to the joy my mother demonstrated in this way, an island of bliss — Paradise regained.

Back in my native city, I learned that another Arab school was being opened, also funded by private contributions. One of my cousins attended it; she took me there. I was disappointed. The buildings, the timetable, the modern appearance of the masters, made it no different from a common-or-garden French school . . .

I understood later that in the village I had participated in the last of popular, secular teaching. In the city, thanks to the Nationalist movement of "Modernist Muslims," a new generation of Arab culture was being forged.

Since then these *medrasas* have sprung up everywhere. If I had attended one of them (if I'd grown up in the town where I was born) I would have found it quite natural to swathe my head in a turban, to hide my hair, to cover my arms and calves, in a word to move about out of doors like a Muslim nun!

After the age of ten or eleven, shortly before puberty, I was no longer allowed to attend the Quranic school. At this age, boys are suddenly excluded from the women's Turkish bath — that emollient world of naked bodies stifling in a whirl of scalding steam . . . The same thing happened to my companions, the little village girls, one of whom I would like to describe here.

The daughter of the Kabyle baker must, like me, have attended the French school simultaneously with the Quranic school. But I can only recall her presence squatting at my side in front of the Sheikh: side by side, half smiling to each other, both already finding it uncomfortable to sit cross-legged! . . . My legs must have been too long, because of my height: It wasn't easy for me to hide them under my skirt.

For this reason alone I think that I would in any case have been weaned from Quranic instruction at this age: There is no doubt that it's easier to sit cross-legged when wearing a *seroual;* a young girl's body that is beginning to develop more easily conceals its form under the ample folds of the traditional costume. But my skirts, justified by my attendance at the French school, were ill adapted to such a posture.

When I was eleven I started secondary school and became a boarder. What happened to the baker's daughter? Certainly veiled, withdrawn overnight from school: betrayed by her figure. Her swelling breasts, her slender legs, in a word, the emergence of her woman's personality transformed her into an incarcerated body!

I remember how much this Quranic learning, as it is progressively acquired, is linked to the body.

The portion of the sacred verse, inscribed on both sides of the walnut tablet, had to be wiped off at least once a week, after we had shown that we could recite it off by heart. We scrubbed the piece of wood thoroughly, just like other people wash their clothes: The time it took to dry seemed to ensure the interval that the memory needed to digest what it had swallowed . . .

The learning was absorbed by the fingers, the arms, through the physical effort. The act of cleaning the tablet seemed like ingesting a portion of the Quranic text. The writing — itself a copy of writing which is considered immutable — could only continue to unfold before us if it relied, clause by clause, on this osmosis . . .

As the hand traces the liana-script, the mouth opens to repeat the words, obedient to their rhythm, partly to memorize, partly to relieve the muscular tension . . . The shrill voices of the drowsy children rise up in a monotonous, sing-song chorus.

Stumbling on, swaying from side to side, care taken to observe the tonic accents, to differentiate between long and short vowels, attentive to the rhythm of the chant; muscles of the larynx as well as the torso moving in harmony. Controlling the breath to allow the correct emission of the voice, and letting the understanding advance precariously along its tight-rope. Respecting the grammar by speaking it aloud, making it part of the chant.

This language which I learn demands the correct posture for the body, on which the memory rests for its support. The childish hand, spurred on — as in training for some sport — by willpower worthy of an adult, begins to write. "Read!" The fingers labouring on the tablet send back the signs to the body, which is simultaneously reader and servant. The lips having finished their muttering, the hand will once more do the washing, proceeding to wipe out what is written on the tablet: This is the moment of absolution, like touching the hem of death's garment. Again, it is the turn of writing, and the circle is completed.

And when I sit curled up like this to study my native language it is as though my body reproduces the architecture of my native city: the *medinas* with their tortuous alleyways closed off to the outside world, living their secret life. When I write and read the foreign language, my body travels far in subversive space, in spite of the neighbours and suspicious matrons; it would not need much for it to take wing and fly away!

As I approach a marriageable age, these two different apprenticeships, undertaken simultaneously, land me in a dichotomy of location. My father's preference will decide for me: light rather than darkness. I do not realize that an irrevocable choice is being made: the outdoors and the risk, instead of the prison of my peers. This stroke of luck brings me to the verge of breakdown.

I write and speak French outside: The words I use convey no flesh-and-blood reality. I learn the names of birds I've never seen, trees I shall take ten years or more to identify, lists of flowers and plants that I shall never smell until I travel north of the Mediterranean. In this respect, all vocabulary expresses what is missing in my life, exoticism without mystery, causing a kind of visual humiliation that it is not seemly to admit to . . . Settings and episodes in children's books are nothing but theoretical concepts; in the French family the mother comes to fetch her daughter or son from school; in the French street, the parents walk quite naturally side by side . . . So, the world of the school is expunged from the daily life of my native city, as it is from the life of my family. The latter is refused any referential rôle.

My conscious mind is here, huddled against my mother's knees, in the darkest corners of the flat which she never leaves. The ambit of the school is elsewhere: My search, my eyes are fixed on other regions. I do not realize, no-one around me realizes, that, in the conflict between these two worlds, lies an incipient vertigo.

82

SIMI BEDFORD

Growing Up in Nigeria

This selection is excerpted from a novel about a young girl growing up in Nigeria. What does this selection suggest to us about Nigeria, large wealthy families in the port city of Lagos, the history of slavery, Christianity, and life in modern Africa? How typical do you think this young girl is? In what ways is the life of this girl similar to that of the teenage girl in the previous selection?

Thinking Historically

What would be one problem with basing a theory about the life of young girls in Africa on this story? Did any ideas come to you after reading this piece that might be generalized into a theory? Can you think of a theory that would explain a difference in the lives of Simi Bedford and Assia Djebar (see selection 81)?

Both this selection and the previous one discuss language and religion. What are some of the similarities and differences in their approaches to these topics? Formulate a theory about the importance or meaning of language or religion for young women in Africa.

"Africans can talk oh!" Aunt Rose often said.

She was right, in our house we spoke four languages, and two of them were English, loudly from morning till night, so it was a mystery to us, the foster children and me, that Grandma and Grandpa never

Simi Bedford, "Growing Up in Nigeria," in *Yoruba Girl Dancing* (New York: Penguin, 1992), 1–10.

spoke to each other at all. It was a mystery too that I didn't wake up dead every morning, because unless I was cross with her, I slept with Grandma in her big brass bed. There were twelve pillows on it, six on either side, and if I hadn't slept practically standing up, spreadeagled against them with my head angled back over the top one for air, I would have suffocated for sure under the covers.

Grandma was asleep; I liked to look at her in the morning when she was sleeping, because then her eyes were tight shut. When they were open they were black and shiny like pebbles under water and knew what you were thinking. Her face was smooth and peaceful. I stroked her white hair, soft as duck down, back from her forehead and tugged at her plait but she didn't wake up; so I left her and ran next door to my nurse Patience and she dressed me. I was ready and waiting in my grandmother's sitting room for James when he arrived to escort me up to breakfast on the top floor. James was Grandpa's steward.

"Well madam, I see you ready," he said, knocking on Grandma's bedroom door, which was in the right-hand corner of the sitting room.

"Can we go now?" I was impatient to leave this morning, I had a choice piece of news.

"Yes yes, we dey go now," he replied, laughing down at me.

"Do I look pretty?"

"You are fine, fine," he said, as always.

Grandma's arm, plump and sepia coloured, appeared around the door with a white note folded in her hand and James plucked it from her fingers, sketched a small bow to the rest of her invisible behind the door, and ushered me out in front of him.

Grandpa was already in his armchair sorting through his post, which scattered onto the floor as, taking a running jump, I settled myself in his lap and lay back against his shirt front which appeared dazzlingly white in the darkened room. I had hoped for a glimpse of Grandma's note — Grandpa had taught me to read when I was three — but he raised his arms above my head and read the letter safely out of reach. Frustrated, I slipped from his knee to fetch the Bible, which I'd left on the table next to his desk the day before, I didn't expect to find it there though, because both table and desk were heaped with books. The walls of Grandpa's sitting room were painted cream but you couldn't see them either, they were lined with books filling the shelves from floor to ceiling. Books spilled out of the shelves ruckling up the rugs on the polished wooden floor, vying for space with mounds of newspapers and periodicals, old and new. I found the Bible on the floor at the same time as a shout of laughter from Grandpa signalled that he'd come to the end of Grandma's note and brought James's head enquiringly around the door of the next room, where he was busy preparing breakfast. Hopefully I turned around too, but the joke was not to be shared.

"Come here," Grandpa said and hugged me close so that my nose was filled with the scent of his cologne and coconut hair pomade. "Where did we finish yesterday?"

We were working our way day by day through the Old Testament, Grandpa had little truck with the New, that the meek should inherit the earth had no place in his philosophy.

"God killed all the firstborn," I said, opening the Bible with the green leather marker, "and the Pharaoh was just about to let all the Israelites go."

Frankly I thought the Pharaoh had brought his troubles on himself. Moses had told him in no uncertain terms that unless he was allowed to lead the Israelites out of Egypt, God would smite every firstborn in the land and Pharaoh had been given plenty of proof with the nine plagues already visited on him that God would keep his word. It was horrifying all the same, though, because, as I pointed out to Grandpa, that would have been me, I was the firstborn child in my family. Grandpa assured me he would not have allowed it to happen. I believed him, he would have made a deal and got the best of it.

"Begin now!" he said, gesturing towards the page.

Keeping my place by moving my forefinger carefully beneath each word, I began reading. But Grandpa was not in the mood; no sooner were the Israelites safely across the Red Sea and the pursuing Egyptians drowned in their chariots, than he called out to James that we were ready to eat.

I wasn't ready to let the Israelites go just yet though. I waited until James had finished wrapping me in a big white napkin in order to protect my dress and then I said, "Aunt Rose says that we used to be slaves, like the Israelites."

"Aunt Rose talks too much. What will you eat?"

"Did we, Grandpa?"

He spooned up his pawpaw and didn't answer; after a pause and another mouthful, he said testily, "Yes, in America, but that was a long time ago. The important thing for you to remember is that our family came back."

"To Lagos?"

"Not initially, they settled in Sierra Leone to begin with."

"Where Uncle Marcus and lots of the cousins live?"

"That's right. Are you not eating this morning?"

"Were you a slave, Grandpa?"

"Of course not! Do I look like a slave? However it is a fact that my grandfather was one. You know he was a very brave man: He fought, along with many other slaves, on the side of the British in their war against the Americans and in return for his help he was given his freedom. Afterwards the British brought all the freed slaves to Sierra Leone. They crossed the Atlantic Ocean in a big ship and it arrived just in time for my father, your great-grandfather, Elias Foster, to be born a free man in Africa again. When he became a grown man he came home: to Nigeria. He settled in Lagos and began trading in palm oil. He was very successful too."

"Like Moses!"

"Exactly."

"How did great-grandpa Elias know that this was his home?"

"Well he knew that according to our family tradition we came originally from the area around Abeokuta, so he made a journey up there and when he arrived he immediately recognised the tribal markings on the faces of the people, they were identical to the pattern handed down to his father by his grandfather in America. We are home for good now, I promise you."

"I don't think I'd like to go to America."

"But you would like to go to England some day, wouldn't you, to study?"

"Like Papa and Aunt Harriet? Some day maybe."

"Now! What are you going to eat?"

I looked at the bowl on the table, it was hard to choose from the mangoes, pawpaws, guavas, oranges, pineapple, grapefruit, and melon. I asked James, who'd been standing by, to cut me an avocado in half and sprinkle it with salt. We ate in silence and it wasn't until I was halfway through my second slice of pineapple — I loved pineapple — that I remembered my news for Grandpa. I felt sorry for Grandpa — he never knew anything, because he only ever left his eyrie to go to the Chamber of Commerce and to church on Sunday.

"Sisi Bola's getting married," I said, looking at him sideways.

"Don't speak with your mouth full. Who is she marrying?"

"Akin Ojo."

Grandpa raised his eyebrows, "She only recently left for England, are you sure?"

"Oh yes. She came back last week and Nimota says — you know my nurse Nimota? — she says that it must have been love at first look."

Grandpa roared with laughter. "Indeed."

"And Patience says — "

"Which one is Patience?"

"Grandpa you know my nurse Patience very well."

"Do I?"

"Yes! She says that the food in England have plenty magic, because Sisi Bola only stick out de back when she go, but she stick out the front too like a elephant when she come back."

My grandfather laughed again. "You are a disgraceful child! Eat up, eat up now."

"Don't you want to know when the wedding is?"

"I'm sure you will tell me."

"It's in three weeks' time. I'm to be a bridesmaid. Aunt Delma has asked Grandma."

Aunt Delma was Grandma's sister and Sisi Bola's mother.

Sisi Bola was to be married from our house and Aunt Rose said that Aunt Delma was exceedingly lucky to have a sister like Grandma who was not only generous but who was also wife to the richest man in Lagos. The wedding, she said, would be the wedding of the decade, we should mark her words. I repeated this to Yowande, the youngest of the foster children, who, although three years older than me, was my best friend in the house. She didn't know what wedding of the decade meant either, but she did know that Nimota, my second nanny, was planning to put a curse on Yetunde, her rival in love, so that she would be too sick to attend any of the celebrations. I must be careful not to say anything, she said, because if Grandma found out she would beat us all.

"I won't tell her," I said. Yowande looked sceptical. It wasn't fair, just because I was the youngest in the house. Even I knew how fanatical Grandma was about that kind of thing. She considered it a blasphemy against the Christian Religion. And anyway I never told tales now.

We all, the Fosters that is, lived a stone's throw from the Marina in the residential area off Broad Street: Broad Street, Aunt Rose said, was the commercial centre, whatever that meant, of Lagos, where, she said, men of substance like Grandpa had built their mansions in the European style. Nimota said that that simply meant Grandpa was a big man. Where she came from, up country, he would have been, she said, a Paramount Chief. It was a fact that Grandpa's warehouses, which we passed nearly every day on our constitutional along the Marina, stretched for half a mile around the bay, I'd been inside many times of course with Grandpa. Aunt Rose, who frequently accompanied Nimota and me, said that Grandpa's warehouses were filled with all the riches of the continent, but actually they contained quite ordinary everyday things, as Grandpa said. Palm oil, leather, timber, and stuff like that. You name it, Aunt Rose said, and Grandpa sold it. He had branches and factories throughout the country, even where Nimota came from, and that was very remote. Aunt Rose counted them up on her fingers, there were twenty-three in all, branches, that is, not fingers, Aunt Rose had the normal number, but you wouldn't think so, Nimota said, they were into everything. Our house was four storeys high and painted a bright strawberry pink with a cream pattern of whirls and fancy flourishes around the windows and doors. The Lagos sun which, Grandma said, can wreck such havoc with pink complexions, had been kind to this one and aged it gently, so that with time the colour had mellowed and become discreet. Long rows of windows each with its own wrought-iron balcony looked out across the front, and large double doors opened directly onto the street. At the back there was a large paved courtyard with a well in the centre. A huge avocado provided shade, as did the mango, pawpaw, guava, and banana trees; broad-leaved ferns masked the hot glitter of the paving stones.

During the day we liked to sit pleasantly and peacefully, on the benches under the trees; the light filtering down through the leaves was always green and forest cool. At night the courtyard was lit by the fires of the servants cooking their food in the outside kitchen and loud with the sound of crickets. The smoke from the fires kept the mosquitoes at bay.

We were a miniature village, thirty people lived in our house. Grandpa lived on the top floor and was attended by his own servants. He and Grandma had been effectively separated for fifteen years; he never came downstairs. Even so he ruled us all, his word was law and his power was absolute. Aunt Rose said that people were equally terrified of him outside the house, including the score of Europeans he employed. I heard her tell Patience that she herself was so in awe of him she had only dared to address him directly three or four times in the twenty years since she had been living under his roof. I thought that was pretty silly of Aunt Rose. I wasn't scared of Grandpa and he certainly wasn't frightening to look at. The neat whorls of his hair had turned to grey, but his moustache was marvellously black and glossy and so was his skin which had an almost metallic sheen. It seemed to me that he was always laughing and, unlike Grandma, who complained of the smell that clung to me when I came back down after breakfast upstairs, I liked his cigars. He was seldom without one, either clenched in his teeth or drifting smoke from between his long fingers. It was all right for me, Aunt Rose said, I was the favoured grandchild, the little princess.

My grandmother, Grandma Loretta, ruled the rest of the household from her sitting room, which served as another courtyard inside the house. All the other rooms on the first floor opened onto it. Stationed in her rocking chair in the corner by her bedroom door, no coming or going escaped her notice. I loved Grandma, she was fat and marvellously comfortable to sit on, her brown skin was soft to touch and she wore her hair plaited in a crown around her head. Any impression of cosiness however was dispelled by a second glance at her eyes, it was impossible to look into them and lie.

With the exception of my father Simon, all Grandpa and Grandma's children were still living at home. My father Simon was the eldest and my Aunt Harriet was next. In fact, however, they were not Grandma's children at all: They were Grandpa's two children by the Fante princess. So she was my real grandmother, but I never knew her, she was never seen in Lagos, and she died in Ghana which was her country long before I was born. Grandma brought up the two children as if they were her own. Aunt Harriet, who resembled her mother and kept a photograph of her locked in her drawer, was considered a great beauty. The photograph showed a magnificent woman with bare shoulders wrapped in a length of Kente cloth, which, so Aunt Harriet told me and I told Yowande, could only be worn by royalty. If the picture were in colour the cloth would be glowing red, green, and gold,

like the stained-glass windows in Lagos cathedral. Her jet black hair
was pulled up in a fan shape over a wooden frame and fastened with
solid gold nuggets as befitted a Fante princess. Grandma said, and I
heard her say it many times to Aunt Rose when they were sitting taking
a glass of home-made ginger beer, that though Aunt Harriet, who was
a barrister, was brilliant, she was too highly strung. Grandma was worried that Harriet might even be a little unstable. After all it was common knowledge that there was ... well, instability, in the Fante
princess's family. There was no denying Aunt Harriet was sensitive, because as Aunt Rose said, she had a habit of bursting into tears at the
least little thing and rushing from the room.

Aunt Sylvia, Grandma's own elder daughter, was brilliant too, she
was going to be a doctor. As Aunt Rose said, making sure that
Grandma heard her, there was nothing unstable about that one. She
was my father's favourite, he liked to hold her up as a perfect model of
African womanhood. According to my father Aunt Sylvia was serious,
clever, modest, and good. Nobody was perfect, Aunt Rose said. Aunt
Grace, the youngest of my father's brothers and sisters, was my
favourite, Yowande and I loved to play with her hair which was thick
and shoulder length and watch her maid straightening it and curling it
in the latest styles from England. Aunt Grace's eyebrows were two perfect arches, she was destined to be a film star. We knew it.

Grandma's only son Uncle George would normally have been at
home too, but he had gone to England to fly aeroplanes and fight in the
war. According to Patience he was a source of great pride, anger, and
anxiety for my grandmother, not necessarily in that order. Opinion in
the house was divided about Uncle George: We children thought he
was a hero but Aunt Rose, and Patience too, believed he was downright
foolhardy to get involved in dem white people war. They didn't say this
to Grandma. Everyone had to be careful too on the subject of Uncle
Henry. He was Grandpa's son by an outside wife and the spitting
image of Grandpa. Yowande and I knew from listening to conversations around the house (we had our eyes to every keyhole and our ear
to every door, Aunt Rose said, but she was no better, in Nimota's opinion) that Uncle Henry was one of the reasons Grandma never spoke to
Grandpa, but no one explained why. Aunt Rose would only say that
certain tenets of the Christian faith appealed to Grandpa more than
others and one man one wife was not among them.

Aunt Rose had been living with my grandparents for twenty years,
ever since she had arrived for a short holiday in her teens. Even the servants referred to her as poor Aunt Rose, not because she was a poor relation, which she was, but because she had never married, and even
worse, Nimota said, she had no children. She was given to wearing
dark coloured dresses with pale collars; thin and spindly, she hugged
the corners of the house, delicate yet durable, like a cobweb.

Aunt Sylvia said that we made Aunt Rose's life intolerable. There were ten of us, nine foster children and me. The foster children were the sons and daughters of poor relations, like Aunt Rose; their parents sent them to live in Grandpa's house so that they could advance themselves. Yowande was the youngest, she was nine; Morenike was the eldest, she was fifteen and would be going home soon. In fact she would be leaving the CMS[1] just as I was beginning. Alaba who was my third nanny would miss her most, they were the same age. Aunt Rose said that when one of the foster children left, another appeared to take its place, miraculously, like shark's teeth. And then there was me: Everybody knew who I was. I was Remi Foster, the eldest of Simon Foster's three children, and Grandpa and Grandma's first grandchild. I lived with them because, as Grandpa said, Grandma would have been sad without a baby growing up in the house, and so would he. I was on permanent loan: It was the custom with the eldest grandchild and anyway, as Aunt Rose said, I was only a girl. She also said that no child required three nannies to trail after her all day long. I would be spoiled for life, we should mark her words. Well, the foster children certainly didn't spoil me, if I told tales they beat me up, and Grandma beat me too just to be sure. My life wasn't easy, like Aunt Rose thought. I couldn't tell her though, my lips were sealed.

83

CAROLINA MARIA DE JESUS

From *Child of the Dark: The Diary of Carolina Maria de Jesus*

This selection is from the diary of a common — and extraordinary — woman in Brazil in 1958. Carolina Maria de Jesus was born in 1913 in a small town in the interior of Brazil. Her mother, unmarried and unemployed, insisted that Carolina attend school, which she hated until the day she learned to read. She remembers reading out loud every sign

---

[1] School.

Carolina Maria de Jesus, *Child of the Dark: The Diary of Carolina Maria de Jesus,* trans. David St. Clair (New York: NAL Penguin, 1962), 32–34, 42–47.

and label she could find. It was the beginning of a lifetime fascination with words. But she was forced to leave school after the second grade.

When Carolina was sixteen, her mother moved to the suburbs of São Paulo. Carolina worked in a hospital, ran away to sing in a circus, and was employed in a long succession of jobs as cleaning woman and maid when, in 1947, she became pregnant. Her lover had abandoned her, and the family she worked for refused to let her into their house. Desperate, she moved into a *favela* (slum) in São Paulo, building her own shack with cardboard and cans taken from a Church construction site. In the next ten years she had two more children. In order to keep from thinking of her troubles, she wrote. Poems, plays, novels, "anything and everything, for when I was writing I was in a golden palace, with crystal windows and silver chandeliers." She also kept a diary that reveals the actual details of her daily life. It is a life still lived by many women in the *favelas* of Brazil.

What does the diary tell you about the lives of the poor in Brazil?

Thinking Historically

Of course, there are poor women in Africa and rich women in South America. And it need hardly be said that the poor outnumber the wealthy in Africa and Latin America as well as in China and the United States. Yet, it is difficult to imagine such desperate poverty as that described by Carolina Maria de Jesus. She is an articulate and thoughtful woman whose writing has helped her shape her own ideas. If you asked her what caused such poverty in her country, what might she say? Does she offer any theories about this? What is your theory for the existence of such poverty?

May 2, 1958 I'm not lazy. There are times when I try to keep up my diary. But then I think it's not worth it and figure I'm wasting my time.

I've made a promise to myself. I want to treat people that I know with more consideration. I want to have a pleasant smile for children and the employed.

I received a summons to appear at 8 P.M. at police station number 12. I spent the day looking for paper. At night my feet pained me so I couldn't walk. It started to rain. I went to the station and took José Carlos with me. The summons was for him. José Carlos is nine years old.

May 3 I went to the market at Carlos de Campos Street looking for any old thing. I got a lot of greens. But it didn't help much, for I've got no cooking fat. The children are upset because there's nothing to eat.

May 6 In the morning I went for water. I made João carry it. I was happy, then I received another summons. I was inspired yesterday and my verses were so pretty, I forgot to go to the station. It was 11:00 when I remembered the invitation from the illustrious lieutenant of the 12th precinct.

My advice to would-be politicians is that people do not tolerate hunger. It's necessary to know hunger to know how to describe it.

They are putting up a circus here at Araguaia Street. The Nilo Circus Theater.

May 9 I looked for paper but I didn't like it. Then I thought: I'll pretend that I'm dreaming.

May 10 I went to the police station and talked to the lieutenant. What a pleasant man! If I had known he was going to be so pleasant, I'd have gone on the first summons. The lieutenant was interested in my boys' education. He said the *favelas* have an unhealthy atmosphere where the people have more chance to go wrong than to become useful to state and country. I thought: If he knows this why doesn't he make a report and send it to the politicians? . . . Now he tells me this, I a poor garbage collector. I can't even solve my own problems.

Brazil needs to be led by a person who has known hunger. Hunger is also a teacher.

Who has gone hungry learns to think of the future and of the children.

May 11 Today is Mother's Day. The sky is blue and white. It seems that even nature wants to pay homage to the mothers who feel unhappy because they can't realize the desires of their children.

The sun keeps climbing. Today it's not going to rain. Today is our day.

Dona Teresinha came to visit me. She gave me 15 *cruzeiros* and said it was for Vera to go to the circus. But I'm going to use the money to buy bread tomorrow because I only have four *cruzeiros*.

Yesterday I got half a pig's head at the slaughterhouse. We ate the meat and saved the bones. Today I put the bones on to boil and into the broth I put some potatoes. My children are always hungry. When they are starving they aren't so fussy about what they eat.

Night came. The stars are hidden. The shack is filled with mosquitoes. I lit a page from a newspaper and ran it over the walls. This is the way the *favela* dwellers kill mosquitoes.

May 13 At dawn it was raining. Today is a nice day for me, it's the anniversary of the Abolition. The day we celebrate the freeing of the slaves. In the jails the Negroes were the scapegoats. But now the whites are more educated and don't treat us any more with contempt. May God enlighten the whites so that the Negroes may have a happier life.

It continued to rain and I only have beans and salt. The rain is strong but even so I sent the boys to school. I'm writing until the rain goes away so I can go to Senhor Manuel and sell scrap. With that money I'm going to buy rice and sausage. The rain has stopped for a while. I'm going out.

I feel so sorry for my children. When they see the things to eat that I come home with they shout:

"Viva Mama!"

Their outbursts please me. I've lost the habit of smiling. Ten minutes later they want more food. I sent João to ask Dona Ida for a little pork fat. She didn't have any. I sent her a note:

"Dona Ida, I beg you to help me get a little pork fat, so I can make soup for the children. Today it's raining and I can't go looking for paper. Thank you, Carolina."

It rained and got colder. Winter had arrived and in winter people eat more. Vera asked for food, and I didn't have any. It was the same old show. I had two *cruzeiros* and wanted to buy a little flour to make a *virado*.[1] I went to ask Dona Alice for a little pork. She gave me pork and rice. It was 9 at night when we ate.

And that is the way on May 13, 1958, I fought against the real slavery — hunger!

May 15 On the nights they have a party they don't let anybody sleep. The neighbors in the brick houses near by have signed a petition to get rid of the *favelados*. But they won't get their way. The neighbors in the brick houses say:

"The politicians protect the *favelados*."

Who protects us are the public and the Order of St. Vincent Church. The politicians only show up here during election campaigns. Senhor Candido Sampaio, when he was city councilman in 1953, spent his Sundays here in the *favela*. He was so nice. He drank our coffee, drinking right out of our cups. He made us laugh with his jokes. He played with our children. He left a good impression here and when he was candidate for state deputy, he won. But the Chamber of Deputies didn't do one thing for the *favelados*. He doesn't visit us any more. . . .

May 22 Today I'm sad. I'm nervous. I don't know if I should start crying or start running until I fall unconscious. At dawn it was raining. I couldn't go out to get any money. I spent the day writing. I cooked the macaroni and I'll warm it up again for the children. I cooked the potatoes and they ate them. I have a few tin cans and a little scrap that I'm going to sell to Senhor Manuel. When João came home from school I sent him to sell the scrap. He got 13 *cruzeiros*. He bought a glass of mineral water: two *cruzeiros*. I was furious with him. Where had he seen a *favelado* with such highborn tastes?

---

[1] A dish of black beans, manioc flour, pork, and eggs.

The children eat a lot of bread. They like soft bread but when they don't have it, they eat hard bread.

Hard is the bread that we eat. Hard is the bed on which we sleep. Hard is the life of the *favelado*.

Oh, São Paulo! A queen that vainly shows her skyscrapers that are her crown of gold. All dressed up in velvet and silk but with cheap stockings underneath — the *favela*.

The money didn't stretch far enough to buy meat, so I cooked macaroni with a carrot. I didn't have any grease, it was horrible. Vera was the only one who complained yet asked for more.

"Mama, sell me to Dona Julita, because she has delicious food."

I know that there exist Brazilians here inside São Paulo who suffer more than I do. In June of '57 I felt sick and passed through the offices of the Social Service. I had carried a lot of scrap iron and got pains in my kidneys. So as not to see my children hungry I asked for help from the famous Social Service. It was there that I saw the tears slipping from the eyes of the poor. How painful it is to see the dramas that are played out there. The coldness in which they treat the poor. The only things they want to know about them is their name and address.

I went to the Governor's Palace.[2] The Palace sent me to an office at Brigadeiro Luis Antonio Avenue. They in turn sent me to the Social Service at the Santa Casa charity hospital. There I talked with Dona Maria Aparecida, who listened to me, said many things yet said nothing. I decided to go back to the Palace. I talked with Senhor Alcides. He is not Japanese yet is as yellow as rotten butter. I said to Senhor Alcides:

"I came here to ask for help because I'm ill. You sent me to Brigadeiro Luis Antonio Avenue, and I went. There they sent me to the Santa Casa. And I spent all the money I have on transportation."

"Take her!"

They wouldn't let me leave. A soldier put his bayonet at my chest. I looked the soldier in the eyes and saw that he had pity on me. I told him:

"I am poor. That's why I came here."

Dr. Osvaldo de Barros entered, a false philanthropist in São Paulo who is masquerading as St. Vincent de Paul. He said:

"Call a squad car!"

The policeman took me back to the *favela* and warned me that the next time I made a scene at the welfare agency I would be locked up.

Welfare agency! Welfare for whom? . . .

May 27 It seems that the slaughterhouse threw kerosene on their garbage dump so the *favelados* would not look for meat to eat. I didn't

---

[2] Like most Brazilians, Carolina believes in going straight to the top to make her complaints.

have any breakfast and walked around half dizzy. The daze of hunger is worse than that of alcohol. The daze of alcohol makes us sing, but the one of hunger makes us shake. I know how horrible it is to only have air in the stomach.

I began to have a bitter taste in my mouth. I thought: Is there no end to the bitterness of life? I think that when I was born I was marked by fate to go hungry. I filled one sack of paper. When I entered Paulo Guimarães Street, a woman gave me some newspapers. They were clean and I went to the junk yard picking up everything that I found. Steel, tin, coal, everything serves the *favelado*. Leon weighed the paper and I got six *cruzeiros*.

I wanted to save the money to buy beans but I couldn't because my stomach was screaming and torturing me.

I decided to do something about it and bought a bread roll. What a surprising effect food has on our organisms. Before I ate, I saw the sky, the trees, and the birds all yellow, but after I ate, everything was normal to my eyes.

Food in the stomach is like fuel in machines. I was able to work better. My body stopped weighing me down. I started to walk faster. I had the feeling that I was gliding in space. I started to smile as if I was witnessing a beautiful play. And will there ever be a drama more beautiful than that of eating? I felt that I was eating for the first time in my life.

The Radio Patrol arrived. They came to take the two Negro boys who had broken into the power station. Four and six years old. It's easy to see that they are of the *favela*. *Favela* children are the most ragged children in the city. What they can find in the streets they eat. Banana peels, melon rind, and even pineapple husks. Anything that is too tough to chew, they grind. These boys had their pockets filled with aluminum coins, that new money in circulation.

May 28 It dawned raining. I only have three *cruzeiros* because I loaned Leila five so she could get her daughter in the hospital. I'm confused and don't know where to begin. I want to write, I want to work, I want to wash clothes. I'm cold and I don't have any shoes to wear. The children's shoes are worn out.

The worst thing in the *favela* is that there are children here. All the children of the *favela* know what a woman's body looks like. Because when the couples that are drunk fight, the woman, so as not to get a beating, runs naked into the street. When the fights start the *favelados* leave whatever they are doing to be present at the battle. So that when the woman goes running naked it's a real show for Joe Citizen. Afterward the comments begin among the children:

"Fernanda ran out nude when Armin was hitting her."

"Oh, I didn't see it. Damn!"

"What does a naked woman look like?"

And then the other, in order to tell him, puts his mouth near his ear. And the loud laughter echoes. Everything that is obscene or pornographic the *favelado* learns quickly.

There are some shacks where prostitutes play their love scenes right in front of the children.

The rich neighbors in the brick houses say we are protected by the politicians. They're wrong. The politicians only show up here in the Garbage Dump at election time. This year we had a visit from a candidate for deputy, Dr. Paulo de Campos Moura, who gave us beans and some wonderful blankets. He came at an opportune moment, before it got cold.

What I want to clear up about the people who live in the *favela* is the following: The only ones who really survive here are the *nordestinos*.[3] They work and don't squander. They buy a house or go back up north.

Here in the *favela* there are those who build shacks to live in and those who build them to rent. And the rents are from 500 to 700 *cruzeiros*. Those who make shacks to sell spend 4,000 *cruzeiros* and sell them for 11,000. Who made a lot of shacks to sell was Tiburcio.

May 29 It finally stopped raining. The clouds glided toward the horizon. Only the cold attacked us. Many people in the *favela* don't have warm clothing. When one has shoes he won't have a coat. I choke up watching the children walk in the mud. It seems that some new people have arrived in the *favela*. They are ragged with undernourished faces. They improvised a shack. It hurts me to see so much pain, reserved for the working class. I stared at my new companion in misfortune. She looked at the *favela* with its mud and sickly children. It was the saddest look I'd ever seen. Perhaps she has no more illusions. She had given her life over to misery.

There will be those who reading what I write will say — this is untrue. But misery is real.

What I revolt against is the greed of men who squeeze other men as if they were squeezing oranges.

---

[3] Forced by land-parching droughts and almost no industry, the poor of the north swarm into cities like São Paulo and Rio looking for work. Needing a place to live, they choose the *favelas* and end up worse off than they were before.

84

JENNIFER HARBURY

From *Bridge of Courage*

After graduating from Harvard Law School in 1978, Jennifer Harbury became engaged in human rights work that took her to Guatemala in 1985 and 1986. She returned to Guatemala in 1990 to record the oral history interviews that are the basis of the book from which this selection is excerpted. In Guatemala she met and married Commandante Everardo, who was later captured and disappeared. In 1995 her multiple hunger strikes forced the CIA to admit that her husband was dead, murdered by one of its paid agents.

U.S. policy in Guatemala switched from one of support to opposition in 1944 with the downfall of the dictator Jorge Chico and the election of a popular nationalist president, Jacobo Arbenz, who redistributed land to the poor, threatening the interests of U.S.–owned tropical fruit companies and U.S. investors. After securing his downfall in 1954, the United States trained the Guatemalan military and insured the continuance of conservative military regimes. In the 1980s these efforts were part of the U.S. campaign against neighboring Nicaragua and its support for the right-wing "death squads" of El Salvador. In 1999, an international Historical Clarification Commission issued a nine-volume report, "Guatemala: Memory of Silence," which held that the Guatemalan military, with the backing of the United States, engaged in a policy of genocide against the local population of Mayan Indians; 200,000 were tortured and murdered in a thirty-four-year war that ended in 1996.

This is the story of Anita, a physician who joined the Guatemalans and fought against this military regime. How did Anita become involved in the revolution against the government? Was her involvement unusual for an urban woman and for a physician?

Thinking Historically

How might Anita explain her various identities and activities? If you asked her if she had any theories about how a woman could become involved in all of these things, what might she say?

Compare Anita with Carolina from selection 83. How might you explain why Anita became a revolutionary and Carolina did not? Formulate a theory that generalizes and explains their differences.

Jennifer Harbury, "Anita," in *Bridge of Courage: Life Stories of the Guatemalan Companeros and Companeras* (Monroe, ME: Common Courage Press, 1995), 36–38, 103–106, 109–13.

Compare Anita with one of the African women you read about. What makes their experiences so different from Anita's? Formulate a theory that explains these differences.

I joined the underground during my last year of medical school. I had just finished a rotation up in the jungle areas with the peasant cooperatives, and had learned a lot. What an eye opener that year was! It had been very difficult. My school supervisor hated women medical students and had sent me to the most remote regions in hopes that I would give up. Instead, though, I thrived, and came to love the villagers who took me in and cared for me. I loved their gentle ways, and their generosity, and I saw the unfairness and repression that they suffered. I never forgot it, even after I returned to the capital for my last year of study. And with my new awareness, I saw the things in the city that, perhaps, I hadn't wanted to see before.

I lived not far from a small union office, and on the way to the hospital each morning, I saw the fresh black ribbons on the union door, the new photographs, signaling yet another member dragged off to an ugly death in the middle of the night. And I saw the morgues. The tortures that had been inflicted on those poor people, the expressions on those dead faces, I will never forget. It is because of the morgues, I am positive, that so many of us medical students, and yes, even professors, joined up with the underground that year. Look, here is my graduation photo. See the two men handing me my diploma? They are both dead now; they were part of the city underground, but I didn't know it then. The two students next to me? They were with the guerrillas, too. I think they went to the mountains. None of us knew about each other, for security reasons. But I know now, and when I look at this photo, I feel doubly proud. Proud of the diploma and my completed studies, proud of all of us in the group, and proud of the courage represented in this image. It makes me happy to show it to you. I want these people remembered.

At first I worked in the city, with another medical student named Melissa. We had many small tasks: treating a wounded person brought in from the mountains, hiding medicines and passing them on, working in the clandestine clinics. It was all very dangerous. To be caught with medicines outside of the hospital meant death by torture. To be found treating a wounded combatant meant an immediate bullet. We both understood this, but we gave each other so much support, so much love. We were more than sisters. I still weep when I think of Melissa.

I don't know how she was found out, but she was. Things had grown so terrible in the city. Every day, our people were captured and tortured. And under that kind of torture, if people do not die quickly, they will talk.

They cannot help it. So perhaps someone spoke of her, described her, gave away her next meeting point. Who knows — it doesn't matter. I found her in the morgue with so many others. She was naked and battered, her face bluish from strangulation, small razor cuts and cigarette burns up and down her arms and legs. Her autopsy report showed vaginal slashes, as if her captors, once finished with her themselves, had raped her with a broken bottle. Her eyes were gone, the sockets filled with mud. Looking down at her, I felt all my physician's arts were useless. It is so strange — it was not her injuries that hurt me the most. She was the same as all the others, there on the metal slabs that day. I had grown used to it. The pain was just from the loss of her, the loss for all of us left living.

That was the day I left for the mountains. I knew they would be coming for me soon. But that wasn't the real reason I left. I knew I could die just as quickly in the mountains. I could have fled the country to safety, but I chose not to. I had made a decision — I had decided to fight. I had decided that when those animals came looking for me, to kill me in that way, by God they were going to find me with a gun in my hands.

. . . I loved my work. I was the unit physician, but I was also responsible for physical fitness programs in the morning and for political education. The fitness program was often comical, especially when we got some macho young *compas* straight in from the city. I would always tell them to take it easy the first few days, to take things gradually and build up their bodies with time. But of course, they would always want to keep up with the women, even those of us who had been up there for months and months. After a heavy session of squats and abdominals, let alone the mountain climbing it takes just to get from tent to tent, it was not unusual to see some proud newcomer limping around sheepishly for a few days. But you must never laugh at a beginner. They learned for themselves, just as they learned that cooking and sewing and washing were no longer only women's work. All of us had a lot to learn, or unlearn, up there in the mountains.

It was the political work that I loved the best. We would all sit together in a big circle and talk about our heritage, the conquest, the problems of land distribution in our country, the racism. Most of our people were Maya from small villages, taught since birth that they were inferior. My goal, in teaching, was to convince them that they counted, that they had equal value, that they had much to say and much to give. My goal was to tell them that the new world, after our triumph, would be theirs. My reward was the expression on their faces. And you should hear the things they had to say, once they believed that they would be listened to with respect. So many ideas, so much wisdom these gentle people had stored up in their minds. Our country will be in good hands, some day. This much I know.

I would have stayed up in the mountains forever. I was happy enough with my work and my life, even though it was dangerous and often sad. I was in love with another young *compa,* Mario. We fought side by side in combat, and we could talk about anything. He had little formal education, but he was very intelligent, and respected women as revolutionaries and as equals. He was very quiet and kindly, and completely dedicated. That is why we are not together now. When I was hurt later on, he could have stayed in the city with me while I recovered. But he chose to go back to combat. He knew how much he was needed in the mountains, and so that was the end of that. I respected his decision and I still do, but that doesn't mean it wasn't painful at the time. Most of the story I am going to tell you now is about painful memories, but I want to tell it anyway. I want you to write about it for us.

The day I was shot started out like any other day. I was on kitchen duty that morning, washing pots at the edge of the river. Some other *compas* were swimming nearby, getting cleaned up after hauling supplies from the bottom of the volcano, splashing water at me. What we didn't know was that one of our new people, a young *compa* named Marcelino, had slipped away during the night to head back towards his village. He had a serious alcoholism problem which he had not told us about, and in a moment of despair, he had decided he could not handle the situation, and had left all alone. We would have escorted him down, to safety, but he had been too ashamed to tell us of his problem. He did not get far before the army caught and tortured him, and it did not take long to make him talk. I am sorry for him, when I think of this. He only wanted to go home. Instead he met a bad death and almost took the rest of us with him.

I was bending over a large iron cauldron when the first hail of bullets hit us. It took me completely by surprise. I heard the explosion of gunfire, from so many, many guns and saw a river of blood pouring from my face. For a moment, I couldn't feel much and was able to crawl to safety behind some big rocks at the river's edge. Our *compas* had appeared instantly on the ledge above us, and fought back against the soldiers with so much strength that we were protected. It is thanks to them that I and the others in the river that day were neither killed nor captured. I lay behind the rocks for a long time while they fought. The bullet had taken off the right half of my jaw, and I was bleeding heavily, but all I could do was wrap up my face in the bandana I had been wearing and lie still. I knew the injury was very serious, and thought I would probably die, except that it hurt like hell. I had always been told that when you are truly close to death, there is no pain. So I lay there feeling cheated and mad — mad that not only was I going to die, but that this "no pain" stuff was just an old fairy tale. The worst part, though, was listening to the other wounded ones crying out for help. I was their doctor, but I couldn't even move a finger to help them.

I could only lie there and listen, and wonder who was hurt, and how badly. This was the worst.

The battle went on for a long time, but I don't know how long. I fainted off and on, but I lived through it. I woke up to the sound of someone whispering my name nearby, and I tossed some pebbles to attract their attention. Then I saw the anxious faces of my friends leaning over me, gentle hands pulling me upright, checking my body for other injuries. People had seen me go down and thought I had been shot through the head, so they were really happy to find me not only alive but conscious, as well. They hauled me away from the river back to a hiding place where the rest of the *compas* were waiting. . . .

It took us ten days to get out of the mountains. . . .

On the tenth day . . . we staggered into a small village. It was a Mayan community, but you must not tell the name. Can you believe that the entire village came running to help us? There we were, ragged, bloody, armed and in uniform, and they still took us in and cared for us, even though the army was searching for us everywhere. I collapsed completely as we arrived. My legs had kept moving for as long as they had to, but once we reached safety, I had nothing left. A gray-haired, old *campesino* picked me up and carried me into a hut. His wife cleared off the bed for me, and they dressed me in clean clothes and washed my wounded face. Then — I will always remember this — she fixed me a good, strong soup that I could drink through the IV tubes. It was my first real food in so many days. I swear that this soup saved my life. Mario came to the hut, too, and stayed with me until I was taken away to the city.

Everyone was taken in and hidden. For most of our *compas,* hiding was easy. Dressed in civilian clothes, they became the Mayan *campesinos* they had been before the war. No one would know they had not been born there. They rested and helped work in the fields, while the villagers took care of the wounded and brought us food and news about the army activities nearby. The villagers also smuggled messages for us to the capital to help us reconnect with another platoon and to arrange medical care for us. The entire village could have been wiped out for this, but no one ever spoke of us, no one ever gave us away. A community commitment had been made to take care of us, and that commitment was honored by every single villager. Few words were spoken, and they never asked for thanks or payment. To me, it is people like these who are the true heroes of this war. Even though you must not tell the name of this village, you must tell what these people gave to us, what they risked for us.

I think we were there for close to a month while arrangements were made. Mario had made contact with his brother, Alejo, in the capital, and I was to stay with him in one of our safe houses while I received medical treatment. Alejo was the older one, and had brought Mario into the movement. The two brothers were incredibly close. I was happy to think that I would have a chance to know him, but when the car came to take me away, it was very difficult. I knew what Mario was going back to, and that we would probably never see each other again. And in fact we never did. Maybe this part I will not talk about. I arrived safely in the capital, which was no small achievement given my marked face and all the army roadblocks. Alejo took me in and cared for me as his own sister.

I wish this story had a happier ending, but it doesn't. It was early 1982, when the terror in the capital was at its height. The *compas* in our urban front fought bravely to the very end, but they came close to extermination. In the mountains, you stand a chance, but in the city there was just too much surveillance, too many terrified informants trying to get their own family members out of torture cells. We had a number of houses in the capital, but we watched them fall, one by one. Sometimes it was on television, the footage of tanks and bazookas destroying a quiet, middle-class home on a tree-lined street. Sometimes it was in the papers. There were many pictures of the dead, our *compas,* sometimes shot to death, often tortured. We all knew that our time was not far off.

85

AUNG SAN SUU KYI

From *Letters from Burma*

The author of these letters heads the democratic political party that won election in Burma in 1980. In consequence, she was placed under house arrest by the brutal military junta (SLORC, for State Law and Order Restoration Council), which has continued to rule. Despite her receipt of the Nobel Prize in 1991 and continued devotional support from the Burmese people, the generals have refused to let this daughter of Aung San — Burma's national hero who was assassinated in 1947 just before Burma achieved independence — take office and sometimes even leave her house.

In these letters, written to a Japanese newspaper in 1996, Suu Kyi reveals an unusual combination of the personal and political, some might say the patriotic without the patriarchal. Is this a view of politics that a male politician would be unlikely to hold?

Aung San Suu Kyi, *Letters from Burma* (New York: Penguin, 1996), 19–21, 55–57.

Thinking Historically

Is there such a thing as women's politics? Do women vote differently than men? If so, what is that difference? Construct a theory that explains it.

Some people have pointed to the relatively large number of women presidents and prime ministers in South Asia in recent years. Women have been elected to govern India, Pakistan, Sri Lanka, as well as Burma. Can you formulate a theory that might explain this?

Many would say that particular women who have governed South Asia — Indira Gandhi of India, Benizar Bhutto of Pakistan, Sirimavo Bandaranaike of Sri Lanka — have not governed any differently than men. Perhaps politics has more to do with social background, interests, wealth, and class than it does with gender. Try to formulate a theory about women in politics that is based on the readings of this chapter.

The Peacock and the Dragon

The tenth day of the waning moon of the month of Tazaungdine marks National Day in Burma. It is the anniversary of the boycott against the 1920 Rangoon University Act which was seen by the Burmese as a move to restrict higher education to a privileged few. This boycott, which was initiated by university students, gained widespread support and could be said to have been the first step in the movement for an independent Burma. National Day is thus a symbol of the intimate and indissoluble link between political and intellectual freedom and of the vital role that students have played in the politics of Burma.

This year the seventy-fifth anniversary of National Day fell on 16 November. A committee headed by elder politicians and prominent men of letters was formed to plan the commemoration ceremony. It was decided that the celebrations should be on a modest scale in keeping with our financial resources and the economic situation of the country. The programme was very simple: some speeches, the presentation of prizes to those who had taken part in essay competitions organized by the National League for Democracy, and the playing of songs dating back to the days of the independence struggle. There was also a small exhibition of photographs, old books, and magazines.

An unseasonable rain had been falling for several days before the sixteenth but on the morning of National Day itself the weather turned out to be fine and dry. Many of the guests came clad in *pinni*, a hand-woven cotton cloth that ranges in colour from a flaxen beige through varying shades of apricot and orange to burnt umber. During the independence struggle *pinni* had acquired the same significance in Burma as *khaddi* in India, a symbol of patriotism and a practical sign of support for native goods.

Since 1988 it has also become the symbol of the movement for democracy. A *pinni* jacket worn with a white collarless shirt and a Kachin sarong (a tartan pattern in purple, black, and green) is the unofficial uniform for "democracy men." The dress for "democracy women" is a *pinni aingyi* (Burmese style blouse) with a traditional hand-woven sarong. During my campaign trip to the state of Kachin in 1989 I once drove through an area considered unsafe because it was within a zone where insurgents were known to be active. For mile upon mile men clad in *pinni* jackets on which the red badge of NLD [National League for Democracy] gleamed bravely stood as a "guard of honour" along the route, entirely unarmed. It was a proud and joyous sight.

The seventy-fifth anniversary of National Day brought a proud and joyous sight too. The guests were not all clad in *pinni* but there was about them a brightness that was pleasing to both the eye and the heart. The younger people were full of quiet enthusiasm and the older ones seemed rejuvenated. A well-known student politician of the 1930s who had become notorious in his mature years for the shapeless shirt, shabby denim trousers, scuffed shoes (gum boots during the monsoons), and battered hat in which he would tramp around town was suddenly transformed into a dapper gentleman in full Burmese national costume. All who knew him were stunned by the sudden picture of elegance he presented and our photographer hastened to record such an extraordinary vision.

The large bamboo and thatch pavilion that had been put up to receive the thousand guests was decorated with white banners on which were printed the green figure of a dancing peacock. As a backdrop to the stage there was a large dancing peacock, delicately executed on a white disc. This bird is the symbol of the students who first awoke the political consciousness of the people of Burma. It represents a national movement that culminated triumphantly with the independence of the country.

The orchestra had arrived a little late as there had been an attempt to try to "persuade" the musicians not to perform at our celebration. But their spirits were not dampened. They stayed on after the end of the official ceremony to play and sing nationalist songs from the old days. The most popular of these was *Nagani*, "Red Dragon." *Nagani* was the name of a book club founded by a group of young politicians in 1937 with the intention of making works on politics, economics, history, and literature accessible to the people of Burma. The name of the club became closely identified with patriotism and a song was written about the prosperity that would come to the country through the power of the Red Dragon.

Nagani was sung by a young man with a strong, beautiful voice and we all joined in the chorus while some of the guests went up on stage and performed Burmese dances. But beneath the light-hearted merriment ran a current of serious intent. The work of our national movement remains unfinished. We have still to achieve the prosperity promised by the dragon. It is not yet time for the triumphant dance of the peacock. . . .

A Baby in the Family

A couple of weeks ago some friends of mine became grandparents for the first time when their daughter gave birth to a little girl. The husband accepted his new status as grandfather with customary joviality, while the wife, too young-looking and pretty to get into the conventional idea of a cosily aged grandmother, found it a somewhat startling experience. The baby was the first grandchild for the "boy's side" as well, so she was truly a novel addition to the family circle, the subject of much adoring attention. I was told the paternal grandfather was especially pleased because the baby had been born in the Burmese month of *Pyatho* — an auspicious time for the birth of a girl child.

In societies where the birth of a girl is considered a disaster, the atmosphere of excitement and pride surrounding my friends' granddaughter would have caused astonishment. In Burma there is no prejudice against girl babies. In fact, there is a general belief that daughters are more dutiful and loving than sons and many Burmese parents welcome the birth of a daughter as an assurance that they will have somebody to take care of them in their old age.

My friends' granddaughter was only twelve days old when I went to admire her. She lay swaddled in pristine white on a comfortable pile of blankets and sheets spread on the wooden floor of my friends' bungalow, a small dome of mosquito netting arched prettily over her. It had been a long time since I had seen such a tiny baby and I was struck by its miniature perfection. I do not subscribe to the Wodehousian view that all babies look like poached eggs. Even if they do not have clearly defined features, babies have distinct expressions that mark them off as individuals from birth. And they certainly have individual cries, a fact I learned soon after the birth of my first son. It took me a few hours to realize that the yells of each tiny vociferous inmate of the maternity hospital had its own unique pitch, cadence, range, and grace-notes.

My friends' grandchild, however, did not provide me with a chance to familiarize myself with her particular milk call. Throughout my visit she remained as inanimate and still as a carved papoose on display in a museum, oblivious of the fuss and chatter around her. At one time her eyelids fluttered slightly and she showed signs of stirring but it was a false alarm. She remained resolutely asleep even when I picked her up and we all clustered around to have our photograph taken with the new star in our firmament.

Babies, I have read somewhere, are specially constructed to present an appealingly vulnerable appearance aimed at arousing tender, protective instincts: only then can tough adults be induced to act as willing slaves to demanding little beings utterly incapable of doing anything for themselves. It is claimed that there is something about the natural smell of a baby's skin that invites cuddles and kisses. Certainly I like both the shape and smell of babies, but I wonder whether their attraction does not lie in something more than merely physical attributes. Is it not the thought of a life stretching out like a shining clean slate on which might one day be written the most beautiful prose and poetry of existence that engenders such joy in the hearts of the parents and grandparents of a newly born child? The birth of a baby is an occasion for weaving hopeful dreams about the future.

However, in some families parents are not able to indulge in long dreams over their children. The infant mortality rate in Burma is 94 per 1000 live births, the fourth highest among the nations of the East Asia and Pacific Region. The mortality rate for those under the age of five too is the fourth highest in the region, 147 per 1000. And the maternal mortality rate is the third highest in the region at the official rate of 123 per 100 000 live births. (United Nations agencies surmise that the actual maternal mortality rate is in fact higher, 140 or more per 100 000.)

The reasons for these high mortality rates are malnutrition, lack of access to safe water and sanitation, lack of access to health services, and lack of caring capacity, which includes programmes for childhood development, primary education, and health education. In summary, there is a strong need in Burma for greater investment in health and education. Yet government expenditure in both sectors, as a proportion of the budget, has been falling steadily. Education accounted for 5.9 per cent of the budget in 1992–3, 5.2 per cent in 1993–4, and 5 per cent in 1994–5. Similarly, government spending on health care has dropped from 2.6 per cent in 1992–3, to 1.8 per cent in 1993–4, and 1.6 per cent in 1994–5.

Some of the best indicators of a country developing along the right lines are healthy mothers giving birth to healthy children who are assured of good care and a sound education that will enable them to face the challenges of a changing world. Our dreams for the future of the children of Burma have to be woven firmly around a commitment to better health care and better education.

REFLECTIONS

Can there be a history of women, even a history of women during the last half of the twentieth century? Or are the lives of women too diverse — globally, economically, politically, culturally — to make a single, coherent story? Is the history of women during the last fifty years markedly different from the history of men or the history of humanity?

This chapter gives only a hint of the diversity of women's lives. We included China's hopeful marriage law at the beginning of the chapter but nothing about the failures to observe it, or about women who were forced out of work to make room for men, or about girls who were sold into virtual slavery, or about young women forced to work long hours in sweatshops. Nor did we include any discussion of glamorous models in Shanghai, rich capitalists and poor sex workers in Hong Kong, or ordinary mothers, wives, and workers for whom the law of 1950 *did* make a difference.

While Betty Friedan verbalized the feelings of many American women in 1963, how many women today, exhausted by working long hours that barely cover the costs of child care and commuting, would consider returning to a fifties world of motherhood and housework? How can two African novelists speak for poor, illiterate, rural women in areas devastated by civil wars or AIDS? How important are national differences? In what sense, if any, does an Algerian woman who is Muslim speak for a Muslim woman in Egypt or Iran or Pakistan, or for a Christian woman in Algeria? We have not even considered women from the Middle East, India, Russia, and Europe.

These questions are not meant to be an exercise in what literary critics call "deconstructing the text"; rather, they are intended to point out the enormous variety of women's experiences. Of course, the historian is forever seeking patterns and process, but finding even the general direction of change is not as simple as it might seem.

Have the lives of women improved over the course of the last hundred or the last fifty years? It is commonly thought that the twentieth century was extremely important in freeing women from the bonds of patriarchal limitations. Often, this process is divided into two stages, the first consisting of gaining the vote in the early decades of the century in Europe and America, and the second, the successes of the women's movement since 1960. This second wave broadened the feminist critique from concerns about elections to issues of equality in the workplace and patriarchy as a social and cultural force, ultimately resulting in a cohesive movement, improved public awareness, and specific legislation regarding women's rights. In this way, the movement of the sixties became public policy.

Yet, this history belongs only to women from Europe and North America. Is it accurate for women from Asia, Africa, and Latin America? To a certain extent, ideas about equal rights and the rights of women that were first instituted in Europe and North America have surfaced in less prosperous regions of the world, sometimes through the pressure of international organizations or the persuasion of Western-trained elites. Still, adoption of Western ways has not always benefited women. As nations in Asia and Africa became independent after World War II, male-dominated political bureaucracies often replaced more informal networks that had previously given greater prominence to women. In some cases, as in Algeria, women were given full equality with men during the national struggle, but as soon as independence was won they were forced out of the public realm, domiciled and veiled, becoming mute signs of male authority.

For most women today, the world has been shaped less by political struggles and more by the expanding global market. Poor women in Brazil, Indonesia, China, and the Philippines have seized the opportunity to escape the authority of fathers and village elders to work in modern factories that pay far more than they ever imagined, but barely enough to survive in distant cities after sending money home. The victory of market forces in former "command economies," like Russia, Poland, and Lithuania (countries where most doctors were women), has been accompanied by drastic declines in the employment of women and men, as well as declines in the percentage of professional women.

If there is not a single history of women that is different from a single history of humanity, there are millions, indeed billions, of histories of women, women's acts, women's worlds. The selections in this chapter hint at just a few of those histories. Perhaps the most useful service our brief discussions here can serve is to encourage you to explore women's stories further. In your studies, branch off in different directions: Study women in Algeria, maybe Muslim women or women in Africa, for example.

All of the women featured in this chapter are writers. Assia Djebar and Carolina Maria de Jesus give us especially poignant accounts of what their writing means to them. You might study the ways in which women use their writing as witness, mirror, and tools. After rereading the selections in this chapter and contemplating the role of writing, you might formulate a theory about women and words, or the link between writing and women's liberation. You might also notice that in many of these selections women refer to their bodies or their appearance. After carefully rereading the selections and giving the topic some quiet contemplation, you might ask yourself whether men and women write differently. You might ask yourself any number of questions and begin to formulate new theories that will help improve your level of understanding.

14

Globalization

1960 to the Present

HISTORICAL CONTEXT

Globalization is a term used by historians, economists, politicians, religious leaders, social reformers, business people, and average citizens to describe large-scale changes and trends in the world today. It is often defined as a complex phenomenon whereby individuals, nations, and regions of the world become increasingly integrated and interdependent, and national and traditional identities are diminished. Although it is a widely used term, globalization is also a controversial and widely debated topic. Is globalization really a new phenomenon or is it a continuation of earlier trends? Is it driven by technological forces or economic forces, or both? Does it enrich or impoverish? Is it democratizing or antidemocratic? Is it generally a positive or negative thing?

Some limit the definition of globalization to the global integration driven by the development of the international market economy in the last twenty to forty years. Worldwide integration dates back much further, however, and has important technological, cultural, and political causes as well. In fact, all of human history can be understood as the story of increased interaction on a limited planet. Ancient empires brought diverse peoples from vast regions of the world together under single administrations. These empires, connected by land or maritime routes, interacted with each other through trade and exploration, exchanging goods as well as ideas. The unification of the Eastern and Western hemispheres after 1492 was a major step in the globalization of crops, peoples, cultures, and diseases. The industrial revolution joined countries and continents in ever vaster and faster transportation and communication networks. The great colonial empires that developed during the eighteenth and nineteenth centuries integrated the populations of far-flung areas of the world. The commercial aspects of these developments cannot be divorced from religious zeal, technological innovations, and political motives, which were often driving factors.

The current era of economic globalization is largely a product of the industrial capitalist world, roughly dating back to the middle of the nineteenth century. We might call the period between 1850 and 1914 the first great age of globalization in the modern sense. It was the age of ocean liners, mass migrations, undersea telegraph cables, transcontinental railroads, refrigeration, and preserved canned foods, when huge European empires dramatically reduced the number of sovereign states in the world. The period ended with World War I, which not only dug trenches between nations and wiped out a generation of future migrants and visitors, but also planted seeds of animosity that festered for decades, strangling the growth of international trade, interaction, and immigration.

Since the conclusion of World War II in 1945, and increasingly since the end of the Cold War in 1989, political and technological developments have enabled economic globalization on a wider scale and at a faster pace than occurred during the previous age of steamships and telegraphs. The collapse of the Soviet Union and international communism unleashed the forces of market capitalism as never before. Jet travel, satellite technology, mobile phones, and the World Wide Web have revived global integration and enabled the global marketplace. The United States, the World Bank, and the International Monetary Fund led in the creation of regional and international free-trade agreements, the reduction of tariffs, and the removal of national trade barriers, touting these changes as agents of material progress and democratic transformation.

Multinational companies are now able to generate great wealth by moving capital, labor, raw materials, and finished products through international markets at increasing speeds and with lasting impact. This economic globalization has profound cultural ramifications; increasingly the peoples of the world are watching the same films and television programs, speaking the same languages, wearing the same clothes, enjoying the same amusements, and listening to the same music. Whether free-market capitalism lifts all boats, or only yachts, is a hotly debated issue today. The first selection in this chapter is a proglobalization advertisement from Exxon/Mobil that touts the importance and advantage of training tomorrow's young people to compete in the market economy. In the second selection Sherif Hetata derides the mass materialism that he sees sweeping his native Egypt as a type of cultural imperialism. Philippe Legrain counters Hetata by arguing that cultural globalization is a rich exchange among cultures, and not a process of homogenization. Globalization has produced mixed results in the lives of ordinary workers around the world, as seen in a selection by Miriam Ching Yoon Louie that explores the unique and universal struggles faced by Mexican women working in transnational factories.

While some debate the positive and negative aspects of economic and cultural globalization, Benjamin Barber argues that globalization not only creates a unified world of consumers; it also reinforces "tribal" identities and stokes nationalistic grievances. Mark Juergens-meyer explores such tendencies in religious fundamentalist movements that rail against the amorality of the global marketplace.

The images of the global environment included in the chapter re-mind us that we all share one planet and its resources. The modern world is lit, driven, and warmed by fossil fuels — coal, gas, and oil — a legacy hundreds of millions years old. But these images also show that the earth's inheritance is not shared equally, either among, or within, nations. What does globalization mean for rich and poor, north and south, industrial and agricultural, rural and urban, coast and interior, island and continent, sea-level and mountainous areas? Does globaliza-tion create one world, or two, or many?

We conclude the chapter with two pieces that address the effect the terrorist attacks of September 11, 2001, have had in reshaping the global order. As the single superpower in the world since the collapse of the Soviet Union, the United States has become the principal propo-nent and symbol of global integration, for good or ill.

THINKING HISTORICALLY
Understanding Process

What are the most important ways in which the world is changing? What are the most significant and powerful forces of change? What is the engine that is driving our world? These are the big questions raised at the end of historical investigation. They also arise at the beginning, as the assumptions that shape our specific investigations. Globalization is one of the words most frequently used to describe the big changes that are occurring in our world. All of the readings in this chapter as-sume or describe some kind of global integration as a dominant driver of the world in which we live. This chapter asks you to think about large-scale historical processes. It asks you to examine globalization as one of the most important of these processes. It asks you to reflect on what globalization means, and what causes it. How does each of these authors use the term? Do the authors see this process as primarily com-mercial and market-driven, or do they view it as a matter of culture or politics? Does globalization come from one place or many, from a cen-ter outwards, from one kind of society to another? Is globalization lin-ear or unidirectional, or does it have differing, even opposite effects? What do these writers, thinkers, and activists believe about the most important changes transforming our world? And what do you think?

86

EXXONMOBIL CORPORATION

Free Markets and the Global Classroom

Like many international corporations, ExxonMobil takes an active interest in public issues, expressing corporate positions in paid newspaper advertisements. The following Exxon advertisement, from December 2002, applauds the advances of economic globalization and praises a worldwide education program that supports the development of the global marketplace. What do you think the company hopes to accomplish with this advertisement? Who might be the target audience? What would be the advantage of preparing future generations to be "workforce-ready and savvy about free enterprise"?

Thinking Historically

This advertisement presents an interpretation of the way the world is changing. According to the advertisement, what have been the main drivers of global change over the last two decades? What have been the effects of these developments? What stake does ExxonMobil hold in furthering these developments? What does the company propose to do to aid this process?

One of the most impressive trends of the past two decades has been the expansion of international trade. Economic globalization is a market-driven phenomenon accelerated by advances in technology.

But economic restructuring and the transition to open markets in former state-dominated economies have produced uneven results. In some of these countries corruption has undermined progress while underground markets flourish.

The extent to which economic reforms work will depend almost entirely on whether a country's young people understand how open markets function and whether they gain the skills they need to succeed.

A worldwide educational initiative, spearheaded by Junior Achievement (JA), is helping to do just that. Its objective is to reach 10 million students annually by 2005, and a total of at least 100 million over the next two decades.

Founded in the United States in 1919, Junior Achievement is the world's oldest and largest nonprofit economic education organization.

JA's time-tested programs provide the education and practical skills that can empower future generations to be workforce-ready and savvy about free enterprise in a global economy. Its classroom delivery network includes business volunteers who teach economics and business skills. JA courses today reach 6.2 million young people annually in 36 languages and are adapted to reflect cultural norms in the 112 countries that have welcomed Junior Achievement. In Russia alone more than 350,000 students will participate in programs this year.

JA programs are primarily designed for grades K-12 and range from board games for elementary schools to simulated companies for older students. The GLOBE program for high school students, for example, is a cross-border initiative in which students from different countries form a company, develop a product to manufacture and market, hire staff, elect officers, sell stock, distribute dividends, and eventually liquidate the company. By the time students complete the course they have an excellent understanding of business plans, marketing strategies, tariffs, and taxation systems.

Emerging markets and restructured economies will only succeed if today's young people understand the importance of openness, honesty, and ethical behavior as key contributors to economic success.

The door to that understanding is education. Junior Achievement provides access to the knowledge, tools, and skills that will enable students everywhere to prosper under free markets.

87

SHERIF HETATA

Dollarization

Sherif Hetata is an Egyptian intellectual, novelist, and activist who was originally trained as a medical doctor. He and his wife, the famous feminist writer Nawal El-Saadawi, have worked together to promote reform in Egypt and the larger Arab world. In the following address Hetata outlines the global economy's homogenizing effects on

---

Sherif Hetata, "Dollarization, Fragmentation, and God," in *The Cultures of Globalization,* ed. Fredric Jameson and Masao Miyoshi (Durham: Duke University Press, 1998), 273–74, 276–80.

culture. Through what historic lens does Hetata view globalization? What links does he make between globalization and imperialism? What do you think of his argument?

Thinking Historically

What, according to Hetata, is the main process that is changing the world? Has it changed since his youth, or is the same force of change becoming stronger? What is the likely outcome of the changes that he describes? What critique might Hetata have of the ExxonMobil statement in the previous selection?

As a young medical student, born and brought up in a colony, like many other people in my country, Egypt, I quickly learned to make the link between politics, economics, culture, and religion. Educated in an English school, I discovered that my English teachers looked down on us. We learned Rudyard Kipling by heart, praised the glories of the British Empire, followed the adventures of Kim in India, imbibed the culture of British supremacy, and sang carols on Christmas night.

At the medical school in university, when students demonstrated against occupation by British troops it was the Moslem Brothers who beat them up, using iron chains and long curved knives, and it was the governments supported by the king that shot at them or locked them up.

When I graduated in 1946, the hospital wards taught me how poverty and health are linked. I needed only another step to know that poverty had something to do with colonial rule, with the king who supported it, with class and race, with what was called imperialism at the time, with cotton prices falling on the market, with the seizure of land by foreign banks. These things were common talk in family gatherings, expressed in a simple, colorful language without frills. They were the facts of everyday life. We did not need to read books to make the links: They were there for us to see and grasp. And every time we made a link, someone told us it was time to stop, someone in authority whom we did not like: a ruler or a father, a policeman or a teacher, a landowner, a *maulana* (religious leader or teacher), a Jesuit, or a God.

And if we went on making these links, they locked us up.

For me, therefore, coming from this background, cultural studies and globalization open up a vast horizon, one of global links in a world where things are changing quickly. It is a chance to learn and probe how the economics, the politics, the culture, the philosophical thought of our days connect or disconnect, harmonize or contradict.

Of course, I will not even try to deal with all of that. I just want to raise a few points to discuss under the title of my talk, "Dollarization,

Fragmentation, and God." Because I come from Egypt, my vantage point will be that of someone looking at the globe from the part we now call South, rather than "third world" or something else.

A New Economic Order: Gazing North at the Global Few

Never before in the history of the world has there been such a concentration and centralization of capital in so few nations and in the hands of so few people. The countries that form the Group of Seven, with their 800 million inhabitants, control more technological, economic, informatics, and military power than the rest of the approximately 430 billion who live in Asia, Africa, Eastern Europe, and Latin America.

Five hundred multinational corporations account for 80 percent of world trade and 75 percent of investment. Half of all the multinational corporations are based in the United States, Germany, Japan, and Switzerland. The OECD (Organization for Economic Cooperation and Development) group of countries contributes 80 percent of world production. . . .

A Global Culture for a Global Market

To expand the world market, to globalize it, to maintain the New Economic Order, the multinational corporations use economic power and control politics and the armed forces. But this is not so easy. People will always resist being exploited, resist injustice, struggle for their freedom, their needs, security, a better life, peace.

However, it becomes easier if they can be convinced to do what the masters of the global economy want them to do. This is where the issue of culture comes in. Culture can serve in different ways to help the global economy reach out all over the world and expand its markets to the most distant regions. Culture can also serve to reduce or destroy or prevent or divide or outflank the resistance of people who do not like what is happening to them, or have their doubts about it, or want to think. Culture can be like cocaine, which is going global these days: from Kali in Columbia to Texas, to Madrid, to the Italian mafiosi in southern Italy, to Moscow, Burma, and Thailand, a worldwide network uses the methods and the cover of big business, with a total trade of $5 billion a year, midway between oil and the arms trade.

At the disposal of global culture today are powerful means that function across the whole world: the media, which, like the economy, have made it one world, a bipolar North/South world. If genetic engineering gives scientists the possibility of programming embryos before

children are born, children, youth, and adults are now being pro-
grammed after they are born in the culture they imbibe mainly through
the media, but also in the family, in school, at the university, and elsewhere. Is this an exaggeration? an excessively gloomy picture of the
world?

To expand the global market, increase the number of consumers,
make sure that they buy what is sold, develop needs that conform to
what is produced, and develop the fever of consumerism, culture must
play a role in developing certain values, patterns of behavior, visions of
what is happiness and success in the world, attitudes toward sex and
love. Culture must model a global consumer.

In some ways, I was a "conservative radical." I went to jail, but I
always dressed in a classical, subdued way. When my son started wearing blue jeans and New Balance shoes, I shivered with horror. He's
going to become like some of those crazy kids abroad, the disco generation, I thought! Until the age of twenty-five he adamantly refused to
smoke. Now he smokes two packs of Marlboros a day (the ones that
the macho cowboy smokes). That does not prevent him from being a
talented film director. But in the third-world, films, TV, and other
media have increased the percentage of smokers. I saw half-starved kids
in a markeplace in Mali buying single imported Benson & Hedges cigarettes and smoking.

But worse was still to come. Something happened that to me
seemed impossible at one time, more difficult than adhering to a left-
wing movement. At the age of seventy-one, I have taken to wearing
blue jeans and Nike shoes. I listen to rock and reggae and sometimes
rap. I like to go to discos and I sometimes have other cravings, which so
far I have successfully fought! And I know these things have crept into
our lives through the media, through TV, films, radio, advertisements,
newspapers, and even novels, music, and poetry. It's a culture and it's
reaching out, becoming global.

In my village, I have a friend. He is a peasant and we are very close.
He lives in a big mud hut, and the animals (buffalo, sheep, cows, and
donkeys) live in the house with him. Altogether, in the household, with
the wife and children of his brother, his uncle, the mother, and his own
family, there are thirty people. He wears a long *galabeya* (robe), works
in the fields for long hours, and eats food cooked in the mud oven.

But when he married, he rode around the village in a hired Peugeot
car with his bride. She wore a white wedding dress, her face was made
up like a film star, her hair curled at the hairdresser's of the provincial
town, her finger and toe nails manicured and polished, and her body
bathed with special soap and perfumed. At the marriage ceremony,
they had a wedding cake, which she cut with her husband's hand over
hers. Very different from the customary rural marriage ceremony of
his father. And all this change in the notion of beauty, of femininity, of

celebration, of happiness, of prestige, of progress happened to my peasant friend and his bride in one generation.

The culprit, or the benevolent agent, depending on how you see it, was television.

In the past years, television has been the subject of numerous studies. In France, such studies have shown that before the age of twelve a child will have been exposed to an average 100,000 TV advertisements. Through these TV advertisements, the young boy or girl will have assimilated a whole set of values and behavioral patterns, of which he or she is not aware, of course. They become a part of his or her psychological (emotional and mental) makeup. Linked to these values are the norms and ways in which we see good and evil, beauty and ugliness, justice and injustice, truth and falseness, and which are being propagated at the same time. In other words, the fundamental values that form our aesthetic and moral vision of things are being inculcated, even hammered home, at this early stage, and they remain almost unchanged throughout life.

The commercial media no longer worry about the truthfulness or falsity of what they portray. Their role is to sell: beauty products, for example, to propagate the "beauty myth" and a "beauty culture" for both females and males alike and ensure that it reaches the farthest corners of the earth, including my village in the Delta of the Nile. Many of these beauty products are harmful to the health, can cause allergic disorders or skin infections or even worse. They cost money, work on the sex drives, and transform women and men, but especially women, into sex objects. They hide the real person, the natural beauty, the process of time, the stages of life, and instill false values about who we are, can be, or should become.

Advertisements do not depend on verifiable information or even rational thinking. They depend for their effect on images, colors, smart technical production, associations, and hidden drives. For them, attracting the opposite sex or social success or professional achievement and promotion or happiness do not depend on truthfulness or hard work or character, but rather on seduction, having a powerful car, buying things or people. . . .

Thus the media produce and reproduce the culture of consumption, of violence and sex to ensure that the global economic powers, the multinational corporations can promote a global market for themselves and protect it. And when everything is being bought or sold everyday and at all times in this vast supermarket, including culture, art, science, and thought, prostitution can become a way of life, for everything is priced. The search for the immediate need, the fleeting pleasure, the quick enjoyment, the commodity to buy, excess, pornography, drugs keeps this global economy rolling, for to stop is suicide.

88

PHILIPPE LEGRAIN

Cultural Globalization Is Not Americanization

Philippe Legrain, an economist, journalist, and former advisor to the
World Trade Organization, takes aim at what he calls the myths of
globalization in the following article. He argues that globalization
brings cultural enrichment, not monotonous conformity, and that the
intermixing of cultures is an old story with many happy results. What
do you think of his argument? How might Sherif Hetata respond to it?

Thinking Historically

Does the author believe the driving force of globalization is economic
or cultural? How important does he think globalization is? How, according to the author, is globalization changing the world? What examples does he cite? How does Legrain's view of America differ from
Hetata's?

Fears that globalization is imposing a deadening cultural uniformity
are as ubiquitous as Coca-Cola, McDonald's, and Mickey Mouse. Europeans and Latin Americans, left-wingers and right, rich and poor —
all of them dread that local cultures and national identities are dissolv-
ing into a crass All-American consumerism. That cultural imperialism
is said to impose American values as well as products, promote the
commercial at the expense of the authentic, and substitute shallow gratification for deeper satisfaction.

. . . If critics of globalization were less obsessed with "Coca-
colonization," they might notice a rich feast of cultural mixing that belies fears about Americanized uniformity. Algerians in Paris practice
Thai boxing; Asian rappers in London snack on Turkish pizza; Salman
Rushdie delights readers everywhere with his Anglo-Indian tales. Although — as with any change — there can be downsides to cultural
globalization, this cross-fertilization is overwhelmingly a force for good.

The beauty of globalization is that it can free people from the
tyranny of geography. Just because someone was born in France does
not mean they can only aspire to speak French, eat French food, read

Philippe Legrain, "Cultural Globalization Is Not Americanization," *The Chronicle of Higher
Education,* 49, no. 35 (May 9, 2003): B7.

French books, visit museums in France, and so on. A Frenchman — or an American, for that matter — can take holidays in Spain or Florida, eat sushi or spaghetti for dinner, drink Coke or Chilean wine, watch a Hollywood blockbuster or an Almodóvar, listen to bhangra or rap, practice yoga or kickboxing, read *Elle* or *The Economist,* and have friends from around the world. That we are increasingly free to choose our cultural experiences enriches our lives immeasurably. We could not always enjoy the best the world has to offer.

Globalization not only increases individual freedom, but also revitalizes cultures and cultural artifacts through foreign influences, technologies, and markets. Thriving cultures are not set in stone. They are forever changing from within and without. Each generation challenges the previous one; science and technology alter the way we see ourselves and the world; fashions come and go; experience and events influence our beliefs; outsiders affect us for good and ill.

Many of the best things come from cultures mixing: V. S. Naipaul's Anglo-Indo-Caribbean writing, Paul Gauguin painting in Polynesia, or the African rhythms in rock 'n' roll. Behold the great British curry. Admire the many-colored faces of France's World Cup–winning soccer team, the ferment of ideas that came from Eastern Europe's Jewish diaspora, and the cosmopolitan cities of London and New York. Western numbers are actually Arabic; zero comes most recently from India; Icelandic, French, and Sanskrit stem from a common root.

John Stuart Mill was right: "The economical benefits of commerce are surpassed in importance by those of its effects which are intellectual and moral. It is hardly possible to overrate the value, for the improvement of human beings, of things which bring them into contact with persons dissimilar to themselves, and with modes of thought and action unlike those with which they are familiar. . . . It is indispensable to be perpetually comparing [one's] own notions and customs with the experience and example of persons in different circumstances. . . . There is no nation which does not need to borrow from others."

It is a myth that globalization involves the imposition of Americanized uniformity, rather than an explosion of cultural exchange. For a start, many archetypal "American" products are not as all-American as they seem. Levi Strauss, a German immigrant, invented jeans by combining denim cloth (or "serge de Nîmes," because it was traditionally woven in the French town) with Genes, a style of trousers worn by Genoese sailors. So Levi's jeans are in fact an American twist on a European hybrid. Even quintessentially American exports are often tailored to local tastes. MTV in Asia promotes Thai pop stars and plays rock music sung in Mandarin. CNN en Español offers a Latin American take on world news. McDonald's sells beer in France, lamb in India, and chili in Mexico.

In some ways, America is an outlier, not a global leader. Most of the world has adopted the metric system born from the French Revolution; America persists with antiquated measurements inherited from its British-colonial past. Most developed countries have become intensely secular, but many Americans burn with fundamentalist fervor — like Muslims in the Middle East. Where else in the developed world could there be a serious debate about teaching kids Bible-inspired "creationism" instead of Darwinist evolution?

America's tastes in sports are often idiosyncratic, too. Baseball and American football have not traveled well, although basketball has fared rather better. Many of the world's most popular sports, notably soccer, came by way of Britain. Asian martial arts — judo, karate, kickboxing — and pastimes like yoga have also swept the world.

People are not only guzzling hamburgers and Coke. Despite Coke's ambition of displacing water as the world's drink of choice, it accounts for less than 2 of the 64 fluid ounces that the typical person drinks a day. Britain's favorite takeaway is a curry, not a burger: Indian restaurants there outnumber McDonald's six to one. For all the concerns about American fast food trashing France's culinary traditions, France imported a mere $620 million in food from the United States in 2000, while exporting to America three times that. Nor is plonk[1] from America's Gallo displacing Europe's finest: Italy and France together account for three-fifths of global wine exports, the United States for only a twentieth. Worldwide, pizzas are more popular than burgers, Chinese restaurants seem to sprout up everywhere, and sushi is spreading fast. By far the biggest purveyor of alcoholic drinks is Britain's Diageo, which sells the world's best-selling whiskey (Johnnie Walker), gin (Gordon's), vodka (Smirnoff), and liqueur (Baileys).

In fashion, the ne plus ultra is Italian or French. Trendy Americans wear Gucci, Armani, Versace, Chanel, and Hermès. On the high street and in the mall, Sweden's Hennes & Mauritz (H&M) and Spain's Zara vie with America's Gap to dress the global masses. Nike shoes are given a run for their money by Germany's Adidas, Britain's Reebok, and Italy's Fila.

In pop music, American crooners do not have the stage to themselves. The three artists who were featured most widely in national Top Ten album charts in 2000 were America's Britney Spears, closely followed by Mexico's Carlos Santana and the British Beatles. Even tiny Iceland has produced a global star: Björk. Popular opera's biggest singers are Italy's Luciano Pavarotti, Spain's José Carreras, and the Spanish-Mexican Placido Domingo. Latin American salsa, Brazilian lambada, and African music have all carved out global niches for themselves. In most countries, local artists still top the charts. According to

---

[1]British slang for cheap, low-quality alcohol. [Ed.]

the IFPI, the record-industry, bible, local acts accounted for 68 percent of music sales in 2000, up from 58 percent in 1991.

One of the most famous living writers is a Columbian, Gabriel García Márquez, author of *One Hundred Years of Solitude*. Paulo Coelho, another writer who has notched up tens of millions of global sales with *The Alchemist* and other books, is Brazilian. More than 200 million Harlequin romance novels, a Canadian export, were sold in 1990; they account for two-fifths of mass-market paperback sales in the United States. The biggest publisher in the English-speaking world is Germany's Bertelsmann, which gobbled up America's largest, Random House, in 1998.

Local fare glues more eyeballs to TV screens than American programs. Although nearly three-quarters of television drama exported worldwide comes from the United States, most countries' favorite shows are homegrown.

Nor are Americans the only players in the global media industry. Of the seven market leaders that have their fingers in nearly every pie, four are American (AOL Time Warner, Disney, Viacom, and News Corporation), one is German (Bertelsmann), one is French (Vivendi), and one Japanese (Sony). What they distribute comes from all quarters: Bertelsmann publishes books by American writers; News Corporation broadcasts Asian news; Sony sells Brazilian music.

The evidence is overwhelming. Fears about an Americanized uniformity are over-blown: American cultural products are not uniquely dominant; local ones are alive and well.

89

MIRIAM CHING YOON LOUIE

From *Sweatshop Warriors: Immigrant Women Workers Take On the Global Factory*

Sherif Hetata and Philippe Legrain highlight the impact of globalization on consumers, but it is also important to examine how it affects workers. Free-trade policies have removed barriers to international trade, with global consequences. An example of such change can be witnessed along the border between Mexico and the United States, es-

---

Miriam Ching Yoon Louie, *Sweatshop Warriors: Immigrant Women Workers Take On the Global Factory* (Cambridge, MA: South End Press, 2001), 65–71, 87–89.

pecially in the export factories, or *maquiladoras*, that are run by international corporations on both the U.S. and Mexican side of the border. In the following excerpt, Miriam Ching Yoon Louie, a writer and activist, interviews Mexican women who work in these factories and explores both the challenges they face and the strength they show in overcoming these challenges. What is the impact of liberalized trade laws on women who work in the *maquiladoras*? What is neoliberalism and how is it tied to globalization? Why are women particularly vulnerable to these policies?

Thinking Historically

According to Louie, how far back do neoliberalism and economic globalization date? How does Louie's assessment of economic globalization differ from the views expressed in the ExxonMobil advertisement? Would Junior Achievement programs provide effective solutions to the problems faced by the *maquiladora* workers?

Many of today's *nuevas revolucionarias* started working on the global assembly line as young women in northern Mexico for foreign transnational corporations. Some women worked on the U.S. side as "commuters" before they moved across the border with their families. Their stories reveal the length, complexity, and interpenetration of the U.S. and Mexican economies, labor markets, histories, cultures, and race relations. The women talk about the devastating impact of globalization, including massive layoffs and the spread of sweatshops on both sides of the border. *Las mujeres* recount what drove them to join and lead movements for economic, racial, and gender justice, as well as the challenges they faced within their families and communities to assert their basic human rights. . . .

Growing Up Female and Poor

Mexican women and girls were traditionally expected to do all the cooking, cleaning, and serving for their husbands, brothers, and sons. For girls from poor families, shouldering these domestic responsibilities proved doubly difficult because they also performed farm, sweatshop, or domestic service work simultaneously. . . .

Petra Mata, a former seamstress for Levi's whose mother died shortly after childbirth, recalls the heavy housework she did as the only daughter:

> Aiyeee, let me tell you! It was very hard. In those times in Mexico, I was raised with the ideal that you have to learn to do everything — cook, make tortillas, wash your clothes, and clean the house — just the

way they wanted you to. My grandparents were very strict. I always
had to ask their permission and then let them tell me what to do. I was
not a free woman. Life was hard for me. I didn't have much of a childhood; I started working when I was 12 or 13 years old.

Neoliberalism and Creeping Maquiladorization

These women came of age during a period of major change in the relationship between the Mexican and U.S. economies. Like Puerto Rico,
Hong Kong, South Korea, Taiwan, Malaysia, Singapore, and the
Philippines, northern Mexico served as one of the first stations of the
global assembly line tapping young women's labor. In 1965 the Mexican government initiated the Border Industrialization Program (BIP)
that set up export plants, called *maquiladoras* or *maquilas,* which were
either the direct subsidiaries or subcontractors of transnational corporations. Mexican government incentives to U.S. and other foreign investors included low wages and high productivity; infrastructure; proximity to U.S. markets, facilities, and lifestyles; tariff loopholes; and
pliant, pro-government unions. . . .

Describing her quarter-century-long sewing career in Mexico, Ce-
leste Jiménez ticks off the names of famous U.S. manufacturers who
hopped over the border to take advantage of cheap wages:

> I sewed for twenty-four years when I lived in Chihuahua in big name
> factories like Billy the Kid, Levi Strauss, and Lee *maquiladoras.* Every-
> one was down there. Here a company might sell under the brand name
> of Lee; there in Mexico it would be called Blanca García.

Transnational exploitation of women's labor was part of a broader
set of policies that critical opposition movements in the Third World
have dubbed "neoliberalism," i.e., the new version of the British Liberal Party's program of laissez faire capitalism espoused by the rising
European and U.S. colonial powers during the late eighteenth and nineteenth centuries. The Western powers, Japan, and international financial institutions like the World Bank and International Monetary Fund
have aggressively promoted neoliberal policies since the 1970s. Mexico
served as an early testing ground for such standard neoliberal policies
as erection of free trade zones; commercialization of agriculture; currency devaluation; deregulation; privatization; outsourcing; cuts in
wages and social programs; suppression of workers', women's, and indigenous people's rights; free trade; militarization; and promotion of
neoconservative ideology.

Neoliberalism intersects with gender and national oppression.
Third World women constitute the majority of migrants seeking jobs
as maids, vendors, maquila operatives, and service industry workers.

Women also pay the highest price for cuts in education, health and housing programs, and food and energy subsidies and increases in their unpaid labor. . . .

The deepening of the economic crisis in Mexico, especially under the International Monetary Fund's pressure to devaluate the peso in 1976, 1982, and 1994, forced many women to work in both the formal and informal economy to survive and meet their childbearing and household responsibilities. María Antonia Flores was forced to work two jobs after her husband abandoned the family, leaving her with three children to support. She had no choice but to leave her children home alone, *solitos,* to look after themselves. Refugio Arrieta straddled the formal and informal economy because her job in an auto parts assembly *maquiladora* failed to bring in sufficient income. To compensate for the shortfall, she worked longer hours at her *maquila* job and "moonlighted" elsewhere:

> We made chassis for cars and for the headlights. I worked lots! I worked 12 hours more or less because they paid us so little that if you worked more, you got more money. I did this because the schools in Mexico don't provide everything. You have to buy the books, notebooks, *todos, todos* [everything]. And I had five kids. It's very expensive. I also worked out of my house and sold ceramics. I did many things to get more money for my kids.

In the three decades following its humble beginnings in the mid-1960s, the *maquila* sector swelled to more than 2,000 plants employing an estimated 776,000 people, over 10 percent of Mexico's labor force. In 1985, *maquiladoras* overtook tourism as the largest source of foreign exchange. In 1996, this sector trailed only petroleum-related industries in economic importance and accounted for over U.S. $29 billion in export earnings annually. The *maquila* system has also penetrated the interior of the country, as in the case of Guadalajara's electronics assembly industry and Tehuacán's jeans production zones. Although the proportion of male *maquila* workers has increased since 1983, especially in auto-transport equipment assembly, almost 70 percent of the workers continue to be women.

As part of a delegation of labor and human rights activists, this author met some of Mexico's newest proletarians — young indigenous women migrant workers from the Sierra Negra to Tehuacán, a town famous for its refreshing mineral water springs in the state of Puebla, just southeast of Mexico City. Standing packed like cattle in the back of the trucks each morning the women headed for jobs sewing for name brand manufacturers like Guess?, VF Corporation (producing Lee brand clothing), Gap, Sun Apparel (producing brands such as Polo, Arizona, and Express), Cherokee, Ditto Apparel of California, Levi's, and others. The workers told U.S. delegation members that their wages averaged U.S. $30 to $50 a week for 12-hour work days, six days a week. Some workers reported having to do *veladas* [all-nighters] once or twice a week. Employees often stayed longer without pay if they did not finish high production goals.

Girls as young as 12 and 13 worked in the factories. Workers were searched when they left for lunch and again at the end of the day to check that they weren't stealing materials. Women were routinely given urine tests when hired and those found to be pregnant were promptly fired, in violation of Mexican labor law. Although the workers had organized an independent union several years earlier, Tehuacán's Human Rights Commission members told us that it had collapsed after one of its leaders was assassinated.

Carmen Valadez and Reyna Montero, long-time activists in the women's and social justice movements, helped found Casa de La Mujer Factor X in 1977, a workers' center in Tijuana that organizes around women's workplace, reproductive, and health rights, and against domestic violence. Valadez and Montero say that the low wages and dangerous working conditions characteristic of the *maquiladoras* on the Mexico-U.S. border are being "extended to all areas of the country and to Central America and the Caribbean. NAFTA represents nothing but the *'maquiladorization'* of the region."

Elizabeth "Beti" Robles Ortega, who began working in the *maquilas* at the age of fourteen and was blacklisted after participating in independent union organizing drives on Mexico's northern border, now works as an organizer for the Servicio, Desarrollo y Paz, AC (SEDEPAC) [Service, Development and Peace organization]. Robles described the erosion of workers rights and women's health under NAFTA:

> NAFTA has led to an increase in the workforce, as foreign industry has grown. They are reforming labor laws and our constitution to favor even more foreign investment, which is unfair against our labor rights. For example, they are now trying to take away from us free organization which was guaranteed by Mexican law. Because foreign capital is investing in Mexico and is dominating, we must have guarantees. The government is just there with its hands held out; it's always had them out but now even more shamelessly. . . . Ecological problems are increasing. A majority of women are coming down with cancer — skin and breast cancer, leukemia, and lung and heart problems. There are daily deaths of worker women. You can see and feel the contamination of the water and the air. As soon as you arrive and start breathing the air in Acuña and Piedras Negras [border cities between the states of Coahuila and Texas], you sense the heavy air, making you feel like vomiting.

. . .

Joining the Movement

Much of the education and leadership training the women received took place "on the job." The women talked about how much their participation in the movement had changed them. They learned how to analyze working conditions and social problems, who was responsible for these conditions, and what workers could do to get justice. They learned to speak truth to power, whether this was to government representatives, corporate management, the media, unions, or co-ethnic gatekeepers. They built relations with different kinds of sectors and groups and organized a wide variety of educational activities and actions. Their activism expanded their world view beyond that of their immediate families to seeing themselves as part of peoples' movements fighting for justice. . . .

. . . Through her participation in the movement, [María del Carmen Domínguez] developed her skills, leadership, and awareness:

> When I stayed at work in the factory, I was only thinking of myself and how am I going to support my family — nothing more, nothing less. And I served my husband and my son, my girl. But when I started working with La Mujer Obrera I thought, "I need more respect for myself. We need more respect for ourselves." (laughs) . . .
>
> . . . I learned about the law and I learned how to organize classes with people, whether they were men or women like me.

90

BENJAMIN BARBER

From *Jihad vs. McWorld*

Not everyone views the world as coming together, for better or worse, under the umbrella of globalization. Benjamin Barber, a political scientist, uses the terms *Jihad* and *McWorld* to refer to what he sees as the two poles of the modern global system. *McWorld* is the force of Hollywood, fast-food outlets, jeans, and Americanization. *Jihad* (the Arab word for "struggle") is used to symbolize all the nationalist, fundamentalist, ethnocentric, and tribal rejections of McWorld.

Benjamin Barber, *Jihad vs. McWorld: How Globalism and Tribalism Are Reshaping the World* (New York: Ballantine, 1995), 3–8.

Barber's argument is that these forces have largely shaped modern culture and that despite their opposition to each other, they both prevent the development of civic society and democracy: Jihad by terrorist opposition to discussion and debate, and McWorld by turning everyone into complacent, unthinking robots. What do you think of his argument? Is it persuasive? What sort of future does he predict?

Thinking Historically

Barber argues that Jihad originated in opposition to McWorld and that the two play off each other in a way that gives them both substance and support. Jihad thrives on the insensitivity, blandness, and oppression of McWorld; McWorld needs ethnic realities to give substance and soul to its theme parks and entertainments. Thus, according to Barber, they make each other stronger by struggling against each other. The gains of these two extreme positions come at the expense of a genuine, democratic civic culture. How useful is Barber's model for understanding the world today? How does it relate to globalization?

History is not over. Nor are we arrived in the wondrous land of techné[1] promised by the futurologists. The collapse of state communism has not delivered people to a safe democratic haven, and the past, fratricide and civil discord perduring, still clouds the horizon just behind us. Those who look back see all of the horrors of the ancient slaughterbench reenacted in disintegral nations like Bosnia, Sri Lanka, Ossetia, and Rwanda and they declare that nothing has changed. Those who look forward prophesize commercial and technological interdependence — a virtual paradise made possible by spreading markets and global technology — and they proclaim that everything is or soon will be different. The rival observers seem to consult different almanacs drawn from the libraries of contrarian planets.

Yet anyone who reads the daily papers carefully, taking in the front page accounts of civil carnage as well as the business page stories on the mechanics of the information superhighway and the economics of communication mergers, anyone who turns deliberately to take in the whole 360-degree horizon, knows that our world and our lives are caught between what [Irish poet] William Butler Yeats called the two eternities of race and soul: that of race reflecting the tribal past, that of soul anticipating the cosmopolitan future. Our secular eternities are corrupted, however, race reduced to an insignia of resentment, and soul sized down to fit the demanding body by which it now measures its

[1] Technology.

needs. Neither race nor soul offers us a future that is other than bleak, neither promises a polity that is remotely democratic.

The first scenario rooted in race holds out the grim prospect of a retribalization of large swaths of humankind by war and bloodshed: a threatened balkanization of nation-states in which culture is pitted against culture, people against people, tribe against tribe, a Jihad in the name of a hundred narrowly conceived faiths against every kind of interdependence, every kind of artificial social cooperation and mutuality: against technology, against pop culture, and against integrated markets; against modernity itself as well as the future in which modernity issues. The second paints that future in shimmering pastels, a busy portrait of onrushing economic, technological, and ecological forces that demand integration and uniformity and that mesmerize peoples everywhere with fast music, fast computers, and fast food — MTV, Macintosh, and McDonald's — pressing nations into one homogenous global theme park, one McWorld tied together by communications, information, entertainment, and commerce. Caught between Babel and Disneyland, the planet is falling precipitously apart and coming reluctantly together at the very same moment.

Some stunned observers notice only Babel, complaining about the thousand newly sundered "peoples" who prefer to address their neighbors with sniper rifles and mortars; others — zealots in Disneyland — seize on futurological platitudes and the promise of virtuality, exclaiming "It's a small world after all!" Both are right, but how can that be?

We are compelled to choose between what passes as "the twilight of sovereignty" and an entropic end of all history, or a return to the past's most fractious and demoralizing discord; to "the menace of global anarchy," to [John] Milton's capital of hell, Pandaemonium; to a world totally "out of control."

The apparent truth, which speaks to the paradox at the core of this book, is that the tendencies of both Jihad *and* McWorld are at work, both visible sometimes in the same country at the very same instant. Iranian zealots keep one ear tuned to the mullahs urging holy war and the other cocked to [Australian media mogul] Rupert Murdoch's Star television beaming in *Dynasty, Donahue,* and *The Simpsons* from hovering satellites. Chinese entrepreneurs vie for the attention of party cadres in Beijing and simultaneously pursue KFC franchises in cities like Nanjing, Hangzhou, and Xian where twenty-eight outlets serve over 100,000 customers a day. The Russian Orthodox church, even as it struggles to renew the ancient faith, has entered a joint venture with California businessmen to bottle and sell natural waters under the rubric Saint Springs Water Company. Serbian assassins wear Adidas sneakers and listen to Madonna on Walkman headphones as they take aim through their gunscopes at scurrying Sarajevo civilians looking to fill family watercans. Orthodox Hasids and brooding neo-Nazis have both turned to rock music to get their traditional messages out to the new generation, while fundamentalists plot virtual conspiracies on the Internet.

Now neither Jihad nor McWorld is in itself novel. History ending in the triumph of science and reason or some monstrous perversion thereof (Mary Shelley's Doctor Frankenstein) has been the leitmotiv of every philosopher and poet who has regretted the Age of Reason since the Enlightenment. [W. B.] Yeats lamented "the center will not hold, mere anarchy is loosed upon the world," and observers of Jihad today have little but historical detail to add. The Christian parable of the Fall and of the possibilities of redemption that it makes possible captures the eighteenth-century ambivalence — and our own — about past and future. I want, however, to do more than dress up the central paradox of human history in modern clothes. It is not Jihad and McWorld but the relationship between them that most interests me. For, squeezed between their opposing forces, the world has been sent spinning out of control. Can it be that what Jihad and McWorld have in common is anarchy: the absence of common will and that conscious and collective human control under the guidance of law we call democracy?

Progress moves in steps that sometimes lurch backwards; in history's twisting maze, Jihad not only revolts against but abets McWorld, while McWorld not only imperils but re-creates and reinforces Jihad. They produce their contraries and need one another. My object here then is not simply to offer sequential portraits of McWorld and Jihad, but while examining McWorld, to keep Jihad in my field of vision, and while dissecting Jihad, never to forget the context of McWorld. Call it a dialectic of McWorld: a study in the cunning of reason that does honor to the radical differences that distinguish Jihad and McWorld yet that acknowledges their powerful and paradoxical interdependence.

There is a crucial difference, however, between my modest attempt at dialectic and that of the masters of the nineteenth century. Still seduced by the Enlightenment's faith in progress, both [G. W. F.] Hegel and [Karl] Marx believed reason's cunning was on the side of progress. But it is harder to believe that the clash of Jihad and McWorld will issue in some overriding good. The outcome seems more likely to pervert than to nurture human liberty. The two may, in opposing each other, work to the same ends, work in apparent tension yet in covert harmony, but democracy is not their beneficiary. In East Berlin, tribal communism has yielded to capitalism. In Marx-Engelsplatz, the stolid, overbearing statues of Marx and [Friedrich] Engels face east, as if seeking distant solace from Moscow: but now, circling them along the streets that surround the park that is their prison are chain eateries like T.G.I. Friday's, international hotels like the Radisson, and a circle of neon billboards mocking them with brand names like Panasonic, Coke, and GoldStar. New gods, yes, but more liberty?

What then does it mean in concrete terms to view Jihad and McWorld dialectically when the tendencies of the two sets of forces initially appear so intractably antithetical? After all, Jihad and McWorld operate with equal strength in opposite directions, the one driven by parochial hatreds, the other by universalizing markets, the one re-creating ancient subnational and ethnic borders from within, the other making national borders porous from without. Yet Jihad and McWorld have this in common: They both make war on the sovereign nation-state and thus undermine the nation-state's democratic institutions. Each eschews civil society and belittles democratic citizenship, neither seeks alternative democratic institutions. Their common thread is indifference to civil liberty. Jihad forges communities of blood rooted in exclusion and hatred, communities that slight democracy in favor of tyrannical paternalism or consensual tribalism. McWorld forges global markets rooted in consumption and profit, leaving to an untrustworthy, if not altogether fictitious, invisible hand issues of public interest and common good that once might have been nurtured by democratic citizenries and their watchful governments. Such governments, intimidated by market ideology, are actually pulling back at the very moment they ought to be aggressively intervening. What was once understood as protecting the public interest is now excoriated as heavy-handed regulatory browbeating. Justice yields to markets, even though, as [New York banker] Felix Rohatyn has bluntly confessed, "there is a brutal Darwinian logic to these markets. They are nervous and greedy. They look for stability and transparency, but what they reward is not always our preferred form of democracy." If the traditional conservators of freedom were democratic constitutions and Bills of Rights, "the new temples to liberty," [literary critic and philosopher] George Steiner suggests, "will be McDonald's and Kentucky Fried Chicken."

In being reduced to a choice between the market's universal church and a retribalizing politics of particularist identities, peoples around the globe are threatened with an atavistic return to medieval politics where local tribes and ambitious emperors together ruled the world entire, women and men united by the universal abstraction of Christianity even as they lived out isolated lives in warring fiefdoms defined by involuntary (ascriptive) forms of identity. This was a world in which princes and kings had little real power until they conceived the ideology of nationalism. Nationalism established government on a scale greater than the tribe yet less cosmopolitan than the universal church and in time gave birth to those intermediate, gradually more democratic institutions that would come to constitute the nation-state. Today, at the far end of this history, we seem intent on re-creating a world in which our only choices are the secular universalism of the cosmopolitan market and the everyday particularism of the fractious tribe.

In the tumult of the confrontation between global commerce and parochial ethnicity, the virtues of the democratic nation are lost and the instrumentalities by which it permitted peoples to transform themselves into nations and seize sovereign power in the name of liberty and the commonweal are put at risk. Neither Jihad nor McWorld aspires to resecure the civic virtues undermined by its denationalizing practices; neither global markets nor blood communities service public goods or pursue equality and justice. Impartial judiciaries and deliberate assemblies play no role in the roving killer bands that speak on behalf of newly liberated "peoples," and such democratic institutions have at best only marginal influence on the roving multinational corporations that speak on behalf of newly liberated markets. Jihad pursues a bloody politics of identity, McWorld a bloodless economics of profit. Belonging by default to McWorld, everyone is a consumer; seeking a repository for identity, everyone belongs to some tribe. But no one is a citizen. Without citizens, how can there be democracy?

$$91$$

MARK JUERGENSMEYER

From *Terror in the Mind of God*

It is hard to deny the power and influence of the global market economy, the driving force behind Benjamin Barber's "McWorld." Many find this power threatening because it is not guided by a specific moral creed. In the following selection Mark Juergensmeyer, a political scientist who focuses on international studies, argues that religious fundamentalists (the embodiment of Barber's *Jihad*) are increasingly trying to fill the moral void created by the amoral global economy, and are threatening the future of the secular nation state. According to Juergensmeyer, why might religious fundamentalism be appealing to some? How important a cause is secularism? Why is it increasingly important to understand the causes and consequences of religious fundamentalism?

Thinking Historically

Juergensmeyer frames his argument in the post–Cold War era. What specific developments since the fall of the Soviet Union does he cite as precipitating factors in the rise of religious terrorism? How does his

Mark Juergensmeyer, *Terror in the Mind of God: The Global Rise of Religious Violence* (Berkeley: University of California Press, 2000), 225–29.

assessment compare with that of Benjamin Barber, who describes *Jihad* and McWorld as "the central paradox of human history"? Do you think the tensions between these two forces are age-old, or are they the result of recent political, cultural, and economic developments?

The moral leadership of the secular state has become increasingly challenged in the last decade of the twentieth century following the end of the Cold War and the rise of a global economy. The Cold War provided contesting models of moral politics — communism and democracy — that have been replaced by a global market that has weakened national sovereignty and is conspicuously devoid of political ideals. The global economy became characterized by transnational businesses accountable to no single governmental authority and with no clear ideological or moral standards of behavior. But while both Christian and Enlightenment values were left behind, transnational commerce transported aspects of Westernized popular culture to the rest of the world. American and European music, videos, and films were beamed across national boundaries, where they threatened to obliterate local and traditional forms of artistic expression. Added to this social confusion were convulsive shifts in political power that followed the breakup of the Soviet Union and the faltering of Asian economies.

The public sense of insecurity that has come in the wake of these cataclysmic global changes has been felt not only in the societies of those nations that were economically devastated by them — especially countries in the former Soviet Union — but also in economically stronger industrialized societies. The United States, for example, has seen a remarkable degree of disaffection with its political leaders and witnessed the rise of right-wing religious movements that feed on the public's perception of the inherent immorality of government.

Is the rise of religious terrorism related to these global changes? We know that some groups associated with violence in industrialized societies have an antimodernist political agenda. At the extreme end of this religious rejection of modernism in the United States are members of the American anti-abortion group Defensive Action, the Christian militia and Christian Identity movement, and isolated groups such as the Branch Davidian sect in Waco, Texas. When Michael Bray and other members of the religious right cast aspersions at "the new world order" allegedly promoted by President Bill Clinton and the United Nations, what he and his colleagues feared was the imposition of a reign of order that was not just tyrannical but atheist. They saw evidence of an anti-religious government program in what they regarded as a pandering to pluralist cultural values in a society with no single set of religious moorings.

Similar attitudes toward secular government have emerged in Israel — the religious nationalist ideology of the Kach party is an extreme example — and, as the Aum Shinrikyo movement demonstrated, in Japan. Like the United States, contentious groups within these countries became disillusioned about the ability of secular leaders to guide their countries' destinies. They identified government as the enemy. In Israel, for instance, Hamas and the Jewish right have been in opposition not so much to each other as to their own secular leaders. This fact was demonstrated by the reaction of Jewish settlers in Gaza to a Hamas suicide bombing attempt in 1998, soon after the Wye River accords, in which an activist attempted to ram a car loaded with explosives into a school bus filled with forty of the settlers' children. One of the parents immediately lashed out in hatred — not against the Arabs who tried to kill her child, but against her own secular leader, Netanyahu, whom she blamed for precipitating the action by entering into peace agreements with Arafat. Her comments demonstrated that the religious war in Israel and Palestine has not been a war between religions, but a double set of religious wars — Jewish and Muslim — against secularism.

The global shifts that have given rise to antimodernist movements have also affected less-developed nations. India's Jawaharlal Nehru, Egypt's Gamal Abdel Nasser, and Iran's Riza Shah Pahlavi were once committed to creating versions of America — or a kind of cross between America and the Soviet Union — in their own countries. But new generations of leaders no longer believed in the Westernized visions of Nehru, Nasser, or the shah. Rather, they were eager to complete the process of decolonialization and build new, indigenous nationalisms.

When activists in Algeria demonstrating against the crackdown on the Islamic Salvation Front in 1991 proclaimed that they were continuing the war of liberation against French colonialism, they had the ideological rather than political reach of European influence in mind. Religious activists such as the Algerian leaders, Ayatollah Khomeini in Iran, Sheik Ahmed Yassin in Palestine, Sayyid Qutb and his disciple Sheik Omar Abdul Rahman in Egypt, L. K. Advani in India, and Sant Jarnail Singh Bhindranwale in India's Punjab have asserted the legitimacy of a postcolonial national identity based on traditional culture.

The result of this disaffection with the values of the modern West has been what I have called a "loss of faith" in the ideological form of that culture, secular nationalism. Although a few years ago it would have been a startling notion, the idea has now become virtually commonplace that secular nationalism — the principle that the nation is rooted in a secular compact rather than a religious or ethnic identity — is in crisis. In many parts of the world it is seen as an alien cultural construction, one closely linked with what has been called "the project of modernity." In such cases, religious alternatives to secular ideologies have had extraordinary appeal.

The uncertainty about what constitutes a valid basis for national identity is a political form of postmodernism. In Iran it has resulted in the rejection of a modern Western political regime and the creation of a successful religious state. Increasingly, even secular scholars in the West have recognized that religious ideologies might offer an alternative to modernity in the political sphere. Yet what lies beyond modernity is not necessarily a new form of political order, religious or otherwise. In nations formerly under Soviet control, for example, the specter of the future beyond the socialist form of modernity has been one of cultural anarchism. The fear of a spiritual as well as a political collapse at modernity's center has, in many parts of the world, led to terror.

Both violence and religion have emerged at times when authority is in question, since they are both ways of challenging and replacing authority. One gains its power from force and the other from its claims to ultimate order. The combination of the two in acts of religious terrorism has been a potent assertion indeed. Whether or not the perpetrators of these acts consciously intended them to be political acts, any public act of violence has political consequences. Insofar as they have been attempts to reshape the public order, they have been examples of what José Casanova has called the increasing "deprivatization" of religion. In various parts of the world where attempts have been made by defenders of religion to reclaim the center of public attention and authority, religious terrorism is often the violent face of these attempts. . . .

From Algeria to Idaho, . . . small but potent groups of violent activists have represented growing masses of supporters, and they have exemplified currents of thinking and cultures of commitment that have risen to counter the prevailing modernism — the ideology of individualism and skepticism — that has emerged in the past three centuries from the European Enlightenment and spread throughout the world. They have come to hate secular governments with an almost transcendent passion. These guerrilla nationalists have dreamed of revolutionary changes that would establish a godly social order in the rubble of what the citizens of most secular societies have regarded as modern, egalitarian democracies. Their enemies have seemed to most people to be both benign and banal: modern, secular leaders such as Yitzhak Rabin and Anwar Sadat, and such symbols of prosperity and authority as the World Trade Center and the Japanese subway system. The logic of this kind of militant religiosity has therefore been difficult for many people to comprehend. Yet its challenge has been profound, for it has contained a fundamental critique of the world's post-Enlightenment secular culture and politics.

For this reason these acts of guerrilla religious warfare have been not only attempts at "delegitimization," as Ehud Sprinzak has put it, but also relegitimization: attempts to purchase public recognition of the legitimacy of religious world views with the currency of violence. Since religious authority can provide a ready-made replacement for secular leadership, it is no surprise that when secular leaders have been deemed inadequate or corrupt, the challenges to their legitimacy and the attempts to gain support for their rivals have been based on religion. When the proponents of religion have asserted their claims to be the moral force undergirding public order, they sometimes have done so with the kind of power that a confused society can graphically recognize: the force of terror.

92

GLOBAL SNAPSHOTS

Cartogram of Global Warming

Satellite Photo of the Earth at Night

At the heart of many debates surrounding globalization is the natural environment. It is difficult to ignore the vast problems endangering the planet — global warming, acid rain, species extinction, rainforest depletion. These environmental issues require global cooperation to be solved, and they also require a certain global consciousness, or understanding, that all people are part of a global community and that what people do in one part of the world affects those in another part.

These two images remind us that despite our differences we all share one planet. In addition, they provide a graphic measure of the integration and imbalances of the world today. Specifically, these images show how the consumption of energy resources — heat and light — is distributed throughout the world.

"Global Warming" from Dan Smith, *The State of the World Atlas,* 7th ed. (Brighton, U.K.: Myriad Editions, 2003). "Earth at Night" by Craig Mayhew and Robert Simmon (NASA/GSFC), NOAA/NGDC, DMSP Digital Archive, November 27, 2000.

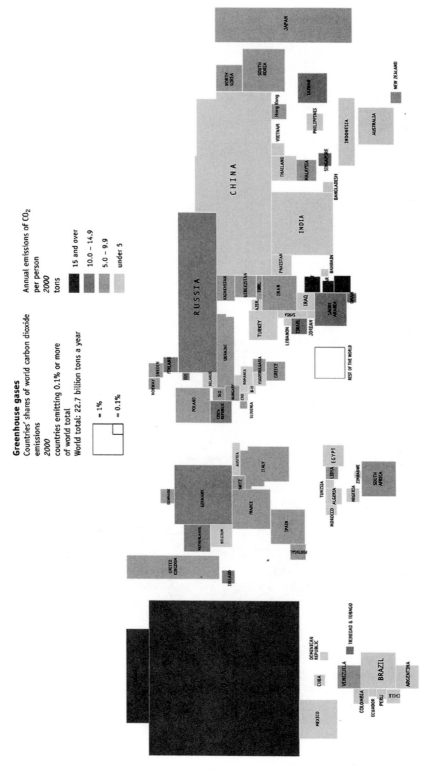

Figure 14.1 Cartogram of Global Warming. Emissions of carbon dioxide, one of the main greenhouse gases.

Source: Reproduced from *The State of the World Atlas*, 7th edition, by Dan Smith @ Myriad Editions Limited/www.myriadeditions.com.

Greenhouse gases

Countries' shares of world carbon dioxide emissions
2000
countries emitting 0.1% or more of world total
World total: 22.7 billion tons a year

Annual emissions of CO_2 per person
2000
tons

15 and over
10.0 – 14.9
5.0 – 9.9
under 5

= 1%
= 0.1%

543

Figure 14.2 Satellite Photo of the Earth at Night.

Source: The Earth at Night. Courtesy of C. Mayhew and R. Simmon (NASA/GSFC), NOAA/NGDC, DSMP Digital Archive. Downloadable at http://antwrp.gsfc.nasa.gov/apod/ap001127.html or http://antwerp.gsfc.nasa.gov/apod/ap020810.html for the nights of November 27, 2000, and August 10, 2002, respectively.

The first image is a cartogram, which is a stylized map in which countries are not represented to scale, but are sized to reflect a specific measurement. This cartogram measures relative emissions of greenhouse gases by country, so the largest countries on the map emit the most gases, and the smallest emit the fewest. Which countries produce the most greenhouse gases? Which countries produce the least? What accounts for these differences?

The satellite photograph of the Earth at night shows that energy use is no more uniform within countries than it is from one country to another. What areas of countries use the most light? Why? Does the photograph correspond to the cartogram in every respect? What does the photograph tell you about the relationship between energy use, transportation routes, urban centers, and general population density? What else can you deduce about global energy use from the photograph?

Thinking Historically

A snapshot is hardly the proper format to display process since it captures only a moment in time. Nevertheless, what long-term global trends can you extrapolate from these images? Can you see evidence of any of the historical processes discussed in this chapter? What historical processes do these snapshots capture most dramatically?

93

JEAN-MARIE COLOMBANI

We Are All Americans

"Nous Sommes Tous des Americains" declared the headline of the French daily *Le Monde* on September 12, 2001, the day after nineteen hijackers flew two passenger airliners into the World Trade Center towers in New York, crashed a third into the Pentagon in Washington, D.C., and commandeered a fourth, supposedly bound for the White House, before the flight was fatally aborted by its passengers over Pennsylvania. In the signed article that follows, *Le Monde's*

Jean-Marie Colombani, *"Nous Sommes Tous des Americains,"* Le Monde, Paris, France (12 September 2001). From *World Press Review*, 48, no. 11 (November 2001).

editor, Jean-Marie Colombani, expressed the shock and outrage felt by many around the world. What did he mean by his declaration that all were Americans? What explanations does he offer for the terrorist attacks? Which does he argue is the most significant cause? How does he propose to counter the "barbarian" forces behind the attacks?

Thinking Historically

Within what historical context does Colombani place the events of 9/11? How does his editorial relate to Juergensmeyer's and Barber's selections, which were written before the attacks? Some historians, journalists, and politicians believe that 9/11 was a turning point in modern history. Have we entered a new phase of history? How do we decide? How might the events of September 11, 2001, affect how people think about globalization?

In this tragic moment, when words seem so inadequate to express the shock people feel, the first thing that comes to mind is this: We are all Americans! We are all New Yorkers, just as surely as John F. Kennedy declared himself to be a Berliner in 1962 when he visited Berlin. Indeed, just as in the gravest moments of our own history, how can we not feel profound solidarity with those people, that country, the United States, to whom we are so close and to whom we owe our freedom, and therefore our solidarity? How can we not be struck at the same time by this observation: The new century has come a long way.

September 11, 2001, marks the ushering in of a new age that seems so far from the promise of another historic day, November 9, 1989 [the breaking of the Berlin Wall], and a somewhat euphoric year, 2000, which we thought might conclude with peace in the Middle East.

And so a new century moves ahead, with powerful technology, as shown by the sophistication of the war operation that struck America's symbols: those of its enormous economic power in the heart of Manhattan [and] of its military might at the Pentagon. The beginnings of this century defy understanding unless you promptly and indiscriminately subscribe to the cliché that is already the most widespread: the triggering of a war of the South against the North.

But to say this would be to credit the perpetrators of this murderous madness with "good intentions," or with some plan, whereby the oppressed peoples would be avenged against their sole oppressor, America. That would have allowed them to claim "poverty" as their authority, thus committing an affront to it! What monstrous hypocrisy! None of those who had a hand in this operation can claim they intend the good of humanity. Actually, they have no interest in a better world. They simply want to wipe ours off the face of the Earth.

The reality is more certainly that of a world with no counterbalance, physically destabilized, and thus more dangerous since there is no multipolar balance. And America, in the solitude of its power, in its status as the sole superpower, now in the absence of a Soviet countermodel, has ceased to draw other nations to itself; or more precisely, in certain parts of the globe, it seems to draw nothing but hate. In the regulated world of the Cold War, where the various kinds of terrorism were more or less aided by Moscow, a certain degree of control was still possible, and the dialogue between Moscow and Washington never stopped. In today's monopolistic world, it is a new barbarism, apparently with no control, which seems to want to set itself up as a counterpower. Perhaps, even in Europe, from the Gulf War to the use of F-16s by the Israeli army against the Palestinians, we have underestimated the intensity of the hate, which, from the outskirts of Jakarta to those of Durban, among the rejoicing crowds in Nablus and Cairo, is focused against the United States.

But the reality is perhaps also that of an America whose own cynicism has caught up with it. If bin Laden, as the American authorities seem to think, really is the one who ordered the September 11 attacks, how can we fail to recall that he was in fact trained by the CIA and that he was an element of a policy, directed against the Soviets, that the Americans considered to be wise? Might it not then have been America itself that created this demon?

Be that as it may, America is going to change. Profoundly. America is like a large ocean liner, sailing for a long time on the same course. When the course is changed, it is changed for a long time. And, even though the expression may be overworked, the United States has suffered an unprecedented shock. Pearl Harbor marked the end of isolationism, so deeply rooted that it was not even moved by Hitler's barbarity. After Pearl Harbor, everything changed. And America accepted it all, from the Marshall Plan to sending GIs to every point of the globe. Then came the Vietnam debacle, which led to a new doctrine, that of the rare but massive use of force, accompanied by the dogma of "zero casualties" for the United States, as illustrated during the Gulf War. All of that has now been swept away. There is no doubt that every means will be employed against enemies who, up to now, have remained elusive.

The new hand that has begun to be dealt out in blood, at this stage, will bring with it at least two foreseeable consequences. Both have to do with alliances: It is certainly the end of an entire strategy conceived in opposition to Russia, the Soviet Union at the time. Russia, at least in its non-Islamic areas, is going to become the main ally of the United

States. Perhaps it is also the end of an alliance that the United States had traced out in the 1930s and soundly established in the 1950s with Sunni Muslim fundamentalism, such as it is defended particularly in Saudi Arabia and Pakistan. In the eyes of American public opinion and its leadership, Islamic fundamentalism, in all its forms, risks being designated as the new enemy. Indeed, the anti-Islamic reflex, immediately after the attack on a federal building in Oklahoma City, resulted in statements that were ridiculous, if not downright odious.

Beyond their obvious murderous madness, these latest attacks nonetheless follow a certain logic.

Obviously it is a barbarous logic, marked by a new nihilism that is repugnant to the great majority of those who believe in Islam, which, as a religion, does not condone suicide any more than Christianity does, and certainly not suicide coupled with the massacre of innocent people. But it is a political logic, which, by going to extremes, seeks to force Muslim opinion to "choose sides" against those who are currently designated as "the Great Satan." By doing this, their objective might well be to spread and deepen an unprecedented crisis in the Arab world.

In the long term, this attitude is obviously suicidal, because it attracts lightning. And it might attract a bolt of lightning that does not discriminate. This situation requires our leaders to rise to the occasion. They must act so that the people whom these warmongers are seeking to win over and are counting on will not fall in step behind them in their suicidal logic. This we can say with some dread: Modern technology allows them to go even further. Madness, even under the pretext of despair, is never a force that can regenerate the world. That is why today we are all Americans.

94

MARGARET ATWOOD

A Letter to America

Days after the terrorist attacks of September 11, 2001, U.S. President George W. Bush declared a global war on terror. This unconventional war was to be waged against terrorists themselves and any nation that harbored or supported them. Simultaneously, the U.S. Congress quickly passed the Patriot Act, a comprehensive bill that aimed to give law enforcement more resources to investigate and prevent terrorism but was criticized for possibly impinging on civil liberties.

Canadian novelist and poet Margaret Atwood wrote the following "letter to America" in the midst of Operation Iraqi Freedom, a military intervention to depose Iraqi dictator Saddam Hussein that the United States pursued under the umbrella of the war on terror. France, Germany, Russia, China, and much of the Arab and Muslim world opposed the war as a unilateral display of American power and a flouting of the United Nations. According to Atwood, what problems does America face today? How does she suggest that the Iraqi war was a symptom of a larger problem?

Thinking Historically

Atwood's letter stands in stark contrast to Colombani's editorial: In effect, she says "we *were* all Americans." What has changed? Although she feels that she no longer understands America, she also feels more vulnerable to U.S. policies. Why? Does Atwood's letter suggest we are living in a "post-9/11" world? What, according to Atwood, is America's place in world history?

Dear America:

This is a difficult letter to write, because I'm no longer sure who you are. Some of you may be having the same trouble.

I thought I knew you: We'd become well acquainted over the past fifty-five years. You were the Mickey Mouse and Donald Duck comic books I read in the late 1940s. You were the radio shows — Jack Benny, "Our Miss Brooks." You were the music I sang and danced to:

Margaret Atwood, "Letter to America," *The Nation*, 276, no. 14 (April 2003).

the Andrews Sisters, Ella Fitzgerald, the Platters, Elvis. You were a ton of fun.

You wrote some of my favorite books. You created Huckleberry Finn, and Hawkeye, and Beth and Jo in *Little Women,* courageous in their different ways. Later, you were my beloved Thoreau, father of environmentalism, witness to individual conscience; and Walt Whitman, singer of the great Republic; and Emily Dickinson, keeper of the private soul. You were Hammett and Chandler, heroic walkers of mean streets; even later, you were the amazing trio, Hemingway, Fitzgerald and Faulkner, who traced the dark labyrinths of your hidden heart. You were Sinclair Lewis and Arthur Miller, who, with their own American idealism, went after the sham in you, because they thought you could do better.

You were Marlon Brando in *On the Waterfront,* you were Humphrey Bogart in *Key Largo,* you were Lillian Gish in *Night of the Hunter.* You stood up for freedom, honesty, and justice; you protected the innocent. I believed most of that. I think you did, too. It seemed true at the time.

You put God on the money, though, even then. You had a way of thinking that the things of Caesar were the same as the things of God: That gave you self-confidence. You have always wanted to be a city upon a hill, a light to all nations, and for a while you were. Give me your tired, your poor, you sang, and for a while you meant it.

We've always been close, you and us. History, that old entangler, has twisted us together since the early seventeenth century. Some of us used to be you; some of us want to be you; some of you used to be us.

You are not only our neighbors: In many cases — mine, for instance — you are also our blood relations, our colleagues and our personal friends. But although we've had a ringside seat, we've never understood you completely, up here north of the 49th parallel. We're like Romanized Gauls — look like Romans, dress like Romans, but aren't Romans — peering over the wall at the real Romans. What are they doing? Why? What are they doing now? Why is the haruspex eyeballing the sheep's liver? Why is the soothsayer wholesaling the Bewares?

Perhaps that's been my difficulty in writing you this letter: I'm not sure I know what's really going on. Anyway, you have a huge posse of experienced entrail-sifters who do nothing but analyze your every vein and lobe. What can I tell you about yourself that you don't already know?

This might be the reason for my hesitation: embarrassment, brought on by a becoming modesty. But it is more likely to be embarrassment of another sort. When my grandmother — from a New England background — was confronted with an unsavory topic, she would change the subject and gaze out the window. And that is my own inclination: Keep your mouth shut, mind your own business.

But I'll take the plunge, because your business is no longer merely your business. To paraphrase Marley's Ghost, who figured it out too late, mankind is your business. And vice versa: When the Jolly Green Giant goes on the rampage, many lesser plants and animals get trampled underfoot. As for us, you're our biggest trading partner: We know perfectly well that if you go down the plug-hole, we're going with you. We have every reason to wish you well.

I won't go into the reasons why I think your recent Iraqi adventures have been — taking the long view — an ill-advised tactical error. By the time you read this, Baghdad may or may not be a pancake, and many more sheep entrails will have been examined. Let's talk, then, not about what you're doing to other people but about what you're doing to yourselves.

You're gutting the Constitution. Already your home can be entered without your knowledge or permission, you can be snatched away and incarcerated without cause, your mail can be spied on, your private records searched. Why isn't this a recipe for widespread business theft, political intimidation, and fraud? I know you've been told that all this is for your own safety and protection, but think about it for a minute. Anyway, when did you get so scared? You didn't used to be easily frightened.

You're running up a record level of debt. Keep spending at this rate and pretty soon you won't be able to afford any big military adventures. Either that or you'll go the way of the USSR: lots of tanks, but no air conditioning. That will make folks very cross. They'll be even crosser when they can't take a shower because your shortsighted bulldozing of environmental protections has dirtied most of the water and dried up the rest. Then things will get hot and dirty indeed.

You're torching the American economy. How soon before the answer to that will be not to produce anything yourselves but to grab stuff other people produce, at gunboat-diplomacy prices? Is the world going to consist of a few mega-rich King Midases, with the rest being serfs, both inside and outside your country? Will the biggest business sector in the United States be the prison system? Let's hope not.

If you proceed much further down the slippery slope, people around the world will stop admiring the good things about you. They'll decide that your city upon the hill is a slum and your democracy is a sham, and therefore you have no business trying to impose your sullied vision on them. They'll think you've abandoned the rule of law. They'll think you've fouled your own nest.

The British used to have a myth about King Arthur. He wasn't dead, but sleeping in a cave, it was said; and in the country's hour of greatest peril, he would return. You too have great spirits of the past you may call upon: men and women of courage, of conscience, of pre-science. Summon them now, to stand with you, to inspire you, to de-fend the best in you. You need them.

REFLECTIONS

The present can be more perplexing than the past. Our modern world can be the hardest to understand because it is an unfinished story. And yet the present has little meaning bereft of history, and the surer our historical footing, the less likely we will be surprised by tomorrow. When confronted with dramatic change we search the recent and dis-tant past for explanations, for clues that we are moving in a new direc-tion or that we are returning to an old trend. For example, in Margaret Atwood's "Letter to America," in trying to make sense of the changes in the United States Atwood alludes to its glorious past — its cultural icons, its identity as "the city on the hill," its founding principles of freedom, honesty, and justice — and tries to put recent changes in broad historical context. She even alludes to the fallen Roman empire, perhaps as a cautionary note to overgrown U.S. power.

When the United States was attacked on September 11, 2001, Jean-Marie Colombani was hardly the only commentator to declare the be-ginning of a new era and a new barbarism. But seeing only what is new is to be caught without history, as the editor of *Le Monde* well knew. Thus, he searched for historical explanation: Was it the end of the Cold War? political compromises with Saudi Arabia? or the U.S. support of Muslim fundamentalism in Soviet Afghanistan in the 1980s?

When considering the causes and consequences of 9/11 and Amer-ica's war on terrorism, the process of globalization cannot be ignored. But what exactly is this force of globalization? Is it the driving force shaping our present and future? Is the force of globalization the spread of market capitalism: free-trade agreements, multinational corpora-tions, international finance? If so, what are its effects? How is this process changing our lives? Can we expect commerce, consumerism, and capital markets to erode national boundaries, traditional values, folk culture, and religion? Will the world become one gigantic shop-ping mall? Or, as Benjamin Barber and Mark Juergensmeyer suggest, is religious fundamentalism the result of exploding capitalism? Are the pieces of the world becoming more alike or more different? Are we be-coming more cosmopolitan or more tribal?

Finally, is globalization good for us, or bad? Or does it depend on who the "us" is? Philippe Legrain sees cross-fertilization and liberation where Sherif Hetata sees hegemony and homogenization. Who is right? Are they talking about the same things, or the same people? Life is clearly hard for third-world women working in the sweatshops of multinational corporations, as Miriam Ching Yoon Louie reminds us, but is globalization responsible for their suffering, or does it provide them with opportunities? And what of the next generation? Are they better off learning how to play the games of the future or accepting the roles of the past? Does it matter that those games are funded by international corporations intent on smoothing their own path to future profits from compliant workers and customers?

Understanding the process of change is the most useful "habit of mind" we gain from studying the past. Although the facts are many and the details overwhelming, process only appears through the study of the specific. And we must continually check our theories of change with the facts, and revise them to conform to new information.

More important, understanding change does not necessarily mean that we must submit to it. Of the processes of globalization discussed in this chapter — trade and technological transfers, cultural homogenization and competition, commercialization, and market expansion — some may seem inevitable, some merely strong, some even reversible. Intelligent action requires an appreciation of the possible as well as the identification of the improbable.

History is not an exact science. Fortunately, human beings are creators, as well as subjects, of change. Even winds that cannot be stopped can be deflected and harnessed. Which way is the world moving? What are we becoming? What can we do? What kind of world can we create? These are questions that can only be answered by studying the past, both distant and recent, and trying to understand the overarching changes that are shaping our world. Worlds of history converge upon us, but only one world will emerge from our wishes, our wisdom, and our will.

Acknowledgments

Chinua Achebe. Excerpt from *Things Fall Apart*. Copyright © 1958 by Chinua Achebe. Reprinted with the permission of Heinemann Educational Publishers, a division of Reed Educational & Professional Publishing, Ltd.

Abigail Adams. "Letters from Abigail Adams to John Adams, March 31–April 1776, 7–9 May 1776," and "Letter from John Adams to Abigail Adams, April 14, 1776." From *Adams Family Papers: An Electronic Archive,* Boston, Massachusetts Historical Society, 2002. www.masshist.org. Reprinted by permission.

Benedict Anderson. "The First Filipino." Excerpts from *The Spectre of Comparisons: Nationalism, Southeast Asia and the World.* Copyright © 1998. Reprinted by permission of Verso, an imprint of New Left Books, Ltd.

Bonnie S. Anderson and Judith P. Zinsser. "Women and Science." From *A History of Their Own,* Volume II. Copyright © 1988 by Bonnie Anderson and Judith Zinsser. Reprinted by permission of HarperCollins Publishers, Inc.

Margaret Atwood. "Letter to America." From *The Nation,* April 14. 2003. Copyright 2003. Reprinted by permission.

Benjamin Barber. Excerpt from *Jihad vs. McWorld: How Globalism and Tribalism Are Reshaping the World.* Copyright © 1995 by Benjamin R. Barber. Used by permission of Times Books, a division of Random House, Inc.

Simi Bedford. "Growing Up in Nigeria." Excerpt from Chapter 1 in *Yoruba Girl Dancing.* Copyright © 1992 by Simi Bedford. Reprinted with the permission of Viking Penguin, a division of Penguin Group (USA) Inc.

Ralph Blumenthal with Judith Miller. "Japan Rebuffs Requests for Information about Its Germ-Warfare Atrocities." From *The New York Times,* March 4, 1999. Copyright © 1999 by the New York Times Company. Reprinted by permission.

Simon Bolivar. "A Constitution for Venezuela." From *Selected Writings of Bolivar,* Vincent Lecuna, comp., and Harold A. Bierck Jr., ed. Colonial Press/Banco de Venezuela (1951). Reprinted by permission.

S. V. Britten, Hugo Muller, Bill Bland, and Kande Kamara. "Witness of Soldiers." Diary entries for April 17, 22, and 23, 1915, from 1914–1918 in *Voices and Images of the Great War.* Copyright © 1988 by Lyn Macdonald. Reprinted with permission of Pollinger, Ltd.

Ghislain de Busbecq. "The Ottoman Empire under Suleiman." From *The Turkish Letters of Ogier Ghislain de Busbecq, Imperial Ambassador at Constantinople, 1534–1562,* translated by Edward Seymur Foster. Copyright © 1927. Reprinted by permission of Oxford University Press Ltd.

Iris Chang. Excerpt from *The Rape of Nanking: The Forgotten Holocaust of World War II.* Copyright © 1997 by Iris Chang. Reprinted with the permission of Basic Books, a member of Perseus Books, LLC.

Jean-Marie Colombani. "We Are All Americans." From *Le Monde,* Paris, France, September 12, 2001. Later published in the 11/01 issue of *World Press Review* (Volume 48, No. 1). Copyright © 2001, Le Monde. Reprinted by permission.

Theodore F. Cook Jr. "Zheng He and Chinese Expansion." From *What If?* Vol. 2, edited by Robert Crowley. Copyright © 2001 by American Historical Publications, Inc. Used by permission of G. P. Putnam's Sons, a division of Penguin Group (USA) Inc.

Deng Yingchao. "The Spirit of the May Fourth Movement." Adapted from the translation by Liu Xiaochang in *Women in China,* published in May 1989.